Teoria: 20th Century Polish Thought

Freud's emissaries II

Lena Magnone

LENA MAGNONE

Translated by Tul'si Bhambry

FREUD'S EMISSARIES II

the transfer of psychoanalysis through the Polish intelligentsia to Europe 1900-1939

sdvig press

GENÈVE | LAUSANNE

Publication financed by the Polish Ministry of Science and Higher Education within the National Programme for the Development of the Humanities 2018-2021, agreement 0266/NPRH6/H21/85/2017

NATIONAL PROGRAMME FOR THE DEVELOPMENT OF HUMANITIES

ISBN: 9782940738090
DOI: 10.19079/9782940738090

sdvig press
Place de la Louve 3, 1003 Lausanne
www.sdvigpress.org

Original edition: Lena Magnone, *Emisariusze Freuda. Transfer kulturowy psychoanalizy do polskich sfer inteligenckich przed drugą wojną światową. Tom I-II*, Warszawa, Universitas, 2016

Table of contents

Part 4

Eugenia Sokolnicka

A PIONEER OF PSYCHOANALYSIS IN FRANCE

"KUTNERKA"

According to the marriage certificate issued to Michał Sokolnicki and his bride, née Eugenia Kutner, the future psychoanalyst Eugenia Sokolnicka was born in Warsaw in 1876.[1] Throughout her career, however, she claimed a later date of birth, namely 1884, which figures in many reference works on psychoanalysis.[2] 1884 also happens to be Helene Deutsch's date of birth – a coincidence that calls for a comparative reading of their lives. The two women grew up in different partitions and had very different experiences once they became affiliated with the Freudian movement, but the years of their youth show a number of telling parallels.

Eugenia's parents Maurycy Kutner and Paulina Kutner, née Flejszer, were well-to-do liberal Jews. Supporting Poland's independence was part of the family tradition. The men on the father's side had fought in the uprisings of 1830-31 and 1863-64; Paulina was an activist in the Women's Patriotic Society[3] and was imprisoned in the Warsaw citadel in 1863.[4] It is

1 Archiwum Państwowe w Warszawie, Akta stanu cywilnego parafii rzymsko-katolickiej Wszystkich Świętych w Warszawie, 72/1219/0–/122 (I used the electronic version available on <metryki.genealodzy.pl> [accessed on 24/08/2020]). Eugenia and Michał Sokolnicki both have individual entries in the *Polski Słownik Biograficzny* (vol. 40). On Sokolnicka's biography see also E. Pichon, "Eugénie Sokolnicka", *RFP* 1934, no. 4, pp. 590–603; A. Clancier, "Eugenia Sokolnicka (1884–1934)", *RFP* 1987, vol. 51, no. 1, pp. 427–429; E. Roudinesco, "Tragique varsovienne: Eugénie Sokolnicka", in *Histoire de la psychanalyse en France*, vol. 1 (Paris: Fayard, 2003), pp. 279–289.

2 E. Mühlleitner, *Biographisches Lexikon der Psychoanalyse*, pp. 304–305; *International Dictionary of Psychoanalysis*, pp. 1663–1664; E. Roudinesco, M. Plon, *Dictionnaire de la psychanalyse*, pp. 1014–1015.

3 The Women's Patriotic Society [Żeńskie Towarzystwo Patriotyczne] was a secret organisation formed during the January Uprising (1863-64). Each basic unit consisted of five women, which is why the organisation was also called "Piątka," from *pięć* [five]. See M. Bruchnalska, *Ciche bohaterki: Udział kobiet w powstaniu styczniowym* (Miejsce Piastowe: Tow. św. Michała Archanioła, 1933), pp. 69–75.

4 J. Maliszewski, *Powstanie styczniowe: Notatki biograficzne uczestników z oryginalnemi ilustracjami* (Warsaw: [Self-Published], 1932), pp. 97–98.

unclear what school Eugenia attended. Perhaps it was a public girls' gymnasium in Warsaw (in the late nineteenth century one out of three female gymnasium students in the Kingdom of Poland were Jewish) or a private boarding school for girls, such as the one run by Jadwiga Sikorska, where Jews represented about 20% of the student body.[5] Having com-pleted her secondary education, the ambitious young woman left for Paris.[6] She studied natural sciences at the Sorbonne and took extra courses with Pierre Janet, Théodule Ribot and Jean-Martin Charcot at the Collège de France. It was during her student days that she met Michał Sokolnicki (1880–1967), who had come to Paris in 1898 to study at the École Libre des Sciences Politiques.

Sokolnicki went on to become a distinguished career diplomat. He published his memoirs, *Czternaście lat* [Fourteen Years], in 1936. Astonishingly, he never mentions his wife Eugenia, not even in the passages about his formative years in France. Perhaps they had met at the Polish student society "Spójnia," which Sokolnicki describes as follows:

> The association "Spójnia" [...] was one of the oldest, biggest and wealthiest Polish student societies. As was typical of émigré Poles in those days, outside their educational institutions they established no private or family ties with the French; they generally showed little interest in their French fellow students but kept to their own little unions and circles and lived in what they called the Polish colony. Their groups of friends took on the role of the family, while the association and its slogans replaced the distant fatherland – and there is no doubt that sometimes their minds and souls were sharpened, irritated and confused by their inner turmoil, rooted in their families' misunderstandings and squabbles, and their emotional state, marked by an overwhelming longing amid the difficulties of adjusting to new people.[7]

---

5 H. Datner, *Ta i tamta strona: Żydowska inteligencja Warszawy drugiej połowy XIX wieku*, pp. 113–114.

6 The exact date could not be established. It is certain that in 1899 Eugenia Kutner was already in Paris; on 2 September 1899 Kazimierz Kelles-Krauz wrote to his wife that she was temporarily staying in Warsaw but was due to return to Paris in late September or early October. K. Kelles-Krauz, *Listy*, ed. by F. Tych (Wrocław: Zakład Narodowy im. Ossolińskich, 1984), vol. 2, p. 267.

7 M. Sokolnicki, *Czternaście lat* (Warsaw: Instytut Badania Najnowszej Historii Polski, 1936), p. 13.

Eugenia Kutner could have been one of the women friends he mentions – "students of medicine living under the care of 'mama' [Witolda] Rechniewska" (p. 31). According to Stanisław Koszutski, a contemporary in Paris, both Rechniewska and Kutner were among the closest associates of philosopher and sociologist Kazimierz Kelles-Krauz in Paris; Michał Sokolnicki is also mentioned in this context. They frequently dropped in at a flat rented by Polish socialists on Boulevard Arago; other visitors included Bolesław Motz and his wife Zofia, Hieronim Kon, Bronisława Neufeldówna and Regina Przeciszewska.[8] As a socialist activist Eugenia used the pseudonym "Pietruszyńska". In January 1900 she joined the Foreign Section of the Polish Socialist Party in Paris, where her husband was already a member.[9]

Having completed his studies in 1901, Sokolnicki moved to Lviv to write a thesis on his great-grandfather's brother, General Michał Sokolnicki. His supervisor was Prof. Szymon Askenazy, but he also attended lectures by other professors, such as Kazimierz Twardowski. In 1902 he enrolled at the University of Berlin, sending correspondence articles to the Polish press (*Kurier Warszawski*, *Przedświt*, *Ogniwo* as well as *Prawda*).

Eugenia also left university at this time. Her diploma, issued in 1902, confirms that she completed two years of study, allowing her to enrol as a doctoral student (and take the examination after three years) or to study for a degree in medicine.[10] Kelles-Krauz mentions "Kutnerka," his nickname for Eugenia Kutner, in a letter to his wife. He describes a visit to Saint-Quentin, where Bronisława Neufeldówna's sister was living; "Kutnerka" was staying there as well. "She has finally passed her exams, which makes her very happy; she is now a *licenciée es sciences* and has been offered a position for 1000 roubles per annum in a private home in Częstochowa. She is due to set off any day now and in Vienna she's planning to stay with you; she was hesitant, not wanting to make a nuisance of herself – but I encouraged and invited her to stay."[11] He adds in the same letter:

8 S. Koszutski, *Walka młodzieży polskiej o wielkie ideały: Wspomnienia z czasów gimnazjalnych i uniwersyteckich* (Warsaw: Dom Książki Polskiej, 1928), p. 146.

9 K. Kelles-Krauz, *Listy*, p. 268.

10 Cf. J. Hulewicz, "Materiały do studiów Polek w Paryżu i Genewie w latach dziewięćdziesiątych XIX wieku", *PHO* 1962, no. 2, p. 313.

11 K. Kelles-Krauz, *Listy*, p. 649.

> Kutnerka is the only person from the former colony who is still friends with Michaś [Michał Sokolnicki] and it's because of Michaś that she and Motz are on pretty bad terms. But Mr and Mrs Pióro never mention Michaś to her and I also keep to the same tactics, which, of course, is not to say that you should do the same. (p. 650)

It seems that the young woman declined the offer in Częstochowa. In early December Kelles-Krauz informed his wife that "Kutnerka" was planning to stay in Paris for another three months, "studying bacteriology at the Pasteur Institute" (p. 661). From the French capital she probably went directly to Berlin, joining Sokolnicki; it is there that the banns of marriage were published. They returned to Warsaw together, and on 27 October 1903, following Eugenia's conversion to Catholicism, they were married in Warsaw.

Sokolnicki writes in his memoirs that he spent the summer semester 1904 in Zurich and used the library of the Polish Museum in Rapperswil. From there he went to Zakopane, where he formed a relationship with the intellectuals affiliated with the Public Reading Room and Library; he met Stefan Żeromski and Józef Piłsudski. In March 1905 he travelled to Italy and Switzerland on a mission related to the National Treasury [Skarb Narodowy], which Piłsudski wanted to secure for the war effort; next he went to Paris. In April he became a student in Heidelberg, contributing articles to Wilhelm Feldman's *Krytyka*. In August he spent some time in his parents' village, then in Warsaw and, briefly, in St. Petersburg. During the Revolution he was in Warsaw, leaving in 1907 with no legal right to return to any region under Russian rule. In 1908 he went back to Switzerland to enrol as a doctoral student at the University of Bern.

Sokolnicki's memoir suggests that he was alone during all these years. He never uses the plural "we"; what is more, he emphasises his loneliness, for instance when he writes about his time as a student in Bern. The early 1910s are described as "a time of illness and meandering;" he adds, enigmatically, that he was "unsettled and restless," "in the grip of storms – my own and other people's".[12] About his travels he writes:

> Reflecting on the past today I find it hard to explain or account for what was drawing me, once more, to foreign paths, why I left my homeland for

12 M. Sokolnicki, *Czternaście lat*, pp. 371–374.

> yet another length of time, what forces and what reasons kept compelling me to set off on another journey, what restlessness I expressed in these changes of place, the vagaries of my destiny, in this search for something of elusive contours, of unreal content. (pp. 374–375)

The following passage can be read as an allusion to something beyond politics:

> The common Polish diseases followed me on the different paths of my wanderings across Europe. Layers of bitterness gradually accrued from the events I experienced, from unfulfilled desires. To attain my life's goal never seemed possible without liberating my country. [...] this biting feeling intensified in my life, tossed onto the world's various roads, without even a home to call my own. (p. 381)

This period is a white patch in Eugenia's biography. We only know that in March 1904 she was staying in Berlin again, for *Ogniwo* published her correspondence article "Niemcy spółczesne" [Contemporary Germany].[13] In Congress Poland she must have worked in teaching, as suggested by the fact that she authored a two-volume textbook titled *Kurs elementarny zoologii, botaniki i mineralogii* [Elementary Course in Zoology, Botany and Mineralogy]. The book, published by Wydawnictwo Pedagogiczne Księgarni Ludwika Fiszera in 1906, was a great success, going through seven editions by 1921. In December 1906, the Sokolnickis' flat in Wróbla Street in Warsaw became a safe house for independence fighter Walery Sławek, who feared a renewed arrest after a court order had reversed his prison sentence for a failed combat operation near Milanówek. Eugenia helped him escape by taking him from Warsaw to the Russian-German border.[14]

From 1910 onwards Sokolnicka was based in Zurich and practiced under Carl Gustav Jung at Burghölzli.[15] In March 1912 she was accepted into the Zurich group of the International Psychoanalytical Association,

13 E.S. [E. Sokolnicka], "Niemcy spółczesne", *O* 1904, no. 12, pp. 281–282, no. 14, pp. 329–331. The pseudonym is identified in *Ogniwo 1902–1905: Bibliografia zawartości*, ed. by M. Lipska, R. Loth (Wrocław: Zakład im. Ossolińskich, 1957), p. 147.

14 Cf. W. Pobóg-Malinowski, "Niedoszła akcja bojowa na linii Milanówek–Grodzisk", *NPD* 1933, vol. 8, p. 267.

15 A. Wieser, *Zur frühen Psychoanalyse in Zürich 1900–1914*, pp. 193–194.

which also included Mira Gincburg, Jan Nelken and Herman Nunberg. She was a member until the group dissolved in 1914. Her husband was with her in 1910, as he recalls in his memoirs:

> In Switzerland I found myself faced with an entirely new method that was opening up new horizons. In Vienna a professor of the local university, Sigmund Freud, had just published his groundbreaking studies on childhood psychology, on the paramount importance of instincts and complexes, on the roots of mental illness.[16]

Sokolnicki was fascinated with Freud's "ambition to transform the world of the soul, of sounding the deficiencies of contemporary human society," as well as the fact that psychoanalysis promised "mysterious and enticing ways to influence the soul, to transform it, to shape it to correspond to the truth of the instincts, the depth of nature itself," and its "yet unexplored and unlimited therapeutic possibilities" (p. 386). Zurich being "one of the centres of the Freudian movement," Sokolnicki writes, he returned there "several times" (p. 387) in the years 1901-12. It is hard to tell if he was trying to downplay his wife's role in bringing him to Burghölzli, or if he had a genuine interest in psychoanalysis – after all, it is possible that he inspired Eugenia to explore Freudianism. Zurich had been a refuge for Polish and Russian political activists for decades, and other socialists' autobiographies also mention that they went through a phase of being interested in Freud. In 1906-10, the economist Adam Pragier, who had only enrolled in medicine in Cracow to appease his parents, was completing his course in Zurich while also working on a doctorate in economics. He would later write about his time in the city:

> Unexpectedly, I became interested in psychiatry and devoted much more time to it than was strictly necessary. The psychiatric clinic in Zurich, directed by Prof. Bleuler, was at the time the only one where Freud's psychoanalysis was (cautiously) being applied. The docent at that clinic was Carl Jung, who later came to fame. One of the assistants was a Pole, Jan Nelken, subsequently a renowned psychiatrist in Warsaw. I attended a few psychoanalyses, usually as a witness and a few times as the subject of investigation. This was something entirely new, somewhat sensational and heretical in relation to the accepted norms of psychiatry, which was

16 M. Sokolnicki, *Czternaście lat*, p. 385.

> wandering around in the dark, but was, nonetheless, already very sure of itself. On the margins of the psychoanalyses performed at the clinic there emerged among the students (not all medics) a popular sport of mutual psychoanalysis, which meant in practice that we told each other our dreams (sometimes made them up) and tried to decipher their symbolism according to Freud's discoveries; we also caught each other's slips of the tongue and other errors that Freud relates to certain "complexes".[17]

Sokolnicki's understanding of psychoanalysis is remarkably Jungian. For instance, he writes:

> Conscious life was becoming a mere part of great unconscious nature; and, despite all individualistic theories, the entirety of the individual's life, conscious or unconscious, was turning out to be connected, by a general pulsation, with the mental world of generations and collectives.[18]

His memoir suggests that he hoped psychoanalysis might alleviate his political despair. He admits that in his "wandering around Europe at the time, the axis of all efforts was the search of a mental cure" (p. 383). A few pages later he adds: "Above all, Freud's theory struck me as a path toward deeper insight into the self, a chance to resolve my troubling internal puzzles on my own" (p. 387). He was convinced – and said so repeatedly – that Poland would not become independent without a European war; he condemned pacifism, believing its goal was to "perpetuate the existing state of affairs in Europe, which has been built on social violence and national injustice, permeated by the materialism of wealth and indulgence" (p. 119). In this context he recalls a discussion with "a smart and strong Swiss man, [...] Dr Jung":

> In my dream interpretation I came to manifestations of the dark qualities of violence and battle in human nature. I felt regretful about some of the illusions about a clement way of being together, a mutual tolerance for each other's flaws and sins, which are inextricably linked to the eighteenth-century philosophy which had been instilled in all of us. My master guided me mercilessly towards the ultimate levels of logical thinking: in this mutual tolerance, this compliant character, these polite manners there

17 A. Pragier, *Czas przeszły dokonany* (London: B. Świderski, 1966), p. 41.

18 M. Sokolnicki, *Czternaście lat*, p. 386.

> is falsity and weakness mixed with falsity; true human nature, freeing itself, will demand sacrifices; but truth, paid for with sacrifices if need be, is still better than living with the prospect of internal decay, with constant doubt, erring in the dark, not finding oneself and missing others. "But this leads us [...] straight into a widespread war," I replied to this argument, which was opening up before me the abyss of violent resolutions. That's how it is, if there is no other way. (pp. 389–390)

In 1912 Sokolnicki was in Paris; from there he returned to Cracow just before the outbreak of the first Balkan War. He gave up his plan to write a habilitation thesis in Switzerland and interrupted his archival research on Polish émigrés. He also mentions "sacrificing other life plans" (p. 419). Perhaps he was thinking about his wife, who was still in Zurich at the time, when he wrote that he "abandoned human relationships and affairs, sometimes important ones, often dear and cherished ones. A new kind of duty was calling and other issues became the proper task of my life" (*ibid.*). Sokolnicki was going back and forth between Warsaw, Vilnius and Vienna, where he founded a provisional commission of federated independence parties. Recalling the spring of 1913 he writes:

> I was contacted from afar, from entirely different lands, where life was marked by quiet certainty and highly developed cultural systems, with a tempting proposition. This was perhaps the last time in my life that I wavered in the choice of my path, standing at the crossroads between my own personal development and my duty to the cause I was serving. (p. 447)

Could this enigmatic statement be related to Eugenia and psychoanalysis? Sokolnicki's memoirs end with the following words: "These were the meandering ways of my life: on one side of the valley in which I walked there were my personal adventures, my spiritual dilemmas, moods, doubts, nagging disbelief, the sad depths of pessimism, while on the other side [...] there was only this one path, with no snags and no hesitation whatsoever" (p. 464).

Sokolnicka arrived at Burghölzli just before the break between Freud and Jung. When the relationship between the two great theorists cooled, she sided with Freud. In 1913 she moved to Vienna to undergo analysis with the master. The therapy lasted 68 hours in total, beginning on

Thursday, 19 March, and ending on Friday, 12 June 1914, with sessions taking place six times a week.[19] In April 1914 Sokolnicka became a guest listener at the meetings of the VPS. She was accepted as a member in November 1916, two years before Helene Deutsch.

Sokolnicka's biography brings to mind that of another Jewish woman psychoanalyst, namely Sabina Spielrein from Rostov-on-Don in Russia. She was Jung's first patient between 1904 and 1911. Just like Sokolnicka, during the conflict between Jung and Freud she sided with the latter, entering the VPS as one of the first women and working on child psychotherapy in later years.[20] If the two women's paths had not crossed earlier, they must have met at the 6th International Psychoanalytical Congress in The Hague in September 1920. Sokolnicka gave a presentation titled "Zur Symptomatologie und Diagnostik in der psychoanalytischen Neurosenlehre" [Symptomatology and Diagnostics in Psychoanalytic Studies of Neuroses],[21] while Spielrein talked about language development in a paper titled "Zur Frage der Entstehung und Entwicklung der Lautsprache" [On the Question of the Origin and Development of Articulated Language]. This was also Helene Deutsch's first international congress; her paper was titled "Über das Mißtrauen" ["On the Psychology of Suspicion"].

In 1914 Freud encouraged Sokolnicka to move to Munich on a mission to establish a psychoanalytical circle, but at the outbreak of the war she left the city and returned to her homeland. Perhaps it was at this stage that the Sokolnickis' long-drawn-out divorce proceedings began. The dispute was only settled in 1920. In February that year Sándor Ferenczi wrote to Freud that the case was on track although the couple were having bitter arguments about their assets. The court case did not end well for Eugenia.[22] Their separation must have been an annulment, for in 1920 Sokolnicki had another Catholic wedding with Irena Podoska, with whom he would spend the rest of his life. The judicial separation left Eugenia in financial straits, which meant she was unable to continue her analysis with Freud. She would never forgive him for ending her therapy because she could not afford his fees.

19 U. May, "Freud's Patient Calendars", pp. 153–201.

20 See A. Carotenuto, *A Secret Symmetry: Sabina Spielrein between Jung and Freud*, trans. by A. Pomerans, J. Shepley, K. Winston (New York: Pantheon Books, 1982).

21 The presentation was not published, an abstract appeared in *IZP* 1920, no 4, pp. 398–399.

22 *The Correspondence of Sigmund Freud and Sándor Ferenczi*, vol. 3, p. 23.

During World War I Sokolnicka saw patients in Warsaw (in 1914 she lived on Hoża Street 39; in 1919-20 on Polna Street 46). During this time she stayed in touch with the VPS, attending at least one meeting in February 1919. At the same time, she worked to establish a Polish Psychoanalytic Society. On 19 January 1918 Freud wrote to his closest collaborators, Karl Abraham and Sándor Ferenczi, that on Sokolnicka's initiative a new psychoanalytic society was being founded in Warsaw.[23] A notice appeared in *Internationale Zeitschrift für Psychoanalyse*, announcing a group called "Gesellschaft für psychopathologische Forschungen" [Society for Psychopathological Research] that was affiliated with the Institute of Psychology [Instytut Psychologiczny] headed by Edward Abramowski. According to the unnamed contributor, there were grounds for hope that this group would eventually give rise to a new section of the International Psychoanalytical Association.[24]

Sokolnicka and Otto Rank became acquainted in Vienna. Following her return to Warsaw they met several times, as Rank was doing his military service in Cracow. His letters to Freud are a valuable source on her efforts to promote psychoanalysis in Poland. In June 1918 Rank reported that Sokolnicka complained about the obstacles she encountered in her mission, and that she was wondering if Freud might call her back to Vienna. Rank also pointed out what she had accomplished in the short time since her arrival in Warsaw: she had inspired many people to take an interest in psychoanalysis, she organised a lecture series and seminars, and she had also conducted a number of therapies which she described as successful. Rank greatly admired these achievements, especially since he had gained firsthand experience of the "wall of closed-mindedness and meanness" that one had to break through when it came to psychoanalysis in Poland.[25]

According to a note in *Internationale Zeitschrift für Psychoanalyse* of 1919, the society in Warsaw already counted twelve members, all medical doctors.[26] It foundered, however, in unspecified circumstances. Perhaps it was bad timing: Poland's newly regained independence meant that an autonomous Polish administrative and educational system had to be

---

23 *The Complete Correspondence of Sigmund Freud and Karl Abraham*, p. 369; *The Correspondence of Sigmund Freud and Sándor Ferenczi*, vol. 2, p. 259.

24 *IZAP* 1916/1917, no. 6, p. 348.

25 *Inside Psychoanalysis: The Letters of Sigmund Freud & Otto Rank*, p. 84.

26 *IZP* 1919, no. 5, p. 228.

established from the ground up, so that even the most engaged supporters might have decided to postpone the project. Abramowski's death on 21 June 1918 must also have put a damper on the new society. It is possible that Sokolnicka had met the great psychologist long before her return to Warsaw, when he was still a member of the Union of Polish Socialists Abroad. In any case, when their shared interest in psychoanalysis caused their paths cross (again), Abramowski was already gravely ill and barely able to support Sokolnicka in her undertaking. One contemporary, Konstanty Krzeczkowski, remembers this time as follows:

> The last year of his life was filled with tremendously intensive work, without a break, almost day and night. It was as if Abramowski already felt life was leaving him; he regretted every wasted moment. Besides his own work he was constantly in consultations with someone or other, running various tests and experiments. He was always surrounded by people: stakeholders, friends, patients seeking psychological advice, students. He organised reading groups for students, was active in book clubs and at the same time conducted his research and experiments, singlehandedly turning a tiny room into a metapsychological laboratory; he supervised building work and installations at the Institute, gave readings and took part in discussions – tireless, unremitting – he was entirely on fire and was burning himself out quickly. Sometimes he was extremely weary and exhausted.[27]

Perhaps Abramowski did find time to meet with Sokolnicka and discuss the new society that had roused such hopes in Vienna, but no sources survive to confirm the announcement in the psychoanalytical periodical; no newly founded association was reported in the Polish press, nor do Abramowski's biographers mention anything of the sort.

Abramowski had developed an interest in psychology while he was working in Geneva. This discipline, he reckoned, was able to support philosophy by furnishing information on the process of cognition.[28] His first work in the field was *Teoria jednostek psychicznych* [The Theory of Mental Units], written in 1895 and published four years later. He continued to explore the subject, mostly referring to Bergson's theory in an article titled

27 K. Krzeczkowski, *Dzieje życia i twórczości Edwarda Abramowskiego* (Warsaw: Spółdzielczy Instytut Naukowy, 1933), p. 61.

28 See U. Dobrzycka, *Abramowski* (Warsaw: Wiedza Powszechna, 1991), pp. 13–30.

"Dwulicowy charakter postrzeżeń" [The Two-Faced Nature of Perceptions], published in *Przegląd Filozoficzny* in 1898. Between 1908 and 1912 Abramowski worked in laboratories in Belgium and Switzerland, describing his findings in the three-volume *Badania doświadczalne nad pamięcią* [Experimental Research on Memory]. The book appeared in France in 1914, titled *Le subconscient normal*.[29] He also contributed to the Polish journals *Sfinks* and *Przegląd Filozoficzny*, as well as to the French-language press (nine articles in *Revue psychologique*, *Journal de psychologie normale et pathologique* and *Archive de psychologie*). Under the auspices of the Polish Psychological Association [Polskie Towarzystwo Psychologiczne] Abramowski opened the first psychology laboratory in Warsaw in 1910; it was later renamed the Psychology Institute [Instytut Psychologiczny]. A synthesis of his work of twenty years was published in 1914 with the title *Źródła podświadomości i jej przejawy* [Sources of the Subconscious and Its Manifestations]. It was at this time that he tried to establish the first Polish psychology journal. Three issues of *Prace z Psychologii Doświadczalnej* [Studies in Experimental Psychology] appeared between 1913 and 1915, mostly featuring articles by Abramowski and his collaborators, such as Adam Cygielstrejch and Józefa Kodisowa. The second issue contains Abramowski's treatise "Metody badania podświadomości" [Methods to Study the Subconscious]. In 1915 Abramowski was appointed Chair in Psychology at the University of Warsaw.

Abramowski's early work was received with some interest in psychoanalytical circles.[30] Still, his theory decidedly differs from Freud's.[31] Above

---

29 Abramowski's *Le subconscient normal* gained considerable popularity in France; according to Maria Dąbrowska it even functioned as a psychology textbook (M. Dąbrowska, "Non omnis moriar", *NKU* 1958, no. 28, p. 11). Writers who have drawn on this work include Jean-Paul Sartre in *The Imaginary: A Phenomenological Psychology of the Imagination*, trans. by Jonathan Webber (London: Routledge, 2004), p. 89.

30 Reviewing an article by Abramowski published in *Revue Psychologique*, namely "Dissociation et transformation du subconscient normal" [Dissociation and Transformation of the Normal Subconscious], Ludwika Karpińska wrote in *Przegląd Filozoficzny*: "it is a personal pleasure to acknowledge this writer's work especially since its assumptions are based on the work of Freud, whose writings are still hard to come by on the Polish market, although over time they will no doubt become tremendously stimulating for various branches of regular psychology." *PF* 1911, no. 1, p. 117.

31 My outline of Abramowski's theory is based on Anna Dziedzic's work ("Edwarda Abramowskiego koncepcja podświadomości", *KR* 2007, no. 3, pp. 196–208 and *Antropologia filozoficzna Edwarda Abramowskiego* (Wrocław: Uniwersytet Wrocławski, 2010), pp. 123–168). See also B. Dobroczyński, *Idea nieświadomości w polskiej myśli psychologicznej przed Freudem*, pp. 241–250.

all, Abramowski – unlike Freud but in line with Wilhelm Wundt and many other nineteenth-century writers, such as Théodule Ribot, Theodor Ziehen, Hugo Münsterberg or Franz Brentano – did not believe in unconscious mental phenomena, i.e. ones that would be inaccessible to introspection. A process in the brain that cannot be experienced is not a mental phenomenon that a person must become aware of. Hence, Abramowski did not explore the *un*conscious but the *sub*conscious, which can be described as consciousness of a different kind: the subconscious is sensory and non-intellectual but still accessible to the subject in their inner perception of the body, their "self-feeling" or coenaesthesis.

Abramowski had already remarked in *Teoria jednostek psychicznych* that initially, the data of internal experience consists of mere feeling, unspecified and "nameless". Only the effect of attention, which confronts impressions with representations (memory patterns), allows the subject to develop a preliminary orientation in their environment and then to identify attributes of objects and form concepts and judgements. The scope of this attention is narrower than the wealth of impressions that fill the field of consciousness at any given time, i.e. the impressions that make up the mental moment. Intellectual cognition always works to minimise these possibilities and eliminate the openness of the intuitive state. Apperception is the level of closed and intentional systems of thought, of intersubjective knowledge that can be expressed in judgements, whereas the pre-thought, intuitive level is an emotional state that is essentially individualised.[32] Expanding this theory of external perceptions to introspection, Abramowski develops the notion of a latent memory (cryptomnesia). He proposes that what is stored in memory is not apperception (intellectualised memory images) but the intuitive side of perceptions; memory is a collection of all that has either never entered the field of attention or that has already disappeared from it, turning into emotional equivalents. Thus reality "first manifests itself to us in a nameless, emotional, non-intellectual form, and later it is reduced back to it, taking on the shape of memories".[33]

Abramowski proposes the term agnosia to describe the moment when attention is suspended, when mental activity is reduced almost to zero. Mystical and aesthetic states would be particular cases of agnosia. For

32 Cf. S. Borzym, "Abramowski, filozof epoki modernizmu", in E. Abramowski, *Metafizyka doświadczalna i inne pisma*, ed. by S. Borzym (Warsaw: PWN, 1980), p. xiv.

33 A. Dziedzic, *Antropologia filozoficzna Edwarda Abramowskiego*, p. 129.

Abramowski, all that is pre-thought is unconditionally beautiful, "each moment of the suspension of the intellect [...] is also the moment of the birth of beauty".[34] A child perceives the world in a purely aesthetic way, looking at it for the first time, and this is also how we experience all new or sudden impressions as well as dreams and memories. Art is associated with recollecting the unconscious: "A work of art, in the psychological definition, is therefore always a trapped memory," it is a memory which "to a greater or lesser extent has found its lost world of representations and ideas, but never completely".

The distinction between apperception and intuition inclined Abramowski to differentiate between intellectual and non-intellectual consciousness. The latter, which we might describe as subconsciousness, is called "pseudo-unconsciousness" in his early writings. For Abramowski, impressions that go unnoticed, that never transform into a perception but elude the effect of attention, can be described as subconscious. The same applies to memories – forgotten perceptions that take on a nameless, non-intellectual form. He identifies three layers of subconsciousness: the shallowest one refers to states which (in favourable conditions) it is always possible to call back into consciousness; the middle layer stands for those states that become intellectualised only sometimes and with effort, while the deepest layer represents states that cannot cross the threshold of consciousness.

Based on this theory, Abramowski developed the experimental metaphysics that he lectured at the University of Warsaw a year before his death.[35] Agnostic states had turned out to be synonymous with things-in-themselves (noumena):

---

34 I obtained permission to quote from this forthcoming publication: E. Abramowski, "The Sources of Subconsciousness and Its Manifestations", trans. by Michelle Granas, in *Metaphysics of Cooperation: Edward Abramowski's Social Philosophy With a Selection of His Writings*, ed. by Bartłomiej Błesznowski, Cezary Rudnicki (Leiden: Brill, forthcoming 2023).

35 Abramowski never turned this material into a manuscript for publication. His students' handwritten notes were edited and published in 1980 (E. Abramowski, "Metafizyka doświadczalna", in *Metafizyka doświadczalna*, pp. 515–624). In 1917 one of his students, the writer Maria Dąbrowska, published a short outline of his theory ("Metafizyka doświadczalna: Odczyty prof. Abramowskiego", *GS* 1917, no. 70, p. 2). She writes that her synopsis was "corrected by professor Abramowski himself" (M. Dąbrowska, "Abramowski jako psycholog", *WL* 1924, no. 18, p. 1). In 1924 she asks with indignation: "Why are experts not writing about him? Let this equivocal ring of silence surrounding his person be shattered. Where are his students, his followers, his critics? A few reviews twenty years ago and before that, commenting on his books in sociology, is this all that Polish scholarship has gained from its flag-bearer?" (*Ibid.*).

> Original, complete experience is never completely intellectualised – there is always a certain part that does not belong to our mind, but which, however, enters, as a constituent part, into all mental products, beginning with concrete perceptions, down to the most purified abstractions.

Intellectual cognition or apperception is related to phenomena, while intuitive cognition is associated with noumena. A noumenon is the object of pre-thought feeling, a reality that is given in experience, although it is only partially or not at all accessible to intellectual consciousness.

For Abramowski, psychology, being an experimental science, ought to leave behind its habitual intellectualism and turn to "a pre-thought realm of the soul that cannot be equated with what we know as concepts" (*ibid.*). Kant's mistake, he argues, was to build on the false assumption that we could grasp transphenomenal reality by analysing concepts. Speculation, Abramowski proposes, forsakes its relationship with experience, which is why the knowledge it provides is fictional. By proving the existence of a consciousness beyond the intellect, psychology discredits rationalist metaphysics and should – in as far as contemporary epistemology adapts to its findings – bring about the development of "experimental metaphysics".

When Sokolnicka arrived in Warsaw just after the outbreak of World War I, Abramowski was the most prominent researcher in psychology across the Polish-speaking lands. It is unsurprising, therefore, that – irrespective of their shared socialist ideals and the fact that they might have met in the past – she should have turned to him to solicit his support in setting up a Polish Psychoanalytical Society. It is unlikely that she would have contacted Julian Ochorowicz, who was ostracised by the scientific community ever since his presentation on *X*x rays at the first Congress of Polish Neurologists, Psychiatrists and Psychologists. In the meantime, Ochorowicz had also developed an original theory of the mental apparatus; unlike Abramowski, he did not exclude the possibility of the unconscious, which would have made his position more compatible with Freud's.[36]

In contrast to Abramowski, Ochorowicz saw psychology not as a branch of philosophy but as an "empirical science" that "needs observers in

36 For an outline of Ochorowicz's theory see B. Dobroczyński, *Idea nieświadomości w polskiej myśli psychologicznej przed Freudem*, pp. 200–219.

the first place, and only then theorists".[37] In *Dziennik Psychologa* [Diary of a Psychologist], published as early as 1873, he had already made a distinction between conscious and unaware mental processes, insisting that "consciousness is but a passing state of mental processes, but not their stable or inextricable attribute, which means that the general sum of conscious processes represents but a minuscule proportion of the ones of which we remain unaware" (p. 145). What Ochorowicz calls "unawareness" can be seen as an equivalent of Freud's "unconscious" as defined in the second topic: in his later work *Pierwsze zasady psychologii* [The First Principles of Psychology, 1916] Ochorowicz's defines "unawareness" in opposition to the subconscious, which comprises – just like the unconscious in Freud's first topic or the subconscious in Abramowski's work – content that had once already been conscious and that can become conscious once again. "Unawareness," meanwhile, consists of material that has never been conscious and that is very unlikely to ever enter into consciousness.[38]

Ochorowicz's experiments in the field of mediumism made him conclude that there is not only a quantitative but also a qualitative difference between consciousness and unconsciousness. He discussed this in his polemical review of Théodule Ribot's *La vie inconsciente et les mouvements* [Unconscious Life and Movements]. He criticises Ribot for portraying the unconscious as "always just a fragment of our personality, nothing more," and he asks, rhetorically: "And what if it turns out that it is the other way around, that consciousness is but a little fragment of the non-conscious?...".[39] He wonders why all the thinkers cited by Ribot "tried so hard to reduce life to some single form known to the conscious mind":

> And why Ribot, having presented two possible theories – the identification of the non-conscious with brain activity, or viewing it merely as another form of consciousness – did not propose a third as still possible, namely to acknowledge that the non-conscious is a separate entity with types that are as variegated as those of consciousness itself? (p. 264)

---

37 J. Ochorowicz, *Z dziennika psychologa: Wrażenia, uwagi i spostrzeżenia w ciągu dziesięciu lat spisane* (Warsaw: W. Dębski, 1876), pp. 5–6.

38 Cf. J. Ochorowicz, *Pierwsze zasady psychologii* (Warsaw: Gebethner i Wolff, 1916), p. 329.

39 J. Ochorowicz, "Th. Ribot: La vie inconsciente et les mouvements", *PF* 1915, no. 3/4, p. 267.

Ochorowicz clearly indicated that beyond the forms that can become active in consciousness, the sphere of unawareness also contains other forms, "unknown to us, which we will only understand over time" (*ibid.*). This represents an obvious difference between his concept and that of Abramowski, who saw the subconscious above all as a collection of forgotten impressions, a sort of stand-by consciousness, principally accessible to every normal subject, while phenomena such as the ones observed and documented by Ochorowicz were for him, at most, manifestations of "pathological consciousness," of an excessive intensification of normal symptoms.

In 1915, *Przegląd Filozoficzny* featured Ochorowicz's review of Abramowski's *Prace z Psychologii Doświadczalnej* [Studies in Experimental Psychology], published by the Instytut Psychologiczny. In this article, which spans more than fifty pages, Ochorowicz criticises Abramowski and his colleagues:

> They have a very limited understanding of the subconscious as something less important, secondary, always ready to be "created". They still ignore that unawareness is the vastest and richest sphere of the animal spirit, that it contains the prototypes of all forms proper to consciousness – what is imagined, felt or desired – and that consciousness is but the visible surface of these invisible depths accumulated over the ages of animal evolution.[40]

For Ochorowicz, consciousness is the last and strictly human psychological form, which evolved out of the more ancient unconscious:

> If our conscious life appears to exhaust the scope of our life of the mind, then it is only because we do not grasp anything else directly; on closer examination, with an indirect view, it turns out that the conscious mind is only a small part, the last developmental form of unawareness, which encompasses much broader and deeper spheres at lower stages and phases of animal development.[41]

The animal world makes it plain that consciousness is not a necessary condition for psychological phenomena – it is, rather, built on them. We

40 J. Ochorowicz, "Wydawnictwo Instytutu Psychologicznego w Warszawie: Prace z psychologii doświadczalnej, wychodzące pod kierunkiem Edwarda Abramowskiego, tom I i II, rok 1914 i 1915", *PF* 1915, no. 1/2, p. 30.

41 J. Ochorowicz, "Th. Ribot", p. 172.

are related to the animal order by alternative, unaware memory, a sort of collective unconscious, which Ochorowicz theorised in his book *Bezwiedne tradycje ludzkości: Studium z psychologii historii* [Unaware Traditions of Humanity: A Study in the Psychology of History, 1898]. Arguing that history is "a collective psychological processes,"[42] he introduced the concepts of "eternal memory," "inherited memories" and "the unaware tradition". The latter may seem "unlikely, strange, suspicious, unclear, fantastical, forgotten" (p. 221), but it lives in people and exerts a considerable influence on them: "the unaware traditions are stronger than conscious progress" (p. 176). Ochorowicz identified the pressure of this collective unconscious in myths, legends and fairytales: "I am firmly convinced that no one could either spread or even invent such a fairytale that would not be a collage of fragmentary symptoms against the backdrop of unaware traditions. The most original individual cannot but plagiarise humanity as a whole" (p. 79).

In *Pierwsze zasady psychologii*, Ochorowicz proposed the term "synthetic personality," encompassing a person's consciousness, their unconscious as well as their physiology. If a person is a vessel in which a transformation of energy constantly occurs, then there must exist a supreme instance that ensures that the ever-changing self maintains an identity. The synthetic personality delineates the roles of each of the three levels of existence while also welding them together; this process, however, remains unconscious, accessible only during the deeper stages of hypnosis or during sleepwalking. Still, Ochorowicz, believed that it was possible to communicate with it – indeed, that individual synthetic personalities communicated with each other and influenced each other without the participation of the conscious mind. It seems that when he applied magnetic sleep in his practice as a doctor, he tried to address his patients' synthetic personality. He believed that it was this, and not organic processes, that had a decisive impact, and that the healing of the body depended on healing the soul, restoring its equilibrium. The synthetic personality, in his view, mostly consists of strong drives: "its attributes are what used to be called life force as well as what used to be known as healing power, and what we call the instinct of self-preservation, or rather the instinct to propagate the species."[43] At the same time, the synthetic

42 J. Ochorowicz, *Bezwiedne tradycje ludzkości: Studium z psychologii historii* (Warsaw: K. Kowalewski, 1898), p. 7.

43 J. Ochorowicz, *Pierwsze zasady psychologii*, p. 337.

personality is for Ochorowicz external to and independent of the subject, imposing its own laws, directing the subject's most intimate core and ensuring their sense of self-identity – almost like Lacan's Other, the guarantor of the subject's coherence.

Ochorowicz was familiar with Freud's work, at least his *Introductory Lectures on Psycho-Analysis*. In September 1916, when he decided to include his essay "Choroby i uczucia" [Afflictions and Emotions] in the second volume of *Psychologia i medycyna* [Psychology and Medicine], he added a footnote to a passage lamenting his contemporaries' limited interest in the topic:

> I wrote this in 1892. Things began to get better within a few years [...]. Still, this improvement was so slow that even now, 24 years later, Dr Sig. Freud, the creator of "Psychoanalysis," was able to address medical doctors as follows: "Your earlier education has given a particular direction to your thinking, which leads far away from psycho-analysis. You have been trained to find an anatomical basis for the functions of the organism and their disorders, to explain them chemically and physically and to view them biologically. But no portion of your interest has been directed to psychical life, in which, after all, the achievement of this marvellously complex organism reaches its peak. For that reason psychological modes of thought have remained foreign to you. You have grown accustomed to regarding them with suspicion, to denying them the attribute of being scientific, and to handing them over to laymen, poets, natural philosophers and mystics."[44]

In this footnote, Freud appears as one of many pioneers of psychotherapy.[45] Ochorowicz did not consider him to be an important theorist; for instance, he omitted his name in the above-mentioned review of Théodule Ribot's book, where he refers to a number of theories of the unconscious that Ribot, in his view, ought to have considered.[46]

---

44 J. Ochorowicz, "Choroby i uczucia", in *Psychologia i medycyna*, pp. 332–334. The quotation is from Freud's *A General Introduction to Psychoanalysis*, SE XV, pp. 19-20.

45 Unfortunately Ochorowicz's outline of the history of psychiatry ("Z dziejów psychiatrii," in vol. 2 of *Psychologia i medycyna*) ends with Charcot, making it impossible to tell what place he would have foreseen for Freud. The third volume, announced as a continuation, never saw the light of day.

46 The journal's editors compensated for this gap, placing A. Cygielstrejch's article "Psychika podświadoma" – which refers to Freud – in the same issue (*PF* 1915, no. 3/4, pp. 229–257).

Reviewing books from the series "Prace z psychologii doświadczalnej" [Works in Experimental Psychology] edited by Abramowski, Ochorowicz sharply criticised the philosopher's occasional mentions of the psychoanalytical technique. He ridicules Abramowski's "method of associating clouds with cabbages" and dismisses dream analysis and especially the cathartic method as useless.

> For many years I have been performing observations, still unpublished, on how the content and form of dreams relate to wakeful states of life, and I can assure the esteemed director of our laboratory that an open-minded, neutral observation leads us to discover so many factors exerting an impact on dreams and so many types of dreams that to attribute the dreams' content to "pent-up emotions," as does the amateur psychologist Freud, with this erotic bee in his bonnet and his obsession with curing neuroses by "bringing pent-up emotions to consciousness," which, as Mr A[bramowski] assures us, "destroys both the basis and the source of the illness" – is nothing but a shallow and doctrinaire pastime.[47]

Ochorowicz went so far as to reach for the most hackneyed phrase of the time and diagnosed Freud with pansexualism: "the dream is [...] amoral only in the degenerate views of Freud with his erotic obsession" (p. 42).

Ochorowicz, an active participant in the French scientific community, could not have thought of Freud as a pioneering or even particularly important thinker. Being thoroughly versed in the history of magnetism, Ochorowicz knew that all its practitioners, beginning with Mesmer himself, had taken into account the unconscious. His own teacher, Charles Richet, explored post-hypnotic suggestion and discovered unrecognised memories that were absent from consciousness but determined the individual's behaviour. The fact that emotions experienced in childhood, even if they are inaccessible, can give rise to various pathologies had also been discussed by Gabriel Tarde. The notion of repression, meanwhile, on which Freud based his first topic, had already been introduced as *réduction* in Hippolyte Taine's *De l'intelligence* [On Intelligence] in 1870. Ochorowicz was a careful reader of Taine's work; Taine also inspired Ribot and Janet, while Freud read the book in 1896, between the publication of his *Studies on Hysteria* and *The Interpretation of Dreams.* This was a key

47 J. Ochorowicz, *Prace z psychologii doświadczalnej*, p. 60.

phase; he was constructing the foundations of psychoanalysis, bidding his last farewell to neurology and entering metapsychology. He wrote to Fliess that Taine's vision suited him "extraordinarily well".[48] Both Ochorowicz and his French colleagues were familiar with the idea that the unconscious is an active and stable part of the human psyche and at the same time a collection of emotions and forgotten or repressed facts; that the unconscious can in certain circumstances impact a person's behaviour or provoke pathological symptoms, and that these emotions and facts may become accessible by means of suggestion. In principle these ideas overlap with Freud's theory.[49]

Ochorowicz's review of his younger colleagues' achievements, written towards the end of his life, is marked by bitter disappointment about the lack of appreciation he received for his work. Time and again he stresses that he had studied the unconscious as early as the 1860s, before the Polish research community had shown any interest in it whatsoever; he also insists that present-day scholars ought to return to his books. His sharp criticism of Abramowski might be due to his resentment and his deepening conviction that he was a precursor. The same issue of *Przegląd Filozoficzny* that featured Ochorowicz's review also contains a response by Adam Cygielstrejch, who remarks that the review had become for Ochorowicz "an ardently desired occasion to talk about himself".[50] Abramowski, meanwhile, declined to take up the gauntlet:

> With an opponent like this, all discussion is aimless and of no value [...]. To play with common insults, with arguments, for instance, that the only achievement of my research on memory is the discovery that memory exists [...] – I openly confess that it does not attract me in the least. I prefer to yield to my opponent, giving him the satisfying illusion of an effortless triumph.[51]

48 *The Complete Letters of Sigmund Freud to Wilhelm Fliess 1887-1904*, trans. and ed. by Jeffrey Moussaieff Masson (Cambridge, MA: The Belknap Press of Harvard University Press, 1985), p. 172.

49 Cf. L. Chertok, R. de Saussure, *The Therapeutic Revolution: From Mesmer to Freud*, trans. by R. H. Ahrenfeldt (New York: Brunner/Mazel, 1979), pp. 165–172.

50 A. Cygielstrejch, "Odpowiedź (Z powodu recenzji p. J. Ochorowicza o *Pracach z Psychologii doświadczalnej*, wychodzących pod kierunkiem Edwarda Abramowskiego)", *PF* 1915, no. 1/2, p. 141.

51 E. Abramowski, "Odpowiedzi ciąg dalszy i zakończenie", *PF* 1915, no. 1/2, p. 165.

Abramowski also suggested that Ochorowicz's violent reaction itself could furnish interesting material for a psychoanalysis. This is the only documented exchange of opinions between these two prolific researchers.

We should not forget that Ochorowicz, derided and marginalised as he often was in his home country, was considered an authority in France. In 1900 he was a co-founder, alongside Charles Richet and Pierre Janet, of the international centre for psychological research, L'Institut Psychique, later Institut Psychologique International, becoming its secretary in 1906. Ochorowicz's feature article "Hypnotisme et mesmérisme" appeared in the *Dictionnaire de Physiologie*, edited by Richet, in 1909.[52] From 1905 onwards he also sat on the editorial board of the *Annales des Sciences Psychiques*, established by Richet in 1891, and it is in this journal that he published reports on his experiments with Stanisława Tomczykówna in the years 1909–12. These reports were illustrated with numerous photographs purportedly demonstrating the Polish medium's capacity for "photographic ideoplasty"; in 1913 he was awarded a premium from the Parisian Society for Transcendental Photography (Société de photographie transcendantale) for these photographs.[53] In 1912 the Académie des Sciences de Paris honoured his lifetime achievements. In 1923, a few years after Ochorowicz's death, a seven-day International Congress of Psychological Research (Congrès International des Recherches Psychiques) was organised in his honour in Warsaw. The scientific committee included Władysław Witwicki, while participants arrived not only from Poland but also from the United Kingdom, the US, France, Italy, Germany, Switzerland, Denmark, Sweden, Iceland, Hungary, Belgium, the Netherlands, Finland, Russia and India. The event had been masterminded by Charles Richet, who wrote in his introduction to the conference proceedings, published the following year:

> The Warsaw Congress was held under the patronage of Julian Ochorowicz. He was one of my closest friends; I admired his character and talent in equal measure. How thrilled he would have been to be able to join us, here, in his beloved city – finally free, finally truly Polish – and to participate in this congress where his ideas had gained such wonderful consecration.[54]

---

52 J. Ochorowicz, "Hypnotisme et Mesmérisme", *Dictionnaire de Physiologie* (Paris: Felix Alcan, 1909), vol. 8, pp. 709–778.

53 See *RF* 1913, no. 2, p. 48.

54 C. Richet, "Introduction", in *L'état actuel des recherches psychiques d'après les travaux du II*me *Congrès International tenu à Varsovie en 1923* (Paris: PUF, 1924), p. vii.

Ochorowicz and Abramowski, the two Poles whose theories of the unconscious represented alternatives to Freud's model, both died before Sokolnicka managed to establish a Polish Psychoanalytical Society. Ochorowicz, having passed away on 1 May 1917, probably never lived to hear about her efforts, although it is hard to determine when she started her campaign. As for Abramowski, we might surmise that had he not succumbed to tuberculosis, conflicts would have arisen earlier or later on account of the fundamental differences between his concepts and psychoanalysis, which Freud and his followers were treating in an increasingly dogmatic manner. Sokolnicka's mission was doomed from the start. It was not until the 1930s that another campaign would be launched to establish a Polish branch of the Freudian movement, this time by Gustav Bychowski, another one of Freud's emissaries. His efforts would be equally unproductive, although for entirely different reasons.

From Budapest to Paris

Sokolnicka left Warsaw soon after the end of World War I and never visited independent Poland. Still, her practice there left one significant trace in the form of an article published in *Internationale Zeitschrift für Psychoanalyse* in 1920.[55] It is an early example of child analysis, preceding any of Anna Freud's works and appearing simultaneously with Melanie Klein's earliest articles. In 1919 Klein talked about her analysis of five-year-old "Fritz" (her son Erich) at the forum of the Hungarian Psychoanalytical Society. It is there, in Budapest, that the two pioneers of child psychoanalysis must have met, for Sokolnicka, having spent a short while in Zurich after the war, had settled in Budapest. Profoundly depressed on account of her unsuccessful campaign in Warsaw she started a therapy with Sándor Ferenczi, who had also been Klein's analyst (from 1914 until 1917).

Ferenczi, born in Miskolc, Austria-Hungary, in 1873, was the son of Jewish immigrants from Poland. His father, the bookseller Bernát Ferenczi, was born Baruch Fränkel in Cracow in 1830. Today Sándor Ferenczi is considered to be one of the most gifted clinicians in the history of the

55 Two years after the original publication in German ("Analyse einer infantilen Zwangsneurose", *IZP* 1920, no. 3, pp. 228–241) the text was translated into English (E. Sokolnicka, "Analysis of an Obsessional Neurosis in a Child", *IJP* 1922, no. 3, pp. 306–319). I will discuss this article in detail in the following sub-chapter.

Freudian movement, especially thanks to his discovery of counter-transference, about which he wrote in a letter to Freud dated as early as 1908. The father of psychoanalysis soon came to treat Ferenczi as an important collaborator. In 1909 Ferenczi and Jung accompanied Freud on his journey to America; he enjoyed Freud's complete trust almost from the beginning, was one of the five members of the "secret committee" and the only disciple who was invited to vacation with the Freuds.

Unlike many other of Freud's earliest followers, Ferenczi never moved to Vienna. The short distance – just over 130 miles – between the two capital cities of Austria-Hungary allowed him to be in touch with the VPS while also promoting psychoanalysis in medical circles at home. This was no easy task. During his first presentation at an assembly of the Budapest Medical Society he met with such vehement criticism – one member of the audience demanded the speaker should be arrested – that Freud decided the case was not worth pursuing.[56] A Hungarian Psychoanalytic Society was only established in 1913; besides Ferenczi, the earliest members included only one other medical doctor, István Hollós. One of the laypeople in the Society should be named, however, and that is Hugó Veigelsberg, the writer behind the pen name Ignotus who was also the founder and editor-in-chief of the bimonthly *Nyugat* [The West], established in 1908. Ferenczi was responsible not only for implementing Freudianism in Hungary, but, more importantly, also for the remarkably early reception of psychoanalysis in Hungarian literature. Between 1908 and 1939, *Nyugat* published fifty articles touching on psychoanalysis, including twenty-seven by creative writers.[57] In this period, so important for Hungarian modernism, Ferenczi published many of his own works in *Nyugat*. He formed close friendships with members of the editorial team and their associates, whom he initiated into the arcana of Freudianism during long evenings at the Café Royal. Besides the editor-in-chief, his circle of friends also included Dezső Kosztolányi (following the International Psychoanalytical Congress held in Budapest in 1918 Kosztolányi authored a humoristic report titled "Freud szivarja" [Freud's Cigar] for *Pesti Napló*), Frigyes Karinthy (he immortalised Ferenczi in his novel

56 E. Brabant-Gerö, *Ferenczi et l'école hongroise de psychanalyse* (Paris: Éditions l'Harmattan, 1993), p. 56.

57 G. P. Hárs, "Pszichoanalízis a Nyugatban", *MEJ* 2008, no. 1. I draw on C. Royer, *Le Royaume littéraire: Quêtes d'identité d'une génération d'écrivains juifs de l'entre-deux-guerres. Hongrie, Slovaquie, Transylvanie* (Paris: Honoré Champion, 2011), p. 214.

Kötéltánc [Tightrope Walking] in 1923), Milán Füst, who was analysed by both Ferenczi and Georg Groddeck, as well as Gyula Krúdy, Ferenczi's favourite writer, the author of *Álmoskönyv* [A Book of Dreams, 1925], for which Ferenczi acted as a sounding board. By the 1930s, the majority of these writers were distancing themselves from psychoanalysis, but the impact of Freud's theories on early-twentieth-century Hungarian modernism is indisputable and inexorably linked with Freud's first Hungarian disciple.[58]

Ferenczi was also the prime mover and co-founder of the International Psychoanalytical Association. After Jung and Abraham, he became its third president, being elected unanimously during the fifth congress in Budapest in September 1918 – an event he had organised. This first assembly after the break imposed by the war represented the crowning moment of Ferenczi's efforts. His hope was to awaken an interest in Freud's theories among his compatriots and to convince Freud and his followers about Hungary's potential. The discussions, which focused mostly on war neuroses, took place in the meeting room of the Hungarian Academy of Sciences. Leading national and municipal officials greeted the participants with unprecedented pomp. This made such an impression on Freud that he began to think about relocating the movement's centre to Budapest. Eventually, however, it turned out that this moment of optimism did not stand for the beginning of a glorious history of psychoanalysis in Hungary. Instead, it represents the zenith of its popularity.

The development of Freudianism in Hungary after World War I was linked to the violent political upheavals in the region. Following the collapse of the Austro-Hungarian Monarchy, formed in 1867, a short-lived democratic republic was established; the Bolshevik Revolution swept the country, followed by a wave of White Terror, until, in 1920, Miklós Horthy became regent of the kingdom and turned Hungary into Europe's first right-wing dictatorship. In the spring of 1919, the University of Budapest founded a chair in psychoanalysis and a psychoanalytical university clinic for Ferenczi (the order was signed by Commissar György Lukács, later a fierce opponent of psychoanalysis). Ferenczi's department

58 See P. Ádám, "Présentation", in M. Babits, G. Csáth, M. Füst, F. Karinthy, D. Kosztolányi, G. Krúdy, *Cure d'ennui: Ecrivains hongrois autour de Sándor Ferenczi*, trans. by S. Képès, ed. by M. Moreau-Ricaud (Paris: Gallimard, 1992), pp. 7–22. Cf. also C. Royer, "L'invasion de la psychanalyse en littérature hongroise" in *Le Royaume littéraire*, pp. 213–218.

survived Béla Kun's Hungarian Soviet Republic only by a few months. Both the chair and the clinic were dissolved in 1920, with Ferenczi being stripped not only of his position but also of his membership of the Budapest Medical Society. With right-wing forces coming into power, many Hungarian psychoanalysts emigrated to Berlin, fearing repercussions related to their former political activities – Sándor Radó, Jenő Hárnik, but also Melanie Klein and Michael and Alice Balint (or Bálint). Instead of Budapest, it was Berlin that became the centre of the psychoanalytical movement in the 1920s (as I will discuss in more detail in part V). Ferenczi remained in Budapest until his death from pernicious anaemia in 1933 (*Nyugat* published an obituary by his friend Dezső Kosztolányi). Dying only months after Hitler came to power, he was spared the experience of Hungary striking an alliance with Nazi Germany.

Sokolnicka's analysis began in early 1920. A detailed, though one-sided account of the sessions can be found in Ferenczi's letters to Freud.[59] Sokolnicka told her analyst about her three most pressing problems right at the outset. One was her conflict with Freud and her inability to come to terms with the sudden rupture of their therapeutic contract. Another reason for her unhappiness was her romantic attachment to Otto Rank: Sokolnicka had developed unrequited feelings for him when they were both in Vienna, but did not fully acknowledge this when he was single; once he married Beata Münzer, however, she realised just how much she loved him. Most importantly, despite her work with Freud, she had not managed to overcome her most important neurotic symptom and remained unable to achieve full sexual satisfaction with a man, which is why she resorted to "immature" acts of self-pleasure.[60]

According to a letter by Ferenczi to Freud, Sokolnicka blamed Freud for terminating her analysis and thereby precipitating the end of her relationship with Rank. In his work with her, Ferenczi developed his idea of the "active" technique, which he first presented at the sixth congress in

59 I draw on the following edition: *The Correspondence of Sigmund Freud and Sandor Ferenczi*, ed. by Eva Brabant, Ernst Falzeder, Patrizia Giampieri-Deutsch, trans. by Peter T. Hoffer (Cambridge, MA: The Belknap Press of Harvard University Press, 1993), vol. 3, 1920-1933. On Sokolnicka's therapy see also T. Bokanowski, "Entre Freud et Ferenczi, leurs patients: Un aspect de leur correspondance", *RIH* 1989, no. 2, pp. 219–220.

60 *The Correspondence of Sigmund Freud and Sandor Ferenczi*, ed. by Eva Brabant, Ernst Falzeder, Patrizia Giampieri-Deutsch, trans. by Peter T. Hoffer (Cambridge, MA: The Belknap Press of Harvard University Press, 1993), vol. 3, *1920-1933*, p. 49.

The Hague (his paper was titled "Weiterer Ausbau der aktiven Technik in der Psychoanalyse" [Further Development of the Active Technique in Psychoanalysis]).[61] His intervention was to encourage his patient to refrain from masturbating for the duration of the analysis, which led to a transferential renewal of a minor childhood obsession accompanied by an intense animosity towards her analyst. Sokolnicka reportedly compared Ferenczi to Adler and Jung (a serious insult to any Freudian in 1920); she called him a sadist and was on the lookout for his "active technique" in his every word and gesture. Her most important defensive response, however, was to reverse their roles and to start analysing Ferenczi, maintaining that even though she allowed him to help her, any therapeutic success was exclusively hers.

Ferenczi initially complained to Freud that his patient was so bold as to diagnose him during their sessions. For instance, she suggested that he was unfulfilled in his marriage and that he suffered from complexes resulting from his relationship to his overly strict mother – complexes that he was projecting onto her. Be that as it may, it was during Sokolnicka's therapy that Ferenczi developed his theory of "mutual analysis,"[62] a term borrowed from George Groddeck. This concept, which Freud never accepted, hinged on a reciprocal analysis between two persons engaged in a psychoanalytical process; the rigid division between the roles of patient and analyst was suspended, acknowledging that the analyst also learns from the analysand, who is not an object of analysis but an active participant and an alert commentator on the analyst's processes. This working system, which Ferenczi quickly adopted as his own, was all but imposed on him by Sokolnicka.

In one of his letters to Freud, Ferenczi writes how upset Sokolnicka was when he received an "ordinary" lady patient immediately after their session. As they passed at the door, the other lady could have assumed that Sokolnicka was just another neurotic or that she was an analyst in training, whereas she, a student of Freud's, had nothing to learn from "some Ferenczi". The Hungarian analyst reported that Sokolnicka had little respect for her colleagues and would not describe anyone besides Freud as

61 Cf. M. Stanton, *Sándor Ferenczi: Reconsidering Active Intervention* (London: Aronson, 1991).

62 On Sokolnicka and Ferenczi's mutual analysis and its influence on the Hungarian psychoanalyst's practice see P. L. Rudnytsky, *Reading Psychoanalysis: Freud, Rank, Ferenczi, Groddeck* (Ithaca: Cornell University Press, 2002), esp. p. 180.

a psychoanalyst, at the same time thinking herself to be better than her peers. She accused Ferenczi of trying to get ahead of her, criticised his publications and pointed out technical errors in his analysis of her.

Describing his patient to Freud, Ferenczi mentions that she was remarkably gifted but very difficult. He remarked on her pathological oversensitivity and fits of anger (the names she called him included "idiot," "ass" and "washcloth"; she also said he was "characterless" (p. 25)). Ferenczi was sure that she suffered from depression and had suicidal tendencies. She had already tried to take her own life on two occasions: as a child she had jumped into boiling water, and after the abrupt end of her analysis with Freud she had tried to poison herself. Ferenczi identified paranoiac symptoms (she often dreamed of spies; in her everyday life she was constantly preoccupied by what other people might think of her), as well as a homosexual or rather "masculine" sexual component. Her strong penis envy reportedly mostly expressed itself in her dreams (she had "a penis-like long growth in place of each nipple"). Ferenczi believed that Sokolnicka tried in vain to compensate her masculinity complex through excessive femininity (a diagnosis that was often applied to patients of the "new woman" type, as I argued in the part on Helene Deutsch). He concluded that a kind of erotomaniac conceit about her feminine seductiveness had expressed itself from the very beginning; she apparently tried to make him believe that he had been in love with her during their Vienna days, and was quite surprised when he cleared up the misunderstanding.[63]

Ferenczi recounted two more of Sokolnicka's dreams to Freud, asking for help in their interpretation. In the first she dreamed of an older gentleman lying on a couch while two spies stood in the same room. The gentleman behaved as if he were her friend, but at the same time he gave the impression of colluding with the spies. The second dream was set in Sokolnicka's boarding house in Budapest, where Melanie Klein was her next-door neighbour and where, according to Ferenczi, she had only made enemies. She dreamed that she realised that her liquor bottle was half empty, as if someone had been helping themselves to it. She saw many funny-looking liqueur glasses that did not seem to belong to her set. On the couch she saw Ludwika Karpińska, smiling, which made her so angry that she made a scene.

---

63 *The Correspondence of Sigmund Freud and Sandor Ferenczi*, p. 24.

Freud's response to his colleague's questions does not survive, but Ferenczi presents Sokolnicka's interpretation of her dreams, supplementing it with his own thoughts. According to the patient, the gentleman on the couch was Ferenczi himself, because he was the one who was neurotic in her eyes, quite like her cousin's fiancé, who often slept on the couch at her place (here Ferenczi points out to Freud that Sokolnicka reversed the analytical situation, placing her therapist on the couch, as if she were analysing him). Ferenczi also remarks that in the second dream it is Sokolnicka who is lying on the couch – the different Polish surname being a simple case of substitution (it is unclear if Karpińska was visiting Budapest at the time), and that she was the one who was guilty of stealing. In the end, he proposes, Sokolnicka was not quite sure who was ill – she or her analyst – and who was consequently guilty. In a postscript Ferenczi adds that a breakthrough had occurred in the analysis: the patient admitted that her violent reactions against him were rooted in the masturbation ban, and she accepted his interpretation of her dreams.

Freud acknowledged his colleague's work and expected this exemplary analysis to give good results. At the same time he warned Ferenczi about Sokolnicka: "she won't let go of you so soon" (p. 29). He insisted that he must not, under any circumstances, take her along on his vacation, but Ferenczi did just that, convinced that a longer hiatus in the therapy would be impermissible.

The correspondence between Ferenczi and Freud indicates that the Hungarian therapist was doing his best to bring Sokolnicka back into the master's favour. He was perfectly aware that otherwise she would find it hard to work as a psychoanalyst. Friendly relations between Sokolnicka and Freud were, however, impossible to establish. Freud's remarks about her are nothing but cruel: "She has always been repugnant to me, despite her undeniable talent. [...] I don't consider her a paranoia [sic] but a basically disgusting person" (*ibid.*). Her main problem, he believed, was that she failed to come to terms with ageing, and since there was little to be done about that, one could only expect that her "crazy [*meschuggener*] traits" (*ibid.*) would worsen over time.

During her stay in Budapest, Sokolnicka not only underwent analysis but also took part in the sessions of the Hungarian Psychoanalytic Society, which were held in German on her account. As I already mentioned, the Hungarian society was marked by exceptional interdisciplinarity. At Sokolnicka's arrival its members included not only doctors but also writers and poets (Ignotus, Géza Szilágyi), the literary publisher Manó Dick, the ethnographer Géza Róheim and the wealthy businessman Anton von Tószeghi-Freund. (Tószeghi-Freund was a generous benefactor of the movement; he endowed the International Psychoanalytic Press.) Above all, the Hungarian school at the time was characterised by Ferenczi's influence, for instance his fascination with the life and work of George Groddeck; this explains why many of its members studied the mother-infant relationship. Ferenczi himself was working on his most important book, *Thalassa*, which would appear in 1924. Here he suggests that the wish to return to the womb symbolises a longing for the aquatic beginnings of all life.

On 4 March 1920, Sokolnicka overcame her fear of public appearances and presented a first draft of her case study of a child to the Society in Budapest. On 21 November she gave another paper, this time on Selma Lagerlöf's novel *The Tale of a Manor*, but this was not published and is probably lost. Both presentations were seen as confirmations of her talent as an analyst. Her place of residence in the Society's documentation is consistently listed as Warsaw, as if she still considered returning to Poland. It was only in early 1921, after she had quarrelled with both Freud and Ferenczi, that Sokolnicka moved again. Disappointed with her failed mission in Warsaw and aware that her German was insufficient to allow her to practice in that language, she joined her brother in Paris.

Concluding Sokolnicka's year-long therapy, Ferenczi did not consider her cured (for instance, her suicidal tendencies remained). In his opinion it was Sokolnicka herself who was to blame. He saw her as an extremely unpleasant patient with a discomfiting manner, who resisted making any sort of progress during her analysis. Although he was unhappy with the results of the therapy, in his letters to Freud and to the "secret committee" he tried to convince the master that she must be offered some support. He urged Freud to write her letters of recommendation addressed to French sympathisers of psychoanalysis (including Samuel Jankélévitch, a translator of Hegel and Schelling who was at that time toying with the idea of translating Freud's *Traumdeutung* for the publishing house Payot – a project that never materialised); Ferenczi also encouraged his colleagues to refer patients to her in Paris. He vouched: "Intellectually, she has flourished here. She was always very smart, but here she has developed into a capable force in the Society, as well as through her own work and by sloughing off a certain hardness in her character" (p. 44). Ferenczi also requested Freud to persuade Rank to mention her arrival in Paris in the *Internationale Zeitschrift für Psychoanalyse* and to apologise to Sokolnicka for his behaviour during the congress in The Hague, (details about the incident, which had deeply offended Sokolnicka, are unknown). Freud agreed to talk to Rank but he added: "we both don't like her, whereas you evidently have a weakness for this disagreeable person" (p. 45). Ferenczi argued back that he was simply impressed with his patient's unusual psychoanalytical talent. He boldly told Freud that an analysand's unpleasant character traits ought to be treated as dispassionately as any neurotic symptoms (p. 48). He never ceased to prevail upon Freud to reach out to Sokolnicka and offer his support, without which – that much was clear to Ferenczi – her move to France could end in a dramatic fiasco.

The later turn of events rather confirm Ferenczi's predictions. Not being Freud's official emissary to France (a few years later this role would be played by Princess Marie Bonaparte, a favourite student of Freud's), nor even a medical doctor, Sokolnicka faced immediate difficulties adapting to the French psychiatric community, which had barely heard of psychoanalysis at the time. No one in Paris was practicing the new therapeutic method. The earliest French-language articles on psychoanalysis had appeared in Switzerland, and it is there that translations of Freud's works were first published. Freud's American lectures, rendered into Polish as early as 1911, were only published in French in a 1920 issue of *La Revue de Genève*; two years later, this translation by Yves Le Lay appeared in France titled *Cinq leçons sur la psychanalyse.*

The history of psychoanalysis in France merits a digression here. One might say that everything had started in Paris; after all, Freud developed his theory on the basis of Charcot's discoveries, which he encountered during his internship at the Salpêtrière, and he published his earliest works in French. In fact, the text in which he names the new technique for the first time also appeared in French ("*la psychoanalyse*" – the letter "o" was later dropped to form the current term, *psychanalyse*).[64] Nonetheless, France was, next to Germany, the country where Freudianism met with the most stubborn resistance. This was due to the purportedly derivative nature of psychoanalysis. It seemed to borrow from French psychiatry, especially the work of Freud's main rival, Pierre Janet. Other reasons include anti-German sentiments that prevailed after World War I as well as the fact that Freud's concept of sexuality and its role in the inner life of the

64 S. Freud, "L'Hérédité et l'étiologie des névroses", *RN* 1896, 4 (6), pp. 161-169.

individual found no acceptance in France.[65]

The very first French publication on psychoanalysis, *La Psychoanalyse des névroses et des psychoses, ses applications médicales et extramédicales* [Psychoanalysis of Neuroses and Psychoses, Its Medical and Extra-Medical Applications] by Angelo Louis-Marie Hesnard and Emmanuel Régis (1914), was already characterised by an intellectual balancing act that would become typical of many works to come. Justyna Zych describes this delicate manoeuvre as an attempt "to apply Freud's theory to the puritan and rationalist requirements and claims of what used to be called *le génie latin*":

> [This] term was supposed to identify the love of logic, reason, clarity and decency proper to the Latin nations – including of course the French, being their noblest representatives. For many French propagators of psychoanalysis, including Hesnard, Freud's theories were simply incompatible with the *génie latin* and unacceptable to the critical French mind. In their opinion one ought to approach Freudian notions carefully, taking on any relevant and useful elements but recognising without fail and consistently avoiding all manifestations of what Hesnard called *l'envoûtement judéogermanique* [Judeo-Germanic sorcery] […]. It is unsurprising that many passages of *La Psychoanalyse des névroses et des psychoses* misconstrue or distort Freud's concepts and that he criticised the book.[66]

Parisian writers and artists tended to be more familiar with psychoanalysis, which was already in vogue among the surrealists.[67] The group's leader, writer and poet André Breton, had encountered Freud's works in 1916 and counted himself among his admirers; in 1921 he visited him in Vienna to conduct an interview for the review *Littérature*.[68] This meeting turned out to be a comedy of errors. Freud openly admitted that he felt no affinity

---

65 Cf. E. Roudinesco, *Histoire de la psychanalyse en France*, esp. pp. 181–269. For a Polish comparison between Freud's theory with the work of French psychopathologists see A. Dryjski, "Geneza i technika metody psychoanalitycznej", *WCL* 1929, nos. 27–30. Dryjski, too, concludes that "what makes [Freud's] theory of the unconscious stand out is its sexual character. All other elements can be found in earlier researchers" (no. 27, p. 638).

66 J. Zych, "Sześciokąt antyfreudowski, czyli o recepcji psychoanalizy w międzywojennej Francji", *PH* 2011, no. 2, pp. 39–48.

67 J. Poirier, "Psychanalyse et avant-garde", in *Littérature et psychanalyse*, pp. 161–229.

68 A. Breton, "Interview du Professeur Freud à Vienne", *LIT* 1922, no. 1, p. 19.

with surrealism, that he could not understand the avant-garde's artistic propositions and failed to see what links they should have with psychoanalysis. This did not deter Breton and his followers, who often referenced Freud as their patron, even if he consistently disowned it.[69] Until this day, Breton's *Surrealist Manifesto* (1924) is seen as an important example of the early impact of psychoanalysis on literature.[70]

Breton's work bespeaks an engagement with psychoanalysis that predates Freud's general popularity in France, but he cannot be said to be the first French writer to introduce the theme. Here, credit is due to Paul Bourget, the author of the 1918 novel *Némésis*. As Jacques Poirier has noted,[71] it seems ironic that the first mention of Freud's name in French literature is not attributable to a representative of the avant-garde but to Paul Bourget, a member of the Académie Française and one of the most popular writers of his era. Bourget was associated with nineteenth-century realism, and his works, which started to appear in the mid-1880s, soon came to be seen as the finest examples of the French psychological novel.

Bourget had always been interested in psychology (his famous *Essais de psychologie contemporaine* [Essays in Contemporary Psychology] appeared as early as 1883), especially in states that diverged from the norm. In 1913 Guillaume Apollinaire wrote that Bourget "had a passionate interest in the insane".[72] This passion lead him to Freudianism, but since no French translations of any works on psychoanalysis existed at the time, he most likely learned about Freud's theories from his acquaintances who worked in psychiatry. His *Némésis*, the very first novel in which psychoanalysis is mentioned, tells the story of a strange encounter between two ex-lovers, a colony officer and a young countess. Little by little, memories of their romance surface; at the same time (just as in Jensen's *Gradiva*), an archeologist searches Etruscan graves and discovers a statue of the goddess Nemesis. The central secret, it turns out, is that the heroine had an abortion:

69 Cf. A. de Mijolla, "La psychanalyse en France (1893–1965)", in *Histoire de la Psychanalyse*, ed. by R. Jaccard (Paris: Hachette, 1982), vol. 2, p. 36.

70 D. Steel, "Les débuts de la psychanalyse dans les lettres françaises: 1914–1922", *RHL* 1979, no. 1, p. 63. Steel ranks George Groddeck's novel *The Soul-Seeker*, Italo Svevo's *Zeno's Conscience* as well as Thomas Mann's *The Magic Mountain* on one level, followed by André Breton's *Surrealist Manifesto* and André Gide's *The Counterfeiters*.

71 J. Poirier, "Paul Bourget archeologue", in *Littérature et psychanalyse*, pp. 102–106.

72 G. Apollinaire, "La vie anecdotique", *MDF* 1913, no. 396, p. 862.

> The young woman had experienced one of those blows for which one of the most original modern psychiatrists, Freud from Vienna, has coined the barbaric but expressive term of affective trauma. [...] Having observed that such traumas most often result in neurosis, he identifies the entry of an individual who has been tried too hard into illness with the effort with which the artist, the mystic or the philosopher turn away from a reality that is too harsh. They escape into the dream, while the morally wounded person escapes into illness. Freud calls this *Flucht in die Krankheit*. This profound conviction extends to the entire psyche an idea from pathology, namely that illness is but a defensive manifestation of life.[73]

Bourget's collection *Anomalies*, published two years later, contains the short novella "Ma Maison de Saint-Cloud" in which he again refers to Freud's theory. This time the narrator, Dr Courriolles, is a psychiatrist. He tells the story of a poor tailor called Dupin who happens to see a beautiful property for sale near Saint-Cloud. He goes to view the house as if he had the means to purchase it and develops an obsession. Dupin resolves the conflict by splitting into two and creating a dual personality: he is at once a poor tailor in his abject abode and the owner of a house in Saint-Cloud, which he decorates and furnishes in his dreams. Finally he breaks free from his madness with the help of Dr Courriolles. The medical procedures described have nothing in common with psychoanalysis. Soon after being cured, however, he returns to the doctor and tries to kill him, then, stricken with shame, he leaves for the province. The psychiatrist now becomes aware of his guilt, having deprived his patient of an illusion that had made him happy and sending him back to his dismal life. The idea that psychoanalysis threatened the imagination – and thus also literary creativity – was reiterated again and again in the 1920s, not only in French literature but wherever writers were faced with the expansion of Freud's ideas.

Writing his novella, Bourget consulted Prof. Ernest Dupré, who also served as a model for Dr Courriolles. The passage on repression, where the narrator tries to explain the Freudian term in his own words ("It is the constraint imposed by circumstances or by our will on our feelings, and which risks ending in a fiasco"), is furnished with the following comment in a footnote:

---

73 P. Bourget, *Némésis* (Paris: Plon-Nourrit, 1918), pp. 198–199.

> Freud defines *Verdrängung* as the repression of undesirable, painful memories into the unconscious. This repression most often happens automatically or thanks to a kind of censorship, rooted in educational and social factors, which represses […] the harmful elements of affective memory. These elements, repressed into the unconscious, can, in a sort of internal conflict, contend with elements from real, objective life, be it in dreams, daydreams or in morbid crises of an anxious, sometimes delirious nature whose true origin is not understood but which can be revealed by a psycho-analytical examination.[74]

Bourget's familiarity with Freudianism had no impact on the basic themes or form of his works; it did not enrich his characterisations, nor did it alter the way he developed his narratives. He describes his characters' behaviour, then gives retrospective explanations, using terms that roughly correspond to Freud's. We find no interior monologues in his fiction, not to mention free association or the use of dreams (p. 80). Still, his novels were so popular that we can assume that for years, many readers learned about psychoanalysis from Bourget.[75]

Sokolnicka and Paul Bourget met in Paris in the spring of 1922 at the latest. At this point she was giving a series of four lectures on psychoanalysis at the School for Advanced Studies in the Social Sciences (École des hautes études sociales).[76] The novelist introduced her to his psychiatrist friends, Georges Hueyer and Ernest Dupré, and used his influence to arrange a position for her at the hospital Sainte-Anne, where she conducted psychoanalytical therapies for children in the winter of 1922/23. On 26 October 1922 Max Eitingon, who was visiting Paris, wrote to Freud:

> Sokolnicka has enjoyed a superficial and probably short-lived success here. She is a smart wench, you know her well yourself. But she is irritable, moody and lacks stamina; and to top it all: she is all alone, with no support from a man and a doctor and with no perspective that she and analysis should gain a man to stand by them any time soon. It seems rather

74 I quote from D. Steel, "Les débuts de la psychanalyse dans les lettres françaises", p. 79.

75 L. Wachholz, *Psychopatologia sądowa: Na podstawie ustaw obowiązujących w Rzeczypospolitej Polskiej* (Warsaw: Gebethner i Wolff, 1923), p. 115.

76 Cf. *IZP* 1922, no. 2, p. 236.

> unlikely that such a person should emerge from French soil in the foreseeable future, and Russian or Polish Jews transplanted here soon turn very French as far as their mentality is concerned.[77]

Indeed, despite Bourget's recommendation, Sokolnicka was soon forced to leave Sainte-Anne on account of having no medical training.

It was also thanks to Bourget that Sokolnicka was introduced into the circle of writers affiliated with *La Nouvelle Revue Française*. Founded in 1909 by André Gide, Jean Schlumberger, Jacques Copeau and Henri Ghéon, this literary magazine is now recognised as the most distinguished and influential review in twentieth-century France. In the interwar period it was already an important institution of the literary scene. The celebrated critic Jacques Rivière was editor-in-chief from 1919 until his untimely death in 1925 (he reportedly said on his deathbed that the only things that really interested him were love and Freudianism[78]). Regular contributors included André Gide, Jean Schlumberger, Roger Martin du Gard, Albert Thibaudet, Gaston Gallimard, Georges Gabory and Jules Romains; the magazine published Marcel Proust, André Breton, Antonin Artaud, André Malraux, Jean-Paul Sartre and other notable writers. Sokolnicka attended the editorial board's Wednesday meetings and became close friends with Rivière. She hosted a weekly Freudian seminar called "Club de refoulés" [Society of the Repressed] in her flat on rue de l'Abbé-Grégoire, which was sometimes attended by most members of the editorial team.

In April 1921, soon after Sokolnicka's arrival in France, the *NRF* published its first article on the possibilities of applying psychoanalytical tools to literary works.[79] In early 1922, Jules Romains had noticed that psychoanalysis had become fashionable in the capital's salons, and he quipped that after the fad for Einstein, "I'm afraid the coming winter is going to be Freud's season".[80] Psychoanalysis also figured in a hugely successful play, Henri-René Lenormand's *Le Mangeur de Rêves* [The Dream-Devourer]. Staged in Geneva and then at the Comédie des Champs-Elysées in Paris, it presents a tragic love story between a psychoanalyst and his neurotic patient. Many years later Lenormand wrote in his autobiography, *Confessions d'un auteur dramatique* [Confessions of a

77 S. Freud, M. Eitingon, *Briefwechsel 1906–1939*, p. 299.

78 D. Steel, "Jacques Rivière et la pensée psychanalytique", *RHL* 1987, no. 5, p. 901.

79 A. Thibaudet, "Psychanalyse et critique", *NRF* 1921, no. 91.

80 J. Romains, "Aperçu de la psychanalyse", *NRF* 1922, no. 100, p. 5.

Playwright], that he had learned about Freud's theory from the actress Rose Vallerest, his romantic partner at the time. She had been friends with Sokolnicka in Switzerland, and Sokolnicka had recommended Vallerest should see Jung after she survived a suicide attempt.[81] Over the years to come, Freudian themes and terminology kept finding their way into the columns of the *NRF*, especially the texts written by the editors of the literary critical section.[82] Jacques Rivière referred to Freud while commenting on Jean Cocteau, François Mauriac and above all Marcel Proust, who, in his view, was exploring and explaining the human psyche at the same time as Freud. Psychoanalysis was also a fixture in the surrealists' publications, such as *Le Minotaure* and *La Révolution surréaliste.* That said, it was not unusual for surrealist writers to contribute to the *NRF* as well; this was the case, for instance, with the cubist painter and later practicing psychoanalyst Jean Frois-Wittmann (p. 75).

In the summer of 1921 André Gide, encouraged by Sokolnicka, contacted Freud with the proposition to publish a translation of *Die Traumdeutung* in *La Nouvelle Revue Française.*[83] This idea was not realised; the first French edition of a work by Freud was *Introduction à la Psychanalyse* [*Vorlesungen zur Einführung in die Psychoanalyse*], translated by Samuel Jankélévitch and published in 1922. In 1923, however, the *NRF* was able to publish Blanche Reverchon-Jouve's translation of "Trois essais sur la theorie de la sexualité" [*Drei Abhandlungen zur Sexualtheorie*] in an inaugural edition of the series "Documents Bleus".[84]

In December 1923 Sokolnicka, heartened by this success, wrote to Ernest Jones that the growing interest in Freud made her seriously consider whether a psychoanalytical society could be set up.[85] The mission that had failed in Warsaw could be realised in Paris. She had not just established contact with psychiatrists who were sympathetic to her cause, namely René Laforgue and Eduard Pichon, but she was also analysing

81 J. Poirier, *Littérature et psychanalyse: Les écrivains français face au Freudianisme 1914–1944*, p. 36. Cf. also D. Steel, "Les débuts de la psychanalyse dans les lettres françaises", p. 80.

82 Cf. J. Zych, *L'influence de la psychanalyse sur la critique littéraire en France (1914–1939)* (Warsaw: WUW, 2014), pp. 23–34.

83 *Die Rundbriefe des "Geheimen Komitees"*, vol. 2, p. 226.

84 A contemporary Polish overview of the reception of psychoanalysis in French literary circles can be found in Mieczysław Brahmer, "Życie umysłowe zagranicą", *PWS* 1923, vol. 7, pp. 123–132.

85 *Die Rundbriefe des "Geheimen Komitees"*, pp. 319–320.

them and training them in the new technique. Other analysands included Paulette Erickson, René Allendy, Blanche Reverchon and Sophie Morgenstern (a Polish-Jewish medical doctor from Grodno who shared Sokolnicka's interest in child analysis and later analysed and trained Françoise Dolto, a pioneer in the field in France) as well as Jacques Lacan's future analyst, Rudolf Loewenstein from Łódź. Besides Marie Bonaparte, who was analysed by Freud himself, all representatives of the first generation of French psychoanalysts were introduced to Freudianism by the now forgotten Eugenia Sokolnicka. In November 1926 she was among the founding members of the Société Psychanalytique de Paris, where she acted as vice president for two years. Still, Freud's antipathy towards her meant that the role of leader of the psychoanalytical movement in France eventually fell to Marie Bonaparte, a princess who used her own fortune and connections to protect the Freudian cause (in 1938 she ensured that Freud and his family were able to leave Vienna and settle comfortably in London). Slowly but surely, Sokolnicka's influence was curtailed.

The journal *Revue Française de Psychanalyse* was founded in 1927, but Sokolnicka only contributed a few very short notes and one article. Titled "Quelques problèmes de technique psychoanalytique" [Some Problems in Psychoanalytical Technique], it discusses psychoanalysis as a therapeutic technique that should be judged on its ability to bring relief to patients with mental illnesses. The minimal goal of every analysis is to make the patient's life more bearable. The maximum goal, meanwhile, is the complete liberation of the patient's libido; for Sokolnicka, this meant that the patient would become able to make one and the same external object the object of their love and sexual fulfilment; in this way, not only the symptoms are cleared but also the conflicts behind them.[86]

In September 1928, journalist Zofia Kramsztyk contacted Sokolnicka to ask for an interview for *Ewa*. This Jewish women's weekly, founded a few months before, was a sister edition of *Nasz Przegląd* [Our Review], which will be discussed in detail in part VI; Paulina Appenszlakowa was the editor-in-chief of *Ewa*, while her husband Jakub was in charge of *Nasz Przegląd*. The magazine, whose declared goal was to "reflect the opinions, thoughts, problems and aspirations of

86 E. Sokolnicka, "Quelques problèmes de technique psychoanalytique", *RFP* 1929, no. 1, pp. 1–49. Sokolnicka presents a similar argument in "Le dynamisme des névroses et la psychanalyse", published in 1931 in *La Prophylaxie mentale*, the organ of the National League of Mental Hygiene (Ligue nationale d'hygiène mentale).

Jewish women today,"[87] could not have overlooked the growing visibility of female Freudians. Kramsztyk's article, "O pierwszej uczennicy prof. Freuda (wywiad z p. Sokolnicką, znaną psychoanalityczką)" [On Prof. Freud's First Female Student (An Interview with Mrs Sokolnicka, the Renowned Psychoanalyst] is illustrated with a photograph of Sokolnicka, but its focus is actually on women psychoanalysts.[88] Kramsztyk begins by reminding her readers that an earlier issue of *Ewa* contained a brief introduction to psychoanalysis.[89] This is how she explains this editorial decision:

> To gain an exact understanding of psychoanalytic theory is, no doubt, a rather difficult and very serious task. But this difficulty and people's ignorance of this theory certainly present no excuse for the rude mockery of psychoanalysis, or the cheap, stupid jokes, which only bespeak the jester's uncouthness, but which can be heard all over Warsaw even as the city prides itself on being Poland's intellectual centre.[90]

This state of affairs made Poland look bad not only in comparison with Austria, the birthplace of psychoanalysis, but also in relation to other countries such as Germany, "where a major psychoanalytical clinic has been established in Berlin"; France, "where, notwithstanding the great number of opponents, psychoanalytic theory is slowly gaining recognition," or the United States, "from where a multitude of patients are travelling to Europe to seek healing at the sources of psychoanalytical research" (*ibid.*).

Questioned on the medical training of psychoanalysts, Sokolnicka told the reporter that "over many years of practice in this field she was able to observe so many patients being cured that she herself was a living example of a layperson able to practice psychoanalysis" (*ibid.*). Once the analyst obligingly summarised the theory and therapeutic assumptions of psychoanalysis, Kramsztyk returned to her central question: "Are women capable of practicing psychoanalysis?" She quotes one of Sokolnicka's male colleagues, "a very famous psychoanalytical doctor," who allegedly told her that women find it harder to suppress their patients' affective moments

87 "From the Editors", *Ewa* 1928 no. 1, p. 1.

88 Z. Kramsztyk, "O pierwszej uczennicy prof. Freuda (wywiad z p. Sokolnicką, znaną psychoanalityczką)", *E* 1928, no. 31, p. 3.

89 "O czem każdy wiedzieć powinien", *E* 1928, no. 24, p. 4.

90 Z. Kramsztyk, "O pierwszej uczennicy prof. Freuda".

because they succumb to feelings related to transference more easily than male doctors; at the same time, however, this male analyst reportedly admitted that a woman's maternal feelings help her empathise with the patient. "Mrs Sokolnicka, most categorically denying both views, claims that a woman with psychoanalytical training, with intelligence and intuition, is no different from a male doctor" (*ibid.*). She added that wherever psychoanalysis was practiced, women "have made a name for themselves and hosts of women analysts are known to be among Freud's best students". Besides "Mrs Deutschowa, also from Poland," Sokolnicka mentions Anna Freud, Karen Horney, Lou Andreas-Salomé, and others; she also paid a surprisingly warm tribute to Marie Bonaparte.

The last question in this interview was probably posed with a view to *Ewa*'s curious readers: "Does a career in psychoanalysis provide satisfaction to a woman?" Sokolnicka replies:

> In the early years of her career she was completely absorbed in it. Just like any other profession, the art of healing through psychoanalysis becomes over time a question of perfecting one's technique; but striving for perfection, when it is founded on one's belief in the great weight and significance of one's work, renders this effort attractive, and the positive results of one's work provide profound satisfaction. (*Ibid.*)

This answer must be seen as a diplomatic one. Sokolnicka was hit hard by the fact that she had been pushed to the margins; she struggled to find clients and faced economic hardship. A few years after this interview, on 19 May 1934, she took her own life by turning on the gas in her flat on rue Chevert.[91] Although after her death one writer claimed that "she will long be remembered as the first person to practice psychoanalysis in France,"[92] her status as a pioneer was repeatedly challenged. Only her student Eduard Pichon campaigned for the recognition she deserved.[93]

How quickly and completely Sokolnicka was forgotten in Poland is evident from a note in the diary of novelist Zofia Nałkowska and its subsequent representation in a recent edition. Nałkowska only learned about Sokolnicka's death three years after the fact, when she was visiting Paris. She

91 After Sokolnicka's death the *Revue française de la psychanalyse* published E. Pichon's extensive article "Eugénie Sokolnicka", pp. 590–603.

92 *RFP* 1935, vol. 8, no. 2, p. 358.

93 Cf. e.g. E. Pichon, "La réalité devant M. Laforgue", *RFP* 1938, no. 4, p. 669.

writes about the "suicide of an acquaintance,"[94] and she also records a rumour she heard, namely that the retired diplomat Władysław Baranowski, a Piłsudskiite and freemason, had played some role in this matter – he killed himself a short time later. By the 1980s, the leading Nałkowska scholar Hanna Kirchner failed to identify Sokolnicka in her edition of the diary. No footnote gives any background on this Mrs Sokolnicka who committed suicide in Paris, and the only information to be found in the index is that Sokolnicka was "an acquaintance of Nałkowska" (p. 497).

Even if Sokolnicka's role in setting up the foundations of the French psychoanalytical movement was treated as peripheral, her significance for the literary scene was immortalised by André Gide. His 1925 novel *The Counterfeiters* is not just another work of European fiction that mentions psychoanalysis, as Paul Bourget had done in *Némesis* (1918), George Groddeck in *The Soul-Seeker* (1921), Italo Svevo in *Zeno's Conscience* (1923) or finally Thomas Mann in *The Magic Mountain* (1924). Gide's work is groundbreaking in that it gives a detailed account of a psychoanalytical therapy, placing it at the centre of his reflections on the novel itself and using ideas on psychoanalysis to think about literature and vice versa.

Six sessions

André Gide became interested in psychoanalysis around 1920. As I mentioned before, in 1921 he contacted Freud requesting his permission to translate one of his works for *La Nouvelle Revue Française*. He was keen to meet the master in person and was toying with the idea of asking Freud to write an introduction to the German edition of his *Corydon*, an essay in defence of homosexuality.[95] When Sokolnicka arrived in Paris he started an analysis with her, but he terminated the therapy after no more than six sessions.[96]

---

94 Z. Nałkowska, *Dzienniki*, ed. by H. Kirchner (Warsaw: Czytelnik, 1988), vol. 4.2, p. 258.

95 Cf. E. Roudinesco, *Histoire de la psychanalyse en France*, vol. 2, pp. 99–109, and also D. Steel, "Gide et Freud", *RHL*, 1977 no. 1, pp. 48–74.

96 As a clinician Sokolnicka generally preferred short-term therapies (cf. E. Sokolnicka, "Sur un cas de guérison rapide", *RFP* 1932, no. 3, p. 440). In another report she indicates that homosexual men represented a significant part of her clientele. She tried to "cure" them, treating same-sex desire as a neurotic transitional state between masturbation, where the subject represents his or her own sexual object, and heterosexuality understood as the libido's choice of an object that is not only external but also "normal" (E. Sokolnicka, "Quelques problèmes de technique psychoanalytique", p. 34). Perhaps her approach contributed to the failure of Gide's therapy, although no sources survive to corroborate this.

Many years later Gide would often stress that he learnt nothing from Freud that he himself had not already intuited.[97] Indeed, his early fiction, such as *The Immoralist* (1902) or *Strait Is the Gate* (1909), explore how the individual's development is impacted by family structure and early experiences of erotic repression. Although in his journal Gide went so far as to call Freud an "imbecile of genius,"[98] almost all of his interwar writings are imbued with psychoanalysis. *Corydon* (1924), for instance, clearly dialogues with Freud's *Three Essays on the Theory of Sexuality* (the French translation had appeared the previous year), while his play *Œdipe* [Oedipus], written between 1919 and 1930, presents a Freudian reading of the Greek myth. His most important debate with psychoanalysis is *The Counterfeiters* [*Les Faux-monnayeurs*], published in 1925. The novel not only includes a character called Dr Sophroniska, an alter ego of Eugenia Sokolnicka, but most importantly, Gide's fictional little Boris is based on his therapist's case study of a ten-year-old boy whom she had analysed in Warsaw in 1919. In 1927 Gide published the *Journal of "The Counterfeiters"*, a detailed documentation of his sources and the making of the novel. Interestingly, neither Sokolnicka nor her case are mentioned, as if Gide had wanted to erase all traces of this particular inspiration. One source that suggests that Gide must have been familiar with the case is found in the diary of writer Roger Martin du Gard, Sokolnicka's acquaintance from the *NRF*.[99] On 7 January 1922 he recorded a meeting of the "Club de refoulés," which was often attended by the editorial team of the *NRF*:

> Thursday night, a rather interesting session […] at Mme Sokolnicka's […]. She gave us a long presentation on her analysis and cure of a ten-year-old

97 In an entry dated 4 February 1922, Gide writes: "Freudianism… For the last ten years, or fifteen, I have been indulging in it without knowing it." See *The Journals of André Gide*, trans. by Justin O'Brien (New York: Knopf, 1949), vol. II, p. 298. He also wrote to his friend Dorothy Bussy: "To tell the truth, he [Freud] tells me nothing that I haven't already thought, but he clarifies a series of thoughts that remained for me in an undefined state – larval, shall we say". See *Selected Letters of André Gide and Dorothy Bussy*, ed. by Richard Tedeschi (Oxford: Oxford University Press, 1983), p. 67.

98 "Ah, how embarrassing Freud is! And how easily it seems to me we would have discovered his America without him! […] What he especially brings us is daring; or, more exactly, he spares us a certain false and embarrassing modesty. But how many absurd things in that imbecile of genius!" (*The Journals of André Gide*, p. 351).

99 Another piece of evidence is Gide's fictionalised recounting of the same case, which will be discussed below.

> boy from a Polish-Jewish family who suffered from obsession. His nervous disorders resulted from the repression of his sexual instincts when excessive threats were used to stop him from engaging in "onanism".[100]

It seems apt to summarise Sokolnicka's article – "Analyse einer infantilen Zwangsneurose" (1920) or "Analysis of an Obsessional Neurosis in a Child" (1922) in English – before comparing it to Gide's fictional version.

The circumstances in which Sokolnicka's young patient came to her are remarkable. The Polish-Jewish boy, who remains unnamed, grew up in Minsk. Despite the hardships of war, his parents never had reason to worry about his health or academic performance. This changed when the city was taken by the Bolsheviks in January 1919. This event had a profound impact on the family. Their financial situation deteriorated; the boy's grandfather and father were forced to flee, the grandmother was imprisoned and the secret police often came to search their house. The boy started to display obsessive traits, and the mother decided to take him to Warsaw. By April his obsessive behaviour had become so severe that a doctor referred him to Sokolnicka. His initial compulsion had been to constantly stop and check the soles of his shoes in the street; he could not walk more than a few paces without doing this. Next he refused to touch anything, forcing the mother to feed him, to dress him and to hand him all necessary objects while observing a particular ritual. Should she fail to follow the minutiae of the ceremony, the boy would convulse in pain, vomit or have fits of anger that might lead him to bite his mother, to tear at her clothes or even to faint. One characteristic symptom was the boy's use of equivocation, always uttering a sentence along with its negation, such as "give me some tea, don't give me any tea; I will, I will not; I understand, I don't understand".[101] This most basic form of disturbance allowed Sokolnicka to identify the core of the boy's ambivalent feelings.

Using the method of free association Sokolnicka discovered that some of her patient's compulsive behaviours were related to his governess's threat that his growth would be stunted if he was disobedient. His symptoms disappeared when Sokolnicka explained to him that he was not going to be punished in that way. The permanent headaches that had kept him from his schoolwork subsided when Sokolnicka, believing the cause was

---

100 I draw on J. Poirier, *Littérature et psychanalyse*, p. 52, trans. from French by T. Bhambry.

101 E. Sokolnicka,"Analysis of an Obsessional Neurosis in a Child", p. 311.

his repression of sexual knowledge, told him about the facts of life. The next phase of the analysis aimed to draw out the boy's deepest secret. He eventually confessed to his therapist that one of his friends at school had magical powers that would save both families from the Bolsheviks.

Having analysed three of the boy's dreams, Sokolnicka was able to explain that the root of the problem was his repressed hostility towards his father. He blamed him for the birth of his sister and believed that the father was sexually besmirching his beloved mother; at the same time he was envious of the father's sexual prowess. In one of the dreams the boy transformed into a magician whose spell, "Gas, telephone, 100.000 [roubles]" (p. 314) diminished his father's physical strength and gave the boy the power to restore it. Sokolnicka related this dream to the magic that the boy had learned from his friend, and which in her view stood for onanism. This allowed her to recognise the boy's obsessive rituals as a substitute for masturbation. His mother, who had once caught him in the act, had explicitly forbidden it, which triggered his castration complex.[102] For Sokolnicka it soon became apparent that the boy's illness was rooted in a sense of guilt: the last of his dreams suggested an unconscious desire that his father might die in the war so that he might take his place by the mother's side; at the same time the boy believed that his habit of touching himself was linked to his own magical powers and that these had brought on his father's political persecution.

After six weeks of therapy the patient was free of most of his symptoms and was generally doing much better. His mother took him to the countryside for the summer. Sokolnicka hoped to see him again, but he was not brought back to her, which she optimistically interpreted as a sign that he was cured.

The part of *The Counterfeiters* that introduces Sokolnicka's alter ego is set in Saas-Fee, a holiday resort in Switzerland. Edouard, Bernard and Laura meet Boris, a severely neurotic thirteen-year-old from Warsaw. Boris is the child of a Russian student and her former teacher's son. Boris' father died before his birth, and the boy is one of many illegitimate children in the novel. He is in the care of a Polish psychoanalyst, Dr Sophroniska. The Swiss setting allows Gide to avoid an obvious anachronism (the action

102 Julia Kristeva suggests that Sokolnicka was treating the boy for onanism, for which she would later seek treatment with Ferenczi, who also struggled with the same compulsion. See J. Kristeva, "Le contretransfert et les psychanalystes femmes", in *Les femmes dans l'histoire de la psychanalyse*, pp. 98–100.

takes place in 1906, when psychoanalysis was completely unknown in France) and to refer to Jung's theory, which can be gleaned in Sophroniska's vaguely sketched mystical inclinations. The word "psychoanalysis" does not appear in the novel, but the therapist talks about an enigmatic "new method" that she applies working with her young patient:

> Oh, simply in letting him talk. Every day I spend one or two hours with him. I question him, but very little. [...] Boris starts by telling me what he has dreamt the night before [...]. Boris dreams aloud in my presence. Every morning he consents to remain during one hour in that state of semi-somnolence in which the images which present themselves to us escape from the control of our reason. They no longer group and associate themselves according to ordinary logic, but according to unforeseen affinities; above all, they answer to a mysterious inward compulsion – which is the very thing I want to discover.[103]

Just as Sokolnicka's analysis of the boy from Minsk, the therapy presented in the novel is supposed to identify the sources of the patient's neurosis, which lie in his childhood sexuality. Sophroniska notices that her charge gives the impression of being "exceedingly pure" (p. 180) – a motif that clearly recalls Sokolnicka's case study. Both Sokolnicka and the fictional Sophroniska search for "some sort of ugly secret" (*ibid.*) behind their illness, but the most important parallels, however, lie in the details of the patient histories. Both boys – Sokolnicka's patient and Gide's fictional Boris – come from Eastern Europe; their symptoms are remarkably similar, including various obsessive behaviours towards their mothers and an identical linguistic tick of using equivocal expressions. In Gide's novel they are: "Yes, I will. No, I won't," "It's too hot, it's too cold," "Yes. No" (p. 174). Both boys link masturbation to magical thinking, and it is a peer who initiated them into sexuality and superstitious behaviour. Boris believes that it is "magic," i.e. his practice of onanism, that caused his father's death, and his guilt drives him to perform obsessive rituals. Unveiling Boris' secret, Sophroniska also sheds light on the meaning of his talisman, a piece of parchment that he keeps in a sachet with saints' medals. The parchment is inscribed with words: "GAS... TELEPHONE... ONE HUNDRED THOUSAND ROUBLES" (p. 207).

103 André Gide, *The Counterfeiters with Journal of "The Counterfeiters"*, trans. by Dorothy Bussy and Justin O'Brien (New York: Vintage Books, 1973), pp. 178-179.

According to Sophroniska, "these six words were the boys' formula of incantation – the 'Open Sesame' of the shameful Paradise, into which their pleasure plunged them" (*ibid.*).

It was only in 1986 that literary scholars became aware that Gide had taken his inspiration from an article by Sokolnicka, published in 1920 in *Internationale Zeitschrift für Psychoanalyse.*[104] Until then, Boris had been read as an alter ego of Gide himself, following a proposition by Jean Delay in *La Jeunesse d'André Gide* (1956-57).[105] Delay relates Boris' story to Gide's account of his own childhood in his memoir *If It Die…* (*Si le grain ne meurt*, 1926). Here Gide describes his earliest memories of masturbation as well as the sex play with another boy, which shaped his eroticism. Gide lost his father at the age of eleven, soon after he was expelled from school for having been caught masturbating. Delay highlights the fact that, just like Boris, Gide felt guilty for his father's death, which he saw as a punishment for his onanism. However – and this Delay could not have known – Gide also makes a significant change in Boris' case history: Sokolnicka's patient had been initiated into the pleasures of the body by a boy called "Monja" (an unusual name for a boy) whereas Boris' friend in *The Counterfeiters* is called Baptistin Kraft – the name of the boy with whom Gide had his first erotic encounters.[106] In Saas-Fee Boris plays with Sophroniska's daughter Bronja (perhaps an echo of Monja?), whose character is said to be modelled on Gide's cousin Madeleine Rondeaux, whom he married in 1895.[107]

The rediscovery of Sokolnicka's article made scholars reconsider the assumption that the fictional character Boris could be read as the author's portrait of himself as a child. Marianne Mercier-Campiche criticises Delay's work in particularly strong terms, deeming it to be altogether

104 Boris' incantation replicates the one in Sokolnicka's case study. Cf. A. Goulet, *Fiction et vie sociale dans l'œuvre d'André Gide* (Paris: Lettres modernes, 1986). Goulet was drawing on Michel Gourévitch's research as presented in "Eugénie Sokolnicka, pionnier de la psychanalyse et inspiratrice d'André Gide", *MF* 1971, no. 291, pp. 17–22. It is also possible, we might add, that Gide remembered these words from Sokolnicka's presentation at the "Club de refoulés" in Paris 1922, perhaps incorporating notes taken that evening.

105 J. Delay, *La Jeunesse d'André Gide*, vol. 1, pp. 219–289. Jacques Lacan discusses this work in "Jeunesse de Gide ou la lettre du désir" in *Ecrits II* (Paris: Seuil, 1999), pp. 217–243.

106 It is Gourévitsch who discovered this lead. I drew on D. Steel, "Gide et Freud", p. 71.

107 Gide explored their unconsummated marriage in his memoir, *Et nunc manet in te*, 1951.

unfounded, given the obvious impact that the analyst's work had on Gide's creation of Boris.[108] Rather than trying to determine whether Boris really represents young André Gide or if he is simply a fictional version of Sokolnicka's patient, it seems more fruitful to explore if the little Boris from *The Counterfeiters* might not be an avatar of Gide from the time of his therapy with Sokolnicka – in other words, if Boris' analysis with Sophroniska, combined with the case history of Sokolnicka's young patient in Warsaw, might be seen as Gide's portrayal of the therapy he underwent as an adult.

In the novel, the writer Edouard (who comes closest to being the main character of *The Counterfeiters* or Gide's porte-parole) is a close observer of Boris' therapy. Edouard is supposed to be writing his novel, titled *The Counterfeiters*, but feeling blocked, he contents himself with writing a journal and expounding his own theory of the novel to his friends in Saas-Fee. It is through this character that Gide expresses his critique of psychoanalysis. Above all, Edouard finds the analyst's indiscretion distasteful. He often questions whether it is advisable to wrest a patient's hidden secrets from them. For him, the psychoanalytical method is "an inquisition [...] in the nature of an assault" (p. 178), and he suspects that it produces precisely the sort of confessions it demands.[109] He also condemns the way Sophroniska tries to win Boris' trust only to get him "to make a complete confession" (*ibid.*).

It was certainly not out of prudishness that Gide opposed psychoanalysis and its method of wrenching "shameful revelations" (*ibid.*) and intimate details from patients. Rather, his critique of the indiscretion on which the method depends was his care for the integrity of the subject's identity, the subject's right to keep some of the deepest levels of their psyche to themselves only.

Stating that Sophroniska "has succeeded in obtaining a full confession" (p. 206) from Boris, Edouard adds: "The poor child has not got the smallest covert, the smallest tuft left in him, where he can take shelter from the doctor's scrutiny. He has been driven into the open" (*ibid.*). He doubts that denuding the boy's innermost feelings, even if it helps to get rid of physical symptoms, could really cure him:

108 Cf. M. Mercier-Campiche, *Retouches au portrait d'André Gide jeune* (Paris: L'Age d'Homme, 1994), pp. 80–86.

109 A. Gide, *The Counterfeiters*, p. 178.

> Sophroniska goes on repeating that little Boris is cured [...], but I am afraid she is anticipating a little. Of course I don't want to set my opinion against hers, and I admit that his tics, his way of contradicting himself, his hesitations of speech have almost entirely disappeared; but, to my mind, the malady has simply taken refuge in some deeper recess of his being, as though to escape the doctor's inquisitorial glance, and now it is his soul itself which is the seat of mischief. (p. 210)

Unlike Sokolnicka, Gide tells the reader how the young patient fared following his therapy, and as the plot unfolds it becomes clear that Edouard was right. Blinded by her therapeutic success, Sophroniska makes an unforgivable mistake: she thoughtlessly hands Boris' talisman to a certain M. Strouvilhou, the counterfeiter who engages boys from good families in trading with his false coins. Boris is sent to the Parisian boarding school where his paternal grandfather has his lodgings. Meanwhile, his talisman is passed on to Strouvilhou's cousin Ghéridanisol, and then falls into the hands of "The Brotherhood of Strong Men," a gang of Parisian schoolboys. These boys, who happen to be Boris' new classmates, use the talisman to ridicule and humiliate him. Boris relapses into his com-pulsion to masturbate. To stop the bullying he accepts a dare: during a school lesson he shoots himself in the head with a revolver that his own grandfather, unaware of the hazing, had previously loaded. Boris is not the only child who dies in the novel. Sophroniska's daughter, Boris' friend Bronja, also falls ill and dies. Thus the analyst is doubly punished. We might say, moreover, that by killing Boris, Gide not only kills the child he had once been, but he also symbolically takes revenge on Sokolnicka. She is left vanquished. But what is she guilty of, according to Gide?

Pascal Dethurens points out that among the various forms of stealing in the novel, Gide describes a particular variant, namely the stealing of text, or, in other words, reading as transgression.[110] Many key scenes in *The Counterfeiters* hinge on a character discovering the truth, about themselves or another person, through "fraudulent reading" – reading words of which they were not the addressee, which amounts to illicitly assuming

110 P. Dethurens, "L'écriture entre essai et fiction dans *Les Faux-Monnayeurs*: Une poétique du vol", *La Revue des lettres modernes. André Gide 11. L'écriture d'Andé Gide 2. Méthodes et discours*, ed. and introduction by A. Goulet and P. Masson (Paris: Lettres modernes, 1999), pp. 55–79.

ownership of someone else's confession. In the novel's opening scene, for instance, Bernard breaks into a drawer to extract a hidden letter from which he learns that he was born out of wedlock. Bernard then comes into the possession of Edouard's suitcase and the diary in which the writer records not just his literary sketches but also a confession of his love for Georges Molinier, Edouard's nephew and Bernard's friend. Edouard's desire for Georges was sparked when he observed the boy trying to steal a book in a secondhand bookshop. We might also mention that Georges discovers his father's letters to his lover, or the scene in which Sarah shows Edouard her father's diary. We could also see variant of the motif of reading as stealing in the scene where the grandfather gets his hands on a photograph of little Boris that his wife had hidden. In this fictional universe, every most intimate record, especially one that is valuable and concealed with the greatest care, must undergo a sort of violation, it must be stolen and read. The most important thief, however, is the psychoanalyst. Sophroniska surreptitiously gets hold of Boris' carefully hidden talisman and performs a sacrilegious interpretation. Her faith in Freudianism makes her believe that she has managed to uncover not only the meaning of its enigmatic words, but also to master the secret of Boris' inner life. It is psychoanalysis that represents the misappropriating reading par excellence, being a purloining of a person's intimate inner text and a misuse of interpretation.

Sophroniska is not only a thief but also a dealer in stolen goods who indiscreetly passes on knowledge about her patient that she gained by force, just as the boys who distribute Strouvilhou's false coins pass them on as soon as the investigating judge warns Edouard about the planned raid. After all, Sophroniska passes the secret talisman that Boris had entrusted to her to Strouvilhou, who hands it over to Guéridanisol, which then leads to the blackmailing that results in the boy's death.

Thus Sophroniska also turns out to be one of the main counterfeiters in the novel. The wisdom she offers is a counterfeit coin: she promises a cure but brings about her patient's death. The name that Gide uses to conceal Sokolnicka's true identity is also telling: the first part, "Sophro-" (from Ancient Greek σῶς (harmony) and φρήν (mind)) contains both an allusion to her profession as a healer of the soul and a parody of this very meaning.

The intertwining of psychoanalysis with the motifs of stealing and of the gang of counterfeiters of gold coins suggests that in this novel Gide might be settling accounts with Sokolnicka, taking revenge for the theft that she managed to carry out over the course of their six sessions. In a way Gide uses the novel to tell the story of his own analysis, even while maintaining the semblance of a transcription of Sokolnicka's case study of the ten-year-old boy. Gide's representation of Sophroniska's fiasco can be read as his masked vengeance on Sokolnicka, as if she had taken from him a confession, a sort of talisman, a secret related to his childhood and sexuality. In this case, however, the talisman did not fall into the wrong hands – Sokolnicka left no documents concerning her analysis of Gide, nor did she ever refer to *The Counterfeiters.* In fact, she never protested against the way in which Gide portrayed her or her therapeutic method, nor did any of her colleagues comment on her role in his novel. It seems particularly surprising that in 1930, the *Almanach der Psychoanalyse* reprinted the passage on Boris' suicide from *The Counterfeiters*, but Editha Sterba's introduction mentions neither the fictional psychoanalyst in the novel nor its real-life model.[111]

It is remarkable that the section concerned with psychoanalysis is placed right at the centre of the novel, in the part where Edouard talks about his theory of the novel and explains the metaphor of the counterfeit coin that he is developing, even though "of the actual book not a line has been written".[112] It is Sophroniska who introduces herself to Edouard. One day after breakfast she approaches him holding his last book and strikes up a conversation about it – just as he had been "wondering how [to] enter into conversation with her" (p. 176). Edouard records: "Her judgment – both praise and criticism – seemed to me more intelligent than what I am accustomed to hearing, though her point of view is anything but literary" (*ibid.*). In fact, Sophroniska is most interested in the way Edouard captures psychological issues. They both agree that readers usually look for traditional psychology in novels and that it is hard to find a writer who would decide to explore the human mind in a different manner: "'How very little you penetrate into the human soul!' she cried; then she laughed and added abruptly: 'Oh, I don't mean you in particular; when I say you, I mean novelists in general. Most of your characters seem to be built on piles; they have neither foundations nor sub-soil'" (pp. 179-180).

111 E. Sterba, "Der Schülerselbstmord in André Gides Roman *Die Falschmünzer*", *ADP* 1930, pp. 85–99.

112 A. Gide, *The Counterfeiters*, p. 189.

From the moment they meet, Boris' therapy becomes a recurring theme in their conversations about the form of the novel. Edouard puts much store by Sophroniska's opinion, and he tries to convince her about his method. What he envisages is an entirely new type of literary work. But he is only able to point out negative contexts; he knows what his novel should not resemble: he is opposed to Balzac's idea that literature should compete with the civil registry just as much as he resists the naturalists' idea of the novel as "a slice of life". His ambition is not to describe or to imitate reality, as novelists had done before. It is true that he hopes to capture life, but not in the same way: "I should like to put everything into my novel. I don't want any cut of the scissors to limit its substance at one point rather than at another" (p. 187). He admits: "For more than a year now that I have been working at it, nothing happens to me that I don't put into it – everything I see, everything I know, everything that other people's lives and my own teach me" (*ibid.*). But his novel's goal is to represent the writer's struggle with the matter of reality: "My novelist wants to abandon it; but I shall continually bring him back to it" (p. 188).

Edouard has neither a theme for his novel nor a plan or plot. All he has managed to decide on is the main character – a writer – and the title – *The Counterfeiters*. Thus Gide takes the reader right to the bottom of his famous mise en abyme, where Edouard and his novel become an embedded image for the author and his *The Counterfeiters.*[113] It is also striking that instead of writing his work Edouard contents himself with taking notes in his diary of the novel, making daily records of the novel's current shape in his mind – a practice that he describes as a sort of "running criticism of my novel — or rather of the novel in general".[114] Here Gide clearly refers to his own *Journal of "The Counterfeiters"*, which he kept at the same time as he wrote his novel. Edouard's novel is supposed to be at once extremely autobiographical ("in this novelist of yours you won't be able to help painting yourself" (p. 188), Laura reminds him), and to unmask the counterfeiting performed by the subject who tries to record his own experience. "In fact that will be the subject; the struggle between the facts presented by reality and the ideal reality" (*ibid.*). Gide's characters experience delight only while reading what they were not meant to read, when there is a tension between the secret and the revelation of the truth

113 Cf. L. Dallembach, *Le récit speculaire: Essai sur la mise en abyme* (Paris: Seuil, 1977); M. Ron, "The Restricted Abyss", *PTD* 1987, no. 2.

114 A. Gide, *The Counterfeiters*, p. 189.

about its author or owner. Gide uses the very same construction to turn us readers into thieves by letting his own work as a literary writer unfold before our eyes, thus allowing us a glimpse behind the scene.[115]

The emblematic object in Gide's novel is a counterfeit 10 Franc gold coin entered into circulation by Strouvilhou. It comes into Bernard's possession, and he presents it to Edouard at the end of his speech on literature:

> Just hear how true it rings. Almost the same sound as the real one. One would swear it was gold. I was taken in by it this morning, just as the grocer who passed it on to me had been taken in himself, he told me. It isn't quite the same weight, I think; but it has the brightness and the sound of a real piece; it is coated with gold, [...] but it's made of glass. It'll wear transparent. No; don't rub it; you'll spoil it. [...] I thought there couldn't be a better [amateur] than the author of *The Counterfeiters*; and it was to show you that I took it.[116]

The coin embodies the very principle of the novel, which at once creates and confounds the illusion of reality: under the shining gilded surface there is a translucent piece of glass. For Edouard, but also for Gide, to write a novel is to produce counterfeit coins.

115 Several scholars have compared Gide's strategy in *The Counterfeiters* to Karol Irzykowski's design of *Pałuba*. Cf. K. Wyka, "Wstęp do *Pałuby*", in *Modernizm polski* (Cracow: Wydawnictwo Literackie, 1987), pp. 189–219; A. Werner, "Człowiek, literatura i konwencje", in *Z problemów literatury polskiej XX wieku*, vol. 1: Młoda Polska, ed. by J. Kwiatkowski, Z. Żabicki (Warsaw: PIW, 1965), pp. 327–367; W. Krysinski, "*Les Faux-Monnayeurs* et le paradigme du roman européen autour de 1925", in *La Revue des lettres modernes: André Gide 6. Perspectives contemporaines*, ed. by J. Cotnam, A. Olivier and C.D.E. Tolton (Paris: Lettres Modernes, 1979), pp. 233–269 (esp. pp. 245–251). Both novels are basically self-referential, their structure is similar (just as Irzykowski's "Uwagi do *Pałuby*" are an immanent part of *Pałuba*, so Gide produced *The Counterfeiters* along with a *Journal of "The Counterfeiters"*); they also share a concern with the question of dishonesty ("counterfeiting") that is analysed on several levels; finally, and this is most relevant here, the psychological and artistic assumptions of both novels overlap in significant ways with the work of Freud. Just like Gide, Irzykowski often claimed that Freud did not inspire him but rather confirmed his own observations; like Gide, moreover, Irzykowski believed that modern literature and criticism owed a considerable debt to psychoanalysis.

116 A. Gide, *The Counterfeiters*, pp. 192-193.

The critic Jean-Joseph Goux argues that by constructing *The Counterfeiters* in this way Gide tried to indicate that the book we have in our hands is a counterfeit of the "real" (realistic) novel.[117] *The Counterfeiters* exhibits all the external characteristics of a real novel, but under the guise of its plot it secretly calls into question the very form of the novel. Goux also suggests that it is no accident that the crisis of realism in fiction and painting in Europe coincided with the abandonment of the gold standard, which can be seen as a prising apart of the signifier from its economic value or signified. Gide also connected the counterfeiting of money and language to the theme of false paternity. *The Counterfeiters* begins with Bernard's discovery that he is not the child of the man he had always considered to be his begetter, and he begins to talk about him as his "supposed father". Gide quotes Shakespeare's *Cymbeline* in the epigraph to this chapter: "We are all bastards; And that most venerable man which I Did call my father, was I know not where When I was stamped; some coiner with his tools Made me a counterfeit".[118] With these words Gide indicates that Bernard, being an illegitimate child, is a "false coin" himself. He exists outside the system of bourgeois norms and becomes associated with the other youths in search of their fathers in Western literature and culture (Bernard himself talks about Theseus, Telemachus and Hamlet). What is more, Bernard becomes a symbol. As Edouard writes in his journal, "It is to bastards that the future belongs. How full of meaning is the expression 'a natural child'! The bastard alone has the right to be natural" (p. 114). Goux suggests that just as the gold coin used to be a sort of *équivalent général* for objects, so the father played a similar role for subjects. The era of banknotes without reference to gold and illegitimate paternity signifies the transition from a world based on representations considered to be trustworthy, where value is guaranteed by the transcendental meaning or refers to its true counterpart, to a world in which signs (linguistic and monetary) cannot be exchanged for value (transcendental meaning and gold), but where one signifier refers to the next in a never-ending drifting, so that the only meaning that can be gained is local,

117 J.-J. Goux, *Les monnayeurs du langage* (Paris: Editions Galilée, 1984). Cf. also Goux, *Symbolic Economies: After Marx and Freud*, trans. by Jennifer Gage (Ithaca: Cornell University Press, 1990).

118 The last few words, "some coiner with his tools Made me a counterfeit," are missing from the English translation of *The Counterfeiters*. They have been added from Shakespeare's *Cymbeline* (Act 2, Scene 5) to complete Gide's epigraph.

relative and subjective. Seen from the perspective of *The Counterfeiters*, realistic novels – their creation and reception – were legitimate in a world in which people were able to believe in guarantors of truth. With the collapse of this system of references, the illusion of a fiction in which every word has its equivalent in reality and refers to an unshakable meaning turned out to be a mere illusion. This is why Edouard (but also Gide himself) is unable to write a novel that would not be false, a counterfeit.

Goux's argument is convincing, even if we keep in mind, as Derrida has argued,[119] that other writers before Gide had drawn on the analogy between writing fiction and producing fake coins. Gide also has Edouard compare his strategy to Thomas Carlyle's 1836 novel *Sartor Resartus* ("Ideas of exchange, of depreciation, of inflation, etc., gradually invaded his book (like the theory of clothes in Carlyle's *Sartor Resartus*) and usurped the place of the characters"[120]), an even earlier exploration of the idea of clothes as a symbol of language. Just as Carlyle, Edouard aims to portray "the rivalry between the real world and the representation of it which we make to ourselves".[121] Gide's porte-parole writes:

> The manner in which the world of appearances imposes itself upon us, and the manner in which we try to impose on the outside world our own interpretation – this is the drama of our lives. The resistance of facts invites us to transport our ideal construction into the realm of dreams, of hope, of belief in a future life, which is fed by all the disappointments and disillusions of our present one. (*Ibid.*)

Edouard's writing technique resembles psychoanalysis in several ways. When he says that "Sophroniska takes to bits the innermost wheels of [Boris'] mental organism and spreads them out in the broad daylight, like a watchmaker cleaning the works of a clock" (p. 206), he compares the analyst's work not only to Bernard's breaking into the clock drawer in the novel's opening scene, but also to his own creative work as the writer of a journal in which he continually comments on his characters' behaviour. Another aspect that *The Counterfeiters* has in common with psychoanalysis

119 See Jacques Derrida's reading of Baudelaire's short fiction "Counterfeit Money" (1869) in *Given Time: I. Counterfeit Money*, trans. by P. Kamuf (Chicago: University of Chicago Press, 1992).

120 A. Gide, *The Counterfeiters*, p. 192.

121 A. Gide, *The Counterfeiters*, p. 205.

is that both present events not in chronological order but retrospectively. Gide notes in his *Journal of "The Counterfeiters"*:

> Oddly enough, my novel is taking shape in reverse. I mean to say that I am constantly discovering that this or that which has happened previously ought to be included. Thus the chapters are not added one after the other at all; but they are continually pushing back the chapter I originally conceived as the first. (p. 431)

The critic Jean-Yves Debreuille has noted several more parallels between the novel and the structure of psychoanalysis. First, Gide has a tendency to present interpretations of events rather than the events themselves. Laura's extramarital romance, for instance, is initially described from the point of view of her lover Vincent, then by Lady Griffith in a dialogue with another character, and finally by Laura herself in a letter to Edouard. Second, the author often puts his characters in a situation of more or less forced confessions whose mise-en-scène sometimes resembles the setting of a psychoanalyst's office; to tell Vincent about her escape from a sinking ship, for instance, Lady Griffith sits with her back to him, "crouching [...] like an Egyptian statue, with her chin resting on her knees" (p. 62). Third, Edouard's ambivalent relationship with his nephew Olivier and Olivier's friend Bernard recalls the pattern of transference, as the boys vie for Edouard's attention.[122] Finally, we might add, both the writer and the psychoanalyst are dealing not with reality but with the language that constructs it, with a sensitive ear being their greatest asset:

> The poor novelist constructs his characters; he controls them and makes them speak. The true novelist listens to them and watches them function; he eavesdrops on them even before he knows them. It is only according to what he hears them say that he begins to understand who they are. I have put "watches them function" second – because, for me, speech tells me more than action. I think I should lose less if I went blind than if I became deaf.[123]

122 J.-Y. Debreuille, "La psychanalyse en question dans *Les Faux-Monnayeurs*", *SEM* 1994, no. 9, pp. 11–12.

123 A. Gide, *The Counterfeiters*, p. 444.

In the universe of *The Counterfeiters*, Edouard, focused on little Boris, turns out to be a poor novelist, unlike Gide, who transformed the material of the novel into a sort of self-analysis, eavesdropping on different voices, but ones that he heard within himself. If he developed an interest in Sokolnicka's patient, then it was not only, as Delay suggested, because he was thinking about his own childhood, but also because the boy's therapy mirrored his own experience of psychoanalysis, which, though brief, left indelible traces, and with which Gide was trying to come to terms, years later, as a novelist.

A strange history of the avant-garde

The close ties between the literary avant-garde and psychoanalysis in France are obvious and unquestionable. For instance, for the young psychiatrist Jacques Lacan, who joined the Paris Psychoanalytic Society after Eugenia Sokolnicka's death, it was an interest in surrealism that initially drew him to the Freudian movement.[1] Surrealism also became an important channel for the transfer of psychoanalysis into cultural spheres in several Central European countries, particularly Czechoslovakia and Yugoslavia.[2] Czechs,[3] Slovaks,[4] Slovenes,[5] but also Serbs[6] and Macedonians[7] learned about Freudianism thanks to surrealism and along with surrealism. One example is the Czech magazine *Zvěrokruh*, edited by Vítězslav Nezval in the early 1930s, which published Czech translations of Freud next to translations of Éluard, Aragon and Breton;

1 On Lacan's links with surrealism see E. Roudinesco, *Jacques Lacan*, trans. by B. Bray (New York: Columbia University Press, 1997) as well as *Jacques Lacan & Co.: A History of Psychoanalysis in France, 1925-1985*, trans. by J. Mehlman (Chicago: University of Chicago Press, 1990), pp. 3–35.

2 Cf. e.g. S. Jaworski, *Między awangardą a nadrealizmem: Główne kierunki przemian poezji polskiej w latach trzydziestych na tle europejskim* (Cracow: Wydawnictwo Literackie, 1976), pp. 94–96; J. Magnuszewski, "Surrealizm czeski, nadrealizm słowacki", *ML* 1975, no. 8, pp. 47–57; S. Bahun-Radunović, "When the Margin Cries: Surrealism in Yugoslavia", *RDL* 2005, no. 3, pp. 37–52.

3 See *Gegen jede Vernunft: Surrealismus Paris–Prag*, ed. by B. Auer, R. Spieler (Stuttgart: Belser, 2009); L. Bydžovská, K. Srp, *Jindřich Štyrský* (Praha: Argo, 2007); V. Borecký, "Bohuslav Brouk a psychoanalýza v českém surrealismu v letech 1930–1947", in *Český surrealismus 1929–1953*, ed. by L. Bydžovská, K. Srp (Praha: Argo 1996); L. Bydžovská, "Against the Current: The Story of the Surrealist Group of Czechoslovakia", *POS* 2003, no. 1, pp. 1–10.

4 A. Bžoch, "Die Psychoanalyse in der slowakischen Avantgarde des 1930er und 1940er Jahre", *GZF* 2006, no. 2, pp. 197–224; A. Bžoch, *Psychoanalyse in der Slowakei: Eine Geschichte von Enthusiasmus und Widerstand* (Giessen: Psychosozial Verlag, 2013).

5 M. Fedor, *Slovenský nadrealizmus: Anotovaná bibliografia* (Martin: Matica slovenská, 1968).

6 H. Kapidžić-Osmanagić, *Le surréalisme serbe et ses rapports avec le surréalisme français* (Paris: Belles Lettres, 1968).

7 А. Спасов, "Примери на користење на надреалистичкото искусство во современна македонская поезија" [Primeri na koristenje na nadrealističloto iskusstvo vo sovremenna makedonskaja poezija], in *Реферати на македонските слависти за VII Меѓународен Славистички Конгрес во Варшава*, ed. by M. Ѓурчинов et al. (Skopje: Сојуз на друштвата македонски јазик и литература на СРМ, 1973), pp. 147–157.

Nezval explicitly hopedalso wanted to base his new poetics on Freud's theory. It is this wave of interest in Freud that saw the publication of a Czech translation of *The Interpretation of Dreams* (*Výklad snů*) in 1937.

In Poland the situation was different. Polish artists of the avant-garde did not actively reject psychoanalysis, but they were simply not interested in it.[8] This is due to the Poles' particular relationship to surrealism, which never caught foot. Here is how literary historian Jan Prokop puts it:

> To talk about surrealism in Poland [in the interwar period] would be to prove one's lively and creative imagination as a researcher-constructor of the past [...]. There were no followers of surrealism in our country between 1918 and 1939, there was no literary group that referenced the prophet Breton, it was hard to find any more detailed information on this theoretical and artistic movement.[9]

Prokop continues to argue that the artistic community in Poland "cared little about the philosophical roots, the consequences and, generally, the whole theoretical framework of this artistic grouping". At best, we may speak of Polish artists drawing on some aspects of surrealist poetics, such as anti-logical mental connections mirroring the "poetics of dreams" and the free flow of association with sudden leaps from one topic to another (p. 151).[10] The first and rather isolated theoretical affirmation of Breton's programme appeared as

8 Of the many possible definitions of the "Polish avant-garde" I draw on Tadeusz Kłak's, which includes all innovative trends in Polish poetry after 1918, from futurism and formism to the Cracow Group and the second avant-garde. See for instance T. Kłak, *Czasopisma awangardy* (Wrocław: Ossolineum, 1978-79). Despite the arguments put forward by various scholars (e.g. M. Delaperrière, *Les avant-gardes polonaises et la poésie européenne: Étude sur l'imagination poétique*, pp. 18-19), I do not include the Skamander group and their magazine of the same name (published in the years 1920-28 and 1935-39). The editor-in-chief of *Skamander*, Mieczysław Grydzewski, was founder and editor-in-chief of the weekly *Wiadomości Literackie*, which allows us to treat *Skamander* as a forerunner and then an extension of the other magazine. The reception of psychoanalysis in these publications will be discussed in later parts of this study.

9 J. Prokop, "Sprawa nadrealizmu" in *Lekcja rzeczy* (Cracow: Wydawnictwo Literackie, 1972), p. 149.

10 A different view is supported by Małgorzata Baranowska and Maria Cywińska. They argue that these elements suffice to allow us to speak of Polish surrealist poetry. See Małgorzata Baranowska, *Surrealna wyobraźnia i poezja* (Warsaw: Czytelnik, 1984) and Maria Cywińska, *Manufaktura snów: Rozważania o polskiej poezji nadrealistycznej* (Warsaw: PWN, 2007).

late as 1935, when Józef Czechowicz published his "Ewolucja nadrealizmu" [The Evolution of Surrealism] in *Miesięcznik Literatury i Sztuki* [Monthly of Literature and Art]. A presentation of the French surrealists' work appeared another two years later, namely in the December 1937 issue of *Kamena.*[11]

"A TRAVELLING PSYCHOANALYST"

Until recently, Jan Brzękowski was widely considered to be a Polish surrealist.[12] He was a member of the literary group Awangarda Krakowska [Cracow Avant-Garde] and also worked for the group's magazine *Zwrotnica*; in 1928 he moved to Paris, where he edited the journal *L'Art Contemporain – Sztuka Współczesna* (1929–1930). In 1937, Fernand Marc from the Sagesse press published a volume of Brzękowski's poems titled *Spectacle métallique* [Metallic Show]. Brzękowski and Sokolnicka never met. His memoirs, *W Krakowie i w Paryżu* [In Cracow and Paris], suggest that the circles they frequented did not intersect. Brzękowski had few acquaintances in Paris; by his own account he was "known and appreciated only in a small group of poets and painters, not more than one or two hundred people".[13] He surmised: "Age separated me from the poets of Apollinaire's generation, doctrine and apodictic certainty from the surrealists, and from the young ones? I myself have no idea" (*ibid.*).

Brzękowski made one attempt at meeting André Gide, at the behest of Polish theatre director Wilam Horzyca. Here is how he describes his quest, made more difficult by the fact that the French writer had just moved from rue de Varenne to somewhere near the Porte d'Auteil:

> The concierge was unable to give me the exact address; after a long search I found the street she had mentioned, which was more like a tree-lined avenue in the middle of a little park, but, not knowing the number, I was in trouble, as I didn't reckon that other people living in this street would be able to tell me in which house the writer was living. So I started to look around and decided to trust my intuition. One house caught my attention

11 See Z. Ryłko, "Polska recepcja nadrealizmu francuskiego w okresie międzywojennym", *PO* 1975, no. 9, pp. 15–30.

12 Cf. Z. Bieńkowski, "Polski nadrealista", *TW* 1957, no. 6 and "Przypomnienie nadrealisty", *TW* 1959, no. 10.

13 J. Brzękowski, *W Krakowie i w Paryżu* (Cracow: Wydawnictwo Literackie, 1975), p. 291, p. 294.

> as it looked different, more stern than the others; it had something of a protestant spirit. "It's here," I thought and rang the bell at the gate. It turned out I was right. Indeed, Gide did live here, but he had gone away for a longer period of time. This is how it ended, this failed attempt which – I do not recall why – I was not to renew. (pp. 135–136)

There is no remorse in Brzękowski's account of this missed opportunity. Gide was neither important nor particularly interesting to him. He was no more interested in surrealism, which was in full swing.[14] When he met Breton, his attitude to surrealism was already clearly defined. "I had no intention," he recalls, "of adding to the brigades of foreign drudges, those camp followers training behind the surrealists, by establishing a branch of the movement in Poland, the way groups were emerging in Czechoslovakia, Yugoslavia and some South-American countries."[15] The notion of *écriture automatique* struck hims as "the French version of the Romantic cult of inspiration," which he felt "not terribly keen on" (p. 113); finally, he did not sympathise with the group's dependence on Freudianism and unconscious states. In his programmatic essay "Wyobraźnia wyzwolona" [The Imagination Freed], published in *Pion* in 1938, Brzękowski identifies the most important differences between the French surrealists' propositions and his own "metarealism". He rejects *écriture automatique*, which, being based on the psychological processes of dreams, hysteria and trance, evades the responsibility of the creative act. For Brzękowski, alternative states of perception are interesting as long as they are subjected to the work of reason.[16] He applies "the poetics of rigour" to the freed imagi-nation; "the motives of the unconscious function in the framework of the rational world, they do not break through the ceiling set by the poem's construction, they inspire visualisation, but there their power ends".[17] Researchers agree that Brzękowski's aim was "to rationalise the unconscious" and "to maintain – on the level of the poem – a balance between

14 Brzękowski arrived in Paris right between the publications of the first and the second surrealist manifestos. See W.P. Szymański, *Neosymbolizm: O awangardowej poezji polskiej w latach trzydziestych* (Cracow: Wydawnictwo Literackie, 1973), p. 109.

15 J. Brzękowski, *W Krakowie i w Paryżu*, p. 165.

16 See U. Klatka, *Wyobraźnia w czasie: O poezji Jana Brzękowskiego* (Cracow: Collegium Columbinum, 2012), p. 37.

17 J. Prokop, "Sprawa nadrealizmu", p. 154.

'revealing' and 'constructing'".[18] This accounts for the particular tension that marks his work: the lyrical subject distances itself from its own role as the protagonist of unconscious desires.[19]

Brzękowski moved to Paris in 1928, the year that his debut, the novel *Psychoanalityk w podróży* [A Travelling Psychoanalyst], was published in Poland.[20] The main character is Zygmunt, a poet and editor of a literary magazine who feels misunderstood and struggles to make important life decisions.[21] His later works include the novels *Bankructwo profesora Muellera* [Professor Mueller's Bankruptcy] (1932) and *24 kochanków Perdity Loost* [24 Lovers of Perdita Loost] (1961).[22] According to Urszula Klatka, Brzękowski never mentions Freud – neither in his published works, nor in his manuscripts (archived at the Museum of Literature in Warsaw and the Polish Library in Paris) or his voluminous correspondence (from 1927 to 1970) with poet Julian Przyboś. It is unclear, therefore, what inspired the reference to psychoanalysis in his first novel's title. Most likely he first heard about Freud from Witkacy. They met in Zakopane in 1925 and went on to have a brief but intense exchange, documented in a discussion on the theory of pure form in *Głos Zakopiański*.[23]

Witkacy's work had a significant impact on Brzękowski's novel, written between 1922 and 1925. In fact, "A Travelling Psychoanalyst" brings to

18 "A.K. Waśkiewicz, "'Płynnymi dłońmi rozsnuwam twą nagość...': (o erotyce Awangardy krakowskiej)", *T* 1974, no. 1, p. 119.

19 Cf. U. Klatka, *Wyobraźnia w czasie*, p. 68.

20 J. Brzękowski, *Psychoanalityk w podróży* (Warsaw: Księgarnia F. Hoesicka, 1929 [1928]).

21 Brzękowski's novel first appeared in instalments in *Zwrotnica* with the subtitle "Fragments of a Cine-Novel" [Fragmenty powieści filmowej].

22 On Brzękowski's prose see A. Madej, "O filmowej powieści Jana Brzękowskiego", in *Film, sztuka i ideologia*, ed. by J. Trznadlowski (Wrocław: Uniwersytet Wrocławski, 1981), pp. 113–126; T. Kłak, "Filmowa powieść Jana Brzękowskiego (o *Bankructwie profesora Muellera*)", in *Katastrofizm i awangarda*, ed. by T. Bujnicki and T. Kłak (Katowice: Uniwersytet Śląski, 1979), pp. 89–102; A.K. Waśkiewicz, *W kręgu futuryzmu i awangardy* (Wrocław: Atut, 2003), pp. 219–231; A. Wójtowicz, "'Miłość' i cała 'reszta': *24 kochanków Perdity Loost* Jana Brzękowskiego", *PH* 2008, no. 4, pp. 39–57; A. Wójtowicz, *Cogito i "sejsmograf podświadomości": Proza Pierwszej Awangardy* (Lublin: UMCS, 2010); P. Majerski, "Boczny tor awangardowego eksperymentu (O powieściach Jana Brzękowskiego)", *RL* 1999, no. 6, pp. 649–662.

23 J. Brzękowski, "Teoria czystej formy", *GZ* 1925, no. 29, p. 2; S. I. Witkiewicz, "Odpowiedź", *GZ* no. 30, p. 2; J. Brzękowski, "Odpowiedź na odpowiedź", *GZ* no. 31, p. 3.

mind Witkacy's concept of the novel as "a bag into which, without paying any attention to pure form, you can cram everything".[24] Each chapter uses a different genre convention to tell Zygmunt's story. Models include the traditional novel set in a Polish country manor (*powieść szlachecka*), typically recounting a young nobleman's return to the family estate; the sensational detective novel, and finally the cine-novel (*powieść filmowa*) invented by Brzękowski himself. "A Travelling Psychoanalyst" also contains self-referential passages on the future of the novel, attributed to a character called Józef Then, who openly references Witkacy's concept:

> And our novel? A rubbish bin of socio-moralistic tendencies and pornography. Generally speaking we might agree with S. I. Witkiewicz that we shouldn't consider it to be art. Indeed. We are being inundated with reading material suitable for a railway carriage or a pillow at best. Sensation, pornography and rodomontade – these are the principal traits of the contemporary novel. [...]
> – So you reject the novel as a whole, as a work of art? – Zygmunt asked.
> – No. But I believe this is where we're going to end up soon. No one reads artistic novels nowadays. [...]
> – And why is that?...
> – A fallacious understanding of democracy. We're not cultured enough to allow ourselves to be democratic.[25]

Aleksander Wójtowicz suggests that "A Travelling Psychoanalyst" is an avant-garde psychological novel that polemicises with or parodies the *Künstlerroman* of the Young Poland era.[26] I would argue, however, that Brzękowski offers a continuation of Irzykowski's strategy as developed in

24 Witkacy's term *powieść-worek*, translatable as "novel-sack," appears in his "'Wniebowstąpienie' J.M. Rytarda," in *Bez kompromisu* (Warsaw: PIW, 1976), p. 150. I draw on Daniel C. Gerould, *Witkacy: Stanisław Ignacy Witkiewicz as an Imaginative Writer* (Seattle: University of Washington Press, 1981), pp. 268-269. Włodzimierz Bolecki, *Poetycki model prozy w dwudziestoleciu międzywojennym: Witkacy – Gombrowicz – Schulz i inni. Studium z poetyki historycznej* (Cracow: Universitas, 1996), pp. 27-55. See also P. Majerski, "Boczny tor awangardowego eksperymentu", p. 662. K. Jakowska compares the strategies developed by Witkacy and Brzękowski in *Powrót autora: Renesans narracji auktorialnej w polskiej powieści międzywojennej* (Wrocław: Zakład Narodowy im. Ossolińskich, 1983), pp. 69–75.

25 J. Brzękowski, *Psychoanalityk w podróży*, pp. 68–69.

26 A. Wójtowicz, *Cogito i "sejsmograf podświadomości"*, p. 33.

Pałuba, writing "a novel as a critique of the novel".[27] The reference point for his fiction is the conventionalised reality of literature, a reality that is at the same time a falsification, from which the author selects some of the available conventional plot elements. Throughout the novel (which opens with the words "It begins like this:") the narrator plays games with his readers. Recurring parentheses with commentaries suggest his parodic stance towards his own story, and in the end he highlights its fictionality by offering two alternative endings, asking readers to cast their vote.[28] Just as with Irzykowski, Brzękowski is interested in the variability and blurriness of mental processes associated with emotions. This is particularly evident in his last novel, "24 Lovers of Perdita Loost", where Brzękowski – drawing on Irzykowski – places words such as "love" in quotation marks.

Notwithstanding Brzękowski's protests, critics have described "A Travelling Psychoanalyst" as the first Polish psychoanalytical novel.[29] As Aleksander Wójtowicz argues, however, Brzękowski's interest in the inner life of his characters does not mean that he uses the instruments of psychoanalysis, which the Polish avant-garde regarded with "a lot of suspiciousness and sometimes with undisguised aversion".[30] According to Urszula Klatka, "the elaborate layer of Perdita's or Zygmunt's psychology is based on conventional elements, for in most characters the author forgoes a deeper psychological analysis for the benefit of a distinctive type. This reduction of the characters' inner life reflects how Freudianism, which was fashionable at the time, was popularly understood".[31] In "A Travelling Psychoanalyst" Brzękowski frequently distances himself from the strategies of the psychological novel, pronouncing its crisis through his protagonist Józef Then:

> The realistic and naturalistic or psychological novel has given rise to a meticulousness whose secondary results are: long-windedness and the disappearance of important and interesting elements in a deluge of banalities. [...]

27 On the parallels between *Pałuba* and the avant-garde writers' prose experiments see K. Jakowska, *Powrót autora*, p. 74. Discussing *Psychoanalityk w podróży* she points out that "the avant-garde writers' self-referentiality had its roots in the art of the Young Poland movement;" she suggests that in this respect the avant-gardists were "essentially epigones".

28 Cf. A.K. Waśkiewicz, *W kręgu futuryzmu i awangardy*, p. 221.

29 Cf. A.K. Waśkiewicz, "Proza Brzękowskiego", *TW* 1967, no. 12, p. 160.

30 A. Wójtowicz, "'Miłość' i cała 'reszta'", p. 43.

31 U. Klatka, *Wyobraźnia w czasie*, p. 46.

> I'm not surprised that you cannot read 400 pages of psychology […]. A novel cannot be poetry for more than 20 pages […], it cannot be purely psychological for more than 40 pages […] nor sensational for more than 100 pages […]. Three hundred pages maintained in the same formal type are proof of the author's stylistic impoverishment. […] An author's so-called style, essentially stable and unchangeable, is at odds with progress and the twentieth century. Every accumulation of emotion, feeling or fact ought to find the meaning of its own uniqueness not only in the ensemble of the words that express it, but, more powerfully, in their mutual relationship in an artistic form. Formal variety allows one to focus one's thoughts. It enhances the power of one's aesthetic sensibility. It excites one's interest. Formal variety in relation to construction, understood as a unity, symbolises a monistic worldview. And above all: it is the form of the future. The novel should consist of separate formal parts, like a sonata, for instance.[32]

Later in this manifesto-like passage, Then takes a stance against so-called "psychological consistency," which "is possible only with reference to certain moments; with reference to the novel as a whole it is absurd".[33]

In Brzękowski's own words, there is "not an iota of psychoanalysis" in his novel.[34] This would mean that the title is a seemingly random surrealist ploy, "opening the work's meaning up to all possible interpretations, inviting dreams and free associations, submitting to the ludic game of signification and not just refusing to provide readers with information, but purposefully deceiving us".[35] Another trail is, of course, the protagonist's first name, Zygmunt (the Polish version of Sigmund and the one that used to appear in

---

32 J. Brzękowski, *Psychoanalityk w podróży*, pp. 70–71. According to Ewa Szary-Matywiecka, "what the writer [Józef Then] demands of the novelist is the same thing that the actual author, the writer J. Brzękowski, already performs in "A Travelling Psychoanalyst". Through the content and style of the subsequent parts of the novel Brzękowski exemplifies the theses about the novel that are presented discursively within this very novel". See E. Szary-Matywiecka, *Książka–powieść–autotematyzm (od „Pałuby" do „Jedynego wyjścia")* (Wrocław: Zakład Narodowy im. Ossolińskich, 1979), p. 137. Anna Łebkowska considers this to be the weakness of Brzękowski's project: "Brzękowski's novel […], having performed the first *pas*, freezes in a traditional shape". See A. Łebkowska, *Fikcja jako możliwość: Z przemian prozy XX wieku* (Cracow: Universitas, 1998), p. 24.

33 J. Brzękowski, *Psychoanalityk w podróży*, p. 73.

34 A.K. Waśkiewicz, "Od eksperymentu formalnego do powieści – studium moralnego (rozmowa z Janem Brzękowskim)", *NU* 1969, no. 1, p. 22.

35 H. Béhar, "Lieux-dits: les titres surréalistes", *Mélusine*, no. 4, 1983, p. 79.

Polish publications of Freud's work). Perhaps this association with Freud explains why this novel, which presents the peregrinations of the unfulfilled writer Zygmunt, was given the title "A Travelling Psychoanalyst". Aleksander Wójtowicz suggests that the novel was designed to be analogous to a visual artist's collage, whereby "the psychoanalyst's journey" would be a metaphor for Brzękowski's writing method. As is the case with collages, Wójtowicz argues, the title functions as a "constructional tie" revealing the author's intentions: "The juxtaposition of two conventions – the psychological one and the one of travel writing – takes place under the auspices of his polemical stance towards the models [Brzękowski] emulates, but this juxtaposition also contains an element of 'an affirmative programme'".[36]

The only episode in the plot that allows us to associate Zygmunt's journey with Freudianism is when he is committed to a psychiatric clinic because he starts having hallucinations. The advocate of Freudian methods is an unnamed professor with the diabolical attribute of "a sharp, greying beard".[37] He suggests that Zygmunt might be afflicted with "neurasthenic-hysterical phobia"; he places him under observation and indicates that "if paranoia is confirmed, we can try psychoanalysis" (*ibid.*).

Fearing he might be pronounced mad, Zygmunt never tells the doctors about his visions. Brzękowski presents a typical dialogue with Dr Günter:

> – How are you feeling?– Excellent, Doctor.
> – Is our therapy doing you good?
> – Wonderful.
> – Hydropathy?
> – A marvellous cure for the nerves.
> – And your old anxieties, are they still bothering you?
> – They disappeared about a week ago. (p. 192)

The doctor tries hard to obtain a confession, as he plans to describe Zygmunt's case in a scientific journal. He already thinks up "compelling titles" for his article, and feels excited anticipating "the impression he is about to make on his colleagues" (p. 193). Zygmunt, fully aware of this, fantasises about murdering his psychiatrist, but he soon falls into a state of apathy, which the doctor finds to be "of little interest from a psychological point of view" (p. 194). After three months, Zygmunt is pronounced to have

36 A. Wójtowicz, "'Miłość' i cała 'reszta'", p. 54.

37 J. Brzękowski, *Psychoanalityk w podróży*, p. 191.

recovered. He leaves the clinic and returns to his first love, Irena. However, the idyll is not to last: the war breaks out and Zygmunt is sent to the eastern front, where he becomes a pilot and survives a major accident.

Brzękowski proposes two alternative endings. In the first Zygmunt is released from the army and makes a career in banking, but he is soon hit by a car and this time the accident is fatal. The second ending shows Zygmunt recovering physically from his airplane crash, but his mental constitution remains frail. He does not go mad, but he suffers nervous attacks that, once again, leave the doctors helpless. As had been the case before, they struggle to diagnose Zygmunt, considering both amentia and paranoia; "there were also some who suggested a skull shock and the possibility of *melancholia paralytica* on account of his sudden fits of fainting (Westphal disease) as well as apathy with a neurasthenic component" (p. 218). Five years later Zygmunt and Irena are expecting a baby. The specialists are unsure if the patient's offspring might be "burdened with the germ of epilepsy, and if Zygmunt would end up in an asylum for the mentally ill" (*ibid.*). Brzękowski invites his readers to take part in a poll. Upon payment of an administration fee of 1 złoty, every reader may choose whether "Zygmunt succumbs to paranoia, amentia or dementia" and if his children "develop symptoms of a relatively serious mental illness in their later lives" (p. 219). The author pledges to describe his characters' later lives according to the result of the survey. What Brzękowski seems to suggest is that psychiatric diagnoses are as arbitrary and uncertain as the votes cast by the readers of his novel.

While writing "A Travelling Psychoanalyst," Brzękowski was also working on a play, *Dziurek w Elsynorze* [Dziurek in Elsinore]. Completed in 1927, it was never staged in the interwar period and was only published in 1970. Here, too, Witkacy's influence is evident: the list of characters is stylised to look like a list from one of Witkacy's plays; the use of grotesque deformation and anti-psychologism are also clearly reminiscent of Witkacy.[38] The title,

38 Despite the similarities between Brzękowski and Witkacy, the theoretician of Pure Form, scholars have also pointed out their differences:

"[Brzękowski] creates artificial situations, treating his characters like marionettes, excluding all serious psychology – all this indicates that he chose a different path than Witkacy. Reshaping the material of drama, the latter operates with anti-psychologism, thus shattering the entire tradition of verism and symbolism; a psychologism of a novel kind, however, a grotesque and caricatural psychologism, is still at play. Brzękowski, meanwhile, foregoes all kinds of psychological fiction. He constructs his characters like mechanical puppets that stand for given ideas and positions". (J. Pieszczachowicz, "'Dziurek' na tle epoki", *DI* 1970, no. 12, p. 115).

alluding to the setting of Shakespeare's *Hamlet*, is also a reference to the experimental theatre Elsynor in Warsaw where Karol Borowski directed Witkacy's *Pragmatyści* in December 1921.[39]

The play's titular protagonist Dziurek only makes an appearance in the second act. The opening scenes are set in the office of professor Paterek, a specialist in nervous diseases. According to the list of characters, he is "a neurologist, young, handsome (and a professor already!)".[40] His assistant is Dr Klara Czeluściower, stereotyped as a Jewish intellectual with "an aquiline-Semitic nose (otherwise handsome)". The professor is a diabolical figure. His first name is Sobiesław, or Biesio for short – a nickname that brings to mind *bies*, an old Polish word for devil. His cunning also associates him with Mephistopheles; for instance, he hires a certain Dr Karen despite their extreme differences of opinion, for "an enemy under surveillance is far less dangerous than an invisible schemer" (p. 82). Dr Karen is the clinic's most zealous supporter of psychoanalysis. Besides research on "the effect of *hypophysis cerebri* and gland transplantation," he is most interested in "the question, tackled more than half a decade ago by Freud and his school but then forgotten, in how far mental qualities are dependent on the role of the reproductive glands" (p. 81). Prof. Paterek, too, applies methods declared to be "psychoanalytical". Treating a patient for his sexual inhibition he suggests – by means of hypnosis and magnetism – that he should seduce the first woman he encounters after leaving the consultation room. Ironically, the man immediately runs into the professor's wife; she promptly decides to elope with him. The professor's reasoning is that the patient developed his complex when, the night before his wedding, he saw cats mating; this complex could only be substituted with another complex. Paterek does not hesitate to bring about such a complex artificially. This is how Dr Czeluściower explains the procedure to Dr Karen:

> Since you referred to Steinach and Voronoff's forgotten research, we, too, have been using the old method of "no restrain" in psychotherapy, but we

39 Cf. "Elsynor", *NS* 1921, no. 1, p. 31. The troupe was founded by writers from the Skamander group (Emil Breiter, Wilam Horzyca, Jarosław Iwaszkiewicz, Jerzy M. Rytard, Julian Wołoszynowski and Władysław Zawistowski), with logistical support from Arnold Szyfman, who arranged for their use of the small auditorium of the Teatr Polski in Warsaw. The troupe disbanded after no more than four performances. See J. Degler, "'Pragmatyści' w Elsynorze", *PAT* 1969, no. 3, pp. 281–290.

40 J. Brzękowski, "Dziurek w Elsynorze", *DI* 1970, no. 12, p. 78.

> have adapted it to modern requirements by relating it to our own invention, the method of mental compulsion; we have combined thesis and antithesis into one unique synthesis… (p. 89)

The procedure is, of course, entirely fictional. This is unsurprising, as the stage directions early in the text already suggest that we are dealing with psychoanalytical science fiction: the decor in the eminent professor's consultation room is "something like a resistor combined with a chair and a dial gauge, somewhat like the weighing scales you find at railway stations" (p. 79). The device brings to mind an invention from "A Travelling Psychoanalyst," described as a lie detector:

> On the outside the device looks like a regular radio headset that you place on the criminal's temples. It works by detecting vibrations in the inter-psychic arc, which shows distinct reactions to reality and delusion. The clock-like gauge, which is connected to the receiver-aneroid, tells us whether the defendant is telling the truth or lying.[41]

The device, invented by the engineer Goetter, is used to examine Zygmunt:

> He placed the headset on his temples and pressed the button. A mad crunching sound was heard, the cogwheels, big and small, started to whirr, finally the pointer on the gauge dial moved and stopped mid-way between two positions – "highly gifted" and "vengeful instincts that may foster criminal behaviour". Next Goetter asked the defendant if he had played any role in the disappearance of Mr Ł. The prisoner said no, but the unbalanced instrument betrayed him. The pointer on the device stopped at "Yes". (p. 126)

Zygmunt was, of course, innocent.

In the play *Dziurek w Elsynorze*, the device is professor Paterek's invention, based on his studies of yoga. His "psychosexometer" works on the principle of "bringing out ectoplasmic psychosexual abilities".[42] A patient suffering from impotence is placed on a chair that begins to levitate slightly when the doctors move the switch; they are then able to read the angle on the dial: 37.538, which is to say "quite good". This

41 J. Brzękowski, *Psychoanalityk w podróży*, p. 112.

42 J. Brzękowski, "Dziurek w Elsynorze", p. 83.

invention is applied not only in diagnosis. In the first act it helps the professor quieten a mob of rioting patients: the malcontent who raised the uproar is made to sit in the magic chair and then lifted up so high that, to the horror of the remaining patients, he disappears altogether. In the third act the device is transformed into a rocket launcher, for it turns out that it has two buttons, and pressing the second one activates "electro-psycho-motoric forces" (pp. 100–101) that catapult the passenger into space.

Before this happens, however, the second act takes us to Rita Valedemoroza's salon. She hosts snobbish aristocrats as well as the industrial and cultural elite, including the futurist poet Klamor Dziurek. He proposes that the assembled party should gatecrash a ball at the psychiatric clinic. In the final act, the guests set out for the dance. Dziurek, inspired by Edgar Allan Poe's short story "The System of Doctor Tarr and Professor Fether," plans to instigate the patients to revolt and seize control of the hospital.

Meanwhile, professor Paterek's wife returns to him. She is disappointed with her lover, whose sexual potency the professor had not restored completly. But Paterek is already having an affair with an actress. The four of them decide to collectively commit suicide under the guise of a scientific experiment: they will ingest a capsule containing the drug Hesperys H.L.31 ("morphine, cocaine, opium and peyotl taken together are a child's play in comparison" (p. 101)) and then test the machine's effect on themselves. One by one they take a seat in the psychosexometer, rise above the ground and disappear. But they are not transported to the other world or to the moon, as they initially think (a police officer tells them that they are "in the lunar highlands a hundred kilometres from the main canal leading to the Mare Tenebrarum" (p. 103)), nor in the fourth dimension, as the professor believes. In fact, they are in hell. While in "A Travelling Psychoanalyst" the artist is locked up in a psychiatric ward, which makes him lose his gift as a writer and turn into a "simple and uncomplicated human being,"[43] in *Dziurek* it is the psychoanalyst who arrives in a hell designed by an avant-garde poet, with the lost souls reciting futuristic poems ("I have a feeling that some writer put me here"[44]). Just as he did in his novels, Brzękowski constantly draws the reader's attention to the narrative situation, making us aware of the fictionality of the dramatic text. He breaks the theatrical illusion by having his characters comment on their own lines, and they interfere with the events unfolding on stage; when

43 J. Brzękowski, *Psychoanalityk w podróży*, p. 201.

44 J. Brzękowski, "Dziurek w Elsynorze", p. 103.

they want to return to reality they simply walk up to the front of the stage and lower the heavy curtains to conceal the "surrealist decor".

At the clinic, meanwhile, the patients' revolt has been suppressed. Professor Paterek talks about his experience and is declared insane; during the revolt he received a hammer blow on the head – this is presented as the cause for his confusion. Filled with remorse, Dziurek simulates mental illness and has himself locked up along with the professor. Eventually Paterek manages to prove his sanity and tells Dziurek:

> Remember that you must not talk about anything that, from the point of view of our senses and character, might seem impossible to people. You'd be risking the straitjacket. Once upon a time we believed in miracles, now we live in the age of realism. Cursed is every word, deed and gesture that insults our exuberant sense of probability, that contradicts real-life possibilities. We are being drained by the era of consequent vitalism and psychological naturalism. We are propagating, once more, a return back to nature, to faith in miracles of the mind and wishes coming true through faith. We must be children in relation to reality. My current deviations were born of metaphysics. I am a poet, just like you. (p. 112)

The protagonist Klamor Dziurek is a satire, as is obvious in his statements, for instance: "I am an idealist materialist. This school emerged in Paris two weeks ago. I am proud to be its first and so far only representative in our country" (p. 87). He talks about his acquaintance with Marinetti and tries to scandalise conventional society, but no one seems shocked. Quite to the contrary: the futurist poet comes to be seen as fashionable; members of the elite compete for his attention just to outsnob one another. Dziurek ends up being a mascot at their salons. He keeps proclaiming ideological manifestos but creates nothing until he incites the revolt at the clinic – this is where he recites his first poem. Analysing the name of this character, Ewa Guderian-Czaplińska associates Klamor with the Latin *clamor* (shout, outcry) and Dziurek with the Polish *dziura* (hole), so that Klamor Dziurek can be read as one who causes much ado but is hollow inside, "a hole in the shape of a poet". Guderian-Czaplińska suggests that Dziurek is a representation of the Polish avant-garde poet Jalu Kurek (1904-1983), while the professor brings to mind writer and critic Tadeusz Peiper (1891-1969), who was also the editor of *Zwrotnica*.[45]

45 E. Guderian-Czaplińska, *Szara strefa awangardy* (Wrocław: Wiedza o Kulturze, 1998), pp. 101–118.

Guderian-Czaplińska focuses on the mental patients' riot, seemingly orchestrated by Dziurek but in fact controlled by the professor: despite the play's title, it is professor Paterek who is always in charge; he has the "keys to the human soul," he has discovered the secret of extraterrestrial travel and the women all swoon over him. Dziurek strives for art and for power, but next to the professor he is a nobody. Thus the play can be read as a representation of the apparent freedom and actual subservience of a young avant-garde poet who has signed a pact with Mephistopheles; the play also reflects Brzękowski's anxiety: as a protégé of Peiper he is aware that being taken under the wing of a great master is a unique opportunity, but at the same time he has doubts about such a poetic apprenticeship: is it a path that he can truly call his own? According to Guderian-Czaplińska, this play is a warning to all of Peiper's young colleagues at *Zwrotnica*.

Dziurek w Elsynorze has been compared to Witkacy's *The Madman and the Nun* [*Wariat i zakonnica*] and Antoni Cwojdziński's *Freuda teorią snów* [Freud's Theory of Dreams][46] (I will discuss both comedies later). But unlike those plays, which openly satirise psychoanalysis, Brzękowski only mentions Freudianism in the margins, as he did in "A Travelling Psychoanalyst". Like the novel, the play barely shows any influence of psychoanalysis. What is more, as Maria Delaperrière has argued, Freud's research on the unconscious coincided with other developments, such as cubism in art or Ferdinand de Saussure's work on language, which makes it hard to prove that this or that scientific concept had an impact on the avant-garde.[47] In Brzękowski's case we must consider another source of inspiration that seems as important as psychoanalysis, namely film.

What seems most psychoanalytical in "A Travelling Psychoanalyst" is its innovative form, which Brzękowski calls the "cine-novel". This term refers to the technique developed on the basis of the modern medium of film – a technique that Paweł Majerski identifies on several levels of the narrative: "in the construction of the novel as well as on the level of the characters' linguistic imagination; what is more, the characters go to the cinema and are themselves pulled into a new dimension of grasping reality."[48] In particular, this concerns mental states that deviate from the norm. Zygmunt enjoys excellent health, but he is plagued with geometrical hallucinations for which he has no explanation. Brzękowski introduces this motif in the first chapter. The

46 J. Pieszczachowicz, "'Dziurek' na tle epoki", p. 114.

47 M. Delaperrière, *Polskie awangardy a poezja europejska*, p. 273.

48 P. Majerski, "Boczny tor awangardowego eksperymentu", p. 654.

descriptions of Zygmunt's visions recall avant-garde film experiments, assuming a certain film viewer competence on the part of the reader:[49]

> ... Big, big circles. They appear like the hula hoops of childhood, growing out of the earth and chasing each other like cigarette smoke rings. Now there's a succession of smaller circles, ever smaller. They shrink until there's just a dot. Followed by big circles. They merge to form sections of a sphere. New ones keep appearing. A sphere. Spheres. Nothing but spheres. Big and small. They whirl. A whirling planetary system of spheres.
> Space. Empty space. Space whose only dimension is depth. How desper-ately long a fall must take in it! Suddenly the void becomes populated: Dots. Lines. Straight. Crooked. Spiral-like, they gyrate like serpentine streamers. They whirl.
> Cubes. They grow bigger and bigger in a long geometrical order. Like sta-tistics images representing the production of grain or coffee. They stretch upwards, farther and farther...Pyramids grow out of a human head. Triangles of different planes and the sharp edges of hills. They recede into the blue sky.
> Suddenly a cloud appears. Inside there are prisms, deltoids, ellipses, hyper-boles, parabolas. Rhombuses, rhombohedrons. Trapezoids. They place themselves in regular order. A spinning cone. A geometric twisting of space. A big black sphere looms in the periphery. It becomes more and more elongated. A geometric nebula approaches. A black blade reaches the bottom. It cuts through...

Or:

> Red colour. Undulating redness, purple and violet. Intermingling. A diffusion of hues. White colour. Between red and green. Green. Dark → Light → yellow colour → Gold → Blue, azure, steel → An inter-penetration of particles. Osmosis.
> Silver. Living silver, overflowing. You can take it and pour it from one hand into the other.
> Suddenly – wind. A disarray begins to rise from the earth and whirl and spin. The dance of a thousand colours.
> A multi-coloured funnel, rising upwards.[50]

These hallucinations inspire Zygmunt to consult a doctor. He is found to be perfectly healthy, "save for severe nervous exhaustion," which the doctor

49 A. Wójtowicz, *Cogito i "sejsmograf podświadomości"*, p. 208.
50 J. Brzękowski, *Psychoanalityk w podróży*, pp. 44–45.

advises him to treat with a change of scene (p. 47). This recommendation marks the beginning of the travels described in the novel, whose final stage will be Zygmunt's admission into the mental hospital. His visions, meanwhile, change shape a few times. He stays at a seaside spa, reading Conrad and looking out onto the waves (which, incidentally, "very often reminded Zygmunt of film"; "especially in the mid-day sun [the sea] seemed like a screen" (p. 151)). As a result, his dreams lose their original geometric form:

> Now they appeared in a different shape. Sometimes the darkness of his room gave rise to a frightful mass which later stretched into a huge space, like inflated rubber.

Then again he is in an elevator falling into immeasurable depths. Despite his frenzied efforts, he fails to stop it. Before his eyes he sees elements of gigantic cylinders moving, one giving birth to the next, extending into infinity, like the flickering impression of wagons of a fast moving train. Then again there were vast, undulating planes, like bedsheets being shaken out. Or: like the blinding wings of a monstrous bird. (*Ibid.*)

Zygmunt's visions, which initially appeared only in his dreams, start bothering him when he is awake. Gradually he becomes unable to distinguish reality and hallucination. In his psychotic state, "a new abstract reality emerged and shook his nerves by being so life-like" (p. 152). These states seem "like a special effect in a film" (*ibid.*). Zygmunt becomes caught up in the logic of a film narrative; it is as if the hypnotising power of the screen were pulling him in and turning him into "a puppet of his own dreams" (p. 153). During one of these episodes he meets his double, the mysterious Renaldi, who awakens Zygmunt's homoerotic desire. Renaldi owns a coal mine – a legible symbol of the unconscious. Their shared adventures finally allow Zygmunt to experience artistic fulfilment: he writes a long poem, "a great epic about modernity" (p. 162). Renaldi dies in a car accident just after Zygmunt, cured and serene, returns to his previous life and enters a new romantic relationship. Hearing of of his ex-lover's death Zygmunt faints. When he regains consciousness he is "patient number 37".

The origins of cinema and psychoanalysis both date to 1895, but their development followed separate paths until the 1920s. In the 1910s, the discoveries of psychoanalysis gradually began to be popularised on the big screen. German expressionist horror films portrayed demonic psychiatrists. In Robert Wiene's *The Cabinet of Dr Caligari* [*Das Kabinett des Dr Caligari*,

1919], for instance, the director of a mental asylum secretly experiments on his patients, using hypnosis to make them commit heinous murders. Fritz Lang's *Dr Mabuse the Gambler* (*Dr Mabuse, der Spieler*, 1922) portrays a psychoanalyst who masterfully manipulates people. Of course, these films were also screened in Poland. A review by Anatol Stern appeared in *Skamander*. He complained that Lang's film "smothered the screenplay with his parrot-like jabbering, his senseless blathering, his aphorisms on life, death, psychoanalysis and expres-sionism".[51] Enthusiastic reviewers of *Dr Caligari* included Karol Irzykowski[52] as well as Antoni Słonimski, who wrote a lengthy critique for *Kurier Polski*.[53] Literary historians have tried to identify allusions to this film in Jan Brzękowski's poem "Gabinet zbrodni" [Crime Cabinet].[54]

In 1924, the American film producer Samuel Goldwyn approached Freud to propose that, being "the greatest love specialist in the world,"[55] Freud should write a screenplay for a fee of one hundred thousand dollars. Freud declined, but scripts for psychoanalytical films were produced in his immediate circle. One was penned by Siegfried Bernfeld[56]; Karl Abraham and Hanns Sachs wrote another one in Berlin at the same time. *Secrets of a Soul* (*Geheimnisse einer Seele*), based on the script by Abraham and Sachs, premiered in 1926. Directed by Georg Pabst and produced by the Weimar Republic's famous UFA, it was a great success and continues to be seen as a milestone in early history of film.[57] It tells the story of a man who suddenly

51 *S* 1922, no. 25–26, p. 528.

52 K. Irzykowski, *Dziesiąta muza: Zagadnienia estetyczne kina* (Warsaw: Filmowa Agencja Wydawnicza, 1957), pp. 203–205.

53 *KPL* 1920, no. 155. The film also inspired Słonimski's poem "Negatyw" [Negative].

54 On the impact of film on the Polish avant-garde see E. and M. Pytasz, "Poetycka podróż w świat kinematografu", in *Szkice z teorii filmu*, ed. by A. Helman, T. Miczka (Katowice: Uniwersytet Śląski, 1978); W. Otto, *Literatura i film w kulturze dwudziestolecia międzywojennego* (Poznań: PTPN, 2007).

55 Peter Gay, *Freud: A Life for Our Times*, p. 454.

56 Bernfeld's notes on the screenplay of the film *Drei Welten in einem Zimmer* were reprinted in *Siegfried Bernfeld oder die Grenzen der Psychoanalyse: Materialen zu Leben und Werk*, ed. by K. Fallend, J. Reichmayr (Basel: Stroemfeld, 1992), pp. 153–157. Other relevant articles in this book include K. Fallend, J. Reichmayr, "Psychoanalyse, Film und Öffentlichkeit: Konflikte hinter den Kulissen", pp. 132–153, and K. Sierek, "Bemerkungen zu Bernfelds *Drei Welten in einem Zimmer*", pp. 157–163.

57 Cf. P. Ries, "Popularise and/or Be Damned: Psychoanalysis and Film at the Crossroads in 1925", *IJP* 1995, no. 76, pp. 759–791; N. Browne, B. McPherson, "Dream and Photography in a Psychoanalytic Film: 'Secrets of a Soul'" *Dreamworks* 1980, 1, pp. 35–45. This film was known in Poland, see for instance Emil Schürer, "Film treściowy czy abstrakcyjny", *IKF* 1929.

craves to murder his wife and who is cured by an experienced Freudian analyst. This story did more than any other to popularise psychoanalysis.

To present "the talking cure" though silent film – sound was only introduced in 1927 – might seem paradoxical or impossible. But it turned out that film allowed astonishing juxtapositions of images, which could be made overlap, or to fade in and out. The new technique was perfectly suited to illustrate something that had previously been very difficult to represent: dreams, hidden thoughts, fantasies. Film montage was an ideal match for their sensory-visual but discontinuous or fragmented character, so much so that writers and critics constantly repeated and rephrased Paul Valéry's question, "is film not also a dream?".[58] One of the first Polish critics to highlight the fact that cinema offered new means of representation and an alternative to traditional descriptions of mental experiences or states was Wacław Kubacki (1907-1992). In his 1933 article "Zagadnienia psychologiczne w filmie" [Psychological Issues in Film] he argues that, compared to traditional psychology, psychoanalysis "has seen a remarkable shift towards the body," opening ways to "represent the outside world from a psychological point of view" in film.[59] But it seems that it was Brzękowski, in his cine-novel "A Travelling Psychoanalyst," who first became aware of these qualities of film. He would later make this explicit in his influential article "Film a nowa poezja" [Film and New Poetry], identifying the blurred boundaries between thought and its fulfilment as well as the simultaneous representation of many levels of reality as common to both aesthetics.[60]

Towards the end of "A Travelling Psychoanalyst," readers might get the impression that Zygmunt arrives not so much in a psychiatric clinic but in

58 T. Brzozowski, "Gra w psychoanalizę, czyli (de)konstrukcja podmiotu w 'filmowofotograficznym' modelu poezji 'Almanachu Nowej Sztuki'", in *Z problemów podmiotowości w literaturze polskiej XX wieku*, ed. by M. Lalak (Szczecin: Uniwerystet Szczeciński, 1993), p. 57. Paul Valéry is cited in Edgar Morin, *Le cinéma ou l'homme imaginaire* (Paris: Essai d'anthropologie, 1956), p. 15: "N'est-ce pas aussi un rêve que le cinéma?".

59 W. Kubacki, "Zagadnienia psychologiczne w filmie", *WL* 1933, no. 42, p. 7.

60 J. Brzękowski, "Film a nowa poezja", *WL* 1933, no. 28, p. 8. In *Wiadomości Literackie* Brzękowski often wrote about French experimental films such as Jean Epstein's *The Fall of the House of Usher* or Germaine Dulac's *Princesse Mandane* and *The Seashell and the Clergyman* [La Coquille et le Clergyman] with a screenplay by Antonin Artaud. Cf. M. Szpakowska, *"Wiadomości Literackie" prawie dla wszystkich* (Warsaw: W.A.B., 2012), pp. 344–345.

one of the epoch's many films featuring new methods for curing mental illnesses. Zygmunt's doctors, just as the medical practitioners in Brzękowski's play *Dziurek w Elsynorze*, are modelled on the grotesque psychiatrists in German expressionist cinema. Obsessed with advancing their careers, they apply scientifically dubious methods; their credibility is destroyed at the latest when they declare Zygmunt to be mentally healthy, which results in his deployment to the trenches. As Wojciech Otto has remarked, Brzękowski style changes when Zygmunt arrives at the mental asylum. In one of the final chapters, the popular literature conventions that had dominated until then (melodrama, crime fiction, the exotic and adventure novel) give way to the poetics of a film script. Now the writer develops "a montage-like construction, a gradation of film sets, laconic descriptions of characters, places and events, intertitles as well as visualisation, broadly understood":[61]

> An American boxer with thick bundles of muscle, reminding [Zygmunt] of fat Pommeranz, owner of a small shop in his home town, is juggling with red human heads, throwing them up like balls. He is wearing white colonial socks with red drops of sweat dripping onto them.
> The heads are becoming smaller. They become as tiny as pinheads. The tiny heads turn red.
> A battle of red blood cells on the snow of his trousers.
> Squadrons of red, blue and brown bacteria come pouring down. They unfold into chains of streptococcus, cutting through rosaries of staphylo. Vibrio vibrate, spirochaete twist into spirals, bacteria swarming and bacilli like commas. A battle of full stops and commas.
> They occupy his white shorts and his legs, covering his chest, throat, face.
> The man transforms into a heart pulsating with bacteria. Karyokinesis of the heart. A long, painful, amitotic narrowing. Division. Further karyokinesis. The hearts divide. From each muscle, like from a vase, tall, muscular plants start to grow. Their crowns turn into mouths. The growing mouths, stretching upwards, like gum, pierce the horizon.[62]

The visions unfolding before the reader's eyes are all products of the mind of a patient whose only wish is to "have no time to produce figments of the imagination. Unemployment of the brain! Strike of thought!" (p. 193).

61 W. Otto, *Literatura i film w kulturze dwudziestolecia międzywojennego*, p. 173.

62 J. Brzękowski, *Psychoanalityk w podróży*, p. 190.

The similarities between Polish interwar poetry and surrealism or psychoanalysis may partially be rooted in the fact that the poets enthusiastically drew on the oneiric poetics of film. They were most likely inspired by their careful reading of Jean Epstein's essays, which drew on Freud's discoveries.[63] As Tadeusz Brzozowski has shown, this is particularly the case with the group associated with the art magazine *Almanach Nowej Sztuki*, especially the poet and essayist Adam Ważyk (1905-1982).[64] Next to Brzękowski, Ważyk is the Polish writer most often mentioned in the context of surrealism. His work shows many elements of surrealist poetics, such as free association, visualisation and the dream technique, although he does not conceptualise poetry as a stream of the imagination and does not use automatism. Brzękowski assesses Ważyk's work and its links with surrealism in his memoirs: "I don't believe that his poetry meets the demands of Breton's dogmas. Nor do I think that Ważyk was using *écriture automatique*. Today we are well aware that the climate of Polish literature was not favourable to the development of surrealism."[65]

Urszula Klatka remarks that the rejection of surrealism, not only by Brzękowski but by almost all poets of the Polish avant-garde, was mostly due to the young generation's aversion to the legacy of Polish modernism, i.e. the Young Poland movement:

> At the root of [the avant-garde's] distaste for surrealism was their experience of Polish modernism, which became a benchmark defining the poetics that they opposed; this is why the poets of the avant-garde expressly negated the irrational element, why they rigorously rejected the vocabulary sanctified by the poetic tradition, and finally recognised the creative process as a conscious effort and not gusts of inspiration. Metarealism represents a step on the way towards the emancipation of the

63 Z. Czeczot-Gawrak points out that Epstein, who had Polish roots and had spent the first ten years of his life in Warsaw, often refers to Edward Abramowski's theory of the unconscious, for instance in *La poésie d'aujourd'hui* (1921) and in *La Lyrosophie* (1922). See Z. Czeczot-Gawrak, *Jan Epstein: Studium natury w sztuce filmowej* (Warsaw: Wydawnictwa Artystyczne i Filmowe, 1962), p. 93. On the influence on psychoanalysis on Epstein's understanding of film see S. Liebman, "Sublime et désublimation dans la théorie cinématographique de Jean Epstein: 'Le cinématographe vu de l'Etna'", in *Jean Epstein: Cinéaste, poète, philosophe*, ed. by J. Aumont (Paris: Cinémathèque française, 1998), pp. 125–137.

64 T. Brzozowski, "Gra w psychoanalizę", pp. 58-74.

65 J. Brzękowski, *W Krakowie i w Paryżu*, p. 45.

> avant-garde's literary technique; the rejection of the surrealists' spontaneous method restores the rights of the creative subject who constructs the text, struggles with form, and makes decisions on the level of language.[66]

Scholars have discussed the Polish avant-garde artists' inclination towards constructivism, which can be either radical (Peiper, Brzękowski) or moderate (Ważyk).[67] Another factor that explains their general disdain of surrealism is their desire to see contemporary Polish art become independent of French models. Highlighting the remarkable similarities between artistic production in Poland and elsewhere in Europe, Maria Delaperrière points out that immediately after the war, Polish poets had access to all experiences of the avant-garde, though they encountered them with a delay of a decade, more or less.[68] The question of influence was much discussed at the time, most saliently in Karol Irzykowski's article "Plagiatowy charakter przełomów literackich w Polsce" [The Plagiaristic Nature of Literary Innovation in Poland] in 1922. About ten years down the line, Irzykowski still considered his article pertinent enough to include it in his anthology *Słoń wśród porcelany* [An Elephant in a China Shop].[69] He makes the provocative claim that Polish avant-gardists ought to limit themselves to translating and promoting novelties from abroad, without laying any claim to glory as pioneers. The many -isms that appeared in Poland after the war, he argues, "have arrived rather too suddenly, with no justification and no developmental necessity – they immediately found themselves on a certain level of refinement, which is impossible to attain without a longer period of trial and error" (p. 33); this indicates imitation and "a lack of control over influence" (p. 35). Irzykowski accuses Polish culture of its "disgusting atmosphere of parasitism" (p. 36) and

66 U. Klatka, *Wyobraźnia w czasie*, p. 38. For a discussion on this subject in English see Ryszard Nycz, *The Language of Polish Modernism*, (Frankfurt am Main: Peter Lang, 2017).

67 Many years later Brzękowski wrote: "The myth of construction did not allow us to consider ourselves surrealists. But it gave us an effective tool to oppose the post-Romantic traditions of Young Poland." See J. Brzękowski, "O klasycznym i romantycznym widzeniu poezji", in *Wyobraźnia wyzwolona: Szkice i wspomnienia* (Cracow: Wydawnictwo Literackie, 1976), p. 101. Cf. M. Korcala-Delaperrière, "Twórczość Jana Brzękowskiego w świetle francuskich tendencji konstruktywistycznych", *PLI* 1976, no. 2, pp. 83–108.

68 M. Delaperrière, *Les avant-gardes polonaises et la poésie européenne*, p. 53.

69 K. Irzykowski, "Plagiatowy charakter przełomów literackich w Polsce", in *Słoń wśród porcelany: Lżejszy kaliber*, ed. by A. Lam (Cracow: Wydawnictwo Literackie, 1976), pp. 30–65. On Irzykowski's dispute with the avant-garde see e.g. P. Czapliński, *Poetyka manifestu literackiego 1918–1939* (Warsaw: IBL PAN, 1997), pp. 152-175.

its tolerance for plagiarism: "we are camp-followers of the West" (p. 36). Interestingly, he applies psychoanalytical tools to account for the imitators' choices. In a footnote he explains that there is such a thing as unconscious plagiarism, i.e. situations in which one "subconsciously but purposefully forgets" about someone else who came first: "The mechanism of forgetting in such cases has been described in Freud's *The Psychopathology of Everyday Life*. We forget things that might burden our soul with regret or duty" (p. 57).

Irzykowski writes that "those who plagiarise obliterate their traces, for instance by backdating their borrowed material, adding roots to it, which is to say: they try to give it a certain appearance and rationale, so that it might seem to have grown out of this thick soil, the soil of plagiarism, of its own accord" (p. 38). This remark presages the strategy developed by Adam Ważyk in his 1976 memoir *Dziwna historia awangardy* [A Strange History of the Avant-Garde].[70] His version supports three goals, namely to highlight his own generation's precursory status during the emergence of the neo-avant-garde after World War II; to point out the original character of the Polish avant-garde (as not being derivative of European art) and to mark a break with Young Poland, thus raising the profile of the avant-garde poets as the first ones to be truly modern. Ważyk also enumerates three key elements of the poetics of Young Poland that had to be rejected after World War I: first, the poetic vocabulary struck later poets as freakish ("It would have been wrong to borrow it. We had to find a way around it," p. 8); second, the poets of Young Poland had a tendency to disregard all that was empirical and concrete, sensual and material; and third, these poets portrayed human beings by focusing on individual inner conflicts instead of observing people from an everyday point of view (p. 12).

Ważyk's retrospective account emphasises his generation's independent and careful reading of Freud – so much so that some scholars have come to see his book as a sort of chronicle on the reception of Freudianism in Polish poetry before World War II.[71] About the publication of the third issue of *Almanach Nowej Sztuki* in 1925, which featured Apollinaire's portrait on the cover, he writes: "The recently released *Surrealist Manifesto* (October 1924) arrived in Poland, but it failed to capture anyone's attention […]. Meanwhile, the *Introduction to Psychoanalysis* had been

70 A. Ważyk, *Dziwna historia awangardy* (Warsaw: Czytelnik, 1976).

71 See e.g. B. Sienkiewicz, "Poezja z 'Freudowskiego pnia' – w orbicie sporu o polski surrealizm", in *Przez znaki – do człowieka*, ed. by B. Sienkiewicz, A. Legeżyńska, W. Wielopolski (Poznań: WiS, 1997), p. 233.

passed from hand to hand for months, and the debate revolved around the relationship between poetry and the subconscious".[72]

However, Ważyk's claims are not supported by the sources. A search across all major Polish avant-garde publications from 1920 until the mid-1930s (*Nowa Sztuka, Almanach Nowej Sztuki, Reflektor, Zwrotnica, Linia*) produced no results beyond cursory remarks such as "According to Freud, even logic first developed from people's irrational mental lives".[73] If anything, these comments betray the writers' complete lack of familiarity with Freud's theory; their references are based on loose association. Maria Delaperrière proposes that while Freud's discoveries played a significant role in the birth of surrealism, it would be difficult to consider all painters and poets who used dreams and Freudian symbols as surrealists. [74] To this sober remark we might add that it would be difficult to consider references to dreams or eroticism as proof of the writer's familiarity with Freud's work. Despite the thematic similarities that invite psychoanalytical interpretations,[75] the Polish avant-garde did not read Freud or apply his theory in their artistic practice. This can be said not only about the poets involved with the futurist movement or Nowa Sztuka – even the poet and philosopher Debora Vogel (1902–1942) fails to mention Freud. Vogel, a Galician Jew with a German-language education, was involved with the Socialist-Zionist youth movement HaShomer Hatzair and became a protégée of Kazimierz Twardowski, which suggests that she was exceptionally well placed to engage with psychoanalysis. She developed an interest in psychology, which became one of the subjects she taught at a Hebrew

72 A. Ważyk, *Dziwna historia awangardy*, p. 70. A similar statement is found in Aleksander Wat's commentary, written many years later, on his 1919 prose poem "Ja z jednej strony i ja z drugiej strony mego mopsożelaznego piecyka". Wat maintains that he had developed *écriture automatique* "a few years before André Breton, but from the same Freudian inspiration". See A. Wat, "Coś niecoś o 'Piecyku'", in *Antologia polskiego futuryzmu i Nowej Sztuki*, ed. by H. Zaworska, Z. Jarosiński (Wrocław: Zakład Narodowy im. Ossolińskich, 1978), p. 271.

73 J. Kurek, "Valéry o liryźmie", *LI* 1931, no. 1, p. 45.

74 M. Delaperrière, *Les avant-gardes polonaises et la poésie européenne*, p. 204.

75 Cf. e.g. J. Sławiński, "O poezji Jana Brzękowskiego", *TW* 1961, no. 9, pp. 82–101; A.K. Waśkiewicz, "Między śnieniem a nie śnieniem", in *Poeci dwudziestolecia międzywojennego*, ed. by I. Maciejewska (Warsaw: Wiedza Powszechna, 1982), vol. 1, pp. 119–149; "Miejsce Ważyka", in *W kręgu "Zwrotnicy": Studia i szkice z dziejów krakowskiej Awangardy* (Cracow: Wydawnictwo Literackie, 1983), pp. 262–294; Z. Jarosiński, "Poezja ziemi – Anatol Stern", in *Poeci dwudziestolecia międzywojennego*, ed. by I. Maciejewska (Warsaw: Wiedza Powszechna, 1982), vol. 2, pp. 259–291; M. Baranowska, *Surrealna wyobraźnia i poezja*; M. Cywińska, *Manufaktura snów*.

teachers' college in Lviv. In the late 1920s she published several articles combining educational sciences, psychology and pedagogy, but her arguments remained strictly adlerian.[76] Vogel, one of the most interesting avant-garde writers of the interwar years, found no inspiration in Freud, and remained, like Brzękowski, unconvinced by surrealism or the notion that art was related to dreams.[77] Another writer who disparaged the French surrealists' interest in "Bergsonism and Freudianism" was Tadeusz Peiper.[78]

Returning once again to Ważyk's claim, it is also worth asking which edition of the *Introduction* was supposed to have been passed on from hand to hand in avant-garde circles. A Polish translation only appeared in late 1935. Few people were comfortable reading German at the time (Irzykowski writes about this in 1928, suggesting this might be a reason why Freud remained little known in Poland[79]), so it is unlikely that a significant number of poets should have had access to the original *Vorlesungen zur Einführung in die Psychoanalyse* of 1917. It is possible that Ważyk had in mind Samuel Jankélévitch's French translation, *Introduction à la psychanalyse.* After all, he mentions the title of Freud's book was "Wstęp do psychoanalizy" [Introduction to Psychoanalysis] rather than the literal translation of the German title, which would have been "Lectures for an Introduction to Psychoanalysis". This suggests that if the artists really did read Freud, they would have opted for the translation published in France in 1922. It seems more likely, however, that they read about this book in French journals. Ważyk's retrospective account is also called into question by the fact that three Polish translations of Freud were issued in the years 1923-24: Beata Rank's translation *O marzeniu sennem* [*On Dreams*], *Trzy rozprawy z teorii seksualnej* [*Three Essays on the Theory of Sexuality*] translated by Jekels and Albiński, as well as a second edition of Jekels's *Psychopatologia życia codziennego* [*The Psychopathology of Everyday Life*]. Any Polish avant-gardist intending to read Freud in 1925 should have reached for one of these books – there was no need to read either the

76 See e.g. D. Vogel, "Choroba nerwowa i psychiczna w świetle teorii Adlera", *PRZ* 1929, no. 9, pp. 332–340.

77 Cf. K. Szymaniak, *Być agentem wiecznej idei: Przemiany poglądów estetycznych Debory Vogel* (Cracow: Universitas, 2006).

78 Some researchers argue that the key philosophical inspiration for the Polish avant-garde, especially the futurists, was not Freud but Bergson. See W.P. Szymański, *Neosymbolizm*, p. 28 and *Świadomość estetyczna polskiej awangardy* (Cracow: PWN, 1971), p. 15.

79 K. Irzykowski, "Badania Acherontu", *WL* 1928, no. 36, p. 3.

originals or the French translations and reviews. This also applies to Ważyk himself, who, a few pages later, claims that he became acquainted with Freud's theory soon after the publication of his poetry collection *Semafory*, in 1924.

Ważyk's goals and the construction of his book drove him to exaggerate the role of psychoanalysis. He presents Freud's work as antithetical to the metaphysics of the Young Poland movement, which he rejects. "Freud's theory became influential after World War I," he writes. "Many cultured people thought that it was Freud who had discovered the meaning of eroticism and demons. In fact it was the other way around [...]. Freud had chased away the demons and deprived eroticism of its mystery."[80] For Ważyk, the modern psychoanalytical unconscious has little to do with the enigmatic soul in the works of the previous generation:

> The subconscious [*podświadomość*] has ceased to be the seat of formless elements that one might suspect of having something to do with the cosmos [...]. Freud has bestowed on it a structure and the memory of specific events. He has attributed to it a history that is individual and in part also collective. According to Freud's early work, sadism and the destructive drive are childhood fixations serving the adult for pathological self-affirmation. Later Freud believed this perspective was insufficient. His research on war neuroses led him to the risky and convoluted theory of the death drive. Without going into details, we should remark that the cruelty of the twentieth century represents the greatest difficulties for psychoanalysis. (p. 17)

A short summary of Freudianism such as this will always contain inconsistencies and simplifications; for instance, Ważyk's use of the term *podświadomość* [subconscious] is not based on Freud's terminology. But we should highlight the most important upshot of his strategy: in order to play up the difference between the literature of Young Poland and the work of the generation that came of age after World War I, he draws what he calls "the modern line of division" between "a subjective mystical understanding" and "the wave of empirical experience" (p. 18). For this, Ważyk must strip Young Poland of eroticism:

> The traditional notion of the soul as the seat of thought, feeling and will does not contain eroticism. The practice of Przybyszewski and others who

80 A. Ważyk, *Dziwna historia awangardy*, p. 16.

> blended the soul with eroticism ridiculed them in the eyes of later readers. In the work of the same poets we find a model of subjectivity that did not fade away with the end of its era, namely the dynamic model of two drives, two primordial forces. In the work of the naturalist and modernist writers, the instinct that biologists call the instinct to preserve the species took on the shape of a fatalism that wreaks havoc in the life of the individual. In poetry, where it is called desire [*żądza*] or lust [*chuć*], it represented an even crueller force – a force that was biological or, as Ignacy Matuszewski has suggested, even cosmic, and which uses men and women as blind tools. It was complemented by a drive of a higher order, historically derived from the Jena group of early German romanticism, desire without an object, or, according to the language of Young Poland – longing for something unattainable, for the ideal woman who does not exist, for cosmic infinity or for nothingness. The ensemble of these forces collided with the religious moral system. (p. 13)

Throughout this work Ważyk's tone is condescending; he remarks that "for readers accustomed to the ubiquitous eroticism of our century the revelations from 1911 sound amusing" (p. 15); he describes Leśmian's work as "the last demoniacal convulsions in poetry [...]. Never has Lucifer fallen so low"; "against the backdrop of the interwar period, Leśmian has been roving about like Dracula" (p. 19). Eager to present a sharp break and clear definitions, Ważyk presents an argument that is increasingly risky, for instance when he identifies Witkacy – perhaps the only writer besides Irzykowski who was conversant with psychoanalysis immediately after the war – as a straightforward heir of Young Poland: "the fact that he knew Freud made no difference. He used the old model of the two kinds of longing, the metaphysical and the sexual, weaving them into one insatiability" (p. 17).

Ważyk's strategy seems very odd given that *Trzy rozprawy z teorii seksualnej*, the 1924 Polish translation of Freud's *Three Essays on the Theory of Sexuality*, is deeply marked by the language of Young Poland, in particular what is disparagingly called "przybyszewszczyzna," i.e. the style, words and phrases that had entered through the work of Przybyszewski. In their search for Polish equivalents to psychoanalytical terms, Jekels and Albiński chose terms that Ważyk later associated with the erotic fatalism of the Young Poland generation, such as *chuć* for libido. Jekels had already used this word in his first translation, *O psychoanalizie* [*Five Lectures on*

Psycho-Analysis], published in 1911.[81] Bronisław Bandrowski criticised this unfortunate translation in 1912,[82] and no other writer who discussed Freud in the Polish press ever used the word *chuć*, opting for the Latin *libido* or a neutral translation such as "sexual desire" [*pożądanie płciowe*].[83] Perhaps it was Jekels' decision to translate Freud's *Libido* as *chuć* that inspired Przybyszewski to present himself as a precursor of psychoanalysis. In his memoirs, which appeared in 1926, i.e. two years after *Trzy rozprawy z teorii seksualnej* [*Three Essays on the Theory of Sexuality*], he also confesses that his greatest dream had been to become an eminent psychiatrist; finally, he complains that if it had not been for difficult circumstances, he might have attained the fame that had fallen to Freud instead.[84]

In the beginning there was libido?

According to leading expert Gabriela Matuszek, it is not Stanisław Przybyszewski's merit as a writer that makes him worth studying, but his role in shaping Polish modernism. He showed the most original reaction "to the civilisational shock caused by modernity".[85] Przybyszewski's prose poem *Totenmesse* (1893) and its Polish version, *Requiem aeternam* (1904), were, in Matuszek's view, a requiem for the Cartesian subject – the subject that is abstract, free of sexual difference, guaranteeing security, identity, and a coherent world view. His work is marked by a unique tension between aversion to sexuality and a longing for androgyny, in which the fragmented male subject would be made whole again through his union with a woman. The lived reality of the writer's fictional alter ego, however, proves again and again that such a longing could never be fulfilled, as no woman can assure the synthesis of his fragmented self. His search for an androgynous "dual-unity" [*dwój-jednia*] betrays his sense of incompleteness and the instability of the masculine subject which, confronted with the radical difference of the woman, is deprived of its most important support, namely his own untouchable identity. The masculine subject

81 Z. Freud, *O psychoanalizie: Pięć odczytów*, p. 64 and passim.

82 *RF* 1912, no. 7, p. 126.

83 See e.g. W. Sterling, "Istota histerii w świetle nowoczesnych teorii psychologicznych", *MIK* 1910, no. 46, p. 1070.

84 S. Przybyszewski, *Moi współcześni* (Warsaw: Czytelnik, 1959), p. 81.

85 G. Matuszek, *Stanisław Przybyszewski – pisarz nowoczesny: Eseje i proza – próba monografii* (Cracow: Universitas, 2008), p. 9.

discovers in himself a reservoir of otherness that had previously been masked behind a simulated omnipotence. As Paweł Dybel has argued, the horizon of twentieth-century ideas on sex has been defined by Freud's proposition that anatomical sexual difference is less salient in the construction of identity than the meaning attributed to it. By highlighting the significance of unconscious fantasies about the body, Freud overcame the "biologism" of which he was so often accused. His most important discovery is perhaps the recognition of the non-hedonistic nature of sexuality, which contains an inextricable element of aggression. The critics who accused Freud of "pansexualism" tended to under-appreciate the inseparability of Eros and Thanatos in psychoanalysis. In fact, sexuality is a deeply traumatic experience for Freud, and his texts betray his fear of womanhood; he conceals it, but according to later readers it still emerges in his misogyny.[86] In Poland, similar ideas and fears, rooted in the intellectual atmosphere of the fin de siècle, found their clearest – and earliest – expression in the work of Przybyszewski.

Matuszek examines one of Przybyszewski's less well-known articles from the year 1907, namely "Przyczynek do etyki płci" [A Contribution to the Ethics of Sex].[87] Here Przybyszewski accepts that the world and humanity carry the stigma of sex, a purely positive, creative force. In this text his aversion to the sexual act has disappeared – instead, he sacralises it and celebrates it for its beauty. Przybyszewski constructs his own redemptive discourse: the combination of the Platonic Androgyne myth with the metaphysics of lust [*chuć*] "allows him to avoid the trap, characteristic of early modernism, of fear of the body and sexuality".[88] Interestingly, Przybyszewski's text struck readers as anachronistic as soon it was published. In 1908 Karol Irzykowski wrote that this sexual monism was entirely passé:

> We will agree with any equation if only it provides, on either side, a concept that is new, unexpected, valuable, one that in some way makes it easier for us to find our bearings in the world, or that serves as a signpost to find our bearings in life. The world = poetry. The world = art. The world = despair. But

86 Cf. P. Dybel, *Zagadka "drugiej płci"* (pp. 91-145).

87 This is Przybyszewski's Polish translation of his article "Das Geschlecht," published in *Der Sturm* in 1910. The German text was a modification of a previous article, also titled "Das Geschlecht," which had appeared three years before in *Die Fackel* in Vienna.

88 G. Matuszek, *Stanisław Przybyszewski*, pp. 81–82.

> the world = sex? [...] Away with the antiquated symbols that mean nothing to our mind, to our feeling, and can therefore only confound us.

"There was a time," Irzykowski adds, "when we were all enthusiastic about this." He writes about one of Przybyszewski's earliest works, *Totenmesse*:

> One of the most powerful passages in all of erotic literature is a passage in *Totenmesse* [...] that describes the sex act as a sort of sacred mystery whose goal is to uncover the secret of the world. Here the protagonist acts as if he were a priest-scientist; he brings to mind the horror and the gravity of a medieval alchemist who is about to discover gold in his crucible; this gold glimmers towards him from the world beyond, which has jealously guarded its secret but was finally vanquished. This loftiness hovers close to ridiculousness. We have all examined the world in this manner, but we found absolutely nothing.[89]

For Irzykowski, *chuć* is one of those "antiquated symbols" that has served the epoch in the early stages of its development; to refer to it on the verge or the twentieth century, however, can only be as embarrassing as any naive ecstasy.

Summarising his own achievements in his memoirs *Moi współcześni* [My Contemporaries], Przybyszewski presents his theory of sexual difference as directly opposed to the work of his long-time rival August Strindberg (1849–1912). He insists that the Swedish playwright and novelist had no influence on him whatsoever, that "perhaps no two artists' works are as dissimilar as Strindberg's and mine".[90] Although they both look to the natural sciences in their representations of the world and their transgressions of taboos, there is a fundamental distinction in the way they portray the relationship between women and men. For Przybyszewski the two sexes are radically different and mutually incomprehensible:

> Never can a woman know anything about man, nor man about woman – everything that a woman writes about men is a simple and usually quite laughable fiction, while things written by men about women are also

89 K. Irzykowski, "Spojrzenie wstecz ku 'Przyczynkowi do etyki płci' Stanisława Przybyszewskiego", in *Pisma rozproszone 1897–1922* (Cracow: Wydawnictwo Literackie, 1998), pp. 73–75 (originally published in *Nasz Kraj* in 1908).

90 S. Przybyszewski, *Moi współcześni*, p. 146.

> fiction: this is what woman looks like in his soul, a woman created by him, a Venus emerging from the ocean foam of the deepest layers of the fathomless profundity of his soul – and nothing more. (p. 148)

Just as man's "knowledge" of woman is fictional, Przybyszewski argues, so is women's demand for equal rights: it aims to do away with sexual difference and grants, albeit indirectly, that men are superior. Between woman and man there can be no other bridge than love. Unlike Strindberg, Przybyszewski continues, he is no misogynist, no matter what the critics might say. He explains: "as a man I must not and cannot [...] value women as such, because somehow a woman is [...] an entirely different creature than I – neither superior nor inferior, simply different" (*ibid.*). Here Przybyszewski makes the surprising claim that misogynist attitudes result from the femininity of the men in question (such as Strindberg or Weininger):

> A man looks at woman differently than Strindberg and is unable to ascertain if woman really looks just the way that Strindberg presents her, but it is possible that the unique and most ingenious feminine mind, which for me Strindberg's mind represents, has managed to bring out the whole painful truth. Only woman can hate like Strindberg. (p. 147)

Przybyszewski goes on to claim: "The man in me was too strong to be able to fathom or even to sense Strindberg's misogyny; too strongly did I feel the distance that God-Nature has created between the psyche of man and woman to hate her for it" (p. 157).

Przybyszewski proposed that Strindberg, adamant about the inferiority of women, was not just a woman at heart but also a hysterical one: "the key to understanding Strindberg is his hysteria as a creative power" (p. 163). He surmises that his Swedish colleague uses two brains: a masculine brain and another, even stronger one, which is "the maternal brain of the woman-fury, craving revenge for imagined wrongs, raving with hatred at anyone and anything that dares to stand in the way of her will, possessed by a persecution mania that detects conspiracy, scheming and inevitable treason in every most innocent word, in every most innocent deed" (*ibid.*). Strindberg, Przybyszewski continues, was forced to wage a bloody battle with himself for the following reason:

> He had in himself the harshest enemy, one that was monstrous in its demonism: woman. All of his implacability towards womankind, which exuded the venom of a plainly grotesque hatred, must be seen as a sadistic maltreatment of the woman in himself – this whole tooth-grinding, furious battle [...] was a battle with the satanic demon within himself: woman. (p. 165)

Thanks to this battle Strindberg not only grows into the most ingenious woman author (*ibid.*), but also sheds light on the construction of gender in general:

> Every man has in his soul a part of femininity and vice versa – every woman has some part of a masculine soul, and when this a balance is maintained, the division into two separate sexes is accomplished. But a terrible havoc and a terrible dilemma befall the soul when the feminine part prevails in a man or vice versa, the masculine part in the soul of a woman. (pp. 165-166)

He goes on to argue that humans are born with both a masculine and a feminine part, which begin to strive for dominance around the time of puberty.

> The question is which of these parts will prevail. In so-called "anomalous" cases the feminine part prevails in the soul of a growing boy and vice versa: in the soul of a girl the masculine part takes the upper hand, and this sad, desperate victory accounts for the phenomenon called homosexuality, which is incomprehensible for a "healthy" person and so barbarously persecuted [...]. (*Ibid.*)

Homosexuality, Przybyszewski believes, "does not necessarily manifest itself only in sexual matters; most often it becomes noticeable in a person's inner life" (*ibid.*). It is noteworthy that he puts words such as "healthy" and "anomalous" in quotation marks – a strategy that dovetails with the radical interrogation of sexual norms that marked his career.

In *Moi współcześni* he concludes his musings on sex as follows:

> I imagine what a bizarre paradox you all must see in this argumentation of mine, but even mainstream science is beginning to suggest that these theories of mine, which I have been promoting for thirty years already, are

> not at all infertile. It is on the very same canvas of thought that the great psychologist Freud in Vienna has been designing the rich and interesting patterns of his theories. (pp. 166-167)

Indeed it would be hard to overlook the similarities between Przybyszewski's early publications – in the 1890s he was writing in German – and Freud's concept of sexual difference, first published as late as 1905 in *Drei Abhandlungen zur Sexualtheorie* [*Three Essays on the Theory of Sexuality*]. Paweł Dybel recently discussed these similarities, validating the claim that Przybyszewski anticipated some of the findings of psychoanalysis.[91] Wojciech Gutowski and Gabriela Matuszek have reached similar conclusions.[92] But such arguments had already been proposed about a hundred years before: in 1924, Georges Dubujadoux discussed Freud's unpopularity in France and the fact that French writers refused to take notice of his theories. By way of comparison he outlined the use of psychoanalysis in other literatures, and here one of his key examples is Stanisław Przybyszewski. Dubujadoux also presents a detailed analysis of the novel *De Profundis* (1896) because he sees Przybyszewski as a precursor of Freud.[93] In 1910, i.e. even before Dubujadoux, it was Blaise Cendrars who became interested in Przybyszewski's work. He considered translating *Totenmesse* from German to French because he was fascinated with the way in which Przybyszewski's exploration of the subconscious foreshadowed Freud's.[94]

Przybyszewski asserts in his memoir that his "metaphysics of sex" had no connection with Otto Weininger's work, but scholars have pointed out similarities. According to Gutowski, a comparison between these two writers "irresistibly imposes itself"[95] even if it is hard to talk about influence, as

91 P. Dybel, "Przybyszewski – powracający meteor", in *Urwane ścieżki: Przybyszewski–Freud–Lacan*, pp. 47–131.

92 Cf. e.g. W. Gutowski, *Konstelacja Przybyszewskiego* (Toruń: Wydawnictwo Adam Marszałek, 2008), p. 78.

93 G. Dubujadoux, "Les Lettres Françaises et l'Inconscient", *MDF* 1924, no. 615, pp. 600–605.

94 D. Steel, "Les debuts", p. 67.

95 W. Gutowski, "Stanisław Przybyszewski i Otto Weininger – dwie metafizyki płci", in *Konstelacja Przybyszewskiego*, p. 16. Gutowski goes on to argue that the similarities between Przybyszewski and Weininger are only superficial: "compared to Weininger's reductive and singularly dogmatic metaphysics of asexuality, Przybyszewski's proposition must be read as a complex metaphysics of the creative Eros, closely related to the concept of 'new art'" (p. 29).

Weininger's monograph *Geschlecht und Charakter* was published long after Przybyszewski's most important literary works (the German original of Weininger's work appeared in 1903). At the same time, Przy-byszewski's claim that he inspired Weininger is doubtful. In his memoir he writes that many of the ingenious passages in *Geschlecht und Charakter* were no more than paraphrases of his own *Totenmesse.* He also reports having read in "some Galician paper" that the writer and poet Peter Altenberg (1859-1919) attributed Weininger's suicide to his reading of Przybyszewski's *Totenmesse.*[96]

The situation can be explained more straightforwardly when we sidestep the notion of influence: whatever Przybyszewski may have believed, any similarities between his ideas and Freud's only pertain to Freud's earliest theories, i.e. from the time of his friendship with the Berlin-based otolaryngologist Wilhelm Fliess. The two gentlemen first met in 1887. Freud was thirty-one years old, Fliess was two years his junior. They started to meet regularly, calling their get-togethers "congresses" – a tongue-in-cheek hint at their own position outside the scientific mainstream. They also began to exchange letters. Their correspondence, which lasted for seventeen years, documents the birth of psychoanalysis; it was most intense at the very end of the nineteenth-century, from the publication of Freud and Breuer's *Studies on Hysteria* in 1895 until the publication of *The Interpretation of Dreams* in 1899.

Fliess, who ran a successful practice, also studied the relationship between sexual disorders in women and changes in their nasal mucous membranes.[97] He had a tremendous influence on his friend. Most importantly, he was Freud's psychoanalyst *avant la lettre*: it is in his letters to Fliess that Freud performed his self-analysis, which led him to define key elements of his theory, such as the Oedipus complex. Freud also borrowed some ideas from Fliess, such as the notion of innate bisexuality and the logic of sexual attraction. The latter brings to mind Przybyszewski's theory that men with feminine traits find themselves drawn to masculine women and *vice versa*, which means that in a way four people – rather than two – participate in the sexual act. Fliess developed an idiosyncratic concept of biorhythms according to which life follows periodic cycles – 28 days for women and 23 days for men – that reflect the cosmic order of nature. This idea did not find its way into Freud's theory, although he was initially

96 S. Przybyszewski, *Moi współcześni*, p. 173.

97 I wrote about Fliess in the chapter on Zapolska: he performed the failed operation on one of Freud's first patients, Emma Eckstein.

intrigued and thought about ways to integrate it into his own discipline; in his letters Freud provided his friend with detailed observations of his own biorhythm. Their friendship ended in 1904 when Fliess came across one of his own concepts, which he had shared with Freud in confidence a few years before, published in Otto Weininger's *Geschlecht und Charakter.*[98] He read, for instance, that every individual has components of both sexes, or that mathematical rules govern people's choice of partners (sexual attraction peaks when one person has the same number of masculine elements as the number of feminine elements in the other person), with the perfect sexual relationship leading to the creation of a unity: a perfect woman and a perfect man.[99]

Fliess accused Freud of indiscretion, and rightly so: his friend in Vienna had shared Fliess's theory with a patient, Hermann Swoboda, who was in turn a friend of Weininger's (he published a biographical account titled "Otto Weiningers Tod" [Otto Weininger's Death] in 1911). In addition, it turned out that Weininger had consulted Freud, who read the manuscript of *Geschlecht und Charakter* but failed to set things straight and prevent the apparently plagiaristic publication.[100] His omission is probably due to the fact that he himself owed more to Fliess than he was willing to admit. In

98 On Weininger see esp. J. Le Rider, *Le cas Otto Weininger: Racines de l'antiféminisme et de l'antisémitisme* (Paris: PUF, 1982); Chandak Sengoopta, *Otto Weininger: Sex, Science, and Self in Imperial Vienna* (Chicago: University of Chicago Press, 2000).

99 Weininger develops this theory in the first part of *Geschlecht und Charakter*, i.e. "Die sexuelle Mannigfaltigkeit". He does not return to it in the second part, "Die sexuellen Typen". Here his misogyny and anti-Semitism appear; femininity and masculinity are treated from an essentialist perspective. Many recent editions have omitted volume one, often without a comment. See for instance O. Weininger, *Płeć i charakter*, trans. by O. Ortwin (Warsaw: Sagittarius, 1994).

100 Freud's role in this plagiarism has been broadly discussed. See esp. E. Porge, *Vol d'idées? Wilhelm Fliess, son plagiat et Freud, suivi de "Pour ma propre cause" de Wilhelm Fliess* (Paris: Denoël, 1994); M. Schröter, "Fliess versus Weininger, Swoboda, and Freud: The Plagiarism Conflict of 1906 Assessed in the Light of the Documents", *PAH* 2003, no. 2, pp. 147–173. It is also worth noting that Hermann Swoboda drew on some of Fliess's theory, i.e. his idea of the periodic cycles, in *Die Perioden des menschlichen Organismus* (1904); unlike Weininger, however, Swoboda does mention Fliess. The first person to accuse Weininger and Swoboda of plagiarising Fliess was the latter's friend Richard Pfenning in a pamphlet titled *Wilhelm Fliess und seine Nachentdecker O. Weininger und H. Swoboda* (Berlin: Emil Goldschmidt, 1906), reprinted in E. Porge, *Vol d'idées?*, pp. 307–346. Fliess took a stance in a leaflet tilted *In eigener Sache: Gegen Otto Weininger u. Hermann Swoboda* (Berlin: Goldschmidt, 1906), reprinted in pp. 243–289.

The Psychopathology of Everyday Life, also published in 1904, his own involuntarily plagiarism of Fliess's idea appears as an example in the chapter "The Forgetting of Impressions and Intentions":

> One day in the summer of 1901 I remarked to a friend with whom I used at that time to have a lively exchange of scientific ideas: "These problems of the neuroses are only to be solved if we base ourselves wholly and completely on the assumption of the original bisexuality of the individual." To which he replied: "That's what I told you two and a half years ago at Br.[Breslau] when we went for that evening walk. But you wouldn't hear of it then." It is painful to be requested in this way to surrender one's originality. I could not recall any such conversation or this pronouncement of my friend's. One of us must have been mistaken and on the "cui prodest?" principle it must have been myself. Indeed, in the course of the next week I remembered the whole incident, which was just as my friend had tried to recall it to me; I even recollected the answer I had given him at the time: "I've not accepted that yet; I'm not inclined to go into the question." But since then I have grown a little more tolerant when, in reading medical literature, I come across one of the few ideas with which my name can be associated, and find that my name has not been mentioned.[101]

While Freud was sending letters to Fliess in Berlin, Przybyszewski was also staying there (1889-94). At first he studied architecture, then, in 1890, he switched to medicine before setting out to write *Totenmesse*, which appeared in 1893. In his memoirs he writes that he was most interested in psychiatry, and that he spent much of his time on experimental psychology, reading Ribot, Paulhan, Münsterberg, Wundt and others.[102] He also admits that he was having "psychopathic fantasies about a professorship in psychiatry" – a dream that was shattered when, after six semesters, his involvement with the workers' movement led to his expulsion from the university:

> My most cherished dream had been to become a great psychiatrist! I had always loved the madmen, the psychopaths, the degenerates, the derailed, the weak and twisted, those who seek death while death avoids them, in a

101 S. Freud, *The Psychopathology of Everyday Life*, SE VI, pp. 143-144.
102 S. Przybyszewski, *Moi współcześni*, p. 75.

word: the poor, disinherited children of Satan, and they loved me in return. (p. 81)

During that time that Przybyszewski spent in Berlin, Fliess, having graduated in 1883, already ran a successful private practice. To ascertain if the two ever met in person would demand a detailed archival search, but we can assume that Freud's friend and the gifted student from Poland moved in the same circles – Berlin's medical community – and were influenced by the same research publications. Przybyszewski's above-mentioned reading list could not have been much different from the one that Fliess would have had a few years earlier, when he was a student at the same university; they probably had some of the same lecturers and professors, which means they were trained in one and the same school of understanding nervous disorders. In later years Fliess became well known among Berlin's avant-garde, i.e. the writers and artists associated with the magazine *Der Sturm*, with which Przybyszewski also collaborated occasionally;[103] "Dr Fliess" is explicitly mentioned by Salomon Friedländer, who published under the pseudonym "Mynona".[104] According to Karolina Krasuska, who has examined the rhetorics of gender in programmatic literary essays, manifests, social criticism and even illustrations in *Der Sturm*, the magazine presented "a configuration of principles of masculinity and femininity assumed to be universal, arranged in a hierarchical relationship;" thus the magazine's outlook was "in keeping with the masculinist tendencies described as characteristic for German modernism and as a symptom of the crisis of masculinity".[105]

There is no doubt that Freud was most indebted to Fliess in his *Drei Abhandlungen zur Sexualtheorie* [*Three Essays on the Theory of Sexuality*].[106] Published in 1905, it was written just as Freud's conflict with Fliess was unfolding. In the same letter in which he responds to Fliess's accusations by explaining his own role in the whole affair he also writes:

103 *Der Sturm* published Przybyszewski's "Das Geschlecht" (*DS* 1910, no. 31, pp. 243–244 and no. 34, pp. 251–252). This text had appeared in the Vienna-based *Die Fackel* three years earlier. The first edition – but not the second – is dedicated to "the spirit of Weininger".

104 Mynona [S. Friedländer], "Willi Wille", *DS* 1917, no. 8, pp. 124–126.

105 K. Krasuska, *Płeć i naród: Trans/lokacje* p. 85.

106 F.J. Sulloway, *Freud, Biologist of the Mind: Beyond the Psychoanalytic Legend* (Cambridge, MA: Harvard University Press, 1992), pp. 171–237.

> At present I am finishing "Three Essays on the Theory of Sexuality", in which I avoid the topic of bisexuality as far as possible. At two places I cannot do so: in the explanation of sexual inversion [...] [and] when I mention the homosexual current in neurotics. There I plan to add a note that I had been prepared for the necessity of this finding by certain remarks of yours.[107]

In the published text, the announced note reads:

> Psychoneuroses are also very often associated with manifest inversion. In such cases the heterosexual current of feelings has undergone complete suppression. It is only fair to say that my attention was first drawn to the necessary universality of the tendency to inversion in psychoneurotics by Wilhelm Fliess of Berlin, after I have discussed its presence in individual cases. This fact, which has not been sufficiently appreciated, cannot fail to have a decisive influence on any theory of homosexuality.[108]

Freud also admits that he owes the phrase "period of sexual latency" (p. 178) to Fliess.

Another brief mention of Fliess can be found in the first edition – and only the first edition – in the chapter "The Differentiation between Men and Women" in Freud's *Three Essays*. The editors of the Standard Edition have reintroduced this mention in a footnote: "Since I have become acquainted [through Wilhelm Fliess] with the notion of bisexuality I have regarded it as the decisive factor, and without taking bisexuality into account I think it would scarcely be possible to arrive at an understanding of the sexual manifestations that are actually to be observed in men and women" (p. 220). Freud does not mention his friend in his literature review on bisexuality, and the one reference to Fliess from the first edition disappears after their fallout. The second edition of *Three Essays* was published in 1910, when Fliess's treatise had finally appeared as well. Now Freud added the following footnote: "Fliess (1906) subsequently claimed the idea of bisexuality (in the sense of duality of sex) as his own" (p. 143). In the sixth edition of 1924 Freud added another two sentences: "In lay circles the hypothesis of human bisexuality is regarded as being due to O.

107 *The Complete Letters of Sigmund Freud to Wilhelm Fliess*, p. 464.

108 *Three Essays on Sexuality*, SE VII, p. 166.

Weininger, the philosopher, who died at an early age, and who made the idea the basis of a somewhat unbalanced book (1903). The particulars which I have enumerated above will be sufficient to show how little justification there is for the claim" (p. 143).

The Polish edition of *Three Essays* is based on the fifth German edition of 1922, so it contains neither the brief acknowledgement of Fliess from the first edition nor the note about Weininger from the sixth. It is worth noting, however, that the Polish edition pays homage to Fliess indirectly. Freud uses the Latin-based term *Bisexualität*, departing from Fliess's *Zweigeschlechtlichkeit* (from German *zwei* [two] and *Geschlecht* [sex or gender]). Jekels and Albiński return to Fliess's vernacular choice, opting not for the Latin-based *biseksualność* but for the Slavic *dwupłciowość*, from *dwa* [two] and *płeć* [sex or gender]. This translation of *Bisexualität* as *dwupłciowość* not only signifies a return to Fliess's term but also associates the Polish edition of Freud's *Three Essays* with Przybyszewski's style: after all, he frequently references the Platonic myth of the androgyne or *dwój-jednia.*[109]

There is no doubt, however, that the most significant of the translators' choices is that of *chuć*, a very loaded term, for Freud's term *Libido*. In the opening sentences of his work Freud justifies this Latin term. The first of the three essays, dedicated to sexual deviance, begins by juxtaposing two essential drives, namely the sexual instinct and the "instinct of nutrition". While in the case of the latter drive everyday language offers a convenient expression for the need in question (hunger), there is no adequate term for the sexual drive in the German language. One might think of the vernacular *Lust*, but Freud rejected this word as too ambiguous, for besides referring to the state of having a certain need it also describes the experience of having this need satisfied. This is why Freud, who usually avoids jargon, opted for the scientific *Libido*. In a footnote he claims that he found this term in Aleksander Moll's *Untersuchungen über die Libido sexualis* (1898), but it is apparent that this reference to Moll's acclaimed treatise was mostly an attempt to legitimise his own work: in his letters to Fliess, Freud had used the term *Libido* at least four years before Moll published his book. Indeed, the German *Lust* can be translated as both inclination or desire as well as delight or pleasure. The Polish *chuć* does not have this double meaning. *Chuć* indicates – as unequivocally as the term "hunger" – a state of need that demands to be fulfilled. Unlike *Libido*,

109 S. Przybyszewski, *Moi współcześni*, p. 167.

moreover, *chuć* leaves no doubt about its connection with sexuality. If anything, *Libido* leaves more room for ambiguity in this regard (for instance in Jung's interpretation, which Freud repeatedly rejected, most notably in *Three Essays*) and has been understood as a form of psychic energy.

The translators' use of *chuć* can be explained by the fact that the Polish language happened to have the word that Freud was not able to find in German, which is why he had to opt for a Latin term. It is surprising, however, that Jekels and Albiński felt no need to explain their choice – after all, they did add a footnote to the more straightforward translation of *Lust* [pleasure] and *Unlust* [unpleasure] as *rozkosz* and *przykrość* respectively.[110] They must have considered *chuć* an obvious equivalent of *Libido*, so much so that Freud's original term almost disappears from the Polish edition.

Jekels and Albiński's rendering of libido as *chuć* has the effect that, in terms of style, their Polish version of Freud reads almost like a lost work by Przybyszewski. The Slavic *chuć*, moreover, was antiquated even when Przybyszewski used it, suggesting some sort of mythical Old-Polish raunchiness. We must add here that there is a difference between his *Totenmesse* and *Requiem aeternam*, his Polish self-translation, which opens with the words: "In the beginning there was lust" ("Na początku była chuć"). The blasphemous verse that opens the German original *Totenmesse* is "Am Anfang war das Geschlecht" or "In the beginning there was sex".[111] Przybyszewski could have opted for words such as *Wollust* [voluptuousness] or *Begierde* [desire] if he had wanted to evoke sexual appetite, as he later did in the Polish version with *chuć*, but he wrote *Geschlecht*, just as Weininger did in the title of *Geschlecht und Charakter*.[112] As Matuszek has

110 This is the translators' only lengthy footnote in the entire book. The remaining notes point out minor uncertainties regarding terms such as *Vorlust* [fore-pleasure] (translated as *rozkosz wstępna*, see Z. Freud, *Trzy rozprawy z teorii seksualnej*, p. 150). Jekels and Albiński expounded Freud's argument in two places. There is a translators' footnote explaining that "conversion is a transposition of psychic drives into physical symptoms" (p. 67), while the section on the child's choice of an object receives a substantial quotation from a recent work by Freud, "The Infantile Genital Organisation" (1923) (pp. 133–134).

111 Here "sex" [*Geschlecht*] is used in the sense of being male or female, not in the sense of sexual activity.

112 Boy-Żeleński discusses the problems with Przybyszewski's self-translations in *Ludzie żywi: Pisma*, vol. 2 (Warsaw: PIW, 1956), pp. 32–51.

demonstrated, however, Przybyszewski understands *Geschlecht* as "the driving force behind all development [...], recalling the Eros of ancient Greece, the Hindu Kama, Schopenhauer's 'blind will,' Nietzsche's 'will to power' or Bergson's later *élan vital*, the cosmic power that has created the world and directs its evolution".[113] In this sense his understanding of *Geschlecht* is close to Freud's libido, which Freud often compares to Plato's Eros. Perhaps if Przybyszewski had written *Totenmesse* after Freud, his opening sentence would have been "Am Anfang war die Libido" – "In the beginning there was the libido". As it seems, this is how his use of *Geschlecht* resonates with literary scholars today, inspiring us to read Przybyszewski alongside Freud.

Such a reading is also facilitated by the fact that the topics discussed in Freud's *Three Essays* are remarkably close to the themes that interested Przybyszewski. The first essay is in fact a catalogue of various "sexual aberrations," arranged according to the object of desire (here we find inversion, i.e. homosexuality, but also pedophilia and zoophilia) as well as the "sexual aim," which can be more or less remote from what is considered to be the norm, i.e. heterosexual genital intercourse (Freud mentions pleasure from stimulating the mouth, anus or other body parts, as well as fetishism, exhibitionism, voyeurism, sadism and masochism). Freud's goal in providing this list was of course different than Krafft-Ebing's *Psychopathia sexualis*, which the modernists read with great interest: rather than pathologising any sexual practices, Freud aimed to highlight the fact that the relationship between the sexual instinct and its object is no more than arbitrary. The deviations he discusses do not represent for him symptoms of degeneracy or mental illness; instead, they attest to the almost infinite number of forms in which the libido can realise itself, since it is not essentially bound to any object or aim. In a footnote Freud insists (at a time when homosexuality was still prohibited in Austria![114]): "Psycho-analytic research is most decidedly opposed to any attempt at separating off homosexuals from the rest of mankind as a group of special character [...]. From the point of view of psycho-analysis the exclusive sexual interest felt by men for women is also a problem that needs elucidating and is not a self-evident fact based upon an attraction

113 G. Matuszek; *Der geniale Pole?*, p. 22.

114 Helmut Graupnel, "Austria", in *Sociolegal Control of Homosexuality: A Multi-Nation Comparison*, ed. by Donald J. West, Richard Green (New York: Kluwer Academic Publishers, 2002), pp. 269-287.

that is ultimately of a chemical nature".[115] Even the idea of two sexes strikes Freud as questionable: "It is essential to understand clearly that the concepts of 'masculine' and 'feminine,' whose meaning seems so unambiguous to ordinary people, are among the most confused that occur in science" (p. 219). Although Freud uses the words "masculine" and "feminine" in his own text to connote activity and passivity (the libido is "masculine," since "an instinct is always active," *ibid.*), he also voices reservations:

> In human beings pure masculinity or femininity is not to be found either in a psychological or a biological sense. Every individual on the contrary displays a mixture of the character-traits belonging to his own and to the opposite sex; and he shows a combination of activity and passivity whether or not these last character-traits tally with his biological ones. (p. 220).

In the second essay Freud goes on to discuss childhood sexuality (he describes it as "polymorphously perverse" and suggests that it "can be led into all possible kinds of sexual irregularities" (p. 191)). Here it becomes clear that puberty represents a series of losses as the individual lets go of the erotic potential with which they were endowed before they entered the cogwheels of cultural normalisation. The third essay focuses on the Oedipus complex, which Freud describes as the most important complex conceptualised by psychoanalysis. Despite the moral taboo, psychoanalysis has shown "how intensely the individual struggles with the temptation to incest during his period of growth and how frequently the barrier is transgressed in phantasies and even in reality" (p. 225). It is remarkable that several passages of this essay correspond to the successive tragic experiences of the protagonist of Przybyszewski's *Totenmesse*.

Perhaps Przybyszewski was right to call himself a precursor of Freud in his memoirs, *Moi współcześni*, in 1926. The Polish translation of Freud's *Three Essays*, which appeared two years before, suggests as much. Through their elaborate style, which echoed the Young Poland movement and Przybyszewski's work, Jekels and Albiński have planted Freud in a nineteenth-century context. It is hard to imagine a less fortunate choice. According to Włodzimierz Bolecki, if it is possible to identify a dominant factor in the literary consciousness of the interwar generation, then it is their opposition to the aesthetics associated with the previous epoch: "the identification of any

115 S. Freud, SE VII, pp. 145-146.

traces of Young Poland in the unfolding creative work of the interwar period led to the parts of the work in question being placed in the sphere of 'unwanted' literature [...]. The critics of the era were quite certain that they did not want a literature that referred back to that tradition."[116] This is why in Poland, during the first decade after World War I, psychoanalysis was regarded not as an expression of modernity, as it was in the Anglosphere or in France, but as a relict of Polish modernism, an anachronistic kind of symbolism related to the typical obsessions of the fin de siècle, i.e. the unconscious and the trauma of sexual difference. Despite Adam Ważyk's efforts to prove the opposite, in reality the same factors that made Polish avant-gardists weary of French surrealism also explain their rejection of Freudianism. The poets and writers who had their debut in the 1920s identified Freud with fin-de-siècle neo-romanticism, and so, having declared war on its "posthumous reign," i.e. the Young Poland movement, its stereotypical language and the heavy symbolism of the prewar era, they were bound to reject psychoanalysis.

However, while the avant-gardists who distanced themselves from Young Poland remained sceptical of psychoanalysis, the writers whose programmatic statements harked back to the neo-romantics of the turn of the twentieth century did not hesitate to discuss it openly. They were, most prominently, the expressionists associated with the journal *Zdrój* in Poznań, about whom Ważyk remarks that they did not join the mainstream of interwar poetry:

> The expressionists had this old-fashioned way of talking about the banality of life, about the wretchedness of existence, about sin, they had this old-fashioned way of assuming a dualism of soul and body, the separateness of the self that is not directed at any object [...]. The effusive and vague flow of their poetry, which was entirely free of visuality, remained in stark contrast to other trends.[117]

Literary historians agree that Stanisław Przybyszewski was the first Young Poland writer whose work can be described as expressionistic.[118] Today he

---

116 W. Bolecki, "Społeczne ramy lektury: 1918–1939 (Rekonesans)", in *Poetycki model prozy w dwudziestoleciu międzywojennym:* , p. 378.

117 A. Ważyk, *Dziwna historia awangardy*, p. 31.

118 K. Wyka, *Zarys współczesnej literatury polskiej (1884–1925)*, quoted in J. Ratajczak, "Wstęp", in *Krzyk i ekstaza: Antologia polskiego ekspresjonizmu*, ed. by J. Ratajczak (Poznań: Wydawnictwo Poznańskie, 1987), p. 5.

is seen as the godfather of Polish and German expressionism. In late 1916 or early 1917, he helped build the first team to run *Zdrój*, appointing Jan Hulewicz as director. The journal appeared between 1917 and 1920 (plus one issue in 1922), and its outlook was essentially modelled on the Young Poland movement. An advertising pamphlet provides a list of Young Poland pre-expressionist writers who had agreed to contribute to the new journal: Wacław Berent, Jan Kasprowicz, Władysław Reymont, Kazimierz Przerwa-Tetmajer and Stefan Żeromski.[119] Przybyszewski was one of the founders, the signatory of the programmatic statement,[120] and the journal's most important contributor. But he was also responsible for the team's fallout in 1918. A group of poets and painters who called themselves the "Bunt" [Revolt] group disagreed with Przybyszewski's relationship to Young Poland. These artists, who also collaborated with the German groups "Der Sturm" and "Die Aktion," believed that the new art could only emerge from the rubble of the old. But *Zdrój* had no place for those expressionists who rejected the heritage of Young Poland.[121] Its profile remained unchanged even when Stanisław Przybyszewski eventually left. It was Jan Stur who replaced him as a leader; he published his own manifesto, and yet, in his articles he referred to the spiritual patronage of the great modernists, Przybyszewski and Miciński.

Inspired by the Austrian writer Hermann Bahr, the expressionists defined their movement as being associated with "internal seeing," in opposition to impressionism, which they viewed as having an external focus;[122] they related expressionism to the Spirit and rejected Matter. These choices explain their interest not only in mysticism, theosophy, occultism and Hinduism but also in depth psychology.

One member of "Zdrój" was Stanisław Marcus, the author of an important programmatic statement titled "Psychologiczne i filozoficzne źródła ekspresjonizmu" [The Psychological and Philosophical Sources of

119 See *Krzyk i ekstaza* p. 27.

120 See S. Przybyszewski, "Odezwa programowa *Zdrój*", in *Kobiety winny moją trumnę ponieść*, pp. 72–79.

121 Cf. J. Malinowski, "Polska awangarda w Niemczech 1900–1933", in *Między Polską a światem: Od średniowiecza po lata II wojny światowej*, ed. by M. Morka, P. Paszkiewicz (Warsaw: Wydawnictwo Krąg, 1993), pp. 260–271.

122 S. Marcus, *Ekspresjonizm: Rozbiór ze stanowiska estetyki i materializmu dziejowego* (Konin: [self-published], 1921), p. 11; cf. also S. Przybyszewski, "Ekspresjonizm – Słowacki i 'Genezis z Ducha'", in *Krzyk i ekstaza*, pp. 70-77.

Expressionism] from 1921.[123] Marcus opens his programmatic statement by recalling the popular opinion that expressionism is a symptom of degeneracy, and that it brings forth creations that resemble the art work of mental patients. He admits that this view results from the fact that, in principle, expressionism does indeed operate with subconscious states. This sets it apart from the earlier movements from which it naturally evolved:

> It is true that the romantics already had an inkling of subconscious states and that the modernists deliberately worked with them, but they mostly presented it through the prism of conscious states, while expressionism works to reproduce a direct image of subconscious states; its whole uniqueness lies in this directness.[124]

Expressionist art is a "visual reproduction of irrationality," an attempt to render the internal world "*in statu nascendi* " (p. 7). Although Marcus mentions irrationality in a reference to Bergson, the most important authority in his view is the philosopher and psychologist Edward Abramowski. In his article "Wpływ woli w tworzeniu obrazów przedsennych" [The Influence of Will in the Creation of Hypnagogic Images], published in the first volume of the series "Prace z psychologii doświadczalnej" [Works in Experimental Psychology], Abramowski describes the hallucinations sometimes experienced on the brink of sleep. Marcus cites this article to suggest that these hypnagogic visuals are prototypes of expressionist paintings. This similarity allows him to argue that "expressionist paintings have their source in the transformation of the processes of the subconscious, they are their reflections" (p. 12). He concludes by equating the subconscious with Przybyszewski's notion of the "naked soul":

> In (rationalist) classicism and naturalism, the unity of the soul stemmed from intellectualism; romanticism and modernism shattered this apparent unity, drawing their inspiration directly from the emotions, until psychology split the soul into atoms, as it were, leading to the discovery of the unfathomable, the subconscious. Expressionism unites classicism and naturalism with romanticism and modernism: it restores the former unity – not the unity of the intellect but of the soul as a whole. The continuity

123 Passages are reprinted in *Krzyk i ekstaza*, pp. 233–239.

124 S. Marcus, *Ekspresjonizm*, p. 4.

> of the states of the soul is this unity that also dovetails perfectly with the "naked soul," i.e. the subconscious, which the romantics have intuited and which the modernists have tenaciously worked to reveal with the help of psychology. For to recognise the subconscious is a condition of recognising the continuity of the states of the soul. (pp. 16-17)

In his polemic *Zaraza w Grenadzie* [The Plague in Grenada, 1926] the Polish poet and critic Jan N. Miller (1890-1977), who was unenthusiastic about expressionism, describes the movement as "the straggling tail of this declining individualistic fission".[125] He identifies its beginnings in romanticism and its peak in the fin de siècle. In expressionism, he writes, "individualism has attained its extreme and self-destructive culmination" (p. 22). But, he continues, "we have come ashore" (*ibid.*) – the long-awaited collapse of this hegemonic trend has taken place, leading to the democratisation of the different forms of art and the universalisation of art's content. Indeed, what sets Polish expressionism apart from its German counterpart is the fact that the members of the "Zdrój" group constantly reference the tradition of Polish romanticism. (In his manifesto "Czego chcemy" [What We Want] Jan Stur writes: "Expressionism is a continuation of romanticisim."[126]) They were most attracted to a particular version of romanticism, namely the one that is represented by Słowacki's work from his genesic period (Przybyszewski's programmatic article was titled "Ekspresjonizm, Słowacki i 'Genezis z Ducha'" [Expressionism, Słowacki and 'Genesis from the Spirit']). The members of the "Zdrój" group saw all three great Polish romantics (Mickiewicz, Krasiński, Słowacki) as having pre-expressionist tendencies. This is why they read works from the early nineteenth century using methods that roughly corresponded to psychoanalytical theories.

It is worth mentioning for instance Stanisław Marcus's book *Podświadome w "Dziadach"* [The Subconscious in *Forefathers' Eve*], which was published in 1923.[127] It consists of the article "Mickiewicz-Gustaw (szkic psychoanalityczny)" [Mickiewicz-Gustaw (A Psychoanalytical Sketch)] as

125 J.N. Miller, *Zaraza w Grenadzie* (Warsaw: Księgarnia F. Hoesicka, 1926), p. 20.

126 Jan Stur, "Czego chcemy", in *Krzyk i ekstaza*, p. 208.

127 S. Marcus, *Podświadome w "Dziadach"* (Warsaw: Gebethner i Wolff, 1923). Literary scholars strongly disagreed with Marcus's argument. See for instance Ignacy Chrzanowski's "Historia literatury polskiej: Przegląd wydawnictw i opracowań naukowych", in *Slavia: Časopis pro slovanskou filologii*, 1928-1929, vol. 7, p. 389.

well as a short treatise, entirely unrelated to psychoanalysis, titled "Budowa mistyczna Improwizacji" [The Mystical Construction of Improvisation]. In the introduction Marcus writes that "to understand art in general and literary works in particular" requires familiarity with at least a few of the basic issues and methods of what he calls "the psychology of the subconscious" (p. 7). His own methodological inspirations present a rather unusual selection: he refers to two of Freud's works, namely the German original of *Introductory Lectures on Psycho-Analysis* as well as Jekels' Polish translation of *Five Lectures on Psycho-Analysis*; Leo Kaplan's *Grundzüge der Psychoanalyse* and Géza Róheim's short study *Spiegelzauber*, adding works by Abramowski, but also Ochorowicz's *Zjawiska mediumiczne* [Mediumistic Phenomena] and William James's *The Varieties of Religious Experience.* In the first article Marcus uses these tools to analyse "one of the most brilliant psychological scenes in Mickiewicz's work" (p. 12), focusing on the motif of the fir twig that the protagonist Gustaw mistakes for a cypress twig in *Forefathers' Eve*, Part IV. For Marcus this twig is a symbolic representation or externalisation of Gustaw's subconscious. Gustaw's monologue is analysed in depth, as if Marcus were the protagonist's psychoanalyst. Marcus proposes that a therapeutic relationship akin to transference arises between Gustaw and a Uniate priest; he also suggests that while writing this part of the drama, Mickiewicz must have entered "into an autocatalytical state, thus freeing himself from pent-up feelings" (p. 38). Here Marcus proposes an original definition of artistic creativity. He paraphrases Freud's notion of the artist having "an ability to convert internally repressed memories into works of art rather than neurotic symptoms" and adds that in his view, art is a "symptom of psychophysiological self-catalysis" (*ibid.*).

Another champion of expressionism was the Lviv-based Polish literature scholar Karol Klein. He, too, combined his fascination with expressionism and Freudianism with research on romanticism. In the second half of the 1920s he published a series of studies inspired by psychoanalysis: "Moment psychologiczny w mickiewiczowskim przekładzie 'Euthanasii'" Byrona" [A Psychological Moment in Mickiewicz's Translation of Byron's 'Euthanasia'][128] and "Przyroda u romantyków:

128 K. Klein, "Moment psychologiczny w mickiewiczowskim przekładzie 'Euthanasji' Byrona", *PLI* 1924/1925, vol. 21, pp. 217–227. For a detailed discussion see M. Lubański, *Krytyka literacka i psychoanaliza*, pp. 47–51. Stefan Baley's "Psychoanaliza jednej pomyłki Słowackiego" appeared the same year in *Pamiętnik Literacki.*

Zagadnienia podstawowe" [Nature in the Works of the Romantics: Fundamental Issues][129] appeared in *Pamiętnik Literacki*, while "O historii jednego motywu słów kilka" [A Few Words on the History of One Motif][130] and "O 'Stygmatacie' Norwida" [On Norwid's 'Stigma'][131] were published in *Ruch Literacki*. The first of these article is basically a psychological theory of literary translation that contains no direct references to Freud's school (Klein demonstrates that the translator's choice of the work was motivated by internal conflicts that also impacted the translation itself; thus the Polish version of "Euthanasia" can be seen as "Mickiewicz's confession displayed on the canvas of Byron's words"). The second article, by contrast, is furnished with an impressive bibliography. Klein was familiar not only with the German original of Freud's *Introductory Lectures on Psycho-Analysis*, works by Stekel and Adler as well as several issues of *Imago*, where he encountered Hitschmann's psychoanalysis of Schopenhauer, Rank and Sachs's article "The Importance of Psychoanalysis for the Humanities" ["Die Bedeutung der Psychoanalyse für die Geisteswissenschaften"], and Sachs's "Über Naturgefühl" [On the Sense of Nature], which had a particularly strong influence on his own thinking, but also the theories of the Swiss school – works by Jung, Bleuler and Silberer.[132]

Klein argues:

> [In Romanic literature] the emotional element is enhanced and empowered, and in relation to nature it has revealed the great significance of the psychic factors which philosophy had been pushing under the threshold of consciousness – an intellectual effort aimed at discovering objective truths and expressing them in a logically coherent and orderly system […].[133]

---

129 K. Klein, "Przyroda u romantyków: zagadnienia podstawowe", *PLI* 1924/25, no. 1/4, pp. 538–560. This publication represents the introductory part of larger study that was published in Lviv in 1928.

130 K. Klein, "O historii jednego motywu słów kilka", *RL* 1927, no. 8, pp. 228–230.

131 K. Klein, "O 'Stygmatacie' Norwida", *RL* 1928, no. 1, pp. 13–16.

132 Klein was remarkably well read in psychoanalysis, which shows for instance in a remark on the poetry of Elżbieta Drużbacka (1698–1765): discussing the motif of gazing into the sun, Klein refers "the psychoanalyst Freud" who comments on the "autobiography of a certain psychopath, Dr Schreber – who attributed to himself the capacity to gaze into the sun with impunity" (K. Klein, "O historii jednego motywu słów kilka", p. 230).

133 K. Klein, "Przyroda u romantyków", p. 544.

The upshot of this spiritual revolution, he continues, was "a subjective shaping and individual colouring of the irrational world – a world that is to a greater or lesser degree a representation of the human psyche that created it" (p. 545). Klein agrees with psychoanalysis that the symbol in poetry possesses "a value that is not stylistic anymore, not ornamental or arbitrary, but essential, conditioned by the functions of the person's mental system" (p. 556); he refers to Freud's work on the personification of nature by prehistoric humans as a "projection of compressed narcissism onto the external world" (p. 549).

Klein's most important work was the literary historical article "Ekspresjonizm polski: Grupa 'Zdroju'" [Polish Expressionism: The "Zdrój" Group].[134] Here he argues that the expressionism that evolved in Poznań had its sources in Jung's psychology and Bergson's philosophy. Klein believes that they both described the same discovery using terminologies appropriate to their disciplines: what Jung defined as libido was nothing else than Bergson's *élan vital.* For the expressionists, "the chaotic conglomerate of subconscious states" is an artistic object (p. 470), which is why this trend can be described as "philosophical irrationalism, transposed into the realm of art" (p. 472). The "Zdrój" group aimed at "reaching the subconscious content of life and strove to affect another person's feeling through means that were as precise as possible, in order to evoke analogous experiences" (*ibid.*). This is how Klein describes the difference between Young Poland and the "Zdrój" group:

> Over the last thirty years, Polish literature has gone through two phases ushered in by the turn towards the *mare tenebrarum*, which spilled into humankind's non-intellectual sphere. These phases are Young Poland and the expressionism of "Zdrój". In the first phase, the analytical functions of the brain were interrupted and the subconscious was brought to the fore, which had to entail changes in the field of aesthetics: the axis of creative efforts and considerations was the mood, i.e. the factor in art that synthesises the scattered activities of individual images, lines, colours and tones, introducing us into the inexpressible sphere of psychic life. If we eliminate from art the mood as a means to support our advancing towards the subconscious, but at the same time we leave its goal, then there emerges a trend that is subconscious par excellence – expressionism. It represents the objectivisation of psychic tension and the visions that

134 K. Klein, "Ekspresjonizm polski: grupa 'Zdroju'", *PH* 1932, no. 4/5, pp. 457–478.

> impose themselves on a person in intense emotional states, when our thoughts delve into concepts of a higher order, when our mental powers are partially suspended, and finally in states between sleep and half-wakefulness, in so-called hypnotic states that are the prototype of expressionist visions, of that inner seeing whose transformation and reflection is the very essence of expressionism. (p. 470)

Przybyszewska

Another person linked to the "Zdrój" group in the early 1920s was Stanisława Przybyszewska, the illegitimate daughter of Przybyszewski and the painter Aniela Pająkówna.[135] Born in 1901, she lost her mother at an early age and spent several years with relatives in Paris, Zurich, Vienna and Cracow. She only met her father when she was nineteen years old, and he was the one to encourage her to move to Poznań. She had just obtained a diploma from a women teachers' training college; a few days before leaving Cracow she also received her matura or secondary school certificate. In Poznań she found employment as a clerk at the Directorate of Posts and Telegraphs, where she worked from 1920 until 1922; she also taught at the Private Preparatory School and the State Teacher Training Courses. What is more, she studied at the University of Poznań's philosophy department, took violin lessons at the conservatory and devised a programme of self-study in the social sciences. Her father, who had ceased to collaborate with the expressionist periodical, introduced her to his acquaintances. Among them was her future husband, the writer and graphic artist Jan Panieński, a member of the "Bunt" [Revolt] group of painters and a great admirer of Przybyszewski's work. He had previously helped define the principles of the "Zdrój" group. After their marriage in 1923, the couple moved to the Free City of Danzig, where Panieński became a teacher at the Polish gymnasium, whose recent establishment was supported by Przybyszewski. Stanisława Przybyszewska's first publication, "Myśli o malarstwie"

135 This account of Przybyszewska's life is based on T. Lewandowski, *Dramat intelektu: Biografia literacka Stanisławy Przybyszewskiej* (Gdańsk: Morskie, 1982). A note on her official name: She was born Pająkówna and received the name Przyby-szewska when she was 13 years old. Having married Jan Panieński, her official name became Panieńska; as a widow she returned to the name Przybyszewska. For the sake of clarity I will refer to her as Przybyszewska.

[Thoughts on Painting], a translation of a few aphorisms by Marcel Lenoir, appeared in the last issue of *Zdrój* in 1922.[136] Her most important works, however, were written in Danzig. She remained there after her husband's untimely death in 1925 to devote herself entirely to writing. In 1929 she completed the play *Sprawa Dantona* [The Danton Case], her only work to be published before World War II. She wrote two other plays as well as several prose works, but she did not even prepare them for publication. She died in 1935.

Przybyszewska's teenage years were marked by a complex relationship to her father. His status as a cult writer marked the atmosphere in which she was raised, but he was not there for her as a parent. His *Totenmesse* made a very strong impression on the young girl. Many years later she recalled:

> I felt the sun beginning to shine above me for the first time. I was riveted, over the moon. I was discovering the world – and myself. Yes, this was my father – my blood, my sensations, my thoughts – but how much bolder, how much brighter than in my eighteen-year-old brain! Finally I had ceased to be completely lonely. There was one person in the world who lived the same life, one single person who thought the same way as I. This one person could become everything to me – my closest companion, confessor, leader. [...] I had no other desire than to find him and confide in him.[137]

But this mutual understanding turned out to be utopic. In Poznań Przybyszewska experienced "the first confrontations between the truth and the myth about the man and the writer".[138] Their face-to-face meetings, but also Stanisława's maturation as a thinker, revealed profound differences between herself and her father. Within a month of his death in 1927 she wrote to her half-sister Ivi:

> A few years ago my metaphysics used to be the same as his. But this spring, all our views on the most diverse subjects have changed, often becoming diametrically different. One and the same foundation gave rise

136 M. Lenoir, *Myśli o malarstwie*, trans. by S. Przybyszewska, *Z* 1922, vol. 14, p. 119. The aphorisms were taken from Marcel Lenoir's book *Raison ou déraison du peintre Marcel-Lenoir* (Paris: L'Abbaye, 1908).

137 S. Przybyszewska, *Listy* (Gdańsk: Morskie, 1978–1985), vol. 1, p. 130.

138 T. Lewandowski, *Dramat intelektu*, p. 36.

to systems that only have in common – and not even this is necessarily the case – the similarity of contrast.[139]

Przybyszewska's father remains a key figure in her autobiographical narrative, but she mostly presents him as a crook who has been exposed, an overthrown giant, "a cabotin, a mystifier, an impostor".[140] She came to believe that her father had nothing to teach her – an opinion she saw confirmed in his understanding of psychoanalysis.

It is possible that Przybyszewska encountered Freudianism at the University of Poznań, where she attended Stefan Błachowski's lectures in psychology for one trimester.[141] On 7 March 1925, soon after her arrival in Gdańsk, Przybyszewska gave a presentation at the Society of Friends of Science and Art [Towarzystwo Przyjaciół Nauki i Sztuki, TPNiS], founded a few years earlier. Her paper, titled "Zasady psychoanalizy" [The Principles of Psychoanalysis], is lost, and the book of minutes only records the resolutions adopted during the board meeting that took place "after Mrs Panieńska's presentation".[142] According to one historian, the readings organised by the TPNiS were "rather informal talks" aimed at a general audience; presenters usually came forward on their own initiative, and the events "did not have a high turnout, nor did they seem to elicit much interest among the members of the Society".[143] Officially, the Society counted one hundred members, but most of them had joined out of a patriotic impulse to support Polish culture in the Free City; they skipped meetings and sometimes failed to pay their membership fees. Readings usually attracted an audience of thirty to forty. No information survives on the number of attendees at Przybyszewska's presentation. Some two months later, in April, her husband Jan Panieński addressed the Society.

139 S. Przybyszewska, *Listy*, vol. 3, p. 8.

140 E. Graczyk, *Ćma: O Stanisławie Przybyszewskiej* (Warsaw: Morskie, 1994), p. 11.

141 As discussed in Part One, Stefan Błachowski attended both Congresses of Polish Neurologists, Psychiatrists and Psychologists before World War I. His article "Problem świadomości u Freuda" [The Problem of Consciousness in Freud] appeared in *Ruch Filozoficzny* in 1914.

142 "Księga protokolarna zebrań Towarzystwa Przyjaciół Nauki i Sztuki", Archiwum Państwowe w Gdańsku, APG 985/1, p. 79.

143 M. Pielczar, "Zarys dziejów Gdańskiego Towarzystwa Naukowego", in *Pięćdziesiąt lat Gdańskiego Towarzystwa Naukowego 1922–1972: Księga pamiątkowa* (Gdańsk: Zakład Narodowy im. Ossolińskich, 1972), p. 33.

He was among its founding members and the president of the Literary-Artistic Section. His talk, "Artysta a społeczeństwo dawniej a dziś" [The Artist and Society in the Past and Today], caused a scandal. It allegedly revealed his "tendencies to act as an agitator with anti-religious and anti-state motives". The board reserved the right to preventive censorship, should "Prof. Panieński [...] intend to give lectures in Danzig under the banner of the Society of Friends of Science and Art" (pp. 36–37). Neither he nor his wife gave any more presentations at the Society.

Given the absence of any notes on Przybyszewska's presentation or the ensuing discussion (if there was any), her views on the principles of psychoanalysis can only be gleaned from her correspondence. One of the names most frequently mentioned in her letters is Freud, but she never discusses his work as a separate subject. Instead, she mentions him in passing when she picks apart psychological complexities in her own or other writers' fiction, when she discusses works of popular culture (espe-cially Chaplin's films), or when she tries to present a deeper self-analysis.

As a widow Przybyszewska continued to live in barrack no. 12 in the courtyard of the gymnasium in Danzig, but she rapidly slid into poverty. She gave up her occasional tutoring jobs to focus on her creative work. For a few years she lived on grants from the Ministry of Religious Denominations and Public Enlightenment; after that she had to make do with irregular financial support from her aunt Helena Barlińska and her half-sister Ivi Bennet. She did not accept any job offers, convinced that she must devote all her energy to her literary work, even at the cost of loneliness, hardship and the humiliation of asking her relatives for money. She certainly had no big budget to spend on books. Although she was fluent in German, it is very unlikely that she kept up to date with developments in the field of psychoanalysis. In one letter she says frankly: "I'm not rich enough to acquaint myself with its current state of development."[144] No specific publication by Freud is mentioned in her letters, and it remains unclear if she had actually read any of his books; it is also difficult to ascertain in what language she read about psychoanalytical theories. It is possible that what she knew was based on articles in *Wiadomości Literackie*, one of her favourite journals and a major platform

144 S. Przybyszewska, *Listy*, vol. 1, p. 504.

popularising Freud's ideas in the 1930s.[145] In a letter to Ivi Bennet, Przybyszewska writes about the "technical means" used by psychoanalysis; here she mentions only two aspects, namely "the division of the soul into the subconscious, the preconscious and consciousness" as well as "the outline of traumatic complexes, which was for the very first time described by Freud".[146] In her prose works, for instance the novella "Pan En," Jung's name appears, but only in relation to the theory of complexes: "I decided that Mr N. is – a mathematician. Why? – There must be some complex behind it. Ask Jung."[147] Przybyszewska probably never read Jung, although his version of psychoanalysis could have suited her better than orthodox Freudianism, which, as we shall see below, alienated her with its focus on sexuality.

Even if Przybyszewska read only a few of the psychoanalysts' works at most, her idiolect is imbued with their language. In her letters she keeps returning to complexes, trauma, libido and symptoms. Writing about problems with blocked heating pipes she jokingly refers to the English term "chimney sweeping," which is how Bertha Pappenheim, alias Anna O., had described psychoanalytical therapy.[148] Her fiction is also saturated with references to Freud. One of her characters who readily uses the language of psychoanalysis is the protagonist of the novel *Sterylitas*; Eda, a doctor in the novel *Asymptoty* [Asymptotes], is also remarkably familiar with Freudianism.

Przybyszewska herself remarks that if her vision of the world resembles that of any other writer besides Georges Bernanos, then it is Freud. She consistently describes Freud as "a scientist"[149] and goes as far as to say that he represents the highest, ingenious type of the scientific psychologist. This is what she has to say about nineteenth-century psychology and psychoanalysis:

---

145 A separate chapter discusses the role of *Wiadomości Literackie* in Part Six of the present volume. See also L. Magnone, "Psychoanaliza na łamach *Wiadomości Literackich*", in *Dwudziestolecie 1918–1939: Odkrycia, fascynacje, zaprzeczenia*, ed. by A. S. Kowalczyk, T. Wójcik, A. Zieniewicz (Warsaw: Elipsa, 2010), pp. 122–136.

146 S. Przybyszewska, *Listy*, vol. 3, p. 33.

147 S. Przybyszewska, "Pan En", in S. Przybyszewska, *Cyrograf na własnej skórze i inne opowiadania* (Gdańsk: słowo/obraz terytoria, 2015), p. 85.

148 S. Przybyszewska, *Listy*, vol. 1, p. 412.

149 S. Przybyszewska, *Listy*, vol. 2, p. 296.

> Using psychology there was no need for strictly scientific knowledge; everything was vague, a question of "feeling" and not of "cognition". Psychoanalysis is an exact science. As exact as physics, which is based on mathematics. It is true that on account of its sensational character it is being misused in the most horrible way by individuals who are charlatans of science more than writers; this is unsurprising, for it is dreadfully inaccessible and a deeper, merely theoretical understanding of it requires intense study; this is why the dreamers and aesthetes are making it easy for themselves – for themselves and for others – by falsifying science, fishing out of it all the sensations and juxtaposing them at random in barbaric simplification and generalisation.[150]

Przybyszewska believed that her coming of age during World War I, a trauma that closed "the beautiful nineteenth century," had made her "a postwar person". She often uses this expression as a synonym for knowledge, maturity and an absence of illusions, for instance when she writes that "there are passages in Stendhal where he is quite post-war".[151] She also writes in a letter:

> When we, being postwar people, read works by the great minds from a hundred years ago – Goethe or Voltaire – we yawn, sadly aware of our great superiority; it's an awareness of the chasm of progress. From our shores we, the most mediocre of the mediocre, look at the heights of the culture of the past as if it were a long-ago stage in our own early development. The boldest idea of the revolutionaries of those times strikes us as commonplace. They didn't even look for words to describe things that are now accessible to every stenotypist.[152]

Convinced about the scientific nature of psychoanalysis, Przybyszewska had no doubt about the materialism of Freud's theory. As she put it, "today we have no actual metaphysical science".[153] She always worked to

150 S. Przybyszewska, *Listy*, vol. 3, pp. 223–224.

151 S. Przybyszewska, *Listy*, vol. 2, p. 31.

152 S. Przybyszewska, *Listy*, vol. 1, p. 338.

153 S. Przybyszewska, *Listy*, vol. 3, p. 33. The materialism of psychoanalysis was a hotly debated subject at the time, with important contributions coming from Bolesław Miciński, whom I will discuss below.

differentiate between what was mental and what was spiritual:[154]

> How oppressive psychology is, and especially psychoanalysis. But then again, things aren't so bad with us yet; however we look at it, besides this infernal animal-human psychological level there is also a spiritual level, from which sometimes a few rays penetrate even into the most depressed life. And the materialist psychoanalysts know nothing about this level. (p. 152)

For Przybyszewska, psychoanalysis has "explained a lot (those whom it has explained are not to be envied)" (p. 430). Still, she believed that "a person's mental constitution is not utterly and completely made of sticky mud. It also contains ingredients that are insoluble – resisting even such a strong acid" (*ibid.*). On several occasions she demanded that psychoanalytical theory should include a "spiritual" dimension, but then she also accepted that "the horrors that Freud and his followers discovered in our souls are really hidden there" and that "his infernal revelations are by no means just morbid nonsense" (p. 429). She discussed Freud's discovery of "the infernal animal level of the human psyche" with an undisguised fascination: "I can't get over my admiration for Freud's mental resilience, that he's able to cope with being aware of this hell" (p. 152).

Particularly interesting, in terms of the reception of psychoanalysis in Poland, is the fact that Przybyszewska read Freud without paying attention to his theory of sexuality. Applying for a literature fellowship in 1929 she described her two principal fields of interest as being the lives of historical and fictional geniuses as well as "deep psychological phenomena: the processes of mental biology that take place beyond consciousness, their reactions to the outside, internal conflicts of this (unconscious) order," adding that this is "a vision closely related to Freudianism but not identical (for instance I give no credence to pansexualism)".[155] She expressed contempt for "snoopy sexologists who have turned psychoanalysis into a journalistic sensation,"[156] and she complained that journalists have given psychoanalysis "an aura of the most unpleasant odour, which is very attractive to schoolboys and the average reader, but discourages people with highly developed minds in the worst possible manner".[157]

154 S. Przybyszewska, *Listy*, vol. 1, p. 294.
155 S. Przybyszewska, *Listy*, vol. 2, p. 32.
156 S. Przybyszewska, *Listy*, vol. 3, p. 142.
157 S. Przybyszewska, *Listy*, vol. 1, p. 504.

Unlike Przybyszewski's writing, where sexuality plays a prominent role, his daughter's work is characterised by "a disregard for eroticism as a subordinate moment" (p. 131). Commenting on her play *Sprawa Dantona* in her "Samowywiad" [Self-Interview] for *Wiadomości Literackie* in 1929, she writes about "the modern tragedy":

> The erotic motif – even the saddest one, even the most ingeniously represented – will not stir the modern soul with a Dionysian shudder. We expect more. The stakes of personal happiness are too low in our eyes: not enough to be the object of a grave tragedy. The tension to which individual desire can be raised – is too weak for us.[158]

Przybyszewska did not consider eroticism worthy of her attention as a writer, and only introduced love themes when the plot absolutely required them. Her earliest reviewers noticed this difference compared to her father's work. For instance, Władysław Kozicki wrote ahead of the preview of *Sprawa Dantona* in *Słowo Polskie*:

> Stanisława Przybyszewska's play! – a priori there is plenty of literary sensation in this phenomenon. The daughter of an outstanding writer [...], having the same name and surname as her father and making her literary debut within just over a year of her father's death – this looks like a sort of miraculous metempsychosis and reincarnation of the great magus of Young Poland [...]. But anyone who wanted to take the works of Stanisław Przybyszewski and Stanisława Przybyszewska as an example to prove the theory of heredity would be mistaken. Besides their identical name and surname they share nothing in their literary practice. These are two separate worlds, two poles that are as different as can be. Judging solely on the basis of the type of work, a person who is unaware of the actual state of things might assume that Stanisław Przybyszewski is a woman and Stanisława a man. For it is in the father's work that we find this paneroticism and pansexualism that is generally considered to be the dominant trait of the female organisation; in his work, the principal and only important element is emotionality, and his intuitive vision of the metaphysical essence of being is based on emotional premises, while "the miserable brain" with its wretched five senses is an object of contempt and disregard. For the daughter, by contrast, the erotic sphere does not exist as an

158 S. Przybyszewska, "Samowywiad", *WL* 1929, no. 42, quoted in Przybyszewska, *Listy*, vol. 2, p. 550.

> object of creative interest. Situations related to it are admitted only in so far as they are necessary for the fullness and truth of human life. The world of feeling, of passion and instinctual will is reduced to the realm of mediocrity and commonplace concerns. The only valuable inner element is the intellect, and the halo of genius surrounds only the fullest, most perfect awareness of thought, which is free of any ballast of feeling and affect, functioning with a precision that is mathematical, superhuman and therefore full of horror.[159]

In their approach to psychoanalysis, father and daughter represented two different epochs and were bound to disagree. Przybyszewski and his contemporaries viewed sexual difference as the most important issue in Freud's work. For Stanisława Przybyszewska, who saw herself as a modern woman, such an interpretation of Freudianism was compromising and indicated that her father was an anachronistic figure immersed in nineteenth-century superstition. She writes to Ivi Bennet: "with regard to mental phenomena I do have a strong similarity with our father, but not entirely in the way that you suggest. [...] I have developed this issue more broadly and deeply – because I draw on the more advanced culture of the twentieth century, not the nineteenth."[160]

In Przybyszewska's view, her father gives an undue priority to erotic themes, and he is anachronistic because he is unable to describe the unconscious without recourse to "an ornamental orgy of words". She, meanwhile, believes in the scientific nature of psychoanalysis and its methods, and she tries to apply them in her writing. At the same time she also admits that unconscious processes "have not yet been laid bare by literature, they generally go unnoticed, not to mention having been described, which is why literature has been unable to create a language for them" (p. 223). This question was immensely important to Przybyszewska, which is perhaps also why she claims, in the same letter, that she hates her father (p. 225) – a confession she makes while discussing psychoanalysis. What is more, she undertakes to rewrite some of his works, such as his expressionist novel *Krzyk* from 1917;[161] her version is titled *Twórczość*

159 W. Kozicki, "Sprawa Dantona: Przed prapremierą dramatu Stanisławy Przybyszewskiej", *SPL* 1931, no. 78, p. 13.

160 S. Przybyszewska, *Listy*, vol. 3, p. 220.

161 Cf. P. Stasiewicz, "*Krzyk* Stanisława Przybyszewskiego jako powieść ekspresjonistyczna", in *W kręgu Młodej Polski: studia i szkice*, ed. by J. Sztachelska (Białystok: Wydawnictwo Uniwersytetu w Białymstoku, 1998), pp. 191–206.

Gerarda Gasztowta [The Work of Gerard Gasztowt].[162] In a letter to her friend, dated 16 December 1928, she gives a psychoanalytical explanation of this development in her work:

> I have a special sort of complex that can be called the complex of plagiarism […]: the libido that has not been overcome in relation to themes that have been dealt with insufficiently. When I come across a novel or novella that contains an idea or motif to which the author has failed to live up to, that he overlooked or distorted out of stupidity – then I find it hard to refrain from rebuilding the whole thing.[163]

Przybyszewska also planned to write a travesty of her father's novel *Il regno doloroso*, a work that tackles the persecution of witches during the Spanish Inquisition in the seventeenth century. The subject was interesting, she thought, but the narrative was constructed and written "so carelessly that it would discredit [Polish] literature if anyone wanted to translate it".[164] What is more, Przybyszewska occasionally weaved ironic remarks on her father's work into her fiction. For instance, one of the characters in her short story "Pentezylea" tells her colleague: "You could kill yourself, but […] this happens in Przybyszewski's books, since he can't afford more original endings; in real life it doesn't happen".[165]

---

162 An early critic describes her work as follows:
"Like another Robespierre, Gasztowt feels that he must rid himself of everything that is human, that excites vanity and the desire to experience pleasure. Any feeling muddles the icy purity of knowledge, any kindness that is accepted brings about a loss of hardening, any kind of bond or attachment signifies the shackles of slavery. He must kill the individual man in himself, for only then will he become a pure creator. In the name of this idea he forces a woman saved from drowning into suicide – on the spot, brutally and ruthlessly. Some dark and silent night, which was neither fear nor desire but an imperial injunction of certainty, made him decide against humanity and in favour of creative power. Przybyszewska has taken idolatry of art to the ultimate limit. With inexorable consistency she pushes the action towards a tragedy that ends with the madness of Gasztowt drowning in his work, she creates a dogma about the supremacy of art over life with such faith as if there were no other way out of the dilemma". (S. Helsztyński, "Stanisława Przybyszewska", *WW* 1936, no. 1, p. 5)

163 S. Przybyszewska, *Listy*, vol. 1, p. 325.

164 S. Przybyszewska, *Listy*, vol. 3, p. 5.

165 S. Przybyszewska, "Pentezylea", in *Cyrograf*, p. 115.

Formulating her literary programme in the essay "Vita nuova," which survives in manuscript, Przybyszewska also "revealed the anachronism and vanity of the themes of modernist [i.e. Young Poland] literature, which mainly presents erotic conflicts and completely limits itself to penetrating the sphere of an individual's personal life".[166] The actual task for postwar writers, meanwhile, was to act as experts who help shape the "new life" alluded to in the title. Przybyszewska's project was based on universalism, anti-individualism and scientism; it was diametrically opposed to the programme of the Young Poland movement. In the modernist tradition she preferred Irzykowski over Przybyszewski.[167] And indeed, what Irzykowski found most interesting in Freud's theory was not the question of sexual difference, either; he might have agreed with her that Freud's key achievement was that "he discovered and reconstructed the mechanism of the mind in general, with this terribly intricate labyrinth of controls, dams, bolts, camouflage" (pp. 429–430). They also seem to have a shared aversion to what Przybyszewska describes as "the epigones of Freud", who make his discoveries "look ridiculous".[168]

For Przybyszewska, her own familiarity with Freud's work and ability to use his ideas to construct her fictional characters indicated that she was a truly modern writer, and she felt entitled to make condescending remarks about writers of previous generations: "the psychology of the giants of yore (e.g. Balzac) is childish compared to what we know about human personality today."[169] The psychological novel, with prominent representatives such as Bourget, Prévost and Maupassant, was for her a "prewar specialty".[170] She juxtaposed it with the psychoanalytical novel, which she tried to create herself, looking for inspiration in all works of contemporary literature that interested her, irrespective of the system of circulation to which they belonged. Among the writers who, in her opinion, took account of modern psychology were Aldous Huxley, Joseph Conrad and Sherwood Anderson, but also Maurice Dekobra and even Pitigrilli. She noted with regret that she was living in an era in which "Freud's terrible discovery serves any idiot as a toy" (p. 142), and at the same time she believed that the general interest in psychoanalysis had not

166 T. Lewandowski, *Dramat intelektu*, p. 85.

167 Cf. S. Przybyszewska, *Listy*, vol. 1, p. 449.

168 S. Przybyszewska, *Asymptoty* (Gdańsk: słowo/obraz terytoria, 2018), p. 279.

169 S. Przybyszewska, *Listy*, vol. 2, p. 31.

170 S. Przybyszewska, *Listy*, vol. 3, p. 223.

yet given rise to a new type of novel. Discussing her 1928 *Asymptoty*, she claims: "I don't know of any book with a main theme similar to my novel. Not even in the young contemporary writers. But I believe – judging from reviews – that Thomas Mann also tried it in his most recent book, *The Magic Mountain.*"[171] It is remarkable that Przybyszewska mentions Mann, rather than the radical reformers of the novel – Proust, Joyce or Woolf – who are more often associated with psychoanalysis. She certainly did not appreciate the "stream of consciousness" method. As one scholar has argued, her disapproval was rooted in her belief in "the primacy of clarity and conciseness in a work's composition" over "forms of expression that were free from the rigour of logic".[172]

> Przybyszewska placed modes of expression that immediately indicate the form-giving efforts of consciousness above the language of psychological introspection – an introspection that recreates the inertia and randomness of the flow of subconscious experiences. (*Ibid.*)

In her own experiments with fiction Przybyszewska combines a sophisticated reflection on psychological mechanisms with the strategies of popular literature. Literary historians have judged most of her novels and novellas rather harshly, describing them as cheap melodramas that offer naive portrayals of higher society.[173] And yet Przybyszewska reduces the key element of the genre – romance – to a minimum. In her most interesting works, erotic adventures are subordinated to a much more essential desire – "the yearning for money".[174] It is worth noting that the exchange of eros for cash is a concern mostly for female characters, and the protagonist of these works is always an ambitious and intelligent young woman who can be read as the author's alter ego. Having no other resources, she is obliged to work at a bank or office, but she keeps fighting for a more fulfilling life. As one scholar has noted, "many pages in these short stories and novels read like unconscious fictional pendants to Marx's *Economic and Philosophic Manuscripts*".[175] In the

171 On Przybyszewska's feeling of kinship with Mann, to whom she addressed her last, poignant letters, see T. Lewandowski, "Stanisława Przybyszewska i Tomasz Mann czyli dialog pozorny", *TW* 1979, no. 12, pp. 72–85.

172 I. Jokiel, "Nad listami Stanisławy Przybyszewskiej", *PNW* 1998, no. 7, p. 93.

173 E. Graczyk, *Ćma*, p. 135.

174 S. Przybyszewska, "Pentyzelea", p. 99.

175 A. Bojarska, "Andrée Lynne (Proza Stanisławy Przybyszewskiej)", *PH* 1978, no. 11, p. 110.

world of modern capitalism, Przybyszewska seems to suggest, the right to develop one's unique talent, to be creative and to think is the exclusive privilege of the rich who need not worry about their physical survival. Przybyszewska's underprivileged protagonists do not dream about love – what they crave is the financial resources to pull themselves out of their treadmill and to follow their creative or intellectual vocation. This goal sanctifies all means, and often the most accessible way to earn extra money is some form of prostitution. Incidentally, Przybyszewska apparently considered this option for herself, too. In one of the letters in which she asked her half-sister for financial support she writes: "If I had the slightest abilities, I would long since have thrown myself at prostitution. But I am neither pretty nor skilful enough for the job; just as I'd be the last in the queue at the office".[176]

It is important to note that Przybyszewska's heroines are all frigid and detached, seeing sexuality merely as a tool to achieve financial independence. In the short story "Pentezylea" the protagonist Olga, a bank clerk who earns extra cash as an escort, explains to her colleague:

> And you, are you not selling yourself for a meagre 250 marks a month, are you not selling yourself entirely, all your strength, all your time at the office, are you not closing the door, once and for all, to real freedom, that is to the possibility of educating yourself, to soak up all this divine European culture [...]? Are you not wasting your life in a scandalous way, not you – only I, because I spend a few pleasant hours a day with a smart man whom I like – never as much as seven hours – for ten to twenty thousand a month – and with these thousands I am gaining access to happiness and joy in life, access that can only be had with money. – Well, let us examine our systems of selling ourselves. What is more exhausting, what deprives one more of health and flexibility, what ruins the mind and the body more: spending day by day in a dark cave with no exercise, giving a slap-dash performance of mind-numbing drudgery, or, rather, a few hours a day with a friend? [...] What is more humiliating to a person, especially a woman: forced punctuality, barrack-like discipline, humble obedience towards unknown men, jumping when the superior rings the bell, putting up with his bad moods, reprimands, threats, because one word of revolt (should your human dignity, which is perpetually being offended, forget itself) may entail disgrace – the loss of your laughable "salary," which is calculated, for the employer's benefit, to maintain the

176 S. Przybyszewska, *Listy*, vol. 3, p. 237.

> machine in a state fit for use – or perhaps the fancy, nearly rococo-like gallantries which the lover of an elegant and expensive woman lavishes on her.[177]

In Przybyszewska's work, outstanding individuals are capable of this level of reflection. Creative work – for which money can free up the necessary time and conditions – makes their lives meaningful. These characters have no other desires, they are above common human needs, including sexual ones. They remain ascetics even if they are sexually active. This is how the protagonist of "Pentezylea" puts it:

> This is what sets us apart from the rest of humanity, for whom love is a natural instinct unregulated by will. – The moment this instinct is transformed into art it must of course lose all its immediacy; this is the moment that sensitive people find most irritating about us. Every other woman gives herself away spontaneously, acting without thinking, almost without a will of her own, just as her enhanced instinct quietly urges her to do. For us, giving ourselves away is the result of profound political considerations, financial ones in particular; the instinct is completely quiet, and every gesture is directed not by instinct but by conscious will. (pp. 121-122)

A woman such as Olga is "an all but perfect creature – and fiendishly intellectual" (p. 120), but she is also sexually frigid. We may get the impression that all her libidinal energy is directed at her own development; this energy is, literally, the ego-libido – it is self-reflexive and has no object. In Przybyszewska's universe, erotic passion and love are reserved for average, mediocre people. As one scholar has argued, the principal significance of such feelings is to prove the lack of the character's essential attributes as a human being.[178]

This brings to mind a characteristic passage from one of Przybyszewska's letters to Helena Barlińska. She comments on the psychology of the characters in *Sprawa Dantona*:

> This is when I realised that one of the cardinal mistakes of psychoanalysis [...] was to underestimate and neglect the analysis of sublimation. Above all [...] we ought to cross out the naive old sexological division: normal

177 S. Przybyszewska, "Pentezylea", p. 112.

178 A. Bojarska, "Andrée Lynne", p. 108.

people, sadists, homosexuals etc., each of them apart and excluding each other within a single individual. This much we know for sure: that each of the phenomena that used to be known as perversions is really part of sexual human nature – in every human being. Normality only consists of a certain defined system of distribution of these forces, one that ensures that the net force should lead to fertility along a path that is as straightforward as possible, with a minimum net loss of energy. [...] But even within these conditions of normality there is considerable leeway. In every normal person there occurs, as a characteristic trait, as a colouring of the relationship that reaches far beyond the sexual life strictly understood, if I may say so, a marginal predominance of one of those forbidden "component instincts," as Freud calls them [...]. Only: in normal people these component instincts sometimes occur as sexual fission (extremely common are homosexual drives in people who are essentially heterosexual); though sometimes they occur in a sublimated form, and then, I dare suggest, they are beyond being sexual.

The Freudians maintain that any impulse (be it dominant or a component) of this (certainly sexual) group, if it does not strive for full physical satisfaction – is simply pathologically restrained or untypical in its development [...]. Because of this assumption they declined to perform special research on sublimation.

In my view, however, the ability to perform sublimation is one of the most valuable and purely human faculties; a faculty that is entirely pure, thus independent of animalistic life (Freud does not recognise at all the existence of phenomena that are pure in this sense; this is also why psychoanalysis is so hellishly depressing). In my opinion we need to differentiate between apparent and true sublimation [...]. Apparent sublimation, which is of course the more common type, overlaps with the Freudians' view: it remains sexual, even though it takes on appearances that could not be farther from sex [...], while true sublimation represents the instinct's simultaneous disconnection from sex in general; and this is what psychoanalysis refuses to acknowledge.[179]

179 S. Przybyszewska, *Listy*, vol. 1, pp. 504-506. The letter continues with a discussion of the relationship between Robespierre and Camille Desmoulins, with Przybyszewska using her own theory of sublimation; she also explores the preconscious factors that influenced Danton as well as the role of the "censor on the threshold of consciousness". Cf. also S. Przybyszewska, "Komentarz psychologiczny do *Sprawy Dantona*", in *Listy*, vol. 2, pp. 561–574.

Przybyszewska believed that outstanding individuals were capable of this particular form of sublimation, but that Freud had failed to take it into account. As Agata Bielik-Robson recently demonstrated, however, Freud did describe it in *Three Essays on the Theory of Sexuality*: it is sublimation understood not as an elevation of libido (which would suggest a secondary process, where sexual desire is directed at non-sexual goals), but a part of the primary process in which libido maintains its original disconnection; this means it is not a form of substitution, but the actual realm of human drives.[180]

In Przybyszewska's work, libidinal energy is a creative force that must not be wasted on sexual goals. For her, sexuality is related to breeding – an activity entirely devoid of meaning. In one letter she writes about the "infernal vicious circle of nonsense":

> This frightfully complicated, seemingly priceless structure that not just every human being represents but also each of the higher animals; this miracle, if I may use such a banal expression, born and reared at the price of a huge investment of energy, in pain, fear, through the darkest dangers; which matures eventually… only to bring into the world a young one of the species and in turn devote its life, which had only just matured, to nurturing it.[181]

This is why Przybyszewska's work contains what Ewa Graczyk describes as "a prohibition on experiencing natural feelings, a prohibition on emotionality, eroticism, sexuality".[182] Jenny from the novella "Wybraniec losu" [Fate's Chosen One] has prospects of becoming a brilliant historian, but then she falls in love and becomes pregnant. To her, the fact that she succumbed to a temptation proves that she was not an outstanding individual, whatever she might have thought of herself before. Similarly, in *Asymptoty*, the protagonist's aptitudes are called into question when emotions come into play: Eda is a laboratory researcher who loves her work. When her husband leaves her, however, she becomes addicted to morphine (Przybyszewska, herself an addict, offers poignant descriptions) and gives up her academic career. Perhaps this prohibition on feelings and

180 A. Bielik-Robson, *Erros: Mesjański witalizm i filozofia* (Cracow: Universitas, 2012), p. 261.

181 S. Przybyszewska, *Listy*, vol. 2, p. 95.

182 E. Graczyk, *Ćma*, p. 70.

sexuality also explains the writer's aversion to babies. In one of her letters she writes: "having the bodies of children cut open like Gilles de Raiz – that's a questionable pleasure. But I can perfectly well understand the feeling that leads to it. Especially when it comes to babies."[183] Przybyszewska also has what she calls "a weakness for homosexuality"; having read Plato's *Symposium* she calls the "pure, male form" of homosexuality "Platonic love, to contribute to the rehabilitation of this concept".[184]

Przybyszewska's concept of love was modelled on the notion of eros from Plato's *Symposium.* In her eyes this Ancient Greek concept was clearly different from sexuality, which "happens under duress, pressured by desire" (p. 130). Owning up to her "fanatical hatred of Nature," she saw the imperative of "idiotic multiplying"[185] as being opposed to "disindividualisation [*dezindywidualizacja*] in pure thought" (*ibid.*), by which she meant unconstrained intellectual development, "the proper content of human life: the only goal that made it worthwhile to have been born" (p. 99). She identified a fundamental gap in psychoanalytical theory, which, due to its focus on sexuality, overlooks the possibility of the same or similar mechanisms functioning on other levels of psychic life as well. Przybyszewska visualises these other levels as concentric circles. The smallest circle, the sexual instinct, is surrounded by the circle of sublimation as theorised by Freud. They have a common centre, "the bodily orgasm," but sublimation has a "growing radius that reaches farther and farther beyond the original radius" (p. 506). To this reconstruction of psychoanalytical theory Przybyszewska adds another circle where the growth process shifts its centre "at different stages of development, from a concentric arrangement all the way to a non-tangent eccentric one (of the periphery)" (*ibid.*). This "authentic sublimation," which evolved from sexuality, is said to eventually give rise to its own centre, entirely disconnected from physiology.

Przybyszewska considered this to be humanity's actual goal and task. In her opinion both men and women ought to "grow up to be humans," to attain the level of purely mental life where "there is no sexual difference anymore; there is only the human being. Those who have grown up to achieve a self-sustaining and active mental life are still men or women in body and soul, but mentally they are hermaphroditic or, more precisely,

183 S. Przybyszewska, *Listy*, vol. 2, p. 96.

184 S. Przybyszewska, *Listy*, vol. 3, p. 143.

185 S. Przybyszewska, *Listy*, vol. 1, p. 98.

beyond gender and sex".[186] Przybyszewska's notion of hermaphroditism is quite different from the concept of androgyny in her father's early work. Her understanding of hermaphroditism is rooted in G.B. Shaw's anthropological utopia. The Irish playwright foresaw that human mental development would soon attain an evolutionary stage in which the individual would function solely as a pure brain, freed from the bonds of the body, including sex and sexuality.[187] In the drama series *Back to Methuselah*, human beings, having attained perfection, pay their dues to nature over the course of no more than the first four years of their lives (which correspond to the period currently understood as youth); in this short time they experience love and they procreate, while in the remaining time, which is unlimited in principle and should last at least a few hundred years, "it is not nature but the person's own will that determines the phases of being to come".[188] Przybyszewska was fascinated with this vision. She stresses that "the grown-up human beings of this Golden Age have not only broken with sexuality, but the two sexes also assume an identical form. A male form, flat-chested and hairless [...]. Their abilities, psychology, material form, too – everything is identical" (p. 217). These beings, who exist beyond sexual difference, have only one goal: "the desire to free themselves completely from matter: to become living, pure thought without a body" (*ibid.*).

Przybyszewska appropriated this system as a foundation for a new religion; in her own understanding, this associated her with the mysticism of Słowacki's late work – a mysticism she hesitated to call idealism, highlighting its critical aspect and its similarities with "anti-materialism" (p. 94). In a letter to the editors of *Wiadomości Literackie*, written towards the end of her life, she offers the following formulation for her worldview: mentalism – cynicism – mysticism.[189] In this vision there was no space anymore for Freudianism.

186 S. Przybyszewska, *Listy*, vol. 2, p. 241.
187 Cf. T. Lewandowski, *Dramat intelektu*, pp. 228–229.
188 S. Przybyszewska, *Listy*, vol. 1, p. 216.
189 S. Przybyszewska, *Listy*, vol. 2, p. 507.

Part 5

Siegfried Bernfeld and the Bornstein sisters

Educational analysts or analytic educationalists...

Siegfried Bernfeld

One of the most astonishing phenomena in the transfer of psychoanalysis to Polish culture is the resonance that Freudianism had in Zionist circles. The new pedagogy that emerged within the HeHalutz movement, and which was to become the foundation for the communal child rearing propagated in Israel, was profoundly shaped by psychoanalysis. The beginnings of this process are associated with the formation of the secular Jewish youth movement HaShomer Hatzair [The Young Guard]. It came into being as HaShomer (the full name was adopted a few years later) in Lviv in 1913, following the merger of several Jewish scout groups in Galicia as well as the organisation Ze'irei Zion [The Youth of Zion].[1] It aimed to prepare young Polish Jews to settle in Palestine and to work for the cause of Eretz Israel. Until 1918, HaShomer Hatzair was essentially a Galician organisation; it was only with Poland's independence that the movement expanded into the former Russian partition. (In this territory, one of the founders and members of the Chief Command was Henryk Goldszmit, i.e. Janusz Korczak.) In the interwar period it was still associated with Zionist organisations, collaborating, for instance, with the Social Democratic Labour Party Poale Zion [Poalej Syjon].

The earliest members of HaShomer Hatzair were born into the assimilated Jewish upper middle class around 1900. What they had in common, above all, was their disappointment with the older generation's reliance on assimilation and a rejection of traditional Jewish culture, in particular the Hasidism that was dominant in Galicia. Searching for a different, modern identity, they returned to a model of personhood derived from the Torah: the prediaspora heroic Jew who works the land. They wanted to be "new Hebrews," and one path towards this goal, besides

1 H. Sterner, "O organizacji szomrowej przedwojennej", *HA* 1917/1918, no. 9, pp. 193–198.

building up their physical fitness and undergoing agricultural training, was to study Hebrew, which was to become the official language in their new homeland. Special self-study books were published to ensure that the young Zionists who arrived in Palestine spoke at least some basic Hebrew. Few were fluent at the time of emigration, however, and, since Yiddish was programmatically rejected as the language of the orthodox shtetl, the organisation settled on Polish as their primary language. Until 1920 almost all of the movement's publications appeared in Polish. In addition, the movement's ideology was strongly influenced by Polish literature and the notion of national messianism.[2] Mordechai Bentov recalls in his memoir: "In fact I became a Zionist under the influence of Polish literature […]. The great literature of Poland, which had emerged at the time of partition, was saturated with messianic dreams about liberation and independence. We soaked in this atmosphere and these ideals."[3] As for the Marxist element of HaShomer Hatzair, Ryszard Löw argues that it was rooted in Stanisław Brzozowski's socialist and nationalist idealism. His novel *Płomienie* [The Flames], which portrays the members of "Narodnaya Volya," was this generation's cult book. It was read by all the young people who settled in Palestine and had an exceptional place in the pedagogical doctrine of the HaShomer Hatzair movement. The Polish Zionists had it translated into Hebrew in 1940. For the young people of the radical left it portrayed "the spiritual roots of the birth of the 'new man'" (p. 386), as we can read in the unsigned Introduction to the Hebrew edition of Brzozowski's novel. Brzozowski, Löw elaborates, was the most important moral and ideological authority of the era that came to be known as the Jewish revolution, which gave rise to the ethos of the New Hebrew – a type that could not be more at odds with the Jewish intellectual from the ghetto. Brzozowski's philosophy provided the intellectual foundations for the Zionists' project of settler colonialism. They quite literally defined work as the strictly human effort to transform nature into culture, while the economy of the kibbutz appeared to realise Brzozowski's dream of an "agricultural utopia," "working the land together in a harmonious community".[4]

---

2 Cf. E. Margalit, "Social and Intellectual Origins of the HaShomer Hatzair Youth Movement 1913–1920", *JOC* 1969, no. 2, pp. 25–46.

3 Cited in R. Löw, "Stanisław Brzozowski wśród lektur syjonistycznych", in *Kwestia żydowska w XIX wieku*, p. 385.

4 M. Wyka, *Brzozowski i jego powieści*, cited in R. Löw, "Stanisław Brzozowski wśród lektur syjonistycznych", p. 383.

A prospective Shomer had to make the following pledge: "I shall be a faithful pioneer of my nation, culture and homeland, I shall establish and fight for equality, liberty and brotherhood in human society, I shall keep the Shomer commandments". These were:

- A Shomer is a person of truth and stands guard to protect it.
- A Shomer is a pioneer of the rebirth of his nation, culture and homeland.
- A Shomer is a person of action and able to sustain himself or herself through his or her own work.
- A Shomer works to establish and fights for equality, liberty and brotherhood in human society.
- A Shomer is a helpful person and gives assistance to others.
- A Shomer is a faithful member of his or her group and is subject to its leaders' discipline.
- A Shomer loves nature, studies it and is able to survive outdoors.
- A Shomer is brave, energetic and perky.
- A Shomer is a person of strong will and maximises his or her physical and mental abilities.
- A Shomer is pure in speech, thoughts and actions (abstaining from tobacco and alcohol and abiding by the principles of sexual purity).[5]

This new decalogue seems to suggest that the main task envisioned by HaShomer Hatzair was to raise physically and morally healthy young people who would bring about the rebirth of the nation. The appreciation for physical culture, the return to nature and a particular anti-intellectualism were combined with an emphasis on asceticism. Unlike other similar movements, HaShomer was not exclusively a men's organisation, which is why the periodicals it published regularly discussed the relationships between the sexes. The model promoted was one of friendship and mutual respect based on completely equal rights and obligations. The young people's sexual energy was supposed to find an outlet in exercise and work.

By the end of World War I, there were thirty Shomer centres in Galicia.[6] The largest hub, however, was in Vienna, where some 175,000 Galician Jews had found refuge with the outbreak of the armed conflict, including the majority of HaShomer's activists. They anxiously observed

5 T. Guzik, M. Skoczeń, "Żydowskie organizacje skautowe w Polsce w latach 1916–1945", *HAR* 1990, no. 1, p. 39.

6 "Sprawozdanie Rady Naczelnej", *HA* 1917/1918, no. 9, pp. 199–206.

the anti-Semitic riots during the Polish-Ukrainian battles as well as during the Bolshevik war, but also the exclusion of Jewish identities from the newly conceived and ethnically monolithic notion of Polishness. The Vienna-based HaShomer had about 1,000 members at the time, i.e. a third of the entire movement. It was in Vienna that the press Vorwärts published the Polish-language periodical *Moriah* from November 1916 until the end of 1919; *Moriah* had previously appeared in Lviv (in the years 1917–18 it included a special supplement titled *Haszomer: Pismo młodzieży szomrowej* [HaShomer: The Journal of the Shomer Youth]). Its goal was to spread the Zionist idea among young Jews. One of its editors and prolific contributors was Marcin (Martin) Buber, the Polish shomers' most important living authority. The Polish-language *Poradnik dla kierowników szomrowych* [A Guide for Shomer Leaders] was also published in Vienna.[7] Besides a practical section on the organisation of teams and work squads, it also included a lengthy chapter on the Shomer worldview. The authors, members of the Naczelna Rada Szomrowa [Chief Shomer Council], declared in the introduction: "We believe that the future of the nation is in the hands of our youth. We believe that the Jewish nation will be reborn in the most straightforward manner: that youth will rejuvenate it" (p. 4). But most importantly, in Vienna the movement's leaders encountered the youth activist and psychoanalyst Siegfried Bernfeld.

Bernfeld was born in Lviv in 1892, although his parents had already been living in Vienna for a year.[8] His mother, twenty-year-old Hermina Schwarzwald, had insisted on giving birth in a familiar environment. Hermina (or Minka as she was called) did not speak German at the time. It appears that she only learned it many years later; until then she and her husband, who spoke no Polish, communicated in French, which both of them had learned at school.[9] Siegfried was taken to Vienna soon after he was born, but we can assume that for many years his mother only spoke to him in Polish.

7 *Poradnik dla kierowników szomrowych*, published by Naczelna Rada Szomrowa (Vienna: Vorwärts, 1917).

8 Details about Bernfeld's life are based mostly on P. Dudek, *"Er war halt genialer als die anderen": Biografische Annäherungen an Siegfried Bernfeld* (Gießen: Psychosozial-Verlag, 2012).

9 Cf. L. Bernfeld Stoss, "'Sie war ja voll von Geschichten': Ein Brief über Hermine Schwarzwald Bernfeld", in *Siegfried Bernfeld oder die Grenzen der Psychoanalyse*, p. 34.

Bernfeld received an excellent education, first at a classical Gymnasium and then at the University of Vienna, with two semesters at the University of Freiburg. In 1915 his home university awarded him a doctorate in philosophy for his treatise "Über den Begriff der Jugend" [On the Notion of Youth]. Following Gustav Wyneken, the German pedagogue who opposed traditional models of education, Bernfeld believed in the revolutionary power of youth, its moral and spiritual sensitivity as well as its natural ability to stand up against injustice and to create a new society. He envisioned a modern, anti-authoritarian and co-educational type of school that would prepare pupils for life in this new society; the programme would be based on a deep bond between teachers and pupils. Inspired by Wyneken, in 1912 Bernfeld began to work for the Academic Committee for School Reform [Akademisches Komitee für Schulreform]. In the same year he and Walter Benjamin, one of Wyneken's protégés who at that time adopted his master's ideas rather uncritically, founded the yearbook *Der Anfang: Zeitschrift der Jugend* [The Beginning: The Journal of the Young]. Both young philosophers were also regular contributors.[10] The question of sexuality was an important issue even then. Bernfeld opposed "the adults' monopoly on sexuality" and supported adolescents' right to sexual expression.[11] This successful journal did not target an exclusively Jewish audience, but the majority of its editorial team identified as Jewish, and its popularity led to the establishment of a Jewish youth organisation of the same name. As its leader, Bernfeld gave three lectures on youth ["Der Sinn der Jugend", "Der Kampf der Jugend", "Der Sieg der Jugend"] at the concert hall of Vienna's Café Adlon, attracting an audience of up to five hundred young people, mostly gymnasium students, every time (p. 78). To appreciate how revolutionary Bernfeld's ideas were before World War I, we should remember that the era of the Habsburg monarchy had given rise to a culture that valued moderation, steadiness and security, which means it distrusted youth as a matter of course. As Stefan Zweig recalls, during the reign of Franz Joseph, "an eighteen-year-old student at the Gymnasium was treated like a child [...] a man of thirty was also regarded as an unfledged person, and even one of forty was not yet

10 On the relationship between Bernfeld and Benjamin as well as their links with Wyneken see P. Dudek, *Fetisch Jugend: Walter Benjamin und Siegfried Bernfeld – Jugendprotest am Vorabend des Ersten Weltkrieges* (Bad Heilbrunn: Klinkhardt, 2002); see esp. the chapter "Gustav Wyneken – der geistige Mentor Benjamins und Bernfelds", pp. 17–41.

11 P. Dudek, *"Er war halt genialer als die anderen"*, p. 66.

considered ripe for a position of responsibility"[12]; "Young people, who always instinctively desire rapid and radical changes, were therefore considered a doubtful element which was to be held down or kept inactive for as long a time as possible" (*Ibid.*).

Bernfeld first read Freud at the age of fifteen. During the war, when he was already a prominent youth leader, he began to attend the meetings of the VPS, becoming a member in 1919, when he presented an analysis of poems written by young people. He and Otto Rank, whom he succeeded as secretary of the VPS, were at the time the only Freudians without medical training. This often led to conflicts with other members, so much so that Bernfeld – who had not even started practicing as an analyst – considered founding a separate society for lay psychoanalysis.[13] This never came to be, but Freud was impressed with his progress. Helene Deutsch writes in her memoir:

> From the beginning Freud was fascinated by Bernfeld's personality – this man seemed to be the very incarnation of the Don Quichote type, even in his external appearance. He was tall and gaunt, with an ugliness that impressed one as beauty. His fanatical adherence to his Zionist ideals led him at times into opportunistic actions, but also made him a spellbinding speaker who converted many enthusiastic young followers to his ideology.[14]

Bernfeld began to work as an analyst in May 1921, mostly treating troubled teenagers.[15] Helene Deutsch remarks that he "achieved what no other member of the analytic group had done: he became a training analyst without having had regular analytic training himself".[16] To this we may add that Bernfeld did all this before he had even been psychoanalysed himself. It was only in the early 1930s that he underwent two years of psychoanalysis with Hanns Sachs.

---

12 Stefan Zweig, *The World of Yesterday: An Autobiography*, Introduction by Harry Zohn (Lincoln: University of Nebraska Press, 1964), p. 33.

13 Freud writes about this in a letter to Ferenczi dated 21 January 1920. See *The Correspondence of Sigmund Freud and Sándor Ferenczi*, vol. 3, p. 4.

14 Helene Deutsch, *Confrontations with Myself*, p. 161.

15 Cf. A. Freud, "A Short History of Child Analysis", *PSO* 1966, no. 21, p. 7.

16 H. Deutsch, *Confrontations with Myself*, p. 161. Being in charge of training analysts at the VPS, Deutsch was highly sensitive to the question of professional standards. Perhaps this accounts for her slightly piqued tone.

Bernfeld became a believer in Zionist ideals even before World War I, when anti-Semitism was on the rise in Austria. By the time he got in touch with the Polish HaShomer Hatzair he was already the leader of the youth league Jerubbaal, which published a journal with the same title.[17] *Jerubbaal's* contributors included Martin Buber, Max Brod and Eugen Höflich, later known as the Israeli writer Mosheh Ya'akov Ben-Gavriel. In May 1918, Bernfeld organised a major Austrian-Jewish Youth Rally in Vienna. This three-day event attracted more than two thousand people, representing two hundred different Zionist youth organisations, mainly Shomer ones, from across the Empire. In 1917 he also became director of the Jüdisches Pädagogium, a teacher training institution whose mission was to foster socialism and Zionism as the values of the new Hebrew culture; having emigrated to Palestine, its graduates would educate the members of the new society. Bernfeld believed that an appropriate pedagogical model was the only way to transform the Jew of the diaspora into a brave pioneer and revolutionary. Following the Balfour Declaration of 1917, in which the British government announced support for the establishment of a "national home for the Jewish people" in Palestine, the Pädagogium became the centre of the entire movement of young Zionist socialists who would join the third Aliyah (the wave of European Jews immigrating to Palestine between 1919 and 1923). Before their departure they not only took intensive courses in Hebrew and Marxist ideology, but they also attended Bernfeld's classes in psychology and psychoanalysis. (Anna Freud, three years Bernfeld's junior and a close friend at the time, was a frequent visitor.) The young theorist considered Freudianism to be a crucial pedagogical method, one that was steeped in humanism and love, and which allowed for a precise diagnosis and therapy of mental disorders – an essential tool for anyone working with children.[18]

It is mostly thanks to the hundreds of HaShomer Hatzair members educated by Bernfeld that Freud's ideas reached Palestine long before the so-called fifth Aliyah, i.e. the wave of Jewish immigration to Palestine in 1931–1940, which included Max Eitingon and other psychoanalysts from

17 In the Bible (Book of Judges), Jerubbaal ("contender with Baal") is a name given to the young rebel Gideon who destroyed the altar of Baal.

18 See S. Bernfeld, "Die Psychoanalyse in der Jugendbewegung", *I* 1917, no. 4, pp. 283–289.

Freud's inner circle.[19] Bernfeld can also be credited with the fact that in the two decades before the State of Israel was established, Freud ranked third among the writers most frequently translated into Hebrew (following Theodor Herzl and Max Nordau). Eight of his books appeared in Palestine – mostly ones that explored society, culture and religion. The first books to be translated were *Group Psychology and the Analysis of the Ego* (1928), followed by *The Future of an Illusion* and *Totem and Taboo*, and, responding an explicit request by Freud, who was worried about this unusual selection, *Introduction to Psychoanalysis*, which appeared in 1934. What is more, Freud's ideas were discussed in about one hundred Hebrew-language articles.[20] Writing to the "secret committee" in 1920, Ernest Jones recalled Chaim Weizmann, the future first president of Israel, talking about "impoverished immigrants from Galicia who were arriving in Palestine with nothing except Marx's *Capital* in one hand and Freud's *Interpretation of Dreams* in the other" (p. 43). Freud's works, especially *The Future of an Illusion* and later *Moses and Monotheism*, were rejected by the conservative part of the Yishuv (the Jewish residents in the lands that became the State of Israel in 1948), but secular leftist intellectuals drew from it additional arguments for Jewish modernism in Palestine.[21]

Back in Vienna, when the leaders of HaShomer Hatzair were either lecturers or students at Bernfeld's institution, they also welcomed his contributions to their journal, *Moriah*. One of the earliest issues to appear in Vienna (after the offices were moved there from Lviv) contains Bernfeld's article "Niemiecki ruch młodzieżowy" [The German Youth Movement]. In this text, which seems to be his only publication in Polish, Bernfeld argues that the German youth movement deserves the Jewish community's – and especially the Zionists' – particular attention:

> First because a considerable number of Jews are active in this movement, so that we must understand what hopes, wishes and efforts these Jews expect to fulfil there. Only this understanding will show us the way in

19 G. Liebermann, *La psychanalyse en Palestine 1918–1948: Aux origines du mouvement analytique israélien* (Paris: Campagne Première, 2012), p. 146.

20 By way of comparison, Nietzsche, usually the most popular thinker, inspired only about half of the articles. See E. J. Rolnik, *Freud in Zion: Psychoanalysis and the Making of Modern Jewish Identity* (London: Routledge, 1997), pp. 50–51.

21 G. Liebermann summarises the debate on Freud's *Moses and Monotheism* in Palestine in *La psychanalyse en Palestine*, pp. 275–291.

> which these Jews' relationship with German culture can be loosened, and thus also with German nationality, and how their appreciable force can be harnessed to renewing Jewish culture and restoring the Jewish nation to health [...]. Moreover, [...] young Germans have found forms of youth life and educational postulates that can, with certain adjustments, be adapted to the youth of any nation; these are forms that we must get to know in order to learn from them what is essential and unconditionally necessary for us as well.[22]

In this context, Bernfeld identifies and presents the three organisations that he considers most important: *Wandervogel*, *Freideutsche Jugend* as well as *Jugendkulturbewegung*, with which he was affiliated himself. *Wandervogel* promotes "friendship, love of nature and embodied feeling," fostering "a type of young person that is stronger, more beautiful, more independent and nobler than before" (p. 98); *Freideutsche Jugend* allows young people to come together in groups of friends interested in self-education, while *Jugendkulturbewegung* uniquely debates the very idea of youth. According to Bernfeld, the movement's roots are in the theory of Gustav Wyneken, the first to claim that adolescence differs from both childhood and adulthood – not only in terms of physicality but also psychologically, having its very own value and a distinct identity. An adolescent is not merely an "incomplete adult," but is characterised by unique traits that fade and disappear with age. "Young people have more drive, enthusiasm, interest, more devotion and passion for the spiritual and moral moment"; they "have in themselves a drive to realise those absolute criteria which they feel so vividly, their meaningful application in everyday life" (p. 100).

For Bernfeld, this stems directly from the "spiritual transformations at the time of sexual maturation" (*Ibid.*). The young individuals about whom he writes are characterised by a tendency to sublimate the libidinal energy that surges during puberty. His concept, therefore, does not refer to an entire age group but only to those individuals whom he describes, elsewhere, as "*geistig*" or spiritual, i.e. a sort of youthful moral and cultural avant-garde. Still, this ideal is attainable to all who care to work on themselves:

22 Z. Bernfeld, "Niemiecki ruch młodzieżowy", *MO* 1917, no. 3, p. 96. The editors mention no translator or original language, as would usually be the case with translated contributions to *Moriah*. This suggests the text was written in Polish.

> Clearly, not every young person between the age of fourteen and twenty-one actually represents this type, and yet it is there as a germ, and the young person's task is to fully develop this potential, this inclination. These attributes of youth generate its duty towards culture. (*Ibid.*)

A young person's duty is "to create a new type, new forms of life, forms that suit it psychologically, i.e. the actual culture of youth" (*Ibid.*). It will be impossible to realise it as long as adolescents are forced to function in the current educational system, which stifles their revolutionary potential, ridicules their ideals, and imposes adults' materialism on them. The *Jugendkulturbewegung* is a political movement in the sense that it aims to combat these obstacles, striving to allow all youngsters to live their own lofty moral and aesthetic ideals to the full, always and everywhere, without any compromises. Bernfeld indicates that he cannot go into detail about the means that would allow him to attain this goal, he only refers his Polish readers to the journal *Der Anfang*, of which he was the editor in the year 1913/14, as well as his book *Die neue Jugend und die Frauen* [The New Youth and Women], published by Hugo Heller in Vienna in 1914, which is wholly dedicated to new sexual mores.

In the same issue, a certain Z.E. (Zygmunt Ellenberg?) discusses ideas on Jewish education proposed by Bernfeld and Moses Calvary. Drawing on an article by Bernfeld in *Der Jude* (edited by Martin Buber), Z.E. summarises what Bernfeld did not phrase explicitly in his article: the task of educating young Jewish people is key to the movement of national rebirth, but no one other than youth itself is able to tackle it. Young people themselves must become "the builders of the new home of Jewish education [...], only the young generation can raise this building for their own benefit".[23] Z.E. also outlines Bernfeld's detailed plan for the cultural revolution: worthy and noble individuals from the rising generation will spontaneously form groups, each of which will have its own leader, "a creative person" who will give it its own unique stamp. The adults' responsibilities are described as follows:

> To unite these individual groups into one powerful organisation, to supply it with generous material means with the aim of founding a whole series of

23 Z.E., "Z. Bernfelda i M. Calvary'ego poglądy na żydowski problem wychowawczy", *MO* 1917, no. 3, p. 111.

> institutions common to all groups, such as union buildings in the cities, in the mountains and at the seaside, places for playing, games and sports, libraries, museums, courses, workshops, gymnastics facilities [...]. (p. 112)

Adults would also be responsible for "organising youth rallies, group outings and trips to Palestine or the Galut Jewish centres, agreements with shipping and rail agencies" (*Ibid.*). The point is that young people should not waste their invaluable energy on financial and administrative tasks but be allowed to fully dedicate themselves to their actual mission, which is "to devote themselves to the universal human and national ideals, the ideals of beauty, philosophy and religion, far away from the materialism that has all of society in its grip" (*Ibid.*). In Z.E.'s opinion, this should wrest the young Jews away from "the clutches of assimilation" and harness their energy into the national rebirth movement, although, as Z.E. is careful to point out, Bernfeld himself "develops these reflections only from the point of view of youth as such, hoping to integrate their goals and needs with the ideals of the Jewish renaissance at a later stage. His main focus is youth with its youthful life" (p. 113) – rather than the national postulates, which is for Z.E. the most controversial aspect of the young ideologue's work.

In 1919, Julian Rottersmann reviewed Bernfeld's recently published book *Das jüdische Volk und seine Jugend* [The Jewish People and Its Youth] in *Moriah*, referring to Bernfeld as "the spiritual leader of the Jewish youth movement in the West".[24] Rottersmann reconstructs the most important assumptions of Bernfeld's pedagogical utopia, according to which a revolutionary and spiritual (*geistig*) young generation would give rise to a new society in Palestine. In Bernfeld's view, children and young people up to the age of twenty-one should be supported by the work of adults, who must ensure the best possible conditions for the youngsters' full development, and not through classical education but through a progressive school system that makes the most of the young people's creative potential. In Bernfeld's view, young people alone have the ability to devote themselves unconditionally to the highest spiritual and mental values, for as people grow older they lose this power to advance culture. Among adults, only a few exceptional individuals are endowed with a deep understanding of the needs and goals of young people. In his utopian vision Bernfeld attributes a special role to these rare adults, these thinkers who are the young generation's sympathisers and advisors. Bernfeld imagines a Jewish

24 J. Rottersmann, "Das jüdische Volk und seine Jugend", *MO* 1919, no. 2, pp. 78–80.

settlement in Palestine as a federation of agricultural communities ruled by young people (independently of the older generations) in the spirit of feminism, socialist cooperativism, a progressive and collectivist education and psychoanalysis. Rottersmann concludes his discussion as follows:

> I do not know if Jewish education will follow the path outlined by Bernfeld, but we must openly say that this path is the only one and that it alone leads to the goal: to the upbringing of full, authentic Jews, working with devotion on the construction of Jewish culture. And these are the ones we need![25]

Bernfeld did not remain a mere utopian theorist in the field of education. After World War I, the American Joint Distribution Committee provided him with funds to establish an orphanage in former army barracks on the outskirts of Vienna. Kinderheim Baumgarten provided shelter to three hundred Jewish refugees from Poland, aged three to sixteen.[26] The institution, which was active only between August 1919 and April 1920, represents the first attempt to apply psychoanalysis in the practice of pedagogy; the project was also a courageous experiment in collectivist education – an entirely novel approach.

The institution, whose official mission was to prepare its charges to work in agricultural communities in Palestine, was organised strictly according to Bernfeld's programme.[27] Part of its philosophy was that traditional education only teaches obedience towards teachers and other state authorities, thus shaping personalities that are subservient to adults' political and economic interests.[28] Bernfeld's goal was the opposite: to create a com-

---

25 Not all Polish activists were equally enthusiastic about Bernfeld's vision. For instance, Shlomoh Horowitz was critical of "the new trends arriving from Vienna" and opposed all attempts to use Wyneken's approach in Jewish education. Despite appearances, he argues, Wyneken's system was "unsocial and not pedagogical," for it focused on individuals who were morally and materially privileged while promoting complete freedom with nothing to regulate the drives; in fact, the goal of education should be to "shape a human being out of chaos through a certain higher ideal". He concludes: "Our youth must be raised in the spirit of Jewish heroism, not in a sentimental and Romantic spirit!" (S. Horowitz, "Na marginesie zjazdu", *HA* 1918, no. 10/12, p. 231).

26 Cf. D. Barth, *Kinderheim Baumgarten: Siegfried Bernfelds "Versuch mit neuer Erziehung" aus psychoanalytischer und soziologischer Sicht* (Gießen: Psychosozial-Verlag, 2010).

27 See D. Barth, *Kinderheim Baumgarten*, p. 63.

28 P.L. Utley, "Siegfried Bernfeld's Jewish Order of Youth 1914–1922", *LB* 1979, no. 4, p. 350.

munity of young people governed by those principles that ought to govern society as a whole one day. Baumgarten had its own "school council," a sort of direct democratic legislature. The rules that regulated school life, including the teaching curriculum, were devised on the basis of a compromise between the wishes of teachers and the students, all of whom had the same right to vote and took part in debates. Modelled on HaShomer Hatzair, the community consisted of seven subgroups headed by an adult. The executive was a student committee elected by the school community. It was tasked with maintaining order and settling disputes. All teachers were recruited from the Jüdisches Pädagogium; Bernfeld envisaged that they should be role models for the youngsters rather than representatives of power. Free expression of emotions was encouraged at the orphanage, and students attended a sort of group therapy. The education was entirely secular, although Jewish holidays were celebrated. The language spoken between students and teachers was Hebrew, and the greatest emphasis was that students acquire it quickly; Yiddish was to be rooted out (Bernfeld reports that the children intuitively avoided Polish, "the language of the pogromists"[29]).

A conflict with the external administration, which was imposed on the orphanage in April 1920, led to Bernfeld being ousted within less than a year. The school's entire governing board was replaced and the orphanage was now subjected to the same regulations that applied to other children's homes. Bernfeld describes his experiences running the institution in *Kinderheim Baumgarten: Bericht über einen ernsthaften Versuch mit neuer Erziehung* [Baumgarten Orphanage: A Report on a Serious Experiment with a Novel Education], published by Jüdischer Verlag in Berlin in 1921. Here discusses the ways in which he tried to implement the tenets outlined in his previous book, *Das jüdische Volk und seine Jugend*, juxtaposing the reality of the orphanage with his previous ideals. He stresses that in this experiment, his charges were deeply traumatised children from the poorest social strata; they were mistrustful and their behaviour was often aggressive and selfish, whereas in his theoretical work he had envisaged mentally stable young people. Still, Bernfeld considers the experiment a success, even if it was discontinued: the realisation of the Baumgarten project, he argues, proves that the principles of a collectivist utopia were valid, even in such adverse circumstances.

29 S. Bernfeld, *Kinderheim Baumgarten: Bericht über einen ernsthaften Versuch mit neuer Erziehung* (Berlin: Jüdischer Verlag, 1921), p. 104.

It is only in Palestine that these principles would be introduced on a broader scale by members of HaShomer Hatzair, trained by Bernfeld. For the educators of the Shomer movement, *Das jüdische Volk und seine Jugend* would serve as a handbook furnishing a complete educational programme, beginning even before birth (with a system of pregnancy care), throughout childhood and youth all the way up to the entry into adulthood.

In the interwar period, the Shomer movement was established in more than a dozen additional countries, reaching 40,000 members by 1926.[30] In 1928, HaShomer Hatzair had about 16,500 members in the Polish Republic; by 1935 the number had risen to 30,000 while global membership amounted to about 50,000.[31] In Palestine the organisation transformed into an influential political party. Members of HaShomer Hatzair were responsible for founding and developing kibbutz settlements. As early as 1930, the movement had eighteen kibbutzim; most of the settlers were Polish Jews aged 17 to 25. Passionate about the idea of building "the new man," they introduced a system of collective education that reproduced Bernfeld's Baumgarten model.[32] The children were brought up in coeducational peer groups and followed a curriculum approved by HaShomer Hatzair, the same one in every kibbutz. In each of the settlements belonging to the organisation, the children wore identical uniforms, read the same books, watched the same films, sang the same songs. Nothing, not even clothes and shoes, was considered private property – everything belonged to the group as a whole. The children were isolated from the world outside and unfamiliar with its rules. They had little contact with the adults' everyday lives; there was a separate children's house for meals and sleeping. The young kibbutzniks ran their own farm – a miniature of the adults'. They were encouraged to learn the rules of self-government, so that they might later establish an egalitarian, just and self-sufficient society.

The priority was to protect the children from the bourgeois family and to foster the development of "the new man," who would be free from the neuroses born from traditional family structures. This is why the children spent no more than an hour a day with their biological parents. At the age

---

30 J. Walicki, *Ruch syjonistyczny w Polsce w latach 1926–1930* (Łódź: Ibidem, 2005), pp. 330–332.

31 *Leksykon harcerstwa*, ed. by O. Fietkiewicz (Warsaw: Młodzieżowa Agencja Wydawnicza, 1988), p. 154; T. Guzik, M. Skoczeń, *Żydowskie organizacje skautowe w Polsce*, pp. 37–41.

32 G. Liebermann, *La psychanalyse en Palestine*, pp. 185–191.

of twelve, they joined an inter-kibbutz educational establishment where studies were entirely voluntary. No grades were given and all subjects were elective. The assumption was that once the children reached a certain age, they would become adult members of the kibbutz; no arrangements were made for any other future. If a young person expressed a desire to pursue higher education or to hone certain skills, they had to obtain an elected committee's approval for their temporary absence from the settlement, and the committee also chose the degree course depending on its usefulness to the kibbutz; personal ambitions were subordinated to the community's goals. One interesting account written from the point of view of a child born and raised in a kibbutz is Yael Neeman's *We Were the Future.*[33] Neeman describes the cult of work at the kibbutz, the ideal of creativity or productivity inspired by Brzozowski, which translated into permanent competitiveness about transforming the desert into arable land, the youngsters' uninhibited sexuality, including ready access to abortion, as well as routine visits at a pedagogue's office, where a poster of Freud adorned the wall.

Bernfeld never visited Palestine himself, but many of his students and colleagues from the Jüdisches Pädagogium settled there. Bernfeld acted as consultant on all school and educational initiatives in Palestine. He also sat on the editorial committee of החינוך /*ha-Chinuch* [Education], the first Hebrew-language education sciences journal.[34] Until the 1950s psychoanalysis represented the basis for Israel's new education system.[35]

Back in interwar Poland, Bernfeld's ideas were also promoted by Hebrew-language Zionist journals. The Warsaw-based monthly אופקים/ *Ofakim* [Horizons], launched in 1932, is a case in point. It was published by the Board of Directors of the Jewish Cultural and Educational Association "Tarbut" [Zarząd Główny Żydowskiego Stowarzyszenia Kulturalno-Oświatowego "Tarbut"] and its editor-in-chief was Zvi Zohar, a Polish HaShomer Hatzair organiser. Zohar had settled in Palestine in 1926, becoming one of the most fervent proponents of psychoanalysis among the kibbutz activists; he later joined the Palestinian Psychoanalytic Society. Between 1929 and 1934, Zohar lived in Poland, where he oversaw the network of Hebrew schools run by "Tarbut" and published two books – חינוך הדור/*Chinuch haDor* [Raising a Generation] and דרכי חינוכנו/*Darkay*

33 Y. Neeman, *We Were the Future*, trans. by S. Silverston (New York: Overlook, 2016).

34 E. J. Rolnik, *Freud in Zion*, pp. 160–169.

35 G. Liebermann, *La psychanalyse en Palestine*, p. 171.

Chinuchenu [Paths of Our Education], promoting Palestinian collectivism among a broader readership. According to an advertisement in the press, *Ofakim* was "a Hebrew journal on a European level, essential to any Jewish teacher".[36] The editors dedicated a lot of space to Freudianism. Zohar believed that the "New Hebrew" could only emerge if the Jewish nation underwent psychoanalysis, got rid of its inferiority complex and healed the traumata suffered through centuries of living in diaspora. *Ofakim* published articles by leading Freudians and discussed recent publications in the field; Paul Federn, whose psychoanalysis handbook was translated into Hebrew by Izrael Kohn and published in Warsaw in 1932, contributed a regular column.[37]

Once the Baumgarten project was discontinued, Siegfried Bernfeld became Martin Buber's personal secretary in Heppenheim, helping to publish *Der Jude*. In April 1921, the journal folded due to financial difficulties and Bernfeld returned to Vienna, where Freud helped him find work as a psychoanalyst. His first patients were Gustav Bychowski and Felix Deutsch (Helene's husband). Bernfeld withdrew from the Zionist movement and focused on psychoanalysis. In late 1925 he moved to Berlin.

It is important to remember that the geopolitical transformations that took place in Central Europe after World War I considerably impacted the history of the psychoanalytical movement. The Treaty of Versailles reduced Vienna, previously the cultural and political heart of the multinational empire, to the status of capital of the Republic of Austria, an exclusively Germanophonic region whose population represented a mere 12% of the imperial population of 52 million. Vienna's position appeared particularly peripheral compared to the burgeoning metropolis of Berlin, which became the new civilisational centre of the German-speaking world and a hub for the Jewish diaspora.[38] The Weimar Republic's capital was the second largest city in Europe and the third largest in the world. Since 1871, when 800 thousand people lived in the new capital of the German Empire, Berlin's population had risen to 4.3 million by 1920. Many of the

36 An advertisement in *Nowy Dziennik* 1932, no. 278, p. 16.

37 To fully understand this question, one would need to do an exhaustive archival survey of Hebrew-language publications in the Second Polish Republic. It is also worth remembering that in the 1890s, Warsaw was already the centre for modern Hebrew book publishing (see H. Datner, *Ta i tamta strona: Żydowska inteligencja Warszawy drugiej połowy XIX wieku*, p. 81).

38 See the monographic number of *Cwiszyn* (2012, no. 1/2).

new inhabitants were migrants drawn by the democratic reforms introduced by the constitution of 1919, by the dizzying speed of the city's modernisation, and the career prospects offered by the rapid industrialisation.

As the Berlin correspondent for *Ilustrowana Republika* wrote in 1928, one out of eight Berliners were born abroad. Compared to them, the "real Germans" from the provinces who visited their capital in the summer looked like "poor relatives in an elegant home" .[39] The city attracted the world's greatest scientists, such as Albert Einstein. Berlin was a press empire (2,486 different journal titles were published in 1928), a centre for the film industry (UFA was Europe's largest film company) and for avant-garde art, fostering movements such as expressionism, Dada and *Neue Sachlichkeit*, the functionalism of the Bauhaus, the engaged theatre developed by Max Reinhardt, Erwin Piscator, Bertolt Brecht and Paul Hindemith's musical radicalism. At the same time, the hyperinflation of 1923 made Berlin extraordinarily affordable to those in possession of foreign currency, especially Americans (many psychoanalysts, incidentally, benefitted from this situation if they had patients who paid in dollars[40]). Visitors from across the Atlantic took advantage of Berlin's night life, cabaret performances and jazz clubs, and many appreciated the moral and sexual freedom, including a flourishing gay culture. The fight for women's rights was beginning to have a visible impact, with milestone achievements such as universal suffrage and university admission; fashion and leisure (sports!) were also reflecting a greater degree of liberty. Berlin saw a rise in immigration from Vienna. Many Jews left Austria due of the ever more virulent anti-Semitism there, while members of the Freudian movement were often swayed to emigrate in response to internal structural shifts.

The role of Freud's emissary to Berlin was played by the psychiatrist Karl Abraham, the master's first student in Germany. He established a practice in 1907, when Berlin was still the capital of the German Empire under Wilhelm II .[41] Abraham was an accomplished clinician as well as a skilful organiser. He managed to win the support of the German medical establishment, and in 1910 he founded the Deutsche Psychoanalytische

39 J. Mayen, "Prawdziwi Niemcy w Berlinie", *IR* 1928, no. 208, p. 3.

40 Cf. E.D. Weitz, *Weimar Germany* (Princeton: Princeton University), p. 139.

41 On the earliest reception of Freud's theory in Germany see H.S. Decker, *Freud in Germany: Revolution and Reaction in Science*, 1893–1907 (New York: International Universities Press, 1977).

Gesellschaft. The seventh Psychoanalytical Congress in 1920 took place in Berlin. The same year, Max Eitingon opened the Berliner Psychoanalytisches Institut [Berlin Psychoanalytical Institute], the first of its kind worldwide, which served as a model for all institutes founded in the years to follow. (The one in Vienna was headed by Helene Deutsch, who took the post after her apprenticeship and psychoanalysis with Abraham in Berlin.) The institute's goal was not only to ensure continuity in the training of analysts, but also to make psychoanalysis accessible as broadly as possible. To reach an audience outside medical circles, the Berliner Psychoanalytisches Institut held open and immensely popular lectures and funded radio features on psychoanalysis.[42]

Max Eitingon was born in Imperial Russia (in the city of Mohilev, now Belarus) and pursued higher education in Switzerland, like most German-speaking Russians. He was Eugen Bleuler's assistant at the university clinic in Zurich and collaborated with Jung. In 1907 he became the first person from outside the Austrio-Hungarian Empires to approach Freud, expressing his admiration and consulting him on a case.[43] Following his analysis by Freud in 1909, he joined the VPA. In 1910 he left for Berlin. After Anton von Freund's death in 1920, Eitingon joined the "secret committee," and when Karl Abraham died in 1925, Eitingon was promoted from secretary to president of the IPA (Abraham had held this position for the last year of his life). He remained in this position until 1934. Thus the Freudian movement was headed by Berlin-based followers for an entire decade, making Weimar Germany's capital the world's centre for psychoanalysis.[44]

The Berliner Institut was financed by Eitingon's private fortune. On several occasions he baled out Freud's movement as it struggled financially, and was a generous supporter of the Internationaler Psychoanalytischer Verlag. The sources of Max Eitingon's wealth, however, take us first to his father, the Russian "king of furs," Chaim Eitingon, and then to someone very high up in the Soviet government who must have protected the furrier. The business continued to thrive even after the October Revolution, with two new branches opening in Paris and New York in 1917, in

42 Cf. *Zehn Jahre Berliner Psychoanalytisches Institut* (Vienna: Internationaler Psychoanalytischer Verlag, 1930).

43 A. Etkind, *Eros of the Impossible*, p. 245.

44 Cf. L. Sokolowsky, *Freud et les Berlinois: Du congrès de Budapest à l'Institut de Berlin 1918–1933* (Rennes: Presses universitaires de Rennes, 2013).

addition to the flagship stores in Leipzig and Bolshevik Moscow. According to Alexander Etkind, Chaim had another son, Nahum Leonid Eitingon, who climbed the career ladder in the Soviet secret police.[45] Following the money trail, therefore, we might conclude that the psycho-analytical movement received financial support thanks to the Soviet secret police, or, more precisely, that the Soviet secret police turned a blind eye to Chaim's profitable business venture, allowing Chaim's son Max to lavish vast sums on the Freudian movement. That said, Etkind's argument has been contended by scholars who do not believe there were any family ties between Max and Nahum Leonid Eitingon.[46]

Max Eitingon is a complex personality. He has been described as a Zionist and at the same time a typical diasporic Jew, always searching for an identity. As Élisabeth Roudinesco puts it, "in Zurich he is a Viennese, in Vienna he is already from Berlin, in Berlin he dreams of Jerusalem. Wherever he goes, he is a Russian and a Pole, and above all – a Jew."[47] Despite his immense fortune Eitingon – just like Ernest Simmel, his co-director at the Institute – was an outspoken socialist. One of his goals was to liberate psychoanalysis from its reliance on wealthy neurotics, which is why the polyclinic affiliated with the Institute offered therapies to *all* patients – free of charge if need be. Thus Eitingon and Simmel took up an idea first formulated by Freud, who, however, had never actually tried to implement it in reality.[48] Over the course of the next few years, similar clinics opened in ten other cities across seven different countries. By the end of the 1920s, pro bono analysts saw patients not only in Berlin and Vienna but also in London, Budapest, Zagreb, Moscow, Frankfurt, New York, Trieste and Paris.[49]

According to Eran Rolnik, the Berlin Polyclinic "transformed the status of Freud's students":

> From an elite and isolated group of Jewish intellectuals, they became a society whose members volunteered a part of their time and effort to listen

45 A. Etkind, *Eros of the Impossible*, pp. 247-251.

46 Cf. e.g. G. Liebermann, *La psychanalyse en Palestine*, pp. 20–21, as well as J. Chemouni, *Trotsky et la psychanalyse* (Paris: In Press, 2004), pp. 100–127.

47 E. Roudinesco, *Histoire de la psychanalyse en France*, p. 152.

48 Cf. Freud's presentation at the 5th International Psychoanalytical Congress in Budapest in 1918: "Lines of Advance in Psycho-Analytic Therapy", SE XVII, pp. 157-168.

49 Cf. E.A. Danto, *Freud's Free Clinics*.

> to and treat the troubles and sorrows of the downtrodden inhabitants of a big city.[50]

It is in the capital of the Weimar Republic that psychoanalysis overcame its previous limitations. It ceased to focus exclusively on one social group, i.e middle-class Jewish women. The therapies offered at no cost made psychoanalysis accessible to a broad range of patients, which in turn made for more diverse clinical observations and corresponding theoretical developments. (Otto Fenichel reportedly joked about reactionary psychoanalysts who never even considered the fact that a patient might lose his job on account of socio-economic factors, rather than due to the profound conflicts in his subconscious (p. 75).) Psychoanalytical social criticism was developed in Berlin, spearheaded by analysts of the second generation who were much more politically engaged than their older colleagues. It was only in Berlin that psychoanalysis really became a radical social project. This explains Bernfeld's decision to move to the German capital, where he found opportunities to popularise his pedagogical concepts.

Childhood development was one of the psychoanalysts' main fields of interest ever since the publication of Freud's *Three Essays on the Theory of Sexuality* (1905). Bringing childhood sexuality out into the open, Freud was clearly questioning existing notions about education, furnishing new arguments for breaking with the traditional, puritan model. At the centre of the debate was the question of sex education.[51] One contentious topic was masturbation. Unlike the Victorian pedagogues who fiercely combatted it as perverse and a health hazard, the Freudians portrayed it as a natural stage in young people's genital organisation.

In *Three Essays on the Theory of Sexuality*, Freud presents a melancholy view of human sexuality, considering heterosexual genital intercourse between adults to be a biological compulsion related to the reproduction of the species; to realise this goal, the individual must renounce other, equally or even more satisfying forms of gratification. The child is born "polymorphously perverse, and can be led into all possible kinds of sexual irregularities;"[52] there are no limits to its sexual pleasure, while its libido is

50 E. J. Rolnik, *Freud in Zion*, p. 73.

51 Cf. S. Freud, "The Sexual Enlightenment of Children (An Open Letter to Dr. M. Fürst)", SE IX, pp. 129-140 and "On the Sexual Theories of Children", SE IX, pp. 205-226.

52 S. Freud, SE VII, p. 191.

not bound to any concrete object. Growing up represents a series of losses and renouncements. Once the young person reaches adulthood, cultural prejudices are superimposed on the teleology of nature – prejudices that keep watch over feminine virtue as a guarantee of legitimate paternity. In 1908 Freud wrote:

> If this evolution of the sexual instinct is borne in mind, three stages of civilisation can be distinguished: a first one, in which the sexual instinct may be freely exercised without regard to the aims of reproduction; a second, in which all of the sexual instinct is suppressed except what serves the aims of reproduction; and a third, in which only legitimate reproduction is allowed as a sexual aim. This third stage is reflected in our present-day "civilised" sexual morality.[53]

The glossary of psychoanalysis contains no reference to any sexual "norm" nor any sort of negative counterpart, be it sin, crime or illness. Freud also rejects earlier explanations of aberrant sexual behaviour, such as Krafft-Ebing's notion of the heredity of sexual deviance. According to Freudian theory, perverts are persons who in their search for pleasure did not succumb to biological or cultural pressure, who did not let themselves be deprived of the form of gratification that they came to enjoy in their earliest childhood. From this point of view, we could say, a pervert's eros is not immature but heroic. The "negative" of perversion is neurosis; it is the price that a person must pay for the compromises made along the way of libidinal development. Pathological symptoms provide a substitute gratification of the desires that the individual was forced to renounce.

The core of Freud's approach was to point out that mental illness was rooted in overly restrictive sexual mores. In several texts, from *Sexuality in the Aetiology of the Neuroses* (the original German was published in 1898) to *Civilisation and Its Discontents* (original publication in 1930), he blames "'civilised' sexual morality" for the spread of nervous diseases. Some analysts of the younger generation drew radical conclusions from Freud's assumptions: if the repression of childhood sexuality is responsible for the nervous problems that arise in adulthood, for people's inability to attain happiness and fulfilment, then an intervention on the level of education is needed in order to carry through a cultural shift. Instead of treating ever younger children for neurosis (in the interwar period psychoanalytical

53 S. Freud, "'Civilised' Sexual Morality and Modern Nervous Illness", SE IX, p. 189.

journals describe cases of two-year-old toddlers), the reformers proposed that it would be better to change the organisation of society so that it would cease to produce neuroses. The most revolutionary conclusions were proposed by Wilhelm Reich, who translated Freud's discovery into concrete political demands. And thus, in the second half of the 1920s, largely using his private fortune, he set up six clinics of sexual hygiene in Vienna. At that time, Reich was a member of the Social Democratic Party of Austria, and the party leadership supported his projects. In 1930, however, they shut down his clinics. This is when Reich moved to Berlin. In the early 1930s, coinciding precisely with the Great Depression (1930–33), he founded Sexpol, the German Association for Proletarian Sexual Politics, and became a member of the Communist Party of Germany (KPD).[54]

In Berlin, Reich wrote his most important books. Inspired by Bronisław Malinowski, *Geschlechtsreife, Enthaltsamkeit, Ehemoral* [Sexual Maturity, Abstinence, Marital Morality]; *Der sexuelle Kampf der Jugend* [The Sexual Struggle of Youth] as well as *Der Einbruch der Sexualmoral* [The Collapse of Sexual Morality] set up the foundations of what Reich called "Freudo-Marxism". He rejected subsequent modifications that Freud added to his psychoanalytical theory, opposing in particular the notion of the death drive; the dualism of drives, he believed, obscured the essence of Freud's discovery – libido.[55]

Once the harmful psychological effects of sexual repression had been made clear, Reich argued, there was an urgent need to bring about complete erotic liberation. A sexual revolution was the first and necessary step on the way towards social revolution. The right to orgasm comes before and is a condition of all other economic or political rights. Ultimately, unrestricted sexual gratification ought to be accessible to all age groups, as is the case in Trobriand society. What preoccupied Reich more than anything, however, was the sexual life of children and teenagers, who are not yet as burdened by inhibition and neurosis as adults. One of his priorities was children's sex education, of which he had a very broad notion (it entailed them being allowed to watch adults engaging in sexual activities, encouraging children's sexual play and masturbation, and faci-

54 Cf. P.A. Robinson, *The Freudian Left*, p. 40.

55 On Reich's atypical orthodoxy, which in some aspects recalls Helene Deutsch's, see esp. J. Mitchell, "Wilhelm Reich: Sexual Politics", in *Psychanalysis and Feminism* (London: Penguin, 1986) pp. 137-227.

litating erotic initiation as early as possible in puberty). Reich did not reject the notion of collective education, which could circumvent the Oedipus complex, and he was a careful observer of innovations in the field in the USSR, which he visited in 1929, especially Vera Schmidt's experimental nursery school in Moscow.

According to historian Eric Weitz, Reich's sexual revolution project, just as the many other reformatory concepts of sexuality that emerged at the time, were part of the "powerful, utopian visions of transforming society – and humanity – once and for all":[56]

> The reformers believed deeply that their work was of a piece with democratic governance, social welfare programs that protected workers from the vicissitudes of the business cycle, and the construction of well-built, sunlit affordable apartments. No less than the major drafters of the Weimar constitution and the architects of modern housing developments, the sex reformers played a central role in making Germany in the Weimar period a more modern, open, and humane society. (p. 302)

Reich's extravagant ideas would eventually lead to his being ousted from both the KPD and the International Psychoanalytical Association. Nonetheless, it seems that all he did was to draw logical conclusions about the application of psychoanalysis to pedagogy, while the other representatives of the movement stopped short of falling into heresy.

The early Freudians had already engaged in a long discussion on the use of psychoanalysis in pedagogy – a discussion that began with Sándor Ferenczi's presentation "Psychoanalyse und Pädagogik" [Psychoanalysis and Pedagogy] at the International Psychoanalytical Congress in Salzburg in 1908. He proposed that the Freudians' goal ought to be to liberate children from unnecessary repression; to achieve this he proposed that educators should undergo analysis, because their unconscious conflicts threw a shadow on their charges' development. Psychoanalytical pedagogy *sensu stricto*, which focused not only on the child and its development but on the very question of education (especially within educational establishments such as nurseries and schools) and the educators and teachers themselves, only emerged in 1926 as an established field with its own journal. This is when the monthly *Zeitschrift für psychoanalytische Pädagogik* [Journal for Psychoanalytical Pedagogy] was founded, as if to bestow

56 E.D. Weitz, *Weimar Germany*, p. 170. See the chapter "Bodies and Sex", pp. 297-331.

legitimacy on the new research area (it ceased to appear in 1937).[57] In the mid-1920s, Freud recognised that the inclusion of psychoanalysis within pedagogy was its latest important achievement. This is how he concludes his *Autobiographical Study* (1925):

> I myself have contributed nothing to the application of analysis to education. It was natural, however, that the analytic discoveries about the sexual life and mental development of children should attract the attention of educators and make them see their problems in a new light [...]. The application of analysis to the prophylactic upbringing of healthy children and to the correcting of those who, though not actually neurotic, have deviated from the normal course of development has led to one consequence which is of practical importance. It is no longer possible to restrict the practice of psycho-analysis to doctors and to exclude laymen from it. In fact, a doctor who has not been through a special training is, in spite of his diploma, a layman in analysis, and a non-doctor who has been suitably trained can, with occasional reference to a doctor, carry out the analytic treatment not only of children but also of neurotics.[58]

In "The Question of Lay Analysis," published a year later, Freud lists the benefits of psychoanalysis practiced by non-doctors. The possibility of applying its findings in education appears as his final and deciding argument:

> Analysis undeniably still has its enemies. I do not know whether they have means at their command for stopping the activities of these educational analysts or analytic educationalists. I do not think it very likely.[59]

It was Siegfried Bernfeld who had the greatest impact on the emerging discipline in psychoanalytical research. At the eighth Psychoanalytical Congress in Salzburg in 1924 he presented a trenchant critique of the way psychoanalysis was being applied in education. Above all, he called into question the optimism of educators – even those who were familiar with

---

57 Cf. G. Bittner, W. Rehm, "Psychoanalyse und Erziehung", in *Psychoanalyse und Erziehung: Ausgewählte Beiträge aus der "Zeitschrift für psychoanalytische Pädagogik"*, ed. by G. Bittner, W. Rehm (Bern–Stuttgart: Huber, 1964), pp. 11–22.

58 S. Freud, *An Autobiographical Study*, SE XX, p. 70.

59 S. Freud, "The Question of Lay Analysis", SE XX, p. 249.

psychoanalysis – and insisted that "psychoanalysis only allows for a pessimistic pedagogy".[60] Indeed, Freudianism had debunked the notion that childhood was a period of particular plasticity which should allow adults to mould the young person through carefully chosen interventions. Such an approach, Bernfeld adds, would only suggest that educators are more narcissistic than other people.

In 1925, the Internationaler Psychoanalytischer Verlag published Bernfeld's most influential work, *Sisyphos, oder die Grenzen der Erziehung* [*Sisyphus or the Limitations of Education*].[61] He distances himself from the narcissistic idealism of the leaders of the so-called new pedagogy, whose lofty but unattainable goals were out of touch with reality. He also reveals the actual political interests promoted by the process of education. Bernfeld's book is his first – and already impressive – attempt to combine psychoanalysis and Marxism. Freud and Marx are the patrons of the scientific pedagogy that he hoped to advance.[62]

In Bernfeld's opinion, the current stage in the development of pedagogy recalls that of medicine before it became professionalised, when it was magic or witchcraft. If it sometimes managed to attain its stated goal, thens it was only by chance, in ways that would be difficult to replicate or even to explain rationally. What is needed, therefore, is not inspired visionaries but dedicated scientists whose theories, introduced to everyday life, would transform the existing paradigm of education; they would do this objectively, permanently and effectively, through the practical implementation of their concepts by millions of teachers and parents. Bernfeld's most important criteria to evaluate a given pedagogical concept are progress and rationalisation on the one hand, and effectiveness and usefulness on the other. Unlike a great mathematician or poet, a pedagogue cannot be judged merely on the basis of individual achievements, but on the ability to put them into practice. Existing educational projects, such as the ones proposed by Rousseau, Fichte, Herbart, Basedow, Jean Paul or Salz-

60 S. Bernfeld, "Kritik der bisherigen Anwendung der Psychoanalyse auf die Pädagogik", *IZP* 1924, no. 2, p. 224.

61 S. Bernfeld, *Sisyphos, oder die Grenzen der Erziehung* (Leipzig–Wien–Zurich: Internationaler Psychoanalytischer Verlag, 1925). English: *Sisyphus or the Limitations of Education*, trans. by F. Lilge (Berkeley: University of California Press, 1973).

62 Bernfeld's entire output is marked by the conviction that both Freudianism and Marxism are sciences – a view that associates his work with that of Wilhelm Reich. Cf. W. Reich, *Dialektischer Materialismus und Psychoanalyse* (Copenhagen: Verlag für Sexualpolitik, 1934).

mann, lack empirical foundations, Bernfeld argues. The great pedagogues mentioned above had little practical experience working with children – they were like astronomers who just went to sleep every night. Their relationship to their own childhood had not been worked through; it was marked by repression and falsified by the selective procedures of memory; it could only obscure their ideas about growing up, impelling them to idealise childhood and fail to acknowledge infantile urges. Such an idyllic and naive vision betrays unconscious and therefore uncontrolled emotions, which means that its propositions can be neither objective nor scientific. Although some intuitive passages in these writers' works are astonishingly accurate, these are still philosophical and literary texts, based on unverified assumptions; they overlook the psychological and social conditions of education and as such they are unsuitable to form the foundation for an entire pedagogical system. Although each of them projects a universal ideal of humankind, their implementation would fail to bring about social change.

Bernfeld emphasises that school as an institution was not established for didactic reasons but emerged out of a concrete economical and political situation, rooted in received opinions which in turn stemmed from intergenerational relationships and class structure; as such, school serves to maintain the status quo. It introduces an artificial division between learning and living, and it views children only as students, ignoring individual urges, desires and ideals. Bernfeld highlights the difference between didactics and pedagogy: the first is no more than the technology of education, while the second is its theory and philosophy; the first is linked to teaching, the second to bringing up a person. In Bernfeld's opinion, commentators notoriously confuse the two, and they privilege discussions on effective training while neglecting the scientific study of pedagogy. This bias is also apparent in the reception of great educators such as Johann Heinrich Pestalozzi: his life work have been reduced to his method of early teaching, ignoring the context and allowing for deformations of his approach. One reason for these shortcomings is a lack of criteria by which pedagogues are judged: it is easier to check if a child has learned to read, than it is to ascertain if the child has been "educated". The school system, Bernfeld continues, only focuses on the transmission of knowledge; this is the basis on which teachers are evaluated, and this is what its mission boils down to. With measurable results – especially combatting illiteracy – being its principle objective, it is organised in a way that is modern and rational but that makes it all but impossible to educate children in the sense of supporting them in their development. In Bernfeld's opinion, the same rationality ought to be harnessed to the goals of education, to form "the new man" and, as a result, a better society. Reading skills alone will not do: what matters is how the individual will apply them.

Bernfeld, clearly inspired by Émile Durkheim's theory of education as a "social fact," defines pedagogy as a social reaction to the "fact" of childhood and development. The permanent and universal aspect of education is the unavoidably conflict-ridden relationship between the will of the adult and the will of the child – after all, childhood is characterised by striving for pleasure. Since this is not in the interest of any human community, this striving for pleasure must be kept in check. Given that the adult is stronger and unafraid of the child, fear does not restrain the expression of emotions or the imposition of the adult's will on the child through corporal punishment. The moment in which ideological, moral or religious scruples appear signifies that universal, human and psychological aspects come into conflict with historical, social and cultural aspects. Wherever adults are highly inhibited in meeting their own needs by the group on which their physical and psychological survival depends, wherever a culture imposes severe restrictions on them, these adults will take it out on children, thus releasing their own affects. For even the best educators are also the products of an educational system; their devotion to children is a sublimation of a love deficit and of personal fulfilment, while the process of education always reproduces how they were treated by their own parents. For Bernfeld, this mechanism remains stable, whether we are dealing with feelings of aggression (in the case of more authoritarian forms of pedagogy) or love. In fact, "the pedagogy of hate" finds more social approval than the "pedagogy of love," for hate only threatens the individual at whom it is directed, whereas the free expression of love undermines the social order as such.

Education is the result of the parents' primary reaction to the ontogenetic fact of growing up. It is rooted in the mother's possessive affection towards her offspring on the one hand, and the father's yearning to destroy and his fear of revenge on the other hand. Feelings of love protect the young generation and ensure society's biological survival; the paternal incest ban, which awakens a sense of guilt in the child, introduces the child to culture, and as such it is the model for all educational institutions. Bernfeld believes that school has served to bring about the child's ultimate separation from the mother and to facilitate an identification that is not limited to the incestuous triangle, thus guaranteeing the cultural continuity of the social structure. The goal of education, for Bernfeld, is to foster a psychological structure that is able to maintain the stage already attained by society. As society evolves, education and childhood become more drawn-out and detached from the biological process of growing up. In Bernfeld's view, this serves the economy, for the economic system is "a kind of material embodiment and justification of the social unconscious,"[63] something like an ideology of a guilty conscience.

Everything that goes beyond these economic functions of education is, according to Bernfeld, political and related to upholding the current distribution of economic power, no matter what pedagogical idealists, moralists or inspired clergymen may believe. He compares children to sheep that are expected to produce a predetermined amount of wool whose market value exceeds the costs of raising the animal – differences between individual sheep, probably detectable to a caring shepherd (or committed pedagogue), are ignored, just as the means by which the intended goal was achieved. Education is a costly undertaking, and capital is in the hands of the bourgeoisie, which is not going to invest in something that will not pay off. The only thing worth supporting is the satisfaction of its own cultural needs (rather than the development and democratisation of culture) and ensuring its own material welfare through ideology. There is no such thing as progress in education. Even if from a technocratic point of view it leads to better and better results, these only serve the further development of capitalism and the solidification of the class struggle.

The limitations of education are both internal and external. The former result from unconscious conflicts in the educators and their charges – limitations that psychoanalysis can help overcome, while the latter are related to the current socio-economic system, which can be demystified using Marxist theory. The process of education not only exits within this system – it also perpetuates it. For Bernfeld, each system of education is intrinsically conservative, for it reflects the aspirations of a given community and its beliefs about the values worth transmitting to the next generation; it also solidifies and increases the power of the group in charge of education. In the capitalist system pedagogy is one of the ideologies harnessed to serve the interests of a privileged minority, facilitating the exploitation of the lower classes. In education, violence comes to appear as

63 S. Bernfeld, *Sisyphus or the Limitations of Education*, p. 64.

a free expression of love and dedication to higher goals. The education system identifies the interests of one class with values shared by the entire nation, creating a community that does not actually exist and suggesting that this community is threatened by some ominous enemy.

Bernfeld concludes his book on a pessimistic note: if education is society's reaction to the fact of growing up, as he often repeats, then the economic structure of a given society sets the framework for this reaction. The way in which education is organised is completely predetermined by society, and the smallest adjustment requires a revision within the framework of this structure. Never has a radical social transformation occurred thanks to education, and it certainly had nothing to do with visionary pedagogues. Educational reforms have all, without exception, resulted from breakthroughs outside of the field. Even if educators become aware of the psychological and social conditioning of their work, their efforts will remain as fruitless as the labours of the titular Sisyphus. No reform in pedagogy will bring about actual results without a change of the social structure. As long as some teenagers get to attend a gymnasium while others are put to work in a factory, as long as access to knowledge depends on the class into which a person happens to be born, as long as an elite gets to select the works and ideas promoted in schools, all innovative pedagogical visions will come to nothing. Socialism alone can introduce the necessary corrections. Any calls for pedagogical reforms that precede such a revolution will remain idealistic; the efforts of individual educators to support particular teenagers will bring to mind a boulder forever being rolled up a hill only to roll down again. Bernfeld tackles the illusions of his own youth, distancing himself from his earlier belief that a revolutionary educational model would lead to the creation of "the new man". Parting with the tenets of HaShomer Hatzair, his views now bring to mind the pessimism that marked Freud's work at the time.

Soon after the publication of *Sisyphos*, Bernfeld began to withdraw from research in pedagogy, but he continued to teach. In the autumn of 1924, he gave a popular lecture series titled "Psychoanalyse und Erziehung" [Psychoanalysis and Education] at the Berlin Psychoanalytical Institute. Once he moved to Berlin he also assumed the teaching responsibilities of Karl Abraham, who had passed away a few weeks before; for instance, in January 1926, he began to train German educators in psychoanalysis. In the years 1928–32 he gave lectures in psychoanalytical theory at the Institute and headed a research group (Pädagogische Arbeitsgemeinschaft) whose mission was to familiarise non-medical professionals with psychoanalysis.[64] He also taught at the Deutsche Hochschule für Politik and gave lectures to general audiences across Germany and beyond the Republic – wherever progressive organisations invited him.

In the second half of the 1920s, Bernfeld had two main preoccupations: first, to add a social dimension to psychoanalysis by introducing the precise terminology of the social sciences to texts in psychoanalysis (for instance, instead of the unspecific term "reality" that used to figure in the Freudians' works he preferred "social position" [*sozialer Ort*, i.e. position in the social order]), and second, to ground psychoanalysis on a measurable data. Hoping to enrich Freud's theory with quantitative methods, and thereby to bring it closer to the exact sciences, he began to develop a libidometre, a devise to measure a patient's libidinal energy (his efforts bring to mind Wilhelm Reich's work in Scandinavia in the mid-1930s, when he tried to build an orgone accumulator to treat a lack or a surplus of orgone energy). In 1932, before the Nazis burned Freud's books, Bernfeld left Berlin and, after two years in Vienna, he moved to France; in 1937 he spent some time in London and then emigrated to California. Until his death in 1953 he mostly worked on collecting materials for a biography of Freud, which, however, he never wrote.[65]

Bernfeld's work on education was taken up and continued – first in Berlin, then in emigration – by the two sisters Berta and Stephanie Bornstein. They also had a Polish-Jewish background, so their lives and work deserve a closer look in the context of this study.

Berta and Stephanie Bornstein

The sisters were born in Cracow to Gizela, née Haber, and Gustaw (Getzel) Bornstein, a Russian citizen. Gustaw (Getzel) Bornstein was co-director, with Mojżesz Blankstein, of a local company manufacturing cement and concrete

64 There were 117 course attendants in 1929, including 13 social workers, 12 educators, five social assistants and three nurses. See R. Kloocke, E. Mühlleitner, "Lehren oder lernen? Siegfried Bernfeld und die 'Pädagogische Ausbildung der Psychoanalytischen Arbeitsgemeinschaft' am Berliner Psychoanalytischen Institut", *LA* 2004, no. 34, p. 38.

65 It is at Bernfeld's request that Ludwig Jekels recorded the memoirs to which I referred in Part One of this book. Between 1944 and 1953 Bernfeld was preparing a scholarly biography Freud. See I. Grubrich-Simitis, "Siegfried Bernfeld: Historiker der Psychoanalyse und Freud-Biograph", *PSY* 1981, no. 35, pp. 397–434.

products. The business started operating on 1 July 1889.[66] It must have enjoyed a good reputation, for it was awarded the bronze medal at the General National Exhibition in Lviv in 1894.[67] When the city of Cracow launched an intensive modernising endeavour under mayor Józef Dietl in 1897, the council entrusted Blankstein and Bornstein with the construction of the sewers – a key part of the project of building a sewage system in Cracow.[68] The following year, their company tendered for the construction of a reservoir for the new waterworks.[69] In the census of 1900, Getzel Bornstein still figures as the owner of a cement factory at Sebastian Street 17.

So much is known for sure. When it comes to the dates of birth of the Bornstein girls, however, the sources provide contradictory information. According to Elke Mühlleitner, Stephanie (Steff for short) was born in 1891 and Berta (Bertl) in 1896.[70] According to the *International Dictionary of Psychoanalysis*, Berta's true date of birth is 1899, the year listed in her obituaries, while Steff is younger and not older.[71] Materials kept at the police archive in Prague suggest that Stephanie was born in 1893.[72] In the documents that Berta had to submit applying for a visa to the USA in the late 1930s she states that she was born in 1898.[73]

Materials kept at the Leo Baeck Institute in New York indicate that the family moved to Berlin after the father's death in 1905. These documents concern the most prominent member of the family, Joseph Bornstein, the third child born in 1899. Once the family had settled in Berlin, Joseph attended the Sophien-Gymnasium, then he studied history and economics in Berlin and Vienna. In the early 1920s he became involved with the young socialists around Paul Levi, one of the founders of the Communist Party of Germany. There he met Leopold Schwarzschild and Stefan Grossmann, and the three founded the journal *Tagebuch*. Joseph Bornstein's main task was to

66 *GLW* 1894, no. 172, p. 10.

67 *GNA* 1894, no. 254, p. 2.

68 *DP* 1897, no. 26, pp. 3. Cf. K. Dohnalik, *Geneza i rozwój wodociągów i kanalizacji miasta Krakowa 1882–1982* (Cracow: Miejskie Przedsiębiorstwo Wodociągów i Kanalizacji, 1986). See also *GŁN* 1897, no. 156, pp. 4–5.

69 *GNA* 1898, no. 269, p. 3; *GLW* 1898, no. 220, p. 6.

70 E. Mühlleitner, *Biographisches Lexikon der Psychoanalyse*, pp. 49–52.

71 *International Dictionary of Psychoanalysis*, p. 205.

72 C. Ludwig-Körner, *Wiederentdeckt – Psychoanalytikerinnen in Berlin* (Giessen: Psychosozial-Verlag, 1999), pp. 79–84.

73 Leo Baeck Institute, Joseph Bornstein Collection 1917–1952, catalogue number AR 4082/MF 650 < http://findingaids.cjh.org/?pID=121524 > [accessed on 12/01/2021].

report on political and social injustice in the country. In 1927 he became editor-in-chief, a position he maintained until 1931. His reportage work won him several awards, and soon he was talked about as a prodigy of German journalism. He reported on the investigation and trial of Rosa Luxemburg's murderers, as well as the case of Sacco and Vanzetti. He was a member of the German League for Human Rights and was seen as one of the most important journalists of the Weimar era – a strong opponent of the right wing and populist parties long before the Nazis came to power. In 1933 he left Germany for Switzerland and then Paris, where until 1938 he continued his collaboration with Leopold Schwarzschild in *Das Neue Tagebuch*, writing under the pseudonym Erich Andermann. He also contributed to other German émigré publications in France, such as *Montag Morgen* and *Pariser Tageszeitung*, where he was editor-in-chief throughout 1939. At this time he befriended the writer Joseph Roth, who had moved to Paris in 1933. Conscripted into the French army, Bornstein was sent to Africa, from where, following his release from active duty in March 1941, he emigrated to the United States. In January 1942 he joined the US Office of War Information. After the war he worked as a literary agent, specialising in representing European writers such as Hermann Hesse and Alberto Moravia on the American book market. He also published his own analysis of Nazi propaganda (*Action Against the Enemy's Mind*, 1942) and a study of political violence in interwar Europe and the USSR, *The Politics of Murder* (1950). He died in 1952.

The youngest brother, Emil Bornstein, was born in 1901. Little is known about his life before he emigrated to San Francisco in 1938. In the US he worked as a trade journal editor; he used his second name and his wife's surname, figuring as Bernard Wienard. The two Bornstein sisters trained as teachers and were particularly interested in special education.[74] They worked in schools for children with disabilities and were actively engaged in social welfare. Their interest in the new discipline was typical of the epoch. According to Eric D. Weitz, "Weimar as a welfare state was, in part, a woman's state, in terms of personnel as well as policy".[75] Women

74 In Germany, women were admitted to universities in 1908. Jews constituted less than 1% of the population, and yet 18% of the first women students were Jewish; within three years, the percentage rose to 28%. After World War I, 30.6% of the women in Germany worked outside the home – more than in any other country in the world. See H.P. Freidenreich, *Female, Jewish, and Educated*, p. 16, and M. Eksteins, *Rites of Spring: The Great War and the Birth of the Modern Age* (Boston: Houghton Mifflin, 1989), p. 90.

75 Eric D. Weitz, *Weimar Germany*, p. 127.

were becoming more visible in the public sphere, but they were not admitted into the economic departments, defence or the state's internal affairs; instead they "worked as welfare inspectors, child and family counsellors, and health officers" (p. 126).

Starting in 1924, the Bornstein sisters attended seminars at the Berlin Psychoanalytic Institute and underwent analysis themselves – Berta was analysed by Hans Lampl, Stephanie by Josine Müller. They were part of Otto Fenichel's circle of friends, and there was a rumour in the group that Berta and Fenichel were lovers for some time.[76] Fenichel, born in Vienna in 1897, was close friends with Siegfried Bernfeld. They had a shared interest in questions of cultural revolution and educational reform. Fenichel collaborated with Bernfeld at HaShomer Hatzair and other projects within the youth movement. He attended Freud's university lectures in 1915-17, and in 1918 he began to attend VPS meetings, becoming a member the following year. In 1921 he completed his medical studies in Vienna, then soon moved to Berlin, where he became a training analyst at the Berlin Psychoanalytical Institute. A group of younger colleagues, all weary of the psychoanalytical establishment, soon formed around him. Secret meetings of the so-called *Kinderseminar* (children's seminar) – a name derived from the fact that the members, fully aware of their own subversiveness, referred to themselves as "naughty children"[77] – took place from November 1924 onwards. The meetings were neither announced nor documented, but we know that 168 of them had taken place by 1934, drawing between five and twenty attendants. The meetings were attended in varying constellations; besides Georg Gerő, the group consisted almost exclusively of women: the Bornstein sisters, Edith Jacobson, Annie Reich (Wilhelm Reich's wife), Kate Friedländer, Barbara Lantos, Edith Ludowyk Gyömrői, Franziska Deri. Wilhelm Reich and Erich Fromm attended the meetings from time to time.

All members of the *Kinderseminar* came from the wealthy central-European bourgeoisie and were born around 1900. The most important

76 Cf. M. Scharaf, *Fury on Earth: A Biography of Wilhelm Reich* (New York: Da Capo Press, 1994), pp. 249. Fenichel's biographer Mühlleitner also states that Otto and Berta had a romantic relationship throughout the first half of the 1920s. See E. Mühlleitner, *Ich – Fenichel: Das Leben eines Psychoanalytikers im 20. Jahrhundert* (Vienna: Zsolnay, 2008), p. 138.

77 Russell Jacoby, *The Repression of Psychoanalysis: Otto Fenichel and the Political Freudians* (Chicago: The University of Chicago Press, 1986), p. 66.

experiences of their early youth, therefore, were World War I, the collapse of monarchies and rise of parliamentary republics, which entailed the development of social legislation, raising the status of the working class and women's suffrage. Between 1915 and 1920 they took part in leftist political activities, in the early 1920s they received their medical diplomas and/or completed their analytical training, which meant they were able to establish their own practice. By 1930 they all lived in Berlin. Their political views were radically leftist, they were outspoken Marxists, some of them were members of the Communist Party.[78]

As Russell Jacoby suggests, the fact that they were no longer in the same geographical place as Freud allowed the younger generation to develop their new theories more freely, and indeed, many Berlin-based psychoanalysts (such as Karen Horney, Franz Alexander and Melanie Klein) openly distanced themselves from some of Freud's ideas. The mission of the *Kinderseminar* can perhaps be described as follows: to uphold the revolutionary dimension of psychoanalysis. The work of the first generation of Freudians may still have been incomplete at the time, but it was certainly codified; having been institutionalised, the movement was becoming more and more bureaucratic. In this situation the members of the *Kinderseminar* took it upon themselves to rescue psychoanalysis from Freud, as Peter Rudnytzky puts it.[79] They applied a Marxist perspective, aiming to present psychoanalysis as a political tool to foster radical social change. Their ideas are known to us thanks to the so-called *Rundbriefe*, secret circular letters that Fenichel wrote after he left Berlin. He gave his last seminar in 1933, then, following Freud's request, moved to Scandinavia with Jekels. His first *Rundbrief* was sent from Oslo in March 1934, and he edited the last one in 1945, shortly before his death in California in January the following year.[80]

Notwithstanding their activities at the Kinderseminar, from March 1930 the Bornstein sisters attended meetings of the German Psychoanalytic Society. Stephanie gave a presentation titled "Zum Problem der narzisstischen Identifizierung" [The Problem of Narcissistic Identification] in May (discussants included her sister, Otto Fenichel and Karen Horney); in July, Berta presented her paper "Zur Psychogenese der Pseudodebilität"

78 Cf. E.A. Danto, *Freud's Free Clinics*, p. 9.

79 P. L. Rudnytsky, *Rescuing Psychoanalysis from Freud and Other Essays in Revision* (London: Karnac Books, 2011).

80 O. Fenichel, *119 Rundbriefe*.

[On the Psychogenesis of Pseudodebility] in the presence of Anna Freud (whose regular collaborator she had become in 1929), Siegfried Bernfeld and Sándor Radó. They both became members of the society on 7 October 1930 (at the same time as Erich Fromm) and their presentations were published in the same issue of the *Internationale Zeitschrift für Psychoanalyse*.[81] They must have been close on other levels, too, for they also shared a flat, at Kurfürstenstraße 4.

Berta Bornstein's article foreshadows the direction of her later work. It is a case description of a twelve-year old girl with developmental delay. Freud had treated the latency period only cursorily, viewing it as being free of tensions and conflicts. Berta Bornstein, however, would later dedicate her most important theoretical work to this phase.[82] In her first article she highlights the importance of sublimation, presenting it as fundamental to the analysis of children as well as to education informed by analysis. She also proposes that intellectual underdevelopment is no hindrance to analysing a patient – one only need to apply techniques used for working with much younger children. The girl in this case study, having undergone analysis, attained an emotional developmental stage typical of girls her age and even caught up at school. Her developmental delay turned out to be linked to her frustration trying to compete for her father's love; her competitor was her unusually gifted brother, whose role in the family impelled her to take up the diametrically opposed position of "the stupid one". Bornstein also mentions the girl's interest in pedagogy and suggests that she might choose a career path in the field. Her article also contains an outspoken critique of girls' education. In fact, the patient's the mother and female teachers were set on seeing her as a simpleton and a good-for-nothing; her disorder appears to be the result of a conspiracy by adult women who wanted to prevent the girl from becoming a rival – they could not permit her to even dream about becoming as smart as her brother. At the same time, her failure to meet developmental milestones was her revenge, as Bornstein suggests paraphrasing the girl's unconscious logic: "Since I have become a stupid little girl because of my mother, she ought to keep making it up to me for the rest of her life" (p. 390).

81 B. Bornstein, "Zur Psychogenese der Pseudodebilität", *IZP* 1930, no. 3/4, pp. 378–399; S. Bornstein, "Zum Problem der narzisstischen Identifizierung", *ibid.*, pp. 400–416.

82 B. Bornstein, "On Latency", *PSO* 1951, no. 6, pp. 279–285; B. Bornstein, "Masturbation in the Latency Period", *PSO* 1953, no. 8, pp. 65–78.

A summary of the presentation appeared in the *Zeitschrift für psychoanalytische Pädagogik*,[83] the journal that published most of Berta Bornstein's works in the interwar period. One of her contributions was "Beziehung zwischen Sexual- und Intellektenwicklung" [The Relationship between Sexuality and Intellectual Development], another essay on children who struggled academically.[84] She builds on Freud's notion that when a child's curiosity about his or her origin is satisfied, this child will be able to turn to other issues – a pattern that can be seen as a blueprint for all search for knowledge and desire to learn. Bornstein presents cases that suggest that a delay in a child's cognitive development can occur when their curiosity is frustrated. An appropriate sex education is, therefore, a precondition for the child's intellect to develop: sublimation can only occur in the absence of suppression.

Berta's most well-known articles, which have been compared to Freud's case descriptions on account of their literary value, deal with much younger patients. Just a year after her presentation at the German Psychoanalytic Society, she published an article about her cure of a two-year-old's phobia.[85] Bornstein was a pioneer developing techniques to analyse very young children. No one besides Melanie Klein had worked with toddlers until then, since the Freudian school considered the ability to use language an essential prerequisite for analysis. This was the key issue in the debate known as the "controversial discussions" between Melanie Klein's supporters in the UK, who saw the child's free play as an equivalent of free association that could be interpreted in a similar way, and the Viennese group centred on Anna Freud, who argued that an analysis of the child's defence mechanisms and resistances was key to working with children.[86] Discussing the two dominant schools of child analysis, i.e. Anna Freud's and Melanie Klein's, in an article in 1942, Beata Rank consistently discredits the latter. She concedes that at the time when their books were

83 B. Bornstein, "Ein Fall von geheilter Dummheit", *ZFPP* 1930, no. 11/12, pp. 455–461.

84 B. Bornstein, "Beziehung zwischen Sexual- und Intellektenwicklung", *ZFPP* 1930, no. 11/12, pp. 446–454. See also B. Bornstein, "Enuresis und Kleptomanie als passageres Symptom", *ZFPP* 1934, no. 5/6/7/8, pp. 229–237, B. Bornstein, "Ein Beispiel für die Leugnung durch die Phantasie", *ZFPP* 1936, no. 4/5, pp. 269–275.

85 B. Bornstein, "Die Phobie eines zweieinhalbjährigen Kindes", *IZP* 1931, no. 3, pp. 344–367, available in English as "Phobia in a Two-and-a-Half Year Old Child", *TPQ* 1935, no. 4, pp. 93–119.

86 P. H. M. King, R. Steiner, *The Freud/Klein Controversies in the British Psycho-Analytical Society, 1941–45* (London: Routledge, 1990).

published (Anna Freud's *Einführung in die Technik der Kinderanalyse* [*Introduction to the Technique of Child Analysis*] in 1927 and Klein's *The Psycho-Analysis of Children* in 1932), Klein had the advantage of having worked with young children, whereas Anna Freud was still focused on children in the latency period. This shortcoming, however, has been more than compensated by "the excellent papers of Bertha [sic] and Steff Bornstein".[87]

Lisa, the two-year-old whose analysis Bornstein describes in her paper on the relationship between sexuality and intellectual development, had poor verbal skills for her age. The mother had to explain to the analyst that Lisa's "aua" signified hurt, which in turn led to the discovery of the little girl's strong and decidedly precocious castration complex. Little Lisa was blaming her mother for her lack of a penis: "Da Mama Lisa aua, Lisa nein gut!" – roughly translatable as "Mamma ow Lisa here, Lisa not good!". This discovery allowed Bornstein to perform a full analysis of the child and to cure her main symptom – a fear of going to sleep. The phobia was rooted in Lisa's inner tension – the desire to take revenge on her mother for the hurt she believed her mother to have inflicted on her, and at the same time a fear of losing her. The trauma of discovering sexual difference made the child regress to the anal phase of development, so that the revenge took the form of soiling her bed; at the same time the child was defending herself against this by refusing to lie down in bed; she would only fall asleep sitting up, clenching her little fists with a tensed expression on her face.

It was only towards the end of this analysis, when she had already come to these conclusions, that Bornstein learned about an incident that had occurred about half a year before she met Lisa and which probably elicited this childhood neurosis. Having undergone strict potty training before her first birthday, Lisa once wet her bed at night while her mother was away. The grandmother warned her that if she had another accident, her mother would never come back. Chance had it that the mother returned with a severe cold and, trying to contain the infection, she kept a distance from her child. Lisa must have understood this unexpected distance as a punishment for her bedwetting, which led to a violent repression of the anal impulses typical of toddlers. These impulses were reactivated when Lisa discovered the genital difference between boys and girls. Bornstein states that it would have helped her a lot to know about this incident earlier, but

87 B. Rank, "Where Child-Analysis Stands Today", pp. 45–46.

it would have done little to change her conclusions. Still, summing up, this experience inspired her to add a note about the windy paths that analysts sometimes follow to reach relatively simple conclusions, and how complex the inner life even of a two-year-old child can be[88] In the last few sentences Bornstein warns her readers against blaming nature and physiology for problems that are actually caused by external conditions, concrete situations and events. This observation takes on particular weight when we remember its context: the same issue of *Internationale Zeitschrift für Psychoanalyse* contains Freud's essay "Female Sexuality" ["Über die weibliche Sexualität"]. That said, Freud's conviction that anatomy is destiny is not what Bornstein disputes most vehemently; rather, she polemicises against the kind of psychoanalysis whose horizons are restricted to the analyst's office, failing to take into account the patient's social circumstances.

Soon after the war, having settled in New York, Berta published her case study of eight-year-old Sonja.[89] This time the symptoms apparently typical of hysteria (in her twilight states Sonja coquettishly tried to convince random men to take her for a drive in their cars) turned out to be related to sexual abuse. At the age of four-and-a-half, the girl had been sexually exploited by an uncle who promised her a ride in his car if she did not tell anyone. Again, it was not analysis that had allowed Bornstein to ascertain this fact but a medical examination of the whole family, in which the mother's younger brother turned out to suffer from the same venereal disease as Sonja. As an émigré, Bornstein also published the case histories of five-year-old Frankie's phobia and eight-year-old Sherry's obsession.[90] People who knew Berta personally often spoke with admiration about her unusual ability to establish a relationship of trust with children.[91]

Like Berta Bornstein, her sister Stephanie also focused on child analysis. The paper that allowed her to become a member of the German Psychoanalytic Society tackles narcissistic identification in a six-year-old boy. Published in 1930s, it is one of only two case studies by Steff; in 1933

---

88 B. Bornstein, "Die Phobie eines zweieinhalbjährigen Kindes", pp. 367.

89 B. Bornstein, "Hysterical Twilight States in an Eight-Year-Old Child", *PSO* 1946, no. 2, pp. 229–240.

90 B. Bornstein, "The Analysis of a Phobic Child", *PSO* 1949, no. 3, pp .181–226 and B. Bornstein, "Fragment of an Analysis of an Obsessional Child", *PSO* 1953, no. 8, pp. 313–332.

91 Cf. e.g E. Menaker, *Appointment in Vienna: An American Psychoanalyst Recalls Her Student Days in Pre-War Austria* (New York: St. Martin's Press, 1989).

she followed with an account of her therapy of three-year-old Peter.[92] While the first article documents a classic child analysis, focusing on the six-year-old's words (quoted at length) with a view to understanding his repressed desires (he identifies with his mother and has erotic feelings for his father), the second therapy appears more like a description of modern sex education. Above all, Bornstein takes upon herself the parents' task of talking to the boy about matters of sexual difference, which bother him greatly; she helps him overcome his fear of castration, and she tells him about the facts of life (this is why little Peter refers to her as "die Steff von den dummen Sachen" or "Steff of the foolish ideas"[93]). Her visits to the patient's home are reminiscent of a social worker's approach more than a psychoanalyst's. Stephanie observes the child in his everyday life, plays with him, takes him out on walks, sometimes she puts him to bed or feeds him. Anticipating her colleagues' criticism concerning her unorthodox methods she writes that this is precisely how an analytical relationship with a child is established. Only by fostering a close bond with a child will one gain the trust they need to share their secrets. The most important aspect is that the child understands that one is interested in everything that concerns them, that comes from them, their feelings and problems, and that nothing that they may say can make them forfeit the love of their new friend, whose only goal is to help them overcome their difficulties. She concludes: "This created a situation free from fear, quite comparable to the analytic situation in adult analysis" (p. 198).

In *A Short History of Child Analysis*, Anna Freud mentions both Bornstein sisters as pioneers,[94] but unlike Berta, Stephanie soon stopped working with children and turned to training educators in psychoanalysis. In the academic year 1931/32 she attended Siegfried Bernfeld's Pädagogische Arbeitsgemeinschaft at the Berlin Psychoanalytical Institute. A presentation she gave in November 1931 – an introduction to the psychoanalysis of pedagogues – was published in *Zeitschrift für psychoanalytische Pädagogik*.[95]

The goal of analysing pedagogues, Bornstein argues, is to find out in what way sublimation presdisposes an individual to choose a career in education and what unconscious motives incline a given educator towards this

92 S. Bornstein, "Eine Kinderanalyse", *ZFPP* 1933, no. 7, pp. 253–281. Available in English as "A Child Analysis", *TPQ* 1935, no. 4, pp. 190–225.

93 S. Bornstein, "A Child Analysis", p. 225.

94 A. Freud, *A Short History of Child Analysis*, pp. 7–14.

95 S. Bornstein, "Ein Beitrag zur Psychoanalyse des Pädagogen", *ZFPP* 1933, 8/9, pp. 314–321.

or that type of pedagogical work; this information would help the educator understand the problems encountered in their work: knowing what unconscious desires are stopping their conscious ego from their goals and tasks. The case discussed in the article, which was explicitly selected on account of its representative qualities, brings to mind her own path. The analysis focuses on a successful teacher who had always wanted to become an educator, and who nurtured ideas about educational reform as a young woman. A pedagogical journal published her article on necessary reforms in history teaching when she was only sixteen years old, following which she found herself drawn to educational reform activism. In her work with children she focused on those with developmental delays. Bornstein believed that her client's devotion to her work was the result of a particular resolution of the Oedipal conflict. Instead of feeling hostile towards the mother after her younger siblings were born, she came to imagine that she was her younger brothers' actual mother. She never fantasised that she had given birth to them – the sexual function remained entirely with the real mother – but that she was the more adequate mother, having more understanding and love for the children. This happened via her identification with the recently deceased grandmother ("I want to be as good to you as Granny was to me," p. 317), which also allowed the girl to gain something she craved, namely the love of the father, who had been closer to his mother than to his wife. Thanks to the fact that she entered the role not of the father's sexual object but of the object of his love – not of the biological mother but the spiritual one – the girl managed to resolve the Oedipus complex without a sense of guilt. Bornstein cites Freud's *The Ego and the Id* (every sublimation results from identification) and adds that in her case study, the young teacher's identification with her grandmother resulted in a sublimation into pedagogy. The author remarks that this is typical of outstanding teachers, educators and social workers, who do not identify with their own mothers but with other substitute mother figures.

Besides this main argument, Bornstein makes another interesting remark, namely that the work of a pedagogue can be compared to that of a writer. Just as writers cede the realisation of their own supressed desires to their characters, so educators can fulfil their own forbidden dreams through the children in their care. What is more, by allowing their charges to act according to natural urges, the educator proves that the child becomes innocently guilty, just as the playwright demonstrates that the tragic hero, though guilty on an objective level, is subjectively innocent.

Stephanie Bornstein was a precursor in the psychoanalytical interpretation of fairy tales. In 1933 *Imago* published her analysis of Sleeping Beauty.[96] Bruno Bettelheim lists this article in the bibliography to his book *The Uses of Enchantment* (1976),[97] but he does not give due credit to Bornstein and her influence on his own work. In his chapter on Sleeping Beauty he fails to even mention the *Imago* article.[98] Today Bettelheim is seen as a pioneer of the study of fairy tales, while Stephanie Bornstein's name is all but forgotten – despite the fact that psychoanalysis has become the most prominent methodology in this area of research. The three-volume *Greenwood Encyclopedia of Folktales and Fairy Tales*, edited by Donald Haase in 2008, overlooks her contribution in the entry on psychological approaches.[99] The same goes for *The Oxford Companion to Fairy Tales*, edited by Jack Zipes in 2000, and its detailed entry on psychoanalysis,[100] as well as the German *Enzyklopädie des Märchens*, edited by Kurt Ranke and others in 2004.[101] Minor works that mention Bornstein's article do so only in passing.[102]

Bornstein does not cite any of her colleagues' works in her article, but two psychoanalytical studies on fairy tales would have been available to her. One was Franz Riklin's *Wunscherfüllung und Symbolik im Märchen*

---

96 S. Bornstein, "Das Märchen vom Dornröschen in psychoanalytischer Darstellung", *I* 1933, no. 4, pp. 505–517.

97 Bruno Bettelheim, *The Uses of Enchantment: The Meaning and Importance of Fairy Tales* (New York: Knopf, 1976), p. 313, p. 327.

98 "The Sleeping Beauty" pp. 225-236.

99 J. Jorgensen, "Psychological Approaches" in *The Greenwood Encyclopedia of Folktales and Fairy Tales*, vol. 2, ed. by D. Haase (London: Greenwood Press, 2008), pp. 778–779.

100 See D. Haase, "Psychology and Fairy Tales", in *The Oxford Companion to Fairy Tales: The Western Fairy Tale Tradition from Medieval to Modern*, ed. by J. Zipes (New York: Oxford University Press, 2000), pp. 404–408.

101 See G.M. Lehmann-Scherf, "Psychoanalyse", in *Enzyklopädie des Märchens: Handwörterbuch zur historischen und vergleichenden Erzählforschung*, vol. 11 (Berlin: De Gruyter, 2004), pp. 14–23.

102 See e.g. J.M. McGlathery, *Fairy Tale Romance: The Grimms, Basile, and Perrault* (Urbana: University of Illinois Press, 1991), p. 129; H. Neeman, *Piercing the Magic Veil: Toward a Theory of the Conte* (Tübingen: Narr, 1999), p. 150; G. De Vos, A. E. Altmann, *New Tales for Old: Folktales as Literary Fictions for Young Adults* (Englewood: Libraries Unlimited, 1999), p. 279; C. F. Rodríguez, *La Bella Durmiente a través de la historia* (Oviedo: Universidad de Oviedo, 1998), p. 46. This biblio-graphical search was performed by Weronika Kostecka as part of our collaboration on the article "Dwa oblicza 'Cierniowej Różyczki': Baśń o Śpiącej Królewnie w psycho-analitycznej interpretacji Stefanii Bornstein", *Przegląd Kulturoznawczy* 2016 no. 4, pp. 385–403.

[*Wishfulfillment and Symbolism in Fairy Tales*], published in 1908. Riklin was a Jungian, so perhaps she ignored the publication intentionally. The other relevant contribution, however, was Freud's *Märchenstoffe in Träumen* ["The Occurrence in Dreams of Material from Fairy Tales"] from 1913.[103] It is unclear if she read it, but her method – reading a fairy tale as if it were told to her by a hypothetical patient – strongly suggests she was influenced by Freud. Bornstein reads the tale of the Sleeping Beauty as if it were told to her by a girl aged twelve or thirteen.[104] From this perspective, the plot illustrates the fears and desires of a girl at the cusp of sexual maturation – her anxiety about her first menstruation and her fantasies concerning her future sex life. The beginning is a typical "family romance" in which the real parents are elevated to the status of King and Queen, while the girl herself is their long-awaited royal descendant.

Bornstein suggests that this unconscious wishes behind the so-called family romance conceal the adolescent girl's sense that her parents do not love her, that they rejected her the moment she began her painful and unrewarding transformation from a child into a woman. The heroine is clearly not a child anymore, who, as Bettelheim proposes, will only be sexually awakened after a prolonged torpor. As a teenager prone to compulsive fantasising, she seems to have much in common with the adolescents described by Helene Deutsch: on the one hand she is anxious about the sexual initiation that awaits her, on the other hand she is preoccupied with and fascinated by the changes in her body, and she searches for a way to relieve her sexual tension. In the Grimm brothers' version of the tale, just before the key event of the princess pricking her finger and falling asleep for a hundred years, she is climbing the stairs towards the mysterious chamber. Bornstein reads this scene as a description of the girl's desire to touch herself:

> The description of the girl succumbing to her visual curiosity is so detailed that it reminds us that this is how the girl's onanistic desire is represented in the language of dreams.

103 Also in 1913, Otto Rank and Hanns Sachs pointed out that psychoanalysis could be applied to the study of fairy tales and myths. See *Die Bedeutung der Psychoanalyse für die Geisteswissenschaften* ["The Significance of Psychoanalysis for the Humanities", trans. by C. R. Payne, *American Imago*, 1964, vol. 22, pp. 6-133].

104 S. Bornstein, "Das Märchen vom Dornröschen", pp. 505-506.

We may suppose that the fifteen-year-old girl seizes the opportunity of being alone to get a better sense of her complex genitalia. (p. 508)

Meanwhile, the sentence about the fire on the hearth, which "flickered, stopped moving, and fell asleep,"[105] is for Bornstein a metaphor for post-orgasmic bliss. The girl's hundred-year sleep also absolves her from any responsibility for her own sexual activity: being asleep she stays clear of any temptation to transgress the masturbation ban and does not feel guilty if fulfilment happens in a dream.

From this perspective the prick with the spindle – that is, menstruation – becomes a sort of punishment for the girl's onanistic fantasies or actual masturbation. For Bornstein, as for Helene Deutsch, this punishment stems from the mother (the King, having heard the wicked wish of the thirteenth wise woman, ordered all spindles in the kingdom to be burned): "You want to be a grown woman and compete with me? There, look what one must suffer as a grown woman, now you are bleeding, and when the penis penetrates you will be bleeding as well" (p. 509). The girl falls asleep for a hundred years not to avoid the unavoidable, as Bettelheim would later argue, but as a result of the jealous Queen's revenge (whom Bettelheim ignores completely). This negative protagonist first disappointed Brier-Rose by not putting her into this world as a boy (for Bornstein, the twelve wise women's gifts serve to compensate the lack of a male organ), and then she tried with all her might to prevent the beautiful girl from turning into a woman and threatening to take her place in her father's heart:

> The separation of the mother corresponds [...] to a split in the inner life of the child: here is the mother as she presents herself to the child's ego on an everyday basis, but one layer deeper down lives the mother-imago who has already been internalised, who is as sadistic as she is sometimes understood, during the sadistic period of early childhood, by the young child's weak Ego. Brier-Rose's real mother says: "My child, it doesn't matter that you must sleep, look, we are going to sleep as well and we won't wake up before you wake." But the internalised mother says: "I will only love you as long as you are a good girl and an innocent child, once you become sexually active and want a man [...] I will let you die." (p. 515)

105 Jacob and Wilhelm Grimm, "Little Brier-Rose", trans. by D. L. Ashliman. <https://www.pitt.edu/~dash/grimm050.html> [accessed on 31/08/2020].

Drawing on Alfred Winterstein's article "Die Pubertätsriten der Mädchen und ihre Spuren im Märchen" [Girls' Coming-of-Age Rites and their Traces in Fairy Tales] (*Imago*, 1928), Bornstein adds an anthropological context to her reflections. Thus the fairy tale's plot is said to be rooted in the initiation rites that girls undergo in some traditional societies: "That which the individual produces today in unconscious fantasies, and which the fairy tale records like a strange fantasy, used to be, so ethnology tells us, a fragment of reality" (pp. 509-510), she writes, citing genital mutilation customs where growing girls are "castrated" by older women ("mothers"). Bornstein is particularly interested in the form of this practice among South Africa's BagammaNgwato: following the cut, the girls are handed thorny twigs with which they are to chase and beat the boys. Bornstein connects this tradition to the name of Dornröschen or Brier-Rose and to the moment in the story where the castle with the sleeping princess is surrounded by a thorn hedge. Unlike Bettelheim, who sees this as the girl's protection from premature sexual experiences, Bornheim interprets the thorn hedge as a revenge on those who have harmed her:

> Because she has been deflowered, the men must be punished, Brier-Rose [Dornröschen] lures them with her beauty and lets them perish in the snares of her thorn hedge.
> Brier-Rose is divided into the one who sleeps in a cell in the tower, punished and yet happy in her sleep, innocent, knowing nothing, and the other one, symbolised by the thorn hedge, who lives out her sadistic vengeance.
> It says in the story: "The thorns held firmly together, as though they had hands, and the young men became stuck in them, could not free themselves" (*Ibid.*). Brier-Rose, who must acknowledge her femininity and yet fears penetration by a man, forms the fantasy of a *vagina dentata* that will destroy the man's penis.[106]

The thorn hedge reflects the prepubescent girl's ambivalent relationship to sexual activity: Brier-Rose already fantasises about it, but she is still mostly scared and prefers to satisfy herself with narcissistic autoeroticism. In relation to men she only allows herself provocations and seduction ("Look, how sweet, how pretty I am, a little rose, but do not get too close to me, I have thorns, I prick" (p. 506)).

---

106 S. Bornstein, "Das Märchen vom Dornröschen", p. 512.

> [Thus] the girl's fear (my body is to remain intact) collides with the superego's demand that originates from the mother: "You are not to be my rival, you are not to let men near you," and the girl's desire, stemming from the id: I belong to my father alone, his mighty penis, which protects me, makes the young men afraid to approach me. (p. 512)

Once the Prince arrives, the hedge parts: the girl overcomes her genital fear, her clitoral activity transforms into passive, vaginal and mature womanhood. "The fire in the kitchen rose up, broke into flames, and cooked the food" (*ibid.*) – the heroine has experienced sexual satisfaction that will result in motherhood; her initiation rites culminate in a sumptuous feast.

Compared to Bettelheim's interpretation, Bornstein's appears much more audacious. In his account the princess is a child terrified by her first menstruation; afraid to assume the role of a woman, she seeks refuge in sleep, whereas for Bornstein she is an active heroine who decides about her own fate and is interested in her own budding sexuality. The two writers also offer different interpretations of the ending: while for Bettelheim it suggests that the girl has managed to grow into the woman's role, which includes a willingness to accept defloration and motherhood, for Bornstein the wedding represents a return to femininity: the princess does not become a woman, for she had already been one even before she fell asleep. Still, a century of lethargy was necessary for her to reconcile her desires with the reality principle ("but since this [sleep] cannot be the meaning of the life that she dreams of, she imagines a happy end in the form of a fiancée and a wedding" (p. 505)). Bornstein concludes her study as follows:

> But the fairy tale, being a work of art with the function of mediating between the superego and the demands of the Id, is the result of a compromise; to appease the superego, Brier-Rose must succumb to twilight sleep and remain detached from life, but eventually the Id is allowed to proclaim its happy ending with the union of man and woman. (p. 517)

Matrimony, therefore, is not the crowning of a woman's destiny, but the girl's socially sanctioned realisation of her erotic desires: Brier-Rose's maturation is related to her attaining this truth.

When her article was published, Stephanie Bornstein was at the threshold of her career. In the winter semester of 1932 she had already covered for Siegfried Bernfeld at the Berlin Psychoanalytical Institute, teaching his seminar "Praktische Fragen der psychoanalytischen Pädagogik" [Practical Questions in Psychoanalytic Pedagogy] and heading the Pädagogische Arbeitsgemeinschaft; in the summer semester 1933 she taught her own seminar for pedagogues. Any further plans that she might have had were thwarted by Hitler's coming to power. The Berlin Psychoanalytical Institute was incorporated into the Deutsche allgemeine Ärztliche Gesellschaft für Psychotherapie [German General Medical Society for Psychotherapy], founded in September 1933.[107] Its director was the Nazi psychiatrist Matthias H. Göring (Hermann Göring's cousin). Publications in the field of psychoanalysis were kept under lock and key at Göring's institute; Freud's name was not to be mentioned, and the same applied to Freudian terminology (the Oedipus complex and the theory of sexuality were dropped, for instance).

Although the German Psychoanalytic Society was officially disbanded on 19 November 1938, Jewish analysts had been forced to resign as early as 1935. Soon after this, they were also banned from practicing (in other words, Jewish analysts were barred from their profession about three years before other Jewish doctors). Of course, women analysts had already come under pressure in 1933, when the Nazis ran a campaign against so-called "*Doppelverdiener*" households – i.e. families in which husband and wife each had an income. According to state propaganda, if a woman had a working husband or was independently wealthy, she should cede her position to an unemployed male colleague.[108] Thus Jewish women were affected by two kinds of state-sponsored discrimination and repression. Eran Rolnik comments on the Psychoanalytic Society's prompt compliance with the state's anti-Semitic regulations, pointing out that other institutions, such as the German Society of Art Historians, refused to follow the order of the Minister of Education and did not expel its Jewish members.[109] This suggests that things could have worked out differently for Jewish analysts, too, if their more privileged colleagues had been less obedient to the demands of the Nazi regime. Some of the responsibility for the decisions taken at the German Psychoanalytic Society lies with non-

107 In 1936, the Deutsche allgemeine Ärztliche Gesellschaft für Psychotherapie was renamed Deutsches Institut für Psychologische Forschung und Psychotherapie [German Institute for Psychological Research and Psychotherapy.

108 L. Pine, *Nazi Family Policy 1933–1945* (New York: Berg, 1997), pp. 20.

109 E. J. Rolnik, *Freud in Zion*, p. 91.

Jewish analysts (especially with Felix Boehm and Carl Müller-Braunschweig); another practitioner who became notorious in this context is Jung, who undertook to replace "Jewish psychoanalysis" with a new "German" approach. In his lectures and radio interviews he often criticised Freud, giving a platform to the belief that Freudianism was a sort of Jewish psychology that did not apply to "Arians".[110] James and Eileen Goggin have pointed out that psychoanalysis did not survive in the Third Reich – it was neither tolerated nor practiced.[111] Some researchers were deceived by the institutional continuity, which was, however, purely formal and not related to the work performed at the centres in question.[112]

One effect – certainly not intended by the Nazi authorities – of the early expulsion of Jews from the Psychoanalytical Institute and the ban on their practice encouraged them to leave the country, which meant they were more likely to survive the Holocaust. Most German analysts emigrated much earlier than their Austrian colleagues. In 1937, no fewer than 69 members of the VPS were still living in Vienna (by 1945 their number had dropped to three[113]), whereas Berlin had been mostly deserted by Freudians by 1935. Max Eitingon left for Palestine in 1933, right after he was ousted from the position of director of the Berlin Institute. He was a competent organiser and wholeheartedly devoted to Freud. He set up the Palestinian Psychoanalytic Society soon after his arrival, and a year later he founded the Psychoanalytical Institute in Jerusalem. In 1937 Moshe Wulff, who had left Moscow for Berlin in 1927, when psychoanalysis was banned in the USSR, established a second Institute in Tel Aviv. By November 1933, the Jewish psychoanalysts who arrived in Palestine included Martin Pappenheim, Kilian Bluhm, Ilja Schalit, Walter Kluge and Anna Smeliansky. All founding members of the Palestinian Psychoanalytic Society had similar biographies: having studied medicine in Marburg, Freiburg or Heilderberg they practiced in Zurich, Vienna or Berlin. They either had Russian roots or they had spent most of their lives in Russia or

---

110 Cf. S. Frosh, *Hate and the "Jewish Science": Anti-Semitism, Nazism and Psychoanalysis* (London: Palgrave Macmillan, 2005), pp. 91–98.

111 J. E. Goggin, E. Brockman Goggin, *Death of a "Jewish Science": Psychoanalysis in the Third Reich* (West Lafayette, IN: Purdue University Press, 2001).

112 See R. Spiegel, "Survival of Psychoanalysis in Nazi Germany", *JOCP* 1975, no. 11, pp. 479–92 as well as "Survival, Psychoanalysis and the Third Reich", *JAA* 1985, no. 13, pp. 521–536, and especially G. Cocks, *Psychotherapy in the Third Reich: The Göring Institute* (New York: Oxford University Press, 1985).

113 L. Fermi, *Illustrious Immigrants*, p. 147.

the USSR, and besides German they spoke Yiddish and Russian. As *Ostjuden* they shared many attributes with the members of the First Aliyah, thanks to which they easily regained their footing in their new surrounding – unlike the *Westjuden* with whom they formed the Fifth Aliyah.[114] In 1938 they were joined by six members of the VPS who fled Europe following the Anschluss. According to Rolnik, experienced Central-European analysts considered emigrating to Palestine only as a last resort, when all other projects had failed (p. 120). The analysts who found themselves in the Near East were mostly in the early stages of their careers, many of them had not even completed their training analyses.

This was the case for a certain Bertha Grünspan, who had been affiliated with the HaShomer Hatzair movement in her youth. In the first half of 1938, Eitingon had asked Anna Freud to help draw up a list of psychoanalysts who were considering moving to Palestine and who may be well suited to this type of emigration. She wrote:

> Mrs Bertha Gruenspan is a brave and diligent psychoanalyst who worked in the past as a nurse and thus has considerable experience in hospitals. She was not endowed with a great deal of imagination, and she undoubtedly will never be able to teach psychoanalysis. In that sense, she cannot here [in Vienna] offer a great deal of help in the Institute, but she is nevertheless a useful member. She has also already conducted a number of analyses of children. I think that, in terms of her general style, she can suit Palestine well. (p. 122)

Bertha Grünspan's place of birth is something of a mystery. The only source about her early life is an interview that Elke Mühlleitner conducted with Grünspan's Israeli friend Brita Kerbl in the early 1990s, fifteen years after the analyst's death and about a century after her birth in a small Galician town whose name her acquaintances found difficult to pronounce. In Mühlleitner's lexicon it appears as "Niedzybrodrie,"[115] and this placename is repeated in all other sources despite the fact that no such town or village appears to exist. It is not unlikely that "Niedzybrodrie" is a phonetic deformation of Międzybrodzie, which is a rather common placename in the region.

---

114 E. J. Rolnik, *Freud in Zion*, p. 109.

115 E. Mühlleitner, *Biographisches Lexikon der Psychoanalyse*, p. 125.

Perhaps Bertha's family lived in the town of Międzybrodzie near Bielsko in Galicia. Born in late 1890, she was the second of six children of a trader and his wife. The family adhered to traditional Jewish customs.[116] Bertha dropped out of school at the age of fourteen to help around the house, while her older sister was training to become a teacher. At the age of seventeen, she moved to Vienna, where she trained as a nurse at the Rothschildkrankenhaus. During World War I she tended to wounded soldiers on the notorious Serbian front.[117] It was while she was serving as a nurse that she decided to train as a doctor. She obtained her *Matura* as an external candidate in 1917 and enrolled at the University of Vienna's Medical Faculty. She graduated with distinction in 1924 and worked as a doctor at the municipal almshouse (*Versorgungsheim*) for a year. In 1933 she moved on to a private Jewish hospital. She got involved with the socialist and Zionist organisations as well as with the women's emancipation movement, and through these groups she got to know many Vienna-based analysts. In the 1920s she was already familiar with psychoanalysis. She attended the meetings of the VPS and was analysed by Willi Hoffer, one of Siegfried Bernfeld's closest collaborators. In 1932 she became a member of the VPS. She emigrated to Palestine in 1938. This was not her first choice – it followed her failed attempt (her motivation is unclear) to obtain a visa to South Africa. Having settled in Haifa she studied Hebrew intensively for two years before opening a private psychoanalytical practice. She joined the Chewra Psychoanalytith b'Erez-Izrael [Israeli Psychoanalytic Society] under a new name, Betty Beile, as a member and training analyst. She made a valuable contribution to the development of psychoanalysis in Palestine (in the 1950s, the organisation had no more than five training analysts). For the last twenty years of her life she lived at the kibbutz Yfat, where she died in 1975. Until the end of her life she continued to give extremely popular seminars to Israeli psychoanalysts, doctors and pedagogues, and she offered analyses to her colleagues. However, she never wrote for any of the journals in the field.

Most experienced psychoanalysts from Berlin emigrated to Palestine, unlike their Viennese colleagues at the end of the decade, who preferred to follow Freud to the UK or establish themselves in the US. Stephanie

116 Cf. G. Liebermanm, *La psychanalyse en Palestine*, p. 134.

117 Relative to other places affected by the war, the Serbian front had the lowest number of doctors and hospitals and the harshest overall conditions; of all soldiers wounded in the war, the Serbs were the most likely to die. See A. Chwalba, *Samobójstwo Europy*, p. 432.

Bornstein and two of her colleagues chose quite a different path, however. In the autumn of 1933, Bornstein, Franziska Deri and Annie Reich left for Prague. Perhaps Bornstein was swayed by the fact that her mother, probably of Czech descent, had settled in the village of Hronec near Brezno.[118] Since no proper psychoanalytic society existed in the Czechoslovak Republic at the time, the three women analysts founded a working group called "Psychoanalytická skupina" in Prague. In 1934, this group was incorporated into the VPS;[119] Otto Fenichel joined after his return from Scandinavia the following year. Stephanie listed Praha-Bubenec, Ovenecká 73 as her permanent address. In 1935 she spent some time in Milan (long enough to sign articles as "Steff Bornstein, Mailand"), though the nature and purpose of her visit remain unclear.

The Prague group's main occupation was to perform training analyses. Bornstein also offered seminars in psychoanalysis and pedagogy for educators, kindergarten teachers and doctors, who all learned how to apply Freud's theory in their work. A broad range of subjects was addressed, including potty training, sex education and various issues related to puberty (nighttime anxiety, nail biting, eating disorders, masturbation and homosexuality). Responding to the participants' request, Bornstein also prepared a separate course titled "Drei Abhandlungen über Sexualtheorie (für Pädagogen)" [Three Essays on the Theory of Sexuality (for Educators)]. She also gave a series of public readings in Prague, Brno and Teplice: "Essstörungen und Schlafstörungen des Kindes" [Children's Eating and Sleep Disorders], "Das Unbewusste der Eltern in der Erziehung der Kinder" [The Parents' Unconscious in the Education of Their Children] and "Über infantile Sexualität" [On Infantile Sexuality]. Each of them drew an audience of 70 to 150.[120]

Bornstein's most interesting contribution – the one that continues to be cited today – is her article on the role of carers' unconscious in the pro-cess of education.[121] It is based on a presentation given at a parents' meet-ing – no further details are available – in Prague. According to Bornstein, parents do not always know what they do: they cannot rationally explain their methods. This does not only concern mothers who suffer from mood

118 C. Ludwig-Körner, *Wiederentdeckt – Psychoanalytikerinnen in Berlin*, p. 85.

119 See R. Fischer, *Zur Geschichte der psychoanalytischen Bewegung in der Tschechoslowakei.*

120 R. Karpe, "Prager Brief", *ZFPP* 1934, no. 5/6/7/8, p. 274.

121 S. Bornstein, "Unbewusstes der Eltern in der Erziehung der Kinder", *ZFPP* 1934, no. 11/12, pp. 353–362, reprinted in *Psychoanalyse und Erziehung*, pp. 108–119.

disorders or overworked fathers, but also healthy and lucid people who take good care of their offspring, including those who, having undergone psychoanalysis, have already gained some insight into their own unconscious. Nonetheless, analysing parents sheds light on some of the mistakes they make dealing with children. Having a child, she argues, activates repressed memories from one's own childhood, which either leads us to reenact the conflicts we had with our parents, or it makes us try to safeguard our child from this type of conflict, assuring it will receive what we lacked and avoiding what we experienced as painful.

Of the many examples cited by Bornstein, the most representative is probably the case of the mother of an intelligent boy who completely ignored his difficulties at school, and even appeared to discourage him from making any effort at all. When Bornstein came to help the child with his homework, the mother suggested that they should better make use of the beautiful weather and go play outside. The boy suffered, feeling his mother was disinterested. And indeed, when his performance at school improved, the only person who expressed any joy was the cook. It turned out that the mother was the third girl born to her parents. She knew they had hoped for a son, and on top of this she struggled at school, so they made her spend extra time studying and they forced her to have her homework checked. This upset her greatly, as it suggested her parents' double disappointment: not only was she a girl, she was also a stupid one. As a mother, she consciously hoped to spare her child this type of pressure; she wanted him to feel loved no matter if he did well at school or not. But on an unconscious level she helped perpetuate the boy's trouble at school because she was gratified by it. It was like an unconscious message to her parents: look, I was born again, this time as a boy, and I am still a poor student.

Bornstein explains that a parent can also come to regard the child as a reincarnation of a younger sibling – the baby brother or sister who took away their monopoly to the mother's love, and who they hoped would die. For a woman, a son can come to represent a brother whom she envied for his penis and other male privileges. From her current position of power she can now take revenge on him for her feelings of inferiority and incompleteness.

In presentations targeted at parents or pedagogues, Stephanie Bornstein used a very simple, straightforward language, avoiding psychoanalytical jargon and any references to secondary literature. Her goal was to give her audience a practical idea of how Freudian tools could help them in their daily work with children, to sensitise educators to the significance of their own childhood, to encourage them to pay more attention to the motivations behind their own choices.

Bornstein also contributed to methodological debates. In a piece with the humble title "Eine Technik der Kinderanalyse bei Kindern mit Lernhemmungen" [A Technique of Child Analysis in Children with Learning Difficulties] she boldly proposes that in the case of children with poor school performance, analysis should be combined with standard pedagogical support.[122] This mixed technique is not to be seen as a substitute for classic analysis nor its "enhancement," but it should allow to harness the pedagogical work to the analytical process. She compares this approach to a situation in which psychoanalysis accompanies the treatment of a patient's organic ailment. No one would allow an analysand to suffer from a toothache or pneumonia, she argues, and similarly there is no reason to refrain from helping the child with their homework, to practice reading or counting. On the contrary, observing the child's academic challenges allows the analyst to better diagnose their root causes. Bornstein describes her work with little Niels, who had a hard time focusing and feared school. She visited him at home for two hours at a time; for the first hour she helped him with his school work, in the second hour they smoothly transitioned to analysing what she had observed tutoring him. In her view, an analyst takes active part in a child's life, analysing not only their unconscious but also their conscious everyday functioning.

In May 1937 Steff travelled to Budapest for the second *Vierländertagung*, a conference attended by psychoanalysts from Hungary, Austria, Czechoslovakia and Italy. She sat on the panel "Revision der psychoanalytischen Pädagogik" [Revision of Psychoanalytical Pedagogy], which aimed to sum up the achievements of the field since it emerged a decade before. Her paper dealt with the pitfalls of psychoanalytical pedagogy.[123] Bornstein emphasises that the goal of education must be to allow the child to build an *Ego* that is as healthy as possible and able to deal with the contradictory demands of the drives, the external world, and the *super-ego*. Without calling for a return to authoritarian pedagogy she stresses that this

122 S. Bornstein, "Eine Technik der Kinderanalyse bei Kindern mit Lernhemmungen", *ZFPP* 1934, no. 5/6/7/8, pp. 141–154.

123 S. Bornstein-Windholz, "Missverständnisse in der psychoanalytischen Pädagogik", *ZFPP* 1937, no. 2, pp. 81–90, reprinted in *Psychoanalyse und Erziehung*, pp. 75–89.

goal cannot be attained when children are never exposed to things that can scare or upset them, when they are sheltered from all negative experiences or when they are never given boundaries and prohibitions. The effect of such an approach is potentially more harmful to a child than if parents had no analytical knowledge and merely followed their intuition.

The Prague working group had a Marxist profile, which is hardly surprising given its members' political leanings and the dominant role played by Otto Fenichel. This is not to say, however, that the group never experienced episodes of internal friction. One of Steff's surviving letters to Fenichel, dated 9 March 1937, suggests that some of the disagreements were related to the question of psychoanalytical-pedagogical training.[124] Bornstein was adamant about the distinction between child analysis and using psychoanalysis in pedagogy (which she saw as her specialty), but not all of her colleagues understood this distinction or thought it useful. Although Steff addressed Fenichel with a familiar "Lieber Pan Chef" – a multilingual combination translatable as "Dear Mister Boss" – she also admits to feeling nostalgic about the harmonious years of matriarchy, i.e. when Franziska Deri, Annie Reich and herself were the only analysts in Prague. Still, it seems that the members of the group were close to each other. For instance, Fenichel wrote a little poem in honour of Steff's birthday on 12 March 1936:

> Oft widerstrebt so ein kindliches Es
> der Erziehung durch beide Elternteile.
> Sie wenden sich dann an die Steffka bös,
> dass diese die Enuresis heile.
> Mehr Kasuistik, sagt Steff, und mehr Kontrolle,
> der Kongress ist da für die Theorie,
> und wer Kastrationsangst begreifen wolle,
> der schaue auf's Kind, sonst lernt er es nie.[125]

124 Elke Mühlleitner reproduces the letter in "Steff Bornstein, Otto Fenichel und die psychoanalytisch-pädagogische Ausbildung der Psychoanalytischen Arbeitsgemeinschaft v. Č.S.R. (1933–1939)", *Luzifer–Amor* 2000, no. 26, pp. 64–78.

125 *Ibid.* A literal translation: "A child's Id often resists / both parents' pedagogical efforts / in which case they get in touch with the wicked Steffka / so that she might cure this enuresis. / More casuistry, Steff says, and more control, / the Congress is there to do theory / and he who wants to grasp what fear of castration means / should look at the child, or he shall never learn."

In 1937 Stephanie married the psychiatrist Emanuel Windholz, a Slovak Jew born in 1903. He was the first person from Czechoslovakia who trained to be an analyst. As a married woman, Stephanie signed her articles "Steff Bornstein-Windolz". They might have met seven years before, during his training at the Berlin Psychoanalytical Institute. It is also possible that they had known each other much longer: Windholz was born in Hronec, the village where the Bornstein sisters' mother had moved. After his time in Berlin, Windholz settled in Prague and became the editor of the first Czech psychoanalytical yearbook (*Sborník psychoanalytických prací*), which was launched in Příbor on Freud's 75th birthday; Windholz also arranged for a commemorative plaque to be unveiled on Freud's birth house in Příbor that day. Stephanie gave all her lectures and seminars in German, but she also participated in the Czech translation of Freud's *Introduction to Psychoanalysis.*[126] Further research would be required to ascertain how proficient she was in this language. Perhaps she had learned Czech as a child, or she relied on its similarities to Polish.

Her marriage with Windholz allowed Stephanie to become a Czechoslovak citizen, which was important because the Nuremberg Laws of September 1935 had stripped German Jews of their citizenship and civil rights. Although Windholz emigrated to the United States a few months later and joined the San Francisco Psychoanalytic Society, Stephanie remained in Prague, where she was the last head of the working group (succeeding Franziska Deri, who emigrated to Los Angeles in 1935, and Otto Fenichel, who left Prague in 1938). It is unclear if she did not want to leave or if she simply did not manage to leave on time. In March 1939 the Germans occupied Prague. Steff died of a heart attack at work on 15 July.[127] Her siblings all survived the war.

Berta, who left for Austria in 1929 to work with Anna Freud, joined the VPS in 1933. In 1936 she started teaching child analysis and training analysts at the Institute in Vienna. Initially she had intended to return to Berlin, but the political situation in Germany swayed her to remain in Vienna. She opened a private practice there, became a member of the training committee of the VPS and worked as a supervisor. She was also

---

126 C. Ludwig-Körner, *Wiederentdeckt – Psychoanalytikerinnen in Berlin*, pp. 83. See also S. Freud, *O Sobě i Psychoanalyse*, trans. by O. Friedman (Prague: Orbis, 1936). Ota Friedman acknowledges several individuals who helped with the translation, including Steff Bornstein.

127 Cf. the obituaries in *IZP* 1939, no. 4, pp. 491; *IJP* 1940, no. 21, pp. 116.

close friends with the Reichs; when Wilhelm and Annie travelled to Russia in 1929, she took care of their daughters. In 1933 the Reichs separated and Berta sided with Annie, who was convinced that her ex-husband was mentally ill and was worried that the girls were not safe with him. In 1934 Berta began to analyse ten-year-old Eva Reich, who lived with her maternal grandparents in Vienna. When Wilhelm Reich suggested Eva should read Bronisław Malinowski's *The Sexual Life of Savages*, Berta Bornstein used her authority to ensure this would not happen, nor did she let the girl attend her father's seminar. She also decided that Eva should remain in Vienna when Reich left for Scandinavia. In 1938 Annie Reich emigrated to the United States with her daughters and second husband. Only as a fourteen-year-old did Eva write to her father, trying to re-establish their connection. In later years both father and daughter reproached Berta for their alienation. Bornstein is portrayed in a negative light in many of Reich's writings, for instance in the unpublished book *Wie ich Eva verlor* [How I Lost Eva]; without mentioning her name he also vilifies her in the crudest terms in the essay *Rede an den kleinen Mann* [*Listen, Little Man*]:[128]

> If you, Little Woman, by mere chance, without any special qualifications, have become a teacher, simply because you did not have children of your own, you do untold damage. Your job is to handle and educate children. In education, if one takes it seriously, this means correctly to manage the children's sexuality. In order to handle the children's sexuality, one must oneself have experienced what love is. But you are fat, awkward and unattractive. That alone is enough to make you hate every charming, alive body with deep and bitter hatred. What I am blaming you for is not that you are fat and unattractive; not that you have never enjoyed love (no healthy man would give it to you); not that you do not understand love in the children. What I am blaming you for is that you make a virtue out of your unattractiveness and your incapacity for love, and that, with your bitter hatred, you strangle the love in the children, if you happen to work in a "progressive school". This is a crime, ugly Little Woman. The harmfulness of your existence consists in your alienating the affection of healthy children from their healthy fathers; in your considering the healthy love of a child a pathological symptom. It consists in your being barrel-shaped, your going around like a barrel, your thinking like a barrel, your educating

128 M. Scharaf, *Fury on Earth*, pp. 248-252.

> like a barrel; in your not modestly retiring to a small corner of life, but, instead, trying to impose upon this life your barrel shape, your falseness, and your bitter hatred hidden behind your false smile.[129]

Like most Viennese psychoanalysts, Berta Bornstein remained in Austria until the Anschluss. In March 1933 she married local industrialist Leopold Pfaller, who died in 1941. Until her emigration, the two sisters visited each other frequently. Steff would attend seminars in child psychoanalysis in Vienna, while Berta supported the Prague group with presentations and regular training sessions. She emigrated in 1938. After a short stay in London she settled in New York, helping her two brothers move to the United States as well. Not having trained as a doctor, she was unable to work as an analyst in the US, but she found employment as a school psychologist at the progressive Walden School in Manhattan. She became a special member of the New York Psychoanalytic Society and Institute, where she taught courses and seminars until 1960; in the years 1952–55 she was head of the child psychoanalysis section. She trained analysts at the Menniger Clinic in Houston, Texas, and at Yale University in Connecticut. At the Philadelphia Association for Psychoanalysis she gave lectures in child analysis and was an honorary member of the American Psychoanalytic Association. She died in 1971 at her summer home on Vinalhaven, Maine. According to an obituary by Peter Blos she had been a living legend: "The beginnings and the developments of child analysis are so closely linked with her name that they are, indeed, one and the same."[130]

"Doctor Korczak, please speak up!"

In Poland, it was Leopold Wołowicz who first highlighted the importance of Freudian theory for education. In his 1914 pamphlet "Jeden z problematów psychoanalizy Freuda" [One of the Problems in Freud's Psychoanalysis] he remarks that in the preceding four years psychoanalysis had officially stepped out of the field of medicine and entered applied pedagogy.[131] As an educator, he commends his colleagues' great interest in

129 Wilhelm Reich, *Listen, Little Man!*, trans. by T. P. Wolfe (Harmondsworth: Penguin Books, 1975), p. 55.

130 P. Blos, "Berta Bornstein 1899–1971", *PSO* 1974, no. 29, p. 35.

131 L. Wołowicz, "Jeden z problematów psychoanalizy Freuda", pp. 3–6.

Freud and proposes to explore the practical impact of psychoanalysis on education. He begins by examining Freud's psychological assumptions – a topic that comes to dominate his pamphlet. Wołowicz ends by announcing another study – a critique of psychoanalysis from the perspective of pedagogy – but he either never wrote it or it has been lost.

For Wołowicz the fact that "psychoanalysis is making rather vigorous claims on pedagogical issues" is evidenced by several recent publications. These include the article "Entwicklung und Ansprüche der Psychoanalyse" [The Development and Claims of Psychoanalysis] (*Imago* 1913) by Rank and Sachs, or the works of Swiss Lutheran minister Oskar Pfister, such as "Anwendungen der Psychoanalyse in der Pädagogik und Seelsorge" [Applications of Psychoanalysis in Education and Pastoral Care] (*Imago* 1912) and *Die Psychoanalytische Methode* [The Psychoanalytical Method], where Pfister, whom Wołowicz describes as a "fanatical Freudian" (p. 4), summarises his psychoanalytical research in the field of pedagogy and pastoral care. Pfister was an early authority in the new field. His *Psychoanalysis in the Service of Education* [German original: *Die Psychanalyse im Dienste der Erziehung*, 1917] was published in Polish in 1931 (*Psychoanaliza na usługach wychowania*).[132] It was translated by Józef Mirski, who merits a more detailed presentation.

Józef Mirski was the author of a recent study titled *Rozwój i wychowanie płciowe dziecka w świetle freudyzmu (pogląd i krytyka)* [Child Development and Sex Education in the Light of Freudianism (Opinion and Criticism)]. His goal was to popularise Freud's theory, which was "generally little known" in Poland, while it was "on everyone's lips abroad (Austria, Hungary, Germany, Switzerland, France and America)".[133] The book was published by Księgarnia Nauczycielska in 1925, but Mirski had started writing it in 1923, submitting instalments to *Ruch Pedagogiczny* the same year. It is telling that that the journal's editors chose to furnish the first instalment with an introduction to Freud, allowing several pages for a summary (by Maria Maćkowska) of the 1911 translation of the Clark University lectures. Apparently, the readers of *Ruch Pedagogiczny* – published by the Association of Polish Primary School Teachers (Związek Polskiego

132 O. Pfister, *Was bietet die Psychoanalyse dem Erzieher?* (Leipzig–Berlin: Klinkhardt, 1917). Polish edition: *Psychoanaliza na usługach wychowania*, trans. by J. Mirski (Lviv–Warsaw: Książnica Atlas, 1931).

133 J. Mirski, *Rozwój i wychowanie płciowe dziecka w świetle freudyzmu (pogląd i krytyka)* (Lviv: Księgarnia Nauczycielska, 1925), p. 4.

Nauczycielstwa Szkół Powszechnych) – could not be trusted to follow Mirski's detailed argument without such a preamble.[134]

Mirski begins his study by warning readers about Freud's views on childhood sexuality:

> They depart so radically from everything that we generally know about these things, from what is believed and written about them, and they shed such a stark light on this field, they "revolutionise" our habitual notions of childhood so much that we must indeed have […] a great deal of "liberation" or a philosopher's calm or a naturalist's view of the world to stop ourselves from rejecting these views right at the outset and to maintain instead a sober and much-needed critical attitude towards them, which will allow us to separate falsity from truth.[135]

For Mirski, Freud's achievements are also at the root of the principal faults of his theory: his discovery of the child's sex drive led to pansexualism; his focus on the unconscious alienated psychoanalysts from scientific criteria, fostering arbitrary, subjective interpretations and speculation. Here is how Mirski paraphrases the general psychoanalytical methods from a pedagogical perspective:

- Make sure that while you suppress various "uncultural" drives you do not also suppress those that have a right to exist!
- Avoid too harsh or uncritical acts of suppression; instead, weave them as best you can into the whole fabric of your charge's psychology and draw out the self-creating powers from his or her soul, so that suppression may be not defeat and escape but a conscious condemnation and victory!
- Never look down on any natural psychological element! Never reject a force as a useless thing, but strive to use it – through its displacement onto higher goals, by bringing it into a different relationship, in a word: thorough continuous and progressive uplifting – as ready material for the internal construction of character! (p. 101)

In his translator's introduction to the Polish version of Pfister's *Die Psychanalyse im Dienste der Erziehung*, Mirski expresses his hope that Polish

134 M.M. [Maria Maćkowska], "O psychoanalizie", *RP* 1923, no. 7–8, pp. 141–144.

135 J. Mirski, *Rozwój i wychowanie płciowe*, p. 5.

teachers might find the book useful, but he also makes a point of warning them about its shortcomings. He tries above all to discourage "overly literal and hasty" applications of the method:

> Great sensitivity, caution and consideration are generally indispensable in education, but in pedanalysis they are not just a precondition for a positive outcome – transgressions against them can lead to very unfortunate developments when the victims of our clumsiness or excessive zeal are mentally fragile.[136]

Mirski believes that psychoanalysis can be at cross-purposes with education, for the two approaches pursue opposite goals: Freudianism intends to render conscious what has been unconscious, while educators often focus on rendering unconscious what is conscious but in conflict with pedagogical objectives. The tension between psychoanalysis and pedagogy reveals a broader conflict between "health on the one hand and culture, or ethics, on the other":

> Naturalism, generally a characteristic of psychoanalysis, which most often views "health" as its principal therapeutic value, is at odds here with ethical and pedagogical idealism, which considers health [...] to be no more than the necessary condition to realise higher values. (p. 7)

In Poland, the most popular writer in this field was Alfred Adler, the founder of the school of individual psychology. He, too, was a Protestant, having converted from Judaism in 1904, soon after he met Freud and began to take part in the Wednesday meetings.[137] Having broken with the Vienna Psychoanalytic Society in 1911, Adler developed his own version of psychoanalysis and founded his own society in 1912. Just as Jung had

136 J. Mirski, "Słowo wstępne tłumacza", in O. Pfister, *Psychoanaliza na usługach wychowania*, p. 9.

137 See for instance: B.H., "Psychologia indywidualna A. Adlera (z powodu 60lecia urodzin)", *DR* 1930, no. 2, pp. 171–173; L. Chmaj, "Teoria pedagogiczna psychologii indywidualnej (Rzecz o Alfredzie Adlerze)", *RP* 1930, no. 5–7, pp. 201–216, pp. 250–263, pp. 304–319; W. Piotrowska, *Myśli o samowychowaniu na podstawie psychologii indywidualnej* (Warsaw: [no publisher], 1934; J. Prusinowski, "Psychologia indywidualna Adlera, 1870–1937", *WL* 1937, no. 29, p. 4; M. Grzywacz-Kaczyńska, "Podstawowe pojęcia psychologii indywidualnej A. Adlera", *V* 1937, no. 2, pp. 277–304; J. Pastuszka, *Psychologia indywidualna: Studium krytyczne* (Lublin: [no publisher], 1938).

done before him, he toned down Freud's emphasis on sexuality, but while Jung defined libido as a force that was not necessarily related to sexuality, thus associating psychoanalysis with other forms of the philosophy of life (such as Schopenhauer's will or Bergson's *élan vital*), Adler renounced the dominant role of the sexual drives and argued that a more important role is played by the need for recognition and power; in his view, neurosis was rooted in feelings of inferiority. Polish pedagogues travelled to Vienna to attend congresses in individual psychology;[138] the journal *Chowanna*, founded at the Pedagogical Institute in Katowice in 1929, systematically summarised Adler's *Internationale Zeitschrift für Individual-Psychologie*; other Polish periodicals such as *Ruch Pedagogiczny* and *Kwartalnik Pedagogiczny* reviewed Adler's works as soon as they were released (Polish translations were published of his *Menschenkenntnis* [*Znajomość człowieka* in Polish or *Understanding Human Nature* in English], *Das Problem der Homosexualität* [*Homoseksualizm*], *Individualpsychologie in der Schule* [*Psychologia indywidualna w wychowaniu*] and *Der Sinn des Lebens* [*Wiedza o życiu*; English: *The Meaning of Life*] and others. When Adler died, his Polish followers wrote lengthy obituaries. In 1936, Estera Markinówna published an outline of his work titled *Psychologia indywidualna Adlera i jej znaczenie pedagogiczne* [Adler's Individual Psychology and Its Pedagogical Significance].[139]

Besides the fact that Pfister and Adler had renounced Freud's groundbreaking views on sexuality, their reception among conservative Polish pedagogues could also have been eased by the fact that neither of them was Jewish – a fact that is not to be underestimated given the rise of anti-Semitism in the interwar period. Mirski, who converted and changed his name from Kretz soon after World War I, writes in his translator's introduction to *Psychoanaliza na usługach wychowania*:

> Pfister is a Freudian. Nevertheless, he evidently tries to tone down his master's notorious "pansexualism," viewing it more in the spirit of Jungian "libido" and introducing his "organic principle," i.e. the principle according to which all "life junctions and the whole mental organism" work together in every mental

138 S. Skalski, "Kongres psychologii indywidualnej w Wiedniu", *RP* 1927, no. 10, pp. 319–322; "IV międzynarodowy Kongres Psychologii Indywidualnej", *RP* 1930, no. 7, p. 333.

139 For a comparison of Witwicki and Adler see E. Markinówna, "Psychologia dążenia do mocy: Zestawienie poglądów Witwickiego i Adlera", *KPS* 1935, vol. VII, pp. 329–340.

> phenomenon. The fact that the author has a broader and freer relationship [...] to psychoanalysis, perhaps due to his profession as a clergyman, allows him to recognise various "symptoms" as being rooted outside sexuality. From a pedagogical point of view, another rather agreeable characteristic of the author's take on human psychology is his strong emphasis on the function of moral and religious feelings, although, being a Protestant, he has an overly rationalistic understanding of the essence and role of religion.[140]

The leading promoter of psychoanalysis among Polish Protestants was Rudolf Kesselring, a Lutheran pastor and professor at the Protestant Theology department at Warsaw University. In August 1935, he gave a lecture titled "Znaczenie psychoanalizy i psychologii indywidualnej we współczesnym systemie wychowawczym" [The Importance of Psychoanalysis and Individual Psychology in the Modern Educational System] to professionals working with Protestant youth in Poland. The lecture is essentially based on Adlerian psychology, which Kesselring describes as "an intelligent and necessary revision of the teachings and views of psychoanalysis".[141] His key idea is to see psychoanalysis as comparable to the Catholic institution of confession. Having renounced this sacrament, Protestants can turn to analysis to experience the sense of relief that Catholics describe after leaving the confessional.[142]

Catholic clergymen also addressed the similarities between psychoanalysis and the sacrament of penance, which in their eyes confirmed that "confession can and most certainly does comprise all the beneficial qualities of psychotherapy".[143] Naturally, a key difference was that the

---

140 J. Mirski, "Słowo wstępne tłumacza", p. 5. Mirski's quotations from Pfister's book are based on the English translation: *Psycho-analysis in the Service of Education: Being an Introduction to Psycho-analysis* (London: Henry Kimpton, 1922), p. 47.

141 R. Kesselring, *Znaczenie psychoanalizy i psychologji indywidualnej we współczesnym systemie wychowawczym: Referaty wygłoszone w Cieszynie 27–29 sierpnia 1935 r. na kursie pracowników wśród młodzieży ewangelickiej w Polsce* (Warsaw: [no publisher], 1936), p. 14.

142 Freud was aware that in Protestant communities, psychoanalysts could potentially assume the role of secular pastors, but he also stressed the difference between analysis and confession. The general assumption is that the Catholic sacrament of penance is based on the notion that every neurotic has an oppressive secret and that sharing it provides relief, but Freud counters: "In Confession the sinner tells what he knows; in analysis the neurotic has to tell more" (*The Question of Lay Analysis*, SE XX, p. 189).

143 S. Huet, *Psychoanaliza a sakrament pokuty* (Włocławek: [no publisher], 1937), p. 68.

main goal of penance is to allow for "the rebirth of life – eternal life – from grace," whereas "the restoration of the balance, thrown out of kilter in the natural life of the soul and in the functioning of its mental powers" (p. 46), is no more than a welcome side effect. Some of the writers in this group argued that Carl G. Jung was "closest to a Catholic psychotherapy" (*Ibid.*). This was, for instance, the opinion expressed by the priest Stanisław Huet, from whose work *Psychoanaliza a sakrament pokuty* [Psychoanalysis and the Sacrament of Penance] I borrowed these quotations, as well as the educator Jan Andrzej Kuchta. Kuchta's publications include a short book titled *Psychologia głębi* [Depth Psychology],[144] which juxtaposes the theories of Freud, Adler and Jung, as well as a series of articles on the applicability of Jung's theory to education.[145] Kuchta's ideal was to help children build a relationship with God.[146] He writes that Freud's undeniable genius has produced "many valuable working hypotheses, fruitful in various branches of science, but given the [...] one-sidedness of his take on metapsychology he remained far removed from the ultimate truth. He has only paved the way that leads there."[147] Kuchta finds a similar one-sidedness in Adler, whom he blames for overrating the role of the drive for power. Only Jung, he argues, successfully avoided the tendentiousness that marred his colleagues' works.

It is worth stressing that when discussing psychoanalysis, many Polish pedagogues did not reference publications by Freud but a rather curious study, originally published in 1930, by the French Jesuit Jules de La Vaissière. A Polish translation of his book was issued by the Poznań-based Księgarnia Św. Wojciecha, a Catholic publisher, in 1935. La Vaissière promises to present and evaluate Freud's key works up until 1928, but to support his critique of Freud he makes frequent references to Saint Thomas. One chapter is dedicated to the application of psychoanalysis in pedagogy, aesthetics and biography. La Vaissière concludes:

---

144 J. Kuchta, *Psychologia głębi (Z. Freud – A. Adler – K.G. Jung)* (Lviv: Książka, 1939). This book is part of the series "Licealna Biblioteczka Filozoficzna," of which Kuchta himself was the editor.

145 Cf. e.g. J. Kuchta, "Psychologiczne typy C.G. Junga", *RP* 1930, no. 5, pp. 217–224 and his *Dzieci trudne do wychowania w świetle badań psychologii głębi (K.G. Jung – Ch. Baudoin)* (Lviv: Księgarnia R. Schweitzera, 1937).

146 Cf. J. Kostkiewicz, *Kierunki i koncepcje pedagogiki katolickiej w Polsce 1918–1939* (Cracow: Oficyna Wydawnicza Impuls, 2013), p. 527.

147 J. Kuchta, *Psychologia głębi*, p. 42.

> By paying attention to the significance of unconscious tendencies, the determinism of the whole and the psyche's continuity, Freud has rendered an outstanding service to science – one that could have earned him pure glory; however, this glory as a psychologist will remain forever tainted by the accusation, kindled by his temerity as a theorist who, without providing solid evidence, presented our sexual dynamism as the source of our loftiest aspirations and our purest loves.[148]

Another short book that garnered enthusiastic reviews in Poland was Geraldine Coster's *Psychoanalysis for Normal People*. The original appeared in 1926; Nasza Księgarnia published Maria Górska's Polish translation, *Psychoanaliza w zastosowaniu do ludzi normalnych*, a few years later.[149] This popular work is not only based on certain far-reaching simplifications and a rather loose understanding of psychoanalysis; most importantly, it sidesteps or tones down the question of sexuality in Freud's work. These decisions allow Coster to perform the impossible, i.e. to present a theory that combines Freud's ideas with those of Jung and Adler.

A telling example of how psychoanalysis was typically discussed in Polish pedagogical journals is an article published in the first yearbook of *Chowanna* (1929). Despite the promising title, "Nowe kierunki psychologii a pedagogika" [Pedagogy and New Areas of Psychology], the author, Stefan Szuman (a professor at the Jagiellonian University who is now seen as representing the Catholic trend in Polish pedagogy[150]) mentions Freud's theory only briefly, stating that he personally feels "very critical" about "psychoanalytical theory as such".[151] Szuman bemoans the fact that psychoanalysis has become fashionable, which makes it "practically more harmful than useful". "It may greatly benefit the teacher who knows how to assess it critically and to make appropriate use of it," but "in the hands of educators who are unprepared for

148 J. de La Vaissière, *La Théorie psychanalytique de Freud: Étude de psychologie positive*, Archives de philosophie, vol. 8, cahier 1 (Paris: Beauchesne, 1930), pp. 100-101. Translation from French by T. Bhambry.

149 For exemplary reviews of Coster's book see *SZS* 1929–1930, no. 2, pp. 120–122 (review by J. Segał) and *RP* 1930, no. 2, pp. 90–92 (review by J. Kuchta).

150 Cf. J. Kostkiewicz, *Kierunki i koncepcje pedagogiki katolickiej w Polsce*, pp. 308–311.

151 S. Szuman, "Nowe kierunki psychologii a pedagogika", *CHO* 1929, vol. 1, p. 7.

the task it can turn into a very dangerous tool" (*Ibid.*).[152]

The bone of contention was, of course, the question of childhood sexuality – the very clou of Freud's theory. (According to de La Vaissière, "to judge Freud on his sexual theories is to condemn him".[153]) Discussions on what children ought to be told about sex dominated pedagogy in the interwar period.[154] The majority opinion is best expressed in Albert Dryjski's *Zagadnienia seksualizmu dziecka i młodzieży szkolnej* [Problems of Child and Teenage Sexuality, 1934].[155] Dryjski, a remarkably competent reader of Freud, was a psychologist based in Poznań. *Warszawskie Czasopismo Lekarskie* had already published his article "Geneza i technika metody psychoanalitycznej" [The Genesis and Technique of the Psychoanalytical Method]. Here Dryjski presents the birth of psychoanalysis in the context of the work of the French psychopathologists, Freud's predecessors. He also outlines Freud's therapeutic technique, about which he is rather sceptical; he argues that analysts mostly use suggestion, which accounts for any positive effects of the cure.[156] In the years to come, Dryjski published two extensive articles in *Kwartalnik Filozoficzny*. These were "Rozbiór i krytyka głównych założeń psychoanalizy" [An Analysis and Critique of the Key Premises of Psychoanalysis][157] and "Współczesne teorie podświadomości" [Contemporary Theories of the Subconscious].[158]

In the latter article, Dryjski gives an erudite presentation of Freudianism against the backdrop of other nineteenth- and early twentieth-century

---

152 Having examined pedagogues' discussions of psychoanalysis in all interwar issues of *Ruch Pedagogiczny*, *Kwartalnik Pedagogiczny*, *Życie Dziecka*, *Chowanna*, *Szkoła Specjalna* and *Polskie Archiwum Psychologii*, I am inclined to conclude that most writers draw attention to the potentially harmful effects of Freud's theory.

153 J. de La Vaissière, *La Théorie psychanalytique de Freud*, p. 100.

154 Cf. M. Babik, *Polskie koncepcje wychowania seksualnego w latach 1900–1939* (Cracow: Wydawnictwo WAM, 2010), esp. pp. 127–260.

155 A. Dryjski, *Zagadnienia seksualizmu dziecka i młodzieży szkolnej: Biologia, psychologia, pedagogika* (Warsaw: Nasza Księgarnia, 1934). Dryjski had previously outlined his views on psychoanalytical theory of sexuality in an article in *Kwartalnik Pedagogiczny*, the organ of the Sekcja Pedagogiczna Stowarzyszenia Chrześcijańsko-Narodowego Nauczycielstwa Szkół Powszechnych [Association of Polish Primary School Teachers] (A. Dryjski, "Psychoanaliza i wychowanie płciowe", *KP* 1930, nos 1–3).

156 A. Dryjski, "Geneza i technika metody psychoanalitycznej", *WCL* 1929, nos 27–30.

157 A. Dryjski, "Rozbiór i krytyka głównych założeń psychoanalizy", *KF* 1929–1930, vol. 7, no. 4, pp. 419– 465, vol. 8, no. 1, pp. 1–58.

158 A. Dryjski, "Współczesne teorie podświadomości", *KF* 1931, vol. 9, pp. 37–74, pp. 111–152, pp. 219–256.

concepts of the unconscious. He classifies them into three groups: metaphysical interpretations (Hartmann, Myers), physiological ones (e.g. Theodule Ribot) and psychological ones. The psychological concepts are in turn categorised into dynamic theories, which includes Freud's and Jung's psychoanalysis; Edward Abramowski's unique "emotional theory", as well as a series of "pathological theories," developed by researchers such as Janet, Grasset, Sidis, Morton and Prince. Dryjski also develops a system that is particularly well suited to German philosophy, as it distinguishes between two possible propositions: unconscious processes can be said to differ from conscious ones solely in terms of quantity (Leibniz, Herbart, Beneke, Fechner); alternatively, one may insist on a fundamental qualitative difference between the two systems. Here Freud appears as the final link in the chain that begins with Christian Wolff, Friedrich Schelling, Carl Gustav Carus and Karl Fortlage and continues through Arthur Schopenhauer and Eduard von Hartmann. Dryjski capably reconstructs the development of Freud's views, recognising the importance of *Das Ich und das Es* [*The Ego and the Id*] (here Freud departs from his understanding of the unconscious as containing only repressed material and introduces the so-called second topic, i.e. the division of the subject into the ego, id and superego).

In his previous article, which analyses the premises of psychoanalysis, Dryjski outlines Freud's transition from psychopathological empiricism through theoretical psychology to purely metaphysical speculation. Psychoanalysis, Dryjski argues, had started off as a therapeutic technique, then it became a philosophy. He attributes this development to Freud's students, especially the "thinker-fantasist" Otto Rank, whose book *The Trauma of Birth* can be seen as a synthesis of psychoanalytical philosophy, as well as Carl Gustav Jung, the creator of a "new mythology". Dryjski examines a series of Freudian terms – the unconscious, complex, conflict, repression, censorship and dreams – that do not serve to describe observable facts but are "concepts designed to account for facts". Psychoanalysis, he argues, is based on the assumption that neurosis can be correctly explained from a purely psychological perspective, while somatic elements are seen as secondary or derivative phenomena – a choice that conveniently eliminates the need to examine somatic symptoms from a physiological angle. His most important criticism, however, concerns the arbitrariness of psychoanalytical interpretation: "We must always remember that Freudianism is a construct, built on an exceptionally bold and certainly original interpretation of facts that could also be explained differently, and thus lead to different constructs than those offered by Freud" (p. 32). Although he is explicitly critical of the details of psychoanalytical theory, Dryjski concludes his article with the following statement:

> While highlighting some of the negative aspects of Freud's system we must also state that he very successfully illuminated the mechanism and dynamics of neuroses. Freud was the first to demonstrate that neurotics' symptoms have a deliberate character, that they are strategic in a way and that they are closely related to the patient's personality as a whole. Thanks to Freud psychopathology was able to shift from passive observation to planned and creative action.[159]

Dryjski most vehemently opposes Freud's theory of the sexual drive, especially his hypothesis of childhood sexuality; he also criticises the fact that psychoanalysis basically observes individuals with mental illnesses and then draws broad conclusions about the entire population. It is unsurprising, therefore, that in Dryjski's book on child and teenage sexuality the psychoanalysts' emphasis on sex education is subjected to strong criticism – "and rightly so," according to Michał Friedländer's review of the book in *Chowanna.*[160] Dryjski was certain that precocious manifestations of sexuality are, for the most part, based not on physical but on social aspects:

> Freud says that individual personality develops along a path dictated by sexuality. In my opinion the father of psychoanalysis was mistaken and the opposite is the case: our sexuality unfolds in the direction suggested by the evolution of our personality.[161]

This explains why pre-puberty education plays a key role in the formation of the sex drive, which "in its early stages preys mostly on any educational gaps and shortcomings". "Only a well-organised environment is able to [...] curb, to channel the excess of emotional energy, not allowing it to spill over into sexual conduits" (p. 343).

---

159 A. Dryjski, "Rozbiór i krytyka głównych założeń psychoanalizy", p. 57.

160 *Chowanna* 1934, yearbook 5, pp. 466–469. Cf. also Friedländer's review of A. Freud, *Einführung in die Psychoanalyse für Pädagogen: Vier Vorträge*: M. Friedländer, "Psychoanaliza a przeżycia wczesnego dzieciństwa", *ŻD* 1938, no. 6, pp. 183–189.

161 A. Dryjski, *Zagadnienia seksualizmu dziecka i młodzieży szkolnej*, p. 337.

> [The environment must] strive to instil a homogenous world view in the young generation. Should it fail to rouse strong interests in the individual, along with resilience, an ability to fight, to work in the name of some higher principle (such as love of the fatherland) – a principle that focuses the individual's efforts and sacrifices – then his energy will flow along the line of least resistance, i.e. in the direction of sex. (*Ibid.*)

For Dryjski, the goal of sex education was to promote erotic self-restraint, which would in turn contribute to the physical and moral progress and health of society as a whole. The role of the educator was to curb the premature awakening of the eroticism encouraged by psychoanalysis. Telling children about the facts of life – a method applied by the Freudians – drew their attention to issues about which they ought to learn much later. For Dryjski, childhood sexuality is always a sign of pathology. He strongly believes that Freud's teachings have a harmful effect on education, and that psychoanalysts pre-empt children's natural curiosity when they impose sexual topics. The application of psychoanalysis to children and teenagers is a scientific error, Dryjski argues, as well as a grave pedagogical wrong. He describes the epoch as one of excessive sexual stimuli; works of art and popular culture are saturated with explicit material. This is why contemporary sex education ought to balance out the environment's erotic stimulations.

> Its task is to create for the young generation such environmental conditions that make it impossible – or at least much more unlikely – for them to become infected with the harmful influences of sexualism. […] If we desire health for future generations, then we must convince the present one that the sexual functions – unlike other activities – ought to maintain over the course of a lifetime the character of a rare celebration. This can be achieved through sublimation, i.e. turning sexual desire towards higher goals.[162]

One educator in interwar Poland, Ludwika Jeleńska, was recently described as "enthusiastic about modern psychology and psychoanalysis (except Freud)".[163] It seems that the same could be said about most of her

162 A. Dryjski, "Psychoanaliza i wychowanie płciowe", p. 310.

163 J. Kostkiewicz, *Kierunki i koncepcje pedagogiki katolickiej w Polsce*, p. 496.

Polish colleagues at the time. One person who attempted to change this situation was Marian Albiński, the co-translator of Freud's *Three Essays on the Theory of Sexuality* (*Trzy rozprawy z teorii seksualnej*), who also wrote articles on the application of psychoanalysis in the Polish army. In 1930 Albiński wrote an essay on psychoanalysis in education for the quarterly *Polskie Archiwum Psychologii*, founded by Józefa Joteyko and published by the above-mentioned Association of Polish Primary School Teachers:

> For more than a decade, psychoanalysis has played a rather prominent role in the field of education. This science, which is all the rage abroad, is not very popular among pedagogues in Poland; worse, if they are familiar at all with it, is only from hearsay and from the most drastic, superficial per-spective, the one that is accessible to the broad masses eager for cheap and facile emotions.[164]

Albiński argues that "psychoanalysis, offering a better insight into the soul of the child, is closer to the soul of the charge than any other pedagogical science. The pedagogy of the future, based on observation and lessons learned from experience, will be closely related to it" (p. 136). He also postulates an educational reform that would hinge on "an adequate awareness, among teachers and educators, of psychological phenomena as discovered through psychoanalysis" (p. 138). His efforts had little effect. The first well-informed and favourable presentation of psychoanalysis in a Polish pedagogical journal only appeared in 1936, when the popularity of Freudianism in Poland had reached its peak thanks to the translation of Freud's *Introduction to Psychoanalysis* (*Wstęp do psychoanalizy*).[165]

The first person to recommend Freud to an audience of educators was Władysław Rowiński in *Chowanna*. In his article, titled "Psychoanaliza z punktu widzenia psychologii i pedagogiki" [Psychoanalysis from a Psychological and Pedagogical Perspective], he argues that the method has applications in different branches of the humanities and social sciences, including pedagogy: "an understanding of the depths of the child's psychology allows us to avoid many educational mistakes, while using its methods helps us get to know the individual student".[166] Rowiński is clearly familiar with Freud's

164 M. Albiński, "O pedagogicznym zastosowaniu psychoanalizy", p. 133.

165 In *Ruch Pedagogiczny* this translation was reviewed by M. Odrzywolski: *RP* 1936, no. 6, pp. 216–218.

166 W. Rowiński, "Psychoanaliza z punktu widzenia psychologii i pedagogiki", *CHO* 1936, vol. 7, no. 1, p. 11.

works – he even presents a readable outline of Freud's second topic – but unfortunately his text barely touches on pedagogy, focusing instead on Freud's theory from the point of view of child psychology.[167] Rowiński, just like his Polish colleagues, fails to mention any of the "analytical pedagogues".

If the researchers associated with *Zeitschrift für psychoanalytische Pädagogik* had any impact at all in interwar Poland then very few traces of it have survived. A cursory mention in a book review represents one rare piece of evidence that the Bornstein sisters and their colleagues in Berlin presented above had a readership in Poland. The reviewer in question, Leon Langholz, discusses the Polish edition of George H. Green's *Psychoanalysis in the Classroom*, translated by a certain Dr Ziembiński and published in Warsaw in 1928. Langholz hails Green's book as "programmatic" for Polish pedagogy, regretting only that Green fails to consider "abnormal cases, such as stuttering, lying, kleptomania, hatred of the teacher etc. Such symptoms and others have been noticed, described and accounted for in much detail in *Zeitschrift für psychoanalytische Pädagogik*".[168] We must keep in mind, however, that this absence of traces concerns Polish-language publications. As I have argued before, the ideas developed by Bernfeld and his students were also disseminated in interwar Poland's Hebrew-language journals. The most prominent publication in this respect was אופקים/*Ofakim* [Horizons], established in 1932 in Warsaw,

---

167 Józef Mirski outlined the changes that Freud introduced after the end of World War I in a supplement to his book *Rozwój i wychowanie płciowe*, pp. 121–127. Ludwik Bandura's review of *Das Unbehagen in der Kultur* [Civilisation and Its Discontents] appeared in *Ruch Pedagogiczny* in 1930 (no. 7, pp. 330–331).

168 *CHO* 1929, pp. 96–98. Langholz also drew attention to the *Zeitschrift für psychoanalytische Pädagogik* in his review of the Polish edition of Pfister's *Psychoanaliza na usługach wychowania* [*Psychoanalysis in the Service of Education*] in *Ruch Pedagogiczny* (1931, no. 3, pp. 138–140). Here it is worth noting that, compared to his Polish colleagues, Langholz was more sceptical of Pfister, who mitigates "the dynamics of sensitive issues that have provoked such a rich and intense discussion"; there is a hint of sarcasm in Langholz's remark that "Freudianism has disappeared under the priest's cassock, passion has given way to temporary shortcomings that will certainly be fixed by a quiet and intelligent talk with a gentle and patient counsellor" (p. 139). Besides Langholz's remarks, another trace of the impact of the German *Zeitschrift in Poland* is Wanda Jakobson's article "Kara jako środek wychowawczy w oświetleniu teorii psychoanalitycznej" [Punishment as a Pedagogical Tool in the Light of Psychoanalytic Theory], published in *Ruch Pedagogiczny* in 1936. Jakobson discusses an article on the same topic by Fritz Redl, published in *Zeitschrift für psychoanalytische Pädagogik*, as well as the journal's monographic issue on punishment.

which offered an important platform for the new pedagogy. Unlike their non-Jewish colleagues, the Zionist educators rejected Adlerism and promoted orthodox Freudianism, and they welcomed contributions by Bernfeld, Fenichel or Wulff.

In this context it is worth examining Janusz Korczak's relationship with psychoanalysis. Henryk Goldszmit (later Korczak) was born in 1878, fourteen years before Bernfeld, but their biographies overlap in many ways.[169] There are parallels between Korczak's leftist worldview and social engagement and Bernfeld's early work; Korczak's associates were affiliated with the Warsaw-based publishing house Czytelnia dla Wszystkich and with *Głos*; he also taught at the clandestine workers' college in Warsaw (Robotniczy Uniwersytet Ludowy). They both sympathised with the Zionist movement. In August 1899, many years before Bernfeld became interested in Theodor Herzl's ideas, Korczak took part in the third Zionist Congress in Basel. In the aftermath of World War I he co-founded and joined the Chief Command of HaShomer Hatzair in the Russian partition. It is possible that Korczak, being engaged in the Central Children's Relief Committee and representing Jewish institutions at the Polish-American Children's Relief Committee, sent Polish-Jewish orphans to Bernfeld's experimental Kinderheim Baumgarten. After all, the orphanage was established thanks to the same funding sources in the United States.

In 1926 Korczak launched *Mały Przegląd* [Little Review], written by and for children. This was a supplement to *Nasz Przegląd* [Our Review], founded in 1923; the journal was the unofficial organ of the Zionist Organisation.[170] In 1925 Korczak signed a fundraising appeal by the Jewish National Fund. At the 19th Congress of the Jewish Agency, which represented the non-Zionist movement, he was elected deputy of a council member of Keren Hayesod (Foundation for the Rebuilding of Palestine). Although he was not a particularly active member of HaShomer Hatzair, Korczak was regularly in touch with this organisation, especially through Mieczysław Zylbertal (Moshe Zertal). Zylbertal was a frequent guest at the orphanage in Warsaw, and sometimes he would take the children – and Korczak, on occasion – on outings with his shomer group.

169 Biographical information based on M. Falkowska, *Kalendarz życia, działalności i twórczości Janusza Korczaka* (Warsaw: Nasza Księgarnia, 1989).

170 *Nasz Przegląd* was an important platform for psychoanalysis. I will return to this topic in more detail in the section on Gustav Bychowski.

In the 1930s many of Korczak's friends, former charges and co-workers from the orphanage settled in Palestine. His closest colleague at the orphanage, Stefania Wilczyńska, who had a strong interest in the idea of communal child rearing, visited the kibbutz Ein Harod on several occasions. In 1934 Korczak himself travelled to Palestine for the first time, staying for three weeks; he visited again for six weeks in 1936. On both occasions he stayed at Ein Harod, working, making observations and giving lectures; he also designed a course for a rural teacher training college. The kibbutz journal *Mabat Mibifnim* [מבט מבפנים] published his favourable opinion on the Palestinian experiment, whose goal was to renew the Jewish land and people. The kibbutz seemed to Korczak like a realisation of his dreams about communal living: a space free of violence and coercion, ensuring unconstrained development to the entire population through voluntary and shared work and study.[171]

On his return to Poland, Korczak gave readings about Palestine at organisations such as B'nai B'rith, the Polish Association of Free Thinking (Polski Związek Myśli Wolnej) and the Judaic Library (Biblioteka Judaistyczna). In the summer of 1938, he took part in a seminar for HaShomer Hatzair educators in Michalin. In June 1940, the underground organisation "Dror" invited him to give the inaugural lecture, and he spoke about collective upbringing in the kibbutz Ein Harod.[172] We know that he was thinking about emigrating, although he spoke neither Yiddish nor Hebrew. In March 1937 he wrote to the Bund activists Rosa and Salek Lichtensztajn:

> As my depression lifted after many months I decided to try one last time: to move to Palestine, to Jerusalem at first, where I will learn Hebrew, and then, after a year, I will become a kibbutznik. All I have is 1000 złoty. Of my family only my sister survives, she owns about fifteen thousand złoty; she speaks several languages so she'll be able to make a living. My departure would have to happen in a month, but I cannot bear the current state of uncertainty any longer.[173]

171 Cf. J. Korczak, *Listy i rozmyślania palestyńskie*, ed. by B. Wojnowska (Warsaw: Ezop, 1999), pp. 10–11.

172 The title of his unpublished presentation was "O kolektywnym wychowaniu w kibucu Ejn Harod". See M. Falkowska, *Kalendarz życia*, p. 345.

173 Quoted in M. Falkowska, *Kalendarz życia, działalności i twórczości Janusza Korczaka*, p. 312.

As late as August 1938, Korczak was still mulling over his plans to emigrate. He was detained by a series of commitments in Poland and by some health issues. Nonetheless, his journeys inspired him to write children's stories that were published as "Opowieści palestyńskie" [Palestinian Tales] in both Poland and Palestine (in Hebrew translation). They included the short story "Ludzie są dobrzy" [People Are Good], written from the perspective of a girl who, following the death of her father, arrives in Palestine with her mother; another story, titled "Trzy wyprawy Herszka" [Herszek's Three Expeditions], features a protagonist who departs for Palestine three times but never arrives.[174] Korczak's *Ghetto Diary*, written shortly before he and the children were murdered, records his dreams about building a big orphanage in the mountains of Lebanon:

> It will have large barracks-like dining rooms and dormitories. There will be small "hermit huts". For myself, on the terrace of a flat roof I will have one room, not too large, with transparent walls, so that I might not miss a single sunrise or sunset and so that, writing at night, I might be able to look now and again at the stars.[175]

In contrast to Bernfeld, Korczak never had an interest in psychoanalysis. His only mention of Freud appears in his 1918 book *Jak kochać dziecko* [*How to Love a Child*], and its tenor is characteristic of a significant segment of Polish pedagogues in the interwar period. Korczak writes: "Freud's research on the sexual life of children has tarnished childhood, but by the same token hasn't it cleansed youth?"[176] Korczak was one of

---

174 The Polish originals were published in the series "Biblioteka Palestyńska dla Dzieci" as a book accompanying *Mały Przegląd*.

175 Janusz Korczak, *Ghetto Diary*, trans. by J. Bachrach and B. Krzywicka (New Haven: Yale University Press, 2003), pp. 20-21.

176 J. Korczak, "How to Love a Child", trans. by B. Paloff, in *How to Love a Child and Other Selected Works*, selected by Olga Medvedeva-Nathoo, ed. by Anna Maria Czernow, vol. 1 (London: Vallentine Mitchell, 2018), p. 90. Korczak strikes a slightly different tone in a private letter: "I regard Freud as a dangerous monomaniac, but anyone who, thanks to him, has come to understand the subconscious, the undiscovered depths of their own soul, and has come to terms with its unknowability – owes him much" (J. Korczak, "Letter to Józef Arnon 3/ VII 1938", trans. by A. Zaranko, in *How to Love a Child and Other Selected Works*, vol. 1, p. 219). Cf. also D. Danek, "Korczak a Freud", in *Sztuka rozumienia: Literatura i psychoanaliza* (Warsaw: IBL, 1997), pp. 394–399.

many Polish educators who rejected Freud's theory of sexuality – perhaps because he was generally reluctant to accept pedagogical theories other than his own.[177] Besides, his position may have been influenced by his work as an expert witness for the court, where his duties included interviewing young victims of sexual abuse. In "For the Safety of Children" Korczak asserts:

> *Children experience erotic arousal, but do not feel lust and have no conscious sexual sensations.* This is how it has been, how it may still be, but is not always necessarily so. A child may be forcibly drawn in, or deceitfully, implicated in sexual experiences; their corruption may spread and become deeply rooted.[178]

In 1933 a book reviewer urged Korczak to clarify his position on the practices of the psychoanalytical pedagogues in Berlin. The journal *Życie Dziecka*, issued by the Polish Committee for Childcare [Polski Komitet Opieki nad Dzieckiem], published Janina Ryngmanowa's highly positive review of Annie Reich's *Der Verein Das Kreide-Dreieck erforscht die Geheimnisse der Erwachsenen* [The Club The Chalk-Triangle Explores the Grown-Ups' Secrets], a children's book on the body and sexuality that had appeared the previous year at the Verlag für Sexualpolitik headed by Wilhelm Reich. (Ryngmanowa stresses that the book was published before Hitler came to power and that both the publisher, "an outpost of radical-left elements among the working classes," and the book itself have been placed on the index in Germany.) Ryngmanowa admits that despite her degree in child psychology and several years of experience in the field, she always struggles when it comes to answering children's questions about where babies come from. Parents, being entirely unprepared for this task, must

177 "Thanks to theory I know, thanks to practice I feel. Theory enriches the intellect, practice gives colour to the feelings, trains the will. I know – does not mean I act according to what I know. Other people's views, those of strangers, must be refracted through my own living self. I do not take theoretical assumptions and develop ideas at random. I reject – forget – omit – I cheat my way out – I disregard. As a result I obtain my own conscious or unconscious theory, which governs my actions. It is remarkable if anything at all, a fragment of the theory, should remain in me, maintaining its raison d'être, having had a certain influence, some kind of impact. I keep renouncing theory, rarely myself" (J. Korczak, "Teoria a praktyka", *SZS* 1925, no. 2, pp. 69–72).

178 J. Korczak, "For the Safety of Children", trans. by S. G. Bye, in *How to Love a Child and Other Selected Works*, vol. 2, p. 164.

be feeling at a loss even more. Reich's book weaves sex education into the main plot, which focuses on a group of children in a working-class suburb who conspire to find out about the grown-ups' secrets. Once a mother discovers the children's clandestine Chalk-Triangle, she tells them about the facts of life. The reviewer stresses:

> Let us add that these explanations [...] are given in a very good manner; straightforward, clear, without a trace of secrecy, as an explanation of facts that are necessary and normal, and at the same time she does the work so thoroughly that the children even learn about the problem of choosing to become a mother, about contraception and – in a way that is very direct and soothing to the children – about masturbation.[179]

The story, Ryngmanowa argues, is suitable for independent reading by children, while the illustrations and cross-sectional anatomical sketches can be helpful to any Polish parent – or at least they could become helpful if the book were published in translation. Here she addresses the director of the orphanage:

> Indeed, it is worth thinking about publishing this book in Polish, especially if a preface was added or if certain adjustments or adaptations were made by Janusz Korczak. Or perhaps it would be even better if a pedagogue and writer of the calibre of Janusz Korczak, who unfortunately has fallen completely silent recently, were to write an original book on these issues. He would be doing an immense favour to both mothers and children. We are facing great social upheavals and great changes in the mindset of people, also in parents' relationships with their children. It cannot be, it absolutely cannot be, that people such as Korczak remain silent in times such as these. Dr Janusz Korczak, please speak up! (p. 337)

Korczak responded to Ryngmanowa's questions in the same journal, summarising them as follows:

- Should a book published by the pedagogical section of a sexual-political seminar in Berlin be translated into Polish?

179 J. Ryngmanowa, "Zagadnienie seksualne w książce dla dzieci (ciekawy eksperyment wychowawczy)", *ŻD* 1933, no. 11–12, p. 336.

- Would I write a preface?
- Shouldn't an original book be written on these issues?

To the first two questions my reply is: "no".[180]

Korczak has two major reservations about Annie Reich's book. Above all, he sees it as typical of the inauthentic work done by "the intelligentsia and the bourgeoisie for the benefit of the proletariat" – it bespeaks the author's perfect ignorance of the social conditions of her audience. Korczak is adamant that the children of the labouring classes are facing a very different set of problems:

> It may well be that middle-class children, who get more sleep than they need, lie awake at night, tormented by the question of how people are born into this world – bless their little hearts. – But a child who lives in a one-room flat will consider this issue, which is not the most pressing one, only during the day – sometimes more, sometimes less frequently. […] The secret keeps Lotte awake, but these children fall asleep; their sleep is not always carefree, it is disturbed by the whimper of the child in the cradle, a kick from their bedfellow (fighting over the blanket), – a toothache, the mother's illness, the intoxicated father, the quarrelsome subletter, bedbugs, stale air… (*Ibid.*)

This short piece contains several sneering remarks about the book's representation of social conditions. Korczak concedes that it may reflect the realities in the country in which it was written, but the story could never have happened in Poland: "Perhaps things are different in Germany, but here a twelve-year-old boy does not have nocturnal emissions and girls reach sexual maturity later than claimed in the book. This is also why it is unsuitable for translation, with or without a preface" (p. 43). He also rejects the kind of sex education portrayed in the book. For him, "a child wants to know, wants to see and wants to try for themselves if something is truly interesting," so it is useless to preempt this natural curiosity. He also strongly disagrees with Reich's idea that masturbation is natural and harmless. He writes mockingly about mothers who might approach doctors "worried why their child hasn't started to masturbate yet" (p. 42).

The question of masturbation among teenagers had already preoccupied Korczak for a long time. In an article in *Szkoła Specjalna* from the same period he writes:

180 J. Korczak, "Der Verein Das Kreide-Dreieck", *ŻD* 1934, no. 2, p. 41.

> A pamphlet with the title "Masturbation in Boys" has been lying in my desk drawer for twenty years. This is a serious and difficult subject, fraught with sensationalism, stifled by prudishness. These are the reasons why I have been hesitating and holding back; I have been waiting for new contributions, which pour in slowly if we want to examine the material critically, rather than incorporating dubious observations, someone's narrations or (even worse) confessions. The more insistently the one camp clamours for an answer, the more obstinately silent are those who have a right and a duty to provide an answer. The problem has not budged, while the danger is growing.[181]

Korczak believed that onanism had a detrimental effect on the formation of a young person's character, and that it never passed of its own accord. A child prone to masturbation will not benefit from punishment or control but needs support in letting go of the noxious habit. Korczak made careful observations of onanism among the boys at the orphanage, striving to identify the underlying causes in each case and finding unique approaches to help each of his protégés overcome what he saw as a harmful addiction.[182] Looking for Korczak's credo we may turn to the final sentences in his response to Ryngmanowa:

> Our need for a hygiene that takes into account sexuality is a different issue. And here is my answer to the third question: why do I not write it? A few years ago I wrote a little book titled *Prawidła życia* [The Rules of Life]. It was an experiment, I waited for feedback, but the response I got was – silence. There was a chapter titled "Zdrowie" [Health]. It is unsurprising: things that are not fashionable or glaring will find no hearing on the market. But what is one to do, being unable to adapt? One must remain silent, even if it is harder and more burdensome than speaking up. I have no qualifications as a "pundit" on child sexuality, but I know for sure that

181 J. Korczak, "O bezpieczeństwo dziecka".

182 In 1937 *Szkoła Specjalna* [Special Education] published an excerpt of Korczak's case study of a boy whose masturbation was successfully suppressed. J. Korczak, "Obserwacja jednego przypadku (onanizm chłopca)", *SZS* 1936/1937, no. 3, pp. 133–139. Franciszka Baumgarten-Tramer's French translation was published in the Swiss *Zeitschrift für Kinderpsychiatrie/Journal de Psychiatrie Infantine*, 1937, vol. 1.

> Social Darwinism and sexual zoologism are misguided, harmful and dangerous. It is wrong to yank at the child, either to the left or to the right.[183]

Janina Ryngmanowa responded to Korczak by suggesting that Reich's book may not be perfect, but given the lack of other material it must suffice. She defended her opinion that the language and concepts are suitable for working-class children, who are indeed interested in the body and sexual matters – their interest may be even keener than among middle-class children, for they are confronted with sex in their everyday lives from a very young age, and often in a form that is vulgar, brutal and repulsive to them.[184]

The debate between Ryngmanowa and Korczak launched a broader discussion in the journal. Several issues focused on sex education, giving a platform to both supporters and opponents of the idea of applying Freud's discoveries in pedagogy. The first group included Wanda Piotrowska, whose article "Kultura i wychowanie erotyczne" [Culture and Sex Education] outlines the possibilities opened up by the Adlerian school.[185] In her opinion the most valuable contribution of psychoanalysis is the mechanism of sublimation, which makes the erotic functions socially valuable. In the hedonistic postwar era, she writes, "the erotic genre has lost some of its psychological heaviness for young people, they have cast aside all responsibility for their erotic life. These questions are stripped of their proper gravity and seriousness, they are transformed into a field of sheer carefree pleasure".[186] In Piotrowska's opinion, sex education should teach youngsters to forsake pleasure, which is the price to be paid for the entry into culture.

> Today psychology furnishes educators with the means to provide sex education and to attain an erotic culture. These means are: 1) sensual drives that are erotic can be repressed into the subconscious as long as possible. 2) Following puberty, the biopsychological energies linked to

183 J. Korczak, "Der Verein Das Kreide-Dreieck", p. 44.

184 J. Ryngmanowa, "Kompromis w życiu, a odpowiedzialność wobec dziecka", *ŻD* 1934, no. 5, pp. 120–128.

185 W. Piotrowska, "Kultura i wychowanie erotyczne", *ŻD* 1934, no. 4, pp. 105–114; no. 5, pp. 139–153. Cf. also B. Bobrowska, "Kwestie 'drażliwe' na kolonii koedukacyjnej", *ŻD* 1934, no. 5, pp. 153–165.

186 W. Piotrowska, "Kultura i wychowanie erotyczne", p. 109.

> these drives are channeled until the practical ability is attained to realise both the social and the biological function of eroticism in predefined circumstances, in agreement with the erotic culture. 3) Sublimation, i.e. the closest possible association of these drives with the erotic ideal, so that any realisation of these drives beyond predefined ethical, aesthetic and cultural norms should become impossible. (pp. 113–114)

Piotrowska also writes that Freud's psychoanalysis and Adler's individual psychology, which could be so helpful to educators facing these challenges are – this is 1934! – "unfortunately little known and undervalued" (p. 110).

One writer who was overtly critical of *Der Verein Das Kreide-Dreieck* was Jadwiga Balicka.[187] Echoing Korczak, she found Reich's book unrealistic: first, the great majority of young children do not ask their parents for details about sex, as do the characters in this story, and second, the explanations provided by the grown-up characters are excessively detailed and unsuitable for children as young as the ones in the story; what is more, they are too reckless. Balicka worries that young readers, excited in this way, might want to try things out for themselves, after receiving such detailed instructions. In her opinion, the book should be kept away from children as well as from foolhardy educators. Korczak responded once more to say that he had little to add to Balicka's article. He concludes by outlining his approach to sex education:

- Do not make a show of your exasperation, do not slap the child or say "ew" when they wet or soil themselves, when they have a snotty nose, dirty trousers, a torn dress or break a glass.
- Do not overfeed the child (neither with calories nor with vitamins).
- When the child is thirsty do not refuse a drink (water).
- Do not force your child to go to bed or to sleep, do not let them overheat.5) Do not refuse movement and play in a large and interesting outdoor space.[188]

Given Polish educators' lack of interest in the ideas developed by the "pedagogical analysts or analytical pedagogues," the only link between the Berlin-based group and the public in Warsaw was Gustav Bychowski. He

187 J. Balicka, "Niebezpieczny eksperyment wychowawczy", *ŻD* 1934, no. 5, pp. 115–119.

188 J. Korczak, "O fajkę pokoju", *ŻD* 1934, no. 5, pp. 137–138.

was inspired by his German colleagues' work and contributed an article to their *Zeitschrift für psychoanalytische Pädagogik*.[189] His role as the most important actor in the cultural transfer of psychoanalysis in the interwar period deserves a separate chapter.

189 G. Bychowski, "Schwierigkeiten in der Schule und ihre Psychotherapie", *ZFPP* 1930, no. 11/12, pp. 420–430.

Part 6

Gustav Bychowski

A Polish Freudian

The life and work of Gustav Bychowski

There is no doubt that among the key figures of this book, Gustav Bychowski is the only one who can be described as a "Polish Freudian". Of all the members of the VPS only he was a citizen of Poland and worked within the territory of Poland, once it had become independent. His role in the transfer of psychoanalysis to Polish culture in the interwar period can be compared to Ludwig Jekels' role before the war. If Jekels was Freud's emissary to the Polish lands, Bychowski, more than thirty years his junior, can be described as the first ambassador. Jekels managed to place two translations of Freud's books with Altenberg Publishers (Wydawnictwo Altenberga). Similarly, Bychowski convinced Jakub Przeworski to issue a Polish translation of Freud's *Introduction to Psychoanalysis*. In the late 1930s Jekels and Bychowski both found themselves in New York, where the latter died in 1972.

Gustav Bychowski was born into an assimilated Jewish family in 1895. His father, Zygmunt Bychowski, was a prominent neurologist.[1] It is possible that he introduced his son to psychoanalysis, perhaps having encountered Jekels' work; after all, he took part in both prewar congresses also attended by Jekels, and he was active in the Warsaw Medical Association (Warszawskie Towarzystwo Lekarskie), an organisation that had links with Jekels and psychoanalysis, as I discussed in Part One of this book. Young Gustav Bychowski attended the Emilian Konopczyński gymnasium. Established in 1905, it was Warsaw's first gymnasium where boys were taught in Polish (the language had been banned from schools for fifty years following the failed January Insurrection of 1863-64). He went on to spend one year in Saint Petersburg to obtain a Russian school leaving diploma, which would

1 E. Herman, *Neurolodzy polscy*, pp. 168–174; P. Szarejko, *Słownik lekarzy polskich XIX wieku*, vol. 3, pp. 65–66.

allow him to pursue higher education abroad.[2] Next he enrolled to read philosophy at Heidelberg University. He studied medicine in Wrocław, Heidelberg and Amsterdam; in 1915-17 he was in Lausanne, then, following a brief stint in Vienna, he came to Zurich for the summer semester of 1918.[3] The following year he obtained his diploma with a dissertation titled "Zur Psychopatologie der Brandstiftung" [On the Psychopathology of Arson], which was published in the *Schweizer Archiv für Neurologie und Psychiatrie*.[4]

Over the next few years, until 1921, Bychowski was an assistant at the psychiatric clinic in Lausanne, where he was working on his first book, *Metaphysik und Schizophrenie* [Metaphysics and Schizophrenia].[5] This comprehensive and erudite study explores the analogies between the structure of psychotic delusions and the most influential philosophical systems; Bychowski discusses Schopenhauer, Nietzsche, Bergson, Simmel, Durkheim, Jaspers, Nicholas of Cusa and the Upanishads as well as key works in anthropology.

In 1921-23, Bychowski was in Vienna again, working at neurological and psychopathological wards within a number of hospitals. Apparently it is only now that he became an active participant in the psychoanalytical movement, for his name does not appear on the lists of attendees at the archives of the Swiss Psychoanalytical Association (where his Polish colleague Mira Gincburg-Oberholzer was a member). He was a regular

2 M. Wallis, "Gustaw Bychowski, psychoanalityk i humanista (1895–1972)", *RF* 1973, no. 2/4, p. 105. It is worth remembering that in the mid-1880s, the University of Warsaw (as well as publicly funded gymnasiums) introduced a quota to limit the number of Jewish students. This meant that at the turn of the century, the percentage of Jews at this university was only marginally higher than across the whole population. In Western European universities, meanwhile, the proportion of Jews at university was typically several times as high as across the general population. The Russian Empire consistently had the lowest ratio of Jewish students in Europe (cf. H. Datner, *Ta i tamta strona: Żydowska inteligencja Warszawy drugiej połowy XIX wieku*, p. 118).

3 I used the database on < www.matrikel.uzh.ch > [accessed 15 January 2021].

4 G. Bychowski, "Zur Psychopatologie der Brandstiftung", *SAN* 1919, no. V, p. 1. The *Internationale Zeitschrift für ärztliche Psychoanalyse* published a detailed review by Hans Meier-Müller, a Zurich-based psychiatrist and member of the Swiss Psychoanalytical Association (*IZAP* 1919, no. 3, pp. 280–282).

5 G. Bychowski, *Metaphysik und Schizophrenie: Eine vergleichend-psychologische Studie*, Abhandlungen aus der Neurologie, Psychiatrie, Psychologie und ihren Grenzgebieten: Beihefte zur Monatsschrift für Psychiatrie und Neurologie, ed. by K. Bonhoeffer, no. 21 (Berlin: S. Karger, 1923).

guest at the VPS meetings between October 1921 and May 1922. On two occasions (9 November 1921 and 18 January 1922) he was accompanied by "Frau Bychowski". (Bychowski met Ellen, a review dancer, in Vienna. Their son Jan Ryszard was born in 1922. After the divorce the boy lived with his father.[6]) Bychowski gave a few presentations at the VPS: "Zur Psychologie des schizophrenen Verfolgungswahnes" [On the Psychology of Schizophrenic Persecutory Delusions] on 23 November 1921, "Eine buddhistische Mutterleibsphantasie" [A Buddhist Womb Fantasy] on 14 December 1921, and finally "Eine Gesichtsillusion als Ausdruck der ambivalenten Übertragung" [A Facial Illusion as an Expression of Ambivalent Transference] on 10 May 1922. The last of these articles appeared in *Internationale Zeitschrift für Psychoanalyse.*[7]

Bychowski was analysed – presumably in Polish – by Siegfried Bernfeld, who had only started working as an analyst in May 1921, without having undergone analysis himself. Bychowski would have been one of his earliest patients. When Bychowski applied to join the VPS, the secret committee discussed his application in much detail. Surviving circulars by Rank and Freud indicate their reservations about the young Pole's intentions. Initially they had believed he would settle in Vienna, but then it turned out that he was planning to return to Warsaw. They concluded that Bychowski was yet to prove worthy of their trust and should content himself with his guest status. Granting him full membership would have meant legitimising any of his activities in Warsaw, and without concrete evidence of his usefulness to the movement the Society had no intention to bestow on him such a wide-ranging guarantee.[8]

Faced with this defeat Bychowski tried to find employment at the Berliner Psychoanalytisches Institut [Berlin Psychoanalytical Institute]. A friend, who unfortunately remains unidentified, introduced him to Sachs, Abraham and Eitingon, who turned to their colleagues in Vienna to inquire about the Pole (p. 99). Freud and Rank responded by saying, again, that Bychowski's theoretical contributions seem interesting but that

6 Gustav Bychowski took Jan Ryszard back Warsaw and enrolled him at the Stefan Batory gymnasium, where the boy became close with two future writers – poet Krzysztof Kamil Baczyński and essayist Konstanty Jeleński. Cf. J. Olczak-Ronikier, *W ogrodzie pamięci* (Cracow: Znak, 2001), p. 174, pp. 182–184.

7 G. Bychowski, "Eine Gesichtsillusion als Ausdruck der ambivalenten Übertragung", *IZP* 1922, no. 3, pp. 337–339.

8 *Die Rundbriefe des "Geheimen Komitees"*, vol. 3, pp. 86–87.

his analytical experience boils down to three months of analysis with Bernfeld. Given his precarious financial situation and the fact that, for whatever reason, few of his colleagues in Vienna had taken a liking to him, a move to Berlin might be the easiest solution (p. 109). In the second half of 1922 Bychowski relocated to Warsaw, and towards the end of that year he wrote to Berlin again to request permission to open a practice there.[9] Once more Abraham asked Freud if they should give their Polish colleague the benefit of the doubt. This time Freud's reply was less disparaging: "Concerning Dr Bychowski, we see no reason to turn him down, nay, we hope that some rigid discipline would benefit him" (p. 35). Still, the German analysts decided against inviting Bychowski.

Bychowski was not admitted into the VPS until 1931. This is a remarkable delay, especially when we take into account the lax criteria that were previously applied and the earlier members' steep careers. By 1923 the VPS had become a brand that needed to protect itself from potential impostors. It was wary of handing out its recommendation letters to all and sundry. The Freudians suspected that Bychowski was keen on the membership because it would promote his practice in Warsaw, that he cared less about serving the cause than about obtaining a sort of concession.

Following these drawbacks Bychowski finally decided, in 1923, to remain in Poland. He nostrified his medical diploma and dedicated him-self to his academic career, which led him to a habilitation in psychiatry in 1935. In contrast to the other protagonists of this book, for whom a relationship with the Freudian movement signified an irreversible break with the medical and academic establishment, Bychowski would always remain, first and foremost, a psychiatrist. His mission was always to incorporate psychoanalysis into psychiatry, to turn Freudianism into an essential tool for doctors.

Bychowski arrived in the capital of newly independent Poland in the early 1920s – too late to meet Eugenia Sokolnicka. She had abandoned her efforts to establish a Polish Psychoanalytical Society and moved to Paris two years before. It is unclear if they ever became acquainted. They kept missing each other by a few years, in Zurich, Vienna and finally in Warsaw, and when Bychowski attended the International Psychoanalytical Congress for the first time, in 1936, Sokolnicka was no longer alive.

Being based in Warsaw, Bychowski was not able to get deeply involved in the psychoanalytic movement. He attended two international conferences, but apart from that he had no contact with other members and

9 *Die Rundbriefe des "Geheimen Komitees"*, vol. 4, p. 30.

barely ever contributed to the movement's official periodicals. During his early years in Warsaw he sent reports from Poland to the editors of *Internationale Zeitschrift für Psychoanalyse* (at the time these were Max Eitingon, Sándor Ferenczi and Sándor Radó). In 1925, for instance, he submitted a few observations from the psychiatric ward of Warsaw's Jewish Hospital (Szpital Starozakonnych).[10] In 1927 he arranged for the section "Polen" [Poland] to reappear under the rubric of "Psychoanalytische Bewegung" [The Psychoanalytic Movement], three years after the last accounts from Poland had been published under Beata Rank's editorship. Summarising the developments of the last few years, Bychowski was not able to mention more than a few medical doctors' interest in psychoanalysis. Besides his own activity he lists only three events: lectures given by Maurycy Bornsztajn (spelled Bornstein before World War I) at the Free Polish University (Wolna Wszechnica Polska) in the spring of 1924,[11] a presentation by Jan Mazurkiewicz on the application of psychoanalysis in psychiatry at the forum of the Psychiatric Society (Towarzystwo Psychiatryczne), as well as the publication of *Pamiętnik pacjentki* [A Patient's Diary], edited by Adam Wizel. He also brings up Roman Markuszewicz and Władysław Matecki's articles on psychoanalytical topics in "serious academic journals". Unfortunately he gives no details, so that it remains unclear which publications he had in mind. Bychowski's initiative was a one-off. News from Warsaw were published only in this one yearbook[12] The journal did, however, publish three more short contributions by Bychowski: "Ein Fall von oralem Verfolgungswahn" ("A Case of Oral Delusions of Persecution"), "Aktivität und Realität" [Activity and Reality] and "Psychoanalyse im hypoglykämischen Zustand: Versuche zur Therapie der Psychosen" [Psychoanalysis in a Hypoglycaemic State: Experiments with the Therapy of Psychoses].[13] Bychowski's publications in Polish periodicals found no

10 G. Bychowski, "Psychoanalytisches aus der psychiatrischen Abteilung", *IZP* 1925, no. 3, pp. 350–352.

11 These lectures were only published several years later: M. Bornsztajn, *Psychoanaliza (6 wykładów, wygłoszonych na Wolnej Wszechnicy w Warszawie)* (Cracow: Okręgowy Związek Kas Chorych, 1930).

12 *IZP* 1927, no. 1, pp. 86–87.

13 G. Bychowski, "Ein Fall von oralem Verfolgungswahn", *IZP* 1929, no. 1, pp. 96-100 (published in English as "A Case of Oral Delusions of Persecution", *IJP* 1930, no. 11, pp. 332–337), G. Bychowski, "Aktivität und Realität", *IZP* 1933, no. 1–2, pp. 152–169, G. Bychowski, "Psychoanalyse im hypoglykämischen Zustand: Versuche zur Therapie der Psychosen", *IZP* 1937, no. 4, pp. 540–547.

resonance among his international colleagues and his name disappeared from the correspondence among Freud's inner circle. Ernest Jones's biography of Freud, the three-volume monograph that also represents the official history of the psychoanalytical movement, does not mention the Polish psychiatrist at all.

In 1936 Bychowski travelled to Vienna to interview Freud for *Wiadomości Literackie*. That they had not seen each other since 1922. Bychowski writes:

> I confess that on my way to see the master I was greatly moved. It felt as if I were to give my teacher an account of a large part of my life, or in any case a large part of my work. In the same unchanging and not very spacious office, where the galleries of his desk are guarded by an amazing collection of fantastic statuettes – mythical figurines from faraway, exotic cults, no doubt gifted to him by travelling ethnologist friends – I am greeted by Freud's still robust frame; his face appears slimmer and older than all those years ago, but his eyes are, as always, deep, bright and expressive. His initial questions are of a personal nature. The professor is interested to hear about what keeps me busy, he asks if I had any regrets about devoting myself to psychoanalysis and proclaims with verve that this is the type of work from which one cannot pull oneself away, having engaged in it once, and then he immediately turns to professional matters.[14]

Bychowski tells Freud about the advances of psychoanalysis in Poland, including his own achievements, such as giving lectures at the University of Warsaw and various publications. When he brings up the resistance with which the theory is received in Poland, just as in any other country, Freud replies:

> The unconscious is by its very nature inaccessible to the average person, who has neither the sense for it nor the interest. If you were to write a history of sea snakes you could count on huge success, but the unconscious...

Returning to the beginnings of the movement, they discuss the general animosity towards Freud's ideas and his heroic determination. Bychowski

14 G. Bychowski, "Rozmowa z Freudem", *WL* 1936, no. 20, p. 4.

quotes him saying: "Knowing that one has discovered something real, one need not expect immediate recognition. I learned early on not to count on it and not to fear being left alone with my conviction. The courage to be lonely, this slight superiority of character, has given me the strength to persevere."

The first Poles had contacted the VTP in its pioneering days. They rose through the ranks quickly, easily entering the heart of the movement and taking up prominent positions as the power structures were established over the years to come. Once psychoanalysis was fully institutionalised, however, such opportunities were no longer available. In the interwar era, Poland found itself on a distant orbit of the movement. Its focus had shifted to establishing structures in Japan, Palestine or India, rather than collaborating with one of the newly founded small countries. By 1938, ten local societies existed across Europe (covering Austria, France, the UK, Denmark and Norway, the Netherlands, Finland and Sweden, Germany, Hungary, Italy, Switzerland), five in the United States (Boston, Chicago, New York, Washington-Baltimore and Philadelphia), one in Israel, one in India and two in Japan (Sendai, Tokyo). A Polish society was only set up in 1997. Bychowski certainly did work towards that end, as suggested by Otto Fenichel's letter to his colleagues dated 6 September 1936:

> Regarding Poland, B[ychowski] told me that a few university students and doctors, having attended his lectures, formed a group and meet on a regular basis to read Freud together; he hopes they might become the germ of a Polish branch of the society.[15]

Referring to this claim one and a half years later, Fenichel writes that according to a different source "things are not as rosy concerning analysis as Bychowski would have it" (p. 677).[16] The letter ends with Fenichel stating that he hopes to hear more from Warsaw, but this topic does not appear again in the *Rundbriefe*.

---

15 O. Fenichel, *119 Rundbriefe*, vol. 1, pp. 464–465.

16 In a letter from March 1934, Fenichel expressed misgivings about Bychowski's keen interest in the early stages of ego formation, including the trauma of birth (see *119 Rundbriefe*, vol. 1, p. 64). In September 1936, he also alluded to other difficulties: "Various reservations, both professional and personal in nature, may be had against Bychowski himself. I hope to receive more detailed information soon." (Letter dated 3 December 1937, *119 Rundbriefe*, vol. 1, p. 677). In February 1944, he took issue with Bychowski's article "The Spiritual Background of Hitlerism" (see *119 Rundbriefe*, vol. 2, p. 1807).

In 1936 Bychowski wrote a report on the International Psychoanalytic Congress in Marienbad for *Polskie Archiwum Psychologii.* It was his first psychoanalytic conference, and he gave a paper on psychoanalysis in a hypoglycaemic state.[17] It is also worth mentioning that he witnessed Jacques Lacan's first conference paper. He reports: "An interesting presentation by Lacan (Paris) discussed the 'mirror stage' as a phase in the development of the ego and thus gave an outstanding theoretical scope to the problems of early childhood."[18] The way in which Bychowski treats "Polishness" in his report is telling: he describes Jekels as "a Pole who currently lives in Stockholm," while Helene Deutsch ("pani Deutschowa") is described as "our compatriot" and as belonging to "the Viennese school". He goes on:

> While congresses in psychoanalysis are generally very well attended, the last one attracted an exceptional number of people. Some 300 participants from Europe, the United States, even from India and South Africa, a huge number of presentations (the conference lasted for 5 days) – all this testified to the growing reach of the international psychoanalytic movement. The only person from Poland was the writer of these words.

Psychoanalysis and Psychiatry

For the first decade he spent in Warsaw, from 1922 to 1933 (the year he joined the psychiatric clinic of Warsaw University directed by Jan Mazurkiewicz), Bychowski worked at the Jewish Hospital in Warsaw (Szpital Starozakonnych na Czystem). He became a regular at the hospital's research meetings and contributor to its journal, *Kwartalnik Kliniczny.*[19]

---

17 Two years later Bychowski also attended the 15th Congress in Paris, where he gave a presentation, illustrated with examples from his own practice, on the relationship between the ego and the super-ego. Cf. G. Bychowski, "Les relations entre le moi et le surmoi", *RFP* 1939, no. 1, pp. 49–59.

18 G. Bychowski, "XIV Międzynarodowy Zjazd Psychoanalityczny w Marienbadzie (sierpień 1936)", *PAP* 1936/7, vol. 9, no. 3, pp. 175–176.

19 G. Bychowski, "Psychoterapia osobników małointeligentnych", *KKS* 1928, no. 2, p. 164; "Współczesny stan nauki o defektach moralnych", *KKS*, no. 4, pp. 363–369; "O maskach neurotycznych", *KKS*, 1929, no. 3–4, pp. 266–270; "Z badań nad stanami osłupienia", *KKS*, 1930, no. 3, p. 212.

In the story of the transfer of psychoanalysis, the Jewish Hospital and its staff play an interesting role. For a number of years the institution had two psychiatric wards. One was directed by Adam Wizel, who had joined the institution in 1898, the other by Maurycy Bornsztajn, who was in charge from 1908 to 1939. When Wizel died in 1929, Bornsztajn came to be at the helm of both wards. Both doctors had started off as staunch opponents of psychoanalysis, but by the time Bychowski was hired they had changed their minds. Wizel, who had been a fierce adversary of Ludwig Jekels (as previously discussed), developed an interest in Freud, particularly his ideas on schizophrenia.[20] Similarly, Bornsztajn had been critical of Freudianism before World War I, but in the meantime he had tried to establish ties with the psychoanalytical movement, going as far as to apply to join the VPS. He could not have known, but his chances of success were extremely slim. In 1918 Otto Rank reported to Freud on his visit to Warsaw:

> I spoke with various people there, including Bornstein, who is impossible, but who, as a respected neurologist, can discredit analysis the same way as the others can – all the while believing himself to be a supporter. With people like that, one sees how likeable the real opponents are.[21]

The Polish psychiatrist is mentioned in the secret committee's circulars in 1923. In early February, Ernest Jones, whom Bornsztajn had contacted, asks if any of his colleagues were familiar with the name. The reply written by Freud and Rank is straightforward: they concede that Bornsztajn is "the only analyst in Warsaw," and yet "his understanding, as far as we know, is in fact so limited that he does not qualify as one".[22] Bornsztajn managed to publish only two contributions in the *Internationale Zeitschrift für Psychoanalyse*. These were a polemic with Abraham's article on the dream symbolism of the spider in 1923,[23] and, three years later, a piece on schizophrenic symptoms.[24] He had no other contact with the Freudian

20 Cf. R. Markuszewicz, "O działalności naukowej śp. Dra Adama Wizla", *M* 1929, no. 17/18, pp. 261–264; M. Bornsztajn, "Adam Wizel (życiorys)", *KKS* 1929, no. 4, pp. 314–317.

21 *Inside Psychoanalysis: The Letters of Sigmund Freud & Otto Rank*, p. 84.

22 *Die Rundbriefe des "Geheimen Komitees"*, vol. 4, p. 37.

23 M. Bornsztajn, "Zur Frage 'Die Spinne als Traumsymbol'", *IZP* 1923, no. 2, pp. 215–216.

24 M. Bornsztajn, "Schizophrene Symptome im Lichte der Psychoanalyse", *IZP* 1926, no. 1, pp. 95–100.

movement. Still, in Poland he became a champion of psychoanalysis, above all – but not exclusively – among doctors.[25] On the occasion of Freud's seventieth birthday in 1926 he wrote accessible articles for both *Warszawskie Czasopismo Lekarskie*[26] and *Kurier Warszawski*. Thus he ensured that Poland joined in the celebrations of an anniversary that, as Bornszajn puts it, "is being fêted by the entire scientific and cultural world on both hemispheres".[27]

Ten years later, Bornsztajn and Bychowski honoured another decade of Freud's life in *Warszawskie Czasopismo Lekarskie*. On the day the father of psychoanalysis turned eighty the journal published Bychowski's "Istota i możliwości lecznicze psychoanalizy" [The Nature and Therapeutic Potential of Psychoanalysis][28] and a presentation that Bornsztajn had given at the Polish Psychiatric Society (Polskie Towarzystwo Psychiatryczne).[29] While Bornsztajn offers a short history of psychoanalysis, Bychowski sets out to remedy medical doctors' poor understanding of Freudianism and their tendency to confuse it with other forms of psychotherapy, especially suggestion and hypnosis. He argues that of all the methods of working with a patient's psyche, only psychoanalysis truly addresses the cause and not just the symptoms. Highlighting the most important aspects of analytical therapy, he also discusses the difficult role of the doctor who holds the key to its success:

> His attention, always vigilant and impartial, catches the slightest psychological vibration in the patient. Embracing the totality of the patient's psychological situation, the doctor knows what these vibrations mean, what they express, what they herald and what they foretell. He shares this knowledge with the patient: this is easily and simply said, but this sentence contains a large part of the difficulty of psychoanalysis. The psychoanalyst

25 Cf. M. Bornsztajn, "Znaczenie teorii psychoanalitycznej dla psychiatrii", *KKS* 1928, no. 4, pp. 321–332.

26 M. Bornsztajn, "Zygmunt Freud", *WCL* 1926, no. 6, pp. 288–291.

27 M. Bornsztajn, "70-lecie twórcy psychoanalizy", *KW* 1926, no. 123, p. 11.

28 G. Bychowski, "Istota i możliwości lecznicze psychoanalizy", *WCL* 1936, no. 17, pp. 296–299.

29 M. Bornsztajn, "Historia rozwoju psychoanalizy i jej stan współczesny". Władysław Matecki's presentation, given on the occasion of Freud's birthday at the Polish Society of Social Medicine (Polskie Towarzystwo Medycyny Społecznej), would only appear a year later in the same journal. See W. Matecki, "Zygmunt Freud – lekarz – myśliciel", *WCL* 1937, no. 11, pp. 214–218.

> must dose his interpretations carefully and skilfully, and this is not merely a question of experience but also of special tact and intuition.

Seen from the doctor's perspective, Bychowski suggests, psychoanalysis is an art, inexorably related to "the spontaneous ideas and flashes of the psychoanalyst's intuition, who, during the session, is fully and wholly immersed in the mental world of the patient".[30]

Psychoanalytical treatment of psychoses

In the interwar period Bychowski was a frequent contributor to specialist periodicals such as *Warszawskie Czasopismo Lekarskie* [Warsaw Medical Journal], *Rocznik Psychiatryczny* [Yearbook of Psychiatry] and *Neurologia Polska* [Polish Neurology]. Only a few of his articles touched on psychoanalysis.[31] Bychowski's areas of interest were schizophrenia and other psychotic states that challenged clinicians in psychiatry as well as Freudians at the time. Freud himself practically never studied psychosis, limiting psychoanalytical therapy to neuroses and perversions, i.e. disorders of obvious psychogenic origin, where organic causes – including heredity – could be ruled out. Psychosis, an illness related to concrete pathologies of the nervous system, was left to psychiatrists and considered incurable through psychoanalysis. Bychowski seems to disagree, at least initially. Although none of his texts openly addresses the possibilities of psychoanalytical therapy in psychotic cases, he makes clear that the idea of a biological origin and psychoanalytical theory are not mutually exclusive – each of them may simply apply to different types of cases.[32] What we must reject are theories about the origin of mental illness that fail to acknowledge the role of trauma – a factor that has nothing to do with a hereditary

30 G. Bychowski, "Istota i możliwości lecznicze psychoanalizy", p. 298.

31 The following articles accord less or no space to psychoanalysis: G. Bychowski, "O odruchach położenia i ustawienia i o indukcji ruchów", *NPL* 1926, no. 1–2, pp. 58–87; "O postaciach monosymptomatycznych stwardnienia rozsianego w początkowych okresach cierpienia", *WCL* 1928, no. 44, pp. 959–962; "O diencefalozach", *WCL* 1938, no. 5, pp. 81–84, no. 6, pp. 101–103; "Zasady analizy psychiatrycznej zaburzeń ogniskowych", *RPS* 1935, no. 25, pp. 110–135.

32 Only in 1936 did Bychowski concede that psychoanalysis is ineffective when it comes to clinical psychosis. He added that analysis may offer some relief in the early stages of certain mental illnesses but that it must cede to the methods of somatic therapy. G. Bychowski, "Istota i możliwości lecznicze psychoanalizy", p. 299.

disposition; a strictly psychogenetic origin, meanwhile, seems very likely in some cases of psychosis.[33]

The primary reason behind Bychowski's interest in psychoses is that they present compelling evidence for psychoanalytical theory: "Psychosis points to interrelationships within the psyche immediately and often without any interpretation, while the psychoanalysis of neurotic patients usually entails considerable difficulty and effort in their identification."[34] Schizophrenia, Bychowski proposes, has didactic and illustrative significance. In many cases of this disorder the analyst will find that the patient's delusions reveal an enduringly eroticised relationship towards the parents, a regression to primitive forms of non-genital eroticism, as well as infantile sexual theories and fantasies. Only psychoanalysis contributes to understanding the content of psychotic experiences and to explaining the genesis and dynamics of otherwise inexplicable hallucinations. The application of psychoanalysis to the pathogenesis of schizophrenia entails certain theoretical difficulties, and in many cases may not appear necessary, but without Freudianism the symptomatology of schizophrenia eludes our understanding. After all, the course of this illness is nothing but a dramatisation of internal conflicts. In Bychowski's view, the most important feature of schizophrenia is narcissism, the inability to transfer libido to objects: the schizophrenic is always balancing between "a complete regression of libido, a complete detachment from the outside world," and "its transference to the whole world without any differentiation, uniting with it completely, regardless of previous ties. The first of these processes corresponds to an end-of-the-world experience, its complete annihilation; the second is accompanied by a feeling of great bliss, ecstasy, possessing everything."[35]

Bychowski cites Freud's analysis of Daniel Paul Schreber's case, "Psycho-Analytic Notes on an Autobiographical Account of a Case of Paranoia (Dementia Paranoides)" – one of Freud's few publications on psychosis. In contrast to most of his case studies, this one is not based on a therapy but represents Freud's analysis of Schreber's memoirs.[36] Here it is worth noting that while Freud considered paranoia to be a psychosis *par*

33 G. Bychowski, "Schizofrenia w świetle psychoanalizy", *RPS* 1927, no. 5, p. 59.

34 G. Bychowski, "Momenty psychoanalityczne w psychozach", *WCL* 1925, no. 8, p. 340.

35 G. Bychowski, "Schizofrenia", p. 60.

36 Cf. S. Freud, "Psycho-Analytic Notes on an Autobiographical Account of a Case of Paranoia (Dementia Paranoides)", SE XII, pp. 1-82.

excellence, Bychowski held with Eugen Bleuler's theory of schizophrenia. It was thanks to Bleuler and his persistent efforts to integrate psychoanalysis into clinical psychiatry that the term schizophrenia replaced the previous term *dementia praecox*.[37] Freud's text alerted Bychowski to the relationship between psychosis and projection (i.e. the transfer of one's own drives, considered to be incompatible with the rest of one's personality, to other people).[38] Bychowski, like Freud, is particularly interested in the mechanism whereby repressed homoerotic desires are voiced. In the Schreber case, the patient's most important delusion was that he must become a woman in order to submit to God and redeem humanity. In Freud's view, the realisation that "I (a man) love him (a man)" entails an inner conflict that the patient cannot accept. This tension then leads to four possible negations of the unbearable truth, and each negation results in a different delusion. The version "I do not love him – I hate him," which by way of projection becomes "he hates me," ends in persecutory mania; "I do not love him – I love her", projected onto women ("she loves me") leads to erotomania; "it is not I who love the man – she loves him" prompts manic jealousy, while "I do not love at all – I do not love any one" and "I love only myself" culminates in megalomania.

Freud's study of the Schreber case, written in 1911, is rooted in his prewar work, but when Bychowski referred to it twenty years later, he was able to build on ideas that Freud had introduced in the meantime. These were, most importantly, the second topic (i.e. the formalised division of the psychic apparatus into the ego, id and super-ego), introduced in 1923, and two articles written in 1924, namely "Neurosis and Psychosis" and "The Loss of Reality in Neurosis and Psychosis". At this time Freud drew the final line between neurosis and psychosis, arguing that the former is characterised by a conflict within the subject, i.e. between the ego and the id (the ego represses the drives, submitting to the demands of reality and the super-ego, but the repressed returns as a symptom); psychosis, meanwhile, is a disturbance of the relationship between the ego and the external world: if the super-ego, an internal representation of reality, is underdeveloped or weakened, then the relationship between the ego and reality is ruptured, leaving the ego to be controlled by the id. The goal of the delusional stage is to rebuild the external world, but this time in a way that

37 One of the many works in which Bychowski refers to Bleuler's "Dementia praecox oder Gruppe der Schizophrenien" (1912) is his article "Schizofrenia".

38 On projection see also G. Bychowski, "O projekcji", *RPS* 1930, no. 12, pp. 137–146.

mirrors the desires of the id. That which has been negated returns – not in form of a symptom (as in the case with neurosis), however, but as if from outside. Despite subsequent efforts to establish a link with the outside world, in psychosis the subject remains at the developmental stage of narcissism, where the boundary between the ego and the external world, between desire and reality, is still unclear. Male homoerotic desire, too, is but a narcissistic projection: the psychotic patient is turned exclusively towards himself, his own body is his only love object, he cannot transfer his libido to another person.

Examining Freud's article in the light of the latest findings in psychoanalysis, Bychowski concludes that in the case of schizophrenia the ego loses control over the id. The suspension of sublimation and the weakening of the ideal ego result in the super-ego ceasing to pose an obstacle to the drives, which surface in their primary and brutal form: "blind urges begin to take the upper hand and liberate themselves from the psychic hierarchy that had been imposed on them."[39] Seen from this perspective, projection becomes one of the ego's defence mechanisms against the id's unshackled drives. Similarly, the patient's construction of a new reality within a system of delusions and hallucinations – a reality that disregards objective truth – results from the id's desires taking over, and yet it can be understood as a desperate attempt at self-healing, of retrieving reality: the disturbed relationship between consciousness and the outside world causes the patient to rebuild or create, on their own, the reality they had lost. Bychowski follows Freud when he argues that the tendency to be healthy, an expression of the desire to regain reality, also accounts for "the frequent transposition of personal conflicts onto the most general arena".

The most interesting aspect of this publication is that Bychowski highlights the social dimension of Schreber's and other psychotics' alleged homosexuality – a dimension that Freud had overlooked, as several interpreters have pointed out:[40]

> It is only the schizophrenic process with its abolition of suppression and sublimation that makes us irrefutably aware of the great significance of

39 G. Bychowski, "Schizofrenia", p. 70.

40 E. Kosofsky Sedgwick, *Between Men: English Literature and Male Homosocial Desire* (New York: Columbia University Press, 1985). Cf. T. Kaliściak, "Psychotyczny romans Paula Daniela Schrebera: Między psychoanalizą a teorią queer", in *Wokół Freuda i Lacana: Interpretacje psychoanalityczne*, pp. 70–84.

> sexual relations, which, being sublimated and inhibited in terms of their goal, consist to a large degree of bonds of friendship, family, community and society. Naturally, the super-ego contains significant parts of this sublimated homosexual libido. The disintegration of the super-ego leads [...] to its regression back to concrete sources – principally the voices of parents and educators who have imposed certain norms, thus restraining the child's urges – sources with which the child used to be linked through homosexual bonds. These bonds now come to the fore and, projected outside they converge to form delusions of persecution. In this way all of the person's social bonds fall apart, and in their place appears fear, i.e. delusions of persecution, where sublimated homoerotic desires, reduced to their original level, are projected.[41]

For researchers today there is no doubt that Freud's Schreber case illustrates the mechanisms of homophobia and " has everything to do with the foregrounding [...] of intense male homosocial desire as at once the most compulsory and the most prohibited of social bonds".[42] Bychowski relates the disintegration of social norms to the disintegration of logical ones and to the type of schizophrenic reasoning that echoes magical thinking. The exposure of primary layers of the psyche also results in "spontaneous operating with symbolism as a self-motivated return to the ancient tongue of the unconscious".[43] In Bychowski's view, narcissism, with its undifferentiated blurring of boundaries between the ego and external reality, associates schizophrenia with magical thinking, based on the identification of words and things as well as a complete arbitrariness of association. Here he returns to the argumentation proposed in his monograph on metaphysics and schizophrenia, where a key chapter explores the same question.

During his time in Warsaw Bychowski was also interested in drug rehabilitation, which tends to activate psychoses.[44] The increase in substance dependence, esp. relating to morphine and cocaine, is, in his view,

---

41 G. Bychowski, "Schizofrenia", pp. 73–74.

42 Eve Kosofsky Sedgwick, *Epistemology of the Closet* (Berkeley: University of California Press, 1990), p. 187.

43 G. Bychowski, "Schizofrenia w świetle psychoanalizy", p. 71.

44 G. Bychowski, "O zaburzeniach psychicznych i nerwowych w demorfinizacji", in *Księga jubileuszowa Edwarda Flataua*, ed. by M. Bornsztajn et al. (Warsaw Gebethner i Wolff, 1929), pp. 738–753; G. Bychowski, "Współczesny stan nauki o morfinizmie", *WCL* 1927, no. 19, pp. 625–630.

one of the negative outcomes of the war: He refers to statistics from Budapest indicating that the number of regular users of morphine doubled during the war and then doubled again over the next few years. Morphine is able to provide a short respite from feelings of guilt, shame and regret; it alleviates pain and gives the user a sense of being able to overcome their difficulties. One of his patients, for instance, was an officer of the Polish Army accused of spying for Russia; he was suspended from the military and put into detention. This man lost his social position and his closest family, who turned away from him. Having no one to count on for support, his only refuge was morphine. Bychowski highlights the possibility offered by psychoanalysis to address the cause, not just the symptom, of morphine addiction. Curing the habit without getting rid of the underlying psychoneurosis, which the addict is trying to neutralise with the drug, will, earlier or later, result in relapse. Only by changing the foundation on which the addiction had developed can there be hope for lasting effects.

For a short while Bychowski also published on topics that intersect with sexology, but these articles tend to be less accomplished. Examples include "Klinika i terapia zaburzeń czynnościowych potencji" [Diagnosis and Therapy of Functional Potency Disorders] and "Klinika i terapia dyspareunji" [Diagnosis and Therapy of Dyspareunia].[45] The latter in particular appears anachronistic and all but misogynistic, especially when we bear in mind Helene Deutsch's work, which appeared before Bychowski's studies and must have been known to him. In this paper, which he read at the Warsaw Gynaecological Society (Warszawskie Towarzystwo Ginekologiczne) in March 1930, Bychowski distinguishes between dyspaurenia (then defined as a lack of satisfaction during sexual intercourse) and frigidity (a lack of sexual desire) and proposes that "both these disorders are often relative and only represent an exaggerated version of normal sexual reluctance, which is proper to women in general" (p. 660). He also presents the example of a patient whom psychoanalysis cured of frigidity, rooted in her negation of her own femininity and her secret desire to be a man.

45 G. Bychowski, "Klinika i terapia zaburzeń czynnościowych potencji", *WCL* 1930, no. 43, pp. 997–1002 and G. Bychowski, "Klinika i terapia dyspareunji", *GP* 1930, vol. 9, no. 10–12, pp. 656–669.

Psyche and soma

The relationship between *psyche* and *soma* was a topic that Bychowski treated in a separate article in *Warszawskie Czasopismo Lekarskie* a few years later.[46] In his opinion, the history of medicine illustrates the rhythm of Hegelian dialectics: the materialist trend can be seen as the thesis; the antithesis is represented by the spiritualists. The era of synthesis – where the psycho-physical personality is viewed as a whole – was launched by Gustav Fechner and his concept of psycho-physical parallelism; it was later developed by Bernheim and Charcot, and, finally, Freud. Bychowski juxtaposes the history of philosophy with the empirical sciences to demonstrate that "what philosophers have been working on for centuries – the independence, self-sufficiency and realness of the psyche – is now, admittedly in a different form, stripped of its metaphysical veils and comes to preoccupy modern scientists" (p. 723). In Bychowski's view, psychoanalysis has helped bridge the gap between philosophy and the natural sciences, even if Freud is wary of going beyond his usual inquiries and always remains careful and self-critical when it comes to philosophical speculation. All in all, Bychowski concludes, psychoanalysis is a metaphysical system because it identifies the drives it has discovered in all living matter, presenting the sexual drive and the death drive as governing all life processes and ascribing libido to every "germ cell" (*ibid.*).

Bychowski also explores the convergence between contemporary philosophy and the life sciences in his article "Patologia mózgowa a architektonika świata" [Brain Pathology and the Architecture of the World] in *Neurologia Polska.* "The most interesting and perhaps most important moments in the history of science," he proposes, are those where different disciplines intersect, for such moments shed light on "the most essential truths of reality".[47] This can be seen, for example, in research in brain pathology, which offers diagnoses that confirm the essential tenets of psychology, logic and what Bychowski calls philosophical anthropology. In his own clinical work he observed that some of his patients suffered from a

46 G. Bychowski, "Psyche i soma", *WCL* 1933, no. 35–36, pp. 723–732. Bychowski first discussed this subject in "O psychoterapii nerwic narządowych", *WCL* 1930, no. 23, pp. 537–540.

47 G. Bychowski, "Patologia mózgowa a architektonika świata", *NPL* 1937, vol. 20, no. 2–3, p. 340.

troubled sense of geometry, struggling to describing the size and shape of objects, others were diagnosed with disorders of categorical perception as defined by Kurt Goldstein.[48] These problems are related to pathological changes in the brain. Bychowski cites a series of studies that corroborate his thesis – studies that essentially suggest a link between spatiality and thought processes in general.

Bychowski's understanding of the analogies outlined here was due to what he describes as a fortunate coincidence, namely his encounter with a book by the philosopher Benedykt Bornstein'. Bornstein was mostly known as an expert on Kant and the Polish translator of Kant's *Critique of Practical Reason*; he was also the author of an original concept of scientific metaphysics, along with a mathematical theory of absolute principles and their panlogic.[49] Bychowski was probably made aware of his work by his colleague, Maurycy Bornstein, the philosopher's brother. Of all of Bornstein's publications, Bychowski was most most impressed with *Architektonika świata* [Architecture of the World], a three-volume study published between 1934 and 1936. Here Bornstein argues that the instinctive tendency to use spatial metaphors, especially when it comes to the language of logic, indicates that the world of concepts and the spatial world share one foundation. Bychowski summarises this argument in his study on brain pathology, proposing that there exists "an architectonic kinship between the world of sense-perception and the world of thought, sensuousness and reason".[50] For Bychowski, the idea that physical space is governed by the same laws as mental space is Bornstein's most important discovery. He cites the philosopher: "The laws of thinking are the laws of objects, while the laws of objects are the laws of our thinking, for the one and the other are the laws of the world whose categorical scaffolding spans and connects both the realm of the subject and that of the object in itself" (pp. 347–348). Bychowski concludes:

> Our brain [...] is the true substrate for all categoricality. Its basic functions are the source and at the same time [...] the reflection of the architecture of the world. This means that disorders of these functions express them-

48 See G. Bychowski, "O podwójnej genezie i o schemacie ustrojowym zaburzeń psychopatycznych", *NPL* 1932, vol. 15, pp. 46–80.

49 Cf. K. Śleziński, *Filozofia Benedykta Bornsteina oraz wybór i opracowanie niepublikowanych pism* (Katowice: Wydawnictwo Uniwersytetu Śląskiego, 2011), p. 7.

50 G. Bychowski, "Patologia mózgowa", p. 347.

> selves in a variety of disorders of cognitive thought […]. Our brain, as a special part of reality, contains *in nuce* the fundamental laws of that reality, and in its development it reveals these laws – in a way that is painstaking but natural. Illnesses, by way of regression, reduces this recognition – along with the patient's world – to forms that are lower, less differentiated and blurred in structure. (p. 348)[51]

The handbook

In 1928 the publisher Towarzystwo Wydawnicze "Ateneum" issued Bychowski's handbook *Psychoanaliza* [Psychoanalysis] of close to 200 pages. Bychowski begins by arguing that Freudianism is a strictly empirical science. In the introduction he compares recent developments in "the science of the soul" to the progress that "the science of matter" had made in the same few decades. The chapter on metapsychology, titled "Rozwój jaźni" [The Development of the Ego], gives a detailed account of the differences between Freud's two topics.[52] Freud's metapsychology, he insists, is the only aspect of psychoanalysis that is based on speculation rather than empirical studies. For later scholars, Freud's view of the structure of the psychic apparatus, which is not based on any hard evidence, was the radical gesture that led psychoanalysis out of the nineteenth-century paradigm of the natural sciences and established it within the humanities or *Geisteswissenschaften.* Bychowski, however, presents it almost as an accidental slip, a great scientist's momentary whim or intellectual game – at any rate something that has no serious consequences.

It seems that Bychowski was operating on bad faith. He must have been aware of the undeniable consequences of the second topic, introduced in *Beyond the Pleasure Principle* and "The Ego and the Id". Perhaps this is precisely why he seemed so keen to preempt accusations against psychoanalysis as being based on speculation. The fact is that Bychowski

51 Bychowski's article on brain pathology was published in *Neurologia Polska* in 1937, the same year that *Imago* printed an essay on repression by Benedykt Bornstein. B. Bornstein, "Strukturallogischer und ontologischer Aspekt des Freudschen Begriffs der Verdrängung", *I* 1937, no. 3, pp. 371–375.

52 Bychowski translates "das Ich" [the ego], "das Es" [the id] and "das Über-Ich" [the super-ego] as "ja", "ono" i „ponadjaźń", also spelled as "ponad-jaźń" or "ponad jaźń"; he applies this terminology consistently across his works.

was at the time hoping to obtain a lectureship in psychiatry, but his strong interest in philosophy may have compromised his candidacy. Perhaps he was essentially trying to defended himself by making a public credo as a scientist. Ironically, the publication of *Psychoanaliza* established his reputation not as an objective researcher but as an orthodox Freudian. His name is mentioned, for instance, in an article titled "O współpracę psychoanalizy i psychologii" [On the Collaboration of Psychoanalysis and Psychology] in *Polskie Archiwum Psychologii*; the author, G. Jampoler, portrays the Freudians as a sect that refuses scientific criticism and debate:

> For very many psychoanalysts, Freud's theory is not a scientific system built on hypotheses, one that calls for vigilant criticism and constant empirical verification, but a faith and a world view as well as an irrational conviction that Freud's theory reveals the last secrets of the human soul [...].

Jampoler adds in a footnote citing Bychowski's book: "The author repeatedly claims that Freudism is not a faith or conviction, but the book itself tells a different story...".[53]

Bychowski's *Psychoanaliza* provided Polish readers with a competent discussion of psychoanalysis in its historical development. He could not have taken into account later publications, such as *Civilisation and Its Discontents*, which appeared in German in 1930, or *Moses and Monotheism* of 1939, otherwise the book could still be used as a solid outline of Freud's oeuvre. Bychowski does in fact restrict his study to "classic" Freudianism, completely ignoring other branches of psychoanalysis. He begins with the roots of psychoanalysis, which reach back to French studies on hypnotism, but in subsequent chapters he lets go of this strictly chronological approach. This decision greatly benefits the clarity of his argument, allowing him to present information in a way that lets readers construct the edifice of psychoanalysis brick by brick. First he introduces comparatively accessible elements, such as the psychopathology of everyday life and the interpretation of dreams, which he discusses at length to familiarise readers with the psychoanalytical method of interpretation. The next few chapters deal with the controversial foundations of Freud's discoveries, i.e. the theory of sexuality. Finally, he outlines the practical fields in which psychoanalysis can be applied – clinical psychiatry and other branches of schol-

53 G. Jampoler, "O współpracę psychoanalizy i psychologii", *PAP* 1930, vol. 3, no. 2, p. 130.

arship and culture. Bychowski stresses that psychoanalysis is not characterised by its object but by its method: "the existence of unconscious psychic phenomena as the most general postulate of the new psychology allows us to apply psychoanalysis to all the disciplines where the psyche represents the ultimate substrate of creativity and action" (p. 174), be it in the sphere of collective creativity (myths, fairy tales, legends) or in individual creativity (literature, art, music). He also reminds readers of his own field of interest, i.e. the intersection of psychoanalysis and philosophy:

> Disregarding the horror of logicians and antipsychologists, we must also consider logical categories to have evolved and to have their own history. Studies on pathological thinking indicate a disintegration of logical categories, and by way of comparison with primordial forms of thinking they allow us to draw certain conclusions about their historical and individual development. (p. 177)

Similarly, Bychowski sees metaphysical systems, "independently of their objective value," as products of the psyche that "must reflect their creators' hidden inclinations" (*ibid.*).

Bychowski's exposition is in fact a faithful representation of Freud's work. His only original contributions are the four chapters on sexuality. Filling one third of the book, these chapters discuss the different implications of Freud's argument about the significance of sexuality. Bychowski does not explicitly mention the widespread accusations of Freud's "pansexualism," but this part of the book can be read as a defence of psychoanalysis.

Bychowski concedes that "psychoanalytical truth" clashes with "certain habits of our thinking," that it may expose "deep-seated prejudice," prudery and hypocrisy, which is "something we all share, to some extent, belonging to certain social and cultural groups" (p. 2). Bychowski defends Freudianism by stressing that its intention is not to destroy but to examine. "Those who worry that the authorities and ideals of family life are being uprooted should be reminded that science never determines values and that understanding can only contribute to raising ethics to a higher level" (pp. 2-3). He reassures his readers that in his discussion of delicate subjects he is as discreet as possible, but he also adds the disclaimer that his book is certainly "not intended for young ladies" (p. 2). He outlines Freud's theory of sexuality, including the subsequent stages of childhood sexuality, young children's "polymorphous perversity" (p. 62) and the initial bisexual "disposition of every individual" (p. 59) of either sex. In the following chapters he gives a detailed account of the concept of libido (it is worth saying that Bychowski never uses the Polish translation of the term proposed by Jekels and Albiński, i.e. *chuć*). One chapter is titled "Popędy i ich losy" [The drives and their destiny]. The wording echoes Freud's "Triebe und Triebschicksale" (1915) – literally translatable as "the drives and their destiny," although the article appeared in English as "Instincts and their Vicissitudes" (SE XIV). While Freud's article introduces a distinction between self-preserving drives and sexual ones, however, Bychowski summarises *Beyond the Pleasure Principle* in this chapter, acquainting Polish readers with the concept of "repetition compulsion" and the related distinction between life drives and death drives:

> The final end of the life of an organism is death, which is at the same time the state, as we must imagine, that had preceded the formation of living matter in the universe. Thus life strives to return to the preceding state, and the drives that are focused on the centre of the living being – the ego-drives – merit to be called death drives [...]. There is no doubt that the drives of the ego, characterised in this way, would soon lead to the extinction of all life, were it not for the counterweight they find in the form of sexual drives. These strive towards life and extend it even when the individual perishes, ensuring the immortality of the species [...].
> Biological speculation, i.e. the consideration of single-cell organisms, which find a means to rejuvenate themselves and to extend their life through copulation (the sexual act), as well as the study of multi-cell organisms which have certainly evolved through the merging of individual single-cell organisms, leads Freud to broaden the notion of sexual drives to the field of biology most generally speaking. Freud imagines that it is the components of the libido of individual cells that constitute the glue between these elements of the organism, and besides, in their entirety they constitute the libido of the individual as a whole. Thus the libido – as the entirety of sexual drives – is more akin to Plato's Eros, the lord of Gods and humans, the creator and bearer of life. (p. 80)

For Bychowski, this concept is essentially metaphysical. He insists that Freud, himself "an enemy of metaphysics" (*ibid.*), is also aware of this, and that for him this was simply an attempt to develop certain premises to see where they would lead. "Hence it goes without saying that we, too, have cited this whole concept not as a collection of facts or theories but only as a highly interesting speculation, as the great empiricist's only metaphysical digression" (*ibid.*).

The last chapter in this section is titled "Z psychologii miłości" [On the Psychology of Love]. Love represents for Bychowski not only the sum of the drives discussed before but "the expression of the entire individual's orientation," which "to some extent reflects all of their predispositions" (p. 90). There is something compulsive about infatuation, which brings to mind neurotic obsessions, while the choice of an object mirrors the earliest fixation of the given subject's libido. For instance, an attachment to the breast (a fixation in the oral phase) can result in "choosing a love object by leaning on the beloved person, just as a child leans on the mother" (p. 91); it also entails the typical overvaluation of the object, which Bychowski relates to a transference of the subject's own narcissism onto the love object. He most often observes this type of love in men and proposes that women rather tend to attribute special importance to themselves, without transferring their libido to the love object: they desire not to love but to be loved. Bychowski explores the different development of boys and girls as they reach the Oedipal phase and sexual difference begins to play a role. (He cites Helene Deutsch on female sexuality.) He also presents a few common types from works of literature: Don Juan (this type, Bychowski suggests, results from a revolt against the father and his prohibition of sexual freedom on the one hand, and an idealisation of the mother and a search for a pure, almost saintly, girl who is put on a pedestal until she is seduced, which makes her completely uninteresting); the type of woman who is not reconciled to her destiny, who plays out a masculinity complex by seeking revenge against all men (Friedrich Hebbel's tragic heroine Judith) or who treats men as no more than inseminators, viewing the child as "the fantastic substitute for her own thwarted but sublimated masculinity" (p. 106) (Annette in Romain Rolland's *The Soul Enchanted*), and finally the girl who is rejected by her father and therefore "goes from her habitual modesty to fantasising about exhibitionism and prostitution" (p. 107), such as Arthur Schnitzler's Fräulein Else or Victor Margueritte's Monique in *The Bachelor Girl.*

In his conclusion Bychowski repeats that psychoanalysis has left its original field, the treatment of nervous disorders, and begun to cover almost all disciplines of the pure and applied sciences, which may create the impression that it was becoming a philosophy or world view. However, he insists, it would be misguided to treat various writers' "far-reaching metaphysical and historiosophic speculations" as an integral part of psychoanalysis – they are no more than "interesting products of personal fantasy". Psychoanalysis is based on two ideals: love of truth and great courage. Like every other science, "psychoanalysis is a wanderer who chooses a moment of light and certainty over whole centuries of illusion" (p. 178); what distinguishes it from other disciplines is that its adepts must be ready to "rise above themselves in a major way by exploring their own weaknesses and destroying the delusions that everyone holds about themselves" (*ibid.*). Freud has proven that the human psyche and culture have developed out of blind and primitive drives. This is one of humanity's "narcissistic wounds," similar to the ones inflicted by Copernicus and later Darwin, but for Bychowski, "our disappointments contain the source of a new contentment of a higher order" (*ibid.*). He predicts that psychoanalysis will help create a new and wonderful world:

> Knowing the hidden foundations of our psyche and culture we are in a better position to cleanse them of the inclinations that go against the latter, it helps us construct them in a better and more conscious way. Rather than repressing ambiguous drives that are secretly amassing explosive material against our culture and society, we would be better off knowing them and assessing them rationally, trying to harness them to different goals. After all, anyone who looks at our history must be shocked at the great predominance of irrational, destructive and inhumane episodes. Who knows if a dissemination of psychoanalytical understanding across and throughout humanity would not, one day, transform the sort of human we have today? […] When psychoanalytical understanding reaches broader social strata it might turn out that people are able to cope with their own drives, without taking recourse to pathological solutions. This is when psychoanalysis would eradicate neurosis, i.e. its original object of study. (pp. 179–180)

Psychoanalysis in jurisdiction and education

Bychowski sees his own book as a contribution to the psychoanalytical conquest of the world. Considering possible obstacles he writes that "psychoanalysis requires a certain mental fortitude that we cannot demand of just anybody" (p. 180); what is more, psychoanalysis entails a number of sacrifices. This path towards self-knowledge will probably be reserved for outstanding individuals. It comes as no surprise that in his final sentence Bychowski refers to Nietzsche's remark that the person who has climbed the mountain tops and breathed the pure, rarified air will not miss the agreeable atmosphere of the lowlands. This is especially true, Bychowski adds, "since in this more rarefied and purer air everything appears brighter and clearer" (*ibid.*). The role of the psychoanalyst who has experienced such enlightenment is not merely to disseminate this knowledge but also to apply his abilities helping people who will never attain similar heights, who are in some sense weaker or disadvantaged. Here Bychowski mentions Freudianism's significance in the fields of pedagogy and criminology, which would become his main preoccupation in the 1930s.

For a long time Bychowski was preoccupied with the question whether psychoanalysis, which required a lively intelligence on the part of the patient, could also be applied to individuals who were either mentally retarded in some way or simply uneducated. In 1928 *Warszawskie Czasopismo Lekarskie* published his article "W sprawie psychoterapii osobników małointeligentnych" [On the Psychotherapy of Simple-Minded Individuals]. Here he argues that to turn down such patients would put medical doctors in conflict with their calling. The profession's duty was to modify and adjust its methods to such cases. For Bychowski this was a matter of great social significance, for the proportion of neurotics in the underprivileged classes was significantly higher than those in the so-called higher social strata. In his view, the conditions that were necessary to accept a patient were the basic ability to think and to understand explanations. The analysand must fathom the psychological relationship between cause and effect. In cases where this ability is absent, the analyst may begin by elucidating certain psychological concepts, presenting them through metaphors and with simple examples from everyday life. The most difficult cases, Bychowski argues, are those where the patient cannot even imagine a therapy that departs from traditional pharmacology or treatments using specialised equipment. In these cases the anchor point to start a psychotherapy is missing. He admits that as an analyst he is helpless in such situations: before the actual cure can begin, the patient ought to go through a process of "education and awareness-raising" – a process that should also include the patient's social environment, so that the influences that affect the patient would not paralyse the practitioner's efforts. This would, however, draw out the therapy and make it even more expensive. Hence, Bychowski concludes (and here he echoes Freud's presentation at the congress in Budapest), psychoanalysis can only be made accessible to the lower social classes within state-sponsored institutions.

> Viewing the conditions in our country from this perspective, we will realise that we absolutely cannot manage to deal with such neurotics, especially ones from the provinces. It is evident: they are suited neither for the closed psychiatric ward nor for the neurological one, where the doctor expects to work with organic problems and is completely absorbed in them. This indicates the necessity to set up not only psychotherapeutic polyclinics but also special units for neurotics, otherwise the important problem of treating simple-minded people cannot be solved.[54]

Analysts at such clinics would have to modify their methods to a significant degree. The technique ought to be more active, aimed at consolidating transference and the patient accepting an inferior position compared to the doctor's authority. But these efforts will remain fruitless if they are not accompanied by "organising society on a large scale" (p. 555).

Thinking about adapting the methods of psychoanalysis, Bychowski was also aware that the problem of mental health among the working classes required a massive effort in the field of social work. This led him to collaborate with the journal *Szkoła Specjalna*, published under the auspices of the special education department of the Association of Polish Primary School Teachers (Związek Polskiego Nauczycielstwa Szkół Powszechnych). Founded by Maria Grzegorzewska in 1924, the journal was dedicated to special-needs education and teaching. One regular contributor was Janusz Korczak – almost every issue featured one of his texts. In the early 1930s, *Szkoła Specjalna* published a number of minor studies by Bychowski as well as two lengthy analyses of concrete cases, namely "Psychoterapia wieku dziecięcego" [Psychotherapy of Childhood] and "Psychoterapia w szkole" [Psychotherapy at School].[55] These two articles were also published

54 G. Bychowski, "W sprawie psychoterapii osobników małointeligentnych," p. 554.

55 G. Bychowski, "Psychoterapia wieku dziecięcego", *SZS* 1930–1931, no. 3, pp. 133–147; G. Bychowski, "Psychoterapia w szkole", *SZS* 1930/1931, no. 3, pp. 148–158. The latter was published in German: G. Bychowski, "Schwierigkeiten in der Schule und ihre Psychoterapie", *ZFPP* 1930, no. 11/12, pp. 420–430.

under the title *O psychicznem leczeniu dziecka* [On the Psychological Treatment of Children] as volume 17 of the series "Biblioteka Pedagogiki Leczniczej" [Library of Therapeutic Pedagogy], edited by Grzegorzewska.[56] Bychowski's articles in *Szkoła Specjalna* are remarkable because they mention the work of the Berlin group discussed in the previous part of this book, making Bychowski the only Pole to reference their publications. In his introduction to a piece on childhood anxiety he reports that the latest issue of *Zeitschrift für psychoanalytische Pädagogik* was a special issue on this topic; he cites Freud (*Inhibitions, Symptoms and Anxiety* and his study of Little Hans) and he refers to Stephanie Borstein, Helene Deutsch and Edith Sterba.[57] Bychowski also examines the geometrical sense disorder in oligophrenia.[58] In an article on dyslexia, based on a study of 50 children aged 10–15 from special schools in Warsaw, he refers to Berta Bornstein's "Zur Psychogenese der Pseudodebilität" [On the Psychogenesis of Pseudo-debility].[59]

Bychowski's article "Psychoanaliza na usługach wychowania dzieci moralnie zaniedbanych" [Psychoanalysis in the Education of Morally Neglected Children], also published in *Szkoła Specjalna*, highlights the problem of caring for "children who resist guidance, asocial children who are morally and socially derailed" – an urgent problem in the wake of the Great War, especially in relation to crime prevention. [60] Bychowski cites his earlier article, "Przestępca w świetle psychoanalizy" [The Criminal in the Light of Psychoanalysis]. Published in *Rocznik Psychiatryczny* in 1935, this article explores the notion that from a Freudian point of view, criminal acts are not fundamentally different from any other human behaviour; they are viewed as being different on account of social criteria, but their principal mechanism is the same as in all other activities. Every action, Bychowski explains, corresponds to certain conscious intentions, it serves the attainment of actual goals, but at the same time its function is to relieve drives whose essence may remain unknown to the subject. A criminal act has its own unconscious and deeply hidden motivations, they

56 G. Bychowski, *O psychicznem leczeniu dziecka* (Warsaw: ZPNSP, 1931).

57 G. Bychowski, "O lęku dziecięcym", *SZS* 1933/34, no. 3, pp. 140–152.

58 G. Bychowski, "O zaburzeniach zmysłu geometrycznego w oligofrenii", *SZS* 1934/1935, no. 2–4, pp. 180–183. Cf. Bychowski, "W sprawie powstawania oligofrenii", *HP* 1938, no. 1–2, pp. 80–97.

59 G. Bychowski, "O legastenii", *PAP* 1934/35, vol. 7, no. 3, p. 205.

60 G. Bychowski, "Psychoanaliza na usługach wychowania dzieci moralnie zaniedbanych", *SZS* 1934/1935, no. 2–4, pp. 206–215.

are only covered in conscious rationalisations – apparent motives that conceal their true origin.

Crime can be understood as a formation similar to a pathological symptom: both contain an unconscious inner conflict that demands to be discharged. A criminal personality and mental illness develop in similar ways, namely from trauma during early psychosexual development. As Bychowski argues, a young child's drives disregard objective reality; they even assume a destructive position towards it. This happens as early as the oral phase, when sadistic impulses yearn to absorb the source of satisfaction that is the breast. This experience may already entail the child's first disappointments, which later result in the adult's sense of scarcity or of being handicapped. More significant for the development of a perverse and criminal personality, however, it is the next phase, i.e. the anal-sadistic one, which entails the clearest expression of "the ambivalent relationship with reality, the inclinations to destroy or to completely control the object – characteristic reactions of stubbornness, contrariness and anger that may turn out to be the prototype of the individual's later conflicts with reality". [61] Fixations in this phase are usually related to homosexual inclinations, while a rebellious stance towards all authorities, a disregard for the law and morality may satisfy an unconscious need to stand up to a strict, domineering father.

The pathological nature of some crimes can be gleaned from their irrationality and compulsive repetition. In kleptomania, for instance, the desire for material gain is a secondary motivation, of no consequence as far as the origin of the deed is concerned. The act of stealing conceals an earlier hurt, a lack that demands compensation. Symbolically, the stolen objects make amends. This is not to say that economic and environmental factors are to be ignored, Bychowski argues, but without a previously established criminal nature the person in question would not respond to these influences by breaking the law. This is why to understand crime it is necessary to supplement sociological analysis with a psychological perspective that takes into account the question of drives:

> Only here do we shed a proper light on the possibilities of preventing and treating criminality and moral derailing, especially of minors, and, consequently, on the great social and educational task posed by the very existence of criminality. (p. 31)

61 G. Bychowski, "Przestępca w świetle psychoanalizy", *RPS* 1935, no. 24, p. 33.

External circumstances, Bychowski adds, mesh with factors related to drives, using and amplifying them. To support this argument he refers to Siegfried Bernfeld's article on the predicament of Tantalus:[62]

> [This is] the psychological situation of people who, seeing around them all the nice things life has to offer, are themselves deprived of the possibility to satisfy their most basic needs. Such a situation increases the intensity of the possessive and aggressive urges, especially as they are becoming, to some extent, an echo of the growing aggressiveness of entire human masses. Here the crimes that intensify during economic crises and the cruel acts accompanying revolutionary movements, which erupt during such times, can be seen as a telling illustration.[63]

Before the drives can find their ruthless and antisocial outlet in the form of a crime, the super-ego must first be weakened. It must remain at a primitive stage of development, or it must be shaped under the influence of a demoralised environment, turning into a "criminal super-ego," a normative instance that calls for obedience to the principles of a given criminal group's morality. That said, an overdeveloped super-ego can also lead to criminality. As Freud puts it, these are "criminals from a sense of guilt". Plagued by unspecified remorse that is rooted in the unconscious, they transgress the law in order to hinge their own unbearable sense of guilt to a concrete fact, and to provoke a punishment that will bring them relief. But their disturbed psyche will be soothed only for a time. Without resolving their unconscious conflict, the individual will be liable to repeat the same process. Bychowski points out that in this case a punishment not only fails to discourage criminal activity, but that, conversely, it fosters it: by disciplining a criminal of this type we satisfy their greatest need. This is only one example of how penalties fail to re-educate some criminals. Bychowski goes as far as to suggest that punishment has no justification in ethics in the case of neurotics whose lawbreaking is not goal-oriented and conscious but compulsive and irrational.

Besides neurotic criminals and those who are motivated by a sense of guilt, Bychowski also explores first-time offenders. They are in fact neurotics whose pent-up tensions suddenly find an outlet in a crime. This usually happens when the mechanisms that used to keep their aggressive

62 S. Bernfeld, "Die Tantalussituation", *I* 1931, no. 2, pp. 252–267.

63 G. Bychowski, "Przestępca w świetle psychoanalizy", p. 47.

drives in check have momentarily slackened. The subject's adherence to the moral order may collapse due to an experience of injustice (for instance in the case of a noble bandit avenging the common people). In cases of disappointment in love or thwarted ambition, the offence may be authorised by the ideal ego; corrupted by suffering, it allows a transgression to be committed – allegedly to restore the offended order (e.g. when a cuckolded husband kills his wife, or when a subordinate shoots at an abusive superior). At the same time, "privation, easily experienced as a hurt inflicted by fate, by the state or society," can soothe the ideal ego's tension and allow repressed drives to surface; what is more, the subject's underprivileged situation diminishes their fear of punishment, facilitating criminal behaviour. Bychowski observes that the ability to sublimate drives depends not only on individual factors, such as innate or acquired faculties, but also on the subject's social position and level of prosperity, i.e. their means of legally satisfying their desires.

> Thus it turns out that the economic situation is not only a direct aetiological factor in criminal behaviour, but that, by standing in the way of a proper discharging of aggressive drives on the one hand and by intensifying them on the other, it indirectly reactivates violent attitudes which then find an outlet in crime. (p. 47)

In such cases punishment also fails to have the intended effect. Its severity only alleviates the offender's sense of guilt and confirms their persuasion about society's injustice, thus encouraging further transgressions.

But psychoanalysis not only sheds a new light on the criminal, Bychowski continues. It also illuminates the part of society that judges criminals, so that examining the judge's psychology is as significant for improving the judiciary as examining the pedagogue's psychology is for the enhancement of education (*ibid.*). He stresses that the same drives that lead to crime in some cases also suffuse the rest of society, including the judge (here he quotes Nietzsche's *Thus Spoke Zarathustra*: "And thou, red judge, if thou would say audibly all thou hast done in thought, then would every one cry: 'Away with the nastiness and the virulent reptile!'"[64]). The criminal, Bychowski argues, gives free rein to their drives – drives that other people repress. This offends the moral order which stipulates that

64 F. Nietzsche, *Thus Spake Zarathustra*, trans. by Thomas Common (New York: The Modern Library, 1917), p. 54.

everyone must repress them. This is why the collective psyche demands punishment as a satisfaction and compensation for the gratification usurped by one of its members" (p. 48). To guarantee true justice, the legislator and the judge must rise above public opinion and free themselves of their own complexes. They must certainly not misuse the trial as a legal and legitimised means to discharge their own repressed sadism or to discipline their own transgressive id. The punitive approach does not effectively curb criminality and must therefore be re-examined. Unconscious factors play a role on both sides – the criminals and the society that penalises them – and these irrational factors "thwart the achievement of conscious goals" (p. 49).

Bychowski believes that Freud has paved the way for reforms in education and law, and that psychoanalytical criminology naturally follows the success of psychoanalytical pedagogy. He concedes that in criminal proceedings and medical or legal jurisprudence psychoanalysis must not be harnessed solely to the humanist approach, "aiming to acquit the offender by way of confirming their unconscious motives". It can, however, render an invaluable service in evidentiary hearings, in the assessment of clues, testimonies by witnesses and defendants; it can help assess the conscious ego's role in a crime and shed light on the mechanisms that led to it. "As is the case in any disease, this knowledge will have an impact on the choice of the most suitable measures and may help the legal system avoid futile efforts and disappointments" (p. 51). Bychowski reminds readers of the important role that education plays in warding off both criminality and neurotic disorders, but when it comes to crime prevention he remains optimistic only in relation to juvenile delinquency, and only if more therapeutic and educational centres are established (in a footnote he refers to issues of *Zeitschrift für psychoanalytische Pädagogik* dedicated to therapeutic pedagogy, neglected adolescents and youth crime). In the case of an established neurotic criminal it is hard to redirect asocial drives, to reorganise the system to foster sublimation, which is why to protect the community the only solution may be to commit the person to an asylum, as is done with mental patients who pose a danger to others. A minor, meanwhile, ought to undergo careful psychological and social assessment. Their punishment ought to be free of retaliation or revenge and be determined solely with an eye to improving and reforming the offender's personality.

In "Psychoanaliza na usługach wychowania dzieci moralnie zaniedbanych" [Psychoanalysis and the Education of Morally Neglected Children] Bychowski proposes that psychoanalysts ought to work with paediatric clinics. These could collect and assess factors contributing to young people's criminal behaviour, such as any disadvantages they may face in life, for instance if their material or emotional needs are not being met. A doctor trained in Freudian theory would penetrate deeper than a community nurse:

> After all we cannot remain on the surface and stop with ascertaining this or that peculiarity in the child's character or behaviour. We must examine their basic drives and proclivities, the level of their ego and the structure of the super-ego as the carrier of moral norms. We must understand their development and identify the weak spot where the deviance from the proper path has taken place.[65]

Regarding the promise of psychoanalysis he writes:

> Beyond the aggressive behaviour we will reveal hidden fear or an unconscious provocation meant to bring about punishment; it will also allow us to understand disturbances in the development of the super-ego, be it in the sense of its underdevelopment or splitting or in the sense of a pathological development. [...] We shall bring to light depressions, ambivalences and negativism, sadistic and masochistic inclinations, paranoid attitudes, feelings of guilt and, last but not least – the notorious sense of inferiority. (pp. 208–209)

In an outpatient setting, where the child stays in their own conflict-ridden environment, the only thing that can be done is to strengthen their awareness of how they react and to point to more helpful ways of dealing with a difficult reality. To bring about lasting change in a juvenile's behaviour patterns, they must be placed in a suitable institution, with children of the same age and educators who have undergone psychoanalysis. The best way to prevent further criminality is to instil in these young people a new and strong super-ego. This is why educators should be role models with strong leadership qualities:

> The desire to measure up to [the educator], to earn his affection and recognition, must become an important driving force for overcoming

65 G. Bychowski, "Psychoanaliza na usługach wychowania dzieci moralnie zaniedbanych", p. 208.

> present habits and reactions, a driving force towards socialisation. In this way the educator's personality becomes the basis to correct the super-ego. (p. 215)

Just as the educator must become a new and better parent for the disturbed child, so the whole institution, "imbued with the finest spirit of solidarity and mutual support," must take the place of their family, fostering "a positive attitude to all higher collectives," including the state and society (*ibid.*).

Bychowski was convinced that child psychoanalysis was inextricably linked to education. In his above-mentioned article "Psychoterapia wieku dziecięcego" he writes:

> There can be no child psychotherapy without getting to work on their closest environment, and in some cases the child's whole upbringing must be so radically transformed that it is only possible with a complete change of their surroundings as a whole.[66]

The fact that there were no dedicated institutions of this kind in Poland left Bychowski feeling helpless. He had worked at the paediatric clinic of the Society of the Friends of Children (Towarzystwo Przyjaciół Dzieci); for two years he had also been a full-time psychoanalyst at one of Warsaw's co-educational gymnasiums, where he diagnosed and treated pupils who fell behind academically. In his articles he often refers to his observations there, assuming that case studies "are always more telling than any theoretical deductions" (p. 5). But his work with children never entailed proper analyses that would reach back to unconscious inhibitions acquired very early; these were short-term interventions focused on current internal conflicts, where his role was limited to offering the young patient a psychoanalytical explanation of their behaviour. According to Bychowski, this usually led to a quick and full recovery.

Almost all of Bychowski's articles discussed here are based on his presentations. He was remarkably active as a public speaker, popularising psychoanalysis at the Warsaw Paediatric Society (Warszawskie Towarzystwo Pediatryczne), the Warsaw Philosophical Society (Warszawskie Towarzystwo Filozoficzne), the Józefa Joteyko Psychological Society (Towarzystwo Psychologiczne im. Józefy Joteyko) and the Second Polish

66 G. Bychowski, *O psychicznem leczeniu dziecka*, p. 4.

Conference of Special School Teachers (II Polski Zjazd Nauczycieli Szkół Specjalnych). He also joined the debate on sexual education, which, as we know, was a prominent controversy in the interwar period. Speaking at the Polish Eugenic Society (Polskie Towarzystwo Eugeniczne) in 1930, Bychowski argued for the principle of the golden mean: while not allowing children to do anything and everything, their sexuality should not be stifled. Excessive and compulsive masturbation is as harmful as the parents' strict opposition to this normal human behaviour. The same rule applies to all manifestations of the child's sexual urges. In case of doubt, parents should remember that while "education must endeavour to control [the sex drive] and to adapt it in appropriate ways, it is not to smother or distort it".[67] The only issue where Bychowski takes a more restrictive stance is when it comes to the child witnessing adult sexual behaviour. He bemoans how often children are exposed to such scenes, and "not only in places where living conditions might excuse this, but also in more spacious flats, on account of the adults' ignorance or recklessness". This, he argues, may lead to "a major nervous shock" in the child and may have a lasting impact, predisposing the child for neurosis (p. 6). When it comes to sexual education, Bychowski stresses that – as long as it is done properly – it should prevent the widespread split between emotion and sensuality. This type of sexual education requires a correct assessment of "the value of eroticism in the lives of people," instead of "stifling it with ideals of artificial purity" or "debasing it by [...] identifying it with the excretory functions" (p. 9). In this way, he believes, "we may create the foundations for a healthy, unabashed and noble sexual morality" (*ibid.*).

Two papers – two cultures

Bychowski's ambition was to promote Freudianism beyond the medical profession, but at the same time he avoided joining efforts with the local Jewish press and cultural organisations, which had already established a

67 G. Bychowski, S. Bogdanowicz, *O wychowaniu seksualnem*, Biblioteka Eugeniczna Polskiego Towarzystwa Eugenicznego: X (Warsaw: Polskie Towarzystwo Eugeniczne, 1930), pp. 3–4. Bychowski's section of this book, titled "Zagadnienia wychowania seksualnego" [Issues in Sex Education], appeared at the same time as an article in the eugenic quarterly *Zagadnienia Rasy* [Issues in Race] 1930, no. 9, p. 44. On the involvement of Polish psychiatrists in eugenics see M. Gawin, *Rasa i nowoczesność: Historia polskiego ruchu eugenicznego (1880–1952)* (Warsaw: Neriton, 2003), pp. 265–272.

lively practice in this domain. By the time he returned to Warsaw in 1923, several different platforms had been put in place, although he mentions none of them in his reports from Poland for *Internationale Zeitschrift für Psychoanalyse*. Dr Władysław Matecki, an assistant at the city's Jewish Hospital, was lecturing on psychoanalysis at the Zionist Adult Education Center in Leszno, a district of Warsaw. A psychoanalytical club (Koło Psychoanalityczne) was active at the Jewish Academic Association (Żydowskie Stowarzyszenie Akademickie); lectures in psychoanalysis were also offered at several other associations, such as the Zionist youth organisation "Merkaz Haceirim" and the Jewish Writers' and Journalists' Association (Związek Literatów i Dziennikarzy Żydowskich) at Tłomackie Street 13, a very popular venue that was seen as a Yiddish cultural centre, "a fortress defending the Jews against assimilation".[68] Each of the events at Tłomackie 13 drew a crowd of about three hundred Varsovians (p. 100). Members of this Association, such as Dr Gliksman, who gave regular presentations on Freud, were often invited to teach in provincial Poland. According to one account, they would spend up to half a year on such a mission:

> A Jewish shtetl. Our auditorium. Who was in the audience? Mostly young people. Members of all existing parties. Jewish workers and old maskilim. Many of them mispronounced foreign words, but there were also those who caught errors in the lectures of highly qualified speakers. They all were hungry for knowledge. They believed in the power of words. There was much naivety in this faith. Many of them were well read. A large number were autodidacts with a measure of success in their chosen field. These people would not be fobbed off with just anything. (pp. 55-56)

The arrival of a lecturer was occasion for a day of major celebrations in such a town, although some reports indicate that local rabbis used their sabbath preaching to urge attendees to boycott the lectures. Such an ambivalent atmosphere must have accompanied the lectures on Freud that were given in the towns of Szydłowiec, Gąbiń, Ozorków, Zawichość, Kovel, Łuck, Pińsk or Baranowicze (p. 57). Announcements about these events were regularly published in the column "Kronika Żydowska" in *Nasz Przegląd* [Our Review].[69]

68 Z. Segałowicz, *Tłomackie 13. Wspomnienia o Żydowskim Związku Literatów i Dziennikarzy w Polsce (1919–1939)* (Wrocław: Wydawnictwo Dolnośląskie, 2001), p. 61.

69 Cf. *NPR* 1925, 314, p. 12; *NPR* 1925, 126, p. 8; *NPR* 1925, 306, p. 8; *NPR* 1926, 125, p. 6.

Nasz Przegląd

The Polish-language Zionist daily newspaper *Nasz Przegląd*, founded and edited by Jakub Appenszlak and headquartered in Warsaw, often drew on news provided by the Jewish Telegraphic Agency. It played a special role in promoting Freudianism, particularly in the 1920s, before psychoanalysis became a topic of general interest. In 1926 detailed accounts were published about Freud's seventieth birthday celebrations, including reports about a banquet in his honour in Berlin,[70] about his receiving an honorary citizenship of Vienna,[71] and about his flat in Berggasse being visited by "representatives of international psychoanalytical societies, headed by the English [sic] scholar prof. Jones". They handed over a gift, "a large sum of money," which Freud "pledged to the International Psycho-Analytical Press and the establishment of a laboratory of psychoanalysis".[72] When Freud received the Goethe Prize in 1930, one somewhat pompous title read: "Droga profesora Freuda: Zdobycie sławy wszechświatowej" [Professor Freud's Journey: The Rise to Worldwide Fame].[73] Readers were duly informed that Freud had become an honorary member of both the Austrian Medical Association[74] and of the Royal College of Physicians in London,[75] as well as chair of the International League Against Anti-Semitism.[76] Among the stories considered newsworthy was one about the Austrian government's announcement that Freud was a candidate for a new badge of honour;[77] *Nasz Przegląd* also reported on Freud's visit to Rabindranath Tagore, the Indian poet and philosopher.[78] On the occasion of Freud's seventy-fifth birthday in 1931 the paper announced:

> Almost the entire Austrian press is dedicating detailed articles to Freud as a person and to his scientific achievements. Some papers highlight the fact that Freud has remained a faithful Jew despite the persecution he had to

70 *NPR* 1926, no. 126, p. 4.
71 *NPR* 1926, no. 131, p. 5.
72 *NPR* 1926, no. 132, p. 6.
73 *NPR* 1930, no. 253, p. 5.
74 *NPR* 1931, no. 85, p. 3.
75 *NPR* 1935, no. 162, p. 3.
76 *NPR* 1930, no. 337, p. 4.
77 *NPR* 1930, no. 220, p. 5.
78 *NPR* 1926, no. 301, p. 10.

endure throughout his life on account of his Jewish heritage [...].[79]

Nasz Przegląd also mentions the Freiberg City Council's resolution to put up a commemorative plaque on Freud's birth house.[80] In the years 1938–39, the largest bold letters were used in headlines about alarming developments concerning the octogenarian Freud and his family. The articles covered his state of health ("Dr Freud ciężko chory" [Dr Freud Gravely Ill],[81] "Prof. Zygmunt Freud przebył operację" [Prof. Sigmund Freud Underwent Surgery][82]), but most of them focused on the political situation ("Prof. Zygmunt Freud aresztowany?" [Prof. Sigmund Freud Arrested?][83]). Day by day the paper informed readers about efforts to facilitate Freud's emigration to London and his obtaining British citizenship.[84]

Nasz Przegląd often mentioned Freud as an example, next to Einstein or Bergson, of "Jewish genius". In 1923 the editors wondered why Freud was absent from a ranking of "the twelve most famous Jews in the world" published by the *Jewish Tribune* in New York.[85] Five years later they organised their own poll. The question "who is the pride of Jewry" was answered by 6754 readers. The list, titled "Elita dwunastu najwybitniejszych Żydów współczesnych" [The Elite of the Twelve most Prominent Jews Today], includes Prof. Chaim Weizman, Nahum Sokolow, Albert Einstein, Włodzimierz Żabotyński, Hayim Nahman Bialik, Sholem Asch, Yitzhak Gruenbaum, Herbert Samuel, Baron Edmond Rothschild, Dr Leo Motzkin, Louis Marshall, Menachem Ussishkin. Freud was number 16 on the list, ahead of Martin Buber or Henri Bergson.[86] Another type of ranking was published in 1937, when readers were asked to imagine that fifteen Jews living at the time should come alive again a few thousand years later. In the field of mathematics it was Einstein who was deemed worthy of resurrection; in philosophy it was Bergson and in psychology, unsurprisingly, Freud.[87] *Nasz Przegląd* also published a detailed review of Abraham A. Roback's book *Jewish Influence in Modern Thought*, where

79 *NPR* 1931, no. 127, p. 4.
80 *NPR* 1931, no. 240, p. 5.
81 *NPR* 1939, no. 215, p. 4.
82 *NPR* 1938, no. 254, p. 4.
83 *NPR* 1938, no. 78, p. 7; *NPR* 1938, no. 87, p. 5.
84 *NPR* 1939, no. 190, p. 5.
85 *NPR* 1923, no. 187, p. 2.
86 *NPR* 1928, no. 1, p. 6.
87 *NPR* 1937, no. 76, p. 17.

Freud, as the reviewer puts it, is presented as "Hasidic in terms of his approach to the human soul".[88]

The newspaper's strategy is a prime example of the classic contribution narrative. From the late nineteenth to the mid-twentieth century, a popular response to anti-Semitic claims that Jews could never fully integrate into Western societies was to emphasise how much they had already done to advance them. Many Jews resorted to this discourse especially after the Nazis came to power in Germany. Jewish historian Moshe Rosman writes:

> This "contribution discourse" appeared after the formal success of the Jewish political emancipation project, and the incubation of a high degree of Jewish acculturation to general European values and lifestyles. It was a sign of Jewish unease, frustration, and fear in the face of indicators that, despite Jews' "good faith" efforts to conform to the legal, social, and cultural demands of the emancipating societies, and notwithstanding legal guarantees of civil and political equality, their integration was in reality but partial, contingent, tenuous, and even revocable.[89]

These attempts to draw attention to their own value were intended to confirm the Jews' status as full members of society. In an opinion piece titled "Między wierszami" [Between the Lines] the editor-in-chief, Jakub Appenszlak (pen name "Pierrot") wrote in 1931:

> I believe I shall never understand this mystery, why among the Polish Jewry, this great concentration of three million people, not one of the prominent Jews from outside the nationalist camp has ever publicly confessed his identity and stressed with pride that he is a Jew [...]. I do not remember a single incident where a Polish Jew, having reached the pinnacle of his career, should have declared: "I am proud to be a Jew!" On the contrary! Eminent scholars, artists, writers, prominent lawyers or doctors, high-ranking dignitaries sheepishly conceal their Jewishness or discreetly gloss over it.[90]

---

88 *NPR* 1930, no. 194, p. 6.

89 Moshe Rosman, *How Jewish is Jewish History?* (Oxford: The Litman Library of Jewish Civilisation, 2007), p. 111.

90 *NPR* 1931, no. 256, p. 4.

To furnish counterexamples – of Jews who were open about their identity – the author mentions Einstein and Freud.

Nasz Przegląd also defended Freudianism against opponents such as Charles E. Maylan, the author of *Freuds tragischer Komplex* [Freud's Tragic Complex]. The paper's correspondent in Vienna, Nussenblat, paraphrases Maylan rather bluntly: "the main characteristic of the psychoanalytical science is revenge [...], Freud's battle against the papacy, the symbol of Catholicism!"[91] Attacks on the father of psychoanalysis are further described as resembling "a wretched chapter from the infamous *Protocols of the Elders of Zion*" (*ibid.*). Nussenblat also stresses that Freud's theory, while it is the achievement of a Jew, has a universal appeal:

> Deep down we all look more or less the same. The naked soul makes no distinction between better people, lower and higher, casts and nationalities, it only has its own equal rights in everyone, it knows the lower affects and higher feelings that are common to the human race [...]. (*Ibid.*)

For Nussenblat, this discovery represents Freud's most ingenious revenge against anti-Semites.

Given that *Nasz Przegląd* was a Zionist paper, Freud's political views were no trifling issue for the editors. The possibility of harnessing him and his work to their own goals largely depended on his stance on a Jewish state in Palestine. The editors' anxiety is apparent in their response to a meeting of the Union of German and Austrian Jews (Union deutsch-österreichischer Juden) in Vienna: not only did the organisation resolve to distance itself from Jewish national politics, but a letter from Freud to his B'nai B'rith lodge was discussed in which he is said to have stated: "I have always been a faithful Jew, but I never considered myself a Jewish nationalist. Nationalism can only harm our fellow Jews and this is why I would rather have nothing to do with it".[92] *Nasz Przegląd* quotes this sentence in an article that carries the dramatic title "Prof. Freud przeciwnikiem

91 T. Nussenblat, "Z walki o naukę Zygmunta Freuda", *NPR* 1929, no. 191.

92 *NPR* 1926, no. 147, p. 8. This misleading paraphrase is based on a section whose published English translation reads as follows: "I was myself a Jew, and it has always appeared to me not only undignified, but outright foolish to deny it. What tied me to Jewry was [...] not the faith [...] for I was always an unbeliever [...]. Whenever I have experienced feelings of national exaltation, I have tried to suppress them as disastrous and unfair, frightened by the warning example of those nations among which we Jews live." (*Letters of Sigmund Freud 1873-1939*, pp. 366-367).

żydostwa narodowego" [Prof. Freud Opposes Jewish Nationalism]. Four issues later, however, the editors announce with evident relief that a misunderstanding had occurred; they set it right in an article emphatically titled "Profesor Zygmunt Freud jest żydem narodowym" [Professor Sigmund Freud Identifies with the Jewish Nation]:

> We are told that Prof. Freud is indignant about the misleading comments about his letter to the lodge of B'nai-B'rith which were made at the last meeting of the Union deutsch-österreichischer Juden. Professor Freud has never questioned the idea of a Jewish nation – neither verbally nor in writing. In his letter to the B'nai-B'rith lodge Prof. Freud writes that he considers himself to be a believer in the Jewish nation and even though general nationalism, having been misinterpreted, has harmed many European peoples, for the Jews it still represents a path towards a noble humanitarian pursuit of historical and cultural significance.[93]

Two years later the editors were excited to report that the Jewish Agency was considering Freud as a representative of Austrian Jews.[94] *Nasz Przegląd* made sure to inform readers about the fact that Freud had signed a call by prominent Jews to the friends of Jewish labour efforts in Palestine,[95] and it provided a running commentary on the activities of the Yiddish Scientific Institute (YIVO) in Vilnius (then Wilno), where Freud was a member of the honorary presidium.[96] The paper's contributors were also fond of quoting Lord Balfour's words, uttered during the opening ceremony of the Hebrew University in Jerusalem, that "scholars of international renown will lecture here – Henri Bergson, Albert Einstein, Sigmund Freud and others".[97] In 1935 *Nasz Przegląd* reprinted a telegram that Freud had sent on the occasion of Keren Hayesod's fifteenth anniversary.[98] In 1938 an appeal was published to support Freud's emigration to Palestine, backing up an application that the Palestine section of the Jewish Physicians' Association had made to the Jewish Agency for Palestine.[99] Readers were

93 *NPR* 1926, no. 151, p. 7.
94 *NPR* 1929, no. 62, p. 6.
95 *NPR* 1930, no. 259, p. 3.
96 *NPR* 1930, no. 135, p. 4; *NPR* 1938, no. 357, p. 5 (and *passim*).
97 *NPR* 1925, no. 93, p. 6.
98 *NPR* 1935, no. 316.
99 *NPR* 1938, no. 81, p. 1.

also informed that Freud had signed a petition to increase Jewish immigration to Palestine[100] and that he had assumed the honorary presidency of the Advisory Council of the Jewish Health Research institute.[101]

The editors of *Nasz Przegląd* seemed to be more concerned with sensational stories about Freud than with the actual substance of his theory. Tellingly, misspellings of his name as "Freund" can be found as late as 1925.[102] An unsigned note titled "Dr Zygmunt Freud i jego nowa teoria" [Dr Sigmund Freud and His New Theory] also appeared in 1925. It is shallow and peppered with errors (Charcot appears as Charcaux, Breuer as Bauer) and inaccuracies ("love, i.e. libido"; "Freudian theory has such a broad understanding of sexuality that it covers all kinds of pleasure and satisfaction"[103]). Later the same year we find a superficial discussion of *The Interpretation of Dreams*.[104] In a review of Fritz Wittels' book *Sigmund Freud, His Personality, His Teaching, & His School*[105] the anonymous critic mostly focuses on passages that touch on the Jewish identity of Freud and his followers. The review also reiterates an often repeated anecdote that Freud once told Wittels:

> I must have been about ten or twelve years old when my father began to take me with him on his walks [...]. On one occasion, when he wished to show me that I was living in better times than those of his own youth, he said to me: "When I was a lad I went for a walk one Sabbath through the streets of Freiberg, in my best clothes, and wearing a new fur cap. A Christian came by, knocked my cap into the mud, and cried, 'Jew, get off the pavement!' 'What did you do?' — 'I stepped into the roadway and picked up my cap,' said my father quietly. To me, the boy whose father was leading him by the hand, the conduct of the big strong man seemed anything but heroic. In my imagination, I contrasted the situation with one much more to my taste. I recalled the scene when Hannibal's father

100 *NPR* 1938, no. 355, p. 3.

101 *NPR* 1938, no. 238, p. 3.

102 *NPR* 1925, no. 314, p. 12. *Nasz Przegląd* was known for its sloppy typesetting, which often inspired satire. See J. Rogozik, "*Nasz Przegląd*: Między 'hajntyzmem' a 'mechesyzmem'", *ZP* 1997, no. 3/4, pp. 127–128.

103 *NPR* 1925, no. 98, pp. 4–5.

104 Gl. G-g., "Tłumaczenie snów", *NPR* 1925, no. 255, p. 4.

105 F. Wittels, *Sigmund Freud; der Mann, die Lehre, die Schule* (Leipzig: E.P. Tal & Co., 1924). The English translation titled *Sigmund Freud, His Personality, His Teaching, & His School* was published by Allen & Unwin in London the same year.

> had made his son swear upon the altar eternal hostility to Rome. Thenceforward, Hannibal had a place in my fantasies.[106]

A similar tendency to mythicise Freud's early career can be found in Nussenblat's articles, which also introduce a number of errors ("As a young ophthalmologist Freud was the first to introduce cocaine as an anaesthetic for eye procedures, he wanted to devote himself to a career in research. Despite his talent he found the path closed. He did not want to open it for the price of baptism. Essentially anti-religious, he rejected this proposition, wanting only to act in accordance with the voice of the soul. This experience was decisive for his later development."[107]) As late as 1926, on the occasion of Freud's seventieth birthday, *Nasz Przegląd* published no more than a cursory biographical note:

> Prof. Freud was born in 1856 in Freiberg, Moravia. Within a short timespan Freud became famous with his theory of psychoanalysis, which revolutionised the field of treating mental illness. Freud's book *Psychopathology of Everyday Life* enjoys great popularity. Societies for doctors applying Freud's theory in practice exist in every country across Europe and America. The doctors' associations are united in an international organisation, which has a continual outlet in the *Internationale Zeitschrift für Psychoanalyse*. Freud's doctrine also has many opponents in the academic world.[108]

A year later *Nasz Przegląd* published a translation of a short interview with Freud that had previously appeared in the British and German press. The editors comment that "ever since he noticed and felt on his own skin the edge of anti-Semitism in Germany and Austria, he prefers to call himself Semitic and to feel completely Jewish".[109]

---

106 Fritz Wittels, *Sigmund Freud, His Personality, His Teaching, & His School*, trans. by Eden and Cedar Paul (London: George Allen & Unwin Ltd., 1924), pp. 247-248. See "Uczeń o mistrzu: Dzieło Fr. Wittelsa o Z. Freudzie," *NPR* 1925, no. 211, p. 7.

107 T. Nussenblat, "Z walki o naukę Zygmunta Freuda".

108 *NPR* 1926, no. 126, p. 4.

109 "Wywiad z prof. Freudem", *NPR* 1927, no. 256, p. 12. For the original interview see "Sigmund Freud Confronts the Sphinx: Interview with George Sylvester Viereck", *London Weekly Dispatch*, July 28, 1927. For the German version see "Professor Freud über den Wert des Lebens: Ein Gespräch mit dem großen Gelehrten", *Neue Freie Presse*, 28/08/1928 (Morgenbl.), p. 4.

Gustav Bychowski's name appears only once in *Nasz Przegląd*, namely in 1924: his paper "Sny w świetle teorii Freuda" [Dreams in the Light of Freud's Theory] is discussed in the section "Z sali odczytowej" [From the Lecture Hall].[110] According to Bychowski's reports for *Internationale Zeitschrift für Psychoanalyse*, in the first half of the 1920s he gave introductions to Freudian theory at the Jewish Medical Association (Żydowskie Stowarzyszenie Medyków) and the Jewish Academic Association (Żydowskie Stowarzyszenie Akademickie).[111] Choosing these organisations he may have been swayed by colleagues from the Jewish Hospital who were already active in the field, or by his father, Zygmunt Bychowski. Dr Bychowski senior was a prominent Zionist activist, having taken part, for example, in the First Zionist Congress in Basel; in Warsaw he was a member of the *qahal* (an autonomous governments of Ashkenazi Jews) and the General Council of the Committee to Aid Jews (Rada Naczelna Komitetu Pomocy Żydom); he was chair of the Jewish Anti-Tuberculosis Society (Żydowskie Towarzystwo Przeciwgruźlicze) "Brijus – Zdrowie", he lectured at the Institute for Judaic Studies (Instytut Nauk Judaistycznych), founded the Society for the Study of the Past and Present of Polish Jews (Towarzystwo Badania Przeszłości i Teraźniejszości Żydów Polskich) and was an honorary member of the Jewish students' fraternity "Bethavia".[112] Dr Bychowski junior, meanwhile, did not enter the same circles and – with one exception[113] – refrained from publishing in *Nasz Przegląd*.

Interestingly, the long article that *Nasz Przegląd* published to celebrate Freud's seventieth birthday was not provided by Bychowski but by Roman Markuszewicz, who wrote in the name of "us, psychoanalysts".[114] Markuszewicz's career shows some parallels with Bychowski's. Having completed his medical training in Zurich in 1921, he spent a few years in Vienna, working at Julius Wagner-Jauregg's clinic among others. In 1924 he moved to Warsaw, where he nostrified his degree and began to practice as a neurologist and psychiatrist. Markuszewicz had attended meetings of the VPS (naming Zurich as his permanent residence) in the first few weeks

110 *NPR* 1924, no. 346, p. 3.

111 *IZP* 1927, no. 1, pp. 86–87.

112 P. Szarejko, *Słownik lekarzy polskich XIX wieku*, vol. 3, p. 66.

113 G. Bychowski, "Psychoanaliza antysemityzmu" *NPR* 1932, no. 59, no. 66, no. 69, no 73.

114 R. Markuszewicz, "Zygmunt Freud w 70-letnią rocznicę urodzin", *NPR* 1926, no. 127, p. 7. Markuszewicz published a similar text in *Polska Gazeta Lekarska* (R. Markuszewicz, "Myśl przewodnia psychoanalizy", *PGL* 1926, no. 32–33, pp. 614–615).

of his stay in Vienna, between 23 November 1921 and 18 January 1922. Before this, the *Internationale Zeitschrift für Psychoanalyse* published his short article "Beitrag zum autistischen Denken bei Kindern" [A Contribution to Autistic Thinking in Children].[115] It is unclear if Markuszewicz tried to join the Society in Vienna, if he underwent analysis or attended sessions at the training institute that had been established by then. Be that as it may, the fact that he never received Freud's blessings did not stop him from considering himself a psychoanalyst and running his own practice, as suggested by his published case studies.[116]

Markuszewicz not only wrote an article on the occasion of Freud's birthday in 1926. He also published a short book titled *Psychoanaliza i jej znaczenie lecznicze* [Psychoanalysis and Its Therapeutic Significance] the same year.[117] Preceding Bychowski's *Psychoanaliza* of 1928, this is the first interwar Polish-language textbook on Freudianism. It filled the gap left when the two introductions published in 1912 – Ludwig Jekels' *Szkic psychoanalizy Freuda* [An Outline of Freud's Psychoanalysis] and Tadeusz Jaroszyński's *O metodzie psychoanalitycznej Freuda i jego teorii powstawania nerwic na tle zaburzeń płciowych* [On Freud's Psychoanalytic Method and His Theory of the Formation of Neuroses from Sexual Disorders][118] – had gone out of print. What is more, this new introduction accounts for the latest psychoanalytical concepts, including that of the ego ideal, which Markuszewicz, keen to dismantle the stereotype of Freud's "pansexualism," elucidates with particular care.

Unlike Bychowski, Markuszewicz addressed an audience of medical practitioners (his book was published as an issue of the yearly Warszawski Kalendarz Lekarski). In the introduction he writes that "we have omitted all those issues in psychoanalysis – such as the psychology of the masses, of primeval people, the application of psychoanalysis to other fields of knowledge and science that find themselves in no immediate relationship with our chosen topic".[119] He also includes many observations from his own practice, especially analyses of his patients' dreams and parapraxes.

115 R. Markuszewicz, "Beitrag zum autistischen Denken bei Kindern", *IZP* 1920, 3, 248–252.

116 Cf. e.g. R. Markuszewicz, "Ucieczka do choroby a popęd samozachowawczy", *NP* 1930, no. 1–2, pp. 34–57.

117 R. Markuszewicz, *Psychoanaliza i jej znaczenie lecznicze* (Warsaw: Warszawski Kalendarz Lekarski, 1926).

118 Tadeusz Jaroszyński, *O metodzie psychoanalitycznej Freuda i jego teorya powstawania nerwic na tle zaburzeń płciowych* (Warsaw: Gebethner i Wolff, 1912).

119 R. Markuszewicz, *Psychoanaliza i jej znaczenie lecznicze*, p. 5.

Markuszewicz's early writing on Freud can be described as apologetic, but he becomes more critical over the course of the next decade. In the 1930s, *Kwartalnik Psychologiczny* published two articles in which the Polish neurologist and psychiatrist revises the findings of psychoanalysis. His reservations concern seemingly theoretical issues, such as the conflict between the ego and the sex drive. Markuszewicz does not recognise this conflict as fundamental to the aetiology of neuroses; in his opinion this view contradicts the dynamic notion of human psychology as postulated by psychoanalysis itself.[120] He proposes that the conflict discovered by the Freudian school is in fact secondary and overwrites the infantile antagonism between the urogenital drive and the self-preservation drive. The actual stimulus that triggered Markuszewicz's research, however, was his growing disappointment with psychoanalysis as a therapeutic technique. Looking back at his career many years later, he said that for about a decade he had analysed neurotic patients with the tools of orthodox Freudianism. Discouraged by the results he spent the next seven years working out his own theory, which drew on psychoanalysis but also considered the self-preservation drive next to the sex drive.[121] It is only by addressing the infantile conflict, he suggests, that the secondary conflict can also be resolved and a satisfactory reconciliation between the sex drive and the ego can be achieved; this, in turn, allows for a successful therapy. Despite these many modifications, Markuszewicz remained convinced that he was still a psychoanalyst: "just as the theories of van Leeuwenhoek, the inventor of the microscope, must not be confused with bacteriology, which emerged thanks to this invention, so we must not identify Freudianism with psychoanalysis".[122]

Markuszewicz tried to refute accusations about the therapeutic inefficacy of psychoanalysis even as his own faith in it was shaken, and this is symptomatic of a development across psychiatry in Poland. Doctors were

120 R. Markuszewicz, "Rewizja podstawowego pojęcia freudyzmu", *KPS* 1936, vol. 8, pp. 357–394; "Od sadomasochizmu do popędu śmierci (dalsza rewizja teorii freudowskiej)", *KPS* 1938, vol. 10, no. 1–2, pp. 103–143. Cf. also Markuszewicz, "Wstępny zarys psychopatologii popędu samozachowawczego", *RPS* 1933, no. 21, pp. 233–245.

121 R. Markuszewicz, "O nowy kierunek w psychopatologii", *RPS* 1949, no. 1, p. 23. Having realised – independently of Soviet psychiatry – that living conditions have a great impact on mental health, Markuszewicz proposes that the new trend should be described as socio-biological.

122 R. Markuszewicz, "Rewizja podstawowego pojęcia freudyzmu", p. 394.

struggling to accept Freud's realisation, expressed with growing certainty, that his method does not cure and only addresses the interminable challenge of getting to know oneself. Freud's acknowledged defeat de facto meant that he was leaving the field of science and medicine. Practicing therapists found this difficult to tolerate. If they wanted to consider themselves doctors, they had to believe in the benefits of psychoanalysis – anything less than that would fly in the face of their professional code of conduct and they would be forced to abandon the method. The publication of Freud's *Die endliche und unendliche Analyse* [*Analysis Terminable and Interminable*] in 1937 troubled many practitioners. When Maurycy Bornsztajn discussed the book in *Rocznik Psychiatryczny*, he tried to veil its actual message: Freud's scepticism and his conviction that in the end not every patient can be cured are portrayed as no more than an expression of his rigour and high expectations: the father of psychoanalysis "will not be satisfied with just any temporary success".[123] Bornsztajn must have been aware of Ludwig Jekels' therapeutic nihilism, and yet he insists that none of Freud's students shares the master's radical position. He also states that he himself is much more optimistic and goes so far as to claim that "as long as the problem is tackled skilfully and subtly," every analysis "can be brought to a successful conclusion earlier or later" (p. 42). That said, Bornsztajn's translation of Freud's title, *Die endliche und unendliche Analyse* [*Analysis Terminable and Interminable*], is also quite telling. His Polish version, "Psychoanaliza, która daje się zakończyć i taka, która dłuży się bez końca," means as much as "A Psychoanalysis that Lends Itself to Completion and One that Drags on Forever". Thus he manages to distort the original message even in his rendition of the title. For Markuszewicz, meanwhile, Freud's statement is water to his mill. In the following issue of the same journal he proposes that instead of talking about interminable analyses (*analizy nieskończone*), such cases ought to be treated as not-yet-completed analyses (*analizy niedokończone*). In order to complete them one would only have to consider the infantile conflict between the urogenital drive and the self-preservation drive – his own discovery – and a straightforward path to healing the patient would emerge.[124]

Markuszewicz's article on Freud's birthday in 1926 barely touches on his being a Jew: "Some critics disapproved of Freud's Jewishness as if that

123 M. Bornsztajn, "Uwagi z powodu artykułu Zygmunta Freuda pt. 'Psychoanaliza, która daje się zakończyć i taka, która dłuży się bez końca'", *RPS* 1938, no. 33, p. 38.

124 R. Markuszewicz, "O 'niekończącej się analizie' Freuda", *RPS* 1938, no. 34/35, pp. 185–210.

were a 'scientific' claim: clearly, they had no factual arguments. But the Jews can be proud of this emphasis on the fact that Freud is a Jew."[125] A comparable article printed in *Nasz Przegląd* in 1931, when Freud turned seventy-five, makes a much stronger point of the question of identity. The article in question is signed by Mojżesz Kanfer, one of the paper's editors. Kanfer was a Cracow-based lawyer with a prominent position in the city's Jewish cultural circles: he was literary and theatre critic, founder of the Jewish Theatre Society (Żydowskie Towarzystwo Teatralne) as well as a translator from Yiddish.[126] In his view, "at the source of Freud's work there lies the Jew's eternal longing for good, for the realisation of justice". He continues:

> Freud never severed his bonds with the Jewry, [...] he is currently on the honorary committee of the *Żydowski Instytut Naukowy* [Institute for Jewish Research, YIVO] and a member of the Board of Governors of the Hebrew University. We know that Freud sincerely approves of Zionism, because as a psychologist Freud understands how much health Zionism has brought to the Jewish soul.[127]

Looking back to Markuszewicz's article it is hard to overlook his grandiloquent style. His opening sentence reads: "In humanity's unbridled forward thrust, in our unthinking pursuit of the victories of everyday life – there comes a moment of composure, a longing to see this eternal truth that dwells hidden deep inside us, and not beyond us"; he concludes with the words: "today, paying homage to Freud, we must remember that to live means to love – to love with a love as great as the one with which Freud came to love everything that is human".[128] Kanfer's article, meanwhile, shifts the focus to substantive questions. He explicitly leaves the scientific evaluation of Freud's work to experts and concedes that as a layman he is mostly interested in Freud as a scholar of culture. This is how he paraphrases the lessons he learned from works such as *Civilisation and Its Discontents*, published the previous year:

125 R. Markuszewicz, "Zygmunt Freud w 70-letnią rocznicę urodzin", p. 7.

126 M. Kanfer, "Zygmunt Freud z okazji 75-lecia jego urodzin", *NPR* 1931, no. 127, p. 9. On Kanfer see E. Prokop-Janiec, "Mojżesz Kanfer a teatr jidysz" in *Teatr żydowski w Krakowie*, ed. by J. Michalik and E. Prokop-Janiec (Cracow: UJ, 1995), pp. 125–150.

127 M. Kanfer, "Zygmunt Freud z okazji 75-lecia jego urodzin".

128 R. Markuszewicz, "Zygmunt Freud w 70-letnią rocznicę urodzin".

> Culture is violence done to human instincts, which seek vengeance by generating the sense of unease that dominates in modern people. For centuries Eros and Thanatos – the demon of destruction and the demon of creation – have been engaged in conflict. In order to tame the instincts, to keep them at bay, humanity falls into an illness that can be described as an inflation of values. Just as the person's "ego" is no more than a sort of fiction that serves to subdue the chaos within us – the chaos that we call *das Es* – so there exists a social "super-ego" that is perhaps even crueller than the individual "ego". To maintain the minimum, a person is required to do their maximum. Such a maximum is, for instance, the call to love one's neighbour, which is impossible to realise in practice. Even this minimum is very difficult to exact from ourselves, for the history of humanity is a tribunal which states the grim truth that until now Thanatos has been winning, the demon of destruction has been triumphing. Whether Eros shall one day come to take the upper hand – the old wise man gives us no answer to this urgent question, for he is too decent to give us, longing as we are for a new tomorrow, not the truth but another illusion. (*Ibid.*)

On the same page the editors placed translations of two passages from Freud's *Theoretische Schriften* [Theoretical Writings], published in 1931; these were excerpts from "Group Psychology and the Analysis of the Ego" (on the herd instinct) and from "Formulations on the Two Principles of Mental Functioning" (on the artist). [129] The translator remains unnamed; it is possible that it was Kanfer himself.

In 1936, when Freud turned eighty years old, *Nasz Przegląd* published an article by Władysław Matecki:

> Freud will be named next to the developers of the diphtheria vaccine, insulin, and many other people who devoted their genius to the health of humanity. But it would be inaccurate and unjust to talk about Freud only as the inventor of a new therapeutic method. Today psychoanalysis is something more. When it comes to the mind, psychoanalysis has in a way become a part of the air we all breathe in this day and age. No manifestation of the human spirit can be understood without a thorough psychoanalytic examination.[130]

129 Z. Freud, "Dwie uwagi", *NPR* 1931, no. 127, p. 9.

130 W. Matecki, "Zygmunt Freud (w 80-tą rocznicę urodzin)", *NPR* 1936, no. 134, p. 6.

The editors also printed a Polish version of the birthday wishes that prominent writers sent to Freud by telegram. The signatories included Thomas Mann, Stefan Zweig, Romain Rolland, Jules Romains, H.G. Wells and Virginia Woolf:

> We, the undersigned, who cannot imagine our mental world without Freud's bold lifework, are happy to know that this great man with his unflagging energy is still among us and still working with undiminished strength. May our grateful feelings long accompany the man we venerate.[131]

Most of the articles on psychoanalysis that appeared in *Nasz Przegląd* in the 1930s were written by two contributors. One was Paweł Klinger, sexologist and author of *Vita sexualis: Prawda o życiu płciowym człowieka* [Vita Sexualis: The Truth about Human Sexuality], a bestselling book published in 1930 and reprinted several times. The other was journalist Jakub Bleiberg, who also wrote for other Jewish publications such the monthly *Miesięcznik Żydowski* (its editor-in-chief was Zygmunt Ellenberg) as well as the weekly *Opinia* (later *Nasza Opinia*), the leading periodical for readers interested in Polish-Jewish literature.[132]

Klinger used *Nasz Przegląd* as a platform to write about issues such as childhood sexuality or the hidden meaning of dreams.[133] He also offered a rather unfounded diagnosis of a "crisis in psychoanalysis," which he related, ironically, to its excessive focus on sexuality (in the same article, remarkably, he announces his discovery of a "Jewish complex" in anti-Semites – a result of early childhood trauma).[134] He often draws on the metaphor of a slumbering beast that civilisation has pushed down into the depths of the collective unconscious, but that constantly urges us to satisfy our "self-preservation instinct, hatred, desire for revenge and the destruction of those who stand in our way, sexual lust and violence as well as a wish that others may die, often directed against the people who are closest to us" (*ibid.*). At the same time he emphasises the "morality" of

131 This is the English version as cited by Ernest Jones in *The Life and Work of Sigmund Freud* (New York: Basic Books, 1957), vol. 3, p. 206. Cf. "Hołd pisarzy całego świata dla Zygmunta Freuda", *NPR* 1936, no. 134, p. 6.

132 Cf. E. Prokop-Janiec, *Polish-Jewish Literature in the Interwar Years*, trans. by Abe Shenitzer (Syracuse: Syracuse University Press, 2003), p. 22.

133 P. Klinger, "Seksualizm dzieci", *NPR* 1937, no. 324, p. 19 and "Nie ma snów bez znaczenia", *NPR* 1938, no. 65, p. 18.

134 P. Klinger, "Kryzys psychoanalizy", *NPR* 1938, no. 44, p. 20.

psychoanalysis, whose goal is not to give in to those hidden desires but to become aware of them.[135] Klinger was certain about the prophylactic significance of psychoanalysis, i.e. in sexual education, and he believed that "there will come a time when psychoanalysis will be in the hands of every doctor, no matter what specialisation".[136] Perhaps it was also Klinger who wrote unsigned sexological articles for *Nasz Przegląd*, such as the one on Havelock Ellis as a precursor of Freud,[137] or a detailed study titled "Kwestia seksualna pod kątem klasowym" [The Question of Sexuality from a Class Perspective], discussing Wilhelm Reich's *Der Einbruch der Sexualmoral* [The Invasion of Compulsory Sex-Morality].[138]

Much more interesting are the texts written by Bleiberg, whose focus was on the philosophical implications of psychoanalysis. In an article of 1937 he identifies two extreme trends in contemporary psychology that also entail two different world views and notions of what it means to be human. One is psychoanalysis, popular in Europe, which is based on the hypothesis of unconscious dynamics of the psyche, and the other is behaviourism, which dominates in North America, and which examines only what is accessible to outside observation, i.e. human behaviour and the physiological changes that accompany it. While behaviourism, which posits the possibility of a conscious and voluntary formation of personhood, results from Anglo-Saxon optimism, psychoanalysis believes that we do not even control our own thinking and desires, thus echoing the gloomy spirit of Schopenhauer's philosophy.[139] A year later, Bleiberg explored Goethe's influence on Freud, highlighting "the intellectual kinship between these two ingenious analysts of the human soul" as evidence for "literature's precursory role in providing a scientific explanation of the riddles and mysteries of the psyche".[140] Bleiberg also developed an interest in humanism (he wrote two lengthy philosophical articles on the subject for the popular science journal *Wiedza i Życie*[141]), and this also spilled over

135 P. Klinger, "Nie ma snów bez znaczenia".

136 P. Klinger, "Kryzys psychoanalizy".

137 [Anonymous], "Filozof problemu seksualnego", *NPR* 1929, no. 320, p. 6.

138 [Anonymous], "Kwestia seksualna pod kątem klasowym", *NPR* 1935, no. 76, p. 22.

139 J. Bleiberg, "'Behavioryzm' i freudyzm: Dwa sprzeczne kierunki w dzisiejszej psychologii", *NPR* 1937, no. 366, p. 26.

140 J. Bleiberg, "Wpływ Goethego na Freuda (na marginesie przekładu freudowskiej autobiografii)", *NPR* 1938, no. 177, p. 20.

141 J. Bleiberg, "Typy humanizmu", *WIŻ* 1938, no. 7/8, pp. 454–462, no. 9, pp. 553–561; Bleiberg, "Humanizm jako problem kultury", *WIŻ* 1939, no. 3, pp. 157–160.

into his study of psychoanalysis, leading to another article for *Nasz Przegląd*; this text, titled "Humanizm Freuda" [Freud's Humanism], shall be discussed in more detail later.[142] For Bleiberg, a particularly important achievement of psychoanalysis was that it provided insight into the psychology of creativity. This he assessed more highly than the work of Ernst Kretschmer, who had a broad resonance in interwar Poland and notably inspired writers such as Witkacy and Bolesław Miciński.[143] Perhaps Bleiberg's view of the mature phase of psychoanalysis as "a well-developed field in the humanities"[144] is confirmed in one of the last prewar issues of *Nasz Przegląd*, where Meir Balaban, an eminent historian affiliated with the University of Warsaw, discusses Freud's *Moses and Monotheism*; Balaban does mention, however, that he only took the book seriously because it was written by Freud himself.[145]

In this context the question arises why Bychowski did not become a regular contributor to *Nasz Przegląd*. As a doctor at the Jewish Hospital in Warsaw on a mission to popularise Freudianism, he could easily have used the paper as a platform, drawing affiliated writers into the realisation of his own project. It seems, however, that the ambitious psychiatrist saw the clinic as no more than a stepping stone, a place to start work immediately upon his return to Warsaw. He must have had an easy way in, being a Jewish doctor returning from Vienna with experience at the VPS under his belt, but also by mere association with his father. What we know for sure is that the Jewish Hospital was not his final destination. In the 1930s, when he joined the psychiatric clinic at the University of Warsaw (where he would soon habilitate), he severed his ties with Jewish organisations. The fact that he distanced himself from the people who had facilitated his entry into the profession did not go unnoticed in *Nasz Przegląd*; Władysław Matecki's review of Bychowski's book – although certainly positive – concludes as follows:

> Here we are left to wonder why Dr Bychowski does not mention Freud's followers in Poland [...], who have not only studied specialised psycho-analytical issues but who have also contributed, in

142 J. Bleiberg, "Humanizm Freuda", *NPR* 1938, no. 228, p. 14.

143 J. Bleiberg, "Geniusz przed sądem psychiatrii", *NPR* 1938, no. 277, p. 15.

144 J. Bleiberg, "Humanizm Freuda", p. 14.

145 M. Bałaban, "O pochodzeniu Mojżesza i tradycji proroków hebrajskich (na marginesie najnowszego dzieła Prof. Zygmunta Freuda)", *NPR* 1939, no. 232, p. 13.

writing and in their talks, to popularising psychoanalytical theory in this country.[146]

Besides the known members of the VPS – Ludwig Jekels and Herman Nunberg – Matecki mentions Bychowski's colleagues and rivals in the field of psychoanalysis from the Jewish hospital: Bornsztajn, Markuszewicz, Wizel and himself.

Wiadomości Literackie

Rather than writing for *Nasz Przegląd*, Gustav Bychowski affiliated himself with Mieczysław Grydzewski's weekly *Wiadomości Literackie* [Literary News]. The dynamics between these two outlets, both established in 1924, were marked by rivalry. *Wiadomości Literackie* addressed the assimilated Jewish intelligentsia; for Karol Irzykowski, the journal was "the fortress of ingenious mimicry".[147] It tackled anti-Semitism, mocked the National Democrats' campaigns to uncover artists' "non-Aryan" connections and distanced itself from all forms of racism. At the same time it critiqued the Jewish ghetto as being at odds with European modernity. As one recent scholar puts it, "the newspaper fought on two fronts: it defended as an unalterable axiom the Jews' right to assimilation and the belief in the possibility and appropriateness of their complete Polonisation".[148] Politically, *Wiadomości Literackie* was, at least until the Brest trials of 1931/32, associated with the governing camp, not only through various subventions but also by ties of friendship between the Skamandrites (the experimental poets associated with the monthly *Skamander* but also with *Wiadomości Literackie*) and the Piłsudskiites.[149] In the first issue of *Wiadomości Literackie*, however, the editors insisted that the journal's only "ideology" was to be modernity. They wanted it to be bold and progressive, but also "to participate in the action aimed at toppling the wall that divides us

146 W. Matecki, "Uwagi krytyczne o książce dra G. Bychowskiego pt. *Psychoanaliza*", *NPR* 1928, no. 51, p. 4. A year earlier, the same paper had published Matecki's positive review of Markuszewicz's book (W. Matecki, "Na marginesie książki Dra R. Markuszewicza *Psychoanaliza i jej znaczenie lecznicze*", *NPR* 1927, no. 29, p. 7).

147 K. Irzykowski, "Udział Żydów w literaturze polskiej", in *Pisma rozproszone 1936–1939* (Cracow: Wydawnictwo Literackie 1999), p. 255.

148 Eugenia Prokop-Janiec, *Polish-Jewish Literature*, p. 74.

149 M. Szpakowska, *"Wiadomości Literackie" prawie dla wszystkich*, p. 14 and pp. 365-369.

from the centres of contemporary civilisation".[150] The editors also vowed to be "tenacious and ruthless in shattering all kinds of backwardness, lies, hypocrisy, falsehoods – be they social or artistic".[151]

Nasz Przegląd also saw itself as liberal, modern and European, but at the same time it remained deeply rooted in Jewish culture and identity.[152] Although staunchly Zionist, it was independent of any political party and proudly printed its motto under the title: "An Independent Organ". Its language was Polish, which is why it was criticised by more radical groups, such as the Yiddish *Hajnt*, which saw the choice of the Polish language as no less than a form of national treason; contributors of *Wiadomości Literackie*, meanwhile, could not reconcile the notion of a Polish-language Jewish culture and the promotion of "Jewish nationalism" with their own understanding of universalism.[153] According to one historian, *Wiadomości Literackie* was not too graceful in its attacks on *Nasz Przegląd*:

> The magazine was fond of ridiculing works written in these circles, it published lists of awful Yiddishisms that marred their Polish and mocked their limited, nationalist ideology. Publications of this kind often became the butt of satire in [...] the section of *Wiadomości Literackie* dedicated to the worst book of the month, in Tuwim's satirical rubric *Camera Obscura*, but also in serious book reviews. (p. 83)

Conversely, both *Nasz Przegląd* and *Hajnt* regarded Grydzewski and his milieu as a group of *meches*, converted Jews, "epigones of a compromised ideology".[154]

The rivalry between *Nasz Przegląd* and *Wiadomości Literackie* was bitter. They may have been diametrically opposed in terms of ideology, but in fact they were competing for the same target audience – the wealthy bourgeoisie, Polish-Jewish professionals, the cosmopolitan middle class. There was no clear dividing line between the Jewish milieu associated with the weekly *Wiadomości Literackie* and the readers of the Zionist daily *Nasz*

150 Cf. S. Baliński, "Pierwszy numer *Wiadomości Literackich*", in *XXX-lecie "Wiadomości"*, ed. by T. Terlecki (London: Wiadomości, 1957), p. 21.

151 "Od redakcji", *WL* 1924, no. 1, p. 1.

152 J. Rogozik, "*Nasz Przegląd*: Między 'hajntyzmem' a 'mechesyzmem'" *ZP*, no. 1/2, p. 123.

153 M. Opalska, "*Wiadomości Literackie* – dyskusje nad kwestią żydowską (1924–1939)", *PH* 1990, no. 10, pp. 82–83.

154 E. Prokop-Janiec, *Polish-Jewish Literature*, p. 82.

Przegląd; a handful of writers and critics who contributed to both outlets further blurred the boundary.[155] In many ways, statistics about interwar Warsaw's liberal intelligentsia mirror Steven Beller's findings on Vienna's educated population, referred to in the Introduction. According to Eugenia Prokop-Janiec, 90% of the readers of *Wiadomości Literackie* identified as Jewish; Jews also constituted a similar percentage of patrons of bookshops, theatres and other places of cultural production. Thus it was a Jewish audience that set trends and aesthetic standards in literature and beyond.[156] For contemporary observer Artur Sandauer, "at a time of tremendous increase in Jewish participation in Polish culture, the terms 'Jew' and 'member of the intelligentsia' began to mean one and the same thing,"[157] while, as Małgorzata Szpakowska added, "the phenomenon that anti-Semites called 'Jewification' was really related to urbanisation and its reflection in culture".[158] What traditional Poles saw as "Jewish" was modernity itself (*ibid.*).

Nasz Przegląd had a daily print run of about 50,000.[159] *Wiadomości Literackie* was purchased by some 13,000 to 15,000 readers every week, with a record sales number of 19,000.[160] There was doubtless a significant overlap between readers of the two. In 1932 Antoni Słonimski mocked the paper as "the organ of Polish Jewry," thus pointing to the worries that his own readers – assimilated Jews like himself – may have felt:

> I enjoy reading *Nasz Przegląd* [*Our Review*] occasionally, although buying this paper entails certain difficulties. One slightly tipsy newsagent, when asked for a copy of "our review," handed me the paper while muttering haughtily: "It's not *Our Review* [*Nasz Przegląd*] but *Your Review* [*Wasz Przegląd*]." Since that day I have been making a special trip to the Jewish quarter to get *Their Review* [*Ich Przegląd*], and I buy the paper from a poor Hasid vendor, inquiring politely if they have *Their Very Own Review* [*Swój Przegląd*].[161]

155 M. Opalska, "*Wiadomości Literackie* – dyskusje nad kwestią żydowską", p. 83.

156 E. Prokop-Janiec, *Polish-Jewish Literature*, pp. 78-81.

157 Artur Sandauer, *On the Situation of the Polish Writer of Jewish Descent in the Twentieth Century (it is not I who should have written this Study...)*, trans. by Abe and Sarah Shenitzer (Jerusalem: The Hebrew University Magnes Press, 2005), p. 57.

158 M. Szpakowska, *"Wiadomości Literackie" prawie dla wszystkich*, p. 246.

159 J. Rogozik, "*Nasz Przegląd*: Między 'hajntyzmem' a 'mechesyzmem' " *ZP*, no. 3/4, pp. 125–126.

160 M. Szpakowska, *"Wiadomości Literackie" prawie dla wszystkich*, p. 11.

161 as. [A. Słonimski], "Wyczyn seksualny", *WL* 1932, no. 46, p. 5.

It was a strategic decision for Bychowski to associate with *Wiadomości Literackie*. It must have been clear for him that the weekly, which had rapidly become the most popular and influential publication on cultural and social matters, was a better platform to popularise Freudianism than the Jews' "very own" daily, which addressed a more narrowly defined group. Bychowski, recently returned from Vienna, must have seen *Wiadomości Literackie* as an equivalent of *Neue Freie Presse*, a paper edited by Jews and read mostly by the Jewish middle class that simply did not see itself as a "Jewish organ". If anything, it was proof of the Jews' perfect assimilation to Austrian culture.

Just as *Nasz Przegląd*, *Wiadomości Literackie* engaged with psychoanalysis from the outset. In the 1920s, when the journal still had a strictly literary or scholarly profile,[162] the introduction of Freudian themes was entirely due to Gustav Bychowski. Reserving his articles on psychiatry for specialist journals, he regularly contributed literary critical articles to *Wiadomości Literackie*, using Freudian theory to analyse books as well as their authors. Within the first year since the weekly's establishment he reviewed Fernand Crommelynck's play *The Magnificent Cuckold* [*Le Cocu magnifique* or *Rogacz wspaniały* in Polish], which he deemed to be "a masterpiece of psychological art". His review opens with a disclaimer:

> It is imprudent to try and elucidate Crommelynck's play from the point of view of psychoanalysis in a non-specialist journal. But the author's rare psychological depth in this simply unparalleled piece, the uncannily clear light that he sheds right into the most hidden corners of the soul, and finally the incomprehensibility of the play for a spectator who is not used to thinking in psychological terms – all this inclines me to give it a go.[163]

Bychowski begins by discussing the protagonist's feelings about his lover – his fear of losing her and his pathological jealousy, which conceals a desire to share her with other men, as well as the role of homoerotic desire in these dynamics. He draws on Freud's famous formulation from the Schreber case, "it is not I who love the man – she loves him,"[164] but also notes that a similar motive appears in other works of literature, such as

162 M. Szpakowska, *"Wiadomości Literackie" prawie dla wszystkich*, p. 59.

163 G. Bychowski, "'Rogacz wspaniały' w świetle psychoanalizy", *WL* 1924, no. 14, p. 2.

164 Cf. S. Freud, "Psycho-Analytic Notes on an Autobiographical Account of a Case of Paranoia (Dementia Paranoides)", SE XII, p. 64.

Friedrich Hebbel's *Gyges and His Ring* or André Gide's *Le Roi Candaule* [King Candaules]; it is also found, Bychowski continues, "in everyday eroticism". He concludes as follows:

> Psychoanalysis shows how this particular constellation of eroticism emerges from a transformation of childhood experiences, how the desire to share a woman with a male companion is based on a subconscious attachment to the mother, who, after all, also belongs to another man. It would be impossible to explain these relationships in more detail here, too much has already been said anyway on matters that must sound horrid to an ear unaccustomed to this field. (*Ibid.*)

In 1924 the ears of the readers of *Wiadomości Literackie* were certainly unaccustomed. It is true that before the war they would have had a few occasions to hear about psychoanalysis, notably thanks to Ludwig Jekels' translations of Freud's *Five Lectures on Psycho-Analysis* and *The Psychopathology of Everyday Life*, published by Altenberg in Lviv. With the notable exception of Karol Irzykowski, however, the reception of Freud was limited to medical circles. 1924, the year *Wiadomości Literackie* began to appear, also saw the publication of Freud's *O marzeniu sennem* [*On Dreams*] translated by Beata Rank and *Trzy rozprawy z teorii seksualnej* [*Three Essays on the Theory of Sexuality*] translated by Jekels and Albiński. Both key works from the first topic appeared with the International Psychoanalytic Press. Bychowski published a lengthy review titled "Freud po polsku" [Freud in Polish], highlighting the importance of this endeavour:

> This is not the place to explore the groundbreaking significance of psychoanalysis in the history of ideas, let it suffice to say that [...] it is not just medicine but also psychology, sociology, the humanities, the history of religion, ethnology, aesthetics and art criticism that have found new avenues through it, glimpsing previously unknown problems.[165]

According to Bychowski, the Polish editions issued by the International Psychoanalytic Press were prime examples of "the great feats being achieved in this field of study, which is perhaps the newest one" (*ibid.*). He also highlights Poland's remarkable delay:

165 G. Bychowski, "Freud po polsku", *WL* 1924, no. 27, p. 4.

> [There exist] a great number of periodicals and books in all cultured languages, special associations of psychoanalyst doctors along with members of the above-mentioned sciences, in Vienna, Berlin, Budapest, Zurich, London, The Hague, Amsterdam, Kazan, Moscow, New-York and Calcutta, and, finally, some of these cities offer therapies in psychoanalytic polyclinics. (*Ibid.*)

Bychowski welcomes the fact that Polish readers will finally be able to get to know two of Freud's most important books. At the same time he expresses a few reservations about the translations themselves: "We appreciate the difficulty of translating a master of style such as Freud into our language, which lacks the appropriate terminology, but we must express our regret that the language of these translations has not been tailored more carefully" (*ibid.*).

In December the same year, *Wiadomości Literackie* published Bychowski's discussion of a special issue of the Belgian journal *Le Disque vert* – a 200-page volume dedicated to Freud and psychoanalysis:

> Given our compatriots' scant familiarity with psychoanalysis, it may seem untimely to touch on a specialist topic such as the relationship between the French and Freudianism. And yet this issue is so important for the future perspective of psychoanalysis in Poland that we do not hesitate to dedicate a special discussion to one issue of a journal [...] focused on the opinions and thoughts of remarkable Frenchmen and Belgians on Freudianism.[166]

The editors of *Le Disque vert* had asked not only doctors but also writers to describe their own reception of psychoanalysis. This indicates that in their view the new discipline had attained a considerable standing, but that there was at the same time an urgent need to study its main theses and to examine them critically.[167] Those contributors who were critical of Freud are left unmentioned in Bychowski's account. He only summarises a short analysis by French psychoanalyst René Laforgue and Freud's first French

166 gb [Gustaw Bychowski], "Psychoanaliza na Zachodzie: Freudyzm a Francja: Ankieta pisma *Le Disque vert*", *WL* 1924, no. 50, p. 2.

167 Cf. J. Zych, "L'influence de la psychanalyse sur la critique littéraire en France (1914–1939)", pp. 34–52.

translator, Yves Le Lay, who both try to explain why psychoanalysis has met with resistance and reluctance in France; in Bychowski's words these are "a Catholic hostility towards all sensuousness" as well as "the fundamental rationality of the French mind, which opposes the laws – often complex and not always clear – of the subconscious psyche".[168] Bychowski highlights that despite these obstacles, Freudianism has succeeded in gaining a standing in French scientific and literary circles. He quotes a few writers, such as the playwright Henri-René Lenormand: "Freud, who only claims to have develop a method to treat neuroses, has unwittingly opened up a path to understand all subconscious phenomena, in the normal person and in the sick one. He gives us the key that unlocks the secret gates of the soul." Bychowski also cites the Swiss writer Robert de Traz, the founder of *La revue de Genève* (in 1920, this journal published the first French translation of a work by Freud, namely his American lectures, *Five Lectures on Psycho-Analysis*):

> What we owe to Freudian doctrine is a new poignancy: it opens for us the possibility of an internal drama that we had barely suspected. The great conflict used to be the one between humankind and the universe [...]. Freud uncovers for us our conflict with ourselves. [...] But on this internal abyss Freud sheds light, he shows us who populates it. And he explains to us that we have risen out of it."

Bychowski mentions two other writers, namely Jean Hytier, for whom psychoanalysis is "a technique of interpretation, a search for what is concealed beneath appearances, for what transpires or tries to hide," and Georges Duhamel, the only one for whom psychoanalysis is "a potentially effective" tool, although Duhamel also warns his readers that this tool is dangerous, so that its "use ought to be restricted to very competent hands" (*ibid.*).

Another contribution by Bychowski to *Wiadomości Literackie* is a review of *Pamiętnik pacjentki* [A Patient's Diary]. The document, presented as a young female patient's authentic journal, was published by Adam Wizel. In a lengthy commentary he introduces himself as the author's psychiatrist and compares it to a text we have already discussed, namely *A Young Girl's Diary*, submitted for publication by Hermine Hug-Hellmuth. According to Wizel, that diary had also been written "with no intention to

168 gb [Gustav Bychowski], "Psychoanaliza na Zachodzie".

give it publicity; it was discovered by chance and published as an invaluable psychological document by the International Psychoanalytic Press".[169] *Pamiętnik pacjentki* is also a diary. The entries are dated before "Miss M." was put under Wizel's psychiatric care, and yet Wizel proposes a diagnosis: "the main twist in the writer's internal drama is her conflict with her sex instinct, which has been repressed into the unconscious" (p. 3). As was the case with Hug-Hellmuth's *Diary*, psychiatrists treated the Polish *Pamiętnik pacjentki* as an authentic document with no artistic ambition, while reviewers in non-medical journals questioned its authenticity and presented it as "psychological romance recreated with the talent of a novelist" or even as "a remarkable work of art" (p. 4). Wizel stresses that the text was a young woman's honest confession. While acknowledging that she was a gifted writer, he also diagnoses her with advanced psychosis and delusions of grandeur (in one delirium she sees herself bearing a child that would redeem humanity). In his commentary Wizel also mentions that he did not draw much on Freud: "I did not conduct a detailed psychoanalysis of Miss M." (p. 177). Instead, his treatment was based on Bleuler's purely psychiatric theories and Kretschmer's popular typology.

Bychowski did not assess the book from a psychiatrist's perspective but took it as an occasion to discuss, once more, the relationship between psychoanalysis and literature:

> The connections between literature and psychopathology have recently experienced tremendous growth. On the one hand psychopathological themes have been entering literature, on the other hand psychopathology has become more and more interested in literary creativity, exploring not only the creative process but also the characters developed through it. Everyone knows what a leading role psychoanalysis has played here, providing us with the tools to study the hidden but most important motives of people's problems and actions.[170]

For Bychowski, the diary edited by Wizel is clearly a work of literature, while the psychiatrist's efforts ("to illuminate his patient's experiences with the bright light of psychoanalytical understanding") resemble the interpretation of literature.

---

169 A. Wizel, "Przedmowa", in *Pamiętnik pacjentki*, ed. by D. Danek (Cracow: Universitas, 2001), p. 2.

170 G. Bychowski, "*Pamiętnik pacjentki*", *WL* 1926, no. 7, p. 3.

Several years later, Bychowski also combines his interest in literature and psychiatry in an article on Aldous Huxley's 1928 novel *Point Counter Point*. His focus is on a character named Maurice Spandrell, a murderer.[171] Bychowski is fascinated with the fact that Spandrell has nothing in common with Lombroso's criminology, which for many years had inspired writers to portray lawbreakers as born criminals. Spandrell's criminality is not inherited but rooted in "a warping of his character, caused by his experiences" (*ibid.*). Bychowski applies psychoanalytical tools to reconstruct the character's life. He highlights the fact that as a teenager Spandrell suppressed his budding sexual desire in the name of an ideal – his mother, whom he put on a pedestal. He stopped worshipping her when she married a man who, for Spandrell, embodied vulgarity and brute lust. "Gone was the living ideal, all lofty values struck him as parodies and lies. Tradition and good manners now seemed to disguise wickedness" (*ibid.*). For Bychowski, the novel portrays the moral development of children as described by psychoanalysts:

> No abstraction will give rise to ethical norms in a child's soul. This is only achieved through the child's love and respect for the people who convey these norms and who – in the child's mind – embody it. A breakdown in the child's relationship with the adults can shatter this sense of value on which the little savage's character development and socialisation are founded. (*Ibid.*)

In Spandrell's case "his wretched way of life was a constant reproach aimed at his mother's very heart". By depraving sexually inexperienced girls he was wreaking vengeance on her. His destructive impulses, however, soon began to spread beyond his sexual transgressions – they turned against the world and then against Spandrell himself. He commits murder and then allows himself to be shot by the police. In Bychowski's view, the murder is – unbeknownst to Spandrell – a cry for punishment, for the return of a moral order:

> What Spandrell says about his own life is that it was inexorably formed by a series of events of one and the same kind. For him this is a satanic net of damnation, which steered the course of his life, leading him towards the devil. For us all these events – just as the coincidences that determined the

171 G. Bychowski, "Zbrodnia Spandrella", *WL* 1933, no. 13, p. 4.

> nature of the crime and the choice of a victim – are but a series of empty vessels that an inner destiny or psychological determinant keeps filling with the same, ever more potent poison. In our day and age, the tragic Moira transforms into a net of unconscious complexes and compulsions whose course we are always able to understand and sometimes to interrupt and reverse. (*Ibid.*)

Bychowski is not only impressed with Huxley's "masterly" psychological character-building, he also seems convinced that "the author's artistic intuition was supported by his understanding of psychoanalysis" (*ibid.*). Huxley, meanwhile, certainly did not see himself as a follower of Freudian theory. His only explicit discussion of the topic carries the telling title "Our Contemporary Hocus-Pocus"[172] and is dated three years before the publication of *Point Counter Point.* Comparing contemporary writers' interest in Freud to Balzac's fascination with magnetic fluids, Huxley predicts that readers would soon find it similarly droll and anachronistic. He stresses his own "profound disbelief in psycho-analysis" (p. 316) ever since he read *The Interpretation of Dreams.*

Perhaps Bychowski's discovery of a psychoanalytical key to Huxley's novel is related to the fact that many passages in the novel treat themes that preoccupied him in his research. After all, the Polish psychiatrist was looking for ways to harness psychoanalysis to crime prevention. Spandrell's story struck him as "a synthesis of many debaucheries, a consolidation of many issues of judgement and those that have never reached judgement," while Huxley's presentation "of the puzzle of an active and aggressive amorality that makes a life goal of the destruction of all social ties" has much in common with "the image that emerges from psychoanalysing a young lawbreaker".[173] This is why "the depiction of Spandrell's story becomes a sort of psychological reportage on a whole cohort of criminals" (*ibid.*).

The following year Bychowski presented the readers of *Wiadomości Literackie* with the main argument of his presentation at the Conference of Polish Doctors and Naturalists (Zjazd Lekarzy i Przyrodników) in Poznań. In a supplement titled "Prawo, przestępca, życie" [Law, the Criminal, Life] he published a short text titled "Przestępca a psychoanaliza" [The Criminal and Psychoanalysis], where he stressed once more that criminology ought

172 A. Huxley, "Our Contemporary Hocus-Pocus", *TF* 1925, vol. 73, pp. 313–320.

173 G. Bychowski, "Zbrodnia Spandrella".

to take into account the results of psychoanalytical research and that psychoanalysis could help formulate new foundations for social practice: "Psychoanalysis provides information on the structure of the terrain that we intend to plough; at the same time it helps us predict the reactions that we must anticipate and facilitates an effective choice of tools. This is why it must play a key role in the mission to heal humanity".[174]

Another one of Bychowski's contributions in *Wiadomości Literackie* was his participation in a discussion titled "Społeczeństwo i medycyna" [Society and Medicine], which appeared in the same year. Here he joins a lively debate on a short book titled *Zachorowałem…* [I Fell Ill…] by Paweł Gart, a patient who accuses Warsaw's medical establishment of indolence. Bychowski begins by pointing out that the book has no intellectual or literary merit. It cannot measure up to Thomas Mann's *The Magic Mountain* with its "vast diapason of suffering," to "the portrayal of the abyss into which the suffering creature plunges" in Arthur Schnitzler's *Dying*, or to the clarity of Stefan Żeromski's *Promień* [Ray]. The only potentially interesting aspect is the author's resentment towards medicine, although this, too, is no more than an example of a commonly found attitude. Bychowski suggests that the patient's relationship with the doctor usually oscillates between the two poles of blind abandonment or faith on the one hand and suspiciousness and malice on the other, then he tries to explain why the incompetence of doctors is a popular topic, not only among patients who experienced medical malpractice:

> The non-medic, a person who is weak and who suffers, approaches medicine with a particular attitude. It seems as if the thoughts and feelings of primordial man were coming back to life, as if the doctor were a priest and a magus and a sorcerer in one, endowed with immense power that could be harnessed to the poor patient's detriment or benefit. The patient used to place himself in the doctor's hands like a helpless child.[175]

The natural reaction to making oneself vulnerable is a desire for revenge. The patients' anger and outrage result from their difficulty accepting that they momentarily believed in the doctor's omnipotence. For Bychowski, the only purpose of Gart's book – a purpose of which the author is more or less aware – is to discharge his traumatic experience with the world of

174 G. Bychowski, "Przestępca a psychoanaliza", *WL* 1934, no. 30, p. 8.

175 *WL* 1933, no. 42, p. 3.

medicine. "Only such affects can account for the meanness of the author's antics" (*ibid.*).

In the 1920s, when Bychowski arrived in Warsaw, *Wiadomości Literackie* was still working with Karol Irzykowski, the only literary writer who had closely followed the emerging psychoanalytical field before World War I. During the interwar period he often expressed his reluctance about Freudianism, for instance in a 1928 review of Ignacy Jeżower's *Księga snów* [Book of Dreams]:

> I used to be an eager observer of dreams: aesthetically I was enchanted by their strange construction, ethereal, with various nooks and crannies; my own "scientific" research was for me no more than a new way to take delight in this material. Only when I became aware of Freud did dreams cease to bring me such joy; their world now appeared [...] thoroughly deprived of its poeticism [...]. It is not that I disrespect Freud, but for me his whole school has diminished and grossly falsified this world. It is only Jeżower's book that is restoring my former relationship to dreams. On 700 pages only 4 deal with Freud! Bravo![176]

Throughout the interwar period, Irzykowski mentions Freud only in passing, in the context of other topics. The most detailed discussions can be found in his theatre reviews written for the newspaper *Robotnik* in the years 1924-34. In a pamphlet titled *Beniaminek* he gives the following account:

> I wrote these reviews not for the proletariat but for the intelligentsia. *Robotnik* certainly contains articles that aim to raise the worker's awareness, but others – ones that have a diplomatic mission, so to say – were designed to help shape general opinion on an equal footing with other newspapers' voices.[177]

Irzykowski used this unusual platform to popularise Freudianism, frequently mentioning it in passing even in contexts that had little to do with it. Reviewing a performance of *Niedojrzały owoc* ["Unripe Fruit" or *Le fruit*

176 K. Irzykowski, "Księga snów", *WL* 1928, no. 11, p. 1.

177 K. Irzykowski, *Benjaminek: Rzecz o Boyu-Żeleńskim* (Warsaw: F. Hoesick, 1933), pp. 181–182. The spelling of *Benjaminek* was later modernised to *Beniaminek*. I reproduce the old spelling when referencing the 1933 edition.

vert in the original], a play by Regis Gignoux and Jacques Thery staged at Warsaw's Teatr Mały, he explains:

> The famous Viennese psychoanalyst Freud claims that humour is founded on joy about that which is forbidden, senseless, bawdy, wild, chaotic, godless, in a word – all that is covered by strict censorship in practical life. It is the joy of circumventing censorship. Of momentarily disempowering all that which acts as a tough policeman in our social and political life and in our own soul. Of course this joy can only free itself in certain conditions, which are based either on coincidence, producing pure humour, or on jokes – and this is why funny people are so well-liked and sought-after, because they make it easier to attain the ecstasy of that momentary liberation, since for them there is "nothing sacred".[178]

Writing about a performance of James Montgomery's *Dzień bez kłamstwa* [*Nothing but the Truth*], Irzykowski informs his readers: "Freud based his theory of dreams on the idea that the human soul has a need to evade censorship and that it looks for secret valves".[179] Reviewing Osip Dymov's satire *Bronx Express* at the Teatr Ateneum in Warsaw he ventures a comment that brings to mind the tone of his articles from before the war:

> Freud's celebrated dream analysis has revealed even more remote and more complex qualities of dreams; there are different adhesions and knots between several threads in a dream, time changes, displacements, condensations, symbols, abbreviations and so on. In Freudianism, i.e. in its best results – and in my opinion these are only his discoveries about the morphology (study of forms) of dreams – science has not only caught up with poetry but it has overtaken it and opened up new possibilities which, however, are very difficult to apply. Unless the poet wants to be no more than an interpreter (performer, translator) of science. But his whole one-sided sexology is in my opinion not efficient enough when it comes to literature – still, this is the field in which it is most often put to use.[180]

By the late 1930s, Irzykowski was still interested in psychoanalysis. Reviewing *Głębia na Zimnej* [Depths on Zimna], a play by Zygmunt Rylski (pseudonym

178 *R* 1925, no. 165, p. 4.
179 *R* 1926, no. 156, p. 4.
180 *R* 1929, no. 330, p. 2.

of Zofia Rylska) he writes:

> This is a dramatised literary study on adolescence. Over the last couple of years, "the sixteen-year-old girl" seems to have become fashionable, appearing as a heroine in film and theatre. But the interest in her is rather symptomatic. Long gone are the days when a teenage boy or girl could be viewed as a passive tool of the will of adults. Despite Sigmund Freud's attention to childhood and the significance he has attributed to it, we must admit that the social transformations of our day are causing this period to become ever shorter.[181]

Only two of Irzykowski's articles in *Wiadomości Literackie* concern psychoanalysis. These are a review, published in 1926, of Stanisław Przybyszewski's memoir *Moi współcześni* [My Contemporaries], in which Przybyszewski presents himself as a pioneer in relation to Freud,[182] and, two years later, a discussion of Gustav Bychowski's *Psychoanaliza*.[183] In the first of these two, Irzykowski discredits Przybyszewski's claims as preposterous:

> The coincidental analogy with Freud must draw attention to their fundamental differences. Freud is truly a psychologist, he walks the path of introspection, observation and scientific combination, his psychology reaches three hundred metres below the surface of the earth; a thinker such as Przybyszewski is (no more or no less than) a prophet, a visionary, and he reaches right into the centre of the planet. The subconscious as conceptualised by Freud is something different than the naked soul [one of Przybyszewski's key concepts]. Freud spreads a net over the complications of life – Przybyszewski's plays, in as far as they are applications of his theory of the naked soul, show unambiguous, uncomplicated humans.[184]

In a way Irzykowski repeats what he had already written in "Freud i freudyści" [Freud and the Freudians] before Przybyszewski appointed himself the forerunner of Freud. In that article, Irzykowski had described the honesty assumed by psychoanalysis as "bringing the underground life of the psyche to light," but he also added a caveat:

---

181 *R* 1938, no. 293, p. 10.

182 K. Irzykowski, "Pierwszy bilans Przybyszewskiego i jego autorehabilitacja", *WL* 1926, 6, p. 1.

183 K. Irzykowski, "Badania Acherontu", *WL* 1928, no. 36, p. 3.

184 K. Irzykowski, "Pierwszy bilans".

> It is not in the metaphysical sense, i.e. not in the way that Przybyszewski for instance sees it. The mistake used to be that our reach was either too shallow or too deep, i.e. we reached down to where there could not be anything anymore, producing cosmic visions instead of introspecting. I believe that to examine the layer a couple of hundred meters below the so-called surface of the soul might suffice, there is no need to look for the nadir.[185]

Irzykowski's review of Bychowski's book, meanwhile, is written as if psychoanalysis in Poland had seen no developments whatsoever since the Second Congress of Polish Neurologists, Psychiatrists and Psychologists. He predicts that the book should find many readers and fill "the embarrassing gap in the education of our intelligentsia".[186] He also adds that "older handbooks by Jekels and Jaroszyński – I do not know if there were any others – are, I believe, out of print, while the proceedings of the Polish Freudians' congress in Cracow never reached readers beyond professional circles" (*ibid.*). Apparently Irzykowski had not noticed that since 1912, i.e. the publication of the works he mentions, no less than four of Freud's books had appeared in Polish translation, next to several popular introductions to his theory. Irzykowski was aware, however, that "the most ingenious madness of the twentieth century" had in the meantime gained popularity across the globe:

> In Germany, for instance, it is the subject of polite conversation on a par with sports. Young ladies and gentlemen, returning from playing tennis, discuss love in a shockingly cocky manner, drawing on psychoanalytical terminology. In French and German literature the impact of Freud's theory is significant – works are being written that simply illustrate them. (*Ibid.*)

In Poland, meanwhile, "no particular interest in Freudianism" (*ibid.*) was noticeable yet. Irzykowski finds this delay surprising. Given the Poles' "eagerness to show off with exotic news, our passion for mysticism and Kabbalism," psychoanalysis ought to enjoy great popularity.

185 K. Irzykowski, "Freudyzm i freudyści", in *Pisma rozproszone 1897–1922*, vol. 1, p. 178. Here Irzykowski is quoting from his own novel *Pałuba*, published in 1903 (cf. K. Irzykowski, *Pałuba*, p. 361).

186 K. Irzykowski, "Badania Acherontu".

It is worth juxtaposing this statement with an opinion ventured by Władysław Matecki one year before. Reviewing Markuszewicz's book on the therapeutic significance of psychoanalysis, Matecki, a medical doctor, wrote that just like in other countries, in Poland, too, "Freud's science has stepped outside the boundaries of medicine and [...] now often becomes the subject of debate, even passionate discussion, in the daily papers".[187] From the point of view of a doctor at the Jewish hospital affiliated with *Nasz Przegląd*, psychoanalysis was a well-established theory. When Irzykowski says that "our intelligentsia" is unfamiliar with Freudianism, the readers he has in mind are not the ones of "Their Review," to borrow Słonimski's *bon mot*. "Our" intelligentsia, the subscribers of *Wiadomości Literackie*, still knew very little about psychoanalysis. Trying to explain this state of affairs, Irzykowski suggests that it may be a question of anti-Semitism (it is for the same reason, he surmises, that "we care little about Einstein"[188]). He also blames his compatriots' ignorance about Freud on the fact that the German language was not too widely known. Thus he obliquely draws attention to an important phenomenon: before the war, the reception of psychoanalysis had mainly taken place in Galicia. Newly independent Poland established its own schooling system, doing away with the Austrian gymnasiums. Few readers of the younger generation had the language skills to read Freud in the original, nor did they share the same cultural references as the generation of Irzykowski, Freud and his students. Younger Poles failed to see psychoanalysis as a continuation of a well-established Herbartian tradition and suspect it of being a "Jewish science," foreign to non-Jews and uncomfortable to the assimilated Jewish subscribers of *Wiadomości Literackie*, who found themselves reminded of their own background.

Irzykowski's assessment of the "compromising gap in the education of our intelligentsia" carries a bitter note of disappointment related to his own unsuccessful attempts to bring psychoanalysis to a broader audience. Perhaps this is why the Second Congress of Polish Neurologists, Psychiatrists and Psychologists is mentioned several times. Despite the work he had put into the dissemination of Freud's theories in 1912, by the late 1920s most Poles still had no clue about it. Irzykowski gives a positive review of Bychowski's book (he also reminds readers of Bychowski's articles in *Wiadomości Literackie*, especially his analysis of *The Magnificent Cuckold*:

187 W. Matecki, "Na marginesie książki Dra R. Markuszewicza".

188 K. Irzykowski, "Badania Acherontu".

"the argument is entirely valid, although I would not agree that fiction based on Freud's profound system is automatically equally profound"[189]); he presents it as a precise and faithful introduction to Freud's theory, expressing his admiration for the skilful summary of such a vast theme in no more than 180 pages, and he appreciates Bychowski's use of cases from the literary world and the fact that he also considers "Freud's most recent works, which stretch out into the field of philosophy" (*ibid.*).

Irzykowski hopes that Bychowski's next publications would elaborate on applied psychoanalysis, which is barely touched upon. He is also interested in hearing more about Freud's analysis of jokes ("here the psyachiatrist has outdone the aestheticians") as well as about Freud's psychoanalytical interpretations of literature, which, in Irzykowski's opinion, are less successful and sometimes even absurd. Furthermore, "one could consider more broadly the Freudians' studies on folk tales and legends, without necessarily trying to find incest everywhere" (*ibid.*). On this occasion Irzykowski revises his view of Wilhelm Stekel, whom he had criticised vehemently before the war. He still opposes Stekel's "Kabbalism of dreams" and mocks his analysis of Grillparzer's *A Dream is Life*, but he also lauds the way in which "Freud's most interesting student" and "the best writer among the Freudians" applies psychoanalysis to "phenomena of a social nature" (*ibid.*). Among the works by Stekel that Irzykowski had read were two books published in 1920 – one on female frigidity and one on male impotence. He found them both impressive and states that Stekel "analyses the unfortunate problem in the sexes' mutual relationship as no one had done in literature since Strindberg. [...] None of modern literature has reached this level [...], it is childish in comparison with these revelations" (*ibid.*). Irzykowski also admits that he often used Stekel "as a compass when writing reviews about plays with erotic themes" (*ibid.*). Here he agrees with Bychowski that "the very nature of analytical truth can offend some of our mental habits and prejudices, that it throws the gauntlet at prudery and hypocrisy" (*ibid.*).

Irzykowski applauds Bychowski's efforts to bring psychoanalysis to a broader audience and recommends his "excellent compendium" to a wide

189 K. Irzykowski, "Badania Acherontu". Elsewhere Irzykowski puts it succinctly: "Writing about Crommelynck's *The Magnificent Cuckold*, Dr Bychowski is fascinated by how 'profound' the work is – on account of it being an illustration of Freud's theory. In my opinion it is profound only in as far as it is not this type of illustration" (*Beniaminek*, pp. 53–54).

readership of writers and intellectuals, educators, priests and scholars in other fields. Still, he cannot embrace Bychowski as his own successor. This is because "Dr Bychowski writes like a scholar with an orthodox gravity" and as a "believer and follower. This is why he gives importance to various connections and details within the system that a neutral presenter might consider unimportant". Irzykowski acknowledges that "certainly, there are benefits to this, an academic writer inspires greater confidence," but at the same time he believes that "Freudianism can be presented as a modern scientific legend, it can be treated from an anecdotal perspective, so to say, one might use style to highlight all that is striking and exciting in it. This is how a literary writer would go about it."

Irzykowski, Słonimski and Boy-Żeleński

If Irzykowski had hoped to write an introduction to Freud that was more literary than Bychowski's, he never actually tackled the task. Perhaps his silence on the subject can be attributed, at least in part, to the conflict into which he entered, in the late 1920s, with Tadeusz Boy-Żeleński and Antoni Słonimski, the most important contributors to *Wiadomości Literackie.* According to Małgorzata Szpakowska, these two critics determined the paper's tone and were key to its success with readers. They were best able to express what could be described as the worldview of *Wiadomości Literackie.*[190]

Słonimski, the paper's main reviewer, disagreed with Irzykowski about the shape and rank of literary criticism. He was funny, sarcastic and his jokes often culminated in strong points, whereas Irzykowski believed that analysing texts was serious work.[191] Słonimski's incessant and indiscreet taunts, often published in the same issue as Irzykowski's programmatic statements, pushed the latter to stop writing for the paper. It is also worth noting that soon after Irzykowski's positive review of Bychowski's *Psychoanaliza*, Słonimski derided the same book in his weekly column, "Kronika Tygodniowa":

> Now I'm reading Dr Bychowski's book titled *Psychoanaliza* and it keeps making me burst out in loud and indecorous giggles. The most amusing

190 M. Szpakowska, *"Wiadomości Literackie" prawie dla wszystkich*, p. 66.

191 See J. Jakóbczyk, *Szachy literackie: Rzecz o twórczości Karola Irzykowskiego* (Katowice: Wydawnictwo Uniwersytetu Śląskiego, 2005), pp. 97–98.

> and irritating thing about the Freudians, quite like the Marxists, is their terrible arbitrariness and their primitive division of the world into just two categories. Marx boils everything down to a fictional capitalist "system," while for Freud everything is based on sex. It's either the proletariat and capitalism or male and female organs. The entire world of dreams and reality is divided into these two options, and the symbolism is so breathtakingly daring that after a couple of dozen pages of *Psychoanaliza* we get used to the idea that a wardrobe does not signify a wardrobe at all, that a keyhole, shop window, ink pot, plate or elevator are very risqué and exciting to men, while a paint brush, walking stick, pen, key or matchstick are objects of lust and sexual desire for all women. I wonder if it also works the other way around. If I dream about a woman, does it signify a wardrobe? Dr Bychowski also uses psychoanalysis to account for slips of the tongue. It would be interesting to hear him explain the language errors that pepper his own *Psychoanaliza* [...]. Dr Bychowski not only explains linguistic stumbles through psychoanalysis but also actual stumbles. He admits that he stumbled and fell in broad daylight just after "an upsetting and unpleasant thought" about one of his close colleagues had crossed his mind. I fear that his medical colleagues, having read *Psychoanaliza*, will be tripping and eating the pavement at every step.[192]

Wiadomości Literackie had been printing Bychowski's psychoanalytical interpretations for years, but it is only now, as if reacting to Irzykowski's praise, that Słonimski decided to deride the Freudian:

> When a writer applies psychoanalysis we get better results and resultresses [*rezultaty i rezulmamy*] than when a professional psychoanalyst turns to literature. [...] Bychowski has a straightforward explanation for the fact that in Zorrilla's play Don Juan seduces Inés: "The father's main prohibition is the ban on sexual freedom, and this is where the son engages in his fiercest battles. This motif is reflected in his choice of love objects, who always belong to another man and are, like Inés, defended by the father himself." But of course it is not only Inés who has a father but every Spanish woman, and every papá will defend his daughter. Or should Don Juan run after orphans and foundlings? But even this would not help him. Dr Bychowski would tell him that this was also a *Vaterkomplex* and that the silly Don Juan was seeking revenge on the fathers of abandoned

192 A. Słonimski, "Kronika Tygodniowa", *WL* 1930, no. 36, p. 4.

> daughters while he believed himself to be seducing a bonny bird. Dr Bychowski's libido is none of my business. I believe that Freud is a great learned man, and I even acknowledge that Freudianism has had a significant impact on literature, but the method gives too many excuses for balderdash. And there is nothing more dangerous than such universal theories in the mouths of dim-witted people. (*Ibid.*)

Several years later Słonimski criticised psychoanalysis in similar terms:

> I know a few Warsaw-based psychoanalysts, but I would not let any of them try and resolve anything for me. I would rather walk about with unresolved complexes than engage in idiotic conversations. I know I am about to cause great indignation in professional circles, but I dare say that intelligent doctors have been offering treatments based on talking long before Freud and that humour and common sense are more effective here than the mechanical application of Freud's method, even if he is doubtless a great sage. Emulating Freud is a bit like to emulating Twain. It requires wit.[193]

Irzykowski's conflict with Boy-Żeleński was also caused by the latter's attitude to psychoanalysis. Boy-Żeleński's relationship with Freud is best represented by the series "Kurkiewy" (the title will be explained below), published in *Kurier Polski* in the summer of 1924.[194] Boy-Żeleński concedes that "Freudianism offers new perspectives, ingenious flashes even," but in his opinion these are "too hastily generalised and, indeed, they are heavily spiced with charlatanism; Freudianism becomes especially questionable when it leaves the cognitive sphere and wants to enter the sphere of practical action" (pp. 65-66). Boy-Żeleński reduces Freud's method to making patients aware of their repressed erotic desires, and he considers this method to be accessible to basically anyone. For instance, he describes his own adventure as a wild analyst in Krynica. During a visit to the spa town he "healed" a very respectable fifty-year-old lady who suffered from nerves:

> Gazing straight into the patient's eyes I impulsively blurted out that she had the unconscious soul of an apache, a madam and a prostitute, I changed her

193 A. Słonimski, "Kronika Tygodniowa", *WL* 1939, no. 36, p. 6.

194 Reprinted in T. Boy-Żeleński, *Brewerie* (Warsaw: F. Hoesick, 1926), pp. 61–109.

> distinguished name from Maria to Mańka, vulgo Mańka Pryszcz, and in this spirit I set about, painstakingly inducing her indignation. [...] I would see my patient every day and consistently addressed her in this spirit, morally brutalising her with absolute ruthlessness, in the presence of others who were privy to the nature of the cure applied. [...] When I was leaving after a week, the "Mańka" I had improvised declared that she had not felt as well for many years, perhaps ever, and she accompanied me to the train station along with all the other ladies and gentlemen, who were astonished about her miraculous cure, and when I boarded the train car she handed me a basket of the most exquisite flowers and fruit, begging me to maintain her under my medical care via correspondence. (p. 84)

This fact, the author claims, ought to free him from the "rather too rashly assigned" label of "anti-Freudian".

The title of the series "Kurkiewy" is derived from the name of Stanisław Kurkiewicz, an eccentric Cracow-based doctor who, in the early twentieth century, developed a rather outlandish system of sexual nomenclature. In his first contribution to the series, "Na marginesie 'freudyzmu'" [On the Margins of "Freudianism"] Boy-Żeleński describes Kurkiewicz not only as a precursor of Polish sexology but as no less than the nation's own Freud. To compare Kurkiewicz with Freud appears like a harmless pleasantry, but a storm ensued, pulling supporters and opponents of psychoanalysis into the debate, and Boy-Żeleński, it seems, was happy enough to offer his weekly column as a platform for this festival of bad faith, prejudice and, especially, anti-Semitism.

One particularly awkward occurrence was Boy-Żeleński's publication of a letter by Antoni Mikulski, a psychiatry professor at the Stefan Batory University in Vilnius. Mikulski had already spoken against psychoanalysis during the 1912 congress in Cracow:

> None of Freud's conclusions have yet been concluded, for, being based on deduction, they must be constantly verified and juxtaposed with existing facts. Their truthfulness can be measured using the following standards: the doctor's or the patient's subjective feeling that the results attained correspond to the actual state of things; successful treatment results. But both are highly unstable.[195]

195 R. Radziwiłłowicz, "Sprawozdanie z II-go Zjazdu 20–23 grudnia w Krakowie", *MIK* 1913, no. 4, pp. 78–79. On Mikulski see also M. Marcinów, B. Dobroczyński, "Antoni Feliks Mikulski – zapomniany pionier psychologii klinicznej", in *Na drogach i bezdrożach historii psychologii*, vol. 1, pp. 123–134.

In his letter to Boy-Żeleński, Mikulski recalls: "In 1912 the [Freudian] offensive was launched in Poland. This is when I wrote an assessment for *Lwowski Tygodnik Lekarski* [Lviv Medical Weekly], and it seems to me that I made a small contribution to halt the initial momentum."[196] He goes on to claim that Polish psychiatrists are absolutely not to be seen as supporters of Freud and that "fortunately" only a small number of doctors can be counted as Freudians – the majority are opposed to the method. Still, he goes on to claim, the offensive continues, this time supported by "international capital". Mikulski makes sure to draw attention to "an issue that no one in Poland has yet dared to utter": the Jews are responsible for the spread of psychoanalysis. He claims not to be an anti-Semite and then goes on to discuss the reasons why "Freudianism is so close and easily accessible to Jews":

> Above all, Jews reach sexual maturity earlier than we do, which is why their childhood years are doubtless more imbued with sexuality than they are in our case. [...]
> Next, Jews are inclined to scholasticism; their entire religion with the Talmud and the Kabbala proves this, as do their methods of discussion and reasoning.
> Third, the so-called Old Testament is saturated with sexualism. All kinds of perversions, incests etc. are the order of the day, treated with great indulgence [...]. All these horrors have been invented simply out of a sort of fondness. If we add that Freud is a Jew and that as such he naturally awakens the sympathy of his co-religionists, then no one should be surprised that those who promote "the new psychology" are above all the Jews. (p. 86)

A response to this letter was written by Gustav Bychowski. He begins by saying that initially he had no intention of joining the debate, knowing that it was not even about a fair exploration of the issues at hand and that "no one can measure up to Boy's wit" (p. 89). To leave Mikulski's letter unanswered, however, was simply unacceptable in his opinion, for by drawing on racist arguments in a purely scientific question that letter set "a sad precedence in the entire history of international psychiatry" (p. 91).

Bychowski points up the word "international" in the context of Mikulski's expression of "international capital," which alludes to "an anonymous superpower, international financiers and other horrors," whereas the psychoanalytic movement is simply international in the sense that it is

196 T. Boy-Żeleński, *Brewerie*, p. 85.

active wherever Western culture exerts an influence, with an international association and an international press. Bychowski does not respond to the provocation by citing the names of famous non-Jewish supporters of Freud (he only allows himself to remark that the first psychiatrist who introduced psychoanalysis to a clinical setting was Eugen Bleuler), nor does he examine the proportions of Gentile and Jewish analysts ("whichever results such calculations would bring, I fail to see how they should contribute to an assessment of Freudianism"). To compare the racial, religious or national identities of patients, Bychowski continues, would be similarly irrelevant; in any case, the lack of statistics effectively forecloses such comparisons. He reminds readers that Freudianism sheds light on ancient and Germanic myths and that it allows to explain the psychological background in the works of Sophocles, Shakespeare, Ibsen and Słowacki (p. 91). Psychoanalysis is well established in many outstanding psychiatric clinics abroad, it is represented at general medical conferences, it exerts an enormous influence on scientific production, so that it can be described as "one of the strongest scientific currents in the Old and the New World" (p. 92). Bychowski's tone becomes sarcastic when he remarks that the force of psychoanalysis cannot be undermined by "such mighty and subtly selected cannons as Prof. Mikulski is mobilising against it"; he concludes by expressing his curiosity about "the next results of the counter-offensive that the Professor launched with such effectiveness in 1912" (*ibid.*).

This controversy did nothing to hamper Boy-Żeleński's self-confidence. Two years later he included his "Kurkiewy" in the collection *Brewerie*, and in the introduction he framed his humoristic series as an important contribution to the popularisation of psychoanalysis:

> Before my sketches and these "Kurkiewy," Freud's works, omnipresent as they were across enlightened Europe, were known to only a handful of people in Poland; I myself have met many prominent lawyers who had never even heard the name of this Viennese scholar! From the time of this dispute everyone became interested in him. (p. 63)

While "Kurkiewy" were being published, however, they were clearly read as attacks against psychoanalysis. This is attested, for instance, by the support that Boy-Żeleński received from Leo Belmont, who seems to have had no previous dealings with psychoanalysis.[197] In an open letter to Boy-

197 Leo Belmont is the pen name of writer and journalist Leopold Blumental (1865-1941).

Żeleński published in *Echo Warszawskie*, Belmont compares him to the child in Andersen's tale "The Emperor's New Clothes".[198] The motto he wrote for his open letter leaves no doubt as to his intentions: "There will be more joy in the heaven of truth over one journalist converted to anti-Freudianism than over ten psychiatrists who virtuously make a living out of 'psychoanalysis'" (*ibid.*).[199]

Irzykowski's argument with Boy-Żeleński dates back to 1925, when the latter began occasionally to write for *Wiadomości Literackie*. In one of his earliest articles in the journal, Boy-Żeleński praised the timelessness of Molière's *Tartuffe*, which he had translated. Irzykowski replied that the comedy was antiquated trash, shallow, ineffective and primitive. According to Małgorzata Szpakowska, the last three epithets were meant to describe not just Molière's work but also that of his Polish translator.[200]

In 1928, Boy-Żeleński became a regular contributor to *Wiadomości Literackie*. This was roughly at the time when Irzykowski withdrew from the journal. For Boy-Żeleński, the weekly became his exclusive platform, and his name came to be associated with it more than any other. According to Szpakowska, his intellect and temperament were a perfect match to the journal's unwritten rules; in particular, he had an ability to write about important matters in an attractive and accessible manner, providing a mix of information, gossip, jokes and a clear message (pp. 111-113). What is more, he was an outspoken supporter of modern values.

Irzykowski took issue with his colleague's tendency to approach every problem with common sense and humour. He also criticised him for trivialising Freudianism and for using it and many other systems of thought for mere effect or to augment his own popularity. It must be said that of all the idiolects of the interwar era, it is probably Freud's vocabulary that had the greatest impact on Boy-Żeleński's language. The fact that terms such as psychological trauma, sublimation and complex became rooted in Polish is largely attributable to an information campaign he ran with the feminist Irena Krzywicka. The campaign was titled "Życie świadome" [Conscious Life]; a supplement they wrote for *Wiadomości*

198 L. Belmont, "List otwarty do doktora Boya", *EW* 1924, no. 194, p. 4.

199 In a later issue Belmont, returns to the subject claiming that in psychoanalysis "the mask of dull science conceals subtle filth" (L. Belmont, "Świńtuchy", *EW* 1924, no. 204, p. 5).

200 Cf. M. Szpakowska, *"Wiadomości Literackie" prawie dla wszystkich*, pp. 108–109. See also D. Skórczewski, "Sprawa Irzykowskiego i Boya: Wokół głośnego epizodu międzywojennego sporu o krytykę", *TD* 2002, no. 3, pp. 223–231.

Literackie carried the same title. Boy-Żeleński and Krzywicka also worked to promote family planning and sex education for children. With their open attitude to erotic matters, these activists and their supporters were able to translate psychoanalytical theories of sexuality into a programme that called for far-reaching reforms in social mores. Their efforts bring to mind the younger generation of Freudians, especially the Berlin group discussed in Part V. Irzykowski, however, found that Boy-Żeleński's treatment of the subject amounted to an unacceptable simplification. He also found it grossly anachronistic; in *Beniaminek* he writes: "via Boy the Polish intelligentsia is working through Przybyszewski and the problems of his era".[201] Irzykowski found that as a translator, Boy-Żeleński managed to "przybyszewskify" [*sprzybyszewszczył*] even French literature by "exaggerating its sexual character" (p. 42). He goes on to offer a droll prediction:

> The world has evolved in such a way that sexuality, once only discussed in a few medical books, has surfaced as the foremost question in psychology, pedagogy, society; it has been validated and dulled, as it were, in terms of emotions, and soon there will come a time where the gentlemen at the dinner table shall tell the ladies: "Oh, please now, stop talking about this Freud and sexuality, is there nothing more interesting to talk about?" (*Ibid.*)

In Poland, he adds, such a state of affairs is not about to set in, as the subject is only just beginning to gain momentum. Still, "under Boy's influence, Poland's intelligentsia has become more childish by twenty years" (p. 120).

Irzykowski suggests that the reason why Boy only rarely mentions Freud directly is that he hopes to avoid a comparison that "suggests itself too much" (p. 53). Being juxtaposed with Freud would reveal the extent to which his own concepts were borrowed. However, once Boy-Żeleński tackled Freud openly in "Kurkiewy," Irzykowski was irritated that he enlisted the Lviv-based eccentric Kurkiewicz "and his bizarre but conceptually poor books" (*ibid.*) against Freud "for a laugh". He goes on:

> This whole Kurkiewy pseudo-prank is a pathetic intellectual backwater. [...] [Boy] imposes Kurkiewicz on us as a precursor of Freud without offering any evidence. Lechoń has come up with yet another precursor of

201 K. Irzykowski, *Benjaminek*, p. 118.

> Freud; during Boy's anniversary he claimed that "concerning what we call sublimation, 400 years before Freud Mikołaj Rej was aware of things that the gentlemen Psychoanalysts are only now beginning to dream about at night". Oh, what barbarism! You can find hundreds of precursors like that for any thinker. (*Ibid.*)

Reviewing a Polish production of Paul Raynal's comedy *Le Maître de son cœur* [The Master of His Heart], Boy-Żeleński discusses the representation of homosexuality, adding that it would have been better "if this play had been the work of a bold analysis, delving into secrets of the human soul that the theatre has not encountered so far". Irzykowski comments angrily: "But these are no secrets, since you can read about them in any psychology book. A few years from now they will have become utterly banal, analysis will become banalysis" (p. 54). He elaborates:

> Boy is a belated echo of Young Poland when he writes about these things: "This much is certain, that the study of the human soul is entering a new phase... The secret is regaining its dominion over humankind". What secret? This is simply the solution of a charade. You must lack all aesthetic sense and have very little knowledge of psychology to develop any enthusiasm about it. No wonder that the way Boy has used psychology [...] has finally provoked anti-psychologism. Today we are actually seeing the end of something that Boy, having no nose in these matters, is only announcing as a phase of the future. (pp. 53-54)

Irzykowski concludes: "In today's Europe there are two systems of suspicion: Freudianism and Marxism. [...] In Poland, instead of Freudianism and Marxism we have adopted Boyism: it is not based on any psychology or economy, just some popular, mild version of the general trend of innuendo" (p. 78).

In *Beniaminek* Irzykowski also attacks Słonimski, Boy-Żeleński's defender, as well as *Wiadomości Literackie*: "I declare: no one besides Boy and Słonimski is able to establish any kind of literary politics in *Wiadomości Literackie* – they will not be admitted. Others can 'embellish the columns' at best" (pp. 181–182). Responding to Słonimski's accusation that Irzykowski's reviews in *Robotnik* were too difficult for the readers of this paper Irzykowski counters:

> I know very well that Słonimski and Boy would make better contributors to *Robotnik* than I; their impoverished way of thinking is a perfect match for people who are, sadly, impoverished in spirit; unfortunately they are expensive and I am cheap. (*Ibid.*)

It is Irzykowski's irritation with Słonimski and his work which, according to one scholar, represents the key motivation behind two of his most unusual articles, both written in 1937.[202] Published in *Kurier Poranny* and described as anti-Semitic by the author himself, they are titled "Żyd jest to Polak z rezerwą" [The Jew is a Pole with Reservations] and "Udział Żydów w literaturze polskiej" [The Jews' Contribution to Polish Literature]. Irzykowski's conflict with the editorial board of *Wiadomości Literackie* meant that he had to submit these articles to a different paper, and yet, as Małgorzata Szpakowska proposes, they can be read as part of a debate initiated the same year by Mieczysław Grydzewski and his colleagues and titled "Pisarze polscy o kwestii żydowskiej" [Polish Writers on the Jewish Question].[203] Indeed, Irzykowski's opening sentences refer to opinions proposed by the writers who were invited to contribute.

Wiadomości Literackie published a total of thirteen articles. The first was an openly anti-Semitic one by Aleksander Świętochowski, a supporter of National Democracy. (For instance, he defends Ghetto benches, the official segregation of Jewish students in the seating of university lecture halls.) Szpakowska summarises his position:

> The conflict between two nations occupying the same territory, "one of which is stronger in terms of numbers, the other in terms of strategy and economic armament," is a conflict that cannot be resolved. The Poles lack a sufficient "ability to assimilate," to absorb a Jewish minority of three million, but at the same time they cannot tolerate "in their midst" a foreign "influx mass" that differs from them in "race, religion, language, customs". Both communities have a negative attitude towards each other, they feel "mutual disgust and contempt".

---

202 Jan Jakóbczyk, *Szachy literackie: Rzecz o twórczości Karola Irzykowskiego* (Katowice: Wydawnictwo Uniwersytetu Śląskiego, 2005), p. 95.

203 M. Szpakowska, *"Wiadomości Literackie" prawie dla wszystkich*, pp. 252–253. In fact both of Irzykowski's articles appeared as part of the discussion "Kultura polska a Żydzi" [Polish Culture and the Jews] in *Kurier Poranny*.

> Świętochowski saw no possibility for a compromise, the only solution was Jewish emigration.[204]

Irzykowski's argument resembles Świętochowski's in many ways. (It is worth noting that around this time, both of them wrote for the right-wing weekly *Prosto z Mostu*, another competitor of *Wiadomości Literackie*.) Racial arguments and vague notions about a "national spirit" are rejected from the outset, nor does Irzykowski want to enter into the debate on the Jews' cultural contributions – however they may be defined. He is convinced that the theories of Freud or Einstein are above all links "in the chain of our common, pan-European intellectual work" (p. 240). There is nothing particularly Jewish about them, just as Copernicus "is in no way an emanation of Polish culture, even though he was a Pole" (*ibid.*). Irzykowski believes that the so-called Jewish question must be viewed in sociological terms, taking into account certain historical, geographical, political and economical conditions. "The Jew is important not only as a nation. A Jew is a situation" (p. 241). Irzykowski adds that the ways of the Jews as a minority often repulse him: "Every time I'm on a train and I hear Jews jabbering I get the impression that they're conspiring against me and want to sell me to turn me into matzo" (*ibid.*). However, he also says that in their place he would act the same way. "The Jewish question was, is and will be a question of settling into a life together" (p. 245). The one available opportunity has been missed with the failure of the assimilation project. Above all, Irzykowski expresses his regret about the fact that during Poland's partition, when "assimilationism was the leading principle, when it was self-understood" (p. 242) in the Austrian territory, neither the Jews nor the Poles had seized the opportunity. There was a lack of goodwill on both sides, which is why after independence it was impossible for the two nations – only one of which actually identified with the fatherland – to coexist within the same state. For a Pole, Irzykowski continues, "Polishness is an irrevocable fact – I swim or I sink with my ship, I cannot change onto any other" (p. 243). The Jews always have this other option, they can easily cease to be Poles. Hence, following the formulation in the title, "The Jew is a Pole with Reservations".

The parallels between Świętochowski's and Irzykowski's opinions are unexpected, especially when we consider how deeply divided they had

204 K. Irzykowski, "Żyd jest to Polak z rezerwą", *KPO* 1937, no. 222, reprinted in *Pisma rozproszone 1936–1939* (Cracow: Wydawnictwo Literackie, 1999), p. 244.

been in 1912, when Irzykowski was publishing his earliest articles about Freud in *Prawda* and Świętochowski, the magazine's founder, was promoting an anti-Jewish boycott (see the end of the second chapter in Part One of this book). The tone of Irzykowski's "Żyd jest to Polak z rezerwą" recalls the anti-Semitic articles that were printed alongside his study on Freud in *Prawda*. The social context is also similar: rising anti-Semitism, the foundation, in 1937, of the political party Obóz Zjednoczenia Narodowego [Camp of National Unity], calls to boycott Jewish merchants and business people. This time not only Świętochowski, but also Irzykowski proposes that "Poles are linked with their fatherland for better or for worse. Jews can pull out of the company" (*ibid.*). He also considers emigration to be the only solution, although in his eyes such a "dissolution of the knot" (p. 245) manifestly represents a failure. He sees it as the ultimate capitulation before the task of living together as a society, proving that neither side was up to the task.

In the second article, which discusses the Jews' contribution to Polish literature, Irzykowski enters into the debate on the unique talent that supposedly characterises Jews. Within the series in *Wiadomości Literackie*, it is an article by Emil Zegadłowicz that explores this "Jewish genius," presenting Einstein and Freud as key examples. In Irzykowski's view, Jews do not originate new trends – they merely propagate them. They are "fructifiers of others' ideas," but they transport these ideas in "a diminished and childish form," which is why they are "poor cultural colporteurs".[205] At the same time, given that "every nation has the Jews it deserves," and "we have done a very bad job at teaching ours good manners" (p. 253), the most important centres of literary culture, including the press and publishing houses, have found themselves in the hands of Jews. The recipients of culture, Irzykowski believes, are also mainly Jews. The most numerous and most enthusiastic readers and theatre goers tend to be Jewish. It is unnerving to imagine, Irzykowski cautions, what might happen if the Jews, whose businesses were prone to boycotting, retaliated by withdrawing from the cultural industries.

All these arguments are aimed at Grydzewski's *Wiadomości Literackie*. Irzykowski portrays the paper as a literary academy, a self-proclaimed authority that "determines the rank, the issues of interest, one that eliminates, ignores and publicises" (p. 255). What is more, the members of

205 K. Irzykowski, "Udział Żydów w literaturze polskiej", *KPO* 1937, no. 224; reprinted in *Pisma rozproszone 1936–1939*, p. 253.

this academy "play their Jewish role so badly, instead of enlivening, awakening, exciting, they become proponents of backwardness, debasement and common megalomania" (*ibid.*), while their "tendency to succumb to fashion, usually yesterday's fashion, leads to a narrowing of the horizon, to becoming doctrinaire, hen-pecked, gossipy" (p. 254). The many years of collaborating with *Wiadomości Literackie*, Irzykowski claims, have helped him overcome his philo-Semitism. Accounting for his break with the paper he also cites the influential position it granted to Antoni Słonimski, who holds "high justice over Polish literature and writers" (p. 256). Here he mentions a discussion with the editor-in-chief, who reportedly tried to convince Irzykowski to come back but was not willing to promise that vicious attacks by Słonimski would not be printed, too. It is Słonimski, "an intellectual without intellect," who is eventually described as "the kind of Jew we have bred, the kind we deserve" (*ibid.*).

Following his review of Bychowski's book in *Wiadomości Literackie*, Irzykowski would rarely return to the subject of psychoanalysis – certainly not in this paper. Perhaps the fact that *Wiadomości Literackie* championed Freudianism has something to do with his decision to discontinue his efforts to promote it, even if his interest in psychoanalysis did not wane. Irzykowski's turn towards "Aryan psychoanalysis" can be seen as an act of provocation that allowed him to mark his own opposition to *Wiadomości Literackie*, once he stopped collaborating with it. In interwar Poland the most popular representative of "Aryan psychoanalysis" was Adler, whose ultimate ideal, according to Irzykowski, was something between socialism and Catholicism. "How remote this is from Freudianism, whose hidden foundation is the notion of bourgeois, purely hedonistic bliss."[206]

Słowacki's soul

In the 1930s *Wiadomości Literackie* became very active in popularising Freud's ideas, and now it was not only thanks to Bychowski's tireless pen – many different writers tackled psychoanalysis in this paper. For instance, in 1928 Freud's *The Future of an Illusion* is mentioned in an article by religious studies scholar Paweł Hulka-Laskowski.[207] In 1938 Artur Lilien-

206 Cf. e.g. K. Irzykowski, "Adleryzm w kulturze dzisiejszej", *KPO* 1937, no. 197, p. 6 (reprinted in *Pisma rozproszone 1936–1939*, pp. 233–237).

207 P. Hulka-Laskowski, "Erotomagja i grafomancja", *WL* 1928, no. 26, p. 1.

Brzozdowiecki reviewed Freud's latest work, *Moses and Monotheism.*[208] In 1935 *Wiadomości Literackie* printed an enthusiastic response to the first Polish translation of Freud's *Introduction to Psychoanalysis* (*Wstęp do psychoanalizy*),[209] the following year Freud's eightieth birthday was celebrated with a special supplement containing the famous photograph of "a stern, carefully dressed elderly gentleman with penetrating eyes and the inevitable cigar"[210] next to Maurycy Bornsztajn's article "Zasady psychoanalizy" [The Principles of Psychoanalysis], Stefan Essmanowski's "Psychoanaliza a sztuka" [Psychoanalysis and Art] as well as Bychowski's interview with Freud.[211] In 1937 *Wiadomości Literackie* published Antoni Cwojdziński's comedy "Freuda teoria snów" [Freud's Theory of Dreams].[212] The play was staged at the Teatr Mały and became a great success (I shall return to it later). The play's entire text was placed on the front page of the weekly paper, adorned with photos of the actors and a quotation from Freud's *Introduction to Psychoanalysis* as a motto. Throughout this period, themes related to psychoanalysis and Freudian terminology kept appearing in articles on unrelated matters, especially in book and theatre reviews.

A particularly interesting debate took place in *Wiadomości Literackie* in 1930. On the surface it concerned the question in how far psychoanalysis was scientific, but in fact it was about its applicability to cultural production. The trigger was a staging of G. K. Chesterton's play *Magic* at Teatr Nowy; the conservative Catholic playwright juxtaposed knowledge and faith in a way that inspired a discussion of his concept of science. [213] I will present this debate in some detail, as it illustrates the ways in which psychoanalysis was understood within Poland's intellectual elite in the last decade before World War II.

As a preamble we may note that Chesterton's aversion to psychoanalysis had already worried Freud and his inner circle ten years before. On 15 December 1920 Ernest Jones wrote about the situation in Great Britain in his circular to the Secret Committee:

---

208 A. Lilien-Brzozdowiecki, "Czy Mojżesz był Egipcjaninem?", *WL* 1938, no. 14, p. 6.

209 S. Essmanowski, "Wreszcie Freud!", *WL* 1935, no. 28, p. 4.

210 Peter Gay, *Freud: A Life for Our Times* (London: Papermac, 1989), p. 454.

211 *WL* 1936, no. 20, p. 4.

212 A. Cwojdziński, "Freuda teoria snów", *WL* 1937, no. 29, no. 32, no. 35.

213 On the occasion of Chesterton's visit to Poland in 1927, *Wiadomości Literackie* dedicated an entire issue to him (*WL* 1927, no. 18), including Andrzej Tretiak's enthusiastic discussion of *Magic*. The debate of 1930 started with Wacław Borowy's "'Magja', 'Głupstwa rozumu' i 'Sprawy przykre'", *WL* 1930, no. 13, p. 2.

> The indication I gave last week of psa [psychoanalysis] being favoured by notices in the Press has developed into a darkly campaign on the part of seven or eight newspapers. The lower class ones denounce psa in violent language, also appealing to anti-German feeling, but the better class content themselves with warning against its dangers in unskilled hands. It is written by someone with no knowledge of the facts, for ψα [psychoanalysis] is widely identified with telepathy, thought-reading, and other "occult tendencies," against which there is at present also a campaign. I have just been told that Chesterton is probably the instigator of the campaign.[214]

One of the reasons why Chesterton questioned the scientificity of psychoanalysis was that in his opinion, no true science could ever become fashionable: "It is a characteristic of sincere scientific speculation that it cannot at any given moment be applied generally to public affairs except with the utmost caution and the most copious dilutions of common sense."[215]

The writers who defended the notion that psychoanalysis was a science in *Wiadomości* were Antoni Słonimski,[216] Bruno Winawer[217] and Jan Emil Skiwski.[218] Skiwski names psychoanalysis next to the theory of evolution and eugenics – three fields that pose dilemmas for religious people. For Skiwski, Chesterton – the author of the pamphlet *Eugenics and Other Evils* (1921) – exposes himself to ridicule when he attacks these two "new fields of science and their research efforts, which are undertaken heroically in a little-known domain that is full of secrets and dangers".[219] It is unsurprising that the

214 *Die Rundbriefe des "Geheimen Komitees"*, vol. 1, p. 219.

215 G.K. Chesterton, "The Game of Psychoanalysis", *TCM* May 1923, p. 35.

216 as. [A. Słonimski], "'Magja' Chestertona", *WL* 1930, no. 14, p. 5.

217 B. Winawer, "Krzywe uznania", *WL* 1930, no. 7, p. 4.

218 J.E. Skiwski, "Chesterton, poloniści i inne sprawy przykre", *WL* 1930, no. 10, p. 1. Skiwski had already criticised Chesterton's *Orthodoxy* in 1929: J.E. Skiwski, "Metafizyk pospolitości", *WL* 1929, no. 39, p. 2.

219 It is worth noting that Skiwski's views on psychoanalysis shifted; ten years later he wrote a novel with the title *Czad* [Choke-Damp]. Here the anti-Semite Tadeusz Podwicki – probably the author's mouthpiece – describes psychoanalysis as an expression of "the Jewish spirit" and "stupid Jewish faddishness". See M. Urbanowski, *Człowiek z głębszego podziemia: Życie i twórczość Jana Emila Skiwskiego* (Cracow: Arcana, 2003), p. 409.

supporters of psychoanalysis were at the same time in favour of eugenics in 1930. (For instance, Gustav Bychowski worked with the Polish Eugenic Society.) In Poland, eugenics was well received in leftist and feminist circles. The campaigns for a renewal of social mores in *Wiadomości Literackie* referred to eugenic ideas, with the caveat that while the eugenicists focused on notions of a common good that were frequently racist, the liberals associated with *Wiadomości Literackie* were motivated by individualistic ideals – they believed eugenics would improve individual lives.[220] Their calls for sex education, birth control and reforms in the institution of marriage in *Wiadomości Literackie* were written in the name of combatting repressive bourgeois culture and superstition – a mission that was frequently justified by citing Sigmund Freud's authority.

One person who defended the English writer – opposing both eugenics and psychoanalysis – was Wacław Borowy, a literary scholar who had recently published a book about Chesterton's life and work.[221] His article in *Wiadomości Literackie* caused a wave of responses. He replied in turn:

> And now a word about Chesterton's relationship to science. This question cannot be tackled with the example of eugenics, for eugenics is not a science, it is an ensemble of practical applications of science – applications that are to be performed on ourselves and our fellow human beings. To call for restraint in social and moral considerations and to assume a purely contemplative position while eugenicists are carrying out experiments such as the mass sterilisation of men (as in California) would be an exaggeration of this scientific "humility" extolled by my (and Chesterton's) critic. The same goes for psychoanalysis. Many good things can be said about it, but there is no need to empathise with the "investigative agitation" in the mind of a researcher, if this researcher summarises Part IV of [Mickiewicz's] *Forefathers' Eve* with reference to the complex of the "mother's bed". And such are things done by leading psychoanalysers![222]

Gustav Bychowski responded to this passage in a letter to the editor that appeared in the section "Korespondencja" two issues later:

220 M. Gawin, *Rasa i nowoczesność*, pp. 210–240. Cf. also M. Zaremba Bielawski, *Higieniści: Z dziejów eugeniki*, trans. by W. Chudoba (Wołowiec: Wydawnictwo Czarne, 2011).

221 W. Borowy, *Gilbert Keith Chesterton* (Cracow: Krakowska Spółka Wydawnicza, 1929).

222 W. Borowy, "'Magja' w różnych stopniach wesołości", *WL* 1930, no. 16, p. 8.

> It is with sad dismay that I read the latest polemical note by Mr Wacław Borowy. It is difficult to understand why Mr Borowy, a serious scholar in his field, writes with such contemptuous disregard of a science about which – as is apparent – he has insufficient understanding. This, I believe, is not a helpful way of seconding Chesterton, who ridicules arrogant, short-sighted and self-complacent scientificity. Similarly problematic are Mr Borowy's comments on eugenics and psychoanalysis. Eugenics is indeed a branch of science, and the fact that it is an applied science does nothing to diminish the scientific nature of its foundation. The domain of practical application is, of course, subject to debate and concerns questions of immense importance. But when it comes to psychoanalysis, Mr Borowy's irresponsible relationship to the subject is best illustrated by his choice of terms that are either wrong or meaningless. There is a term such as "psychoanalyst" [*psychoanalityk*], but no one has ever heard of a "psycho-analyser" [*psychoanalista*] – or does Mr Borowy perhaps say "analyser" to describe an analyst in chemistry, geometry or literary analysis? "The complex of the mother's bed" exists only in Mr Borowy's mind. It is hard to fathom how a serious literary scholar can attempt to downplay and ridicule a science in this way – a science whose significance for literary studies is now widely recognised. One can combat everything – but first one must know and understand it. Thus Mr Borowy's final remarks seem to be a telling testimony of how dangerous it is to take a relativistic view of a science before comprehending it deeply. Perhaps in Poland it is still too early for Chesterton.[223]

Borowy's last word in this debate was an article titled "Beliza i psycho-analiza" [Belise and Psychoanalysis]. He compares Bychowski to the scholarly Belise, a character in Molière's *Les Femmes Savantes*, who shows herself outraged by the family servant's poor grammar. In his view, Bychowski's critical remarks about his neologism *psychoanalista* was out of place, especially given that the terminology of psychoanalysis was still somewhat vague and pliable. In his own defence he also cites a study published in 1923 where the complex of "the mother's bed" is in fact discussed. This study, *Podświadome w "Dziadach"*, was written by Stanisław Marcus, a member of the expressionist group "Zdrój". As I wrote in the chapter on the avant-garde, Marcus was inspired by eclectic sources that

223 G. Bychowski, "Eugenika, psychoanaliza i Chesterton", *WL* 1930, no. 18, p. 6.

were very remote from psychoanalysis as such, and we may wonder how Borowy could ignore the difference between Marcus' work and that of professional psychoanalysts. Perhaps he anticipated such criticism, for he adds:

> But – someone may say – Mr Marcus is not one of the leading psychoanalysts. Well, the study by Mr Marcus passes as a model of subtlety compared to the ramblings of various leading psychoanalysts. The greatest work in the field of applying psychoanalysis to literature, [Otto] Rank's *Das Inzestmotiv in Dichtung und Sage*, is among the ones most thoroughly rejected. This horrible monster of a book was duly subjected to devastating criticism by Ryszard M. Meyer. Another book, published a few years later, was [Albert] Mordell's *The Erotic Motive in Literature*, and it barely enjoys a better standing. Reading Hamlet's drama through the "Oedipus complex" (contained in [Ernest] Jones's *Essays in Applied Psycho-Analysis*) is generally regarded as fantastic balderdash.[224]

Again, we may wonder why Borowy mentions Rank and Jones, actual collaborators of Freud whose recent works truly represented the psychoanalytic movement, alongside Mordell, a writer whose ties with the movement are impossible to verify. He concludes: "that generally recognised significance of psychoanalysis for literary scholarship identified by Mr Bychowski needs to be discussed at much greater length, and it may transpire that it is not deprived of some dark shadows". To support his argument he refers to Western publications that question the benefits of applying psychoanalysis in literary studies. Borowy was a Polish literature scholar of international renown, and we may surmise that he expressed an opinion that was shared by the majority of his colleagues. Be that as it may, this debate demonstrates that while Poland's cultural elite did not hesitate to voice strong opinions on psychoanalysis, these intellectuals tended to be more familiar with psychoanalytical interpretations of literature than they were with Freud's writings themselves. Psychoanalysis now firmly belonged to the field of literary scholarship. At the same time, it appears that the trend of reading literature through Freud had perhaps already beginning to decline.

Paradoxically, the popularity of psychoanalytic literary criticism coincided with an intense campaign against psychologism by the proponents

224 W. Borowy, "Beliza i psychoanaliza", *WL* 1930, no. 20, p. 5.

of formalism, structuralism, and phenomenology, i.e. the most prominent representatives of the "intrinsic" or "ergocentric" approach.[225] It is worth recalling the chronological context: by 1930 most of Stefan (Stepan) Baley's works had been published. Marian Albiński had already written about Wyspiański for *Pro Arte* and *Przegląd Humanistyczny*, while the "Zdrój" group's publications included Marcus's study on Mickiewicz and Klein's readings of Mickiewicz and Norwid. Another telling example of the state of literary scholarship at the time is Rafał Blüth's article on Mickiewicz's poem "Śniła się zima". A great number of psychoanalytic studies of Romantic literature were published in interwar Poland, but this one remains particularly relevant today and merits a closer analysis.[226]

Blüth published his article in *Przegląd Współczesny*, a monthly journal founded by Jesuit priest Jan Badeni. Blüth's articles were often printed either in this journal or in the Catholic quarterly *Verbum*. Among his essays in *Przegląd Współczesny* were several discussions of the political situation in the USRR[227] as well as two studies on Gogol – literature was, we could say, his third field of interest. In his discussions of Gogol Blüth did not apply psychoanalytical tools.[228] Perhaps it was thanks to Polish historian and literary theorist Juliusz Kleiner that he became acquainted with Freudianism. Before World War I, Blüth studied chemistry at the Lviv Polytechnic, where Kleiner became aware of him and invited him to join his seminar. Blüth did not read German, so his understanding of psychoanalysis must have remain limited.[229] In his article on "Śniła się zima" he only refers to Freud's *On Dreams* (in Beata Rank's translation, *O*

225 Associated with this campaign are Roman Ingarden, Manfred Kridl, Zygmunt Łempicki, as well as Gabriel Korbut, Konstanty Troczyński, Karol Zawodziński, Stefania Skwarczyńska and the Warsaw Circle of Polish Literature Scholars (Warszawskie Koło Polonistów). See R. Pawlukiewicz, "Psychologiczne ujęcie problematyki badawczej w polskiej nauce o literaturze do roku 1939", in *Z dziejów polskiej nauki o literaturze*, ed. by H. Markiewicz, G. Matuszek (Warsaw: PWN, 1987), vol. 1, pp. 75–95.

226 R. Blüth, "Psychogeneza 'Snu w Dreźnie'", *PWS* 1925, no. 37, pp. 288–300. Reprinted in R.M. Blüth, *Pisma literackie*, ed. by P. Nowaczyński (Cracow: Znak, 1987), pp. 19–54. Cf. M. Lubański, "Rafała Blütha spotkanie z psychoanalizą", *TD* 1998, no. 1–2, pp. 109–123 as well as *Krytyka literacka i psychoanaliza*, pp. 53–73.

227 On Blüth see W. Weintraub, "Rafał Blüth", in *Straty kultury polskiej 1939–1944*, ed. by A. Ordęga, T. Terlecki (Glasgow: Książnica Polska, 1945), vol. 2, pp. 273–283.

228 R. Blüth, "Tragikomedia snobizmu w życiu i twórczości Gogola", *PWS* 1929, no. 89; R. Blüth, "Przypuszczalna geneza pomysłu *Rewizora* Gogola", *PWS* 1929, no. 90.

229 W. Weintraub, "Rafał Blüth", p. 282.

marzeniu sennem). His interest in psychoanalysis was no doubt rooted in his own way of reading literature. His younger colleague Wiktor Weintraub recalls:

> For him, the literary work was a psychological document testifying to the writer's inner struggles, his conflicts, a testimony that was generally more telling than letters or diaries, for usually these conflicts and experiences were voiced in it in a form that was pure, more crystalline, free from the ballast of details that are accidental. (p. 279)

One factor that must have distanced Blüth from psychoanalysis was its association with Jewish circles. He was born a Jew and later converted to Catholicism. According to Weintraub, "postwar Poland's Jewish intelligentsia was alien to him with its intellectualism, hedonism, liberalism. His tirades against it were such that even the most vicious anti-Semite would have been proud to use them" (p. 276). Literary historian Józef Marian Święcicki, who examined the psychoanalytic trend that flourished in the literary scholarship of the 1920s, sees Blüth's work as the most interesting example. In Blüth's view, Freud is guilty of "purely psychopathological one-sidedness" because he treats dreams as a mere substitute fulfilment of unconscious sexual desire; Blüth also sees this as an expression of Freud's "medical, extremely materialistic, amoral metaphysics".[230] In this sense Blüth's work almost appears to be anti-Freudian. Święcicki, however, finds it interesting precisely because Blüth undertakes "a very successful" attempt to "broaden Freud's psychoanalysis towards a Christianisation of his concept".[231]

Bychowski's somewhat touchy response to Borowy's criticism and the irritability that became apparent in this debate make more sense when we remember that Bychowski had just submitted his own psychoanalytical interpretation of a work of literature. His book *Słowacki i jego dusza* [Słowacki and His Soul] was published by Wydawnictwo Mortkowicza a short time after this dispute.[232] It is also noteworthy that a pre-publication

---

230 R. Blüth, "Psychogeneza 'Snu w Dreźnie'", pp. 288–289.

231 J.M. Święcicki, "Psychoanaliza w literaturze polskiej", *PPO* 1932, no. 580, p. 83. After World War II, Jerzy Speina recalled Święcicki's work in his essay "Psychoanaliza w badaniach literackich w Polsce okresu międzywojennego", in *Z dziejów nauki polskiej: Księga pamiątkowa Towarzystwa Naukowego w Toruniu*, ed. by A. Hutnikiewicz and L. Janiszewski (Warsaw: PWN, 1975), pp. 19–31.

232 G. Bychowski, *Słowacki i jego dusza: Studium psychoanalityczne* (Warsaw: Wydawnictwo J. Mortkowicza, 1930).

review and a few key passages appeared in *Wiadomości Literackie*.[233]

It is the sheer scale of Bychowski's work that distinguishes it from earlier applications of psychoanalysis to literature.[234] What he offers is not an interpretation of one motif or a contribution to understanding the Romantic poet's personality, but a comprehensive account of Słowacki's life and work. He is clearly aware of the pitfalls of his undertaking: "In contrast to analyses of the fantasies or dreams of a living person with whom we communicate directly, our material is limited. We cannot confirm our constructs, nor can we deny them."[235] To fend off any accusations about his hypotheses being arbitrary, Bychowski introduces two binding methodological criteria: first, his interpretation ought to "conform to the principles of psychoanalysis, which are known from other sources," and second, it should "correspond to the entirely of the psyche of the artist whose work we are analysing" (*ibid.*). The second touchstone means that a psychoanalytic interpretation must be tested against previous findings about the poet's character – findings obtained through different methods. For Bychowski, the ultimate authority in this matter is Kleiner's recently published extensive monograph.[236] Occasionally he also refers to Antoni Małecki's *Juliusz Słowacki: Jego życie i dzieła w stosunku do współczesnej epoki* [Juliusz Słowacki: His Life and Work in Relation to His Era, 1901], to an even older "psychological biography" by Ferdynand Hoesick, and, in the final chapters, to Jan G. Pawlikowski's *Mistyka Słowackiego* [Słowacki's Mysticism]. But his tone conveys the greatest sense of pride when he is able to state that he reached his conclusions "independently of our most prominent specialist on Słowacki".[237]

Bychowski's analysis is based on Słowacki's literary works as well as autobiographical notes from his estate, in particular his vast correspondence and diary. He reconstructs the poet's early childhood in order to

233 "Psychoanaliza Słowackiego", *WL* 1930, no. 31, p. 3.

234 Bychowski's work has recently met with renewed scholarly interest, mostly thanks to Danuta Danek and Marek Lubański. Danek re-edited his study *Słowacki i jego dusza: Studium psychoanalityczne* (Cracow: Universitas, 2002), while Lubański discussed Bychowski in *Krytyka literacka i psychoanaliza*, pp. 107–148. Another discussion of Bychowski's book can be found in A. Nasiłowska, "Psychoanalityk i dusza Słowackiego", in *Persona liryczna* (Warsaw: IBL PAN, 2000), pp. 253–269.

235 G. Bychowski, *Słowacki i jego dusza* (2002), p. 79.

236 J. Kleiner, *Juliusz Słowacki: Dzieje twórczości*, vol. 1–4 (Warsaw: Gebethner i Wolf, 1919–1927).

237 G. Bychowski, *Słowacki i jego dusza*, p. 278.

shed light on his later life and work. The subject that figures most prominently is Słowacki's fixation on his mother, Salomea Bécu. This fixation on the mother as the primary object of affection prevented the poet from entering a mature relationship with another woman and inspired him to cultivate an ideal of sexual purity. Almost all the important female figures in Słowacki's work – but also in his life – can be read as successive embodiments of his mother. Bychowski also identifies Salomea in the traits of two opposing female types (a characteristic feature of Słowacki's dramas). Finally, Salomea Bécu is represented symbolically, especially through aquatic metaphors.

Bychowski also explores Słowacki's relationship to his father and stepfather. One recurring theme, he argues, is the Oedipal triangle, i.e. the rivalry between father and son about a beloved woman; it can be found in the plays *Kordian*, *Mazepa* and *Beatryks Cenci*. Next, Bychowski juxtaposes the poetic novel *Lambro* with some of Słowacki's letters from his travels to Greece and the Near East. What he detects, most importantly, is a hidden "homoerotic streak, which, as we know today, occurs to some extent in the psychosexual development of every individual" (p. 100).

When it comes to analysing Słowacki's mystical phase, Bychowski applies the tools he developed in his work on schizophrenia. In the footnotes he refers directly to Freud's Schreber case and, frequently, to his own *Metaphysik und Schizophrenie*. He discusses Słowacki's late work as being rooted in a pathological state in which the psyche reverts to primordial (prelogical, animistic or magical) forms of thinking. The blurring of the boundary between the self and the world outside is presented in terms of a regression to the stage of primary narcissism, "complete bliss" and "a closeness to the mother in which the child's ego does not recognise itself as such and only feels an undefined, entirely unclouded oneness" (p. 329). For Bychowski, Słowacki's philosophy of Genesis is based on a transposition of the poet's internal struggles to a cosmic level, and it brings to mind "the worldview of some primordial peoples, especially totemic systems where [...] it also corresponds to tendencies to repress impulses rooted in the Oedipus complex" (p. 313).

In these sections Bychowski also refers to Carl Jung (p. 243, p. 299). This is remarkable not only because other Freudians avoided mentioning the Swiss renegade's theories, but also because Jung's work was quite unknown in interwar Polish literary scholarship. The only text that dealt with it exclusively was Artur Górski's article "Psychologia analityczna w sztuce" [Analytic Psychology in Art], published in the quarterly *Marchołt* in 1935.[238] For Górski, the former editor of the Young Poland weekly *Życie*, Freudianism boils down to the theory of libido and its different stages of sublimation; he portrays it as an "archaic phase" in the evolution of psychoanalysis, which is "the upshot of an atmosphere associated with a certain prewar generation that had lost the deeper meaning of life" (p. 143). Next to the "naturalist or rather sensualist novel," Freud's "theory of culture as a sublimation of one drive" is no more than "yet another document of its time" (*ibid.*), "unworthy of a young, unhackneyed nation that sensualism has not eaten through" (p. 144). Jung, meanwhile, impresses Górski with his theory of symbolism, which relates a work of art to the "collective unconscious," the world of "unconscious mythology, whose images, rooted in ancient times, represent the common good of humanity" (p. 148). In the light of Jung's theory, the creative process is an "unconscious revitalisation of the archetype" (p. 152), a translation into contemporary language, while Freudianism sees the writer as just another "clinical case," "one of the common specimens of *psychopathia sexualis*" (p. 145). Górski does not mention Bychowski by name but it is likely that the book on Słowacki was on his mind when he complained about psychoanalytical interpretations of works of art and their being "worthless, shallow and boringly monotonous" (*ibid.*).

One person who appreciated Bychowski's work on Słowacki was Juliusz Kleiner. As I already mentioned, Kleiner habilitated in literary studies at the University of Lviv just before World War I and he took active part in the Polish Philosophical Society (Polskie Towarzystwo Filozoficzne), especially those sessions that concerned psychoanalysis. In 1931 he published a four-volume monograph on Słowacki and an edition of his complete works (*Dzieła wszystkie*). Kleiner wrote an extensive review of Bychowski's book for *Kurier Warszawski*. He finds it quite plausible that "Słowacki must be more attractive to a psychologist than any other Polish writer,"[239] and he is unsurprised that "since new methods are being used to delve into the souls of poets, he has become the first in Poland to inspire scholars to try and tear down the psyche's curtains". Kleiner stressed at the outset that, whatever the results of such experiments may be, Freudianism itself ought to be recognised as "one of the most important achievements of science". In his opinion, Freud was the first to discover a way to

238 A. Górski, "Psychologia analityczna w sztuce", *MAR* 1935, no. 1, pp. 143–155.

239 J. Kleiner, "Słowacki w świetle psychoanalizy", *KW* 1931, no. 80, p. 12. Unless stated otherwise, quotations from Kleiner's article refer to this page number.

methodically study the sphere of the unconscious, which, already recognised by Leibniz, had a particular appeal to the Romantics while remaining inaccessible to scientistic understanding: "How are we to study something psychologically that is said to exist in the ego when it remains hidden, inaccessible to this very ego?" For Kleiner, the fact that Freud managed to overcome this aporia means he will be remembered by the history of science, even if the rest of his system, which "often shakes under pressure of scientific criticism," were to be overturned root and branch.

Kleiner goes on to summarise the key ideas of psychoanalysis, especially the mechanism of repression, where upsetting or shameful elements, forced into the unconscious, return in a disguised or symbolic form. When "the mental structure remains within the boundaries of average normality," the repressed mostly transpires in dreams, free association or jokes. In other cases the consequences can be more extreme:

> Either "complexes" poison the spirit, leading to mental illness – or they will find an outlet in some activity or powerful feeling directed at an object that does not arouse resistance from consciousness (e.g. in some cherished ideals) – or in a crime – or, finally, in the intensification and externalisation of dreams, which artistic creativity is said to be. Art – according to the Freudians – is a way of saving oneself from the abyss of mental illness, it is the self-healing of the ego. This explains the very strange echo that human souls find in it, as they sense in it a medicine, a remedy, an escape.

In Kleiner's opinion, psychoanalysis has reached such popularity because it responds to newly emerging world-views. He goes on to argue that in the early days, when Sigmund Freud was mostly known as a psychiatrist specialising in hysteria, "the idea that the mental mechanism of hysterics represented the key to understanding the mind was well suited for an epoch fascinated with neurosis and happy to accept the neurotic as a model of the normal person". In the interwar period, meanwhile, "trying to identify subconscious motors of behaviour appeals to a generation marked by a blunted sense of ethical responsibility," and "revealing hidden erotic desires suits our era of weakened embarrassment" (p. 13).

Notwithstanding this harsh judgement, Kleiner's tone becomes milder when he moves on to Bychowski's book. He finds it praiseworthy especially when compared to the existing literature in the field, which he deems to be mostly "of little value, guilty of affectedness and exaggeration" (*ibid.*). The authors, "followers and imitators" of Freud, try to identify the Oedipus complex in more and more writers, "offering solutions to difficult problems that are too easy, presenting complicated phenomena too simplistically". Kleiner identifies Baley as Bychowski's precursor in the study of Słowacki and, generally, in literary scholarship rooted in psychoanalysis. He highlights Baley's study of Słowacki's poem "W Szwajcarii" [In Switzerland] and his article "Psychoanaliza jednej pomyłki Słowackiego" [A Psychoanalysis of Słowacki's Slips] as the new method's "happy introductions" in the Polish context.[240] Bychowski's book, Kleiner continues, lives up to its model: "with subtle insight and tactful moderation he strides towards a portrayal of the poet's soul".[241] In Kleiner's view, Bychowski does not limit himself to Freudianism, so that the book, despite its subtitle, is "a psychological analysis, not just a 'psychoanalysis'". This, along with the absence of excessive jargon and Bychowski's discrete approach to sensitive issues, allows the book to avoid the usual "flaws and mistakes with which pioneering explorers of the subconscious often discourage and alienate" their readers. As a result, not all of Bychowski's readers will "come to believe in the new method's conclusive fruitfulness, but none will experience strong psychological resistance to them and all will shake off any aversion or prejudice" (*ibid.*). As a renowned Słowacki specialist, Kleiner bestows an unusual compliment on Bychowski when he writes that "thanks to his subtle psychological and aesthetic sensitivity, he has indeed come to know the poet's soul, shimmering in rainbow colours, as well as his works, and at the same time he has duly become acquainted with the state of research". Professor Kleiner only finds "minor faults and inaccuracies" that have no significant impact on the whole. Bychowski's psychological portrayal of Słowacki, described as "engaging, incisive, carried out consistently," is said to highlight and clarify traits of the poet's personality that earlier scholars had already identified. For instance, Słowacki's egotism, which marks his later, mystical phase, are labelled as narcissism. Kleiner also finds the discussion of the poet's ambivalence towards his mother convincing, and he describes Bychowski's psychoanalytical interpretation of this aspect as "an entirely new and sometimes revelatory light" (p. 14). He summarises the argument:

240 Kleiner's view on Baley's innovativeness is also confirmed by the fact that Bychowski refers to Baley several times: G. Bychowski, *Słowacki i jego dusza*, pp. 50–57 as well as pp. 155–156.

241 J. Kleiner, "Słowacki w świetle psychoanalizy", p. 13.

> There is something more in this duality than a defence against an excessive influence by the beloved person. For Słowacki, the object of love has been his mother, ever since his childhood years; she is the one who truly represents femininity in his eyes. This is why as soon as sensuality begins to enter his awareness, an inner resistance stirs as well. The poet has repressed his sensual desires from the very beginning, he has condemned them, detected evil in them. This is the source of his path towards perfection, but also of his internal quandaries. He unconsciously blames his mother for his quandaries, and the fact that her aspirations and ambitions regarding her son contain elements that are incompatible with his ideals opens the door for the dual sense of the mother's most ideal – and most perilous – influence. It returns later in his mystical phase, but at its height the ultimate harmony is attained – the return to the primal unity converges with the return to the mother.

Bychowski's interpretation of Słowacki's feelings towards his father is less compelling for Kleiner, who describes the passages in question as "a search for complexes that are considered permanent, universal, lacking due justification". This search may be interesting and the findings are certainly not implausible, but the approach remains part of a "scientific fantasy". Kleiner concludes that "the pages dedicated to the mother's significance in the poet's work would have sufficed to confer lasting value on the book – and to legitimate the psychoanalytical method".

Other literary scholars where decidedly less appreciative of Bychowski's book than Kleiner. Most agreed about the "great advantage of applying psychoanalysis to Słowacki,"[242] citing Baley's earlier interpretations as evidence. In *Ruch Literacki*, Mieczysław Giergielewicz cryptically mentions a leading Słowacki scholar who regretted his own inability to draw on the psychoanalytical method, as it "could have turned out to be immensely fruitful for his studies" (p. 210).

Compared to literary studies by other Freudians (such as Otto Rank), Giergielewicz argues, Bychowski's book has the benefit of being clearly rooted in admiration for the bard, so that his Freudian tools do not diminish the Słowacki's worth in his readers' eyes. If anything, Bychowski overexerts himself justifying an approach that is unquestionably legitimate:

---

242 M. Giergielewicz, "Gustaw Bychowski: *Słowacki i jego dusza*" [review], *RL* 1931, no. 7, p. 213.

> Just as our enchantment gazing at a beautiful landscape is not diminished by our awareness that the plants that make up its composition are the product of this or that chemical make-up of the soil, so the study of the elements of an artist's psychology does not impact our adoration for the ensemble of these elements – the artist's individuality, which is something new, as well as the works of art. (*ibid.*)

Giergielewicz takes issue with the fact that Bychowski writes about his love for Słowacki's poetry and thereby undermines himself as a scientist: "it is not the chemist's job to be enthralled with the landscape, [...] it will do if his position is strictly factual, free of prejudice" (*ibid.*). He is unsure about what criteria should be applied to assess the book: should it be judged as a contribution to the field of psychiatry (where the results of a psychoanalysis can be empirically verified by examining the effects of a therapy – something that cannot be done with dead people) or to the field of literary scholarship? In the latter case the question would be whether Bychowski proposes "a system that is coordinated and free of contradictions," and if the book offers "a commentary on [Słowacki's] work that is more pragmatic and consistent than one obtained by other means" (p. 211). Giergielewicz further points out errors that show that Bychowski is no expert on Polish literature; he criticises his selective use of secondary literature and also indicates the overambitious nature of the project as a whole. While certainly "not an exact discussion of [Słowacki's] vast output as a whole," however, Bychowski's book "delineates the path, leaving his successors to examine the terrain in more detail". Giergielewicz regrets that the analyses are cursory and sketch-like, especially when it comes to Słowacki's most productive period (1831-42) as well as the oversimplification of his programmatic conflict with Mickiewicz. Still he concludes:

> The author's method can be compared to a spotlight being fleetingly cast into space. It does not illuminate every detail, it does not shed a uniform light on the whole, but wherever the beam falls, a vast view opens up before our eyes; it may not be very clear but it reaches far into the depths.

The most compelling parts of Bychowski's book, according to Giergielewicz, are the passages on Słowacki's youth before the November 1830 Uprising and the analyses of his mystical work, characterised – here the reviewer agrees – by psychological regression. Between these two phases, Giergielewicz surmises, the poet's experiences and works pose too great a challenge for psychoanalysis, which "turns out to be most fruitful when examining certain basic, simple complexes" but which struggles with "life's intricate conflicts" (p. 213). One great advantage of the book for Polish literary scholarship is that reading it "we cannot help but question the one-sidedness of our common opinions about Słowacki, opinions based on an excessive rationalisation of the creative process". The reviewer concludes that the monograph, despite its "special character" (p. 215), presents a valuable contribution to literary studies and "an important step on the path to a deeper understanding of Słowacki's work" (*ibid.*).

A different opinion was put forward by Marian Piątkiewicz, reviewer for the specialist journal *Polonista*. In his view, Bychowski's findings can only be described as "simply outlandish".[243] He has no doubt that "in the history of literary scholarship on Słowacki's output, Dr Bychowski's book will not represent an important position" (p. 269). The reason is not, as Bychowski himself notes in his introductory disclaimer, that he is a layman in the field of literary studies – although even an amateur ought to feel bound to certain principles, such as accuracy and evidence "based on facts confirmed by documents" (p. 266); the book cannot be taken seriously because the author blindly follows "the questionable theses of psychoanalysis, which reduce genius to the lowlands of mediocrity" (*ibid.*). The reviewer cannot agree with the assumption – underlying not only Bychowski's work but psychoanalysis as a whole – that all human beings should be governed by the same laws; he is outraged by the supposition that Słowacki's soul ought to be "full of the same drives and passions as the soul of every average, normal, common person" (*ibid.*). He further takes issue with the approach of always reading characters and events represented in the works as records of the author's experiences – after all, he argues, the psychology of creativity teaches us that the poet brings them to life by the sheer force of his creative imagination:

> Truly, Słowacki fared better with the old "influencologists" who claimed that everything he wrote was a copy of Byron or Shakespeare than with the new psychoanalysts who make him personally responsible for every character he created and every word, as he is supposed to have experienced

243 M. Piątkiewicz, "Gustaw Bychowski: *Słowacki i jego dusza*" [review], *POL* 1931, no. 5/6, p. 266.

> all this in the days of his childhood, and now he only remembers or becomes aware of it. (p. 267)

For Piątkiewicz, the psychoanalytical portrait of Słowacki is "offensive both in its bold disclosure of stark, often lowly traits, and in the fact that it lacks documentary justification" (p. 269). The reviewer also disagrees with Bychowski about the poet's relationship to his mother, which was, in his opinion, "the most beautiful, purest and most human that literature – and not only Polish literature – has passed on to us" (p. 267); he vehemently opposes the idea of an erotic component as imputed by psychoanalysis. What is more, if Bychowski's goal was to portray the poet's soul in all its complexity, the fact that he limited himself to erotic questions is a mistake in itself; to perform such a feat he ought to have "taken into consideration all of the poet's experiences, his relationships with people, his reading, the intellectual issues that interested Słowacki" (p. 269). Piątkiewicz predicts that Bychowski's book "will not live beyond the demise of the trend that is fashionable today" (*ibid.*). If any of Bychowski's interpretations should have a lasting impact, then it is only some of his insightful and subtle textual analyses, especially of the works from Słowacki's mystical period. The reviewer concedes that "the reader cannot resist the allure of many pages of this book," but "it is a pity that this charm is so often bound to crack when the author returns to hitting the questionable keys of psychoanalytical theory" (*ibid.*). As long as the reader does not lose their "compass of careful criticism" (p. 269), however, the book may be useful.

One reviewer who went farther in his conclusions was Władysław Kozicki, an art history professor from Lviv. In his review for *Nowe Słowo* he describes Gustav Bychowski as a "well-known and outstanding psychiatrist and psychoanalyst,"[244] and advises him to focus on his own specialisation. He describes Bychowski's book as "conscientious and skilful" and applauds that it provides "many subtle observations on Słowacki's poetic ideas and their genesis from the murky depths of the subconscious" (*ibid.*). Like all of Freudian scholarship, however, it is burdened by "the curse of pansexualism," which leads to results that are "pathetic" and "decidedly incorrect" (*ibid.*). Interestingly, Kozicki's opposition is particularly vehement when it comes to the psychoanalytical method's application in the interpretation of stage plays. In the case of poetry he concedes that it reflects the writer's unconscious emotions; drama, however, has a different origin:

---

244 W.K. [W. Kozicki], "Wśród książek", *SPL* 1931, no. 186, p. 4.

> [Plays are] objective constructs, certainly always containing a tiny grain of subjective attitudes and feelings, but they are nonetheless mainly the work of consciousness and generally intellectual factors, guided by the principles of an intentionally chosen fiction, the laws of contrast, conflict etc., and are, therefore, works in which the subconscious has, relatively speaking, the smallest field of action. (*Ibid.*)

Kozicki's conclusion is unforgiving:

> Perhaps the psychoanalysts would do well to confine their method to therapeutic, psychiatric purposes and leave literature and art in peace. The theory of literary and artistic scholarship, meanwhile, can only make use of their work in this field with great caution and very far-reaching reservations. Otherwise it will go astray in a mightily deplorable manner. (*Ibid.*)

A negative opinion about the book was also published by Stefan Szuman, a psychologist, in the journal *Polskie Archiwum Psychologii.* Szuman begins by highlighting the difficulties of assessing Bychowski's work objectively, setting aside the fact that the author is, "from what we can say based on his book about psychoanalysis, not just an ardent supporter but a follower of Freud's teachings, one who accepts his master's psychological system without reservations".[245] Reviewers of *Słowacki i jego dusza*, Szuman argues, will have to take a stand on psychoanalysis as such, even though all readers, whatever their attitude to Freudianism, ought to acknowledge that Bychowski has skilfully fulfilled the task he set himself and, given his assumptions, has produced a consistent and positive discussion of the topic at hand. In this sense, Szuman acknowledges, the book is "very thorough, thoughtful, consistent, interesting and valuable" (p. 45). The answer must be negative, however, when it comes to the question if Bychowski's psychoanalytical portrait of the poet's soul has allowed him to make any contribution to our understanding of Słowacki.

Like Kleiner, Szuman points out that earlier researchers had already drawn attention to the poet's close relationship with his mother. In this sense there would be nothing shocking about Bychowski's findings if only

245 S. Szuman, "Krytyczny pogląd na znaczenie psychoanalizy dla badań twórczości literackiej", *PAP* 1931, no. 1, p. 45.

he did not suggest that there was something "plainly erotic, literally sexual" about Słowacki's feelings for Salomea Bécu. Szuman acknowledges that Bychowski chooses his words carefully and tries not to offend the reader, and yet he cannot agree with Bychowski's interpretation. He mentions the multiple meanings of Freud's term libido, regretting that he could never tell when Bychowski was using it in the general sense of love and when he had in mind sensual love. Szuman is inclined to believe that in most cases the analyst meant the latter, which in his view is not sufficiently founded in the poet's work. Bychowski's interpretations, Szuman believes, only "seek to agree with psychoanalytic doctrine, which actually makes it impossible for him to properly understand the issue in its multifaceted, complex and authentic essence" (p. 47). He is especially outraged about Bychowski's claims that Słowacki had an oral fixation and that generally his entire output can be accounted for by examining his childhood experiences.

Szuman agrees that Bychowski's account of Słowacki's relationship to his mother is supported by biographical facts, but the remaining aspects of his analysis strike him as pure speculation. Like Kleiner he remains unconvinced about the passages concerning the Oedipus complex. He appreciates the theory about the conflict between the pleasure principle and the reality principle as a useful contribution of psychoanalysis. At the same time he disagrees with Bychowski's proposal that the tension between Słowacki's high opinion of himself and the fact that he remained under-appreciated throughout his lifetime can be understood in terms of narcissism. He also argues that while we may assume that poetry is in some measure "a realisation, in the sphere of art, of something that cannot be realised in life" (p. 51), it would still be wrong to reduce it to the sole function of compensation. Instead of "exploring and portraying Słowacki's psyche and his works," Bychowski has only "applied all the teachings of psychoanalysis to the particular case that is Słowacki" (p. 50). Most importantly, Szuman adds, Bychowski has failed to comment on the fact that poetry was not just an escape from reality for the bard but also a way of substituting reality with an ideal, which is also a way of overcoming it.

> The mystical world view that arose from Słowacki's poetic work was not a mere regression into the prelogical, animistic domain of thinking, as the author has it, but the creation of a loftier reality, one that was factual even

> if it was ideal, not solipsistic or autistic but participative, philosophically convincing. (p. 51)

Szuman identifies the same principle in the way Słowacki resolves the conflict between the pleasure principle and the reality principle. The poet's refusal to enter into a compromise with reality aligns him with other thinkers who developed world views and philosophical systems. Słowacki achieved something great:

> [He constructed] not only a poetic and dream-like reality for himself, a rainbow home for his heart, weary of reality, but he erected a new and strong fortress with solid foundations, for the spirit in its eternal struggle with reality. Unable to defend his fatherland through action he went about defending it with the spirit [...], thus he truly became the leader of the nation and realised his calling in the domain of the reality that he himself created through his poetry. (p. 52)

For Szuman, the poet's sexual abstinence represents his "overcoming of sensual reality" rather than a result of early childhood complexes. He also opposes the idea of describing Słowacki's great spiritual achievement in terms of regression. The concept of regression may have a particular meaning in psychoanalysis, but it is still an insult: "the reader will naturally conclude [...] that in the author's view, Słowacki's work, though beautiful, must still be, when it comes to the ideas and views it contains, the product of a mind that has become somewhat infantile" (p. 52). He also objects to Bychowski's reference to notions such as animism and prelogical, primitive or magical thinking. Defending Słowacki's mystical work against the claims of psychoanalysis, he suggests that *Genezis z ducha* has much in common with Darwin's theory of evolution.[246]

Another urgent issue for Szuman is the question if psychoanalysis ought to be applied to literary works in general, and Słowacki's in particular. Psychoanalysis, "the study of methods to interpret symbols,"[247] appears to have much in common with literary scholarship, which involves the attempt to read a work's implicit meaning. The problem with psycho-

246 Here Szuman echoes an argument proposed by philosopher Wincenty Lutosławski as early as 1909. Cf. W. Lutosławski, *Darwin i Słowacki* (Warsaw: Gebethner i Wolff, 1909).

247 S. Szuman, "Krytyczny pogląd na znaczenie psychoanalizy", p. 54.

analytical interpretations of literature, however, is that Freud has established fixed meanings for certain symbols – erotic meanings to boot. For Szuman, Bychowski's analysis of Słowacki also shows that psychoanalytical theory (which presents art as a realisation of hidden desires, a sublimation of drives that save the subject from madness) cannot do justice to the phenomenon of a poet who "even as a young child aspires to poetic creativity, feels his inspiration and knows that he has a calling" (p. 61). Psychoanalytical theory is helpless in the face of such outstanding talent, and it fails to account for the formal crystallisation of the poems' content, "the arduous labour of mining the gold of the spirit from the depths of the poet's womb into the light of truth" (*ibid.*).

Szuman's conclusion is categorical: "I do not consider psychoanalysis to be an appropriate tool to elucidate the psyche of a great poet and his work" (p. 60). At the same time he emphasises that he does not condemn Freudianism as such; on the contrary, he states:

> I see Freud as an exceptional mind and I do not hesitate to acknowledge his genius, while his oeuvre has, in my view, a great significance for the development of psychology and human thought in general. I do not see it, however, as a dogma that we ought to accept uncritically, nor do I count myself among Freud's followers and absolute devotees; among them, as I conclude from both publications I have read, is the author of the book discussed here. (*Ibid.*)

Szuman quips that if Bychowski's book were to be assessed on the sole criterion of its conformity with Freud's theory then it ought to be described as perfect – but only on this condition.

In 1932 the debate on *Słowacki i jego dusza* was crowned by Józef Marian Święcicki in a comprehensive article titled "Psychoanaliza w literaturze polskiej" [Psychoanalysis in Polish Literature] in *Przegląd Powszechny.* As I already mentioned above, Święcicki considers Rafał Blüth most successful in applying psychoanalysis to literature, and it is certainly no coincidence that Blüth is the least strict in his use of Freud. Bychowski, by contrast, described as "*plus freudiste que Freud même,*" does not impress Święcicki. Instead of drawing on psychoanalysis as "a very useful, more or less plausible hypothesis," Bychowski, an "ardent admirer" of psychoanalytical theory, sees in it "something like a new profession of faith".[248] The result is that "Bychowski's

248 J.M. Święcicki, "Psychoanaliza w literaturze polskiej", *PPO* 1932, no. 193, p. 176.

overelaborate work stands and falls with the dogmas of Freudianism" (p. 343). Comparing Blüth's article on Mickiewicz's "Śniła się zima" with Bychowski's analysis of Słowacki's *Sen Srebrny Salomei*, Święcicki highlights the subtlety and "exemplary objectivity" of the former in contrast to Bychowski's fanaticism and hubris.[249] Święcicki adds that he cannot understand why Kleiner published a favourable, even commendatory, review of the book; he is especially baffled about Kleiner's positive assessment of Bychowski's analysis of the poet's relationship with his mother. He finds it much easier to agree with Szuman's reservations and his general opinion about psychoanalysis and its applicability to literary scholarship:

> At least the debate prompted by Bychowski's work has outlined the negative limits of the new method; scholars with a dual appreciation for psychology and literature now have the responsibility to produce a study that would find some modus vivendi between these two undoubtedly related disciplines. Bychowski's book has thrown down the gauntlet. You can criticise it, you can pass over it in silence, but the only worthy response would be a genuine psychoanalysis of Słowacki, one that would be free of the pathological aspects of Freudianism. (pp. 88–89)

249 J.M. Święcicki, "Psychoanaliza w literaturze polskiej", *PPO* 1932, vol. 194, p. 88.

Introduction to Psychoanalysis

A Polish translation of Freud's *Introduction to psychoanalysis*

Bychowski's most enduring contribution to the cultural transfer of psychoanalysis was his involvement in the publication of another Polish translation of a book by Freud, namely his *Introduction to Psychoanalysis* (*Vorlesungen zur Einführung in die Psychoanalyse*). This project, which came to fruition in 1935, had already been envisaged many years before. As early as 1917, an announcement in *Kurier Lwowski* mentioned that Freud's recently published book was being translated by Leopold Wołowicz, but this edition never saw the light of day.[1] *Wstęp do psychoanalizy* appeared in 1935 (postdated 1936). It was translated by Salomea Kempnerówna (the form ending in -ówna designates an unmarried woman from the Kempner family) and a certain W. Zaniewicki; it was edited by Gustav Bychowski.[2] After the long period in which Polish translations had appeared exclusively with the International Psychoanalytic Press, this time it was a newly established local publisher that revived the project of bringing Freud to Polish readers. Przeworski's Press (Wydawnictwo Przeworskiego), founded in 1933, was run by a Jewish family. As was the case with Altenberg Publishers, which had issued Freud's works before World War I, here, too, the publisher's history and position in the market merit a short digression. The press was by founded by Jakub Przeworski in Warsaw. He was an experienced antiquarian book dealer who entered the business in 1900 and came to own two shops in the city. When he died in

1 The section with news from the publishing world contains the following announcement: The psychiatrist Dr Sigmund Freud, professor at the University of Vienna, has presented a complete psychological and medical system known as psychoanalysis, arousing great interest among both supporters and opponents (who are numerous). Polish translations are available of a number of minor works by the Viennese savant; at present, a translation of Prof. Freud's key work *Vorlesungen zur Einführung in die Psychoanalyse*, the second volume of which was issued recently, is being prepared for publication. The person in charge is Prof. Dr Leopold Wołowicz, who has attended a course on the subject in Vienna and is familiar with the relevant literature. (*KL* 1917, no. 16, p. 7)

2 Zygmunt Freud, *Wstęp do psychoanalizy*, trans. by S. Kempnerówna and W. Zaniewicki, ed. by G. Bychowski (Warsaw: Przeworski, 1935).

1935, his son Marek took charge of the firm and established it as one of the region's leading publishing houses.[3] Three hundred titles were issued by 1939. The Prze-worskis focused on previously unpublished works, especially translations in the fields of philosophy, sociology and history, later also bioraphy, fiction and poetry. Besides Freud's *Introduction to Psychoanalysis*, Przewor-ski's Press also issued Polish translations of Freud's *Selbstdarstellung* (*An Autobiographical Study*), i.e. *Wizerunek własny* (1936),[4] as well as of Stefan Zweig's biography of Freud (1933).[5] Their catalogue also included highly successful translations of works by Bronisław Malinowski and Bertrand Russell as well as interwar bestsellers such as Margaret Mitchell's novel *Gone with the Wind* and children's literature by Walt Disney. Their books were prepared with much attention to detail and enjoyed immense popu-larity. Przeworski's commercial success was supported by advertising cam-paigns in the press: upcoming publications were announced in the daily newspapers, prospectuses were distributed with literary monthlies and regularly updated catalogues were available, too. The books were dis-patched to all libraries across the country, and they were stocked by most retailers. Especially trained travelling salesmen offered the books on instal-ments, so the print runs sold out quickly despite the elevated price tag. An advertisement in *Wiadomości Literackie* indicates that in 1936, a Polish translation of Freud's *Theoretische Schriften* [Theoretical Works] was under way;[6] in 1939 the *New Introductory Lectures on Psycho-Analysis* were an-nounced.[7] The Nazi invasion dashed all publication projects. Marek Prze-worski managed to escape the Warsaw ghetto, but he was shot by the Gestapo in 1943.[8]

For a long time the two books by Freud that Przeworski's Press had been able to issue, i.e. *Introduction to Psychoanalysis* and *An Autobiographical Study*, were the only sources available to Polish readers interested in the theoretical development of psychoanalysis. It is, therefore, worth recalling their origin. The *Introduction to Psychoanalysis* was based on

---

3 Cf. *Słownik pracowników książki polskiej*, ed. by I. Treichel (Warsaw: PWN, 1972), pp. 722-723.

4 Z. Freud, *Wizerunek własny*, trans. by H. Załszupin (Warsaw: J. Przeworski, 1936).

5 S. Zweig, *Zygmunt Freud*, trans. by M. Wassermanówna (Warsaw: J. Przeworski, 1933).

6 See *WL* 1936, no. 20, p 5.

7 *WL* 1939 no. 22, p. 42; no. 31/32, p. 42.

8 H. Tadeusiewicz, I. Treichel, *Straty osobowe księgarstwa polskiego w latach 1939-1945* (Łódź: Wydawnictwo Uniwersytetu Łódzkiego, 1993), p. 53.

Freud's lectures at the University of Vienna during the winter semester of the academic years 1915/16 and 1916/17. They were first published by Hugo Heller, initially appearing in three volumes that dealt with parapraxis, dreams and the psychoanalytical theory of neurosis. This tripartite structure was maintained in later editions, even if they presented the lectures as a single volume. By the outbreak of World War II, twelve editions had appeared, eight of them with the Internationaler Psychoanalytischer Verlag. In 1932 Freud published a sequel (this time not based on any actual lectures) titled *Neue Folge der Vorlesungen zur Einführung in die Psychoanalyse* (*New Introductory Lectures on Psycho-Analysis*). His intention was to draw on the book's popular success to give a financial boost to the struggling press established by him and his colleagues.

While the *Introduction to Psychoanalysis* outlined the principal theories of the first topic, Polish readers who wanted to learn about the second topic had no other source but the translation of Freud's *An Autobiographical Study.* Here Freud summarises the key points of *Beyond the Pleasure Principle* and *The Ego and the Id* and discusses *Totem and Taboo* and other works on group psychology and cultural questions. Freud wrote his *An Autobiographical Study* in 1925, responding to an invitation by the editors of the Leipzig-based series "Die Medizin der Gegenwart in Selbstdarstellungen" [Contemporary Medicine in Self-Portraits]. His contribution can be seen as a history of psychoanalysis. Besides a detailed account of its birth and development, Freud's focus is on the gradual establishment of what he sees as the authentic version, the one that he and his faithful students managed to preserve against successive dissidents, such as Jung and Adler. The history of the movement, in Freud's view, can be divided into two stages: before 1907 he mostly worked on his own; after that year his collaborators began to play an ever more prominent role. Two thirds of the book are dedicated to the first stage, as Freud avoided discussing the ways in which his work was developed by his colleagues. Concerning his most recent publications he confesses: "I have given free rein to the inclination, which I kept down for so long, to speculation."[9] He mentions the introduction of the pleasure principle and the reality principle, followed by the division of the self into the ego, the id and the super-ego, and finally, crowning this stage, the antinomy of the two drives Eros and Thanatos. These developments, he writes, merely represent the hull of a future theoretical construct, one at which psychoanalysis ought to arrive

9 S. Freud, *An Autobiographical Study*, SE XX, p. 57.

by means of painstaking observations, just like any natural science. For Freud, these "clear basic concepts and sharply drawn definitions are only possible in the mental sciences in so far as the latter seek to fit a region of facts into the frame of a logical system" (*Ibid.*). But in the natural sciences one must not begin with theories:

> The basic ideas or most general concepts in any of the disciplines of science are always left indeterminate at first and are only explained to begin with by reference to the realm of phenomena from which they were derived; it is only by means of a progressive analysis of the material of observation that they can be made clear and can find a significant and consistent meaning. (p. 59)

Freud writes with regret: "I have always felt it as a gross injustice that people have refused to treat psycho-analysis like any other science" (p. 58). He continues with reference to his most recent works: "Even when I have moved away from observation, I have carefully avoided any contact with philosophy proper" (p. 59). Still, the final chapter deals with psychoanalytical approaches to art and culture. Freud assumes responsibility for the shift in his approach: "Here and there I have gone a little way along the path in order to gratify my non-medical interests" (p. 63). His tone is particularly self-reproachful when it comes to his interpretations of *Hamlet*, *Gradiva*, Leonardo da Vinci's personality or the mechanisms of the joke, but also the anthropological hypotheses in *Totem and Taboo.* At the same time he stresses that a large proportion of current studies on literature, art history, religion, mythology, ethnology or pedagogy – fields that have little in common with medicine – are inspired by his research. Freud concludes that the successful application of psychoanalysis to other fields leads to the necessity of admitting laypeople: "It is no longer possible to restrict the practice of psycho-analysis to doctors"; "a doctor who has not been through a special training is, in spite of his diploma, a layman in analysis, and a non-doctor who has been suitably trained can, with occasional reference to a doctor, carry out the analytic treatment" (p. 70); another consequence is the blurred definition of psychoanalysis, which now takes on several meanings:

> While it was originally the name of a particular therapeutic method, it has now also become the name of a science – the science of unconscious mental processes. By itself this science is seldom able to deal with a

> problem completely, but it seems destined to give valuable contributory help in the most varied regions of knowledge. (p. 70)

The Polish translation of *An Autobiographical Study* was based on the second edition, which appeared a decade later, in 1935, and included a few pages in which Freud reveals that he had written the book soon after receiving a diagnosis of terminal cancer. Assuming he was about to die, he set about putting down an official version of his biography as well as an intellectual testament that would establish orthodox psychoanalysis. A surgical intervention unexpectedly saved his life, so he was able to continue his work for another decade. He admits he was surprised about where his path had taken him since:

> I myself find that a significant change has come about. Threads which in the course of my development had become intertangled have now begun to separate; interests which I had acquired in the later part of my life have receded, while the older and original ones become prominent once more. It is true that in this last decade I have carried out some important pieces of analytical work, such as a revision of the problem of anxiety in my book *Inhibitions, Symptoms and Anxiety* (1926) or the simple explanation of sexual "fetishism" which I was able to make a year later (1927). Nevertheless it would be true to say that, since I put forward my hypothesis of the existence of two classes of instincts (Eros and the death instinct) and since I proposed a division of the mental personality into an ego, a super-ego, and an id (1923), I have made no further decisive contributions to psycho-analysis: what I have written on the subject since then has been either unessential or would soon have been supplied by someone else. (pp. 71-72)

Freud suggests that his recent works, such as *The Future of an Illusion* (1927) and *Civilisation and its Discontents* (1930) went far beyond psychoanalysis and represented a sort of regression: "My interest, after making a lifelong détour through the natural sciences, medicine and psychotherapy, returned to the crucial problems which had fascinated me long before, when I was a youth scarcely old enough for thinking" (p. 72). Indeed, in the opening pages of *An Autobiographical Study*, Freud confesses that he never had any real fondness for medicine:

> I was moved, rather, by a sort of curiosity, which was, however, directed more towards human concerns than towards natural objects [...]. My deep engrossment in the Bible story (almost as soon as I had learnt the art of reading) had, as I recognised much later, an enduring effect upon the direction of my interest. (p. 8)

Darwin's work may have inspired "hopes of an extraordinary advance in our understanding of the world" (*Ibid.*), and Freud acknowledges that he was anything but immune to this great promise. Still, the experience that inclined him to study medicine was not Darwin but the fact that, just before his school leaving exams, he heard "Goethe's beautiful essay on Nature read aloud at a popular lecture by Professor Carl Brühl" (*Ibid.*).[10]

It is with a sense of astonishment that Freud describes the reception of his work. The books that "have perhaps awakened more public sympathy than psycho-analysis itself" (p. 72) are the ones that he sees as marginal; what is more, "they may have played a part in creating the short-lived illusion that I was among the writers to whom a great nation like Germany was ready to listen" (*Ibid.*). In 1930 he was awarded the Goethe Prize. "This was the climax of my life as a citizen. Soon afterwards the boundaries of our country narrowed and the nation would know no more of us" (p. 73). These words conclude Freud's account of his private affairs. What follows is an overview of the movement now fully independent of his person. Freud hopes that psychoanalysis, having proved its viability both as a science and as a therapeutic method, may outlive him.

Wstęp do psychoanalizy (*Introduction to Psychoanalysis*) and *Wizerunek własny* (*An Autobiographical Study*) were the last translations of Freud's book-length works into Polish before World War II. A few minor translations – overlooked by previous bibliographers – also appeared in the press. As I mentioned before, *Nasz Przegląd* published two short pieces from Freud's *Theoretische Schriften.* Titled "Dwie uwagi" [Two Remarks], these were an excerpt from the chapter "The Herd Instinct" in *Group Psychology and the Analysis of the Ego*, as well as a passage on the artist from

10 "Die Natur" is an essay by Georg Christoph Tobler. It is often incorrectly attributed to Goethe, perhaps because Tobler wrote it after repeated conversations with the German poet and thinker. The text first appeared in the *Tiefurt Journal* (1783); an English translation by T. H. Huxley, titled "Nature: Aphorisms by Goethe," was published in the first issue of *Nature* magazine.

"Formulations on the Two Principles of Mental Functioning".[11] Furthermore, an excerpt of the correspondence between Einstein and Freud appeared under the title "Dwugłos wielkich uczonych o wojnie" [Two Great Scholars' Voices on the Subject of War] in *Robotnik* in 1934.[12]

The popularisation of psychoanalysis must have been greatly aided by Zweig's biography of Freud, especially among those readers who felt intimidated by academic publications. As Eustachy Czekalski wrote in the illustrated weekly *Świat*:

> The educated reader nowadays often encounters the name of S. Freud, the eminent Viennese physician and sexologist. Not everyone has the ability or is prepared to study his writings, to gain first-hand familiarity with the texts containing this great researcher's original therapeutic and psychological ideas. Stefan Zweig's book, which is an extremely clear and accessible exposition of this psychiatrist's scientific achievements, acquaints the lay reader with all of the Viennese professor's analytical methods. These are on everyone's lips
> across the world [...]. The term "libido" has even become popular in society, while the "complexes" are part and parcel of the educated European's vocabulary. Thanks to Stefan Zweig's book, these terms are at last going to be used in an intelligent manner! His presentation of Freud's scientific ideas is exemplary and fascinating.[13]

11 Z. Freud, "Dwie uwagi", *NPR* 1931, no. 127, p. 9.

12 "Dwugłos wielkich uczonych o wojnie", *R* 1934, no. 477, p. 4. The correspondence between Einstein and Freud was initiated by the Permanent Committee for Literature and the Arts of the League of Nations in 1931. The idea was that a dialogue between prominent personalities would serve the covenant of nations. The organisation first approached Einstein and asked him to name a partner. Einstein proposed Freud, who readily agreed. In 1933 their letters were published in three languages at the same time, with the English edition carrying the title *Why War?*. In Poland, the project was reviewed by Artur Górski. He used the opportunity to criticise Freud:
Freud, with his notorious pessimism, is able to see only two instincts in humankind: the erotic, sexual instinct and the destructive instinct; all others, in his view, can be reduced to these two. These propositions have already been countered by E. Michaelis, A. Adler and C.G. Jung, who have also defined Freud's place in science. Today the views of this writer, whose publications include titles such as *Die Zukunft einer Illusion* or *Das Unbehangen in der Kultur*, arouse no deep interest where the complex questions of the humanities are concerned. (Artur Górski, *NPOL* 1935, vol. 20, pp. 363-364)

13 E.Cz. [E. Czekalski], "Książka o Zygmuncie Freudzie", *Ś* 1933, no. 35, p. 16.

Zweig's book was published in German in 1931 as part of a three-volume work, *Die Heilung durch den Geist* [*Mental Healers*, 1932].[14] The volume on psychoanalysis was translated into Polish by Melania Wassermanówna and came out with Przeworski in 1933. Two re-editions appeared in 1936 and 1939. The weekly *Myśl Narodowa* published a vicious commentary by Adolf Nowaczyński:

> The more he [Freud] was treated coldly and stiffly in the world of professional scholars, the more passionately he took charge of his advertising campaign, enlisting the literati and the tabloid press. Writers of the second and third rank are ideal material for such an operation, as they are impressionable and under-educated, eager for shiny new terms and truisms, and finally snobbish in the most trivial manner. All sorts of half-talents, quarter-talents, the coffeehouse rabble, Penclub extras, donnas and lady writers, "essayists" and die-hard dilettantes, all of them will come piling in at break-neck speed, delighting in the paper *confetti* and *coriandoli* memorised from fashionable gospels from a department store [...]. The commercial success of this Viennese thinker (*contradictio in adiecto*) has grown and flourished only thanks to the worship and advertising of a few ephemeral fiction-writers who were nothing but shooting-stars, now vanished, non-existent, as well as plain Jericho-like advertising by a ten-thousand-strong trust of scribbling Jewboys from the press around the globe. A phone call went around the world for every Kahan or Cohen to write a minimum of 56 to 165 lines about every new "work" by the brilliant "reformer" (sic) and explorer (sic). And right away, Wasereng and Wasserberger went to their desks, while their colleague Wasserman (Melanie) was already busy translating the latest study on Freud by Stefan Zweig himself (published by the Yid Przeworski of Świętokrzyska Street).[15]

Zweig's biography sold well not only because of the general interest in psychoanalysis but also because he was a writer of immense renown. He was one of the most widely translated German-language writers of his time and several of his books had already enjoyed international commercial

14 To Freud's dismay, the other two parts were dedicated to Franz Mesmer and Mary Baker Eddy. See Stefan Zweig, *Die Heilung durch den Geist* (Leipzig: Insel, 1931). Available in English as Stefan Zweig, *Mental Healers: Franz Anton Mesmer, Mary Baker Eddy, Sigmund Freud*, trans. by Eden and Cedar Paul (New York: Viking Press, 1932).

15 A. Nowaczyński, "Ofensywa: Propaganda Freuda", *MNR* 1933, no. 36, p. 539.

success. When it came to psychoanalytical theories, however, Zweig's *Zygmunt Freud* provided nothing that Polish readers would not have been able to find, even before World War I, in Ludwig Jekels' *Szkic psychoanalizy Freuda* or his translation of Freud's Clark lectures, *O psychoanalizie.* Zweig's book, though published in the early 1930s, deals with the shock that nineteenth-century bourgeois culture experienced when Freud revealed the essential role of the sexual drives in every individual's life and in the aetiology of mental illnesses. In his 1942 memoir *Die Welt von Gestern* (*The World of Yesterday*), Zweig thematises the hypocrisy that marked his upbringing and the permanent sense of guilt which was instilled in him. Reading his biography of Freud alongside this memoir it becomes quite apparent that what he describes as a Freudian revolution must have been an emancipatory experience for him. The promise of liberation not only inspired him to read Freud's works but also to try and get to know him personally; eventually they became friends, and intellectual partners. Zweig tells the story of Freud's heroic journey through the hostile medical world. Nearly half of the book is dedicated to the birth of psychoanalysis, describing Freud's fellowship in Paris, his earliest cases of hysteria, his decision to relinquish hypnosis and his discovery of other methods to tap into the unconscious, such as the interpretation of dreams, parapraxis and free association. Zweig never discusses Freudianism as an institutionalised movement, and he never even mentions any of Freud's students, which creates the image of a lone genius. Freud and psychoanalysis are treated as one and the same thing, so much so that in the chapter on therapy, Zweig – who must have been perfectly aware of the psychoanalytical institutes, the formalised path into the profession as well as the fact that hundreds of Freudian analysts were practicing around the world – questions whether the technique could be taught to anyone at all. Analysis is presented as a matter of vocation, requiring such unique personal and intellectual qualities that its practice by anyone other than the inventor himself could be no more than a pale imitation; it follows that such a treatment is unlikely to be effective. Zweig discusses Freud's most recent works, *The Future of an Illusion* and *Civilisation and Its Discontents*, in no more than a few pages, and he dismisses Freud's pessimism by referring to his old age. Zweig's apparent lack of enthusiasm about Freud's later work raises the question why he mentioned it at all. We know that he consulted Freud while he was writing his biography, so it is possible that he succumbed to some form of pressure; alternatively it might have been his own determination to present a comprehensive account of Freud's output. At any rate, by casting the father of psychoanalysis as the one who saved humanity from the repressive fetters of nineteenth-century sexual morality, Zweig fails to do justice to the theoretical nuances introduced in the second topic and to the scepticism about the emancipatory dimension of psychoanalysis that marks Freud's later work.

Zweig's book had a huge impact on Freud's image in the 1930s, but not necessarily a positive one. Caricaturists took up the discrepancy between the idea of Freud as a disciplined and emotionless researcher and the fact that he spent his time exploring the darkest secrets of human sexuality; the comical idea of a *Herr Professor* heading a sexual revolution was played up mercilessly. By mythicising Freud, Zweig had unwittingly provided fodder for these satires. What is more, Zweig's belief that an analysis carried out by anyone but the master himself was bound to be ineffective most probably discouraged potential patients who might otherwise have seen psychoanalysis as a viable alternative to other kinds of therapy. Zweig also stripped psychoanalysis of its scientific character: a repeatable technique with empirically proven efficacy became something more akin to magic, a sort of shamanism that depended on Freud's personal charisma.

The translators

The two books on Freudianism that appeared with Przeworski's Press were translated by two different individuals. Melania Wassermanówna, who produced the Polish version of Zweig's biography of Freud, was already mentioned. Not much is known about her. Born in 1907, she started her career as a translator, writer and journalist associated with women's magazines in pre-war Poland. Today she is better known as Maria Wisłowska, the name she assumed after the war, when she joined the Polish Workers' Party (PPR) and later the Polish United Workers' Party (PZPR). She worked for the Polish Radio's propaganda and political department, then she became head of the foreign department of Książka i Wiedza [Books and Knowledge], communist Poland's leading state publisher in the fields of politics and history; she also joined the staff of the Polish Press Agency.[16]

16 See P. Libera, "Marcel Reich-Ranicki przed Centralną Komisją Kontroli Partyjnej (1950–1957)", *ZH* 2009, no. 167, p. 276.

The translator of Freud's *Autobiographical Study*, acknowledged in the book as "dr H. Załszupin," was Henryk Załszupin, born in Łódź in 1902.[17] His father Ignacy was a lawyer who sat on the councils of Łódź's Jewish Charity Society as well as the Mutual Credit Union of the Merchants and Industrialists of Łódź; he was also a candidate for the city's delegate to the First Duma. After his death in 1910, his widow Julia Freidenberg, a manufacturer's daughter, went abroad with their children. Henryk finished school in Zurich and went to university in Berlin, Strasbourg, Brussels and Lille, obtaining a PhD in economics and philosophy. When his mother died in 1927, he moved to now independent Poland. He became a journalist and reviewed international politics for the weekly *Prawda*, among others. He also worked for the monthly *Europa*, and, after a time, was appointed secretary of the paper.[18] He was also affiliated with *Auto i Sport*, the monthly publication of the tire manufacturer Dunlop Rubber Company, which appeared between 1930 and 1932 with a print run of 25,000 copies. The magazine boasted contributions by leading experts of the automotive industry, but it also featured pieces by Marian Hemar (an extremely popular satirist, author of song texts and associate of the Skamandrites) as well as illustrations by Jerzy Zaruba (Poland's most prominent caricaturist at the time).

Załszupin translated several other books besides Freud's *Autobiographical Study*. One of these was the eugenicist treatise *We Europeans: A Survey of Racial Problems* (*My Europejczycy: Przegląd zagadnień "rasowych"*) by Julian S. Huxley and Alfred C. Haddon. His translations did not earn the best reviews. According to Bolesław Dudziński in *Robotnik*, Załszupin's version of Freud's book "bespeaks the translator's care and attention but leaves a lot to be desired from a linguistic point of view".[19] Similarly, Stefan Essmanowski wrote in *Wiadomości Literackie* that the translation would have benefitted from stylistic polishing.[20] Not much is known about Załszupin's interest in psychoanalysis. One surviving document suggests that he must have associated with psychiatrist and psychoanalyst Roman Markuszewicz: a signed copy of his *Psychoanaliza i jej znaczenie*

---

17 My portrayal of Załszupin/Tarn is based on M. Prussak, "Posłowie i Nota wydawcy", in S. Mrożek, A. Tarn, *Listy 1963-1975* (Cracow: Wydawnictwo Literackie, 2009), pp. 350-357.

18 A. S. Kowalczyk, "Na spotkanie Europie: Posłowie", in *"Europa" 1929–1930: Antologia*, ed. by A. S. Kowalczyk (Warsaw: Ministerstwo Spraw Zagranicznych, 2012), p. 229.

19 B. Dudziński, "Nowe książki", *R* 1936, no. 177, p. 5.

20 S. Essmanowski, "Wizerunek własny Freuda", *WL* 1936, no. 33, p. 3.

lecznicze [Psychoanalysis and Its Therapeutic Significance] at the University of Warsaw Library is marked with a hand-written dedication to Henryk Załszupin, dated 1929: "as a remembrance of our time together".[21] Perhaps Załszupin had undergone analysis with Markuszewicz, but this hypothesis is not corroborated by any other source.

In 1934 Załszupin published a novel titled *Obraz ojca w czterech ramach* [A Portrait of Father in Four Frames]. The book appeared with Przeworski's Press under the pseudonym Adam Tarn. The last couple of pages advertise the forthcoming publication of Zweig's biography of Freud; there is also a note announcing a translation of Freud's *Introduction to Psychoanalysis* (*Wstęp do psychoanalizy*):

> Long awaited by the educated Polish reader, this fundamental work by the founder of psychoanalysis is a turning point in modern psychology. A lucid presentation, illustrated with striking examples, allows everyone to find the correct approach to all mental processes.

It was certainly no coincidence that these two titles were chosen from the publisher's catalogue. Quite on the contrary – this advertisement indicates a lucid marketing strategy. The Freud biography, *An Introduction to Psychoanalysis* and Tarn's novel, which the critics unanimously identified as psychoanalytical (as I shall discuss below), targeted the very same group of readers.

After the war Henryk Załszupin officially changed his name to Adam Tarn. Having left for Paris in 1937, he found himself in the USA in 1941 and worked for the United Nations for the next eight years, then he returned to Poland once more. While no surviving documents indicate any affiliation between anyone with the name of Henryk Załszupin and the theatre, Adam Tarn became a playwright, worked as a literary manager for several Warsaw theatres, and in 1956 founded the magazine *Dialog*, which still exists today. It featured works by the most important Polish playwrights and translations of contemporary drama from across the world. Tarn himself translated Beckett, Pinter, Saroyan, Ionesco, Volodin and Chekhov. His life changed dramatically in 1968. Having refused to sign a letter condemning the March events in Poland, he was ousted from

21 R. Markuszewicz, *Psychoanaliza i jej znaczenie lecznicze* (Warsaw: Warszawski Kalendarz Lekarski, 1926), copy held at the University of Warsaw Library, reference number 139404.

his posts as editor-in-chief of *Dialog* and literary manager at the Teatr Współczesny. He decided to emigrate once again. His visa application to the US was rejected because in the application form he mentioned having been active as a socialist, but he was successful in Canada. He became a Professor of Drama at the University of Calgary, then he taught at Carleton University, Ottawa. But starting his life all over again at the age of 66, alone and with few resources, was tough. Tarn was facing financial difficulties as well as serious health issues. His letters frequently mention his wife, who apparently stayed in Poland. His source of joy in those years of loneliness and isolation was his correspondence with close friends, artists and intellectuals such as Sławomir Mrożek and Samuel Beckett. He died of lung cancer in 1975, the year he was poised to obtain Canadian citizenship.

The Freud translator who demands the most detailed portrayal is Salomea Kempner (or Kempnerówna in contemporary Polish documents), who produced the Polish version of *Introduction to Psychoanalysis* (*Wstęp do psychoanalizy*). She was born in 1880 to Mojżesz Hersz, a Jewish apothecary, and Ella Ruchla née Margulies.[22] Her father's brother Lejb (Ludwik) Kempner, having taken over the bookshop founded by their parents in Płock, became a veritable bookselling tycoon by the turn of the century.[23] Besides the city's largest and best-stocked warehouse (also when it came to banned books), he also owned the first printing press in Płock. The local newspaper, *Echa Płockie i Łomżyńskie*, published a fiercely anti-Semitic comment about a portrait of Theodor Herzl on the Kempners' business premises in 14 Grodzka Street, claiming that it kept attracting "little clusters of Jews who could not get enough of the sight of their leader".[24]

22 Ludger M. Hermanns, "Unsere letzte psychoanalytische Mohikanerin in Berlin: Die Berliner Jahre (1923–1939) der polnischen Psychoanalytikerin Salomea Kempner (1880–1943) und ihr 'Verschwinden' in Warschau", in: *Im Schatten von Krieg und Holocaust: Psychoanalyse in Polen im polnisch-deutsch-jüdischen Kontext*, ed. by E. Kobylinska-Dehe, P. Dybel, L. M. Hermanns (Gießen: Psychosozial-Verlag, 2019), pp. 90-91.

23 U. Morawska, *Drukarstwo płockie do roku 1918* (Płock: Towarzystwo Naukowe Płockie, 1984), pp. 108-109; B. Konarska-Pabiniak, "Księgarstwo płockie w latach 1863–1890", *KS* 1976, no. 1-2, pp. 71-72. Cf. also A. J. Papierowski, J. Stefański, *Płocczanie znani i nieznani: Słownik biograficzny* (Płock: Książnica Płocka, 2002), p. 263.

24 *EPIŁ* 1900, no. 67, p. 2.

Salomea had a younger sister, Felicja (1882), and the two had a very close relationship with their cousins, Rafał (1875) and Cecylia aka Celina (1881).[25] In fact, more is known about these cousins, who were active in the Polish Socialist Party (the Płock branch was established in 1901) and in illegal educational work.[26] Rafał studied law at the University of Warsaw and then joined the most left-leaning faction of the Polish Socialist Party (Polska Partia Socjalistyczna – Lewica or PPS–L). In 1909 he was arrested by the Tsarist authorities for having participated in the revolution. His worldview did not change when Poland regained independence, and as a lawyer he often defended communist activists. His sister was also active in the socialist movement. Her familiarity with the works of Marx and Engels impressed her friends in Płock. Celina was affiliated with the independence fraction at the PPS and had ties with industrial workers at the agricultural machine manufacturers Sarna and Margulies, the mill and the brewery in Płock. In 1905 she co-organised a workers' march through Płock that ended rather dramatically: at the culminating rally in a park she addressed the crowd, reportedly saying "I am in triple bondage – as a woman, as a Pole and as a labour activist resisting oppression,"[27] when a mounted squad of Cossacks – employed by the Tsar to suppress domestic disorder – showed up out of nowhere and violently dispersed the audience. Some workers escorted Kempner away from the scene and ensured her safe return to the city.

Salomea, Felicja and Celina all graduated from the public Girls' Gymnasium in Płock. In the midst of the raging counter-revolution they left Russian-occupied Congress Poland and enrolled at Cracow's Jagiellonian University for the academic year 1905/06.[28] While Celina initially wanted to study philosophy, the sisters Felicja and Salomea joined the department of medicine. Felicja had already completed six semesters at the medical department of the University of Bern, while Salomea had studied medicine

25 These are the birth dates the sisters gave when they enrolled at the University of Zurich: < www.matrikel.uzh.ch > [accessed on 22/08/2022]. Cecilia's birth year is often said to be 1886, as listed on her marriage certificate from 1935, but dates stated on birth certificates are generally more reliable than those on marriage certificates.

26 Cf. S. Świdwiński, "O udziale Żydów płockich w pracy niepodległościowej: Garść wspomnień", in *Żydzi bojownicy o niepodległość Polski* (Lviv: [n.p.], 1939), pp. 139-141.

27 Cf. K. Askanas, "Paweł Lewinson-Łapiński, działacz ruchu robotniczego", *NPK* 1985, no. 1, p. 34.

28 Cf. M. Kulczykowski, *Żydzi-studenci Uniwersytetu Jagiellońskiego w dobie autonomicznej Galicji (1867–1918)*, p. 339.

and natural sciences at the University of Zurich, but without graduating. She had moved there in early 1899, after obtaining a diploma as a private tutor.[29] In Zurich she attended lectures for three semesters. Felicja and Salomea spent a year in Cracow, then returned to Switzerland, where they both obtained doctoral degrees in the academic year 1908/1909. In Zurich Salomea defended her thesis "Versuche zum Mikroskop: Nachweis der Narkose der Nerven" [Microscope Experiments: Evidence of Anaesthesia of the Nerves] in October 1908, Felicja followed in June 1909 with her dissertation "Beiträge zur physikalischen Chemie der Nierensekretion" [Contributions on the Physical Chemistry of Renal Secretion]. Felicja never married. She worked as a doctor in Zurich, including a stint at Burghölzli in 1910-11,[30] where she was friends with Mira Gincburg.[31] She died prematurely of kidney failure in 1916.

Salomea also stayed in Switzerland, working as a trainee doctor at a cantonal mental asylum in Rheinau between 1912 and 1921.[32] The earliest documents suggesting her acquaintance with psychoanalysis date from this period. She most likely learned about it from Philipp Sarasin, with whom she was romantically involved for many years, although they never formalised their relationship.[33] Sarasin came from an old Protestant family in Basel. After completing his medical studies, he briefly worked under Eugen Bleuler at the Burghölzli clinic, where he underwent his first analysis. From 1916 to 1921 he was a doctor at Rheinau, but he frequently travelled to Berlin for analysis with Hanns Sachs. In 1919 both Sarasin and Kempner joined the newly formed Swiss Psychoanalytic Society, founded by Mira and Emil Oberholzer (I wrote about Mira Gincburg-Oberholzer in the section on Helena Deutsch). In 1920 they attended the International Psychoanalytic Congress in The Hague and met Freud in person. The following year they moved to Vienna. In a letter to Karl Abraham dated 30 March 1922, Freud writes: "at present I have three Swiss people: Sarasin, the Kempner woman and the young Dr Blum from

29 Salomea Kempnerówna appears on the list of persons to whom "the educational authority in Warsaw has just issued [...] certificates for home teachers in subjects listed in the institute's attestation". This list was reprinted in *GH* 1897, no. 189, p. 3 as well as *KW* 1897, no. 227, p. 3.

30 A. Wieser, "Zur frühen Psychoanalyse in Zürich 1900–1914", p. 189.

31 V. von Planta, "Analysiere nie wieder", p. 87.

32 Salomea Kempner is mentioned by B. Schoop-Russbült in *Psychiatrischer Alltag in der Autobiographie von Karl Gehry (1881–1962)* (Zurich: Juris, 1989), pp. 98-99, p. 106.

33 Cf. P. Roazen, *Helene Deutsch*, p. 246.

Zurich".[34] Sarasin was analysed by Freud, after which he returned to Basel in 1924 and opened a private practice. For over thirty years (1928-1960) he headed the Swiss Psychoanalytic Society.[35] Salomea decided to remain in Vienna and join the VPS. In 1923, just a few days before Beata Rank delivered her paper on the role of women in the development of societies at a VPS meeting, Kempner presented a case of neurotic fixation on the oral phase. Her patient is described as a young woman doctor suffering from a "masculinity complex," who rejects genital sexuality as it would reduce her to the feminine role; this patient longs for a pre-Oedipal symbiosis with her mother.[36]

Having initially worked with Sarasin at the Viennese Psychoanalytic Clinic recently established by Helene Deutsch,[37] Salomea Kempner moved to Berlin in autumn 1923.[38] At the psychoanalytic polyclinic there she conducted between nine and thirteen analyses at any given time.[39] Two years later she joined the Berlin Psychoanalytic Institute. Her name appears in Alix Strachey's letters to her husband, written in Berlin in 1924-25. Interestingly, Strachey describes Kempner as "an ex-Pole".[40]

Salomea Kemper and Philipp Sarasin maintained a long-distance relationship and appeared together at various conferences. They both helped organise the international congress in Innsbruck in September 1927; a note thanking them for managing the congress office was printed in the *Internationale Zeitschrift für Psychoanalyse*.[41] In April 1928 the couple went to see Freud, who mentions their visit in a letter to Max Eitingon, affectionately referring to Salomea Kempner as "Sala".[42] Sarasin's only

34 *The Complete Correspondence of Sigmund Freud and Karl Abraham*, p. 455.

35 Cf. P. Roazen, *The Historiography of Psychoanalysis* (New Brunswick, NJ: Transaction, 2001), pp. 167-171.

36 S. Kempner, "Beitrag zur Oralerotik", *IZP* 1925, no. 1, pp. 69-77, an English version appeared the same year: S. Kempner, "Some Remarks on Oral Erotism", *IJP* 1925, vol. 6, pp. 419-429. In many ways this case resembles those described by Helene Deutsch; incidentally, Kempner's text appeared in the same issue of the *Internationale Zeitschrift für Psychoanalyse* as Deutsch's "Psychologie des Weibes in den Funktionen der Fortpflanzung" [Psychology of the Female in the Reproductive Functions].

37 *Die Rundbriefe des "Geheimen Komitees"*, vol. 3, p. 149.

38 *Die Rundbriefe des "Geheimen Komitees"*, vol. 4, p. 103.

39 O. Fenichel, "Rapport statistique sur l'activité thérapeutique entre 1920–1930", in *On forme les psychanalystes*, p. 65.

40 *Bloomsbury/Freud: The Letters of James and Alix Strachey*, pp. 77-78.

41 *IZP* 1927, no. 13, p. 468.

42 S. Freud, M. Eitingon, *Briefwechsel 1906–1939*, p. 597.

important work was an interpretation, printed in *Imago* in 1929, of the character Mignon in Goethe's *Wilhelm Meister's Apprenticeship*.[43] Sarasin mentions that the idea had come to him during his analysis with Freud.

The only one of the three young Kempner women who went to live in independent Poland was Celina, the cousin who had studied philosophy in Cracow. She switched to the department of medicine after two years and completed six semesters. In 1910, her fiancé Józef Kwiatek, a leading PPS activist from Płock, received a crushing medical diagnosis and took his own life. This is when she decided to join her cousins in Zurich for the academic year.[44] She left university when World War I broke out and never completed her degree.[45] Instead, she settled in Warsaw and resumed her political activity. She was treasurer of the Warsaw Women's Division of the PPS, and in 1926 she became personal secretary to socialist politician Ignacy Daszyński (1866-1936), with whom she became romantically involved. When Daszyński became Marshal of the Sejm in 1928, his official residence was an apartment on Jerusalem Avenue 7 in Warsaw. Celina Kempner moved in with him there, and she remained by his side throughout his later years, when his health was failing. One historian describes her as "reserved, intellectually developed, tactful," adding that she "made a positive impression on everyone around her".[46] In early February 1931 she accompanied Daszyński to Bystra. He stayed at what had been Ludwig Jekels' sanatorium, now known as "Dom Zdrowia" [House of Health], while she took a room in a small hotel. It was only after Daszyński's wife Maria, née Paszkowska, had passed away that they formalised their relationship. Celina Kempner converted to Christianity in order to marry Daszyński. The wedding took place at the Church of St Michael the Archangel in Wilkowice near Bystra on 11 April 1935.[47] Daszyński's five

43 P. Sarasin, "Goethes Mignon: Eine psychoanalytische Studie", *I* 1929, no. 3/4, pp. 349-399. This study also appeared as a separate publication with the International Psychoanalaytic Press in 1930.

44 J. Cynarski-Krzesławski, "Józef Kwiatek (1874–1910)", in the appendix titled "Księga życiorysów działaczy rewolucyjnych", *KRR* 1935, no. 1, pp. 6-8; A. Pacholczykowa, "Kwiatek Józef", in *Słownik Biograficzny Działaczy Polskiego Ruchu Robotniczego*, ed. by F. Tych (Warsaw: Książka i Wiedza, 1992), vol. 3, pp. 599-601.

45 Cf. the database on the University of Zurich: < www.matrikel.uzh.ch > [accessed on 22/08/2022].

46 W. Najdus, *Ignacy Daszyński 1866–1936* (Warsaw: Czytelnik, 1988), p. 508.

47 T. Nikiel, "Szczególne wydarzenie w dziejach Wilkowic", *GG* 2007, no. 10, p. 9; see also W. Najdus, *Ignacy Daszyński*, pp. 512-513.

grown-up children by Maria never accepted the relationship.[48] A few days after his 70th birthday, in late October 1936, Daszyński died in Bystra.

A group photograph taken during Celina Kempner and Ignacy Daszyński's modest wedding celebrations suggests that not many members of her family were able to attend. Her father had passed away in 1908, her cousin Felicja in 1916, her mother in 1933. It is likely that her brother Rafał Kempner was present – he had already visited her in Bystra, travelling all the way from Łódź, where he lived with his family and ran a law firm (p. 520). It seems that Salomea, who was based in Berlin at the time, did not come. The photograph shows only one other woman besides the bride, and she was identified as the wife of Romuald Pajerski, a medical doctor who acted as witness (the other witness was Dr Ignacy Spitzer, the director of the "Dom Zdrowia" spa).

After the National Socialists had come to power, the directors of the German Psychoanalytical Society decreed that as "a foreign Jew" [*ausländische Jüdin*] Salomea Kempner was not to see patients at the polyclinic anymore.[49] In 1935 she was banned from the Berlin Psychoanalytic Institute.[50] Still, she continued to perform training analyses in her flat in the Wilmersdorf district until 1938; her name can be found in the records of the city's registration offices until the same year.

It is unclear why she did not leave Berlin. All other Jewish Freudians had emigrated by 1935. Perhaps she planned to go to Switzerland but was delayed by formalities. In 1939 she was arrested and deported to Warsaw Ghetto. Her cousins Rafał and Celina were already there. They all perished during the occupation. The date of Celina's death is unknown;[51] Rafał died in 1941. Salomea contracted pneumonia and died on 29 January 1943. No records survive to tell us who notified Philipp Sarasin of her death. He informed the other members of the psychoanalytical movement.

The reception of two Polish translations of Freud

Kempner's translation of the *Introduction to Psychoanalysis* appeared in late 1935. The title page of the Polish version names a certain Dr W. Zaniewicki – nothing is known about him – as Kempner's co-translator. He

48 W. Najdus, *Ignacy Daszyński*, p. 523.
49 O. Fenichel, *119 Rundbriefe*, vol. 1, pp. 42-45
50 Cf. O. Fenichel, *119 Rundbriefe*, vol. 1, p. 367, p. 388.
51 W. Najdus, *Ignacy Daszyński*, p. 533.

probably joined the project just before its completion, since the announcement that Przeworski's Press printed on the last few pages of Tarn's above-mentioned novel in 1934 refers to the forthcoming translation by Salomea Kempner, "reviewed and completed by Gustav Bychowski".[52]

Despite the efforts of Kempner, Zaniewicki and, presumably, Bychowski, the translation had a number of flaws and was judged quite harshly. The most scathing review, written by Maria Adlerówna (or Adler in modern Polish) for *Polskie Archiwum Psychologii*, is a long enumeration of faults.[53] She criticises many of the Freudian terms chosen by the translators – a vexation that seems odd today, as many of them are now firmly established. Another point, however, certainly seems fair. It concerns the shortcuts in the translation. Whenever an anecdote based on wordplay had no ready Polish equivalent, Kempner either gave a literal translation, thus sacrificing the pun (e.g. the rhyming German *Schwert* and *Pferd* become *miecz* and *koń* in Polish – there is no phonetic similarity), or simply skipped the passage. Some sections, Adler writes, seem to have been omitted "out of consideration for the reader's assumed prudery" (p. 78). Other parts were translated "in a way that was extremely 'free'" (*Ibid.*). She also points out various potentially misleading printing errors (*poglądów* [views] instead of *popędów* [drives]; *estetyczne* [aesthetic] instead of *etyczne* [ethical]). For Adler, these mistakes risk that "some of the author's ideas become incomprehensible or are misrepresented" (p. 77). Her greatest concern, however, is that the Polish edition does not render justice to the quality of Freud's prose: "the linguistic finesse of the original is lost in the translation, which is not appealing, clear, entirely correct or free of Germanisms" (p. 78).

Adler's review in a specialist psychology journal focuses entirely on the quality of the translation, not on the author's contribution. She justifies this as follows: "the debate on Freud's system has been ongoing for a long time and its details are familiar. A critical evaluation of the claims made in the *Introduction to Psychoanalysis* or an exploration of the concepts it presents would be out of place here" (p. 77). Adler's assessment is representative. Reviewers generally agreed that the publication filled a

52 Adam Tarn, *Obraz ojca w czterech ramach* (Warsaw: Wydawnictwo J. Przeworskiego, 1934), advertisement on the last page of the book. It is not clear what role exactly Bychowski played in this translation.

53 M. Adlerówna, "Z. Freud, Wstęp do psychoanalizy" [review], *PAP* 1935, no. 9/11, pp. 76-78.

major gap in the Polish book market, but what they seemed most pleased about was that the book provided an accessible introduction for educated readers who only had second-hand knowledge of Freud; as for specialist readers, they had long ceased to debate the ideas presented in it.

Several months before Kempner's translation appeared in the bookshops, the publisher launched an advertising campaign in both *Nasz Przegląd* and *Wiadomości Literackie*. Both journals informed readers: "The Polish translation of Sigmund Freud's classic *Introduction to Psychoanalysis* is forthcoming with J. Przeworski's Press. Prepayments can be deposited at J. Przeworski's Bookshop, Sienkiewicz Street 2, Warsaw, until 20 May."[54] The exact same advertisement – most probably written at Przeworski's office – was printed in the two competing papers:

> Freud's theory, which revolutionised minds and established opinions at the beginning of the twentieth century, has broadened academic psychology by adding a new and crucial theory of subconscious states. In order to properly evaluate Freud's discovery we must view it in the context of prewar attitudes – or rather the lack of any attitudes – regarding the genesis and essence of human drives. The nineteenth century defended itself fiercely against Freud's attempt to shed light on the depths of the human mind, where these drives originate. The morality of that era ignored sexual matters and boycotted them by passing over them in silence. Thanks to Freud, the unconscious has ceased to be tantamount to the unfathomable and has entered the realm of what can be known about the psyche. Freud has portrayed the unconscious as the pit of consciousness, thus shifting the dimensions and balance of forces in the dynamics of the mind. Freud has demonstrated that the unconscious is not a waste product of the mind but that it is the primordial material of which only a small part surfaces into our consciousness. The unexploited and undisclosed content of the unconscious is not dead, however, but has its own dynamics. It actively influences the way we think, feel and act. Our life is under constant pressure from the unconscious. Freud's vision is one of a continuous struggle between consciousness and the hidden power of the unconscious: our inner life is a constant battle between responsible behaviour and "irresponsible" drives. Freud has opened up new possibilities not only for psychology, but also for psychotherapy. He has proven that drives and traumas brought to the surface from the depths of the subcon-

54 "Zygmunt Freud", *WL* 1935, no. 19, p. 5; "Zygmunt Freud", *NPR* 1935, no. 135, p. 10.

> scious can do no more harm as soon as they are revealed. Hence the therapeutic value of psychoanalysis. (*Ibid.*)

This text not only summarises Freudian theory, it also indicates that the publisher's marketing department had an excellent understanding of their customer base. Readers of *Wiadomości Literackie* and of *Nasz Przegląd* were generally interested in all that was modern, and they were likely to be swayed by the same argumentation: by associating Freud's opponents with the dusty nineteenth century, the publisher was able to enlist anyone who called themselves a progressive.

Once Freud's *Introduction* hit the bookshops, both papers, *Wiadomości Literackie* and *Nasz Przegląd*, published reviews that merit close examination. *Nasz Przegląd*, which championed Freudianism ever since it was founded in 1923, commissioned a review by Tadeusz Heller, a literary scholar rather than a medical doctor.[55] He describes the book as a "vade mecum of Freudianism" and "a psychoanalysis for lay people" that "can be faulted for excessive simplification rather than for inaccessible, esoteric or pedantic jargon".[56] Heller does not count himself among the target audience, i.e. "the general readership" (*Ibid.*), letting slip his insider's knowledge about the fact that Freud was already broadening the scope of his theory and analysing "cultural and religious processes, imbuing them with entirely novel dimensions, applying to them the yardstick of his ideas about latent dynamic forces lying dormant at the bottom of the human subconscious" (*Ibid.*). He regrets that the *Introduction to Psychoanalysis* does not address any of these themes.

Stefan Essmanowski's review in *Wiadomości Literackie* carries the telling title "Wreszcie Freud!" [Freud at Last!]. He maintains that "in Poland there has been an increasingly urgent need for a translation of Freud's works".[57] Apparently Essmanowski was unaware that Freud's *Five Lectures on Psycho-Analysis* – *O psychoanalizie* in Jekels' translation – had appeared with Altenberg many years before. To contextualise the new publication he mentions that "until now we only had the rather poor translation of *The Psychopathology of Everyday Life* and the even more deplorable one of *On Dreams*". He also writes that the introductions by Bornsztajn, Bychowski

55 For a portrait of Heller see Józef Hen, *Nowolipie: Najpiękniejsze lata* (Warsaw: W.A.B., 2011), p. 203.

56 T. Heller, "Psychoanaliza dla laików", *NPR* 1935, no. 178, p. 18.

57 S. Essmanowski, "Wreszcie Freud!", *WL* 1935, no. 28, p. 4.

and Markuszewicz failed to have the impact they deserved. As a result, "most of the cultural and intellectual circles in Poland know Freud 'coffeeshop style,' from oral tradition, from casual mentions in articles, and so on". This is why the translation of the *Introduction to Psychoanalysis*, whatever its shortcomings, must be welcomed:

> The *Introduction to Psychoanalysis* comes very late indeed, but not yet too late. Remarks about classical Freudianism being obsolete can still be countered with Mark Twain's words, quoted by Freud himself: "Report of my death greatly exaggerated." No eclectic introduction to psychoanalysis, even if it were more "up to date," could ever replace the founder's own works. Many accusations have been levied against the intentional or unintentional distortions of Freud's theory, so he must not be denied the right to take responsibility for his own – but only his own – views, for what he said and what he did not say. Freud is a writer we must get to know from his own work. Another consideration, leading to the same conclusion, is the outstanding quality of Freud's writing. Elsewhere we will search in vain for such straightforward creativity combined with stylistic merits such as clarity, vividness, accessibility, accuracy.[58]

Essmanowski admits that Polish readers may not find these qualities in the translation, about which he himself has "serious reservations". Nonetheless, he concludes on an optimistic note:

> This detracts neither from this edition's great importance nor from the publisher's solid merit; we hear that further volumes by Freud are underway. Let us hope that the next one will be *Totem and Taboo*, a book whose momentous significance Thomas Mann has so astutely recognised, a book that opens up broad perspectives and casts the psychoanalytic method as one of the most important tasks in the history of humankind following its banishment from the paradise of illusions. (*Ibid.*)

The critic's hopes about the sequence of translations were dashed, but at least the next year saw a Polish edition of *An Autobiographical Study*, in which Freud devotes a few pages to *Totem and Taboo*. Essmanowski published another review in *Wiadomości Literackie*, describing this addi-

58 *Ibid.* The sentence attributed to Mark Twain is quoted from S. Freud, "On the History of the Psycho-Analytic Movement", SE XIV, p. 35.

tion to the Polish Freud corpus as "an outline of the history of psychoanalysis" that, thanks to Freud's talent as a writer, makes for a "truly pleasurable" reading experience, even for those who are already familiar with his theory and its development.[59] He also discusses the ways in which the field has evolved since 1918, i.e. after the *Introduction to Psychoanalysis*: "In these years Freud formulates new theories; they do not fundamentally overturn his previous achievements, but impose a revision of his concepts, strengthening weak points of his theory and clarifying apparent contradictions" (*Ibid.*). This applies especially to two books – *The Ego and the Id* and *Beyond the Pleasure Principle*. About the former he writes:

> The summary juxtaposition of consciousness and the unconscious gives way to a topical dissection of the mind's setup. Freud now identifies in it an extensive, unconscious domain of drives (id), its external part, which is modified in contact with life (ego), and finally a newly discovered super-ego, firmly rooted in the sphere of the unconscious and growing out of the ruins of the Oedipus complex. (*Ibid.*)

Beyond the Pleasure Principle, Essmanowski writes, presents Freud's interest in the compulsion to repeat, which inclined him to introduce a new type of drive. The opposition between sexual and self-preservation drives was replaced by Eros, i.e. libido, and Thanatos, the death drive, which aims to return to the inorganic state from which life originally emerged. The identification of the super-ego had a profound impact on approaches in psychology and pedagogy that were based on psychoanalysis, but *Beyond the Pleasure Principle*, according to Essmanowski, "demanded a much more radical revision"; its effect was "completely unforeseen, and at the same time desirable" (*Ibid.*). Acknowledging that Freud's new concept was being criticised even by "otherwise orthodox Freudians," Essmanowski refrains from weighing in on the debate whether this new theory of psychoanalysis was still rooted in biology or if Freud had become a metaphysician; he only stresses the momentous significance of this shift for the humanities. His review concludes with a note on the persistent delay that Polish readers faced in relation to the dynamic development of Freudianism:

> In Poland, sadly, little has been said about these things until now. We got the *Introduction to Psychoanalysis*, as I wrote last year, not only with a delay

59 S. Essmanowski, "Wizerunek własny Freuda", *WL* 1936, no. 33, p. 3.

> of seventeen years, but too late altogether, for in that interval several concepts had been extensively revised. In a small way, the publication of *An Autobiographical Study* may compensate for this neglect. This is the book's greatest value for us. Of course, we still hope that the second cycle of *Vorlesungen zur Einführung* [*New Introductory Lectures on Psycho-Analysis*], originally published in 1933, will appear soon. At least that. We dare not dream about a [Polish] edition of the complete works, such as – characteristically – Spain and Russia are producing in Europe. (*Ibid.*)

In *Nasz Przegląd* the same questions were tackled by Jakub Bleiberg. He points out "that psychoanalysis is evolving towards the humanities, closely following its founder's 'spiritual' tastes and inclinations as well as his philosophical and speculative attitude".[60] The same writer had voiced his scepticism about Freud's trajectory not that long before. Only the previous year he had reviewed Albert Dryjski's *Zagadnienia seksualizmu dziecka i młodzieży szkolnej* [Problems in Child and Teenage Sexuality] for *Droga*, praising Dryjski's approach to Freudianism, i.e. the way in which he subjected psychoanalysis to "factual, scientific criticism, free of any ulterior motives or tendentiousness".[61] Such an attitude, Bleiberg argues, was not to be taken for granted in a cultural context in which "psychoanalysis is usually talked about either enthusiastically or ironically, using either uncritical superlatives or ridiculing epithets – i.e. in a manner that is neither objective nor based on science in either case" (*ibid.*). Bleiberg agrees with Dryjski's argument that the theory of libido had transformed psychoanalysis from a therapeutic method into a worldview with a clearly metaphysical colouring, removing it from its empirical sources and propelling it into the slippery terrain of speculation. Going one step farther than Dryjski, Bleiberg also adds that Freud was led astray by his monistic tendency (his attempt to reduce all of reality to a single principle, namely the sexual drive).

A year later, however, Bleiberg was inspired to write another article for *Droga* to explore the duality of psychoanalysis. He had just read volume XII of Freud's *Gesammelte Schriften*, which included *Civilisation and its Discontents* and the *New Introductory Lectures on Psycho-Analysis.* These texts, Bleiberg argues, touch on "several branches of the humanities," with

60 J. Bleiberg, "Dwa aspekty psychoanalizy (na marginesie dwunastego tomu Freuda)", *DR* 1935, no. 10, p. 893.

61 *DR* 1934, no. 11, pp. 1054-1056.

only a loose connection to "the original, empirical source" of psychoanalysis.[62] For Bleiberg, this volume contradicted the views put forward in volume XI. In "The Future of an Illusion" (vol. XI) Freud had described religion as an infantile symptom, a relic that does not speak to mature civilisations. In *Civilisation and its Discontents* (vol. XII), which is supposed to be a continuation, religion is portrayed as an important factor in socialisation and a weapon against the tyranny of the instincts. For Bleiberg, this exemplifies the fundamental contradiction of psychoanalysis, torn between its metaphysical and empirical tendencies:

> The first one, rooted in sexual monism and the study of the unconscious (metapsychology), associated Freud with voluntarist metaphysics and Schopenhauer's pessimism, while the second one, which is the actual starting point of psychoanalysis, endowed him with Baconian confidence and positivist faith in the power of scientific thinking. The metaphysical Freud is a pessimist who judges religion with benevolence, while the empirical Freud is an optimist and a firm opponent of religious infantilism. (p. 894)

For Bleiberg, Freud's latest works carry the mark of this inner struggle, and the texts printed side by side in volume XII epitomise this friction. Freud the specialist in nervous disorders, the radical empiricist and positivist, questions speculative world views and the possibility of creating a philosophical system on scientific grounds "with the passion of an eighteenth-century materialist"; he regards the future of humanity with confidence, bolstered by his trust in the possible reconciliation of nature and culture, instinct and reason. At the same time, Freud the irrationalist, who has founded metapsychology and the psychoanalytical mythology of the complexes, has been deprived of any illusions about human nature, which only renounces its passions and desires when under pressure, and claims that the most tragic fact of civilised humanity is culture itself (*Ibid.*).

In his later review of *An Autobiographical Study* Bleiberg highlights Freud's claim that he chose to study medicine despite his inclination towards the humanities, and that this choice was motivated by an accidental encounter with *Die Natur*, a text attributed to Goethe.[63] Bleiberg

---

62 J. Bleiberg, "Dwa aspekty psychoanalizy", p. 893.

63 J. Bleiberg, "Wizerunek własny Freuda", *DR* 1936, no. 7-8, pp. 647-649. Cf. J. Bleiberg, "Wpływ Goethego na Freuda (na marginesie przekładu freudowskiej autobiografii)", *NPR* 1938, no. 177, p. 20.

suggests that the naturalistic and monistic credo underlying this text had a profound influence on Freud's theory, especially his psychological determinism and the dynamic view of the mind. He cites the essay that inspired the young Freud:

> We obey [Nature's] laws even when we rebel against them; we work with her even when we desire to work against her. […] That which is most unnatural is still Nature […]. Whoso cannot see her everywhere, sees her nowhere rightly.[64]

Similarly, Bleiberg argues, psychoanalysis aims to reveal the method beneath irrational madness; here, too, even that which appears unnatural is still nature. Pointing to Freud's strictly philosophical contributions – the theory of libido as well as the interpretation (*Deutung*) that is central to psychoanalysis – he concludes that Freud's practice of the humanities is not restricted to *Geisteswissenschaft* but also includes *Kulturwissenschaft*.

These ideas are echoed in Bleiberg's articles for *Nasz Przegląd*. In 1938 he portrays Freud as a pure humanist, and, interestingly, he suggests that Freud had been one from the very outset, or at least from the time when he quit neurology and entered the field of psychotherapy to develop "a novel perspective on the essence of the human soul".[65] For Bleiberg, the fact that Freud abandoned hypnosis is due to his humanistic attitude, his aversion to a method that had something in common with "a naturalist's experiment, a mechanical procedure imposed on the patient in an atmosphere of spiritual pressure and compulsion"; the task of psychoanalysis, meanwhile, is to allow patients to explore the roots of their troubles and to gain cognitive distance as a first step towards resolving them. Furthermore, Bleiberg points to the philosophical and speculative – rather than biological – character of psychoanalysis and its parallels with the systems proposed by Schopenhauer and Bergson. He concludes by approving of psychoanalysis:

> Freud's humanism is the leitmotif of all his studies, manifested in his earliest research exploring the subconscious as well as in his latest

64 Johann Wolfgang von Goethe [Georg Christoph Tobler], "Nature: Aphorisms by Goethe," trans. by T. H. Huxley, *Nature: A Weekly Illustrated Journal of Science*, 04/11/1869 <https://mathcs.clarku.edu/huxley/UnColl/Nature/Goet.html> [accessed 14/02/2022].

65 J. Bleiberg, "Humanizm Freuda", *NPR* 1938, no. 228, p. 14.

> works, which have turned his entire output into a consistent and compact whole. (*Ibid.*)

Thus Freudianism should be seen not only as a method to treat nervous diseases, or even as a worldview, but as nothing less than "a wide-ranging field within the humanities" (*Ibid.*).

Prosto z Mostu

In 1935, the same year that the Polish translation of Freud's *Introduction to Psychoanalysis* appeared in the bookshops, a new journal on culture and society also appeared on the market. It was *Prosto z Mostu*, a rightist weekly that was first launched as a supplement to the daily *ABC* and then became an independent publication. The title literally means "straight off the bridge," but as an idiom it could be translated as "straight from the shoulder". It soon became the first real competitor for *Wiadomości Literackie*. As one literary historian recently put it, "the ambition of almost every editor of a newly established literary journal at the time was to 'smash' *Wiadomości Literackie*, which had something like a monopoly on the literature of the Second Republic".[66] Before *Prosto z Mostu*, no new publication managed to have an impact on the print run of *Wiadomości Literackie*, but many readers saw this rightist weekly as an alternative. Its print run came to match that of *Wiadomości Literackie* – somewhere between twelve and fifteen thousand copies. Just like *Wiadomości Literackie*, which was founded, edited and owned by Grydzewski, at *Prosto z Mostu*, too, one man – his name was Stanisław Piasecki – always had the last say. But while Grydzewski rarely wrote articles for *Wiadomości Literackie*, Piasecki was one of the main contributors of *Prosto z Mostu*. When he became editor-in-chief he had no affiliation with any political party and made an effort to bestow on his journal an air of non-partisanship. As a university student, however, he had ties with the National Democracy; he also used to be an activist in two far-right organisations – All-Polish Youth (Młodzież Wszechpolska) and Camp of Great Poland (Obóz Wielkiej Polski). Unsurprisingly, his journal's ideology was clearly legible (as was the case with the leftist *Wiadomości Literackie*). *Prosto z Mostu* stood for the (Polish) nation, (Catholic) religion, (the traditional)

66 M. Urbanowski, "*Prosto z Mostu*", in *Oczyszczenie: Szkice o literaturze polskiej XX wieku* (Cracow: Arcana, 2002), p. 72.

family and discipline.[67] Its readers tended to be "well-educated young ethnic Poles, students at university or secondary school, often from the provinces and often having rightist or nationalist ideas".[68] Piasecki's journal responded to shifts in public opinion, such as rising nationalism and anti-Semitism, often attributed to the economic crisis and the sense of threat – externally from both Soviet Russia and Hitler's Germany, internally from the communists and the Jewish minority. *Prosto z Mostu* was openly critical of the government and the cultural establishment. Attacks on *Wiadomości Literackie* were daily fare. This attracted many writers who had never fit in with that journal, such as Bolesław Miciński, or who had fallen out with Grydzewski like Karol Irzykowski.

For Małgorzata Szpakowska, the success of *Prosto z Mostu* has much to do with its similarity to *Wiadomości Literackie*:

> [*Prosto z Mostu*] was certainly cruder (it was printed on paper of poorer quality, with graphic design that was not very sophisticated and an unattractive layout), but it was published according to a similar formula: a journal on culture and society with a wide range of interests, with similar regular columns and basically the same target readership. One could say that Piasecki's journal entered a well-trodden path [...].[69]

The rivalry between *Wiadomości Literackie* and *Prosto z Mostu*, Szpakowska continues, can be seen as part of "the long history, which goes back at least to the Enlightenment, of disputes about the modernisation of Poland and the Polish model of civilisation" (*Ibid.*). The same camps are pitched against each other:

> Familiarity against foreignness, Sarmatism against Europeanness, tradition against progress, religion against freethought, rigorism against liberalism, community against the individual, and finally an ontological understanding of the nation against a cultural one [...]. Within this matrix, *Wiadomości Literackie* would naturally be on the side of the modernisers, reformers and cosmopolitans, facing the representatives of tradition, the national spirit and unadulterated Polishness. (pp. 439–440)

67 M. Szpakowska, *"Wiadomości Literackie" prawie dla wszystkich*, p. 438.
68 M. Urbanowski, "*Prosto z Mostu*", p. 72.
69 M. Szpakowska, *"Wiadomości Literackie" prawie dla wszystkich*, p. 436.

Piasecki's journal was decidedly pro-Catholic and anti-Semitic from the outset, but it became more radical over time. The very first issue contained inveiglements against the Jewish minority as well as their role in politics, economics and culture; the proposed solution was Jewish mass emigration to Palestine. A few years later, however, the paper's already drastic anti-Semitism went so far beyond what had come to seem acceptable in the interwar press that some contributors resigned in protest. Irzykowski ceased to publish in *Prosto z Mostu* in 1938, along with Bolesław Miciński (discussed below), Jerzy Andrzejewski, Karol Ludwik Koniński and other important writers. Piasecki filled the empty space with such infamous texts as Céline's *Trifles for a Massacre*.[70]

Retrospectively, however, a nuanced assessment is in order. As Maciej Urbanowski argues, "it would be a mistake to ignore the weekly paper's anti-Semitism, just as it would probably be wrong to view it as a journal that was always anti-Jewish".[71] Indeed, the representation of psychoanalysis in *Prosto z Mostu* offers a counterpoint to its anti-Semitism. A lot of space was dedicated to Freud's theory, and it was discussed with an attitude that is noticeably more respectful than what we find in extremist right-wing papers, such as *Myśl Narodowa*, the organ of the National Democracy movement (Endecja). Here, Freud is portrayed as "an apostle of universal ruttishness, staring at the totem of the phallus"; his work is presented as worthless for academics and accused of promoting "the eternal decay" that was "the Jews' revenge" against the Christian world.[72] The nationalists claimed they had shown Freud's goals (as well as those of Marx, Bergson and Einstein) for what they were, namely to destroy the foundations of European civilisation.[73]

---

70 An incomplete Polish version of Céline's *Bagatelles pour un massacre*, translated by Michał Małek and titled "Pogromowe drobiazgi," was serialised in *Prosto z Mostu* from 1938 (issue 44) to 1939 (issue 6). The Polish text corresponds to about half of the French original. The last instalment appeared on 5 February 1939; a continuation is announced, but the second half of the text never appeared. The periodical folded after the German invasion, with the last issue appearing on 10 September 1939.

71 M. Urbanowski, "*Prosto z Mostu*", p. 85.

72 A. Nowaczyński, "Ofensywa: Propaganda Freuda", p. 539. *Myśl Narodowa* also published viciously anti-Semitic opinions about Freud by Władysław Jabłonowski and Michał Wiśniewski.

73 See M. Domagalska, *Antysemityzm dla inteligencji?: Kwestia żydowska w publicystyce Adolfa Nowaczyńskiego na łamach "Myśli Narodowej" (1921–1934) i "Prosto z Mostu" (1935–1939) na tle porównawczym* (Warsaw: ŻIH, 2004), p. 76.

Prosto z Mostu, by contrast, echoed the French Jesuit Jules de La Vaissière, whom I already discussed in Part V. His book *La Théorie Psychanalytique de Freud*, published in Polish translation by Księgarnia Św. Wojciecha,[74] received a positive review in *Prosto z Mostu*:

> By highlighting the role of unconscious tendencies, the determinism of the whole and the continuity of the psychic apparatus, Freud has rendered an outstanding service to science – a service that could have earned him a blameless reputation. His reputation as a psychologist, however, will always be overshadowed by a certain reproach, brought about by his heedlessness as a theoretician, for he has failed to look for strong evidence to support his idea that our sexual dynamism should be the source of our greatest moments of exaltation and our purest loves.[75]

Another example of the attitude towards psychoanalysis promoted by *Prosto z Mostu* is a column by Wojciech Wasiutyński. He reassures readers who wonder if it is appropriate for a Catholic to read Freud:

> There is no harm in exploring any theory as long as you have a compass that tells you where the truth lies. And you need not reason like a Jew: you need not worry about it all being kosher. You may engage with the pantheistic Jew Einstein and find in his works something that will bring you closer to the truth. You may engage with the sexualised Jew Freud and find in his theories something that will bring you closer to the truth.[76]

Needless to say, this compass is the Catholic faith. Those who are firm in the catechism, Wasiutyński argues, can safely indulge in psychoanalysis. It may well be that "Freud is a Jew and an enemy of religion and writes many things that are superficial and blasphemous, and efforts are being made to cast his theories as something like a world view," but Wasiutyński also detects redemptive qualities:

> [Freud's] discovery of the sphere of the subconscious in humankind, of a black pit within the soul that seethes with low instincts, and the fact that

---

74 J. de La Vaissière, *Teoria psychoanalityczna Freuda: Studium z psychologii pozytywnej*, trans. by M. and Z. Ziembiński (Poznań: Księgarnia św. Wojciecha, 1935).

75 "Ruch wydawniczy" [unsigned], *PZM* 1936, no. 34, p. 6.

76 W. Wasiutyński, "Czucie i szkiełko", *PZM* 1935, no. 41, p. 8.

> he has detected a "censor" which guards the soul and prevents many things "from down there" from even rising into our consciousness – this is a first-rate argument proving that the teachings of the Church are true [...]. Just replace "complexes" with "sin" and "the censor" with "the Guardian Angel" and... (*Ibid.*)

Prosto z Mostu also welcomes the publication of *Wstęp do psychoanalizy*, the Polish version of Freud's *Introduction to Psychoanalysis.* In an article titled "Literatura a psychologia" [Literature and Psychology] Kazimierz Czachowski highlights "the scientific achievements of new psychology" and its impact on contemporary literature. He mentions Edward Abramowski and other researchers in the field, insisting that Freudianism, which is "overly one-sided in its understanding of sexually motivated psychological phenomena," is not the only trend worthy of attention.[77] Still, discussing the achievements of psychoanalysis, he writes:

> Many contemporary novels clearly indicate that Freudianism has added psychological depth to literature, although it also often leads to completely arbitrary associations or interpretations. It is not the theory that is at fault, but the fact that it is understood rather too superficially. As far as literature is concerned, the translation of Sigmund Freud's *Introduction to Psychoanalysis* deserves appreciation. (*Ibid.*)

Besides Kazimierz Czachowski's article, the introduction of psychoanalysis to *Prosto z Mostu* can be credited to one person in particular, namely Bolesław Miciński. Two of his four studies on this topic appeared in Piasecki's journal. Within its first year, *Prosto z Mostu* published, in instalments, Miciński's thorough review of the *Introduction to Psychoanalysis.* This article, titled "Metafizyka czy metoda leczenia histerii?" [Metaphysics or a Treatment for Hysteria?],[78] is a more detailed version of the review he placed in *Przegląd Filozoficzny.*[79] The following year he published a review titled "Trzy prace o psychoanalizie" [Three Works in Psychoanalysis],

77 K. Czachowski, "Literatura a psychologia", *PZM* 1935, no. 34, p. 7.

78 B. Miciński, "Metafizyka czy metoda leczenia histerii?", *PZM* 1935, no. 36, p. 2; no. 37, p. 2; no. 38, p. 5. Reprinted in B. Miciński, *Pisma*, ed. by A. Micińska (Cracow: Znak, 1970), pp. 328-348.

79 B. Miciński, "Zygmunt Freud, *Wstęp do psychoanalizy*", *PF* 1936, no. 2, pp. 195-199.

discussing Freud's *An Autobiographical Study* among others.[80] His last piece, "O teoretycznych podstawach psychoanalizy" [On the Theoretical Foundations of Psychoanalysis], appeared in the Catholic *Verbum* – probably because he fell out with *Prosto z Mostu*, like Irzykowski and others.[81]

Miciński's article "Metafizyka czy metoda leczenia histerii?" does not formally appear like a review, even though it was clearly inspired by the Polish edition of Freud's *Introduction to Psychoanalysis* and does not touch on any other topic. Freud's popular lectures, given at the University of Vienna during the final years of World War I, were published within a short time span, and they correspond to the initial phase in the development of psychoanalytical theory. Freud summarises his work on the interpretation of dreams and the psychopathology of everyday life; in the chapter "General Theory of the Neuroses" he discusses the association of mental illness and repressed sexual trauma. This is the same material that Jekels presented in his *Szkic psychoanalizy Freuda* [An Outline of Freud's Psychoanalysis] in 1912, and which Polish experts and critics had since discussed in much detail. A lengthier and more up-to-date presentation of Freud's work became available to Polish readers in 1928, when Bychowski published his *Psychoanaliza*. Miciński did not refer to this book, nor did he draw on other publications by Freud. The main references for his review are Ludwika Karpińska's prewar article in *Przegląd Filozoficzny*, Nikolai Berdyaev's *The Destiny of Man*, which had recently appeared in French translation, as well as a book published the previous year, namely *Filozofia współczesna* [Contemporary Philosophy] by Józef Pastuszka, a Catholic priest and head of the Psychology Department at the Catholic University of Lublin. While Karpińska was a follower of Freud, Berdyaev and Pastuszka were decidedly opposed to his ideas.

Józef Pastuszka's book deals with contemporary philosophy, but the first chapter is dedicated to psychoanalysis and its impact on society.[82] The

80 B. Miciński, "Trzy prace o psychoanalizie", *PZM* 1936, no. 41, p. 7. Reprinted in B. Miciński, *Pisma*, ed. by A. Micińska (Cracow: Znak, 1970), pp. 348-356.

81 B. Miciński, "O teoretycznych podstawach psychoanalizy", *V* 1938, no. 4, pp. 715-724.

82 This chapter had previously appeared in *Ateneum Kapłańskie*: J. Pastuszka, "Psychoanaliza", *AK* 1933, no. 31, pp. 105-121. Miciński followed Pastuszka's work with great interest. In 1939 he reviewed his book on Adler's individual psychology for *Przegląd Filozoficzny* (B. Miciński, "J. Pastuszka, *Psychologia indywidualna*", *PF* 1939, no. 1, pp. 108-110).

pioneers of the movement may present it as no more than a psychological method, Pastuszka argues, but in fact it is nothing less than a world view combining activism, naturalism and pseudo-mysticism. He identifies a number of factors – beyond any clinical success of psychoanalysis – that may explain its immense popularity: first, the "mystical touch" of psychoanalysis satisfies "the human spirit's longing, its search for loftier, suprasensual moments in life"; second, Freud gives a convincing account of the dualism underlying human subjectivity and replaces moral concepts with sophisticated psychological jargon; third, psychoanalysis is characterised by the spirit of negation, which corresponds to the "attitude of the new man, who craves new paths and new ideals, especially after the sudden collapse of some of traditional values". Finally, psychoanalysis capitalises on its highly eroticised elements – an aspect that is "especially dangerous as it appears under the thin guise of scientific research, but it does not stop with merely satisfying curiosity – it goes on to postulate principles that threaten the very foundations of our traditional morality".[83] Pastuszka concludes with a defeatist vision of the triumph of psychoanalysis:

> Despite its conservative poses, psychoanalysis is a movement that supports reform and revolution. It lives to negate the world of ideas as we have known it. [...] By subverting our old hierarchies of knowledge, by destroying religious and moral ideals, by eradicating the spiritual elements in the individual, by proclaiming hedonistic values, i.e. the most extreme sexual liberalism, Freud's psychoanalysis is an attack against the very foundations of the Christian world view. (p. 121)

The title of Miciński's long article, "Metafizyka czy metoda leczenia histerii?" [Metaphysics or a Treatment for Hysteria?], hinges on a rhetorical question borrowed from Pastuszka's book. Miciński suggests that Freud's apparent "method to treat hysteria" conceals "a pansexual metaphysics" that can also be turned into an ideology:

> We have identified the Nietzscheanism that underlies Hitlerism, as well as Marx's historical materialism which has recently shaped what is called 'the face of the new Russia,' and so we must not ignore psychoanalysis as a cosmopolitan and stateless worldview.[84]

83 J. Pastuszka, "Psychoanaliza", pp. 120-121.

84 B. Miciński, *Pisma*, p. 329.

Miciński also draws on Pastuszka for two other elements of his review: first, a bon mot attributed to Richard Downey, Archbishop of Liverpool, who reportedly quipped that what is true in psychoanalysis is not new, and what is new in it is false, and second, the conclusion of Georges Dumas' *Traité de psychologie* [The Treatise of Psychology].[85]

Miciński finds it unsettling that Freud portrays the unconscious as "a separate mental realm, with its own desire, its own expression and its own mechanisms" (p. 344). He dwells on the question of Freud's "astonishing ambition," which makes him search for the ultimate explanation of the relationship between the physical world and the realm of psychology. For the young philosopher Miciński, this is "one of the toughest problems known to humanity" – the one that condemned Descartes' dualism to fail. The way in which Freud tried to solve it reminds Miciński of the theologian and philosopher Nicolas Malebranche, the occasionalist who referred to divine intervention to account for the coherence between mental and physical processes. Freud, Miciński argues, does the same thing, he only exchanges the factor "x" – in the place of God he presents the unconscious. A twentieth-century professor of medicine, however, should not get away with a fallacy that seems forgivable in a seventeenth-century theologian:

> Steeped in the gibberish of dreams, psychoanalysts are searching for complexes, obstinately and with cold fanaticism, just as centuries ago the fathers of the Holy Inquisition searched for the sinister *stigma diabolicum* on a witch's body. The doctor's white smock becomes a priest's robe, while the copy of *Psychoanalysis* into the famous *Hammer of Witches* – this is how we should imagine the ballet in a new version of *The Imaginary Invalid*. In

85 No original source has been identified for Richard Downey's bon mot. The passage quoted from Dumas reads:
"Even though Freudianism contains a part of of truth, we must not overlook the outrageous character of the system […], the deficiencies in the historical and physiological justification of the entire theory of libido, the inadequacy of that theory when it comes to accounting for the causes of psycho-neuroses […], the fantastic interpretations of sexual matters and the logical pitfalls inherent in the symbolism that leads to such interpretations.
Freudianism, having made a global commotion, will undoubtedly confirm Brunetière's view that the enduring values of any system always lie outside the system itself" (Georges Dumas, *Traité de psychologie* (Paris: Librairie Félix Alcan, 1924), vol. 2, p. 1065, trans. from French by T. Bhambry), quoted in B. Miciński, *Pisma*, p. 348.

> Molière's time, the poor hypochondriac was told he had tuberculosis and arthritis, today it would be incest and necrophilia. But poor Argan would be happier today – he would be more than welcome to tell us all about his illness. (p. 347)

The most important point in Miciński's review for *Prosto z Mostu* is what he perceives as Freud's anti-intellectualism. The article has four epigraphs, three of which are taken from classics of Western philosophy: Kant's *Critique of Judgment*, Pascal's *Pensées* and Descartes' *Discourse on the Method*. These mottos, which highlight humankind's special status in the natural world – a status that stems from the ability to think – form a contrasting backdrop for the fourth quotation, taken from Freud's *Introduction to Psychoanalysis* and proposing that "mental processes are in themselves unconscious" (p. 328).[86] In Miciński's view, Freud deprives humankind of that which is essential and unique:

> This reduction of the role of the intellect, subordinated to instincts and embryonic mental states that, smeared with faeces and urine, swirl and roll around in the subconscious, is a hundred times more dreadful than the Oedipus complexes and all the "desires" that Freud finds in dreams. For by attacking the autonomy of the intellect, Freud attacks the foundations of what it means to be human [...]. The silly old joke where *cogito* is turned into *coito ergo sum* only becomes intelligible in the context of psychoanalysis. (p. 340)

Miciński also takes issue with Freud's presumptuousness in comparing himself to Copernicus and Darwin:

> It was Freud who first insulted human dignity. Darwin pointed to our origins in the animal world, but Freud turned us into animals, and not because he smeared us with urine, semen and faeces, but because he unlawfully took away the right to think from one "whose whole essence or nature consists only in thinking"... (p. 330)[87]

86 The English translation of this quotation is taken from S. Freud, SE XV, p. 21.

87 The English translation of this quotation is taken from René Descartes, *Discourse on Method*, trans. by John Veitch (La Salle: Open Court, 1962), pp. 35-36.

Over the years, Miciński's views on psychoanalysis changed, mostly under the influence of his friend Kazimierz Golonka. They first met in Kościan in 1935, when Miciński and his fiancée, Halina Krauze, were spending the summer. Golonka, a psychiatrist, had recently joined the local Institute for Nervous Diseases (Zakład dla Nerwowo Chorych) in Kościan, where he was to practice psychoanalysis. Miciński was impressed by this sophisticated and highly successful therapist. The following year he recommended Golonka to Jarosław Iwaszkiewicz, who was looking for a psychiatrist for his wife. His letters to Golonka, written over the next few years, bespeak a relationship of mutual trust. According to Anna Micińska, who edited their correspondence, Golonka's "extraordinary intelligence and great literary culture" allowed him to became "the most intimate confidant of Miciński's struggles as an artist, and he followed his friend's work not only as a critic but also as a psychoanalyst" (p. 427).[88] As one critic argues, Miciński's fascination with psychoanalysis coincided with two important life events, namely his engagement and a grave relapse of tuberculosis. The young philosopher found himself balancing between life and death, and his "imprisonment between Eros and Thanatos [...] must have brought him close to this dimension of Freud's thought".[89] Miciński admits in his letters that his friend Golonka allowed him to understand how much his own essay collection *Podróże do piekieł* [Journeys to Hell] – saturated as it was with psychoanalytic jargon – had been "cathartic or therapeutic," touching on the most personal issues.[90]

Miciński wrote his article for *Prosto z Mostu* during his stay in Kościan. In late September or early October he posted a letter to the poet Włodzimierz Sebyła, asking him for feedback on the piece and adding: "I have insane 'verve' to write and I've been working a lot on Freud – I've been at it for three weeks, barely ever leaving my desk" (p. 389). It was only in 1938, two years after Miciński's review of Freud's book appeared in *Przegląd Filozoficzny*, that he gave Golonka a copy of his article. He was impatient to hear what his new friend had to say about it; should Golonka reply favourably then he might show his opinion to Witkacy, also a friend,

88 The editor of the correspondence does not mention where the original manuscripts are kept. The published letters (*Pisma*, pp. 427-448) omit passages concerning Miciński's personal problems. Perhaps – though this cannot be verified – Golonka supported Miciński as a therapist.

89 R. Kwiecień, "Bolesław Miciński i psychoanaliza", *TD* 1998, no. 1/2, p. 90.

90 B. Miciński, *Pisma*, p. 436.

but one who found Miciński's review unacceptable ("Witkacy threw himself at me," Miciński wrote to Golonka, "simply roaring with rage" (p. 444)). Golonka, who described himself as a follower of Stekel rather than Freud, responded that Miciński ought to explore the non-orthodox branches of psychoanalysis.[91]

Miciński's review article "Trzy prace o psychoanalizie" [Three Works in Psychoanalysis] for *Prosto z Mostu* presents Jules de La Vaissière's book as well as Freud's *Introduction to Psychoanalysis* and *An Autobiographical Study*. Miciński describes the latter as "simply one more presentation of psychoanalysis, with a few dates, names and a drop of bile," and treats it in a more cursory manner than the other two books; his focus is on Freud's harshness towards his apostates, Jung and Adler.[92] Discussing de La Vaissière's work, Miciński applauds the publisher, Księgarnia Św. Wojciecha, for "complementing the publishing project launched by Przeworski's Press and offering a brilliant counterpoint to the impact of orthodox Freudianism on the readership, which is generally uncritical" (p. 350). Miciński considers de La Vaissière to be not only erudite, clear and concise, but also as neutral as a critic can be, pointing out that this writer even "finds words of praise for Freud, a member of a Jewish freemasonry lodge – words that we would vainly look for in many writings by secular biologists or experimental psychologists" (*Ibid.*). That said, Miciński agrees with de La Vaissière's accusations against psychoanalysis, namely that it underestimates intellectual activities while overrating the sexual instinct; what is more, psychoanalysis misrepresents the problem of willpower and reduces the individual's inner life to a game of drives. Miciński discusses at length his own conclusion from this reading, namely that, unlike other fields of study, "a psychological theory imposed on the collective is able to change the reality which is its object" (*Ibid.*). In physics, no theory will ever affect the material world, but in psychology a theory that is wrong can in time influence its object and become true. The danger of psychoanalysis, for Miciński, is its potential to fundamentally transform the human psyche – a process that is already unfolding. In his conclusion Miciński cites Golonka's piece on Wilhelm Stekel, but he discusses Stekel alongside Jung and Adler. Unlike these two heretics, he suggests, Stekel did not stray into philosophy but remained on the firm ground of medicine.

91 Golonka wrote a detailed article on Stekel for *Nowiny Psychiatryczne*. See K. Golonka, "Psychoanaliza Stekela," *NP* 1935, no. 3/4, pp. 221–239.

92 B. Miciński, *Pisma*, p. 349.

Miciński regrets that Stekel's theory remains "completely unknown in our country" (p. 355); after all, Stekel usefully narrows down the role of sexuality to focus on the conflict between the "cultural self" and the "impulsive self," thus presenting an alternative to Freud's idea about the domination of unconscious forces.

In one of his letters to Golonka Miciński confesses: "All the books on the subject have not given me a tiny fraction of what I've gained from our conversations – instead of looking in books, I reimagine our discussions" (p. 446). Unsurprisingly perhaps, his subsequent works were partly inspired by his friend. For instance, Miciński explores the metaphysical assumptions of psychoanalysis. He even announces his intention to write a work on psychoanalysis and the history of philosophy, which would complement the book Golonka was writing at the time about the history of psychoanalysis. Neither of their books ever saw the light of day, but Miciński's stated goal was to "study all that has been done so far in the field of psychoanalysis and to relate it to spiritualist philosophy" (p. 438). With a playful sense of remorse he states that it was now too late for him to study medicine; unable to become a therapist, he could at least try his luck as a theorist.

Miciński suggests that while Freudianism presents itself in the robe of materialism, when we examine its psychological assumptions it becomes apparent that its spiritualist metaphysics resonate with Leibniz's monadology.[93] In his review of Freud's *Introduction to Psychoanalysis* in *Przegląd Filozoficzny* he had focused on the differences between Leibniz and Freud. By 1937, however, writing for the more popular *Polska Zbrojna*, he portrayed the rationalist philosopher as a precursor of the most recently developed branch of psychology.[94] Initially, Miciński had assumed that Freud's comparison of consciousness and the unconscious to a rider on a rearing horse suggested that "it is best to follow the horse's impulse and lead it where it wants to go".[95] Later, however, he concluded that Freud, like Leibniz, believed the drives ought to be controlled by reason: "everything pathogenic must be reduced to consciousness".[96] Summarising Freud's theory for readers of *Polska Zbrojna*, Miciński echoes the view of

93 B. Miciński, "Psychologia indywidualna", *PF* 1939, no. 1, p. 109.

94 B. Miciński, "Zagadnienia psychoanalizy, 'Polska zbrojna w kulturę'", a supplement to *PZ* 1937, no. 7, p. 2.

95 B. Miciński, "Zygmunt Freud, Wstęp do psychoanalizy", *PF* 1936, no. 2, p. 197.

96 B. Miciński, "Zagadnienia psychoanalizy", p. 2.

Freud proposed by Karol Irzykowski before World War I. His focus, as he illustrates with a series of telling similes, is on the ethical dimension of psychoanalysis, which fosters self-knowledge:

> The conscious mind can be compared to a swift river, the subconscious to a stagnant pond covered in duckweed; hanging over it are the stifling fumes of putrefying detritus. The task of psychoanalysis is to regulate these spheres, to dig waterways connecting the closed pond with the riverbed whose invigorating flow can cleanse the bottom of the pond, silted up and strewn with waste.
> Another example: the conscious mind is a house built on a wetland – the seeping water (subconsciousness) washes away the foundations and floods the cellars, thus damaging the building. The engineer drains the land and finds an outlet for the water; brought to the surface it flows down its designated bed. Similarly, psychoanalysis also brings to the surface tendencies that undermine us and that are contrary to our conscience, tendencies that in our everyday life only emerge from the darkness of our subconscious in the form of nervous disorders (neuroses), dreams and daydreams, irrational reflexes and little slips that we usually do not pay attention to. They are like the traces of damp on the white façade of a house, which allow us to make inferences about the seeping water gnawing away at the edifice. It is by referring to these aspects of our lives that psychoanalysis begins its work. (*Ibid.*)

Miciński understands why Freud's message is rejected: "humans naturally avoid and abhor the truth," while psychoanalysis acts as "a Roentgen apparatus, directed at the soul and revealing truths that are always unpleasant" (*Ibid.*). At the same time he insists that this search for authenticity is a necessary effort:

> If we are to defeat the evil with which we are all burdened, and to subdue our asocial tendencies, then we must come to know them, and psychoanalysis is exactly – drawing on military comparisons – the "intelligence" that breaks into the enemy's headquarters, uncovers their plans and detects their secret codes. (*Ibid.*)

Miciński, previously a fierce critic of Freudianism, later became a fervent supporter. In February 1937 he wrote to his friend: "You should know that I have decided to promote psychoanalysis until the end of my life."[97] In a letter written in the autumn to 1938, he tells Golonka that in order to bolster his income he had taken a position as a philosophy teacher at three different secondary schools in Warsaw: "Instead of experimental psychology, I pound psychoanalysis into 120 brains as the Lord God has commanded; if an inspection comes I'll be fired, but that's fine, I'm not cut out to be a teacher anyway, and at least I'll have saved 120 souls" (p. 447).

Miciński returned to the convergence of monadology with psychoanalysis, which he had touched on in the column, in *Verbum*. The extensive article "O teoretycznych podstawach psychoanalizy" [On the Theoretical Foundations of Psychoanalysis] was his last work on the subject. This time he declared in the opening sentence that "the present piece has no popularising ambitions" (p. 364). Its stated goal, as suggested in the title, is to explore the "foundations of psychoanalysis" and thus to show that Freudians "do not think what they preach". While the majority of commentators focus on the apparent materialism and determinism of this branch of psychology, what can be found at its roots, in its psychological assumptions, are a number of metaphysical hypotheses. Miciński names Georges Politzer's 1928 study *Critique des Fondements de la Psychologie* [*Critique of the Foundations of Psychology*] as an inspiration. He also refers to Ludwika Karpińska, whose pre-war study "O psychologicznych podstawach Freudyzmu" [The Psychological Foundations of Freudianism] is echoed in the title of his own article and cited in the text. Miciński proposes to examine not so much the propositions formulated directly by Freud, but to bring out issues that Freud does not write about and of which he may not even be aware: "The nerve of psychoanalysis is the so-called 'interpretation,' that is, the technique of deepening the meaning of gestures and statements. […] We shall try to apply this method to the works of its founders" (p. 365). He predicts two difficulties in this endeavour. The first stems from the fact that psychoanalysis, being the work of medical practitioners unaccustomed to theorising, is characterised by "conceptual sloppiness"; the second is related to the fact that this field of study is still being developed and not yet a closed system.

Reconstructing the unique "materialist metaphysics" of psychoanalysis, Miciński concludes that Freud did what he could to obliterate its revolutionary dimension. Freud's most important innovation, he continues, was that he created a "psychology in the first person". Previous psycho-

97 B. Miciński, *Pisma*, p. 431.

logical theorists had considered mental facts in isolation from the real, concrete subject, as if in the third person. Instead of writing about phenomena occurring in one individual's consciousness, they wrote about abstract consciousness in general. Psychoanalysts were the first to acknowledge the necessity to study individual subjects. This is best seen in dream interpretation, which assumes that the seemingly meaningless text has been formulated as part of an individual's unique psychological set-up. Unlike the traditional psychologist, the analyst does not detach the phenomenon, but relates it to the subject and "interprets their subjective interpretation" (p. 372). Miciński contends that "whenever Freud goes beyond the assumption that a phenomenon must be apprehended 'in the first person,' he ceases to be a revolutionary and obliterates his own achievements" (*ibid.*). In Miciński's view this happens frequently, as he sees the very idea of the unconscious as an example of psychological abstractionism; when Freud draws on models from other sciences, Miciński accuses him of physiological and biological abstractionism. Psychoanalysis builds on generalisations, it uses extra-psychological premises and replaces teleology with a mechanistically regulated processes, and as a consequence it loses its subversive potential, becoming that which what it had initially opposed.

In Miciński's opinion, the relationship between psychoanalysis and materialism and evolutionism, which both belong to the era, are superficial; "its genealogical line leads towards the philosophy of Schopenhauer and Hartmann on the one hand, and the monadology of Leibniz on the other" (p. 375). Its similarity with the two philosophers may be profound, but they only concern "the theoretical superstructure of psychoanalysis," not its revolutionary core. Both systems have been formulated in the "third person": "the will" and "the unconscious" are "impersonal forces beyond the subject – the inner conflict is not individual but universal in nature. It is a cosmic conflict, not a psychological one" (p. 376). Monadology, meanwhile, develops concepts of unconscious mental life and of its teleology. Here "psychoanalysis can rediscover not only the assumptions of its own psychology, but also the foundations of metaphysics "in the first person" that are concealed in those assumptions (*Ibid.*). Leibniz's system has the benefit that the sources of these dynamics do not lie outside the monad but are part of its inner structure. If Freud only referred back to Leibniz, Miciński suggests, he might save his theory, which is otherwise condemned to inertia. To prove that a psychoanalysis rooted in monadology is possible, he juxtaposes, in a footnote, passages from Maine de Biran's study *Mémoires sur les perceptions obscures* with sections from Freud's works.

In his conclusion Miciński points out a fundamental gap in psychoanalysis. Values, as he states in his closing sentence, "cannot be formulated in the first person" (p. 379). The subject of psychoanalysis is "the human monad, which is incapable of stepping outside of itself," cut off from transcendental reality, finds no support anywhere, hates itself and is gripped by fear. In Freud's view the individual is not self-sufficient. This echoes thinkers such as Saint Augustine, Kierkegaard, and, to mention a contemporary, Heidegger. This is perhaps why Miciński's views evolved "through spiritualism and objectivism" (p. 425) straight to Catholicism. He describes this development at length in a letter to Jarosław Iwaszkiewicz, adding that it is through the work of self-exploration that he had become a believer. Paradoxically, therefore, psychoanalysis was the bridge that led him towards faith.[98]

Miciński's article on psychoanalysis was certainly no popular introduction; it assumed familiarity with Freud's theory on the readers' part, as well as considerable erudition in philosophy. Nonetheless, when it came to choosing a piece of work to present at the Polish Academy of Literature (Polska Akademia Literatury or PAL), Miciński picked his most recent article in *Verbum* on the theoretical foundations of psychoanalysis. As it turned out, his audience completely misunderstood his argument. The reporter for *Wiadomości Literackie*, a certain Stanisław Brucz, praised Miciński's "personal and thorough settling of accounts with Freudianism," acknowledging that he used "the most sophisticated keys to unlock and dismount the Freudian system".[99] In Brucz's opinion, "Miciński is right to call Freud a materialist". He goes on to inform readers that the speaker's main opponent was "the well-known Freudian Dr Bychowski," whose reaction was "characterised by the fervour of a committed student and the defensive zeal of an orthodox believer".

The atmosphere during the meeting, "a major event for Warsaw's intellectuals," was described by Eustachy Czekalski, a reporter for *Tygodnik*

98 J. Błoński, "Przedmowa", in B. Miciński, *Pisma*, p. 10. After the outbreak of the war, Miciński returned to psychoanalysis: in 1941-42, he studied Freud's "Thoughts for the Times on War and Death", written during World War I. He found Freud's ideas so perspicacious and topical that he called him a great moralist (see B. Miciński, "Myśli o wojnie", in *Pisma*, pp. 148-153).

99 S. Brucz, "Zagadnienie psychoanalizy w ujęciu Bolesława Micińskiego", *WL* 1939, 18, p. 6.

Ilustrowany.[100] According to his account, Miciński, "a contributor to the Catholic *Verbum*, stressed the Viennese professor's materialism" and voiced his concerns about "the moral aspect of Freud's psychological work". Besides Miciński and Freud's apologist Bychowski, Czekalski adds, there was a third person who spoke up during the meeting, also attacking Freudianism:

> The academician K. Irzykowski, who questioned the Viennese psychiatrist's "alleged" scientific achievements. K. Irzykowski's remarks were interrupted by applause. The audience reacted with particular enthusiasm when the expert on literature remarked that Freud "has infected the whole world with his theory of dreams, his complexes and sexualism". (*Ibid.*)

This misrepresentation of Miciński's views – both papers portrayed him as an opponent of psychoanalysis – led to a heated debate in *Wiadomości Literackie*. A letter to the editor was submitted by Jakub Bickels, a medical doctor and specialist in mental illnesses from Lviv. To counter the notion of Freud's materialism attributed to Miciński, Bickels refers to Wilhelm Stekel. In *Conditions of Nervous Anxiety and Their Treatment* Stekel describes how astonished he was, having always viewed the human body as a mechanical apparatus, when he discovered a science based on the study of unexpected links between the body and the soul. Bickels also provides a quotation from Stekel: "New and powerful changes await the medical sciences. [...] Youth is pushing forward and demanding a new understanding of how things are related. Materialism, this hard-hearted tyrant, is to be dethroned and thought is to be proclaimed king once more."[101] Another letter was sent by a certain Marek Katl from Cracow. He writes that Freud, who opposed somatic medicine and searched for mental causes, cannot be described as a materialist in the field of medicine; this fact, he adds, is so obvious that to prove it there was really no need to quote Stekel. But it is another matter when it comes to Freud's materialism in a purely philosophical sense:

100 E. Czekalski, "Freud, Weyssenhoff i car Paweł", *TI* 1939, no. 18, p. 352.

101 J. Bickels, "Freud nie jest 'materialistą'", *WL* 1939, no. 21, p. 8. The passage from Stekel was translated from the German by T. Bhambry, since it was omitted from Rosalie Gabler's English translation of Stekel's book. For the original see W. Stekel, *Nervöse Angstzustände und ihre Behandlung* (Berlin: Urban & Schwarzenberg, 1908), p. viii.

> Mr Brucz's argument (the grammatical construction does not suggest whether this was also the opinion proffered by the speaker), supposedly proving the materialism of psychoanalysis, is not very convincing. Mr Brucz writes: "Freud is a materialist, because psychoanalysis, rooted in the assumptions of practical and applicable (?) neurotherapy, is aimed at having a preventive function in society." This would suggest that Buddhism, for instance, or "Christian Science" are materialist concepts. It would be hard to agree with that.[102]

Miciński also joined the debate. In a letter, which the editors provided with the title "Rzekomy materializm psychoanalizy" [The Alleged Materialism of Psychoanalysis] he gave the following justification:

> Regrettably I must state that Mr Brucz's report has completely misrepresented the gist of my presentation, whose only goal was to call attention to the spiritualist assumption at the root of the theory proposed by the ingenious Viennese psychologist. Mr Brucz might have accused me of changing my mind and of disavowing the position I had previously taken. Luckily, "scripta restant" and my presentation at PAL was only a development of my short study "O filozoficznych podstawach psychoanalizy" [On the Philosophical Foundations of Psychoanalysis], which was published in *Verbum* (no. 4, 1938). That study was meant precisely to free psychoanalysis from the superficial associations with materialist metaphysics.[103]

The debate on the philosophical assumptions of Freudianism sounded the final chord to *Wiadomości Literackie* in the interwar period. At the same time in *Nasz Przegląd*, Jakub Bleiberg discussed the place of psychoanalysis within the humanities – not only in the so-called *Geisteswissenschaften* but above all in the field of *Kulturwissenschaften*. Even before that, Leon Chwistek had declared in *Przegląd Współczesny* that "all that is truly great in contemporary philosophy has been created by mathematicians (Poincaré), logicians (Russell), physicists (Mach, Einstein) and doctors

102 M. Katl, "Korespondencja", WL 1939, no. 27, p. 8.

103 B. Miciński, "Rzekomy materializm psychoanalizy", *WL* 1939, no. 30, p. 8. Stanisław Brucz remained unconvinced. In another open letter he insisted on his interpretation of Miciński's lecture: "*Verba volant* – but not as much as Mr Miciński seems to imagine" (S. Brucz, "Materializm psychoanalizy", *WL* 1939, no. 33, p. 8).

(Freud)".[104] On the eve of World War II, Polish readers of Freud were preoccupied with a fundamental problem that would haunt many later critics and scholars. As Szymon Wróbel has pointed out, the uncertainty about whether psychology was a natural science or a part of hermeneutics accompanied the discipline ever since it came into being, and it still continues to divide it into two camps: behaviourism takes on a nomothetic orientation, while humanist psychology opts for the idiographic paradigm. Psychoanalysis, meanwhile, "appears at odds with itself (cracked from within): naturalist [ontological] declarations go hand in hand with anti-naturalist methods,"[105] which is why it seems impossible to resolve the dilemma once and for all. Its continuing relevance is also seen in the debate provoked by Frank J. Sulloway's monumental study *Freud, Biologist of the Mind* in 1979. Sulloway argues that in the twentieth century psychoanalysis came to be treated as part of the humanities, and even of literature; in terms of its scientific aspirations, however, its founder was a psychobiologist, a child of his time, drawing on the same methodological inspirations as Darwin – even if towards the end of his life he chose to remove from his collected works all his studies in neurology and neuroanatomy.[106] Sulloway's argument was a shock to readers who had become attached to the well-established views on psychoanalysis proposed by Jaspers, Habermas or Ricœur, according to whom psychoanalysis, despite Freud's own convictions, did not belong to the natural sciences but was above all part of hermeneutics and the philosophy of culture.

Regardless of the subsequent discussions around the status of psychoanalysis, the last decade of Freud's life was marked by a general agreement that psychoanalysis had left the field of scientism to find itself in the field of culture. This was related to the increasing number of philosophical ("speculative") works by Freud, as well as to a radicalisation in the so-called *Methodenstreit*, the dispute among German-language academics about the ultimate difference between the natural and social sciences. Freud was awarded the Goethe Prize in 1930; five years later, Karl Popper rejected the scientific character of psychoanalysis in his *Logik der Forschung*. Another year later, on Freud's eightieth birthday, Romain Rolland nominated him for the Nobel Prize in Literature. This was a novelty in the

104 L. Chwistek, "Zagadnienia kultury duchowej w Polsce", *PWS* 1930, no. 102, p. 354.

105 S. Wróbel, *Odkrycie nieświadomości: Czy destrukcja kartezjańskiego pojęcia podmiotu poznającego?* (Wrocław: Leopoldinum, 1997), p. 94.

106 F. J. Sulloway, *Freud, Biologist of the Mind*, esp. the Preface to the 1992 edition, pp. xi-xvi.

sense that the Stockholm committee had previously only been asked to consider Freud in the field of medicine.

Nasz Przegląd, *Wiadomości Literackie* and *Prosto z Mostu* were the most widely read and influential magazines in interwar Poland, and they all had very different political profiles. The debate on psychoanalysis, its philosophical foundations and scientific position made its way into them because Polish writers keep a finger on the pulse of developments in the field. A survey of these publications also indicates the debate was held on a remarkably mature level, testifying indirectly to the success of Bychowski's popularising efforts as an ambassador of psychoanalysis in Poland.

Psychoanalysis and fiction

Of the many reviews of Kempner's translation of Freud's *Introduction to Psychoanalysis*, the most puzzling one was penned by the modernist writer Witold Gombrowicz. His article, "Nauka ściga się o prawdę psychologiczną z literaturą" [Science is Racing with Literature for Psychological Truth] appeared in *Kurier Poranny*. Gombrowicz deals with Freud's book only in the very first paragraph:

> A massive volume, 580 pages, but even if it reads easily, this is an extremely difficult book – seemingly objective and yet referring to the reader's intentions, seemingly scientific, and yet not empirically verifiable, profoundly honest and assuming the recipient's honesty, and yet founded on ideas that are so volatile and vague that, more than anything else, it is susceptible to fantasy, and even sheer claptrap. Freud – *Introduction to Psychoanalysis*. There is perhaps no field that is more vulnerable and less protected from chicanery. But is this not precisely why this method is of such high quality and so prolific? Integrity, non-formalistic honesty, are always exposed to chicanery.[107]

Gombrowicz considers himself ill-equipped "to defend the scientific methods of psychoanalysis," so rather than reviewing Freud's book he engages with "the enduring and malicious chicanery" levelled against literature. Conservative literary critics in Poland seem determined to identify Freudian elements in every literary debut, Gombrowicz writes.

107 W. Gombrowicz, "Nauka ściga się o prawdę psychologiczną z literaturą: O brudach i urokach", *KPO* 1935, no. 263, p. 10.

"One only needs to write a book that is more direct and not entirely compliant with traditional norms to be proclaimed right away as being 'under the influence of Freud'. The theory of psychoanalysis is imputed to anyone and everyone who touches on the subconscious" (*Ibid.*).

Perhaps Gombrowicz had more reason to complain than other writers. Two years earlier, his short story collection, *Pamiętnik z okresu dojrzewania* [Memoirs of a Time of Immaturity, published in English as *Bacacay*] was published, and the overwhelming majority of critics proclaimed it to be essentially Freudian.[108] To better understand Gombrowicz's article of 1935, it is perhaps worth looking back at those reviews. The most vociferous critic of Gombrowicz's debut was Leon Piwiński, who argued in *Wiadomości Literackie* that the very title "suggests that we will be dealing here with a genuine contribution in the style of Freud's psychoanalysis".[109] Even though the book is not actually "an experimental psychoanalytic study," Piwiński continues, "the spirit of Freudian psychology permeates it entirely. Each of the seven stories develops or illustrates some complex, and each deals with issues that lie deep in the subconscious" (*Ibid.*). The critic proceeds story by story, presenting a psychoanalytical reading of each one in turn. In "Lawyer Kraykowski's Dancer," he suggests, Gombrowicz explores "the inferiority complex in the context of an obsequious interest in the sexuality of another person, one whom the subject affected by that complex regards as infinitely superior to himself"; "The Memoirs of Stefan Czarniecki" illustrates "an inferiority complex rooted in racial disharmony," while "Dinner at Countess Pavahoke's", "Adventures" and "The

---

108 Gombrowicz continues to be among the Polish writers most intensely read through a Freudian lens. See e.g. E. Fiała, "O początkach i perspektywach psychoanalitycznej interpretacji literatury: Gombrowicz w optyce Freuda i Fromma", *PLI* 2001, no. 4, pp. 75–96; J. Błoński, "*Ślub* jako tragedia psychoanalityczna", in *Forma, śmiech i rzeczy ostateczne: Studia o Gombrowiczu* (Cracow: Znak, 1994), pp. 111–139; D. Danek, "Poetyka snu w *Operetce*", in *Sztuka rozumienia: Literatura i psychoanaliza* (Warsaw: IBL, 1997), pp. 61–104; E. Graczyk, *Przed wybuchem wstrząsnąć: O twórczości Witolda Gombrowicza w okresie międzywojennym* (Gdańsk: słowo/obraz terytoria, 2004); M.P. Markowski, *Czarny nurt: Gombrowicz, świat, literatura* (Cracow: Wydawnictwo Literackie, 2004); P. Dybel, *Mesjasz, który odszedł: Bruno Schulz i psychoanaliza* (Cracow: Universitas, 2017). Only Jan Tomkowski has argued that Gombrowicz "owes much less to Freud than his friends"; see *Pokolenie Gombrowicza: Narodziny powieści XX wieku w Polsce* (Warsaw: Czytelnik, 2001), p. 71.

109 L. Piwiński, "Interesujący debiut", *WL* 1933, no. 32, p. 5. Interestingly, when the same critic reviewed Bruno Schulz's *Sklepy cynamonowe* [*The Cinnamon Shops*] a year later, he did not detect any psychoanalytical elements in it (*WL* 1934, no. 6, p. 3).

Events on the Banbury" structurally resemble a dream. Unsurprisingly, Piwiński also considers the main theme of "Virginity" to be "typically psychoanalytical":

> Alice is a sexually inexperienced and naïve young lady. Her unconscious eroticism finds a substitute expression in the most bizarre desires: she wishes men would throw stones at her, she wishes to be hungry and steal bread rolls, and above all she has a terrible craving for a bone from the rubbish and desires to gnaw at it with her fiancé. (*Ibid.*)

All of these stories, the critic continues, apply "an original but very circular method to give artistic expression to certain dark, complicated, nameless emotional states, mainly so-called psychological 'traumas'". For Piwiński, this inventiveness hinges on Gombrowicz's ability to extract comic value – "very particular" and unexpected though it may be – from psychoanalytical themes: "a combination of horror and the 'uncanny' in the style of Poe with grotesque, dizzyingly caricatured exaggeration and 'unhealthy' dark humour" (*ibid.*).

Another critic who identified Freudian elements in Gombrowicz's short story collection was Ignacy Fik. He went so far as to coin a new word to describe emerging writers whose fascination with psychoanalysis he considered to be unhealthy.[110] The term he proposed was *choromaniak*, based on the surname of Michał Choromański, the author of a novel titled *Zazdrość i medycyna* [Jealousy and Medicine], published in 1932; Choromański's name lent itself particularly well to Fik's purposes because it phonetically resembles the Polish words for illness (*choroba*) and for mania. Several months before the Polish translation of the *Introduction to Psychoanalysis* was published, Fik's article discusses the emergence of an entirely new type of fiction, which he relates to Freud's influence. However, he continues, while Freud saw psychoanalysis as a diagnostic psychiatric tool, "our literary psychoanalysts [...] have turned it into an

110 I. Fik, "Literatura choromaniaków", *TA* 1935, no. 15; I draw on the reprint in *Wybór pism krytycznych*, ed. by A. Chruszczyński (Warsaw: Książka i Wiedza, 1979), pp. 125–135. Gombrowicz compared his work to that of Choromański and Rudnicki in an article titled "Postawa nowych autorów," published under the pseudonym G.K. [G. Kotkowski], *KPO* 1933, no. 328. His direct response to Fik's accusations, although it primarily defended Bruno Schulz, appeared as "O myślach chudych", *KPO* 1935, no. 307, p. 6.

end in itself. They delight in mashing up the worst clinical specimens, they boast of the details of their work and invite us into their torture chambers and séances".[111] Perhaps Choromański's name, besides its obvious phonetic associations, was also chosen as a signifier because his novel enjoyed huge commercial and critical success; it was even awarded the annual young writers' prize by the Polish Academy of Literature.[112] Still, Fik's focus is not solely on Choromański; he refers to many other writers of the generation associated with the radical modernisation of the Polish novel. In Fik's view, Gombrowicz, Witkacy and Schulz align Polish literature with the most prominent global trends of the time. For Fik, however, these are anything but positive achievements, as can be seen in the way he describes contemporary writers:

> [They are] people whose development was arrested at puberty, homosexuals, exhibitionists, psychopaths, degenerates, drug addicts, people with chronic stomach illnesses, people who are permanent residents at hospitals, people who cannot distinguish between dream and reality, hypochondriacs, neurasthenics, misanthropes.[113]

For Fik, the popularity of modernist literature and of psychoanalysis itself is rooted in a sort of conspiracy:

> People who have been providing material for a certain branch of medicine, thus facilitating the development of a certain theory of psychopathology, have also entered into a kind of alliance with it: let us support each other in our careers. And indeed, suddenly we are witnessing certain types of writers surfacing out of psychoanalysis, while on the other hand psychoanalysis is also being promoted as a first-rate *artistic* method and value. (*Ibid.*)

The very choice of a protagonist, Fik argues, can betray a novel's psychoanalytical inspiration. The main character must be "as abnormal as possible," allowing the novelist to explore "the ulcers, shameful places, dirty corners" in the their psyche (*ibid.*). If the subconscious can be

111 I. Fik, "Literatura choromaniaków", p. 127.

112 Cf. S. Wysłouch, "Twórczość Choromańskiego wobec międzywojennego psychologizmu", *PLI* 1975, no. 1, pp. 61–84.

113 I. Fik, "Literatura choromaniaków".

compared to a jungle, then the writer is a traveller-anthropologist who crosses unknown lands in search of ever more exotic specimens. Focused on catching the protagonist red-handed, on identifying traces of "bovine idiocy and cretinism, swinishness and neglect," the novelist proceeds without paying any attention to the characters' social context. The individual thus becomes "the plaything of subterranean and supra-atmospheric currents and blind forces, being tossed from wave to wave" (p. 128); in this system, the individual can never become a creator of culture, self-aware, rational and morally disciplined. Socialisation is only an "insignificant superstructure" (p. 127), "like some flaccid foam, a thin sheet of ice, full of cracks and floating on the turbulent surface of a sea of irrational fluctuations and eddies" (p. 128). The subject, in these novels, is nothing more than the mechanical sum of various psychological phenomena:

> It consists of gestures, grimaces, sputtering, disgusting stench, hackneyed phrases, animalistic urges, mystical ecstasy, rude manhandling and stagnant complexes. All of this piled up in a heap and clumped together like vermin in a dumpster. (p. 129)

In Fik's view, it is Freud who inspired contemporary writers' interest in sexuality and dreams: "the most primitive form of human intellectual vegetation now passes as the most excellent and essential method of creativity" (p. 130). When Gombrowicz's second book, the novel *Ferdydurke*, was published in 1938, Fik wrote another review in which he stated authoritatively: "Gombrowicz's "pupism," i.e. his fascination with immaturity, is a derivative of Freudianism. It is like a literary development of that aspect. Therefore everything that can be said against Freudism can be said against pupism."[114] In 1939 he repeats the same opinion in his study "Dwadzieścia lat literatury polskiej" [Twenty Years of Polish Literature].

---

114 I. Fik, "Miny trudne i miny łatwe", *NW* 1938, no. 3; I draw on the reprint in I. Fik, *Wybór pism*, p. 188. J. E. Skiwski published a similar opinion on the novel:

> I do not know of a book more preoccupied with the child and at the same time so repulsively adult in nature, so alien to child psychology [...]. This is probably a legacy of Freudianism. Freud's individual ideas may be correct, but the spirit of his theory, pushing man from eroticism into sexualism, is a matter not of science but of the discoverer's personality. One could have taken a different path, elevating sexualism. Mr Gombrowicz is an orthodox Freudian, "from below". (See J. E. Skiwski, "Kurza pierś", *KPIŚ* 1938, no. 2; quoted from J. E. Skiwski, *Na przełaj oraz inne szkice o literaturze i kulturze*, ed. by M. Urbanowski (Cracow: Wydawnictwo Literackie, 1999), p. 473)

Discussing Freud's influence on Polish literature, he states that Irzykowski's *Pałuba*, for example, "had vivisected the human soul independently, long before the great wave of psychoanalysis, and was therefore a revelatory and useful thing"; Gombrowicz, by contrast, uses psychoanalytic theories only "for empty play".[115]

But let us return to Gombrowicz's discussion of psychoanalysis and modern literature. He counters critics like Piwiński and Fik by stating that "the intellectual bureaucracy is thrilled to put numbers and labels on thoughts and pigeonhole them"; in fact, however, "contemporary literature is not so much Freudian as Freud himself belongs to the modern era. You don't even need to know Freud – just listen in on the nature of jokes, people's chatter, parables, sayings, observations and reactions, on the tram, at the office, in the café, out in the street, you only need to be among people to find yourself immersed in psychoanalysis."[116]

What Gombrowicz has in mind referring the "Freudian" climate of his time is, as he puts it, a general tendency to "unmask, expose, break down the facade," or, to put it briefly, "to render things ugly rather than pretty" (*Ibid.*). This is his paraphrase of a preface to his short story collection that was removed from the book at the last minute:

> As for my vision of the world, my gloomy, erotic or sensual and downright monstrous vision, I repeat once again that there is no need to worry. I am certainly not denying this vision, which is rightfully mine, but haven't we all experienced the harmless complexes, rebellions and torments of this nasty time of adolescence? [...] Concerning the sexual factor [...], its dominance is due to the spirit of the times, which, unfortunately, is

115 I. Fik, "Dwadzieścia lat literatury polskiej (1918–1938)", in *Wybór pism*, p. 413, p. 505. Another reviewer of *Ferdydurke*, Stanisław Piasecki, similarly described the novel as the best example of the opportunistic, superficial Freudianism that was emblematic of *Wiadomości Literackie*:
"It shows us a very typical spiritual profile of a professional Polish writer, fostered during the last decade by Café Ziemiańska. Literati of this ilk consider themselves sufficiently well-equipped as writers when they have stumbled upon some Freudian novelties or on the idea that so-called sincere realism (the use of foul language) is a necessity; they are indifferent to everything but the problem of the literary market: [...] how to make oneself appear loftier than one is, how to enthral the very esteemed members of the audience". (S. Piasecki, "Czarowanie gałązką w zębach", *PZM* 1938, no. 7, p. 1.)

116 W. Gombrowicz, "Nauka ściga się o prawdę psychologiczną z literaturą".

> putting a more acute focus on the relationship between the sexual sphere and the spiritual sphere; the dominance of cruelty and repulsion [...] is due to the fact that, in my opinion, their role in our lives exceeds our wildest dreams. In this regard I have in mind Hitler.[117]

If modern "Freudian" writers create in order to expose, and if they really relish in filth, Gombrowicz argues, then they are doing so because they must.

> And why must they? Because if they were to pass over these dangerous matters in embarrassed silence, hoping to salvage the rest of their exhausted charms, no enlightened person would believe their writing. Criticism has become enormously fierce, the mechanisms of creativity have been laid bare, the reader's gaze has become suspicious and sceptical, the writer is no longer a statue, but a naked machine. Thanks to the latest achievements of psychology, [...] artists are forced out of their previous positions and must expose, because they themselves have been exposed. This is a wonderful opportunity for a minor chicanery, which assumes [...] that they are doing it deliberately, out of inclination, because they are simply loving it. But how worthless would be the kind of beauty that is cowardly and avoids ugliness. It is only in confrontation with ugliness, only when it, too, is taken into account, that new, meaningful types of beauty and new charms can emerge.[118]

Gombrowicz returned to the same question a year later, when he entered a polemic with Bruno Schulz in *Studio*.[119] In fact, their exchange of open letters can be directly related to Gustav Bychowski. The polemic has come to be known as "the duel for the doctor's wife from Wilcza Street" because it contains a letter by Gombrowicz that refers to the opinion "of a certain doctor's wife whom I once met by accident on Line 18. Bruno Schulz, she said, he's either a sick pervert or a poseur, but most probably a poseur. He's

117 W. Gombrowicz, *Bakakaj i inne opowiadania* (Cracow: Wydawnictwo Literackie, 2001), p. 197.

118 W. Gombrowicz, "Nauka ściga się o prawdę psychologiczną z literaturą".

119 For the entire debate, including more marginal voices such as Jan Emil Skiwski in *Tygodnik Ilustrowany*, Andrzej Pleśniewicz in *Kurier Poranny* and Włodzimierz Pietrzak in *Studio*, see W. Gombrowicz, *Polemiki i dyskusje*, ed. by W. Bolecki (Cracow: Wydawnictwo Literackie, 2004), pp. 30–57.

only pretending. – She said this and got off, for the streetcar had just stopped at Wilcza Street."[120] For a long time, literary historians assumed that the doctor's wife was an entirely fictional personification of priggishness, but recently it was suggested that this could be an oblique reference to Maryla Bychowska, née Auerbach, the psychoanalyst's second wife. The couple lived on Wilcza Street in the 1930s.[121] More important in this context, however, is the fact that Gombrowicz, in his later public statements, returned to Schulz's views on "one of the basic antinomies of the human soul". In Gombrowicz's view, Schulz believed that "our sexuality together with its whole ideological aura belongs to another era of development than our intellectuality" (p. 378). To counter this, Gombrowicz presented his own concept of the interdependence between haughty superiority and insolent inferiority. In his open letter Gombrowicz says that Schulz strikes him as "a man without an aunt" (p. 381), who exists "as if the earth had not known those creatures carrying the memory of our short trousers" (p. 381), a person who only cares about "Human Fate, Love, Death, the Destiny of Humankind and the like" (p. 382). Employing one of his stylistic trademarks, namely the reference to concrete human body parts in lieu of abstract concepts, Gombrowicz presents the calf, associated with young boys in short trousers, as a concretisation of immaturity. His stated goal is to put "on the pedestal concepts such as aunt, calf, leg, shorts and all such compromising, disqualifying, immature, indirect, inferior, slippery and green notions which you call not-yet-human" (p. 381). He would like "to confront Goethe himself with his aunt, with the calf" (p. 381). At the same time, he adds an important caveat: "I know that these days, as soon as one mentions a calf, people say it's Freud and that's the end of it. Of course, when I say 'calf' it does not mean Freud at all, and he who takes it so is very much mistaken" (p. 383).

In contrast to Gombrowicz, incidentally, Schulz read Freud in the original and was quite familiar with his theories. He was comfortable using

120 Witold Gombrowicz, "Open Letter to Bruno Schulz", in *The Collected Works of Bruno Schulz*, ed. by Jerzy Ficowski (London: Picador, 1998), pp. 373-375 (p. 374). For Schulz's reply see *Ibid.*, pp. 376-380; for Gombrowicz's reaction see *Ibid.* pp. 381-383. See also A. Fiut, "Pojedynek o doktorową z Wilczej", in *Czytanie Schulza: Materiały międzynarodowej sesji naukowej "Bruno Schulz – w stulecie urodzin i pięćdziesięciolecie śmierci"*, ed. by J. Jarzębski (Cracow: Instytut Filologii Polskiej UJ, 1994), pp. 154–158.

121 Mirosław Wójcik, "Komentarze i przypisy", in B. Schulz, *Szkice krytyczne*, ed. by W. Bolecki (Gdańsk: słowo/obraz terytoria, 2017), pp. 189–197.

psychoanalytic tools in his literary criticism.[122] In a way, his reviews can be said to realise the demands made by Irzykowski before the war: Schulz never psychoanalyses the author or the protagonist but places the text itself on the analytical couch.[123] Włodzimierz Bolecki explains this as follows:

> In Schulz's conception, psychoanalysis is close to literature when it is stripped of assertiveness, i.e. when the unambiguity (truthfulness) of its claims is replaced by ambiguity, and when a "glimmering" takes the place of precision. Schulz was undoubtedly more interested in the literariness of the mechanisms described by psychoanalysis than in psychoanalytic studies of literature.[124]

Interestingly, Schulz did decide to read Gombrowicz alongside Freud on two occasions at least. Schulz's surviving correspondence contains only one mention of Freud; it is in a letter to his friend Romana Halpern. Discussing *Ferdydurke*, Schulz describes the novel as "pioneering and revelatory"; "as an intellectual exploit," moreover, it ranks "next to such phenomena as Freud or Proust" (p. 415).[125] In his review of *Ferdydurke*, published in *Skamander* in 1938, Schulz portrays Gombrowicz's discoveries as more significant than Freud's:

---

122 See M. Bartosik, *Bruno Schulz jako krytyk* (Cracow: Universitas, 2000), pp. 54–79. Cf. also P. Dybel, "Literatura i prawda, czyli Bruno Schulz i psychoanaliza", in *Schulz: Między mitem a filozofią*, ed. by J. Michalik, P. Bursztyka (Gdańsk: słowo/obraz terytoria, 2014), pp. 177–192. I decided to only touch on this well-researched aspect, rather than develop it it detail, because the physical destruction of a huge part of Schulz's correspondence and other archival materials has made it impossible to examine how he came to read Freud, to determine when and what exactly he read, or to find any other traces of the cultural transfer of Freudianism in this writer's life and work. In these circumstances, to examine the connections between Schulz's work and psychoanalysis would necessarily boil down to searching his literary text for traces of a the reception of Freud, i.e. to presume an influence wherever Schulz's work strikes us as "psychoanalytic". This, of course, is exactly what I am trying to avoid.

123 B. Schulz, "Aneksja podświadomości (Uwagi o *Cudzoziemce* Kuncewiczowej)", *PI* 1936, no. 17; "Ferdydurke", *S* 1938, no. 96–98; "Zofia Nałkowska na tle swej nowej powieści", *S* 1939, no. 108–110. "The Annexation of the Subconscious: Observations on Maria Kuncewicz's *The Foreigner*"; "Review of Gombrowicz's *Ferdydurke*", in: *The Collected Works of Bruno Schulz*, ed. by Jerzy Ficowski (London: Picador, 1998).

124 W. Bolecki, "Psychoanaliza", in *Słownik Schulzowski*, ed. by W. Bolecki, J. Jarzębski, S. Rosiek (Gdańsk: słowo/obraz terytoria, 2003), pp. 295–296.

125 B. Schulz, *The Collected Works of Bruno Schulz*, p. 415. On Schulz and Gombrowicz see also A. Sandauer, "Schulz i Gombrowicz, czyli literatura głębin (Próba krytycznej psychoanalizy)", in *Pisma zebrane* (Warsaw: Czytelnik, 1985), vol. 1, pp. 614–633.

> While Freud, after he had discovered the domain of the subconscious, made a psychological curiosity of it, an isolated island whose incomprehensible manifestations and distinct paradoxical logic he clearly delineated, so likewise, behind the bars of pathology, isolated from the background of normal acts, Gombrowicz directed his speculum at these allegedly normal and mature processes, pointed out that their legitimacy and regularity are an optical illusion of our consciousness that – itself a product of a certain training – accepts only meanings that are adequate to it, but does not recognise the element of immaturity that flows around the tiny lagoon of official meanings [...]. Gombrowicz's grotesqueness is nothing more than a vesicle of defiance and repugnance, adopted for the purpose of recognition. Freud showed a small sector of this subterranean world accessible only to the psychologist's methods, methods with which he neutralised the destructive influence of ridiculousness and nonsense. And so he stays fundamentally on the level of scientific seriousness. A general assault on this position could nonetheless only succeed in total liquidation and sacrifice of the position of seriousness, and an opening up of the front line to the element of laughter for a boundless invasion of the comic. It became evident that the biggest obstacle to a radical unmasking of the mechanisms of thinking lay solely in the scientific seriousness and in the investigator's dignified pose. Driven from their unmasked position, officialdom and hypocrisy took flight in the seriousness of investigative behaviour. This was a blind man's bluff, and Gombrowicz blew it to bits. (pp. 417-418)

In his review of Freud's *Introduction to Psychoanalysis*, Gombrowicz points out a unique characteristic of interwar literary criticism in Poland, namely its obsession with finding Freudian influences in every avant-garde work of literature. In retrospect, one hypothesis to explain this phenomenon would be that Polish critics, even before they got their hands on avant-garde novels written in Polish, already associated experimental trends in European fiction with psychoanalysis. In particular, Polish critics at the time took for granted that Marcel Proust, Virginia Woolf and James Joyce were inspired by Freud.

Proust, Woolf and Joyce in Poland

The critics were particularly inclined to discuss Proust in the context of psychoanalytical interpretations of literary works, even though he could not have been influenced by Freud. Successive volumes of *In Search of Lost Time* began to appear in 1913, with the last volume being published posthumously in 1927.[126] Marcel Proust died in 1922, when psychoanalysis was only beginning to gain ground in France, but as soon as Parisian intellectuals became acquainted with Freud – thanks to Eugenia Sokolnicka's efforts – they anointed Proust a precursor or even co-creator of psychoanalysis.[127] January 1923, *La Nouvelle Revue Française* published Jacques Rivière's article about the overlapping psychological concepts in Proust and Freud.[128] Rivière does not present a psychobiography of Proust – such interpretations would appear over the years to come. Instead, he treats Proust as a psychologist and Freud's kindred spirit. The article was reprinted in Rivière's 1926 essay collection *Quelques progrès dans l'étude du cœur humain* [Some Advances in the Study of the Human Heart], which aimed to identify the contributions that each protagonist had made to psychology. Rivière argues that Proust, just like Freud, had highlighted the role of sexuality in individual identity formation; Rivière also discusses the parallels in Freud's and Proust's innovative understanding of time and memory and their significance in human psychology. Proust's idea, paraphrased by Rivière, that "the primary function of our feelings is to lie to us and that the first duty of the psychologist, of the writer, is to resist the evidence they give concerning themselves and the guise in which they seek to appear before our eyes," is in his view akin to Freud's ideas.[129] For

---

126 In Poland, the writer Boy-Żeleński was among the earliest Proust enthusiasts; he would also go on to translate his monumental work. See T. Boy-Żeleński, "Nowe słońce literatury", *KPO* 1924, no. 45, p. 2. For a comprehensive overview of critical opinions on Proust in Poland see J. Domagalski, "Recepcja krytyczna Prousta w prasie międzywojnia", in *Proust w literaturze polskiej (do 1945 roku)* (Warsaw: IBL, 1995), pp. 7–31.

127 Juliusz Kleiner describes this phenomenon in his review of Bychowski's book on Słowacki; he argues that the popularity of psychoanalysis in France was partially due to "the simultaneous effect of Proust's psychology in his fiction" (J. Kleiner, "Słowacki w świetle psychoanalizy", p. 13).

128 Cf. J. Zych, *L'influence de la psychanalyse sur la critique littéraire en France (1914–1939)*, pp. 27–34.

129 Jacques Rivière, *The Ideal Reader: Proust, Freud, and the Reconstruction of European Culture*, trans. by Blanche A. Price (New York: Routledge, 2017), p. 166.

Rivière, Freud's most important concepts are the unconscious, repression and libido, and he offers an account of their equivalents in Proust's novel. The key difference, he continues is that Freud's goal was to discover the universal laws of the human mind, while Proust always focused on the individual.

In Poland, a similar reading of Proust was proposed by Gustav Bychowski. Having already referred to Proust as "a Balzac in Freud's era" in his book *Psychoanaliza*,[130] in 1930, he dedicated a separate study, published in the monthly *Droga*, to Proust.[131] This article is worth examining in detail. Bychowski begins by explaining the title, "Proust jako poeta analizy psychologicznej," translated for *American Imago* as "Proust as a Poet of Psychoanalysis". He grants that the coupling of pure aesthetics (poetry) with science (psychoanalysis) can seem oxymoronic, but this apparent contradiction is resolved in Proust's ingenious work, described as "endlessly precise and at the same time beautiful".[132] Proust, Bychowski argues, has the temperament of a researcher whose greatest desire is "to maintain the eternal values in the change of mental existence" (*Ibid.*), to establish the principles governing human psychology.

---

130 G. Bychowski, *Psychoanaliza*, p. 157.

131 G. Bychowski, "Proust jako poeta analizy psychologicznej", *DR* 1930, no. 1, pp. 55–66; no. 2, pp. 149–157. Two years later, a German translation (possibly by Bychowski himself) of the article appeared in *Psychoanalytische Bewegung* (G. Bychowski, "Marcel Proust als Dichter der psychologischen Analyse", *DPB* 1932, no. 4, pp. 323–344); after Bychowski's death it was chosen from among his vast output to appear, in English translation, in a special issue of *American Imago* dedicated to Bychowski (G. Bychowski, "Marcel Proust as Poet of Psychoanalysis", trans. by Robert Levengood, *AI* 1973, no. 30, pp. 26–32). This issue also contains Bychowski's last work, based on an unfinished manuscript titled "Marcel Proust and his Mother" (*AI* 1973, no. 30, pp. 8–25).

It is unclear why Bychowski, a long-time contributor to *Wiadomości Literackie*, decided to place this particular article in a pro-government journal edited by Wilam Horzyca, whose ambition was to implement Piłsudski's programme of strengthening Polish statehood through patriotic work in the cultural field (cf. S. Jaworski, "Od *Drogi* do *Pionu* (o kształtowaniu się sanacyjnego programu 'upaństwowienia' literatury)", *RKH* 1967, no. 5, pp. 105–147). This article on Proust is Bychowski's only contribution to the journal, which appeared between 1922 and 1937, while the topic of psychoanalysis did not reappear in *Droga* until the mid-1930s, when the tireless Jakub Bleiberg submitted three book reviews (J. Bleiberg, "Albert Dryjski, *Zagadnienia seksualizmu dziecka i młodzieży szkolnej*", *DR* 1934, no. 11, pp. 1054–1056; "Dwa aspekty psychoanalizy (na marginesie dwunastego tomu Freuda)", *DR* 1935, no. 10, pp. 893–895; "Wizerunek własny Freuda", *DR* 1936, pp. 647–649).

132 G. Bychowski, "Marcel Proust as Poet of Psychoanalysis", p. 26.

> With inexhaustible perseverance and patience, he follows love, jealousy, yearning, and the pain of separation of his heroes and continually asks himself whether he comprehends their lives, understands their ideas [...]. The magnitude of his message is apparent in that he is never satisfied, he always probes and searches, he always remembers and moulds, he always returns to the same mind. And finally, he pursues not only the same feeling in different men but, also, he ferrets it out in all the corners of the mind, observes it from different points of view and in various situations. (*Ibid.*)

Proust did not face the obstacles that typically stand in the way of such an endeavour. Above all, his poor health prevented him from living an active life, and turned his attention to introspection. Besides, unlike "the average mind," which represses everything that fails to correspond to the individual's self-image, Proust shows no tendency to hush up painful thoughts and feelings. On the contrary, he is most passionate when he analyses his own anguish and disappointment. This associates him with Freud, who also proceeded along thorough self-analysis to construct a new psychology. The two also have in common an unusual gift for empathy, which is distinct from indulgent sentimentality. Bychowski associates their work with Schopenhauer's ethics (p. 27). In Proust's novel, moreover, everything he describes becomes bright and beautiful to behold:

> A genius of clarity illuminates all the shadows of the mind; and all, which whirls somewhere in the underworld [...] becomes outstandingly simple and comprehensible, becomes the expression of eternal and profound laws and greater beauty. [...] In the light of this understanding and this presentation from the inner self, all the social, intellectual, and ethical differences become harmonious; the mental changes of barons and lackeys, of princes and cooks, of good and honourable people, as well as insignificant mundane men, of laughable snobs or narrow and primitive egotists become clear and absorbing. (pp. 26-27)

Bychowski highlights the way in which the narrator is steeped in internal time and identifies this experience of time with Bergson's pure duration (*durée pure*). It is not an objective measure of the duration, but mostly depends on how events are experienced.

> Constant awareness of this dependency and the continuity in the time of the self and all of its experiences causes each development of Proust's inner life, whether it might be his own or that of his heroes, [to] be comprehended immediately in the atmosphere of this creative time, in other words, as a stage in the process of mental development, as a reflection of the past and a harbinger of the future. Above all, that means a silent, subtle feeling among the casual relationships, which are bound here to the understanding of the tenderest spiritual emotion; it also means comprehension of the All, the entire world, of each perception, of each contact with the inner reality in the atmosphere of the individual self, of the dynamic yet always constant nucleus in the individual inner time… (p. 28)

Bychowski is most impressed with Proust's analysis of enduring love:

> As is well known, unsatisfied wishes, which are assumed to exist in the unconscious, bind a great deal of energy and thereby determine the kind of later experiences – this is certainly one of the basic premises of psychoanalysis. Among writers, no one expressed this truth so clearly, so penetratingly, and felt it as painfully, as Proust. (pp. 28-29)

Bychowski also highlights Proust's masterful understanding of the mechanism of jealousy, so that the emotion, should it suddenly "disappear from human minds […], remains preserved in Proust's work" (p. 29).

Proust's outstanding psychological intuition allowed him to demonstrate the analogies between a boy's early experiences, related to the figure of the mother, and his reactions as a man. When Proust examines a feeling, he also presents its history, its becoming. Thus, we may say that "the current psychology of the personality, which above all is a genetic psychology, celebrates its highest artistic triumph in Proust" (p. 30). Crucially, he writes about Swann's ideal love in the same way as he does about the inner life of his depraved characters. Representing the dark eroticism of Baron de Charlus's, with scenes such as a flogging in an all-male brothel,

> Proust becomes the discoverer of new worlds for literature, new – as everything he gives – not only in regard to the material. The world of inverse love found here, for the first time, its author, an author, who knew

> how to handle the microscope of the biologist and the scalpel of the anatomist. The joy of discovery, which he feels when he succeeds, to be witness of the baron's courtship of Jupien, this has all the earmarks of the joy of a researcher, who was able to discover a new law of nature or to ferret out a hitherto unearthed secret of nature. (p. 30)

Every character in Proust's novel is at once an artistic creation and a piece of scholarship. What is more, Bychowski continues, Proust seems to presage the application of psychoanalysis to collective experience and the history of civilisations, which Freud only began to elaborate in the interwar period. Thus, some passages in Proust's work, such as his representation of the Dreyfus affair and its impact on the French people, or his analysis of their relationship to the Great War, become significant as sociological documents. Like psychoanalysis, Proust's psychological approach lays bare his characters' hypocrisy. Truth in itself, not serving any particular purpose, becomes the most profoundly ethical factor.

Bychowski concludes by examining Proust's ideas about the creative process, suggesting that passages in the novel that focus on art are rooted in Proust's profound introspection as an artist. The writer not only recognises the desire, inherent to creative minds, to recreate the world perfectly, but he also explains the mystery of this desire itself as related to the artist's love of the divine:

> The art, on whose altar Proust laid all the strength of his heart and thought, which he served with the greatest sacrifice and loyalty, is not only the content of his life, but also the benefactor of an absolute value, an echo of the higher and perfect world: it becomes the source of religious experience. Thus, the author-analyst, who relates human sufferings, opinions, and characters, believes not only in the changing and multifarious reality, but also, in their higher foundation and justice. The inner vision of his individual striving for perfection, perceiving, comprehending and describing men envelopes him with the sensing of higher things. (p. 32)

Bychowski's article, which contains many competent Polish translations of passages from Proust's novel, bespeaks his enthusiasm about this literary confirmation of Freud's theory. A similar tone marks reviews of the Polish translation of the first three volumes of Proust's novel. They only appeared in in 1937, i.e. two years after the Polish version of Freud's *Introduction to*

Psychoanalysis (*Wstęp do psychoanalizy*). The delayed reception of Proust coincided with the peak of Polish readers' interest in psychoanalysis, so perhaps this explains why so many critics associated the French writer's psychological astuteness with Freudianism. Even Proust's translator, the writer Tadeusz Boy-Żeleński, argued:

> And how could there not be constant contradictions in humankind, if our conscious life is only an ever-changing sum of subconscious factors adding up and intersecting, an interplay of manifold heredity, of childhood traumas and complexes! At the same time as Freud, and probably still unaware of him, Proust guessed and mythologised the most important discoveries of Freudianism.[133]

Some reviewers proceeded along the same path. Leon Pomirowski wrote in *Tygodnik Ilustrowany*:

> Proust's analyses of subconscious states often overlap with the processes of Freudian psychoanalysis, but Proust goes beyond physiological sources in characterising human psychology. Where Freud perceives only a traumatic moment in an individual's experience, Proust sees a character trait, an organic symptom of individuality.[134]

The review by Jan Dobraczyński in *Prosto z Mostu* is simply titled "Wstęp do psychoanalizy Prousta" [An Introduction to Proustian Psychoanalysis]. The critic begins by claiming that "Marcel Proust produced an excellent take on and realisation of Freud's thought," but then he qualifies his statement:

> In fact, given that *In Search of Lost Time* and certain works by Freud were written more or less at the same time, it is difficult to maintain that the creator of the Swanns and the Guermantes could have drawn on the theoretical foundations of psychoanalysis. He should probably therefore be considered, along with Freud, as its co-discoverer.[135]

---

133 T. Boy-Żeleński, "Proust po polsku", *KPO* 1936, no. 222, pp. 3–4.

134 L. Pomirowski, "*W stronę Swanna*: Pierwsze tomy Prousta w przekładzie T. Boya-Żeleńskiego", *TI* 1937, no. 9, p. 167.

135 J. Dobraczyński, "Wstęp do psychoanalizy Prousta", *PZM* 1938, no. 25, p. 7.

Summarising the great novel, Dobraczyński consistently juxtaposes it with elements of Freud's theory. He concludes:

> [The novel] has much in common with psychoanalytical therapy. Freud treats nervous diseases by shedding light on the unconscious. He does this through "transference" onto the doctor as a person. Proust transfers his baggage onto his readers, submerging their heads in the murky water in the bathtub of memory.[136]

The publication of Proust's magnum opus in Polish translation was deemed to have arrived much too late. For Leon Piwiński in *Życie Literackie*, the elements of the novel that "can today be described as Freudian" constitute "a dead part of the work," because "Proust's artistic achievements and his psychological discoveries have long since percolated into the awareness of Polish readers, and they have done so along a diversion: through the work of Polish writers who have learned from Proust".[137] A similar diagnosis was put forward by Wacław Kubacki:

> By the time Proust was published in Polish, he had become the common property of writers. Proust's "devices" and "manners" were known to all and sundry, and what is more, they had been made more complex and subtle. Writers had made Proust's individual technical devices and psychological observations the central themes of their own works.[138]

In fact, the Polish writer Zofia Nałkowska discussed Proust in *Wiadomości Literackie* as early as 1926. In an article titled "Pisana rzeczywistość" [Written Reality] she highlights the "pathos of authenticity" and "cult of

---

136 *Ibid.* Incidentally, one recurring point in comparisons of Proust and Freud in the late 1930s was the French writer's alleged Jewish origin, which supposedly accounted for both his egotism and his sexual predilections. One year later, Dobraczyński reviewed the volume *The Prisoner*, the last to be translated into Polish. Although the subject he discusses is the same, his tone has changed dramatically: he now argues that the hideous atmosphere of the book can only be overcome with exorcism; to naïve readers of the novel he recommends that they say "one Hail Mary". See J. Dobraczyński, "Proust na ruinach miast Pentapolu", *PZM* 1939, no. 23, p. 7. Cf. J. Domagalski, *Proust w literaturze polskiej (do 1945 roku)*, pp. 25–28.

137 L. Piwiński, "*W stronę Swanna. W cieniu zakwitających dziewcząt*", *ŻL* 1937, no. 4, p. 146.

138 W. Kubacki, "Proust po polsku", *P* 1937, no. 18, p. 6.

living reality" that dominated French fiction, dubbing Proust the patron of this trend.[139] She did not associate him with psychoanalysis at the time, but critics soon took up the term "authenticity" in the sense of a pursuit of maximal realism in descriptions of the characters' internal experience.[140] Ten years later, Jan E. Skiwski tried to define this concept:

> The authenticity we speak of today, which we have in mind when characterising the works of writers such as Marcel Proust, [...] concerns psychological matters; its ambition is to present the interior of the human soul as honestly as possible, in a way that is at the same time profound and fearless in analytical inquiry.[141]

For Skiwski, this authenticity is not only about content, about "not hiding from the reader's eye those nooks and crannies of the human psyche that we usually conceal out of shame" (*Ibid.*). It also concerns research methods and presentation. To be authentic is to be "unconstrained and sincere in unveiling all areas of a person's inner world, and to be creative in the study of the human soul and in the way the results of this study are made known to the reader". Two factions can be distinguished within this trend: the sensationalists, such as Remarque or Céline, who want to discover unusual things, to reveal "those aspects of life that common sense, convention and social discipline keep hidden" (these writers become most popular and have easier access to mainstream readers and their imagination), and the analysts, who focus on exploring ordinary and everyday matters, aiming to reach "the mental layers where [...] our lives are being put together, [...] the kitchen of our soul" (p. 241). Proust and Joyce belong to the second type, which the critic believes is the most characteristic of the age – if not

139 Z. Nałkowska, "Pisana rzeczywistość", *WL* 1926, no. 51/52, p. 1.

140 See H. Markiewicz, *Polskie teorie powieści: Od początków do schyłku XX wieku* (Warsaw: PWN, 1998), p. 112. Nałkowska's notion of authenticity in fiction was one of three options available at the time; next to her idea, authenticity was also used to denote socially engaged non-fiction, e.g. by the "Przedmieście" [Suburb] group; the same term was also used by Stanisław Czernik, who posited in "Okolica Poetów" [Poets' Neighbourhood] that poetic creativity should be based on the material of the poet's own experiences. Andrzej Chruszczyński examines the last two definitions of the term in his book *U schyłku międzywojnia: Autentyzm literatury polskiej lat 1933–1939* (Warsaw: PIW, 1987).

141 J. E. Skiwski, "Autentyzm w literaturze", *PI* 1937, no. 31–32; I draw on the reprint in *Na przełaj oraz inne szkice o literaturze i kulturze*, p. 240.

in Poland then at least in Western literature. The question of why psychological authenticity does not seem to appeal to Polish writers, is answered as follows:

> An inquisitive attitude to reality, passion for research, the whole atmosphere of slowly ripening reflection – they all find the most fertile ground in societies with an old tradition of prosperity, with a vast elite and heads that are sufficiently free from burning issues related to the existence of the nation; they can devote themselves calmly to their work, which requires lifetime dedication. In our case there is still too much to achieve, we are too torn in different directions by matters that need immediate solutions; at this moment, such oases of silence cannot arise and provide the proper soil for the branching tree of reflection to grow. (pp. 249-250)

Recent scholarship has not corroborated Skiwski's opinion. According to Michał Głowiński, Proust is something of a patron of Polish fiction in the second interwar decade, having influenced most (although perhaps not the best) novels from that period. These novels matched the educated reader's tastes most closely, and they shaped the unique stylistic profile of interwar fiction.[142] We could say that the elements of Polish psychological fiction that appear to be inspired by Freud were largely drawn from Proust. Most importantly, it is Proust who introduced writers to new themes and methods of psychological analysis: he ushered in a rising interest in the characters' internal processes and the appearance of extremely subtle and detailed character descriptions. Jerzy Domagalski also argues that Proust's great novel had the strongest impact on the rise of psychological prose in interwar Poland.[143] Many scholars agree that the best example of this influence is Tadeusz Breza's debut novel *Adam Grywałd*;[144] Zbigniew Grabowski's *Ciszy lasu i twojej ciszy* [To the Silence of the Wood and to Your Silence] and Marian Buczkowski's *Tragiczne pokolenie* [The Tragic Generation] are also seen as "Proustian" works. *In Search of Lost Time* was also cited in debates about innovations in Polish literature. In the 1920s,

142 M. Głowiński, *Porządek, chaos, znaczenie* (Warsaw: PIW, 1968), pp. 215–216.

143 J. Domagalski, *Proust w literaturze polskiej*, pp. 94–98.

144 L. Piwiński, "Powieść", *RLIT* 1936, pp. 74–78. J. Domagalski presents a detailed analysis of Breza's novel in the context of Proust's work J. Domagalski in *Proust w literaturze polskiej*. Cf. also M. Dąbrowski, *Polska awangarda prozatorska* (Warsaw: Semper, 1995), p. 75.

Proust's masterpiece was, to cite Jerzy Speina, "a code standing for literary initiation," "a model to be emulated by writers and critics who wanted to integrate Polish literature into contemporary European currents and trends"; in the 1930s, however, the dominant opinion was that the tendency to imitate Proust in Poland had led to "wreaked havoc on narrative prose" and precipitated a crisis of the novel.[145]

The other writer who was consistently associated with psychoanalysis was James Joyce. Safe for a passage of *Ulysses* translated by Józef Czechowicz and published in *Pion* in 1938, a Polish translation was only published in the late 1960s. Still, some writers were familiar with it before then. For instance, Witold Gombrowicz responded to a survey by *Prosto z Mostu* that *Ulysses* was the most interesting book he had read in 1935.[146] Joyce's scandalous novel was frequently discussed in the Polish press, while its plot was summarised by Stanisław Helsztyński[147] and Tadeusz Świątek.[148] Joyce was generally acknowledged as the most outstanding contemporary writer, often mentioned alongside the most eminent individuals of the time. According to the daily *Chwila*, following the Polish edition of *A Portrait of the Artist as a Young Man*, "Joyce's name becomes as prominent in the literary world as perhaps Einstein's or Freud's in the field of science".[149]

Almost from the beginning of Joyce's literary career, critics were keen to identify influences of psychoanalysis in his work. He, meanwhile, was always dismissive about the method, and after his daughter Lucia was unsuccessfully treated by Jung he became openly hostile to it.[150] Joyce, who lived in Jung's immediate neighbourhood in Zurich for some time, was never analysed, not even when one of his wealthy benefactresses

145 J. Speina, *Literatura w perspektywie psychologii*, p. 90.

146 Witold Gombrowicz, *PZM* 1936, no. 5, p. 5. Gombrowicz, who read Joyce in French translation, stressed it ought to be published in Polish as well. See Witold Gombrowicz, "Małgośka i demon: O przekład Joyce'owskiego *Ulissesa*", *KPO* 1937, no. 16, p. 8.

147 Stanisław Helsztyński, "Joyce i jego *Ulisses*: Skonfiskowana książka", *WL* 1924, no. 15, p. 2; S. Helsztyński, "James Joyce", *WL* 1931, no. 35, p. 1.

148 T. Świątek, "*Przegląd Literacki*. Zagadnienia formalne: James Joyce", *KLN* 1936, no. 19, pp. 8–10.

149 *CHW* 1931, no. 4340, p. 10.

150 R. Ellmann, *James Joyce* (Oxford: Oxford University Press, 1982), pp. 676–680. Cf. also L. Appignanesi, *Mad, Bad and Sad: A History of Women and the Mind Doctors from 1800 to the Present* (London: Virago, 2008), pp. 221–251.

announced she would only continue to sponsor him if he underwent therapy.[151] The writer said of Jung that he was "the Swiss Tweedledum who is not to be confused with the Viennese Tweedledee, Dr Freud," adding that Jung "amuses himself at the expense (in every sense of the word) of ladies and gentlemen who are troubled with bees in their bonnets" (p. 510). The distaste appears to have been mutual. When the third German edition of *Ulysses* was being prepared in 1930, the publisher asked Jung to write a foreword, but the text submitted was deemed unacceptable (Jung presented the novel as evidence for Joyce's schizophrenia, and its literary merits were entirely lost on him – for instance, he wrote that the book might equally well be read back to front).[152]

What is certain is that Joyce was interested in dreams, and that he analysed his own tirelessly. He also made use of psychoanalytical theories on verbal associations.[153] Traces of Joyce's familiarity with psychoanalysis can be found in both *Ulysses* and *Finnegans Wake*, even if most of these passages are satirical. It is likely that he gained a basic understanding of Freudianism from his acquaintances, many of whom were close to the movement. One of his friends was Ottocaro Weiss, whose brother Edu-ardo Weiss was the first Freudian from Italy. In 1907, when Joyce lived in Trieste, the businessman Ettore Schmitz became his student and later his friend. In 1923, Schmitz, better known under his pseudonym Italo Svevo, wrote *La coscienza di Zeno* [*Zeno's Conscience*], one of the first novels that directly deal with psychoanalysis. Joyce's reaction was highly positive.

Joyce always denied having been influenced by Freud, and when he was asked about his inspirations he always mentioned Édouard Dujardin's experimental novel *Les lauriers sont coupés* [The Laurels Are Cut] from 1887. Still, the dominant opinion among critics was that *Ulysses* was rooted in psychoanalysis. In Poland, too, many critics argued that a book such as this one could not have been written without Freud's discoveries. The most telling example is Jerzy Stempowski's review, titled "*Ulysses* Joyce'a jako próba psychoanalizy stosowanej" [Joyce's *Ulysses* as an Attempt at Applied Psychoanalysis], published in *Wiadomości Literackie* in early

151 R. Ellmann, *James Joyce*, pp. 466–467.

152 *Ibid.*, p. 628. Two years later Jung published a revised study in *ER* and sent it to Joyce. It was reprinted in *James Joyce, the Critical Heritage*, ed. by R.H. Deming (New York: Routledge, 1970), vol. 2.

153 R. Ellmann, *James Joyce*, p. 358 and *passim*.

1932.[154] Stempowski took an interest in psychoanalysis when he was a medical student, and he considered the discovery of the unconscious, which he describes as "a roaring monster, drowning out and obscuring the features of the outside world," to be the greatest discovery at the turn of the nineteenth and twentieth centuries, one that puts art before completely new challenges.[155] In his opinion, Joyce was the first writer who managed to find a literary expression for the language of the unconscious:

> Apart from the thoughts that are rooted in our upbringing, traditions and ambitions, there is also, slumbering within us, a whole world of impulses, images and associations that only barely reach our consciousness – a world that is rejected, as it were, by our mental setup. It is only in a fragmentary way that we become aware of it, in the form of snippets of the internal gibberish that we hear when we wake up from sleep, or in moments of absent-mindedness.[156]

For Stempowski, Joyce has raised this internal gibberish to the level of art. Of course, poets used "our vague associations of words, sounds and images" as literary material before, and Rabelais taught us about "that part of our inner life which apparently serves none of our conscious tasks, and which we often ignore in our examination of conscience, considering it unnecessary, intrusive, sometimes obscene" (*Ibid.*). In *Ulysses*, however, the difference is that the unconscious does not appear sporadically, "only serving to render the picturesque turns of our experiences, as if this element were no essential component of our inner life" (*Ibid.*). With Joyce, Stempowski continues, "absent-mindedness, hallucinations, associations, reminiscences, the singing, grinding and stammering of the characters'

154 J. Stempowski, "*Ulysses* Joyce'a jako próba psychoanalizy stosowanej", *WL* 1932, no. 6, p. 2. Andrzej S. Kowalczyk points out:
"The article on *Ulysses* is a rather perfect illustration of Stempowski's notion of criticism. The novel is primarily discussed as an example of how psychoanalysis can be used in literature, whereby psychoanalysis becomes almost as important as literature itself. Only a single sentence – the final one – addresses the novel's artistic merits, stating 'the work's deeply disharmonious general character'". (Andrzej S. Kowalczyk, *Nieśpieszny przechodzień i paradoksy: Rzecz o Jerzym Stempowskim* (Wrocław: Towarzystwo Przyjaciół Polonistyki Wrocławskiej, 1997), p. 58)

155 A. S. Kowalczyk, *Nieśpieszny przechodzień i paradoksy*, pp. 145–146.

156 J. Stempowski, "*Ulysses* Joyce'a jako próba psychoanalizy stosowanej".

thoughts are followed systematically, step by step, and they accompany every word and gesture of the story" (*Ibid.*). This is the first reason why the critic describes the novel as "applied psychoanalysis". The second reason is the similarity that he identifies between the narration and psychoanalytical therapy.

Another critic, Marian Promiński, describes Joyce as the founder of a new "psychoanalytical" school in literary fiction. In his article "Awangarda prozatorska" [Avant-Garde Fiction] he argues that Polish literature has fallen behind European trends.[157] He also proposes that the fate of the novel as an art form "bordering on scientific study" was being decided elsewhere, namely in Western Europe:

> When Sigmund Freud began to publish [...] in the 1880s, when he was mocked and patted on the shoulder, no one could have predicted what results this humble psychiatrist's detailed observations would produce in the field of fiction. It began with the discovery of childhood complexes and the interpretation of dream symbols, and generally with snooping around the peripheries and cellars of the psyche. Thanks to the natural osmosis of such issues into popular consciousness, the psychological novel very quickly adopted these medical novelties, transforming them into exotic flowers of the problem of sex. (*Ibid.*)

Promiński continues:

> This influence of psychiatric medicine had an unprecedented significance for art. The mysteries of how feelings arise and subside and the physiological motivation of human behaviour were immediately revealed to us. The desiccated shell of routine, the so-called rational explanation of actions, was irretrievably abandoned. Before the astonished reader's eyes, the innermost truth of humankind was revealed. (*Ibid.*)

For Promiński, the milestones of the novel as a literary genre were all published in the mid-1920s: Mann's *The Magic Mountain*, Proust's *In Search of Lost Time* and Joyce's *Ulysses*. *The Magic Mountain* already contains a detailed "analysis of morbid and subconscious states," and it can be considered "the highest expression of the traditional psychological novel"; Proust's innovation lies in his references to childhood complexes and his "micro-

157 M. Promiński, "Awangarda prozatorska", *KLN* 1935, no. 2, p. 6.

analysis of mental states"; but it is only Joyce's *Ulysses* that can be called a psychoanalytical novel in the strict sense. This novel presents "a faithful psychiatric record, the most sincere, completely unmasked":

> Those books have advanced composition and selection, they often shed light on facts. Here we have association, randomness, psychological processes as they really are. There we have purposeful artistic organisation, here we have inertia and the purely vegetative state of consciousness. (p. 7)

For Promiński, Joyce is the founder of a new literary school whose adepts, rather than emulating him, continue to build on and advance his technique. *Ulysses*, he adds, is not flawless; "if it were perfect, it would have spawned epigones, but not being perfect, it engendered writers" (*Ibid.*). Polish representatives of the Joyce school, the critic suggests, include Zbigniew Grabowski, Adolf Rudnicki, Adam Ważyk, Bruno Schulz and Adam Tarn. For lack of a better term, Promiński describes their work as "psychoanalytical fiction".[158] This term, although not yet established, indicates that the novel seems to emerge "as dictated naturally by mental states";[159] the novel's goal, meanwhile, is not to name psychological states but to portray them. Such "experimental research" gives rise to an entirely new type of realism, one that is exclusive to literature, impossible to render through any other artistic medium.

158 *Ibid.* Promiński's argument is echoed by Ignacy Fik; for him, "the psychoanalytical novel" (inspired by Proust, Joyce and Mann – just as Promiński had suggested), has become a separate genre that included most avant-garde fiction of the interwar period, from Roman Jaworski's *Wesele hrabiego Orgaza* to Wat's *Lucifer unemployed* and Gombrowicz's *Ferdydurke* (I. Fik, "Dwadzieścia lat literatury polskiej (1918–1938)", pp. 449–450). A retrospective account of "literary psychoanalysis" was provided by Stanisław Burkot. For him, the characteristic traits of this type of fiction are the blurred boundaries of mental illness as well as the autobiographical aspect, with its focus on childhood and adolescence. The works he mentions are Kuncewiczowa's *The Stranger*, Choromański's *Zazdrość i medycyna* [Jealousy and Medicine], Zegadłowicz's *Zmory* [Nightmares], Iwaszkiewicz's *Pasje błędomierskie* [The Passions of Blunderville], Witkacy's *Insatiability*, Gombrowicz's *Memoirs of a Time of Immaturity*, Schulz's *The Cinnamon Shops* and *Sanatorium Under the Sign of the Hourglass*, as well as Breza's *Adam Grywałd* (S. Burkot, "Od psychoanalizy klinicznej do literackiej", *RND* 1978, no. 68, pp. 133–157).

159 M. Promiński, "Awangarda prozatorska", *KLN* 1935, no. 4, p. 5.

Promiński was not the only critic to associate psychoanalysis with "new realism".[160] In 1933, Leon Pomirowski applied the term "new realism" to some Polish fiction writers.[161] Experimental novelists shared an interest in "the sphere of the subconscious, the slumbering kingdom of untapped natural possibilities, in a word – the spiritual underworld" (p. 20). Unlike the "descriptive-sensory" realism rooted in the nineteenth century, new realism is "internal, analytical, psychological and idealistic" (p. 63). Another significant shift in relation to the traditional novel is the fact that the focus is not on the internal experience of outstanding individuals but "the inner states of the most average creature" (*Ibid.*).

Yet another critic who wrote about new realism was Aniela Gruszecka. In the late 1920s and early 30s she published several pioneering literary theoretical articles in *Przegląd Współczesny.* According to literary historian Henryk Markiewicz, her work represents "the beginning of modern theory of the novel in Poland".[162] Just like her above-mentioned colleagues, Gruszecka explicitly relates the genre's recent achievements with Freudianism. She puts a special emphasis on Virginia Woolf, introduced in an article from 1933 as "a writer I discovered by chance a few weeks ago".[163]

Gruszecka's first article, "O powieści" [On the Novel], had appeared in 1927. It opens by associating contemporary novelistic trends with "increased attention, psychological insight," and especially the rise of "the

160 For a discussion of the Polish terms for "new realism," "psychological realism" and "psychologism" see E. Frąckowiak-Wiegandtowa, "Psychologizm – przezwa czy nazwa?", *TD* 1973, no. 4, pp. 193–200. On modernist writers' rejection of classical realism in the name of a "quest for reality" see J. Franczak, *Poszukiwanie realności.*

161 For Pomirowski, the novels that fell into this category were many and diverse, including works by Nałkowska, Kaden-Bandrowski, Rostworowski, Witkacy, Dąbrowska, Choromański, Iwaszkiewicz, Szelburg-Zarembina, Naglerowa, Rudnicki, Kruczkowski and Szemplińska. See L. Pomirowski, *Walka o nowy realizm* (Warsaw: Gebethner i Wolff, 1933). Cf. L. Pomirowski, *Nowa literatura w nowej Polsce* (Warsaw: Gebethner i Wolff, 1933), pp. 103–208.

162 H. Markiewicz, *Przekroje i zbliżenia dawne i nowe* (Warsaw: PIW, 1976), pp. 76–84. Cf. also W. Bolecki, *Modalności modernizmu* (Warsaw: IBL PAN, 2012), pp. 298–302.

163 A. Gruszecka, "Stare i nowe w powieści współczesnej", *PWS* 1933, no. 132, p. 71. This sentence is commonly believed to be the first published mention of Virginia Woolf in Poland (see U. Terentowicz-Fotyga, "From Silence to a Polyphony of Voices: Virginia Woolf's Reception in Poland", in *The Reception of Virginia Woolf in Europe*, ed. by M.A. Caws and N. Luckhurst (London: Continuum, 2002), pp. 127–147. In fact, however, Woolf's work had been discussed before, e.g. by Zofia Kunicka in her review of *Mrs Dalloway* in *WL* 1931, no. 32, p. 2.

psychology of the subconscious".[164] Globally, writers are applying Freud's theory more and more broadly. The discoveries of modern science have allowed novelists to better understand mental mechanisms. As a result, novelistic fiction becomes almost as significant to readers as their own personal experiences (*Ibid.*). The first part of the article tackles the average novel, which, Gruszecka predicts, will soon become obsolete as it is gradually replaced by film. This is not the case with what she calls the artistic novel, where the reader is created in response to the text; what such a novel demands from the reader is not a schematic reaction but a unique equivalent to the reading.[165] Besides this performative quality – and here Gruszecka gives examples from Conrad, Proust and Gide – the modern novel departs from the objectively realistic mode of representation; it seeks to eliminate the author's voice and abandons chronology in favour of "psychological plasticity," focusing on "points of view" and emphasising "the instability, the uncertainty of our view of things".[166]

The novels discussed in Gruszecka's 1927 article can still be seen as continuations of early modernist experiments. It is only the next essay, titled "Stare i nowe w powieści współczesnej" [The Old and the New in the Contemporary Novel], published in 1933, that introduces the names of James Joyce, John Dos Passos, and especially Virginia Woolf. Gruszecka gives a detailed discussion of Woolf's *To the Lighthouse* (1927), and, in order to give her readers a better sense of this model "new novel," she presents her own Polish translations of a few passages. What characterises Woolf's work for Gruszecka is "a new type of realism" which is related to the attainments of modern psychology.[167] Traditional novelists bypassed "the randomness, the entanglement, the simultaneity of psychological themes, the varying degrees of clarity and accessibility at different levels of the mind" (p. 75). For them, all the material that was needed to construct the themes of their novels seemed "accessible and approachable: you give it

164 A. Gruszecka, "O powieści", *PWS* 1927, no. 57, p. 42.

165 A. Gruszecka, "O powieści", *PWS* 1927, no. 58, p. 225. Gruszecka's view of Woolf was echoed by Wiesław Juszczak in his book on the crisis of the nineteenth-century novel: "There was [...] a deeply hidden message in *Mrs Dalloway*, addressed to the reader who was treated as the writer's equal partner. This was a new kind of reader, not required by the works of the 'epoch of the novel' – a reader who co-creates the work through its reception." See W. Juszczak, *Zasłona w rajskie ptaki, albo: O granicach "okresu powieści"* (Warsaw: PIW, 1981), p. 97.

166 A. Gruszecka, "O powieści", p. 232.

167 A. Gruszecka, "Stare i nowe", p. 74.

a name, you arrange it, like pieces of a single, homogenous novelistic substance" (*Ibid.*). Things are different for contemporary novelists:

> They respect [...] the grain, the fibre, the knots of the material. They do not smooth it out, arrange it, or pass over its resistances; they try to preserve all its rime, the fluff of its freshness, the tangle of its knots and currents [...]. The material's deformation lies in the necessity of presenting it successively; it is technically impossible to give a complete cross-section of the mind or a complete stream of consciousness. But what they manage to realise through description has an intention, it "wants" to preserve the expression of this intense diversity. (pp. 74-75)

For Gruszecka, Woolf's originality lies in her ability to "express things that, until now, have not been able to be expressed because we were unable to perceive them" (p. 79). She continues:

> What leads to innovation is the deepening of observation, honing it not in the sense of presenting things more beautifully in traditional shapes, but in the sense of viewing the material without leaning on traditional forms of presentation, "differently". (*Ibid.*)

The source of this originality lies in contemporary novelists becoming acquainted with the recent achievements of psychology, gained, according to Gruszecka, through "the methods of scientific thought" (*Ibid.*).

Gruszecka's final essay is titled "Klasyfikacja a życie na terenie powieści współczesnej" [Classification and Life in the Field of the Contemporary Novel] and was published in 1934. It can be seen as a polemic with Stefan Kołaczkowski, who discussed Maria Dąbrowska's historical novel *Noce i dnie* [Nights and Days] to celebrate the return of realism in interwar literature. Gruszecka opposes the label of realism in the case of Dąbrowska's work. Addressing those of her colleagues who seem to be harking back to the nineteenth-century novel, she explicitly points to Freud, adding that one cannot speak of realism in the case of a book that fails to take into account his findings:

> The new psychology, drawn up by Freud and those who further developed his theory, reveals completely new mental processes. These are not the former "states of mind" but the extraordinary energy of the soul, the

> unforeseeable powers of its ever present motives, which are active every day, the secrets of its makeup, of its grandness, the way it is mastered by consciousness, self-criticism, intelligence. Formerly settled by a conventional scheme or by fantasising, today they are understood, at least in part, which provides a key to resolving the darkness and to achieving a far more accurate, fairer, deeper insight into an individual's values. Concerning the novel, this opens up a completely new prospect of realism, with a new approach to experiences, a sensitivity differently prepared; there is striving for a new sincerity, a delightful purity of the portrayal, without pathos, without the template of literary devices worn out long ago.[168]

Gruszecka critiques Dąbrowska's novels as escapist. In her view, even historical fiction can and must apply Freud's ideas: "it can be a novel about the past, but it must use today's new apparatus to shed light on things that the traditional novel was not able to perceive, that can only be seen from our perspective" (p. 66).

For Gruszecka, Virginia Woolf is a realist of the new type, who makes creative us of the discoveries of psychoanalysis. This claim seems more justified than any imputations of Freudianism to Marcel Proust or James Joyce – after all, for the Bloomsbury Group psychoanalysis was a form of rebellion against Victorian attitudes and values; its members were responsible for the transfer of Freud's ideas to British literary and artistic circles.[169] Virginia Woolf's husband Leonard was the first person without medical training to write about psychoanalysis in Great Britain: in 1914 he reviewed *The Interpretation of Dreams* and *The Psychopathology of Everyday Life* for the *New English Weekly*, suggesting that Freud's works can be read as literature. From 1924 onwards, the Woolfs' Hogarth Press published all of Freud's writings (four volumes of his *Collected Papers* appeared in 1924–25) as well as other works in the series International Psycho-Analytical Library. Their translator, the psychoanalyst James Strachey, was the younger brother of Lytton Strachey, one of the Woolfs'

168 A. Gruszecka, "Klasyfikacja a życie na terenie powieści współczesnej", *PWS* 1934, no. 141, pp. 65–66.

169 Thanks to the Bloomsbury Group, psychoanalysis was always perceived in the UK as a literary discourse rather than a scientific one. This even shows in the composition of the British Psychoanalytic Society, which had the highest proportion of non-medical members in the world (40% in the late 1920s). See E. Abel, *Virginia Woolf and the Fictions of Psychoanalysis* (Chicago: University of Chicago Press, 1989), p. 16. Cf. also D.W. Orr, "Virginia Woolf and Psychoanalysis", *TIR* 1989, no. 16, pp. 151–161.

closest friends. James Strachey's wife Alix was also a psychoanalyst; she was, moreover, a close friend and translator of Melanie Klein. In 1925, Klein gave lectures at a salon hosted by Virginia Woolf's younger brother, Adrian Stephen, and his wife Karin, both of whom were analysts.[170]

At the same time – and this Gruszecka could not have known – Woolf avoided reading Freud until very late in her life.[171] She never underwent analysis and was very critical of the idea of using Freudianism as a literary theme; psychological truth and artistic truth were too incompatible in her opinion.[172] When asked about her familiarity with Freud's theory she maintained that it was superficial.[173] Indeed, the sparse references that have been documented indicate that she thought little of psychoanalysis.[174] When numerous artists and writers sent Freud a telegram on his eightieth birthday in 1936, she probably added her signature out of

170 Polish readers found a brief overview of this network in an article by Andrzej Tretiak, published in *Przegląd Współczesny*. See A. Tretiak, "Psychoanaliza w twórczości J. M. Barriego", *PWS* 1933, no. 127, pp. 310–322.

171 Woolf's *Diary* indicates that she began to study Freud as late as 2 December 1939. She spent a year on his oeuvre. At this time she worked on her autobiographical *A Sketch of the Past*, where she tackles, for the first time, such childhood traumas as sexual abuse by her half-brothers and the death of her mother; she also draws on the results of her self-analysis to discover the principles behind her own fiction. I discussed this in more detail in L. Magnone, "Virginia Woolf i freudowski masterplot", pp. 361–376.

172 V. Woolf, "Freudian Fiction", in *Contemporary Writers* (New York: The Hogarth Press, 1965). This article was originally published in *TLS* 25/03/1920.

173 In a letter to Harmon H. Goldstone, a student at Harvard who had contacted her with this question, she responded: "I have not studied Dr Freud or any psychoanalyst – indeed I think I have never read any of their books; my knowledge is merely from superficial talk" (*The Letters of Virginia Woolf*, vol. 5: 1932–1935, ed. by N. Nicolson, J. Trautmann (New York: Chatto & Windus, 1979), p. 36. Cf. R. Hoops, *Der Einfluss der Psychoanalyse auf die englische Literatur* (Heidelberg: Winter, 1934), pp. 141–147. There are parallels concerning the question of Bergson's possible influence on Woolf. Critics have noticed a certain correspondence between Woolf's work and Bergson's theory; what is more, her sister-in-law, Karin Stephen, wrote a book on Bergson in 1922. Still, Woolf never read Bergson, as Adrian Velicu explains in *Unifying Strategies in Virginia Woolf's Experimental Fiction* (Upsala: Almqvist & Wiksell, 1985), p. 17.

174 In a letter to Alix Strachey, James Strachey described a visit to the Woolfs in May 1925, just before the publication of *Mrs Dalloway* and the third volume of Freud's *Collected Papers*: "Virginia made a more then usually ferocious onslaught upon psychoanalysis and psychoanalysts, more particularly the latter" (*Bloomsbury/Freud: The Letters of James and Alix*, p. 264).

politeness. Allusions to psychoanalysis in some of her works, such as *A Room of One's Own* or *Three Guineas*, are all but cursory. Freud's arrival in London in late January 1939 and the Woolfs' personal acquaintance with him did nothing to change this.[175] In May 1940 Woolf gave a lecture in which she claimed that World War I and Freud's work had put an end to nineteenth-century realism, but at the same time she distanced herself from the writers who explicitly affirmed psychoanalysis; she was only an observer of the transformations, without taking an active part.[176]

The fact that Gruszecka recognised Virginia Woolf's work as a final break with traditional realism puts her apart from other Polish critics, who were either unaware of the British writer or who failed to appreciate her.[177] Even if Gruszecka was alone in this, however, her articles can be seen as part of a trend among interwar critics, namely to associate recent innovations in literary fiction with the birth of psychoanalysis – even if no evidence could be found that a given writer (Woolf in this case) was influenced by Freud's theory; if the writer expressed strong opposition to such an attribution (Joyce) or if the writer simply could not have been inspired by Freud (Proust). Polish writers – those who kept abreast of the transformations in the European novel, those who only followed accounts about them in Polish literary periodicals, and even those who read (belated) Polish translations of those works – formed their opinions about psychoanalysis and its potential artistic applications on the basis of modern European fiction. Next, they used those newly gained ideas in their own work. This is why the Freudianism that reviewers identified in Polish novels at the time was in fact much more likely to be "Proustianism".

175 Cf. V. Woolf, *A Moment's Liberty: The Shorter Diary* (New York: Harcourt Brace Jovanovich, 1980), p. 449.

176 V. Woolf, "The Leaning Tower", in *Collected Essays*, vol. 2 (London: The Hogarth Press, 1924), pp. 162–182.

177 Around the same time, in 1932–1933, the women's magazine *Kobieta Współczesna* serialised Gruszecka's novel *Przygoda w nieznanym kraju* [Adventure in a Strange Land]. Its themes and style recall Woolf, while the protagonist reads Freud and Jung and uses psychoanalysis to interpret her own dreams. This work was juxtaposed with Woolf's by Leon Piwiński (*WL* 1934, no. 15, p. 3). See also E. Kraskowska, *Piórem niewieścim: Z problemów prozy kobiecej dwudziestolecia międzywojennego* (Poznań: UAM, 2003), pp. 101–125; A. Araszkiewicz, "Dotknięcie ciała: Literacka strategia Anieli Gruszeckiej", in *Krytyka feministyczna*, pp. 121–136.

Polish literature after 1935: Zegadłowicz

When it comes to the reception of psychoanalysis in Polish literature, the situation became even more complex after the publication of Freud's *Wstęp do psychoanalizy* [*Introduction to Psychoanalysis*]. Shortly before the outbreak of World War II, Przeworski's Press finally made it possible for Polish readers to read Salomea Kempner's translation – almost twenty years after its original publication. The book recapitulated the state of Freudian theory as it was in 1917 – a historical summary, one might say, given that in the meantime, Freud had proposed the second topic as well as an application of psychoanalysis to cultural phenomena. Polish readers received an account that confirmed what they already knew about Freudianism: an outline of the theory of the unconscious, the interpretation of dreams and parapraxes, as well as the theory – quite familiar by now – of how individual psychology was shaped by sexuality and the complexes established in childhood.[178]

Unsurprisingly, the publication of the Polish translation of Freud's *Introduction* was not seen as an actual event but, rather, as a mere catching up on a certain cultural retardation. By 1935, few writers were unfamiliar

178 A telling example of how widely accepted Freudianism was at the time is Andrzej Tretiak's article "Psycho-analiza w twórczości J. M. Barriego" [Psycho-Analysis in J. M. Barrie's Work], published in *Przegląd Współczesny* two years before the Polish translation of Freud's *Introduction*. Tretiak writes about Barrie's dramatic works after the Great War:
"Naturally, when I discuss psychoanalysis I mean the form it acquired in ordinary life. [...] Every scientific theory goes through such a process: first there is a number of facts, then they are classified, and this results in certain data being established, a certain idea that is common to all these facts, and when the theory becomes detached from the research method, then the general public accepts it – first in the form of a complete work, discussing the theory's historical origin, but then we come to deal only with the theory's core idea, and finally, for the sake of convenience, we enclose it in a formula, most often incomplete and frequently incorrect." (A. Tretiak, "Psychoanaliza w twórczości J. M. Barriego", pp. 310–311)
For Tretiak, only a theory that has been simplified in this way can become a linchpin for a work of literature: "it cannot be otherwise – the artist must face a crystallised formula in order to take up a position, and in fact, this act is the source of the 'idea' behind the work of art" (*Ibid.*). In the case of psychoanalysis, the formula that is available to writers is: "we depend on a subconscious foundation, in this foundation there are various complexes, among them there is libido, sensual desire; the most important among these complexes is the relationship between mother and son" (*Ibid.*).

with Freud, and among those who had never read any actual psychoanalytical publications, the great majority would have encountered the theory at a salon or dinner party, in their favourite weekly or in their colleagues' recent books. Thus it is almost impossible to tell the difference between Freud's direct influence on a given literary work on the one hand, and merely superficial inspiration or deceptive parallels on the other.

Furthermore, while in the early 1930s evidence of a writer's familiarity with psychoanalysis in a novel was associated with modernity and Europeanness, the second half of the decade saw a marked turnaround: now, any trace of the fashionable theory risked that the writer would be accused of repetitiveness, schematism or even opportunism. Many novels were labelled fictional renditions of Freud. One reviewer, for instance, surmised that Rudnicki had written *Szczury* [The Rats] "with Freud in his hand".[179] Another reviewer suggested about Tarn's *Obraz ojca w czterech ramach* that it was written "strictly according to Joyce and Freud".[180] For the critic Emil Breiter, the psychoanalytical elements in Kuncewiczowa's *Cudzoziemka* [*The Stranger*] were clearly detrimental to the work:

> This part of the novel – especially Róża's final conversations with her husband and daughter, in which she seems to give a programmatic conclusion about her life as seen from a psychoanalytic point of view – is the least convincing. [...] in her hatred and revenge she had been true and exciting, but in love and peace she became a character out of a textbook of Freudian psychoanalysis.[181]

Two years later, Kuncewiczowa herself commented self-critically:

> Ever since Freud has put catching labels on his ideas about the subconscious, ever since he combined very old sets of feelings into complexes that he could name, many writers, carried away by the magical atmosphere of academic study, began to deal with their literary work as if they were laboratory technicians or surgeons.[182]

179 J. Życieński, "Wykolejeńcy", *EPO* 1932, no. 10, p. 13.
180 Z. Grabowski, "Wśród nowych książek", *KLN* 1934, no. 47, p. 13.
181 E. Breiter, "Powieść o niezwykłej kobiecie", *WL* 1936, no. 4, p. 4.
182 M. Kuncewiczowa, "Dalszy ciąg rozmowy", *SY* 1938, no. 40, p. 2.

After World War II, the novelist Maria Dąbrowska also critiqued the impact of psychoanalysis on writers in the 1920s: "They began to study all areas and mechanisms of life, forgetting about the most important kind of knowledge – artistic knowledge. Most writers did not know how to manage the baggage of their intellect and experience."[183] One sober account of the influence of Freudianism on Polish literature was given by Stefania Zahorska, who wrote articles for the London-based *Wiadomości* in the 1940s. Recognising psychoanalysis as "one of the leading intellectual achievements of the twentieth century," she also remarked that it had "little resonance in Polish literature."[184] Most Polish writers were not interested in psychoanalysis and knew little about it; some, even the more sophisticated ones, associated psychoanalysis with pansexualism, "which indicates that they only knew it from popular slogans and had no idea about its significance" (*Ibid.*).

Stefan Essmanowski, meanwhile, wrote that psychoanalysis had benefitted literary criticism much more than literature itself. His article "Psychoanaliza i sztuka" [Psychoanalysis and Art] appeared in a special supplement to *Wiadomości Literackie* issued on Freud's eightieth birthday. He argues that Freudianism had failed to have the expected impact.[185] He names writers who used it to enhance the psychological depth of their works: Thomas Mann, Stefan Zweig, André Maurois, Karol Čapek and James Joyce; "for others, snippets caught unsystematically only served as fancy delicacies to use as stuffing for their works; they introduced a little complex here or there that proclaimed the author's glory miles ahead: Look, I know about Freud!" (*Ibid.*). In Poland, this category includes Jerzy Bandrowski, the author of *Pałac połamanych lalek* [The Palace of Broken Dolls] and Adam Tarn and his *Obraz ojca w czterech ramach*. Even a solid understanding of Freud's theories, Essmanowski continues, does not guarantee artistic success; it is, at most, a purely intellectual exemplification of psychoanalytical concepts.

183 M. Dąbrowska, "Jak oceniam literaturę dwudziestolecia", *TW* 1946, no. 12, p. 104.

184 S. Zahorska, *Wybór pism: Reportaże, publicystyka, eseje*, ed. by A. Nasiłowska (Warsaw: IBL PAN, 2010), p. 249. Similarly, when she was awarded the 1956 prize of the Union of Writers Abroad [Związek Pisarzy na Obczyźnie], Zahorska said in her speech: "In [Polish] literary circles, Freud was neither recognised nor understood or re-evaluated. Freud the sexualist, Freud the therapist, and Freudian sectarianism often obscure the superstructure of his theory, which could be of great significance for creative writing." (S. Zahorska, *Wybór pism*, p. 336).

185 S. Essmanowski, "Psychoanaliza a sztuka", *WL* 1936, no. 20, p. 4.

At this point, a writer whose work was associated with psychoanalysis had no reason to feel flattered. Among the heated literary debates in interwar Poland, one of the most intense concerned Emil Zegadłowicz's *Zmory* [Nightmares],[186] and its reception focused on the question of Freudian influences more than any other. *Zmory* appeared in early September 1935 with a print run of 1500 copies that sold out so quickly that a second edition was ready for shipment by the end of the year. This edition, however, was confiscated by court order. Following an appeal, the suppression was approved, but only for passages that were "eminently pornographic, mocking Christian dogmas, beliefs and rites, or deriding the nation and the concept of the fatherland" (p. 101). A purged edition was published in July 1936.

In his introduction to a recent re-edition, Mirosław Wójcik proposes that today it is hard to understand why *Zmory* caused such a scandal; its themes and style were not so different from other novels.[187] In fact, it was a *Bildungsroman*, a rather popular form at the time, and it showed similarities to other autobiographical accounts of childhood as well as countless novels about the school years of a protagonist who brought to mind the author.[188] Zegadłowicz was certainly not breaking new terrain when it came to his critical portrayal of small-town life, his anti-militarism or even his liberal treatment of erotic themes.[189] Wójcik argues that *Zmory* caused such an uproar mostly because of Zegadłowicz's transformation as a writer. He was previously seen as a leading Catholic writer; his publisher was Księgarnia Św. Wojciecha [St Adalbert's Books] in Poznań. *Zmory* is a sequel to his novel series, *Żywot Mikołaja Srebrempisanego* [The Life of Mikołaj Srebrempisany]. Published in three volumes, it tells the protagonist's story from his birth

186 K. Szymanowski, *Narcyz: Rzecz o Zegadłowiczu-powieściopisarzu* (Cracow: Wydawnictwo Literackie, 1986), p. 106.

187 M. Wójcik, "Wstęp", in E. Zegadłowicz, *Zmory*, ed. by M. Wójcik (Wrocław: Zakład Narodowy imienia Ossolińskich, 2006), p. xlix.

188 A reviewer of Gombrowicz's *Ferdydurke* wrote in 1939:

> Thanks largely to Freud, childhood and adolescence now hang ominously over literature. Such a large part of the world lies beyond childhood, life is so full of great and serious issues, and yet here we are still dismantling childish or boyish complexes, and this unwillingly drives the soul into the narrow, primordial courtyard from which we have – or should have – emerged long ago. (W. Turno, "Rzeczywista niedojrzałość *Ferdydurki*", *PWS* 1939, no. 208/209, pp. 373–374)

189 M. Wójcik, "Wstęp", p. xlix.

until the age of eleven.[190] *Zmory* portrays the same character, but the message and style are quite different. The initial series represented a sensitive child with a lively imagination and an interest in mysticism. *Zmory*, meanwhile, draws on naturalistic and expressionist prose to portray Mikołaj's time at a Galician gymnasium and his sexual maturation. Readers – especially those who had enjoyed Zegadłowicz's previous novels – may have been offended by the explicit erotic scenes and the accusatory, almost pamphlet-like treatment of the prewar secondary school. Following the publication of *Zmory*, the Catholic press removed all of Zegadłowicz's previous works from their catalogue and even destroyed any copies that remained in stock. The writer's earlier supporters were also discomfited by his critique of the Church's hypocrisy and the caricature of provincial life, marked by superstition and religious obscurantism. More outraged than anyone else were the inhabitants of Wadowice, where the writer had been a pupil twenty years before. Reading the fictional Wołkowice as a representation of their small town, they were so aggrieved that the town authorities revoked Zegadłowicz's honorary citizenship, conferred on him during a pompous celebration of the 25-year-anniversary of his debut in 1933; a street named after him on the same occasion was renamed back to Tatrzańska.[191] The writer's old teachers saw themselves represented in the novel's characters, while former pupils responded to Zegadłowicz's "libel" by writing letters to the press, stressing that their own memories were quite different.[192]

---

190 The original three volumes of *Żywot Mikołaja Srebrempisanego* [The Life of Mikołaj Srebrempisany] were titled *Godzina przed Jutrznią* (The Hour before the Morning Prayer, 1927), *Spod młyńskich kamieni* (From Under the Millstones, 1928) and *Cień nad falami* (The Shadow over the Waves, 1929). The second edition of the series appeared in 1936; it was now titled *Uśmiech* [Smile], passages on religion had been removed and some sections were rewritten to connect the plot to the sequel, *Zmory*.

191 See M. Siwiec-Cielebon, "Nieskutecznie wyklęty, skutecznie niewykorzystany: Aktywność artystyczno-polityczna Emila Zegadłowicza a Wadowice i Wadowiczanie w latach 1935–1939", in *Emil Zegadłowicz: Daleki i bliski*, ed. by H. Czubała, K. Kłosiński, K. Latawiec and W. Próchnicki (Katowice: Uniwersytet Śląski, 2015), pp. 115–131.

192 See for instance S. Witkowski, "Gimnazjum wadowickie pół wieku temu", KLN 1939, no. 7; Z. Żygulski, "O dawnej szkole galicyjskiej (Na marginesie *Zmór*)", *NC* 1936, no. 2; A. Ryniewicz, "*Zmory* i przedwojenna szkoła w Małopolsce", *PPE* 1936, no. 3; A. Nowaczyński, "W obronie 'belfrów'", *PLA* 1939, no. 4030. Cf. W. Studencki, "C.K. Gimnazjum Wadowickie w opinii pisarzy", *ZN* 1962, Historia Literatury, no. 2, pp. 161–170.

For literary critics, the autobiographical aspects of the novel were so self-evident that some discussed the real Wadowice, not the fictional Wołkowice, and treated Mikołaj as a straightforward alter ego of the author. In what appears to be the first review of the novel, Alfred Jesionowski describes *Zmory* as the author's "horrifying memoir" built from "autobiographical elements that have been broadened, deepened – or blurred through the creative imagination"; the author is said to be bitter about his "disappointments in life" and his "wasted youth"; and above all, he is accused of being gratuitously provocative – "*pour épater le bourgeois*".[193] The critic is outraged at the fact that the town – and especially the gymnasium – are "painted as a modern-day Sodom":

> It is rather a nightmarish vision, some kind of madhouse, a house of criminals, ignoramuses, where the professors are, with few exceptions, drunkards, sadists, abnormal types [...]. The students are precocious and sexually active at a young age [...]. Their main concern is sex. (*Ibid.*)

The portrayal of Wadowice recalls Karl Emil Franzos' *Aus Halb-Asien* [From Half-Asia], where the author tackles his Galician birthtown, Czortków, through his fictional Barnów; another literary context in which to read *Zmory* is the Galician satire, with such writers as Jan Lam and Michał Bałucki, which caricatured provincial towns with fictional place-names designed to sound funny. As far as the main theme of *Zmory* is concerned, Robert Musil's novel *The Confusions of Young Törless*, published twenty years earlier, comes to mind. Zegadłowicz's contemporary critics, however, identified quite different literary affinities.

One interesting aspect of the reception of *Zmory* is that it was placed alongside women's writing – a contextualisation that was intended to discredit the author. One critic associates Zegadłowicz's "tendency to constantly wallow in sexual images" with women's fiction.[194] Another critic compares *Zmory* to the novels of Gabriela Zapolska:

> There is the same brutal, exaggerated and repulsive naturalism, the hatred of reality, the negation, "the refusal of the world" [...], and then the ellipses, the internal experiences, the pure, idealistic raptures approaching

193 A. Jesionowski, "Lata gimnazjalne Mikołaja Srebrempisanego", *PZM* 1935, no. 42, p. 3.

194 A. Grzymała-Siedlecki, "Diagnoza *Zmór*", *KW* 1935, no. 314, p. 4.

> the threshold of mysticism. In Zapolska's work, readers would skip the pages between the ellipses, longing for brutal, lurid naturalistic scenes, and readers do the same in *Zmory*.[195]

The critics of *Prosto z Mostu* compared Zegadłowicz to Nałkowska. In his article "Trzy powieści trzech pisarek" [Three Novels by Three Women Writers], Wincenty Lutosławski leaves out the writers' surnames, discussing novels by "Maria" (Kuncewiczowa), "Zofia" (Nałkowska) and "Ewa" (Szelburg-Zarembina).[196] He indicates parallels in the plots of Nałkowska's *Granica* and *Zmory*; the only difference being that "Emil [Zegadłowicz] is less well-mannered and exposes himself through his coarse use of obscene words, while the subtle and refined Zofia [Nałkowska] describes the same things, and worse, in a manner that is equally clear but requires the reader to do a little more guesswork" (*Ibid.*). He also discusses thematic similarities such as the two novels' anti-clericalism, as well as their general tendency "to scour the human experience for such a powerful dominance of lust that little else remains besides"; novels such as *Granica* and *Zmory*, he argues, "encourage readers to act, without inhibitions, on whatever their blood demands, since that is supposedly a universal right about which no one needs to feel embarrassed" (*Ibid.*).

The second critic in *Prosto z Mostu* who associates *Zmory* with women's fiction is Włodzimierz Pietrzak. In his article "Kobieta i perspektywa literatury" [Woman and the Perspective of Literature] he claims that before World War I, the feminist movement galvanised enthusiastic idealists, but women gained neither happiness nor liberation once their emancipatory goals were achieved. Contemporary women writers were producing evidence of women's egocentrism and materialism, and their focus on the theme of love was simply offensive. He concludes: "The atmosphere of Zegadłowicz's *Zmory*, of Boy's erotic perfumes, the physiological backdrop of love, which contemporary literature throws at our feet – this is precisely the problem faced by those who care about what path literature takes in the future."[197]

Some critics – apparently unaware that they were doing Zegadłowicz a favour by mentioning him in the same breath as Joyce and Lawrence –

195 K. Zawodziński, "Blaski i nędze realizmu powieściowego w latach ostatnich", *PWS* 1936, no. 176, p. 419.

196 W. Lutosławski, "Trzy powieści trzech pisarek", *PZM* 1936, no. 18, p. 1.

197 W. Pietrzak, "Kobieta i perspektywa literatury", *PZM* 1936, no. 31, p. 4.

tried to demean him by comparing him to writers deemed scandalous. In *Prosto z Mostu*, for instance, Alfred Jesionowski wrote:

> I have not read Joyce's *Ulysses* or *Lady Chatterley's Lover* by Lawrence – I only know these books from reviews – but I believe that when it comes to a certain type of description Zegadłowicz is the record holder. After all, it is not just that these descriptions exist in his novel – they actually make up almost all of its content, and as a result [...] everything is but the product of an excessive and sick imagination.[198]

Similar contextualisations also appear in the most positive reviews of *Zmory*. For Paweł Hulka-Laskowski (in *Tygodnik Ilustrowany*), for instance, Zegadłowicz's novel "is one of the most beautiful and intelligent in world literature"; he discusses it alongside works by Joyce, Lawrence, Čapek, Huxley, Céline and Proust.[199] Similarly, Kazimierz Wyka (in *Droga*) compares Zegadłowicz with Lawrence, Joyce, Céline and Witkacy. In his view, however, Zegadłowicz differs from these writers in that there is no higher goal behind his use of shocking language or his repulsive representations of

---

198 A. Jesionowski, "Lata gimnazjalne Mikołaja Srebrempisanego", p. 3. Zegadłowicz was again compared to Joyce by later literary scholars such as Egon Naganowski, for whom the explicitly erotic scenes in *Ulysses* are phenomena "with which we are certainly unfamiliar in fictional characters, with the exception, perhaps, of Mikołaj Srebrempisany in *Zmory*"; see *Telemach w labiryncie świata* (Warsaw: Czytelnik, 1962), p. 96. Kornel Szymanowski, meanwhile, proposes that the most important influence on *Zmory* was the Polish translation of Joyce's *Portrait of the Artist as a Young Man*, published a few years earlier, in 1931. He identifies both thematic and narrative or stylistic similarities in the two crypto-autobiographical novels:
Stephen Dedalus' development, his alienation from his family, his struggle with his obsession with sex, freeing himself from religious practices and realising his vocation as an artist, is clearly parallel to that of Mikołaj's ideological and mental maturation. Echoes of Joyce can often be heard in *Zmory* – literally from the novel's first sentences to the last. Zegadłowicz's cosmological prologue, which leads the reader from a vision of the universe, through the Solar System and the Earth, to the microcosm of Mikołaj's psyche, finds its pendant in Stephen Dedalus' reflections on his hometown, while the euphoric ending of *Zmory* – the joy felt by Mik[ołaj], the future poet, who greets the morning with the words "Good morning! Good morning to the Earth and to Heaven!" – clearly corresponds to Stephen similar mood and his "Welcome, O life!" at the end of *Portrait*. (K. Szymanowski, *Narcyz*, p. 98; the quotation is taken from James Joyce, *A Portrait of the Artist as a Young Man* (Oxford: Oxford University Press, 2000), p. 213).

199 P. Hulka-Laskowski, "*Zmory*", *TI* 1935, no. 41, pp. 805–806.

erotic scenes – they exist just for their own sake. What appears to be courageous at first sight does not actually enhance our understanding of the human psyche. For Wyka, Zegadłowicz is no psychologist – a label frequently applied to innovative novelists at the time; rather, he takes on the role of a patient undergoing psychoanalysis. *Zmory*, he continues, is "a liberating reckoning, a psychoanalytic act of shedding complexes by becoming aware of them";[200] at the same time it is a stage in Zegadłowicz's development as a writer. Wyka compares him to the novel's protagonist Mikołaj, who turns to religion to overcome his obsession with sex: "Something similar happened with Zegadłowicz. After his failed attempt to escape into the world of devotional objects, church fairs and religious feelings, stifled attitudes broke out into the light and demanded an even stronger expression, a harsh reckoning with reality" (*Ibid.*).

While for Wyka *Zmory* represents a sort of self-therapy, other critics saw it as evidence for the writer's opportunism. One critic who made such a claim was Jerzy Wyszomirski in *Gazeta Polska*:

> This writer used to be poetic and strait-laced, inspiring readers to follow in the footsteps of Saint Francis, who saw God in every creature; his books were not too popular, some even considered him a graphomaniac. Now, overnight, he decided to become […] a Priapus in order to acquire […] crowds of outraged, offended or enthusiastic readers who will have different opinions on why […] the author uses nine phallic terms or seven definitions of "sleeping with a wench".[201]

Zmory, Wyszomirski continues, represents nothing but another level of Zegadłowicz's hypocrisy. Since his portrayals of folklore and religious customs did not deliver the expected outcome, now it remains to be seen how successful he might be with macabre and erotic scenes. "Freudianism being in vogue at the moment," the critic writes, Zegadłowicz "read a lot of the fashionable literature in pedagogy and sexology […] and uncritically took into account all the deviations invented by contemporary youth psycho-pedagogy" (*Ibid.*).

The critic for *Prosto z Mostu*, having remarked on the idyllic tone and absence of any sexual issues in the previous three volumes of *Żywot Mikołaja Srebrempisanego*, poses a rhetorical question that also suggests

---

200 *DR* 1935, no. 11, p. 1001.

201 J. Wyszomirski, "Artyzm i spekulacja", *GPL* 1935, no. 305, p. 3.

that Zegadłowicz was acting out of opportunism: "Is it only now that these terrible memories have surfaced from his subconscious?"[202] Similarly, one of the greatest admirers of Zegadłowicz's earlier work, Karol H. Rostworowski, hopes that the writer was only profiteering because otherwise he would need a doctor.[203] Adam Grzymała-Siedlecki also wonders what – besides a desire to cause a scandal or to please a certain wing of the literary scene – could have induced Zegadłowicz to "immerse himself gleefully in such an abomination"; he continues to argue that if the main character was rooted in introspection and if Zegadłowicz took his own secondary school years as a model "then the matter is much more profound and painful, but we should also feel sorry for him".[204] This critic describes *Zmory* as "a document about the author's psychology," where pent-up hatred gushes forth, as well as revenge for the humiliations he endured at school: "It is a hysterical fury" (p. 4). The critic Rafał Blüth comments on Zegadłowicz's anti-clericalism and anti-militarism as rooted in trauma, as well as the fact that the writer has not come to terms with his "complexes of Galician servility".[205]

Kornel Szymanowski, a contemporary literary scholar, reads *Zmory* alongside Albert Dryjski's *Zagadnienia seksualizmu dziecka i młodzieży szkolnej* [Problems in Child and Teenage Sexuality] from 1934 as well as Stefan Baley's *Psychologia wieku dojrzewania* [The Psychology of Adolescence], published two years earlier. He has no doubt that Zegadłowicz "only fictionalised some of the ideas put forward by Freud or his followers".[206] In fact, Baley himself had warned of such a development:

> Recently, literary works have taken adolescence as a special theme [...]. [...] in some cases writers apparently draw on the existing scientific literature on adolescence and on its basis hypothetically construct experiences as they should have taken place [...] according to the theory in the book.[207]

---

202 A. Jesionowski, *Lata gimnazjalne Mikołaja Srebrempisanego*, p. 3.

203 K. H. Rostworowski, "Metamorfoza...", *KPOZ* 1935, no. 521, p. 5.

204 A. Grzymała-Siedlecki, "Diagnoza *Zmór*".

205 R. M. Blüth, "*Zmory* i ich kariera społeczna: Uwagi w związku z polemiką literacką", *V* 1935, no. 4. Cited after the reprint in *Pisma literackie*, pp. 298–299.

206 K. Szymanowski, *Narcyz*, pp. 164–165.

207 S. Baley, *Psychologia wieku dojrzewania* (Lviv: Książnica Atalas, 1932), pp. 60–61.

Zegadłowicz did not renounce this influence. In his play *Pokój dziecinny* [The Nursery], which can be read as a commentary on *Zmory*, Freud's name appears side by side with Jesus, Marx and Einstein,[208] while creativity is referred to as "auto-therapy" (p. 33). Discussing the writing process in a letter he reflects that the novel "is essentially about the years when consciousness awakens with the pressure of adolescence (it was impossible to get around psychoanalytical probing)".[209] Raised in Galicia and fluent in German, he could have read Freud in the original. Jekels and Albiński's Polish version of Freud's *Three Essays on the Theory of Sexuality* had also been available for ten years. The idea that he may have read this translation is suggested by overlapping terms in his work and that of Przybyszewski.[210]

These terminological echoes were highlighted early on: in 1934, for instance, the critic Jan Emil Skiwski wrote that Zegadłowicz "has not realised in which epoch he lives. He dwells in Young Poland as if nothing had ever happened".[211] But a direct influence of Przybyszewski on Zegadłowicz is not the most likely explanation, even if the author of *Zmory* had worked with the Expressionists from the Greater Poland region since 1918, and became acquainted with the members of Zdrój during a short

---

208 E. Zegadłowicz, *Pokój dziecinny* (Gorzeń Górny–Czerniowce: Biblioteka Gorzeńska, 1936), p. 63. In a debate printed in *Wiadomości Literackie* in 1937, Zegadłowicz also names Jesus, Freud, Marx and Einstein to exemplify Jewish genius (E. Zegadłowicz, "Poza dyskusją", *WL* 1937, no. 20, p. 2).

209 Cited in M. Wójcik, *Pan na Gorzeniu: Życie i twórczość Emila Zegadłowicza* (Kielce: Akademia Świętokrzyska, 2005), p. 336.

210 Cf. e.g. K. Szymanowski, *Narcyz*, p. 240. Szymanowski also identifies striking similarities in the lives of Przybyszewski and Zegadłowicz:
"Although Zegadłowicz did not set the tone for his epoch and did not play as prominent a role as [Przybyszewski] [...], he became famous for similar literary and non-literary scandals, using his own complex sexuality as material in his works [...]. Both of them often posed as prophets and succumbed to their moods; in both of them, the ease of writing went hand in hand with an unwillingness to chisel down their works. They also shared financial troubles [...], and even Zegadłowicz's unbelievable unpredictability in political affairs brings to mind Przybyszewski's episode as editor of *Gazeta Robotnicza*. The careers of both writers are marked by great popularity during their lifetime, but it is remarkable how quickly they were forgotten, or at least the voices that were critical of their work soon came dominate. Last but not least, Przybyszewski and Zegadłowicz shared a fascination with sex in their writing (and in their lives). Both went beyond the moral norms of their times and shocked contemporary readers." (pp. 317–318)

211 J. E. Skiwski, "Zegadłowicz żyje", *P* 1934, no. 15, p. 9.

stay in Poznań. The linguistic similarities are particularly prominent in descriptions of sex, and this suggests that Zegładowicz picked up on Przybyszewski's language through the Polish translations of Freud. As we know, Jekels and Albiński drew heavily on Przybyszewski, e.g. in their rendition of libido as *chuć*. Szymanowski describes Zegadłowicz's style as "a modernised Przybyszewski filtered through Freudianism".[212] I would argue the opposite, however: Zegadłowicz's style is Freudianism filtered through Przybyszewski.

Zegadłowicz was probably introduced to psychoanalysis by the above-mentioned Stefan Essmanowski, the essayist and critic who reviewed translations of Freud, as I discussed above. Before he moved from Poznań to Warsaw, Essmanowski wrote for the *Tęcza* [Rainbow], a Catholic journal on culture and society of which Zegadłowicz was editor-in-chief. Essmanowski also associated with the expressionists from the "Zdrój" group.[213] Zegadłowicz describes Essmanowski as his friend, "an exceptional linguist, psychoanalyst, scholar and intellectual".[214] Essmanowski, meanwhile, penned one of the most favourable reviews of *Zmory*.

In his review, published in *Bunt Młodych*, Essmanowski presents a psychoanalytical reading of the novel and concludes that Zegadłowicz was much more radical than other writers who had tackled their school years. Previous novels may have been written "according to modern postulates of realism and psychologism," but their approach to adolescent sexuality had the sickly-sweet and artificial scent of the conventional village idyll.[215] Zegadłowicz, by contrast, courageously broke with this hypocrisy, challenging not only his readers but also himself:

> From behind the powerful bolts of internal censorship, he is able to free experiences that even the bravest people try to forget, which they erase or at least distort into symbols beyond recognition. Zegadłowicz, meanwhile, presents us not with symbols or vague allusions, but with clear, bold, sometimes brutal facts. (*Ibid.*)

---

212 K. Szymanowski, *Narcyz*, p. 240.

213 See J. J. Lipski, "eses: Stafan Essmanowski (1898–1942)", in *Warszawscy "pustelnicy" i "bywalscy"*, vol. 2: *Felietoniści i kronikarze 1900–1939* (Warsaw: PIW, 1973), pp. 432–433.

214 E. Zegadłowicz, *Pokój dziecinny*, p. 49.

215 S. Essmanowski, "Obsesje i gwiazdy", p. 9.

According to Essmanowski, none of the characters in the novel are fictional, but this is not to say that they are identical with their real-life models; Zegadłowicz exaggerates their faults while leaving out their positive qualities. This strategy is legitimate from an aesthetic point of view, the critic continues, and it can be associated with "what is called *sekundärer Krankheitsgewinn* in psychoanalysis, and which is justified above all in terms of psychology":

> The book emanates the scent of little Mikołaj's reprisal against adults. This could also explain a stylistic clash, namely the Pantagruelian naming of genitals and their functions […]. Is this not what Ferenczi identified (in *Bausteine zur Psychoanalyse*) as the child's view of "indecency" as an adult privilege? (*Ibid.*)

Essmanowski disagrees with other critics who describe Zegadłowicz as an exhibitionist. "If *Zmory* is an expression of certain inclinations and drives, then it is especially the aggressive drive. Love has been made to focus on the self, which is why everything that the self experiences as unpleasant is felt all the more keenly. This smacks slightly of narcissism" (*Ibid.*). This sheds light on the writer's ideological transformation and his attacks on the Church and religion, his rebellion against all authorities that stand in the way of individual freedom.

It is likely that Essmanowski also introduced Zegadłowicz to Gustav Bychowski, perhaps suggesting that he contact the psychoanalyst. After all, Bychowski had a strong interest in literature and was likely to appreciate *Zmory*. Be that as it may, Bychowski's name figures on a list of twenty individuals to whom the author first sent a copy of his latest work.[216] Zegadłowicz's archive contains a part of his correspondence with Gustav Bychowski from the years 1936 to 1938. The analyst addresses the writer using forms that express sincere affection and respect; he inquires if Zegadłowicz was making good progress with his work,[217] expresses his wish to meet in person,[218] asks for a copy of Zegadłowicz's recently published *Pokój dziecinny*.[219] In a letter dated 24 April 1936, as Freud's eightieth birthday was approaching, Bychowski attached a letter with birthday greetings by "The International Writers' Committee" (including

216 M. Wójcik, *Pan na Gorzeniu*, pp. 336–337.
217 Biblioteka Uniwersytecka w Kielcach, 113.33.2.
218 Biblioteka Uniwersytecka w Kielcach, 113.33.4.
219 Biblioteka Uniwersytecka w Kielcach, 113.33.5.

Thomas Mann, Stefan Zweig, Romain Rolland, Jules Romains, H. G. Wells, Virginia Woolf and others), hoping (in vain) that Zegadłowicz, too, would add his signature.[220] Zegadłowicz published an article in his own defence after he felt misrepresented by Tadeusz Grabowski and his study *Historia literatury polskiej* [The History of Polish Literature];[221] Bychowski, having read Zegadłowicz's response, writes to express his "joy about the vigour" of the writer's "ripostes and attacks".[222] In yet another letter he requests a copy of Zegadłowicz's sold-out translation of *Faust*, hoping to inspire a love of Goethe in his son.[223]

Bychowski and Zegadłowicz grew closer when the former stepped up in defence of *Zmory*. He became active when reviewer Jan N. Miller called for a competent Freudian reading, explicitly naming the psychoanalyst as a suitable discussant:

> With its special focus on childish eroticism, the book presents invaluable material for psychoanalysts, who will easily detect processes of sublimating (elevating) the erotic instinct in the protagonist's life, as well as that instinct's gradual transformation into a creative instinct, into artistic work. From this point of view, the book should be tackled by a professional Freudian like Dr Gustav Bychowski.[224]

On 14 November 1935, their friend Stefan Essmanowski and the Union of Polish Writers – as if they were responding to Miller's appeal – organised a soirée dedicated to Zegadłowicz's novel. Tadeusz Breza wrote about the event for *Kurier Poranny*, describing a tightly packed main room at the organisation's Warsaw branch and a discussion that lasted late into the night:

> No one was spared. Supporters of each view were grilled [...] in turn. The range of perspectives was astonishing, as was the breadth [...] of contradictory opinions, expressed in every possible way – whether in intelligent words, insightful thinking, or [...] in nonsense and banality.[225]

220 Biblioteka Uniwersytecka w Kielcach, 113.33.1.

221 E. Zegadłowicz, "Dwie pary", *WL* 1937, no. 18, p. 5.

222 Biblioteka Uniwersytecka w Kielcach, 113.33.4.

223 Biblioteka Uniwersytecka w Kielcach, 113.33.2.

224 J. N. Miller, "Zmory dzieciństwa", *R* 1935, no. 358, p. 3.

225 tb [T. Breza], "Burza wokoło jednej książki: Freud, *Zmory* i przedmiotowość", *KPO* 1935, no. 349, p. 3. Breza wrote another positive review of *Zmory*: T. Breza, "Wielka przygoda i znakomita książka: Mikołaj czyżby pisany – srebrem...", *KPO* 1935, no. 301, pp. 3–4.

Bychowski gave the keynote that night, and Zegadłowicz selected this paper, titled "Katarsis poety" [The Poet's Catharsis], for publication in *Piszemy listy* (1937), a collection of texts by himself and his readers.[226]

Bychowski's goal in his keynote was to give a conclusive answer to the question if *Zmory* was a fictionalisation of Freud's *Three Essays on the Theory of Sexuality*, or if it was a psychologically necessary eruption. Most critics' assessment of Zegadłowicz's controversial novel depended on how they answered this question. For Bychowski, *Zmory* is not a popular version of Freud's work but a confirmation of its accuracy. Zegadłowicz's earlier work, meanwhile, was governed by suppression and sublimation. *Zmory* can be seen as a real act of purification and self-therapy, and this is why it is so violent and drastic.[227] The novel's disturbing language, described by critics as "coprolalia," is a reaction to "the seraphic purity of his previous vocabulary" (p. 71). Bychowski also contextualises *Zmory* with James Joyce's novel. Just as the great form of *Ulysses* approaches the flow of free association, "the actual language of a psychoanalytical session," so the Polish writer creates "a restless form". The novel's chaotic composition and the jagged rhythm of its sentences can be attributed to the pressure of suppressed material, which was so urgent that it was impossible for the writer to polish the form. An important proof of Zegadłowicz's sincerity, Bychowski goes on, can be found in the scene in which Mikołaj masturbates using his mother's nightgown. While most critics suspected that this scene was only meant to scandalise readers, Bychowski stresses that Zegadłowicz's fascination with the mother, who is largely absent from Mikołaj's life, was already clear in previous parts of the cycle; there was even a dream in which the father appears in the guise of Don Quixote as little Mik's erotic rival. *Zmory* cannot, therefore, have been written out of expediency but emerged from an internal, irresistible compulsion.

226 G. Bychowski, "*Zmory* – katarsis poety", in Emil Zegadłowicz et al., *Piszemy listy* (Warsaw: Księgarnia Powszechna, 1937), pp. 64–79. Among others, the following individuals took part in the discussion after the lecture: Rafał Blüth (he called Zegadłowicz a graphomaniac who deliberately placed "Freudian raisins" in his novel), Artur Prędski (he refers to Zegadłowicz as a lewd coprophagus) and Stefania Zahorska (unlike Irzykowski's *Pałuba*, she claims, *Zmory* is not Freudian). These opinions are quoted in *Piszemy listy*, pp. 56–59.
Zegadłowicz believed that the reactions to his novel reflected the state of Polish culture, which is why he initially intended the volume to be titled "Zwierciadło kultury polskiej" [A Mirror of Polish culture] (see K. Szymanowski, *Narcyz*, p. 118). His publisher was Marceli Tarnowski, the translator of D.H. Lawrence's *A Propos of "Lady Chatterley's Lover"*.

227 G. Bychowski, "*Zmory* – katarsis poety", p. 70.

For Bychowski, Zegadłowicz's work mirrors the process of psychoanalytical treatment:

> Starting out with what we generally see as the highest fabric of personality, character and personal ideals, the patient descends deeper and deeper, down to the most primitive psychological layers, which consist of spontaneous drives which are essentially antisocial and sometimes remarkably animalistic. (p. 67)

Similarly, some readers' resistance to the novel, Bychowski argues, brings to mind a relatively common stage in the therapeutic process, where patients feel that their very humanity is threatened. There is no reason to speak of immorality, neither in the case of psychoanalysis nor in *Zmory*. Bychowski goes so far as to stress the ethical dimension of Zegadłowicz's project: only when repressed matter is discharged can we make a truly free choice about our life's path, and an authentic morality emerges in the place of a false morality that only veils repressed sensuality.

Interestingly, Bychowski argues, Zegadłowicz is still under the sway of a certain necessity:

> Like a wave on the stormy sea, the catharsis of *Zmory* throws precious stones onto the shores of creativity, but also the murky sediment of ancient and impure matters. Who can say what will remain on the beach when the storm subsides and the poet's soul, cleansed of the ghosts of the past, gains profound wisdom and maturity. It will certainly be a new kind of harmony – different from the harmony of years gone by, more human, more familiar and dearer to us, rich and straining towards the future. (p. 79)

In 1937, soon after *Zmory*, Zegadłowicz published his next novel, *Motory* [Motors]. His archived correspondence contains a postcard from Bychowski, thanking him for "the beautiful book" and saying how pleased he was that Zegadłowicz was getting on so well with his work.[228] In fact, Bychowski was one of the novel's very few readers, as it was confiscated two days after its release. It is also worth noting that Bychowski is mentioned by name in *Motory*. He appears at the very beginning, in a passage that can be read as a key to the entire novel. The protagonist, Cyprian Fałn (pronounced [faʊn]), is in solitary confinement in a hospital

228 Biblioteka Uniwersytecka w Kielcach, 113.33.3.

in Cracow when he has a dream or hallucination. His thoughts revolve around his own name and its supposedly Greek, mythological etymology. He sees himself as a faun (also pronounced [faʊn] in Polish) surrounded by muses who look like the women he had loved. But modern-day images keep interrupting this ancient idyll: Fałn sees two men – professor Jerzy Kowalski, a classicist, and Gustav Bychowski – but he cannot keep the two apart, they seem to merge into one figure. Now Fałn sees himself sitting with the analyst; between their leather armchairs there is a small table with a soda water siphon and cakes. The doctor's "fat, lecherous fingers are playing with his pocket watch" and he explains: "anyway, it is clear that the way dreams are constructed is generally simple – it's only that we, when we're awake, are too complicated and artful; that's all".[229] The doctor also shows Fałn a few paintings by mental patients, but "the pages of the book are completely white, no text, no illustrations, nothing; only the doctor sees anything at all in them" (*ibid.*). This passage echoes a section in Bychowski's book *Psychoanaliza*, where dreams are compared to modernist painting: both express "a whole range of thoughts, entire constellations of feelings and deep internal conflicts in one intricately constructed picture".[230]

It would be far-fetched to claim, based on this one conjunction, that Zegadłowicz may have been psychoanalysed by Bychowski. But Krzysztof Kłosiński is certainly right when he describes *Motory* – mostly read as pornographic – as a psychoanalytical novel:

> Creativity is exposed as instrumental, as a compensation for fears that threaten impotence, as a sublimation of the desire to please, the desire to evoke desire, a sublimation of the longing for the domination of the masculine element that was either lost or perhaps never achieved in the first place.[231]

In this sense *Motory* appears to be more "decent" (using the criteria applied by critics at the time) than *Zmory*; the fact is that Zegadłowicz tackles his

229 E. Zegadłowicz, *Motory* (Łódź: Wydawnictwo Łódzkie, 1981), p. 17.

230 G. Bychowski, *Psychoanaliza*, p. 32.

231 K. Kłosiński, "Jak czytać *Motory*", in *Szkice o twórczości Emila Zegadłowicza*, ed. by Z. Andres (Rzeszów: TN, 1985), p. 97. Cf. K. Kłosiński, "Od *Zmór* do *Motorów*: Czy jest możliwa literatura erotyczna?", in *Studia o Zegadłowiczu*, ed. by J. Paszek (Katowice: Uniwersytet Śląski, 1982); in the same volume, see also J. Paszek, "*Motory* i pornografia", pp. 99–111.

own journey as an artist, including the motives behind the shifts in his world-view, which have given rise to so many interpretations.

Only one review of *Zmory* went beyond the question that obsessed most other critics, i.e. whether Zegadłowicz was authentic or opportunistic. This one review, titled "Odważna książka" [A Brave Book], was written by Emil Breiter, a lawyer and prolific contributor to *Wiadomości Literackie*.[232] In his detailed first-page article he proposes that the novel's most important contribution is the way it introduces a language about sex into Polish literature. It is "a voice of lively vitality, of spontaneous truth with a Rabelaisian impetus, with a creative vocabulary, constantly born anew, courageous to the point of blindness, true to the point of pain. The voice of a man who is alive, who wants to live and to convince others to do the same".[233] Breiter's impulse to compare Zegadłowicz to Rabelais is – just as was the case in Stempowski's above-mentioned association of Joyce and Rabelais – mediated through Freud. Zegadłowicz, Breiter argues, explores ways to address sexuality "under the influence of the upheavals in our attitude to sex," which is to say thanks to psychoanalysis. The critic continues to question why "many words, phrases and images that we all use every day have been banished and marginalised in literature"; it is because, "for reasons that have nothing to do with art, an organised social conspiracy has placed an enormous sphere of experiences, sensations and emotions outside the realm of etiquette, morality and ethics" (*Ibid.*). Breiter also refers to Stanisław Brzozowski's argument that Polish society's stance towards sex is symptomatic of its inhibitive culture:

> Keeping silent about the most important matters has been raised to the level of a social duty. A taboo was created that could not be touched with impunity, nor could it be demystified. Stanisław Brzozowski already shed light on the damage done to humanity and culture by the fact that half of life was veiled in secrecy, that the whole world of erotic and sexual experiences was viewed – at best – as an object of clinical research, accessible only to ordained specialists. How many things were thus deformed, how many misunderstood, how many were left completely unexplored! (*Ibid.*)

232 M. Szpakowska, *"Wiadomości Literackie" prawie dla wszystkich*, p. 260. In 1935, *Zmory* was also shortlisted for the readers' prize for the best novel sponsored by *Wiadomości Literackie*. See "Nagroda czytelników *Wiadomości Literackich* za najwybitniejszą książkę roku 1935", *WL* 1936, no. 3, p. 1.

233 E. Breiter, "Odważna książka", *WL* 1935, no. 40, p. 1.

For Breiter, Freudianism and its legacy could be a boon to Polish culture, which relies on repression and hypocrisy. This can be seen especially in *Zmory*. It changed the etiquette of literature as radically as psychoanalysis revolutionised society's norms (*ibid.*).

This celebration of *Zmory* as a "heroic book" was opposed by several critics, such as Jan E. Skiwski and Rafał Blüth, who attributed its popularity to "thoughtlessness, literary snobbism or tolerance driven to the brink of insanity," but also to "ill will and destructive tendencies".[234] Blüth critiqued Breiter in *Verbum*, pointing out that the supposedly revolutionary elements of *Zmory* had long been accepted as obvious and were now almost out of date:

> In this day and age – as sexology experiences an unprecedented increase in popularity, risking to overshadow other psychological disciplines – is it not strange to combat silence on these matters, a silence allegedly raised to the level of a social duty; today, as the bibliography on this subject alone contains thousands of items [...]; to speak about a "taboo" when pedagogues, too [...], have established special sections of sexological pedagogy; in an era where more and more fields are overcoming Freudianism; in the era, finally, of Lawrence, Proust, Joyce...[235]

Blüth's argumentation deserves careful attention. He seems to criticise *Zmory*, but he actually highlights the fact that while the press was engaged in a hot debate over the novel, the transfer of psychoanalysis to Polish culture was a done deal. For Blüth, the campaign for *Zmory* was breaking down an open door.

Psychoanalysis on the stage

When Bychowski interviewed Freud for *Wiadomości Literackie*, he stated that "today, the basic tenets of psychoanalysis have simply entered the language of the intelligentsia as a social class".[236] This was in 1936, no more than eight years after Irzykowski had complained in the same journal that ignorance about psychoanalysis represented "a compromising gap in

---

234 J. E. Skiwski, "*Zmory* trzeba załatwić", *P* 1935, no. 46, p. 4.

235 R. M. Blüth, "*Zmory* i ich kariera społeczna", p. 301.

236 G. Bychowski, "Rozmowa z Freudem", *WL* 1936, no. 20, p. 4.

the education of our intelligentsia".[237] Even Antoni Słonimski, known for his critical attitude towards Freudianism, admitted that "this theory has made an impressive career on the purely verbal level", introducing new words such as 'complex,' 'subconscious' and 'inhibition'.[238] A similar statement was made by a critic in *Nasz Przegląd*: "Notions of psychoanalysis, complexes and the subconscious have now become so fashionable that we encounter them almost every day – not only in literature but in our daily lives and in the average educated person's everyday speech."[239]

From the mid-1930s on, no active effort was required to learn about the basic concepts of psychoanalysis: "Every one of us, reading a contemporary novel or even just the daily paper, has come across concepts such as complexes, repressed feelings, libido, transference, [...]"[240] The Polish term *kompleks* was established especially quickly. It was introduced relatively late, because the translators of Freud's *Three Essays on the Theory of Sexuality* had chosen the Slavic term *zespół* for "complex," so that the Oedipus complex, for instance, was presented as *zespół Edypowy* or *zespół Edypa*.[241] However, the term *zespół* never really caught on. Bychowski's *Psychoanaliza*, published in 1928, attests that the concept and the term *kompleks* were widespread at the time. The author even feels compelled to argue that the main task of psychoanalysis "is by no means to search for so-called complexes".[242] Similarly, the scientific term *libido* soon displaced *chuć*, proposed by Jekels and Albiński and rooted in the language of the Young Poland movement.[243]

The fact that Polish intellectual circles had fully assimilated psychoanalysis by the end of the 1930s is also evidenced by the appropriation of Freudian themes in the theatre. The trend of incorporating such themes culminated in the extraordinary success of a comedy by Antoni Cwoj-

---

237 K. Irzykowski, "Badania Acherontu", *WL* 1928, no. 36, p. 3.

238 as. [A. Słonimski], "Dialog Cwojdzińskiego w Teatrze Małym", *WL* 1937, no. 21, p. 6.

239 P. Klinger, "Kryzys psychoanalizy", *NPR* 1938, no. 44, p. 20.

240 R. Kesselring, "Znaczenie psychoanalizy i psychologji indywidualnej we współczesnym systemie", p. 9.

241 Z. Freud, *Trzy rozprawy z teorii seksualnej*, p. 185.

242 G. Bychowski, *Psychoanaliza*, p. 166.

243 That said, the term *chuć* also continued to be used. For instance, Władysław Matecki writes in his discussion of Freud's notion of the death drive: "For at the beginning of life there was not lust [*chuć*], as Przybyszewski has it, but death." See Władysław Matecki, *Zygmunt Freud – lekarz-myśliciel* (Warsaw: [no publisher], 1937), p. 12.

dziński titled *Freuda teoria snów* [Freud's Theory of Dreams]. Staged by Szyfman at Warsaw's Teatr Mały in 1937, this play did not rely on facile mockery but presented psychoanalysis quite sincerely. Bolesław Miciński wrote to his friend Kazimierz Golonka, a psychiatrist in Katowice:

> What a shame you can't see Cwojdziński's *Theory of Dreams* – it's a really good play. I went with some prejudice, worried that psychoanalysis would be the butt of Cwojdziński's jokes, but his attitude to psychoanalysis is entirely positive, and the play, despite its apparent "lightness," is solid.[244]

The link between psychoanalysis and theatre was exploited on many levels. In the early decades of the twentieth century, it was common to use theatrical metaphors to discuss Freud's discoveries. One example can be found in an article in *Nasz Przegląd* form 1925:

> A person is like a theatre. Both the person and everyone around them see only what is happening on stage. The spectator has no idea about what is going on backstage, about the whole technique and the director's work. Just as art is created behind the scenes, so our lives are created without us, behind our backs. Behind the scenes, we carry all the experiences, dreams and longings […], all our thoughts, desires and impressions […]. […] Above it all there is the director, i.e. love – love in the broad sense: sexual love, neighbourly love, love of humanity, self-love. Love, or libido, as it is called in psychoanalytical language, propels us to action and life. But on the other side of the stage there is an audience. All the actors, and, most of all, the director, are afraid of this tribunal, of the court's verdict – because the audience, in this case, personifies social mores […]. Morality rules over all: it is found in our consciousness and it stands at the threshold of the subconscious, not allowing any inappropriate thought or feeling. This is the Freudian "censor".[245]

Freudianism also became a treasure trove for playwrights in need of plots. Irzykowski points out:

> Freud's theory and method contain a dramatic element, dividing people into the guessers and those who are guessed about, just as the characters in

244 B. Miciński, *Pisma*, p. 432.

245 "Dr Zygmunt Freud i jego nowa teoria", *NPR* 1925, no. 98, p. 5.

> a detective story are agents and thieves. The course of psychoanalytic treatment basically represents a play: the unmasking doctor must be aggressive, the unmasked patient must resist – these are spiritual wrestling matches; another predetermined element is the moment when the patient must transfer their erotic drives to the doctor, which is when the doctor – in the third act of the comedy designed by Freud himself – must sublimate them. This dramatic element makes Freudianism so popular.[246]

Across Europe, theatre made a significant contribution to the popularisation of Freudianism. In France, the reception of psychoanalysis was facilitated, in 1922, by the staging of Henri-René Lenormand's *Le Mangeur des Rêves* [The Dream Eater] at the Comédie des Champs-Elysées. The play deals with the tragic consequences of a psychoanalyst's romance with a neurotic female patient. Following the premiere, Jules Romains wrote: "This winter, I'm afraid, is going to be Freud's season."[247] It was at the theatre that many Parisians learned about psychoanalysis. The successful production turned Freudianism into a major dinner conversation topic, and to lie down on an analyst's couch was considered a sign of good taste.[248] The Hungarian writer Ferenc Molnár, wanting to parody popular representations of Freud's ideas, outlined a play for which he thought he had an excellent idea:

> How it should be developed, I don't yet know, but the fundamental deal is quite simple, as in all great tragedies: Young man – happily married to his mother – discovers that she isn't his mother at all – and shoots himself.[249]

Witkacy

Freuda teoria snów was not the first Polish play to build on psychoanalytic motifs, but the performances of the 1920s mostly took place in avant-garde theatres, unbeknownst to mainstream audiences. As we have seen before, psychoanalysis features in Jan Brzękowski's play *Dziurek w*

246 K. Irzykowski, "Scena czy sala odczytowa", in *Pisma teatralne* (Cracow: Wydawnictwo Literackie, 1997), vol. 4, pp. 292–293.

247 J. Romains, "Aperçu de la psychanalyse", *NRF* 1922, no. 100, p. 5.

248 Cf. J. Zych, *L'influence de la psychanalyse sur la critique littéraire en France*, p. 18.

249 Cited in P. Gay, *Freud: A Life for Our Times* (London: Papermac, 1989), p. 457.

Elsynorze, which was never staged. It also features prominently in Witkacy's *Wariat i zakonnica* [*The Madman and the Nun*]. One might say that Witkacy's entire oeuvre is strewn with allusions to Freud. In *Nadobnisie i koczkodany* [*Dainty Shapes and Hairy Apes*], for instance, one character boasts: "I know the *Kamasutra* and Weininger, Freud and the Babylonian sexologists."[250] Still, *The Madman and the Nun* is his only play where a psychoanalytic therapy is presented on stage.[251] This play was a great success, moreover, while Witkacy's other theatrical works from the period 1918-1925 only enjoyed moderate popularity. (It was only with *Szewcy* [*The Shoemakers*], written in the early 1930s, that he made another successful appearance as a playwright.) Janusz Degler writes:

> Few Polish playwrights of the interwar period received so many scathing reviews, few were so ruthlessly mocked, ridiculed and discredited, subjected to such sharp and abusive accusations, so many contradictory opinions and judgments. Witkacy had few supporters besides Boy[-Żeleński] and we could count on the fingers of one hand the number of critics who evaluated his plays favourably or who tried to justify their accusations with factual arguments.[252]

With its prominent representation of psychoanalysis and remarkable reception history, *The Madman and the Nun* merits a detailed discussion. The titular madman is Mieczysław Walpurg, "dark-complexioned, very handsome, and perfectly built"; he is a poet diagnosed with *dementia praecox*.[253] The audience first sees him straitjacketed, in a cell adapted to raving lunatics. Critics were quick to note that some of the protagonist's features bring to mind the playwright himself: they share a sense of guilt about the death of a betrothed who ended their sadomasochistic rela-

250 Stanislaw Ignacy Witkiewicz, *Seven Plays*, trans. and ed. by Daniel Gerould (New York, NY: Martin E. Segal Theatre Center Publications, 2004), p. 113.

251 Łucja Iwanczewska presents a psychoanalytical reading of Witkacy's plays in *Muszę się odrodzić: Inne spotkania z dramatami Stanisława Ignacego Witkiewicza* (Cracow: Księgarnia Akademicka, 2007). See also E. Łubieniewska, *Czysta forma i bebechy* (Cracow: Universitas, 2007).

252 J. Degler, *Witkacy w teatrze międzywojennym* (Warsaw: Wydawnictwa Artystyczne i Filmowe, 1973), pp. 18–19.

253 Stanislaw Ignacy Witkiewicz, *The Madman and the Nun and Other Plays*, trans. and ed. by Daniel C. Gerould and C.S. Durer (Seattle: University of Washington Press, 1968), p. 11 and p. 13.

tionship through suicide; they both had been to Ceylon; finally, they share a compulsion to create and an unshakable sense of their own grandeur. For a long time, the play was read as autobiographical. For Boy-Żeleński, for instance, Walpurg's tirade about the machine in his head expresses "the most dramatic state of the soul of this poet-painter-thinker [i.e. Witkacy], possessed as he is with the fury of creation, the fury of thinking".[254] Emil Breiter, who believed Witkacy had no talent for playwriting, suggested:

> It seems that [Witkacy] has a complex that is mercilessly pushing him in one direction – towards self-definition. This is why psychological analyses [...] suggest that each of his plays is a monologue into which he has dumped so many oddities that it is difficult to guess. – To guess what? Obviously, the psyche of the playwright, who is always the protagonist of the action on stage. His personality and psychology are certainly very interesting, rich and complex. An outstandingly artistic individual. But this is not enough to build a new theatre from such material [...].[255]

At the lunatic asylum called "At the Sign of the Jugged Hare," Walpurg is first under the care of Dr Jan Bidello, a "Non-Freudian psychiatrist" who prescribes a pharmacological treatment.[256] When it fails, the patient is sent to the psychoanalyst Dr Ephraim Grün. According to the character list he is a 32-year-old "swarthy cherub in the Semitic style" (p. 11) and a "psychoanalyst of the Freudian school" (*Ibid.*). His methods, however, are as unorthodox as Witkacy's own treatment with Karol de Beaurain. In order to resolve Walpurg's "complex" (p. 13), Grün engages a nun who must try and get through to "the dark spot in his soul, the forgotten place, the 'psychic wound,' as they say" (p. 13). The madman, who had not seen a woman in two years, seduces the young nun. At first, this appears to benefit them both, since her life choices were motivated by the same loss as the poet's: she, too, had lost a lover. After a night together, Walpurg declares that he wants "to get out of here, write, work, shave off my beard and moustache, dress well again" (p. 20). He wants "to live, to live a

254 T. Boy-Żeleński, *Flirt z Melpomeną: Wieczór siódmy i ósmy* (Warsaw: PIW, 1964) (*Pisma*, vol. 22), p. 84.

255 E. Breiter, "Teatry Warszawskie", *Ś* 1926, no. 23, p. 12.

256 S. I. Witkiewicz, *The Madman and the Nun and Other Plays*, p. 11. The psychoanalyst who treats Athanasius Bazakbal, the protagonist of *Farewell to Autumn*, carries the same name.

perfectly ordinary life" (p. 20); the nun expresses a similar desire. Now he is prepared to undergo analysis, which is supposed to confirm Grün's initial hypothesis that the poet suffers from "a twin sister complex dating back to the time when he was still an embryo" (p. 23):

> GRÜN:– Walpurg, what's the first thing you associate with "sister"?
> WALPURG [...]:– Sinister – a cave – two orphans on a desert island – Vere Stacpoole's novel *Blue Lagoon*.
> GRÜN:– Can you follow all that, Sister? The cave is the mother's womb. So is the desert island. I've resolved his complex. Now, on the second level, the novel – by the way, Sister, have you read it? – has penetrated into his already developed psychic placenta. Walpurg, in two weeks' time you'll be fit as a fiddle. (p. 23)

The plot takes a tragic turn when Grün frees the madman from his straitjacket and hands him a pencil so he can write poetry. Walpurg jams the pencil into Bidello's temple, killing him just as he was mocking psychoanalysis; the madman then tells Grün that the gesture was a manifestation of "a healthy instinct for life" (*Ibid.*) and that it was necessary for him to play out his inner conflict: "First I identified him with my sister, and then I killed them both with one blow. I'm sure she died at that very moment" (*ibid.*). Grün accepts this explanation. At first he is thrilled about the patient, who "resolved his complex all by himself, just as easy as falling out of bed" (p. 24), but then he recalls having read about a similar case in Jung. "His patient became a model husband and an excellent architect after he butchered his aunt when she came to visit him. He had an aunt complex, and he resolved it. Psychoanalysis alone enabled him to do that" (p. 25). Grün already envisions describing Walpurg's case in a book-length study that would secure his fame; after all, the "old psychiatric school" (*Ibid.*) refuses to acknowledge that "dementia praecox [...] can in fact be cured by resolving complexes" (p. 26). But now the patient disappoints him, allowing himself to be caught in an erotic encounter with the nun:

> Put him in the straitjacket! I'll show him! He concealed from me a complex I didn't know about. And he pretended that he had a sister complex. But there must be repressed truth even in lies. That's Freud's fundamental position. (p. 28)

Walpurg, feeling threatened, commits suicide by hanging himself using his straitjacket. "We've lost our guinea pig" (p. 29), Grün says with regret. But one question remains: "Did he die a sick man, or was this, so to speak, the final action of a sick man whereby he would have become cured? Or perhaps he hanged himself already cured? That would be dreadful!" (*Ibid.*)

The final scene suggests Walpurg's victory over the psychoanalyst. With the poet's dead body still hanging from a window crate, a resurrected Walpurg, shaved and well dressed, goes into town with Bidello (also restored to life) and the nun (in an evening gown). Before leaving, Walpurg locks the analyst in a cell and utters a mocking farewell: "Keep well, Grün. And after this, analyse yourself thoroughly" (p. 30). But the ending can also be read as the opposite of what it seems to be at first sight – the poet leaves defeated, having encountered that "something worse" announced in the play's subtitle ("There is Nothing Bad Which Could Not Turn into Something Worse"): he has been cured, i.e. normalised, forced into a socially acceptable form and deprived of the source of his creativity (his latest poem is embarrassingly bad).[257] He appears to be alive, but in fact, Walpurg is essentially dead when he declares that he is "really completely sane now: sane and happy".[258] This explains the presence of his dead body, which, in the final scene, is pulled into the melee during the clinic assistants' collective punishment of Grün. Jan Błoński proposes another interpretation: since neither psychoanalysis nor traditional psychiatry can solve Walpurg's riddle or stop his murderous impulse, the ending must include "two Walpurgs, one for the traditional psychiatrist, the other for the psychoanalyst".[259]

Thanks to Janusz Degler, the interwar reception history of Witkacy's play is well known. *The Madman and the Nun*, completed in January 1923, was published in *Skamander* two years later.[260] Prior to its appearance in print it was premiered at the Teatr Miejski in Toruń. The ambitious new artistic director, Mieczysław Szpakiewicz, directed it himself on 26 April 1924. But Szpakiewicz's courage had certain limits: fearing a backlash from clerical circles, he changed the play's title to

257 Such a reading is proposed by E. Łubieniewska in *Czysta forma i bebechy*, p. 92. See also M. Skwara, *Motyw szaleństwa w twórczości Witkacego i Conrada: Studium porównawcze* (Wrocław: Uniwersytet Wrocławski, 1999), p. 224.

258 S. I. Witkiewicz, *The Madman and the Nun and Other Plays*, p. 30.

259 J. Błoński, *Witkacy na zawsze*, p. 338.

260 *S* 1925, no. 39, pp. 160–181.

"Wariat i pielęgniarka" (The Madman and the Nurse), introducing corresponding changes in the plot. What is more, the number of spectators was limited; the upper balconies were blocked off, and no tickets were sold to school and university students or soldiers.

The premiere was a success. There was a large crowd and the playwright was called to the stage and applauded several times. Still, the performance was repeated only twice more (on 29 April and 2 May).[261] The psychoanalyst was played by Wacław Malinowski, who had previously directed Witkacy's *W małym dworku* [*Country House*]. Sadly, little is known about the acting or the overall staging idea; only two journals – *Głos Robotnika* and *Słowo Pomorskie* – published reviews, and these were all but cursory.[262] Based on these two reviews, Jan Degler suggests that the director probably aimed at a realistic acting style, instructing the cast to get into character.[263] Both reviewers praised Malinowski's facial expressions and characterisation as well as the way he embodied the transition from grotesqueness to tragedy in the final scene.

A year later, on 21 March 1925, the play was staged by an amateur troupe in Zakopane. In this version, too, the nun was substituted. Witkacy himself supervised the actors; he also designed the scenery and costumes. The production did not fare well. Local audiences disliked it; what is more, disagreements led to a split within the troupe, and it soon disbanded.

It is apparent that theatre directors were concerned about negative reactions from church authorities, but this alone does not predict how Witkacy's plays, or indeed psychoanalysis, were received in Poland. In fact, one representative of the clergy, Father Henryk Kazimierowicz, was a great admirer of Witkacy's plays.[264] This remarkable man merits a closer examination. Born in Warsaw in 1896, Kazimierowicz studied at the Theological Seminary in Włocławek, where he was ordained shortly after World War I. He continued his studies in Lublin and Warsaw, eventually

---

261 Cf. J. Degler, "Noty do dramatów", in S. I. Witkiewicz, *Dzieła zebrane: Dramaty*, vol. 3, p. 636.

262 *GR* 1924, no. 62, p. 4, and Sato [Z. Święcicka-Guzowska], *SPM* 1924, no. 104, p. 3–4. For Witkacy's response to the latter review see "Wariat i pielęgniarka i pani Sato", *PTIM* 1924, no. 4, p. 2.

263 J. Degler, *Witkacy w teatrze międzywojennym*, p. 70.

264 Despite Kazimierowicz's remarkably positive references to psychoanalysis, Paweł Dybel, discussing the Catholic Church's aversion to Freud, mentions him as one of the writers of "philippics of holy indignation, intended to put off all potential followers of psychoanalysis". See P. Dybel, *Urwane ścieżki*, pp. 40–41.

obtaining a doctorate in philosophy and theology in Rome in 1923. On his return to Poland, his unruly character and "immoderate desire to study"[265] caused conflicts with the church authorities. Kazimierowicz was transferred from one parish to another. He was also chastised for his eccentric behaviour, recklessness, a thoughtlessness that led to various gaffes as well as his enthusiasm for the latest trends in painting and poetry.[266]

Kazimierowicz was parish priest successively in Łachnów, Stolin, Mielnik, Śledzianow and Brest-on-the-Bug (now Belarus). In 1936, he returned to the Diocese of Włoclawek; first he was entrusted with the parish of Bronisław, then Tłokinia, where he published a weekly newspaper. Between 1931 and 1934, he wrote for *Przegląd Katolicki*. Some of his articles in this Catholic magazine concern psychoanalysis: "Katolicyzm w świetle psychoanalizy" [Catholicism in the Light of Psychoanalysis] was also published as a separate pamphlet;[267] "Psychoanaliza w konfesjonale" [Psychoanalysis in the Confessional],[268] meanwhile, was announced as part of a monograph titled *Psychoanaliza w zastosowaniu duszpasterskim* [Psychoanalysis Applied to Pastoral Care]. I was not able to retrieve any publication of that title; perhaps it never saw the light of day. Father Józef Pastuszka's response in *Ateneum Kapłańskie* indicates that in general priests were unlikely to share Kazimierowicz's interest in psychoanalysis.[269]

An account of Kazimierowicz's time in Mielnik can be found in the London-based *Wiadomości*. In 1971, a certain Jerzy Pieńkowski, describes his encounter with the parish priest:

> He was short, unimposing, his face badly scarred by smallpox and scruffy, he wore horn-rimmed glasses, a cassock like a Cambridge student's gown, sleeves torn, trousers in tatters [...]. His study – a large room with black cases, about a metre long, piled along the walls all the way up to the

265 S. Librowski, *Ofiary zbrodni niemieckiej spośród duchowieństwa diecezji wrocławskiej 1939–1945* (Włocławek: Księgarnia Powszechna, 1947), pp. 61–62.

266 For a reconstruction of the conflicts on the basis of archived material at the diocesan curia of Włoclawek see Marta Skwara, "Kim był ksiądz Henryk Kazimierowicz", in *Szczecińskie Witkacjana* (Szczecin: Książnica Pomorska, 1999), pp. 32–54.

267 H. Kazimierowicz, "Katolicyzm w świetle psychoanalizy", *PK* 1931, nos 29–31; H. Kazimierowicz, *Katolicyzm w świetle psychoanalizy* (Warsaw: [no publisher], 1932).

268 H. Kazimierowicz, "Psychoanaliza w konfesjonale", *PK* 1932, nos 30–34.

269 J. Pastuszka, "Psychoanaliza", *AK* 1933, no. 31, pp. 105–121. I discussed this text in Part VI, chapter 2, "Introduction to Psychoanalysis".

> ceiling, in one corner there was a couch, separated from the rest of the room by a double wall of cases, and above the couch a futuristic Christ by [Jerzy] Hulewicz, no less. In the middle there was a long table covered with papers and books [...]. I was quite well-read for a young landowner at that time, so we had things to talk about, and when the priest found out that I had read [Witkacy's] *The Pragmatists* and knew who Freud was, the ice broke; my visit ended in the morning and was the beginning of a very close friendship.[270]

Pieńkowski repeatedly highlights Kazimierowicz's two passions, describing him as "enthusiastic about the avant-garde and an avid Freudian" (*Ibid.*). He also recalls that one summer, the priest gave lectures to the holiday makers at the Pieńkowskis' guest house. There were "two excellent presentations, one on Freud, the other on Witkacy's plays, and both raised a furore" (*Ibid.*).

Kazimierowicz is also described by Witkacy's wife, Jadwiga Witkiewicz. She remembers "a priest looking rather unkempt" who visited their flat on Bracka Street in Warsaw in 1932:

> He had read all of Staś's [Witkacy's] plays that existed in print – which weren't many – and was eager to get to know the rest, claiming that he had never read anything as amazing. Staś was very reluctant to part with manuscripts or copies of his plays, but Father Kazimierowicz turned out to be such an enthusiast that eventually Staś agreed to lend him a few plays at each visit, which the priest would return after typing them out [...]. In this way, Father Kazimierowicz came to have a set of Staś's plays at home [...].[271]

Recognisant of Witkacy's generosity, the priest invited him to Stolina in Polesia, where, in June 1932, an amateur group of parishioners was to perform *Wariat i zakonnica* under his direction. The playwright came, and, what is more, he gave a lecture titled "Dlaczego powieść nie jest dziełem Sztuki Czystej" [Why the Novel is not a Work of Pure Art] at the local Science Circle of the Catholic Intelligentsia (Koło Naukowe Inteligencji

270 J. Pieńkowski, "Ksiądz i Witkacy", *W* 1971, no. 41, p. 3.

271 J. Witkiewiczowa, "Wspomnienia o Stanisławie Ignacym Witkiewiczu", in *Spotkanie z Witkacym*, ed. by J. Degler (Jelenia Góra: Teatr im. Cypriana Kamila Norwida, 1979), p. 94.

Katolickiej). The unlikely friendship between Father Kazimierowicz and Witkacy lasted for several years and included intense correspondence.[272]

Besides the unusual performance organised by Kazimierowicz, the last staging of *Wariat i zakonnica* before World War II took place in 1926, when Arnold Szyfman was in charge of Warsaw's Teatr Mały. Szyfman was not afraid to challenge his actors, who had refused, two months previously, to perform in Witkacy's *Tumor Mózgowicz*. Directed by Karol Borowski, *Wariat i zakonnica* opened two weeks after the May Coup, on 28 May 1926. Another play by Witkacy, *Nowe wyzwolenie* [*The New Deliverance*], was performed as part of the same show. It was billed for two weeks and was sold out; the final performance took place on 13 June, responding to popular demand. The show turned out to be a major event for the capital's cultural elite as well as one of the most commercially successful productions of the season.[273]

Most reviews were positive to euphoric.[274] Boy-Żeleński wrote in *Kurier Poranny*: "Perhaps Witkiewicz [Witkacy] has not yet said his last word in the theatre; still, I do not hesitate to declare him one of the strongest and most original dramatic talents – and not only within Poland."[275] He also writes: "Here an enormous talent is erupting from the stage, something absolutely new is coming to be, and from now on it would be a crime on the part of our theatres not to let this man express himself fully" (pp. 87–88). Some of Witkacy's former critics, such as Adolf Nowaczyński for instance, now called him a genius, while sceptics applauded what they saw as his departure from the theory of Pure Form – supposedly a concession to the audience's sense of good taste.[276] In this context, a remark by Wiktor Brumer is exemplary: "Let us hope he frees himself entirely from his dazzling but unrealistic theory, and the Polish theatre will no doubt gain a great and brilliant writer."[277] Disparaging reviews appeared in the right-wing journals *Polska Zbrojna* and *Myśl*

272 Only few of these letters survive. They were edited and published by Marta Skwara in *Szczecińskie Witkacjana*, pp. 38–54.

273 J. Degler, *Witkacy w teatrze międzywojennym*, p. 112.

274 Cf. J. Lorentowicz, *EXP* 1926, no. 150; A. Nowaczyński, *GWP* 1926, no. 145; J. Frühling, *KPL* 1926, no. 150; T. Kończyc, *KW* 1926, no. 145.

275 T. Boy-Żeleński, *Flirt z Melpomeną*, p. 85.

276 Listing his theatrical works, Witkacy himself describes this piece as more realistic than based on the theory of Pure Form. See S. I. Witkiewicz, "Spis sztuk" in *Teatr i inne pisma o teatrze*, ed. by J. Degler (Warsaw: PIW, 1995), pp. 267–269.

277 W. Brumer, *DPL* 1926, no. 124, p. 5.

Narodowa.[278] Among the more influential critics, only Antoni Słonimski, writing for *Wiadomości Literackie*, expressed reservations:

> Both of Witkiewicz's plays go so much against my subjective notion of literature that only the playwright's undeniably great intelligence and the fact that he must have strained his brain very much, plus his large dose of demonic humour, induce me to take these trivial sketches seriously.[279]

Słonimski concludes by describing *Wariat i zakonnica* as "a boring satire on Freud" (*Ibid.*).

The label of "a satire on Freud" became attached to the performance and to the play itself, regardless of how it was assessed. For instance, Jakub Appenszlak, the editor-in-chief of *Nasz Przegląd*, applauded Witkacy as "the only true revolutionary" in Polish theatre, and a writer of "uncommon, flourishing talent". At the same time, he asserts that *Wariat i zakonnica* is "a brilliant, and formally almost conventional, satire on psychoanalysis".[280] For him, the piece only presents "an example of psychoanalytic therapy in which smug doctors are pilloried with a kind of humour that is almost Molièresque" (*ibid.*). Appenszlak, who often promoted Freud's ideas, cautions his readers:

> It is, of course, irrelevant in how far Witkiewicz's position on psycho-analysis is valid. Psychoanalysts would be ill-advised to attack him now from their position of learning. The interesting thing here is the impetus to challenge a certain intellectual trend; what is impressive is the satire's sharpness and virulence, and what is puzzling is this mental exuberance that makes Walpurg go crazy. (*Ibid.*)

For Władysław Zawistowski, a reviewer at *Nowy Kurier Polski*, the play was "clearly a satire where the grotesque becomes a parody of a medical drama from the Grand-Guignol".[281] Boy-Żeleński agrees that "there is something of the grand-guignol in this theatre of horrors, but a grand-guignol whose puppets are played by a smart and wickedly funny artist".[282] This comparison

278 *PZ* 1926, no. 145, p. 5; *MNR* 1926, no. 24, pp. 346–347.

279 *WL* 1926, no. 23, p. 4.

280 *NPR* 1926, no. 148, p. 5.

281 Władysław Zawistowski, [no title; review in the theatre section "Dookoła teatru"] *NKP* 1926, no. 122, p. 9.

282 T. Boy-Żeleński, *Flirt z Melpomeną*, pp. 85–86.

echoes one by literary scholar Jan Błoński: "Walpurg's melodramatic romance with Anna is intertwined with a mockery of psychoanalysis (i.e. with a comedy à thèse), only to coalesce in the finale, which comes straight out of the grand-guignol, the Parisian theatre of horrors".[283] Karol Borowski's staging was one of the main reasons why this view became established. According to Degler's reconstruction, the director "had the play performed at a frenetic pace, buffo-style like in a typical farce, multiplying anti-naturalistic effects and comic gags to intensify its fantastic and grotesque atmosphere".[284] Also part of this concept was Janusz Warnecki's over-the-top acting style; his exaggerated gestures in the role of Grün are captured in the few surviving stills from the performance, and they are pointed up in many reviews. The production also seems to have endowed the doctor with stereotypically Jewish features, following the playwright's descriptions in the character list. Witkacy comments:

> In *Wariat i zakonnica* I took the type of an uncritical and not too intelligent psychoanalyst of Jewish origin because this, with the exception of the last characteristic, was an absolute necessity on account of the madman. In the director's and the critics' flawed interpretation of the play, this turned into an anti-Semitic satire on psychoanalysis. I solemnly declare [...] that I am not and never have been an anti-Semite by creed.[285]

Wariat i zakonnica was also read as a satire on Freudianism by Witkacy's longtime opponent, Karol Irzykowski.[286] While most reviewers presented

283 J. Błoński, *Witkacy na zawsze*, p. 322.

284 J. Degler, *Witkacy w teatrze międzywojennym*, p. 120.

285 S. I. Witkiewicz, "Beznadziejne porachunki z niepowrotnej przeszłości", *ZT* 1934–35, nos 18–20, cited in *Teatr i inne pisma o teatrze*, p. 354.

286 In the late 1920s, Irzykowski published his book *Walka o treść* [Fight for Content], which includes a detailed critique of Witkacy's theory of Pure Form The two writers had already argued about the state of the theatre before. Commenting on a survey about Polish dramaturgy carried out by the weekly magazine *Świat*, Irzykowski stated in 1923 (positioning himself against Formism), that the current crisis of the theatre was due to its growing similarity with film: the abandonment of the dramatic plot, the director's growing power, the "cult of the bagatelle" and "the supremacy of the actor over the author" (see K. Irzykowski, "Uwagi o tzw. upadku twórczości dramatycznej w Polsce", *SCP* 1923, nos 4–6). Witkacy replied that Poland, dominated by realist ideology, had not yet seen any artistic dramatic creation (see S. I. Witkiewicz, "Krytyka artykułu Karola Irzykowskiego pt. 'Uwagi na temat tzw. upadku twórczości dramatycznej'", *EIS* 1924, no. 3–6. For Irzykowski's last word see: "W odpowiedzi S. I. Witkiewiczowi", *EIS* 1924, no. 8/9).

Wariat i zakonnica as an excellent and hilarious parody of psychoanalytic therapy, Irzykowski proposed that although Witkacy had tried to write "something like a satire on psychoanalysis," he failed in fact to "go beyond simple mockery". What is more, Grün, the discipline's representative, "appears like a downright idiot".[287] Irzykowski, an expert on Freudianism, admitted that this theory was perfectly suited for comedy, but it should have been done quite differently:

> If, for example, [the nun] were to really question the madman, if he, pretending to be mad, were to answer her so skilfully that she fell in love with him and even Grün would be seduced. But this would require actual accomplishment, detailed elaboration, which involves meticulous and diligent writing, and perhaps Witkiewicz, in accordance with his theory, looks down on that as an outdated psychological method. His method is the fashionable "shortcut," which – the way he applies it – does not shorten anything at all, it only brutalises life, and it is somewhat schematic and dry. (*Ibid.*)

Ten years down the line, a comedy just like the one imagined by Irzykowski was indeed staged in Warsaw. Antoni Cwojdziński's *Freuda teoria snów* [Freud's Theory of Dreams], which I will discuss in detail, harnesses the comedic potential inherent in Freudianism – especially the method of unmasking hidden intentions. It speaks to the man in the street (providing an enjoyable education on Freud's theory) as well as to the educated reader. Still, Irzykowski did not approve. Perhaps it was just too popular.

Witkacy tried many times to counter such opinions. Even ten years after the premiere he wrote:

> If I had wanted to criticise psychoanalysis or satirise it, I would have written a pamphlet; having plenty of space and not being constrained by the form of a play, and not being concerned with theatre at all, only with psychoanalysis, I would have been able to "meticulously" present dialogues which on stage would take up 48 hours. In a play, life is presented in abbreviated form for artistic purposes [...].[288]

287 K. Irzykowski, "Sprawozdanie teatralne", *R* 1926, no. 148, reprinted in *Pisma teatralne* (Cracow: Wydawnictwo Literackie, 1995), vol. 1: 1896–1926, pp. 541–542.

288 S. I. Witkiewicz, "Beznadziejne porachunki z niepowrotnej przeszłości", p. 354.

Witkacy quotes his character Dr Bidello to define his own views on Freud's work: "As far as psychoanalysis is concerned, I acknowledge its diagnostic techniques, but have no confidence whatsoever in its therapeutic value. It is fine for those people who can devote their entire lives to being cured".[289]

Indeed, Witkiewicz – who had expressed major reservations about psychoanalysis when he was treated by Karol de Beaurain, the "wild analyst" from Zakopane in 1912 – fundamentally changed his mind about it in the 1920s. This can be seen in *Niemyte dusze* [Unwashed Souls], written in 1936. This work, which remained unpublished (with the exception of a few passages printed in *Skawa* in 1938/39) until the 1970s, was dedicated to the memory of de Beaurain.[290] Besides repaying his debt to his friend and psychiatrist in the extensive dedication quoted above, Witkacy also claims that he earned the right to utter painful truths because he had undergone a thorough analysis himself. That said, he does not believe that de Beaurain succeeded in curing him, which is perhaps a good thing:

> If I had "resolved" (as the psychoanalysts say) all my complexes, I would probably have had to give up work in my specialities, i.e., in literature,

---

289 S. I. Witkiewicz, *The Madman and the Nun and Other Plays*, p. 13.

290 This dedication was cited before:
"I owe my familiarity with Freud's method [...] to a friend of my parents (who was in a sense also my friend, despite the age difference), Dr Karol de Beaurain, to whom I dedicate this work with profound gratitude, respect, admiration and affection. For many years I had failed to appreciate what he, perhaps the first pioneer of Freud's ideas in our country, had indirectly done for me. Having taken an interest in my dreams in 1912, he offered me a systematic "practical course" in psychoanalysis, which I accepted enthusiastically as a "novelty" of sorts; but I approached this experiment with some suspiciousness and a critical attitude. At present I shan't go into detail about the course of the "treatment," which, incidentally, was not meant to cure me of any concrete ailment, since – notwithstanding the opinion of Rita Sacchetto (the first wife of the sculptor August Zamoyski), who always refers to me as "dieser geisteskranke W." [this deranged W.] – I am quite sane. I believe Dr de Beaurain was quite fond of me, but I was also an interesting "guinea pig" [...] and what is more, this exceptional man, who remains under-appreciated by his compatriots, wanted to give me something of himself, of his deep understanding of humanity and of life, enhanced a hundredfold by the mighty apparatus of the theory of Freud, who does not always receive the recognition he deserves as one of the greatest geniuses and humanity's benefactors in our era". (S. I. Witkiewicz, *Narkotyki*, pp. 191-192).

> painting, and philosophy, or at least change its nature radically – stop being myself to some degree.[291]

Like many writers who hesitated to undergo psychoanalytical therapy, Witkacy assumed that "all work known pompously as 'creative' stems from complexes which have not been disentangled and that it dies down once they are resolved, the way a mountain stream dries up in its riverbed in summer" (p. 311). For "people considered 'normal'" (p. 312), however, psychoanalysis could only be beneficial, provided they were treated by a competent specialist:

> In fact, it is easy enough to pry into someone's psyche, but the real trick is to ease his suffering and make a proper synthesis of the exploratory analytical work. It was just this part of the programme that I did not pursue to the very end with Dr de Beaurain, for reasons beyond our control, and that is perhaps why my psychoanalysis (so far) did not have as beneficial an effect on me as in principle one might have expected. This was made clear by certain events in my life that happened immediately afterward and that for many years distracted my attention from this field; and when I took it up again intellectually, it was rather in a somewhat ironic manner, which is immediately evident even in some of my plays. But it is not true that I ever totally disparaged psychoanalysis, as has been imputed to me along with anti-Semitism and god knows what else. (p. 312)

Statements such as this allow Witkacy to preempt accusations of hypocrisy or opportunism in his paeans to psychoanalysis in *Niemyte dusze*. He admits that for a long time he had disregarded the fact that his psychoanalyst taught him the art of introspection and interpretation that makes Freud both a genius and a benefactor of humanity.

It is remarkable that Witkacy's renewed interest in psychoanalysis was sparked by his reading of Ernst Kretschmer's *Körperbau und Character* [*Physique and Character*]. The "unwashed souls" in the title are souls that

291 S. I. Witkiewicz, *The Witkiewicz Reader*, trans. by Daniel Gerould (London: Quartet Books, 1993), p. 311. This reader contains a translation of a short section of *Niemyte dusze* [Unwashed Souls]. In this study, quotations from *Niemyte dusze* that have not found their way into this reader are presented in T. Bhambry's translation with references to the Polish edition.

have not been "made aware," "Freudianised and Kretschmerised" (p. 210). For Witkacy, Freud and Kretschmer are two thinkers of the same rank:

> From Kretschmer we learn roughly in which pigeonhole we belong and under what number to look for to locate ourselves; what we gain from Freud is a deeper understanding about who we are in a dynamic sense, in the very progress of events: what are our inner dangers and pitfalls, where we risk deviating, becoming insincere or collapsing. From this we gain a clear sense of ourselves and of others, and certainly an ability to take control of our lives more consciously and rationally than we could do before our "soul-washing," when most of the time we were just playthings of bovine emotions, especially where life's most important issues were concerned, the ones on which everything else is based. (p. 216)

The first chapter of Witkacy's book presents Kretschmer's assumptions, i.e. the classification of humans into schizoids and endomorphs. The second chapter outlines "the general principles of Freud's theory," although the author states openly that he never finished the *Introduction to Psychoanalysis*, which "is unfortunately not a good book to disseminate the author's wonderful main idea: from the beginning, it is too boring and long-winded" (p. 212).[292] His only source, therefore, was "a practical course" completed twenty-four years before with Dr de Beaurain.

One interesting aspect here is Witkacy's definition of what he calls "the subconscious" [*podświadomość*]. He warns his readers against hypostasising it, which risks turning psychoanalysis into "a sort of metaphysics and mythology". Such a tendency can be observed in "some of the psychoanalysts" (p. 232). In his view, this part of the psyche should no be seen as a separate entity; there is no strict boundary between consciousness and the unconscious. Referring to Hans Cornelius' notion of the unnoticeable background, Witkacy proposes that content which remains subconscious represents an unnoticeable backdrop, like film music, and therefore it does not exist apart but "in the way it affects conscious content" (p. 223). Freud's most important achievement, in his view, is that he developed a way for us to free ourselves of "subterranean and sexual currents" and "their dark, uncontrollable effects" (p. 217). Once we understand the

---

292 Instead of Freud, Witkacy recommends the short book by Geraldine Coster, *Psychoanalysis for Normal People*; Maria Górska's Polish translation, *Psychoanaliza w zastosowaniu do ludzi normalnych*, was published in 1927.

mechanisms of sublimation, we can apply them to our own ends: the processes that had been taking place unconsciously now become "transformers" subjected to our will. Similarly, analysing complexes can free us from slavery to "stunted reactions, pent-up reflexes, repressed feelings, long-forgotten spectres" (p. 226). It was Freud, "the great hero of the subterranean thickets of the human soul," who gave us "a weapon against the monsters and reptiles that secretly inhabit our cellars and basements, poisoning the upper floors of our [...] truly amazing spirit" (*Ibid.*).

Witkacy dedicates a separate chapter to the inferiority complex. Naturally, he refers to Adler, although he does not seem to be entirely aware of the methodological differences between these two trends within psychoanalysis; he admits with characteristic disdain that he is "unfamiliar with Adler's main work," while the Polish translation of *Menschenkenntnis* [*Znajomość natury ludzkiej*] struck him as "so primitive" that he could not get through the book (p. 234). The theory of the inferiority complex, however, seems to him an apt description of the Polish national character. Witkacy avows that psychoanalysis allowed him to develop a less emotional approach to Polish history, which had always made him feel shame and indignation. It is noteworthy that his views on the demise of the First Polish Republic have much in common with the Cracow school of Polish historiography.[293] For Witkacy, the nobles' democracy resulted in the typically Polish hubris and hypocrisy: "this is a poorly resolved mass inferiority complex, i.e. a subconscious sense of one's own inferiority, combined with consciously puffing oneself up to the desired level, and it takes the place of taking relevant action in real life".[294] The enduring wish to appear better than others, false ambition, the desire to impress, as well as a reluctance to face the truth, internal falsity and mental laziness – these are not only the sources of all of Poland's calamities but also the characteristics that mark the Second Polish Republic. Boozing, dance halls (Witkacy's great peeve), bridge and the radio – these were ways of dealing with "the unpleasant subconscious sense of one's own smallness" (*ibid.*), a

293 The Cracow school of history emerged in the second half of the nineteenth century; its key figures were Jozef Szujski, Stanislaw Smolka and Michal Bobrzynski. They attributed the decline of the Polish-Lithuanian Commonwealth to its internal instability; in their view, a defective social structure with no hierarchy prevented the emergence of lasting power. For a discussion of Witkacy's opinions on this issue see M. Król, "Polska w twórczości St. I. Witkiewicza", in *Studia o Stanisławie Ignacym Witkiewiczu*, pp. 301–315.

294 S. I. Witkiewicz, *Teatr i inne pisma o teatrze*, p. 369.

modern version of the forays and duels of the past. Witkacy hopes that his book may help raise awareness of the Poles' complex of "puffed up idlers" (p. 279) so that this complex could be resolved.

The pessimism inherent in Witkacy's worldview has been discussed many times.[295] What is pointed out less frequently is its emancipatory potential. At a time when Freud himself had lost faith in the therapeutic effectiveness of his method and its potential to bring about significant social change, Witkacy steadfastly continued to believe that Polish society could be restored to health through psychoanalysis. Progress, he continues, would be achieved if everyone became "thoroughly cleansed" after having gained a "deep understanding of this book" (p. 311). He encourages his readers to urge others to seek the benefits of analysis, even if they resisted. His wife recalls that he did the same:

> [He] kept accusing his friends and acquaintances of not doing enough self-analysis, telling them that if they resolved their "complexes" they would be able to avoid many misunderstandings [...] and their lives would become much easier and more pleasant. Around 1930 he even wrote the so-called "morning song" about this: "Analyse yourself at once, I say – If not immediately, but by the way. And if you don't, and if you don't, you are a lazy mastodont".[296]

Witkacy goes so far as to tell his readers to take others to task for their complexes, if necessary "with the help of terrible, positively inquisitorial psychoanalyses;"[297] his book contains two exemplary scenarios, calling readers to apply them each time that an interlocutor betrays a complex. He boasts about his own success:

> Not long ago I saw a fellow who for two years had behaved like a pig towards me, refused to acknowledge this, lied to himself, hurled insults at Freud and generally put up a fight like an anteater pressed against a wall.

295 See e.g. M. Szpakowska, *Światopogląd St. I. Witkiewicza* (Wrocław: Zakład Narodowy im. Ossolińskich, 1976); B. Danek-Wojnowska, *Stanisław Ignacy Witkiewicz a modernizm: Kształtowanie idei katastroficznych* (Wrocław: Zakład Narodowy im. Ossolińskich, 1976); L. Gawor, *Katastrofizm konsekwentny: O poglądach Mariana Zdziechowskiego i Stanisława Ignacego Witkiewicza* (Lublin: UMCS, 1998).

296 J. Witkiewiczowa, "Wspomnienia o Stanisławie Ignacym Witkiewiczu", p. 102. The lyrics of the song are originally in English.

297 S. I. Witkiewicz, *Narkotyki. Niemyte dusze*, p. 353.

> Today he is an admirer of Freud, to whom (along with me, indirectly) he owes his new life; he is not resisting anymore, he is now on his path towards perfection. (pp. 311–312)

Freud's opponents may see his method as "a needless wallowing in muck," but for Witkacy, refusing to undergo psychoanalysis is akin to not wanting to "wipe one's ass after going to the toilet" (pp. 324–325).

> The well-known principle, "don't touch it or it'll stink" is being applied too often in our country. Without mucking it up, we must scratch and pick at everything, unless we want to turn, in no time, into a society of mental failures, of psychological and social shitheads. (p. 325)

Given the "mass and individual hypocrisy," however, a slow and careful approach is needed: "our society would not be able to cope if all of Poland were to be set right suddenly and unexpectedly" (p. 328). The basic prerequisite to analyse another person is of course a thorough self-analysis and ridding ourselves of pride (p. 312).

Many passages in *Niemyte dusze* deal with the ways in which psychoanalysis has replaced religion:

> Few people can manage without psychoanalysis today, just as in the past few were able to live without confidences and confessions – to unload one's subconscious and to disentangle its seemingly hopeless knots is a necessity. The means to achieve this are provided by the Great Confessor of Humanity, Sigmund Freud. (p. 226)

Witkacy calls psychoanalysis a "redemption" for our times:

> Everything has its limits, we have performed miracles, but we cannot rush on like this, because that risks ending in a disaster: the unleashed changes in external conditions are overwhelming the plasticity of our bodies and organs so much that the whole may collapse into primordial nothingness, into spiritual darkness, which amounts to the darkness of a totemistic clan – a darkness from which back then, long ago, there was only one single exit – through authority and the suffering of the masses to the heights of today's civilisation. But we cannot go on in circles like this forever. (p. 227)

For Witkacy, the history of civilisation has reached a breakpoint:

> [We are at] the limits of how much the human central system can endure in relation to the demands of modern civilisation. We are, I believe, not far from the tipping point and we must consider how best to defend ourselves against the impending catastrophe [...]. There is nothing that can relieve us from dealing with this as intensively as possible right now. (p. 228)

Witkacy explains why it is exactly at this moment in history – a time marked by disenchantment, alienation, oppressive market economy and mob rule – that Freud is so urgently needed:

> Someone may say that it can only be a complete lack of values that allows writing about such things at a time when the world is falling apart, when a gang of degenerate emanations of a tumour in the putrefying pseudo-democratic system are perpetrating, in the name of dead or dying fictions, horrendous lawlessness against millions of people. I swear, this is not the case – these problems are damn important, and the failure to resolve them will lead to the poisoning of valuable individuals within any social structure. (p. 317)

It is time, therefore, "to punch them in the faces, to scrub their foul mugs and give their heads a good shaking, to bang their shitty heads against the walls of a pigsty as best we can, because really, when things begin to happen that surpass our present epoch [...] what they'll find may be not a nation any longer, but a pile of liquid decay" (p. 281).

A quarter of a century after his unfinished psychoanalytical therapy in Zakopane, Witkacy apparently begins to resemble the demonic psychoanalyst he created in his play *Wariat i zakonnica* in 1923. According to his own statement, he was sceptical and tended to agree with his character Dr Bidello, the conventional psychiatrist. In *Niemyte dusze*, however, it is Dr Grün's ecstatic profession of faith that could have been reprinted verbatim to represent Witkacy's personal opinion: "Only psychoanalysis will free mankind from the atrocious nightmare of the lunatic asylum. What I'm saying is that prisons would be empty if every one – from childhood on – were subjected to compulsory analysis which would eradicate all complexes."[298]

298 S. I. Witkiewicz, *The Madman and the Nun and Other Plays*, pp. 22-23.

The fact that the Warsaw premiere of *Wariat i zakonnica* inspired so many theatre critics to focus on the question of psychoanalysis was an irritation to Stefania Zahorska. Right at the outset of her article "Psychoanaliza i Teatr Mały" [Psychoanalysis and Teatr Mały] in *Nowy Kurier Polski* she claims that her intention is not to make a case for Freud:

> I am by no means defending psychoanalysis, which the Teatr Mały condemned with devastating force when they staged Witkiewicz's play *Wariat i zakonnica* [...].
> I am not defending it, because that would be a long overdue and therefore ridiculous thing to do. Twenty or thirty years ago there were so many adventurous opponents of psychoanalysis, while its adventurous defenders were rare and precious; today, however, it can afford simply to ignore its opponents if their arguments are based on ridicule.
> When psychoanalysis was first described as "nonsense" and a "German-Jewish invention" in our country, it was actually quite normal and could count on quite considerable support from Western Europeans. Since then, however, the political constellation has changed profoundly.
> If we were to attack psychoanalysis today purely on the basis of its being "obvious" gibberish (it is a different matter in the case of a scientific counter-argument), if public opinion in Poland were passively to resist this scientific theory (or hypothesis), which is undoubtedly one of the most interesting and profound theories to have emerged in Europe over the last few decades – by now such resistance would condemn us to *splendid* – or not so *splendid* – *isolation*. We would be facing not only Germany and Switzerland but above all England, then America, Italy, Hungary, etc., etc. – And finally – given the events of the last few years – our closest ally, France.[299]

299 S. Zahorska, "Psychoanaliza i Teatr Mały", *NKP* 1926, no. 130, p. 8; the words printed in italics appear in English in the original. The previous year, Zahorska had reviewed an exhibition of paintings by Witkacy and Tymon Niesiołowski at Czesław Garliński's Salon Sztuki for *Przegląd Warszawski* (1925, no. 45). Many years later, Witkacy responded to her critique in "Et tu Zahorska Stefania contra me? (Dawny porachunek)", *ZT* 1935, no. 4, p. 6). He also mentions the critic in his play *Szewcy* [*The Shoemakers*], where the First Apprentice says to the Second Apprentice: "Listen, Andy, I know all about Kretschmer's theory of the different physical and psychological types. I took a course with that intellectual slut Zahorska at our Free Workers College" (*The Madman and the Nun and Other Plays*, p. 229). Zahorska profiled Witkacy for the volume *Straty kultury polskiej*, (Glasgow: Książnicka Polska, 1945), vol. 1.

Zahorska stresses that even France, so tenacious in its resistance against Freudianism, "cannot serve us as a shield anymore when it comes to our own obscurantism in this matter" (*Ibid.*). In 1926, Poland was the last country in Europe to ridicule itself by ridiculing psychoanalysis. "Of course," Zahorska adds, "you can turn any subject, however serious and important, into a satire, a comedy, a farce." There is no harm in this, either for the subject in question or for the comedy, as long as one requirement is met:

> The ideology behind the subject must not be the butt of the joke; the comedy must be about some interpretation of it, some of its consequences, be they psychological or situational. But the untouchability of the ideology itself must be guaranteed. (*Ibid.*)

According to Zahorska, the playwright was not to blame for the shortcomings of the production at the Teatr Mały. Witkacy "had no intention and did not in fact write a satire on psychoanalysis," she argues; the problem lay in the director's decisions. Borowski sacrificed what was most significant while "blowing up" less important or random material (material used by the playwright to demonstrate his concept, i.e. psychoanalysis in this case) until it appeared to be "the core of the thing itself". "I don't know what Witkiewicz thinks about psychoanalysis, and when it comes to his play, this is a rather irrelevant question," Zahorska continues. After all, in *Wariat i zakonnica* he proceeds in the same way as in his other plays:

> He interrogates psychoanalysis, all of psychiatry, life and death, reality as such; for him these are no more than perspectives that are full of uncertainty, material through which he gives shape to his ideas, through which he embodies the only thing that is real for him, i.e. his artistic concept, and through which he constructs his only reality – the life on stage. (*Ibid.*)

This is why, the review concludes, "if Witkiewicz's ideas were understood, psychoanalysis would never be seen to stand at the centre of his play" (*Ibid.*).

Winawer

Zahorska's analysis, though insightful, is missing one important key to the reception of *Wariat i zakonnica*, and this is the Polish theatre goers' previous experience with Freudian themes. One likely reason why Witkacy's play was generally seen as a satire in 1926 – and this aspect has not been discussed before – was the fact that audiences saw it as a continuation of another immensely popular play, namely Bruno Winawer's *R.H. Inżynier* [The Engineer R.H.], staged in 1923.

Winawer was one of the most popular repertory writers. His debut coincided with the crisis of both the bourgeois comedy of manners and the moody psychological drama; at the same time, it overlapped with the rapid surge in performance arts focused on entertainment, such as cabarets, musicals and revues.[300] His plays tend to disregard verisimilitude in plot and character portrayal; linguistic humour modelled on G. B. Shaw always takes precedence. The comic effect usually derives from scripted dialogues that make no attempt at being life-like. One reviewer wrote:

> As a humorist Mr Winawer is solid. If we are to laugh, then let us do it in a way that makes the theatre's walls tremble. [...] Every one of his jokes hits the target immediately and is extremely short-lived: the audience is made to giggle at a joke, but the next one follows close on its heels, then the third one and so on. This is why Winawer's comedies are so funny, so hilarious, so much fun![301]

Winawer's plays enjoyed immense success on stage, but they also make for interesting reading because the scripts usually contain detailed stage directions and comments, such as forewords and annotations.[302] Most plays share the same pattern: a brilliant scientist or scholar, naive and inept to manage his everyday life or to make the world recognise his genius, gets into trouble when he falls in with people who try to take advantage of him. Most plays end with the protagonist's triumph, which he owes to a

300 For a discussion of Winawer's comedies in the context of the cabaret see S. Olechowska "Komedie Brunona Winawera", *DI* 1957, no. 6, pp. 117–125.

301 X, "Z Bagateli", *ND* 1923, no. 83, p. 3.

302 For a discussion of these paratexts see A. Krajewska, *Komedia polska dwudziestolecia międzywojennego: Tradycjonaliści i nowatorzy* (Poznań: UAM, 2004), p. 53

practical-minded female partner, usually a wife whose wealth allows him to pursue his intellectual or scientific endeavours.[303]

The comedy *R.H. Inżynier* also presents an honest fellow exposed to the cruel mechanisms of real life. The protagonist is Ryszard Heyst, an engineer, inventor and mathematician. He inherits a flat from his grandmother, who left her testament in a strongbox hidden in that flat. When Heyst visits the apartment, he finds it occupied by a psychiatrist, professor Jan Pistjan. The doctor notices Heyst's strange behaviour: he gazes at the wallpaper, visibly moved, he counts the floor tiles and he claims that "under this floor something is hidden that will make him rich". Pistjan proposes that Heyst commit himself to a clinic to get treated for obsession and *pseudologia phantastica*. The engineer agrees, mostly because of his hopeless situation on the postwar housing market. Pretending to be mad, he is provided with a roof above his head and shelter from the chaotic external world. The sanatorium for nervous diseases turns out to be a dream come true, and Heyst is finally able to think and work in peace. The curtain rises when he has already spent four years at the institution. He tells another patient:

> Please, Sir, just think about it. Is there any place in the world where you'd be more comfortable than here? There, beyond these walls, something is tumbling, simmering, falling apart – while we just sit here quietly, pleasantly, without anything to worry about. […] Imagine yourself leaving this place today, as a normal person. No later than tomorrow, Sir, your maid is going to come with a bill, followed by the concierge with some formality, then the tax collector, then a clerk from the electricity provider, the man from Cedergren installing the telephone, some advertising agent – you're going to go through hell and back. You'll be supposed to remember your date and place of birth, who witnessed your wedding, how much you were earning in 1920, who is cabinet president, where Yugoslavia is and the route of tram number 18. And here? Peace and quiet, Sir, peace and quiet. You can give nonsense answers to all the questions. No one has a right to complain. If anyone gets on your nerves you can just shoot them. The court is going to admit extenuating circumstances…[304]

303 Cf. E. Wysińska, "Uczony marzyciel i pechowiec", *DI* 1964, no. 4, pp. 129–134.

304 B. Winawer, *R.H. Inżynier: Komedia w trzech aktach* (Lviv: Odrodzenie, 1924), p. 10.

According to Winawer's stage directions, the sanatorium is located "somewhere on the outskirts of Warsaw". The director is "an authority in the field of nervous diseases," and his therapies are based on "the method of Freud and Pistjan" (p. 3). Heyst simulates a series of nervous ticks, such as a twitch in his left cheek and a half-shut eye. Sometimes his moves approximate those of the knight in a chess game (three steps forward, one step left or right), he pretends to have a compulsion to count things such as the floorboards, shirt buttons or flowers on the plafond, while the dreams he reports appear in alphabetical order. He is diagnosed with neurosis. Mary, Pistjan's daughter and a medical student, explains to him: "You are subject to certain compulsions which, according to Freud, arise by pushing the erotic drive out of consciousness [...]. Your libido shows certain deficiencies" (p. 7). His therapy consists of daily meetings with Pistjan, who encourages him to open up ("I am to confess my most secret thoughts, dreams and desires – supposedly the first condition for a successful treatment"). The term "psychoanalysis" is mentioned twice. Heyst complains: "I'm sick of psychoanalysis, eurhythmia and mimeoplasty" (p. 22). Throughout the comedy, the names of real-life nervous disease specialists are interwoven with those of fictional characters, which tend to sound funny (for instance, Heyst says, "I'm cuckoo according to Janet, Pistjan, Freud and Wąchockier" (p. 8), with Wąchock being the name of a fictional town that often appears in Polish jokes); one doctor mentions a case described by "Breuer and Kanarjenfogel" (the latter, a Polish spelling of German *Kanarienvogel* (canary), parodies Jewish occupational names); an allusion to Freud's ideas about jokes can be seen in her reference to the "Witzmethode" by a certain Canter-Ebbinghaus (p. 34), where the patient is told jokes about Jews. Fictional experts such as Ganser and Krawuczke (p. 48) and fictional therapeutic methods such as the one by Fajgenblat and Chareet (p. 34) appear in close proximity to the names of Freud's real-life students – Karl Abraham and Sándor Ferenczi (p. 33). Professor Pistjan expects that his published description of Heyst's case would assure his fame in the international psychoanalytical community, that he would be mentioned in *Centralblatt*, *Presse médicale*, and in the Japanese *Papers* (p. 25) – again a mix of real and fictional publications. A certain Dr Córuś, a zealous Freudian who applies "the latest Viennese method" (p. 21), tells Heyst:

> I read about you a lot, Mr R.H. Our dear professor has made you quite famous. The entire medical press has been celebrating you. They read about you in England, in Japan. You are more popular than most of our

> contemporaries. You have one of the most interesting forms of mental deviation – congrats! (p. 13)

Córuś attends meetings at the fictional Psychoanalytical Association – Warsaw Division (p. 59), located at Miodowa Street 23, i.e exactly where Gustav Bychowski was seeing his patients.[305]

For Krajewska, this mix of fact and fiction is typical for Winawer, who tended to address both the theatre-going public looking for light entertainment, and any potential connoisseurs, who "will read the comedy as a sort of self-parody".[306] It is difficult to gauge, however, how many people would have been amused by these reference in 1923, especially when the play was performed not in Warsaw, Lviv or Cracow but in provincial towns.[307] At one point Mary, impatient with Heyst's resistance, tells him: "How can you be so stubborn? The most talented people have made it clear to you – using methods by Pistjan, Freud, Ferenczi, Shones, Ostrich and Champagne that there is no strongbox – daddy wrote a whole tract on this. And you're still going on about it."[308] For most members of the audience, the names of Ferenczi and Jones/Shones (Bżons in the original) must have sounded no more and no less amusing than the invented names of Pistjan, Ostrich and Champagne (Struś and Kieliszek in the original). It is safe to assume that the only name that was universally recognised was that of Freud. If most jokes were lost on the majority of the audience, it is no wonder that many reviewers emphasised how much the success of the performance depended on the actor in the leading role. For a large part of the audience, the humour was entirely situational. At Warsaw's Teatr Rozmaitości, for instance, the engineer was played by the celebrated Józef Węgrzyn:

> He pretended to be a lunatic, he distorted his mug, contorted his legs, blabbered, rolled his eyes, twitched his ears, his antics bringing to mind a playful and beloved kid that enchanted the whole audience; he immediately created such a fun atmosphere that Winawer's experiment went crazy, turned into a circus, a cabaret, a madhouse hosting a ball.[309]

---

305 Cf. *Cała Warszawa*, a directory from 1930, p. 8.

306 A. Krajewska, *Komedia polska dwudziestolecia międzywojennego*, p. 49.

307 See *OO* 1923, no. 102, p. 2.

308 B. Winawer, *R.H. Inżynier: Komedia w trzech aktach*, p. 57.

309 K. Makuszyński, *RE* 1923, no. 84, p. 6.

Heyst leaves the clinic at the end of the first act, when the general interest in his case stops him from pursuing his own scientific work and the two young women doctors vie for his attention. He then finds himself investing in the construction of institutes for the mentally ill and comes to sudden wealth, which allows him to delve into his research in mathematics. Despite this success, he continues to be seen as a madman. He comments:

> There are two hundred thousand ways to prove to you that you're nuts. They've come up with the method of Freud, Piltz, Kraepelin, Ostrich, Champagne, Franaszek, Herse, Dombala, Żmigryder, Harding, Szyfman, Isadora Duncan and Richard Strauss. But there is no method, not even one, to convince everyone that everything is fine with a person. (p. 88)[310]

Eventually, Heyst manages to find the strongbox, which, he hopes, would prove that he is of sound mind. In the finale, having asked Prof. Pistjan for the hand of his daughter, he also proposes a wager to his future father in law: if the future son of Heyst and Mary does not graduate with a first-class degree and become prime minister, then Heyst will admit defeat and acknowledge his madness. Prof. Pistjan remains unconvinced: "Prime minister? – And what is that supposed to prove?". Here the curtain falls.

The play tackles broadly psychoanalytical themes in only one of the three acts, but this did not stop most reviewers from describing it as a satire on Freudianism. In 1923, a reviewer of the production directed by Aleksander Węgierka at the Teatr Bagatela in Cracow wrote: "Winawer sourced the 'joke' of his latest comedy from the medical world, the branch of science that is most exposed to mockery: [he] ridiculed Freud's theory of psychoanalysis."[311] Following the play's performance at the Teatr Rozmaitości in Warsaw the same year, Zygmunt Kisielewski wrote in *Robotnik* that the playwright, being "a science-buff, makes fun of scientists' thoughtlessness, the thoughtlessness of the medical sect, which, having taken Freud's theory as gospel, has become a thoughtless supporter of psychoanalysis".[312] Even reviewers who were sceptical about the play as a

310 Some of these names belong to prominent individuals or families. For instance, the Herses owned a famous fashion house, while Arnold Szyfman was a well-known theatre director.

311 X, "Z Bagateli", p. 3.

312 Z. Kisielewski, *R* 1923, no. 84, p. 4.

whole tended to appreciate what they presumed to be its key theme. For instance, Artur Ćwikowski wrote in his harsh assessment of a production in Lviv that "the playwright's inventiveness, which never exerts itself too much throughout the so-called plot, is exhausted by the end of act II,"[313] i.e. when the characters leave the clinic; still, he finds Winawer's use of psychoanalytical therapy interesting and amusing.[314]

Examining later reviews it becomes apparent that *R.H. Inżynier* did not age well. When the comedy was staged at the Teatr Narodowy in September 1932, Tadeusz Boy-Żeleński wrote that it was "a revue of past forms of life, of which we have retained only a faint memory".[315] He acknowledges that Winawer's comedy, "even though it was written only yesterday, ought to mention the date on the poster: The play takes place in the year… Performed as if it took place today it becomes absurd" (pp. 77–78). The reviewer is most concerned with the play's social context (housing shortage, inflation, speculation, improvised careers, obsessions with hierarchies, rising divorce rates after the war), but he also sees the representation of psychoanalysis as anachronistic; he regrets that when the

313 A. Ćwikowski, *DL* 1923, no. 52, p. 6.

314 Winawer only confessed what he thought of Freud's theory in one of his columns in the series "Ziemia w malignie". Influenced by Freud's *An Autobiographical Study*, he wrote: "The human brain is a kind of immensely complicated apparatus, very difficult to understand. In the past, philosophers used to deal with it – as well as with the rest of the psyche; they delivered sonorous platitudes, but didn't investigate, didn't put their theorems to the test, didn't run experiments – they just talked. And it is only in Freud's small book *An Autobiographical Study* that we learn how the insightful, careful doctor, a neurologist, came upon a thread of yarn by chance and how he spent several decades persistently searching for the ball. He began with the machines and apparatuses of the "infirm," with the nervous systems of sick people, with hysterics, and little by little […] he worked out clever and more generally applicable methods of investigation; he found a window through which we can sometimes get a glimpse of the great *mare tenebrarum* of mental processes. Psychoanalysis still has all the unpleasant characteristics of emerging sciences, it overwhelms us with numerous Latin words, terms, theories, explanations, caveats, but… it now embraces certain horizons. Freud tackles "humour" and "dreams," primordial religion and poetic creativity, he explores the meaning of totems and taboos and he wonders who wrote Shakespeare's plays. He knows where the *Unbehagen in der Kultur* comes from – perhaps this is not much, but it is something. After so many centuries of idle chatter, we are finally on a scientific, experimental path, humanity is trying to acquire the highest wisdom, to gain an – approximate – understanding of itself." (B. Winawer, *Ziemia w malignie* Warsaw: Rój, 1937, pp. 119–120)

315 T. Boy-Żeleński, *Ludzie i bydlątka (Wrażenia teatralne)* (Warsaw: [no publisher], 1933), p. 82.

protagonist is "examined using the method of psychoanalysis, he improvises fantastic associations drawn straight from the Egyptian Dreambook" (p. 80). This, Boy-Żeleński continues, represents no more than a revival of the eternal satire on doctors and medicine à la Molière.

Cwojdziński

A few years later, Antoni Cwojdziński's *Freuda teoria snów* was performed at the Teatr Mały, and this time Boy-Żeleński was delighted; he wrote that in his new play, the dramatist "has presented more than an outline of Freudianism – he has presented a real comedy, intelligently and skilfully carved from the material. At the same time he endowed Freud's theory with something that its old creator never dreamed of: humour and charm."[316]

Winawer and Cwojdziński had much in common. Both were trained as physicists and started academic careers before dedicating themselves to writing comedies. Both enjoyed popular as well as critical success.[317] Compared to Winawer, however, Cwojdziński was better prepared for the theatre business: he had studied directing under Leon Schiller at the National Institute of Drama (Państwowy Instytut Sztuki Teatralnej), and he had experience acting at Juliusz Osterwa's experimental Reduta theatre. His comedies presented the theories that were most widely discussed at the time in an accessible way, although Cwojdziński did not see himself as a writer of introductions. In the foreword to a collected edition of his plays many years later he wrote that "two hours of giggles cannot give a popular presentation even of the multiplication table".[318] Instead, he believed that since the twentieth century was turning out to be an era of scientific progress, contemporary drama ought to reflect this development. He was interested not so much in transposing scientific achievements onto the stage, but in the question how "the intellectual heights that form our

316 T. Boy-Żeleński, "Straszliwe mroki podświadomości", in *Murzyn zrobił… Wrażeń teatralnych seria siedemnasta*, *Pisma*, vol. 27 (Warsaw: PIW, 1970), p. 102.

317 For comparative readings of Winawer and Cwojdziński see e.g. K. Kapuścińska, "Twórczość komediowa Winawera i Cwojdzińskiego", *Łódzkie Towarzystwo Naukowe, Sprawozdania z Czynności i posiedzeń naukowych*, 1968, vol. 22, no. 1, pp. 1–8; S. Wójcikowska, "Świat komedii naukowych B. Winawera i A. Cwojdzińskiego", *PH* 1979, no. 2, pp. 133–140; A. Krajewska, "Nauka – temat nie komediowy", in *Komedia polska dwudziestolecia międzywojennego*, pp. 42–79.

318 A. Cwojdziński, "Od autora", *Komedie naukowe* (Warsaw: PIW, 1968), p. 7.

culture" manifest themselves in "less elevated minds". This was in his view an excellent theme for comedy: "theory against the backdrop of what we call common sense – this is an underexplored source of humour, and not a stupid one, for it spans both theory and – despite appearances – humankind, human nature" (*Ibid.*).

Besides his comedy about psychoanalysis, Cwojdziński also wrote two other plays in the interwar period. They were *Teoria Einsteina* [Einstein's Theory] and *Temperamenty* [Temperaments], which tackled Kretschmer's ideas. After his emigration to the USA in 1941 he wrote *Obrona genów* [In Defence of Genes], *Hipnoza* [Hypnosis] and a piece dealing with cybernetics, *Sprzężenie zwrotne* [Feedback]. As one critic has argued, of all these theories, Freudianism was best suited for a comedy, as it allowed to merge the scientific comedy with romantic or sexual themes which traditionally propel the action on stage.[319] Before the war, Cwojdziński enjoyed growing popularity. *Teoria Einsteina* was staged at the Reduta theatre (1934), and *Freuda teoria snów* became a blockbuster at the commercial Teatr Mały (1937). The director of this production was Edmund Wierciński; the main roles were played by Janina Romanówna and Mariusz Maszyński.

Soon after the premiere, the play was printed, along with photographs of the actors and a quotation from Freud's *Introduction to Psychoanalysis*, in *Wiadomości Literackie.*[320] The journal also published a positive review by Antoni Słonimski, who was usually critical of Freudianism.[321] The rival publication, *Prosto z Mostu*, which had printed *Teoria Einsteina* less than a year after it was founded, also praised the production. The editor-in-chief himself expressed his admiration: "Cwojdziński handled the risky details of Freud's theory with admirable restraint; the comedy never once crosses the line into the drastic and crude, which, given the subject matter, was by no means easy."[322] For Piasecki, "a person who has never encountered Freud's ideas will learn from Cwojdziński's comedy what they are generally about," but above all he welcomes the fact that these ideas, "clearly disconfirmed by more recent scholarship," have been tackled through "discrete satire". In fact, he continues, Freudianism, known for its

319 L. Eustachiewicz, "Komedie Antoniego Cwojdzińskiego", *DI* 1970, no. 12, p. 124.

320 A. Cwojdziński, "Freuda teoria snów", *WL* 1937, no. 29, pp. 1–2; no. 32 pp. 4–5; no. 35, pp. 2–3.

321 as. [A. Słonimski], "Dialog Cwojdzińskiego w Teatrze Małym", p. 6.

322 *PZM* 1937, no. 21, p. 7.

"pansexualism," had been asking for such a satirical treatment, just as "our mushrooming home-grown psychoanalysts"; Cwojdziński's comedy, the critic argues, offers both (*Ibid.*).

The most positive review is perhaps the one written by Kazimierz Wierzyński for *Gazeta Polska*:

> An excellent new play has appeared in the world of Polish drama. It is a huge success for our culture. There is nothing more delightful than to be able to say this and to give the play an enthusiastic welcome. We rarely get the opportunity to celebrate the work of playwrights in this country, but even if this were so, *Freuda teoria snów* would earn our special attention. It is a work of real talent, full of intelligence, culture, wit and creativity [...]. It would be hard to imagine a more interesting and enjoyable scientific lecture, while in terms of entertainment, it has been a long time since we had anything as tasteful.[323]

Karol Irzykowski was the most sceptical reviewer. Of course, by 1935 it would have been hard to impress him with any kind of cultural production that popularised the basics of psychoanalysis. He accused Cwojdziński of taking the theatrical stage for a lecture platform and described *Freuda teoria snów* as "a play for illiterate people": "a person familiar with Freud's theory and with Freudianism in general, its advantages and disadvantages, will not be able to listen to this boring and quite superfluous lecture without irritation".[324] Irzykowski was clearly not part of Cwojdziński's target audience, but in this review he shows particular ill will – after all, the play conforms astonishingly well to the guidelines he himself had given, in his criticism of *Wariat i zakonnica*, to playwrights who draw on psychoanalytical motifs.

The comedy's opening scene shows a male writer, "educated, serious and even profound," and a young actress reading out the dialogue of a new play. The man does not want the attractive woman to know that he is its author. The audience sees them reading the final lines of the play: "*Third kiss, long and amorous. She touches her lips, treated so rudely*: There is oral sadism, after all! *Curtain.*"[325] The comedy's conclusion reveals that the writer and the actress in the play have been reading *Freuda teoria snów*, and

323 *GPL* 1937, no. 120, pp. 3–4.

324 K. Irzykowski, "Scena czy sala odczytowa", p. 292.

325 A. Cwojdziński, *Freuda teoria snów* (Cracow: Universitas, 2004), p. 7.

that the words cited in the beginning also conclude Cwojdziński's comedy itself.

The first act shows the actress unconvinced about the play; in fact, she calls it "idiotic nonsense". The reason is mainly that she cannot understand the female lead, which she is supposed to play. Does the heroine love her fiancé or not? On the one hand, she professes her love for him throughout the three acts, but on the other hand she eventually misses their rendezvous and spends the evening with another man. The writer, who recently read Freud's *Introduction to Psychoanalysis*, begins to explain that the play is built on the tension between the conscious and the unconscious:

> The truth does not lie in words that are spoken consciously. What really steers our thoughts, opinions and, above all, our behaviour, are unconscious drives. Hidden desires and a variety of complexes, unknown to our consciousness and independent of our will. It's the "Id," as the Freudians say, and this "Id" is the unconscious psychic life at the service of the powerful primitive force of libido, not logic! (p. 9)

The actress resists this idea: "Maybe some amoral fellow who has… that libido in the place of logic, or some hysteric with drives of that sort could play that part – but me? […] I am an honest, simple and innocent girl" (p. 10). That said, she finds the writer's explanations so fascinating that she forgets about her rendezvous with her fiancé Władek, a military man. She calls him at the Ziemiańska café, where he has been waiting for her, and they agree to meet a little bit later; just as she is about to leave, however, the writer tells her that according to Freud, every such seemingly meaningless act of forgetting is in fact intentional; it is not that she forgot about her date, but she was evading her fiancé on purpose. It then transpires that the actress had agreed to have sex with Władek for the first time that night, and that she was actually keen to avoid the situation.

Initially the actress is indignant at the writer's interpretation, but she soon accepts it. She realises that as a married woman she would have to give up her stage career, and that she has little desire to devote herself to family life. Further evidence à la Freud is provided by a dream in which Władek tried to make her go on a boat trip ("But what's so risqué about it? […] – Almost everything!" (p. 19)); she plays with her engagement ring until it gets lost; she keeps glancing at a watch that is not working; trying to reach her lover at the café she dials the wrong number and, instead of

Ziemiańska, ends up talking to a psychoanalyst, Professor Ziemiański; most importantly, she fiercely resists the writer's interpretation. Suddenly she realises that she is late for her date; she calls Władek again, but this time she cannot even apologise because the writer accidentally disconnects the phone. The actress and the writer send Władek a letter of apology and an invitation to a party.

The second act takes place the following day. The three characters are due to meet for the party, but Władek does not show up. It turns out that the writer had addressed the envelope to himself by mistake. The two of them begin to analyse the young woman's dreams. The writer suggests that in reality she is not in love with Władek, whom she unconsciously wishes dead, but with himself, as indicated by her dream about a dog (i.e. him, the writer), which she was pulling up a ladder – symbolically indicating her desire to have sexual intercourse with him. The actress is outraged and leaves, taking with her the writer's copy of *Introduction to Psychoanalysis*.

When the actress comes to see the writer again in the third act, she has not only read the book and several other works in the field, but she has also consulted Dr Ziemiański. Hearing about the writer's dilettantish analyses, the specialist reportedly said that "if this were psychoanalysis, he would immediately resign from the Psychoanalytic Society!" (p. 86). With the professor's guidance, the woman takes her revenge on the wild analyst. She proves to him that he was in fact in love with her and desired to castrate her fiancé. He had thus regressed to the "pregenital phase of sadistic-oral instincts" (p. 100). After all, he had shoved her ring into a drawer along with some papers, he "accidentally" interrupted her conversation with Władek and with his cigarette he burned a hole in Władek's photograph (in the place of his nose!); finally he had sent the letter to his own address. These were no coincidences but symptoms of hidden feelings: "an active subconscious was indeed there all along – but it was yours!" (p. 91).

That said, the actress must admit that she was so preoccupied reading about psychoanalysis that she found no time to meet Władek when he was in town for a few days. The accelerated course in Freudianism also made her realise that they were not on the same wavelength ("What should I talk to him about? Probably about his horse's inferiority complex, because the only thing he cares about is horses" (p. 100)). Finally she misses her last chance to mend her relationship with Władek and stays with the writer. She was right in fact when she discovered that she was the object of his love, and he had guessed correctly that she loved him. After their third passionate kiss they say the same words that concluded their reading in the opening of the comedy: "And where is that castr… complex of mine…? She (*touching her lips*): There is oral sadism, after all!" (p. 123)). Just before the curtain falls, she must admit that the play *Freuda teoria snów* was "not the stupidest at the end of the day" (*ibid.*).

One contemporary reviewer, having outlined the plot for *Gazeta Polska*, adds:

> In a summary it is impossible to reproduce even a tiny part of the playful mood of Cwojdziński's comedy. It is light, free, completely unforced. Fine dialogue climbs fearlessly up the steps of Freud's pyramid, again and again offering hilarious views of the two wanderers merrily erring through their dreams, only to wake up with their arms reaching for each other.[326]

It is true that Irzykowski found reason to complain:

> If only he offered her a flower, if only he talked about something other than Freud, if awkward pauses arose in their conversation, or if at least they were embarrassed to find themselves talking about Freudian sex symbols – if only they breathed the warm and disturbing fluid of love. But no, they discuss "swinishness" like fifth-year medical students from the department for venereal diseases. The playwright shows us no symptoms of falling in love other than those à la Freud […] – to believe that love manifests itself only in this way, one must already be a dogmatic Freudian.[327]

Boy-Żeleński, however, appreciated Cwojdziński's inventiveness. He argued that the tension between conscious and unconscious desires was a traditional element in theatrical comedy, not just since Freud; Cwojdziński's innovation is that: "a third partner comes into play, namely the illusion of scientific self-control," his characters try to deceive the subconscious only to become its victims, and this, eventually, is "even funnier".[328]

---

326 Kazimierz Wierzyński, *GPL* 1937, no. 120, pp. 3–4

327 K. Irzykowski, "Scena czy sala odczytowa", p. 294.

328 T. Boy-Żeleński, "Straszliwe mroki podświadomości", p. 105.

It is interesting to compare Cwojdziński's comedy with the satires about psychoanalysis discussed before. *Freuda teoria snów* does not reference Jews, nor does it feature a clinic. Instead, it is set in the writer's "refined and modern" flat;[329] instead of a compromising attempt to cure a supposed madman with Freudian methods, Cwojdziński explores a young Varsovian's attempts to use psychoanalysis to further his romantic and sexual goals. Freudianism is no dubious therapeutic method applied by a grotesque Jewish scientist anymore. It has now become a sort of parlour game, a modern equivalent of flirting.

It is also striking that the two protagonists of *Freuda teoria snów* are the only characters to appear on stage. This comedy about psychoanalysis is, therefore, the only one that manages without the psychoanalyst, previously an indispensable source of entertainment. The analyst Professor Ziemiański, who only talks to the writer on the phone and treats the actress between two acts, is presented as an intellectual authority, not a charlatan. According to Boy-Żeleński, the play only satirises "dilettantish psychoanalysis by amateurs and under-educated Freudians"; in fact, the critic finds that a more far-reaching mockery – one that also ridiculed the "true psychoanalyst" Professor Ziemiański – would have been justified: "While Freud's fundamental achievements are groundbreaking and brilliant discoveries, their practical application in medical casuistry sometimes verges on farce."[330] Cwojdziński does not go this far. He even has the actress utter a warning against hasty attempts at analysis: pointing to the *Introduction*, she exclaims that "getting down to practice after reading this primer is the height of insolence".[331] She then tells the writer that "dream analysis is not about identifying ready-made symbols left and right" (p. 88). What is more, the character of Professor Ziemiański, who is never seen or heard on stage, cannot be discredited by an actor who, contrary to the playwright's intentions, might make the analyst appear dubious, give him a ridiculous accent or otherwise turn him into a caricature of a Jew. His surname, with the ending in -ski, does not have the mocking aspect of the names that other playwrights used to give their Freudian characters, although "Ziemiański" is obviously associated with the real café Ziemiańska in Warsaw and alludes to the artistic milieu of the Skamander group, where psychoanalysis was most popular at the time.

329 A. Cwojdziński, *Freuda teoria snów*, p. 7.

330 T. Boy-Żeleński, "Straszliwe mroki podświadomości", pp. 105–106.

331 A. Cwojdziński, *Freuda teoria snów*, p. 86.

Irzykowski, who was in conflict with the Skamandrites, seems to have sensed this allusion as well; in his review he mentions that the characters in the play, who seem to subscribe to the Skamander ideology, also conform to the associated principles of "easy living" [*życie ułatwione*], which foregrounds sexual tension over any kind of intellectual attraction.[332] Besides, the fictional Professor Ziemiański is said to be a member of the Psychoanalytic Society. The only Warsaw-based member of the VPS at the time was, of course, Gustav Bychowski, professor at the University of Warsaw. Several details suggest that he might have been on Cwojdziński's mind. First, the most important prop on stage is the Polish edition of *Introduction to Psychoanalysis*, which the writer borrowed from Dr Ziemiański before passing it on to the actress. Second, the writer uses a short book about psychoanalysis; its title is not mentioned, but the actress says that it was written by a lecturer at the University of Warsaw. Finally, the dreams discussed by the protagonists show several similarities with Bychowski's case studies in his *Psychoanaliza* (e.g. a St. Bernard dog as a recurring motif). It is also telling that reviewers compared Cwojdziński's success with Gustav Bychowski's efforts to spread Freudianism. For instance, according to Antoni Słonimski, the playwright wrote a comedy based on Freud's theory because "he realised correctly that the lively and attractive Romanówna would be more entertaining than a stuffed owl, and that Maszyński can speak better than Dr Bychowski".[333]

As I mentioned before, Cwojdziński was more interested in the dissemination of scientific theories than in the actual science itself. When major concepts, inevitably complex, reach ordinary people, they are usually simplified and distorted. Cwojdziński explored this process and built the comic effect of his plays on these deformations. He always chose theories that were fashionable and familiar enough to be understood without any additional explanation. After all, the comic genre presupposes a sense of superiority in the audience – there is nothing funny about watching a situation on stage that one does not understand. In Cwojdzinski's comedies, the audience is always slightly more familiar with a given theory than the character to whom it is explained. Krajewska puts it clearly:

332 K. Irzykowski, "Scena czy sala odczytowa", p. 295.

333 as. [A. Słonimski], "Dialog Cwojdzińskiego w Teatrze Małym".

> Education in comedy can only be [...] funny if the process of explanation itself remains superficial, within the horizon of what the audience already knows, and if the portrayal of the theory does not deviate too much from how it is popularly seen. As soon as an actual scientific dialogue begins to take place on stage, the comedy of the situation is lost.[334]

Freuda teoria snów is a vehicle for cultural transfer. Boy-Żeleński suggests that anyone who has seen the play will be keen to take on the role of an analyst: "the triumph of the play is that the frenzy of psychoanalysis imparts itself to the audience. Everyone engages in psychoanalysis – between the acts and during dinner, at the theatre and after the theatre".[335] At the same time, however, the play's creation and success prove that such a transfer has already taken place.

Cwojdziński's comedy – and its success on the stage of Warsaw's Teatr Mały – can be seen as the final phase in the transfer of psychoanalysis into the milieu of the Polish intelligentsia. One critic put it succinctly in 1939:

> Psychiatry is probably the only field that is as rigorous as medicine and yet familiar to the average educated person. When we were young, we read Lombroso's *Genio e Follia* [Genius and Madness], a book that made the greatest impression on several generations of readers, or, to put it in today's terms, that was most sensational. Later came Freudian psychoanalysis. Zweig's biographical novel *Freud* became an iron ration in any reading room subscriber's rucksack. Dr Gustav Bychowski's lucid presentation of Freudianism, *Psychoanaliza*, primarily targeted lay readers. In *Freuda teoria snów*, Cwojdziński took his lecture about psychoanalysis to the theatrical stage, having us examine it from the comfortable and costly seats on the ground level as well as from the popular benches in the gallery. The result was that people who had long forgotten about the classical *Oedipus Rex* or who had never come across Sophocles' tragedy at all now can't stop talking about the "Oedipus complex" and a thousand other possible and impossible complexes.[336]

334 A. Krajewska, *Komedia polska dwudziestolecia międzywojennego*, p. 49.

335 T. Boy-Żeleński, "Straszliwe mroki podświadomości", p. 106.

336 M. Wadyas, "Pokompleksujmy sobie trochę", *NPR* 1939, no. 162, p. 20.

The play was so popular that it continued to perform at Teatr Mały in 1938. In 1939 it was staged again at the Żydowska Scena Kameralna, a Jewish theatre hosted by the Judaic Library (Biblioteka Judaistyczna) at Tłomackie Street 5, starring Jonas Turkow and Diana Blumenfeld.[337] After the outbreak of the war, the ensemble Nowy Teatr Kameralny revived Cwojdziński's comedy with the same cast but under a different title, namely "Dialogi komiczne Żyda Zygmunta Freuda" [The Comical Dialogues of the Jew Sigmund Freud]. This production was premiered at the same location, now in the Warsaw ghetto, on 8 November 1941.

In the late 1930s, the play's success in Poland coincided with the branding of psychoanalysis a "Jewish science" in the Third Reich. This synchrony becomes abundantly clear when we leaf through issues of *Nasz Przegląd* from the period: in 1938, announcements of a performance at the Teatr Mały are printed side by side with reports on Freud's arrest and his escape from annexed Austria.

337 Cf. *NPR* 1939, no. 32, p. 15.

A NEW DIASPORA

After the Nazis publicly burned books on psychoanalysis on Berlin's Opernplatz on 10 May 1933, Freud wrote that "Berlin is lost".[1] The Austrians, however, felt safe. In Freud's immediate circle, only Ludwig Jekels predicted that the Jews of Vienna would suffer the same fate as those of Berlin. Anna Freud discusses Jekels' position in a letter to Ernest Jones, adding that she and her father did not share his views.[2] In the early 1930s, Hermann Nunberg was practically the only Viennese psychoanalyst who had already emigrated; he had remained in the United States following an invitation by the University of Pennsylvania in 1931. As he notes in his memoirs, Freud did not understand this decision:

> He did not see the threatening danger. When I visited Vienna again in 1934, and implored Freud to leave Austria, he tried even then to convince me that there was no real danger, that the existing government of Austria would protect the Jews and not yield to the Nazis.[3]

In 1935 Freud reportedly begrudged Helene Deutsch's departure for Boston.[4] Even in 1937, a few months before the Anschluss, he is said to have told his French colleague René Laforgue that he was more worried about the Catholic Church than the Nazis.[5]

1 E. J. Rolnik, "Freud in Zion", pp. 82–83. An extensive report on this event appeared in *Wiadomości Literackie*: A. Sobański, "W Niemczech po przewrocie: Cywile, Reichstag, książki", *WL* 1933, no. 29, p. 3. Cf. also Z. Nowakowski, *Niemcy à la minute* (Warsaw: Gebethner i Wolff, 1933).

2 Cited in R. Steiner, "'It is a New Kind of Diaspora…'", *TIR* 1989, no. 16, p. 45.

3 H. Nunberg, *Memoirs: Recollections, Ideas, Reflections*, p. 60.

4 P. Roazen, *Helene Deutsch*, p. 368.

5 R. Laforgue, "Personal Memories of Freud", in *Freud as We Knew Him*, ed. by H. M. Ruitenbeek (Detroit: Wayne State University Press, 1973), p. 344. Robertson argues that Freud was alluding to Wilhelm Schmidt, a Verbist priest and prominent anthropologist who had criticised *Totem and Taboo* in *Ursprung und Werden der Religion* (1930); in the second half of the 1930s, Schmidt played an important role in the clerical-fascist Bundesstaat Österreich (Ständestaat). See R. Robertson, "My True Enemy: Freud and the Catholic Church 1927–1939", in *Austria in the Thirties: Culture and Politics*, ed. by K. Segar and J. Warren (Riverside: Ariadne Press, 1991), pp. 328–344.

The situation changed in March 1938, after Hitler marched into Vienna.[6] Otto Fenichel wrote to his colleagues that Freud remained unaware of the looming calamity:

> The professor is doing well, a rampart of love has been built around him, and he sits behind it and plays tarot with Jekels [...]. Anyhow, everyone is going on walks in this lovely spring weather, living, like the two Jews on a desert island, off mutual loans.[7]

Still, the members of the VPS held a special meeting and voted that the society must move its headquarters to wherever Freud would emigrate. According to Jones, the movement's first historian, this decision initiated a process that Freud compared to the dispersion of the Jewish people after the destruction of the Temple in Jerusalem – a process he referred to as the "new diaspora".[8]

Most Freudians managed to escape the Holocaust.[9] Of the 150 members of the VPS, ten were deported to ghettos or camps. One of them was Isidor Sadger: unable or unwilling to emigrate, he was sent to Theresienstadt in September 1942, where he died the same year.[10] The remaining 140 psychoanalysts managed to emigrate. Freud and his household went to London, thanks to the financial support of Princess Marie Bonaparte, in early June 1938.

Ernest Jones, president of the IPA and the British Psychoanalytical Society at the time, supported his Central European colleagues with their emigration procedures. His influence would grow significantly over the years to come. For Jones, psychoanalysis was a pure science and had no cultural or social implications. In his opening speech at the International Psychoanalytical Congress in Lucerne in 1934 he stressed:

---

6 Thomas Mann wrote: "But what is such hatred compared with that which the protagonist of the unconscious must feel for knowledge and mind? I have a private suspicion that the élan of the march on Vienna had a secret spring: it was directed at the venerable Freud, the real and actual enemy, the philosopher and revealer of the neuroses." See Thomas Mann, "That Man is My Brother," *Esquire*, 01/03/1939, p. 133.

7 O. Fenichel, *119 Rundbriefe*, vol. 2, p. 759.

8 E. Jones, *Sigmund Freud*, vol. 3, p. 236.

9 Riccardo Steiner writes that "one major difference should [...] be kept in mind, in comparison with the Holocaust in general: that very few psychoanalysts, comparatively speaking, end up dying in a concentration camp". See R. Steiner, "'It is a New Kind of Diaspora...'", p. 42. On psychoanalysis in Austria after 1938 see W. Huber, *Psychoanalyse in Österreich seit 1933* (Vienna: Geyer, 1977).

10 E. Mühlleitner, J. Reichmayr, "Following Freud in Vienna", p. 79.

> The master of our school, though well known to be strongly imbued with humanitarian desires for the betterment of human life, has always known how to keep these strictly apart from his scientific work, which has therefore never suffered in its purity. In this, as in so many other respects, he has set us an example we should do well to follow. There are not wanting among us signs of impatience with social conditions and eagerness to engage in the changing of them. From what I said it follows that whoever yields to such impulses becomes by so much the less a psychoanalyst. And to attempt to propagate his particular social ideas in the name of psychoanalysis is to pervert its true nature, a misuse of psychoanalysis which I wish firmly to denounce and repudiate.[11]

Jones made this statement as part of the debate on Wilhelm Reich, the Marxist and former member of the German Communist Party, who had just been expelled from the IPA. It did, however, touch on the core of psychoanalysis; all socially committed Freudians would have seen it as a clear warning. In fact, it has been suggested that Jones' speech in Lucerne can be seen as an early harbinger of what Freud's teaching would become in the United States.[12]

Jones was one of the few Freudians who had no Jewish background, and this enabled him to throw his weight behind large-scale rescue missions to get his colleagues out of Nazi-occupied areas and into the UK. The Isakowers are an exemplary case.[13] Anna Freud described Salomea Isakower as "very quiet and withdrawn, but one of the most brilliant and critical analytic minds".[14] She was born in Oświęcim in 1888 as the daughter of a teacher, Szymon Rettich. She received her secondary school leaving certificate in 1907 at the private Queen Jadwiga Girls' Gymnasium (Prywatne Gimnazjum Żeńskie imienia Królowej Jadwigi) in Cracow and enrolled at the Jagiellonian University's medical department in 1907; in the academic year 1910/1911 she spent one semester at the University of

11 E. Jones, "Opening Speech at the International Psychoanalytical Congress", *IJP* 1934, no. 15, pp. 486–487.

12 R. Jacoby, *The Repression of Psychoanalysis: Otto Fenichel and the Freudians* (Chicago: The University of Chicago Press, 1986), p. 84.

13 Cf. D. Kirsner, "Saving Psychoanalysts: Ernest Jones and the Isakowers", *PAH* 2007, no. 9, pp. 83–91.

14 Cited in D. Kirsner, "Saving Psychoanalysts", p. 83.

Vienna. She received her medical diploma and specialisation in nervous diseases in 1914 in Cracow.[15] While still a student in 1911, she married a doctor, Felix Gutmann, whom she divorced in 1921. At this time she relocated to Vienna, where she worked in psychiatric clinics. She opened a private practice in 1928, the year she met the Viennese physician and psychoanalyst Otto Isakower. He was affiliated with the VPS, and Salomea soon began to attend their meetings, becoming a full member in 1933. By 1934, she was already a training analyst at the Vienna institute. In a letter dated 9 May 1938, Anna Freud asks Ernest Jones to facilitate the couple's escape; they had just married, which meant that "two problems have become one".[16]

At first, Jones tried to obtain licences for his exiled colleagues to practise medicine in the UK, but it soon became apparent that, unlike in the United States, immigrants who declared they were psychoanalysts were more readily accepted than psychiatrists or physicians. The British Medical Association was reluctant to accept refugees. In fact, between 1933 and 1939 only one hundred Jewish doctors obtained an accreditation to practice in Britain.[17] *Wiadomości Literackie* published Maria Morska's report on the structural hurdles placed in their way:

> It would seem that the world should be snatching up the German-Jewish medical elite [...]. Meanwhile... when news of the Viennese doctors' ordeal reached London, the British government decided to grant 500 visas out of several thousand applications. Of the 500 lucky ones, only 50 were able to resettle, the reason being that the British Medical Association protested against the "foreign invasion". As if that wasn't enough, it was decided that these newcomers, many of whom had trained British doctors, were to serve a two-year internship in a hospital before being granted the right to practice in the British Empire.[18]

---

15 See J. Suchmiel, *Żydówki ze stopniem doktora wszech nauk*, pp. 33–34, M. Kulczykowski, *Żydzi-studenci Uniwersytetu Jagiellońskiego w dobie autonomicznej Galicji*, p. 395. Suchmiel refers to Salomea Rettlich-Gutmann; Kulczykowski presents her surname as Rettichówna. Cf. *Corpus Studiosorum Universitatis Iagellonicae 1850/51–1917/18*, ed. by K. Stopka (Cracow: Historia Iagellonica, 2013), vol. 3, part 6, p. 146.

16 Cited in R. Steiner, "'It is a New Kind of Diaspora...'", pp. 104–105.

17 *Ibid.*, pp. 12–13. Cf. also B. Wasserstein, *Britain and the Jews of Europe, 1939–45* (Oxford: Clarendon Press, 1979).

18 M. Dawn [Maria Morska], "Wrażenia z Anglii: Imigracja Żydów do Imperium", *WL* 1939, no. 26, p. 3.

Morska also writes that by closing Britain to these Jewish migrants, the Chamberlain government "has done an irreparable injury not only to them but also to its own people"; after all, the Jewish doctors from Germany and Austria were highly qualified and had made "enormous contributions to medicine". One of the names she mentions is that of Freud, who "laid the foundations of modern psychotherapy" (*ibid.*).

In the psychoanalytic community, the continental émigrés were not welcomed with open arms, either. The British Psychoanalytical Society prioritised its own economic and programmatic interests. The London-based psychoanalysts were facing an underdeveloped market, which explains why they were not particularly welcoming towards new competitors; what is more, their continental colleagues tended to represent orthodox Freudianism, while on the British Isles the tone was already being set by Melanie Klein. She had arrived fifteen years earlier and set up her own school of psychoanalysis, which differed from classical Freudianism in terms of theory and of the techniques applied in therapeutic practice. As her biographer puts it, "Melanie Klein might have been afraid of German bombs, but she was still more afraid of the invasion of German-speaking analysts and their occupation of her territory".[19] In many of his letters Jones stresses that, besides the difficulties with the British authorities, the mission to save Jewish psychoanalysts was hampered by their British colleagues' mixed feelings about the incoming wave of immigrants.[20] They were generally empathetic and willing to help, but sometimes they criticised Jones for being overly active. Having previously witnessed how analysts from Berlin found it difficult to adjust to how things were done in America, Jones was determined to make sure his Austrian colleagues would not try to introduce a central European atmosphere into British psychoanalytic institutions.[21] He realised that foreigners would find their bearings more easily in the United States, a nation of immigration, than in Great Britain, where prejudices against people who spoke with a foreign accent were deeply entrenched. This is why candidates for emigration to the UK were carefully screened even before they left Vienna. Those who were

19 P. Grosskurth, *Melanie Klein: Her World and Her Work* (New York: Knopf, 1986), p. 281.

20 See for instance Jones' letter to the Isakowers dated 17 May 1938 as cited in D. Kirsner, *Saving Psychoanalysts: Ernest Jones and the Isakowers*, pp. 83–84.

21 Jones's letter to Eitingon dated 3 July 1934 is cited in R. Steiner, "'It is a New Kind of Diaspora…'", p. 64.

selected were fluent in English and they tended to be young; the assumption was that they would be able to integrate more easily.[22] Jones' personal sympathies were another important factor. For instance, he effectively discouraged the Lampls and Waelders. Reckoning that there was room for no more than eight new analysts in London, where almost all his British colleagues were practising at the time, he proposed to bring Freud and his daughter, Dorothy Burlingham, Edward Hitschmann, the Krises and either the Bibrings or the Hoffers, leaving the final choice to Anna Freud.

The Isakowers were persuaded to settle in Liverpool. They tried to establish their own practice there and even set up a psychoanalytic training group in collaboration with Michael Bálint and Alfred Gross, who had moved to Manchester. Their sojourn in England must have been trying, for two years after their arrival they decided to move on to the United States. Their medical degrees offered a prospect of being able to practice psychoanalysis there. In 1940, they arrived in New York, where Hermann Nunberg was already working. Salomea became a training analyst and supervisor at the New York Psychoanalytic Society, where she continued to practise for over thirty years; her husband was elected chair of that institute's Educational Committee.

The New York Psychoanalytic Society also became a haven for Ludwig Jekels, Berta Bornstein and Gustav Bychowski, who joined in 1943. He and his family arrived after a veritable odyssey: after the outbreak of the war, Bychowski and his second wife, Maryla (née Auerbach), fled to Lithuania with fifteen-year-old Krystyna, Maryla's daughter from her first marriage, and their two-year-old Monika (later Monica).[23] Otto Fenichel reports that Bychowski intended to continue his psychoanalytic practice in Vilnius.[24] According to a relative, however, the living conditions were absolutely inadequate: "They had no means of subsistence, they shared one room, winter was approaching, there was a fuel shortage, and, stuck between the German occupiers and Russia, they felt trapped".[25] As soon as Bychowski's teenage son Ryszard managed to join, the family decided to emigrate to the United States. The American Psychoanalytic Society arranged visas and money for their onward journey, to be picked up in Sweden. The family arrived in Stockholm in the early spring of 1940. By

22 D. Kirsner, *Saving Psychoanalysts*, p. 86.

23 See J. Olczak-Ronikier, *W ogrodzie pamięci*, pp. 264–266.

24 O. Fenichel, *119 Rundbriefe*, vol. 2, p. 1306.

25 J. Olczak-Ronikier, *W ogrodzie pamięci*, p. 269.

now, however, it was no longer possible to travel directly to the United States; the only way was to apply for help from the Japanese Ministry of Foreign Affairs, which supported Jews from Russian-occupied territories of eastern Poland. The Bychowskis took the Trans-Siberian Railway and reached Vladivostok in February 1941; from there they crossed to Tsuruga in Japan on board a fishing boat. The Polish ambassador Tadeusz Romer helped them obtain tickets for a ship to San Francisco. They arrived on the Pacific coast of the United States in April, where the family parted ways. While the parents and younger children continued on to New York, nineteen-year-old Ryszard stayed in California. He enrolled at the University of Berkeley's Department of Sociology and Political Science. Having completed his first year, he became a volunteer for the Polish Armed Forces and trained as a pilot in Canada. He was deployed to the UK and joined the RAF, attaining the rank of senior navigator sergeant. He was killed in action on 22 May 1944.

A few months before his death, Ryszard Bychowski sent his father a letter announcing that "there are things I need to tell you. I want you to know my point of view on certain key issues. On the night of the second to third of October I had a serious crash, it was a miracle that I got out, and now I'm back to flying again. This letter is supposed to make sure that if I have another accident and the outcome is not so lucky, you'll know what I should have liked to tell you if we could speak to each other today."[26] Ryszard describes his bitter experiences in the Polish army. His observations there and in émigré political circles led him to believe that "Poles have not yet reached the necessary maturity for independence and sovereignty" (p. 113); he also wrote that Polish Jews who had emigrated had no reason to return after the war and ought to stay abroad. Apart from the devastating news from his homeland, Ryszard's opinion was shaped by the anti-Semitism he encountered in the Polish squadron, especially his colleagues' reactions to the liquidation of the Warsaw ghetto: there was indifference, and many of his comrades even approved of the massacre. Ryszard describes anti-Jewish excesses he witnessed in military and political circles, and he passes on information he read in reports by the Ministry of the Interior regarding Poland's situation; other documents mentioned by Ryszard deal with the Anders army in ways that suggest that "if that army ever entered Poland, its first act, just as Haller's army had

26 J. R. Bychowski, "List do ojca", *ZLI* 1991, no. 34, p. 113.

done after the previous war, would be an anti-Jewish pogrom" (p. 115). Ryszard warns his family about returning to Poland:

> I shudder at the thought of what I'm writing to you here, and no one would be happier than me if all this turned out to be untrue. Unfortunately, these are facts to which we must not close our eyes. I want you to keep your eyes open, you especially must not fail to see this reality; you may have a chance to return and to take up a prominent position. [...] A return would be very harmful to you, to Monika. A return would be harmful to those fellow Jews who will have saved themselves, and who will only be able to live and forget, at least to some extent, once we pull them out from among those walls and from among those people, where every moment they will remember what they've been through.
>
> I hope to come out of the war unscathed. I'm quite determined already not to go back to Poland. I don't want to be a second-class citizen ever again, and I don't want my son not to have the same opportunities as others. But above all, I tremble to hear the whole truth about Polish soci-ety's reaction to the extermination of the Jews. I cannot live, talk or work with people who may have turned their backs on Jews in need of help, who may simply have shrugged at their liquidation, who had no qualms to occupy Jewish homes or to denounce or blackmail survivors. (p. 117)

It is hard to tell to what extent this letter persuaded Gustav Bychowski to remain in the United States. Like many of the key figures of this study, he spent the second half of his life practicing psychoanalysis in America. Once his medical degree was recognised, he opened a private analytic practice in New York, performed training analyses and worked with war veterans. He taught at the Albert Einstein College of Medicine, Bellevue Medical Center, Downstate Medical School and Mount Sinai School of Medicine.[27] His daughter Monica, who also became a therapist, married the geriatric psychologist Douglas Holmes in 1959. The couple published a number of works on therapy for elderly people and intergenerational dialogue.

Bychowski's first English-language book, *Dictators and Disciples from Caesar to Stalin: A Psychoanalytic Interpretation of History*, appeared soon after the war, in 1948; it was dedicated to the memory of his son

27 J. Ehrenwald, "Gustav Bychowski a Memorial Issue: An Appreciation", *AI* 1973, no. 30, pp. 1–7.

Ryszard.[28] Chapters on Julius Caesar, Oliver Cromwell, Maximilian Robespierre and the emergence of Hitlerism were first printed in the *Journal of Clinical Psychopathology* (in 1945 and 1946), but the book included new analyses of the personalities of Adolf Hitler and Stalin. In the preface, Bychowski recalls his interview with Freud, conducted for *Wiadomości Literackie* in 1936. Curious about the master's prognosis for culture he asked: "Waves of hatred will shake the foundations of the human world, or will it be able to hold out against them?"[29] At that time Bychowski was hoping to elevate collective life through psychoanalysis, influencing entire nations and their leaders, and he tried to get Freud to agree; Freud, however, was doubtful that psychoanalysis could be combined with politics and offered no hope for a better society. Bychowski, unconvinced, commented in his interview that these were only "the Professor's private views". Now he thinks about this exchange somewhat differently; he shares Freud's scepticism, but remembers him to be more optimistic:

> When, in 1935, I paid my last visit to Sigmund Freud, I asked him what contribution he thought psychoanalysis might eventually make to the solution of the appalling crisis with which our civilisation was threatened. "How can we," I said, "devote our time and energy to curing a few individuals at a time like this when our entire civilisation, our very existence, is imperilled?" Freud replied that in his opinion we could not hope to save mankind, but could best help by advancing and popularising our psychoanalytical knowledge, so that eventually it would become public property, a part of universal thought, so to speak. Then, in the distant future, the day might come when these horrifying reactions of the collective psyche would no longer be possible.[30]

Bychowski must have started working on the book during the war. This is suggested by the fact that he gave a lecture on the same subject shortly after reaching the United States, on 17 February 1943, at the Polish

---

28 The dedication reads: "To the ever mourned memory of my only son Jan Ryszard, Navigator in the R.A.F. Polish Squadron, killed in action on May 22, 1944, who gave his young life fighting for a better world." See G. Bychowski, *Dictators and Disciples* [no page number].

29 G. Bychowski, "Rozmowa z Freudem", p. 4.

30 G. Bychowski, *Dictators and Disciples*, p. 9.

Institute of Arts and Sciences in New York. A summary was published (in English) in the quarterly *Bulletin of the Polish Institute of Arts and Sciences in America*.[31] The University of Warsaw is listed as Bychowski's affiliation. Perhaps this indicates that at this time he was still hoping to return, or perhaps he felt that, despite his emigration, he continued to be part of Warsaw's academic community.

In the opening of the lecture Bychowski identifies dictatorship as the central problem of the time. He explains that it can be seen as a form of interpersonal relationships, and as such it can be studied by psychologists and psychopathologists. Bychowski also mentions that the problem has a personal dimension for him, as the war, having forced him to leave his country and his usual occupations, also made him reflect on its causes. He builds on Freud's *Group Psychology and the Analysis of the Ego*, published twenty years before; from today's perspective, his conclusions also bring to mind Erich Fromm's *Escape from Freedom*, written around the same time. For Bychowski, dictators gain power because of deficiencies in the collective identity, which is weakened by fear, misery, disillusionment after a lost war or an exhausting revolution. Such conditions make a group regress to the most primitive stages of development. Fearful and in search of relief, the group is willing to be governed by a powerful individual who promises to take charge of its destiny. The collective identity attributes an almost divine omnipotence to this leader, trusting and worshipping him in the same way as children naively believe in their parents' magical powers. The dictator's veneration results from his over-idealisation. Group members identify with him and internalise his image, which becomes the super-ego of the collective psyche. What is more, the dictator enthrals crowds and imbues them with his own desires and ideals, his hatred and resentment – quite like a hypnotist. His delusion of grandeur and, later, his persecution complex are reinforced by accumulated collective emotions. The leader and the group incite each other to ever more delusional views. Bychowski concludes by exploring prevention. He points to the role of education in democracy, but the most important aspect, in his view, is economic prosperity. Impoverishment is the key factor that predisposes people to accept dictatorship and to place their faith in impostors. In addition to humanitarian considerations, he stresses, the need for social progress can also be demonstrated on the grounds of psychology. Here Bychowski

31 G. Bychowski, "Dictators and Their Followers: A Theory of Dictatorship", *BPI* 1943, no. 3, pp. 455–458.

returns to his research focus from the interwar period. These issues also reappear in his subsequent books, most prominently in his 1968 study *Evil in Man*.[32]

The Polish Institute of Arts and Sciences in America (PIASA), where Bychowski gave his paper on dictators, became his new intellectual home. The institution was founded in May 1942 in New York by exiled members of the Polish Academy of Arts and Sciences (Polska Akademia Umiejętności or PAU).[33] One of them was Bronisław Malinowski, who was based in London but joined the PAU as an international member in 1930. Shortly after the outbreak of the war he became a visiting professor at Yale University. At PIASA's official opening ceremony he was elected president of the council. He reportedly said to Kazimierz Wierzyński: "Well, Sir, one more year here, and then we shall all go back to Poland" (p. 75). A few hours later, the prominent anthropologist suffered a heart attack and died.

Bychowski was an active member of the PIASA from the beginning. In 1942 he was one the four signatories of a letter protesting against the appointment of the institute's new chairman of the educational research department, Professor Wojciech Świętosławski, previously Minister of Religious Affairs and Public Education. The signatories recalled that as a minister, Świętosławski had overseen the persecution of the Union of Polish Teachers and the introduction of the bench ghetto. He "supported reactionary and fascist trends among young people and professors, was the promoter of the Camp of National Unity [Obóz Zjednoczenia Narodowego] in Polish education," and therefore "offers no guarantee of working in the name of the principles we are now fighting for, the principles of freedom and democracy" (p. 81). When their protest was left unanswered, the daily *Nowy Świat* published Bychowski's open letter to Świętosławski, urging him to publicly disavow his former persuasion:

> While Poland's worst enemy was preparing to invade, you, Sir, were supporting the moral poisoning of Polish youth and Polish university circles. If your Jewish fellow Poles are now dying of hunger and deprivation behind ghetto walls in Polish cities, dying at the hands of an enemy who is

32 G. Bychowski, *Evil in Man: The Anatomy of Hate and Violence* (New York: Grune and Stratton, 1968).

33 For an excellent overview of the institute's work see B. Dorosz, *Nowojorski pasjans: Polski Instytut Naukowy w Ameryce: Studia o wybranych zagadnieniach działalności 1939–1969* (Warsaw: Towarzystwo "Więź", 2013).

> theirs as much as it is the enemy of Christian Poles, then you, Professor, are infamous for giving currency to the concept of the ghetto; during your tenure this concept became acceptable for the first time in modern, reborn Poland, which also became the first country of our era to allow this. This is how your name became associated with the infamy of Poland, with the infamy of Polish culture. (p. 82)

Świętosławski soon stepped down, but Bychowski and seven other PIASA members issued a memorandum demanding that the institution become more democratic. They argued that the PIASA's structures perpetuated the worst features of the PAU in Cracow: disciplinary casteism, formalism, and rigid hierarchies. Instead, the signatories demanded that the Institute should admit all Polish researchers who had emigrated to the United States and that it abandon forms that "had already been relics before the war and that are plainly unacceptable in present-day conditions".[34]

When the Institute's council rejected these demands, six of the signatories left PIASA. Bychowski, persuaded by Florian Znaniecki, was one of the two signatories who remained.[35] He was an active member of PIASA until the end of his life.[36] Bychowski showed a remarkable interest in events that focused on literature. For instance, he took part in a discussion of Jerzy Kosiński's novel *Malowany ptak* [The Painted Bird] in February 1966; he also spoke at a meeting with Sławomir Mrożek in March 1969, and a month later he gave a lecture at an event held in honour of Kazimierz Wierzyński.[37] Finally, according to an obituary by Damian S. Wandycz, the Institute's Director from 1965 to 1969, Bychowski was set to talk about the psychology of Polish history at the Institute's Second Scientific Congress in 1971.[38] Wandycz describes several anecdotes, one of which is worth recounting in this context:

> When Grotowski came to New York with his experimental theatre, it was extremely difficult to get tickets, so Bychowski called him. Hearing his name,

34 This memorandum can be found in the appendix to B. Dorosz's book *Nowojorski pasjans*, pp. 553–557.

35 B. Dorosz, *Nowojorski pasjans*, p. 93.

36 Until 1945, the PIASA was subsidised by the Polish government-in-exile; it became fully independent after the Yalta Conference, when the council refused to submit to the communist government.

37 B. Dorosz, *Nowojorski pasjans*, p. 514, p. 521, p. 428.

38 D.S. Wandycz, "Wspomnienie o Gustawie Bychowskim", *W* 1972, no. 21, p. 3.

> Grotowski asked if he was related to the author of a book on Słowacki published in Poland before the war. He was delighted to learn that he was speaking with the author and informed him that the book was still on his troupe's reading list until that day. And, naturally, he reserved a ticket. (*Ibid.*)

Many of the Polish émigrés in New York were artists and writers, which allowed Bychowski to keep up many of his relationships from prewar Poland. One of his old friends was the poet Jan Lechoń, a close affiliate of the Institute. He suffered from acute depression, so his friends counted on Bychowski to provide professional support. Kazimierz Wierzyński's letter to Mieczysław Grydzewski, written after Lechoń's suicide in June 1956, indicates that a friend had taken Lechoń to a psychoanalyst's office only a few days before, on a Tuesday. The next session was booked for the following Thursday, but Lechoń was no more by then.[39]

Lechoń's diary contains a few references to Bychowski, usually in the context of parapraxes or disturbing dreams.[40] These are rarely described. Even in his private notes Lechoń, who never felt at ease about his homo-sexuality, only makes vague allusions. On 27 September 1950, for in-stance, he notes:

> The dream was obviously sexual and almost unambiguous. A surge of anger at myself and the world, just a sickening wave that suddenly inundates me. My nerves are so tense that I flinch every time someone touches me or utters a livelier word. They say my face is grim. I'd go to see Bychowski if I wasn't afraid it would do me even more harm. (Vol. 1, p. 417)

When he visits the psychoanalyst, it is always on social occasions ("A night at the Bychowskis'. Too much food and booze" (Vol. 3, p. 833)). Lechoń's diary contains several references to Freudian therapy and his doubts about it – always during moments of crisis:

39 See *Z listów do Mieczysława Grydzewskiego 1946–1966*, ed. by R. Habielski (London: Polonia, 1990), p. 77. See also B. Dorosz, "Nowojorskie tajemnice życia i śmierci Jana Lechonia", *TD* 2004, no. 3, pp. 193–208.

40 Lechoń mentions that he appeared in a radio discussion about Belloc: "Somehow I got through it, only instead of Belloc I said Chesterton a couple of times. I wonder what Bychowski would make of that." See J. Lechoń, *Dziennik* (Warsaw: PIW, 1993), vol. 3, p. 174. He also describes "a dream so disgustingly Freudian and unambiguous that I should simply give it to Bychowski for some textbook" (p. 345) as well as "a dream so classic that old Freud must have been rolling over in his grave with joy. Bychowski would have rejoiced as well" (p. 190).

> Half the night I kept tossing and turning, not just because of the heat and humidity, but also because of my personal struggles, which are painfully sharp now, as if they were working up towards the decision I've been putting off for two years. As soon as I fell asleep for a moment, exhausted by this restlessness, I dreamt of a scene between my parents, very long forgotten, but very important to me, I think now. Only I have no idea how to glue it together with what I'm experiencing now. To visit Bychowski – which I don't believe would do me any good – would be like going to Canossa and would only lead to self-disgust. (Vol. 2, p. 467)

Lechoń's association of psychoanalysis with Henry IV's supplication before Pope Gregory VII suggests how reluctant he was to talk about himself openly. Even the prospect of recovery from depression did not sway him to address his tormenting secrets – an act he perceived as a humiliation and a great risk. It also implies that Lechoń saw Bychowski more as an enemy than a friend, or at least as a potential danger, should he be able to see through Lechoń's masks and act indiscreetly. Lechoń seems to prefer to talk to Freud himself. Now dead for more than twenty years, Freud visits him in his dreams and advices him to turn to literature:

> I had a dream today that seemed so beautiful and perfect that I imme-diately telephoned to share it with Gustav Bychowski, and I think it made the same impression on him. I saw a huge train station hall, now I'm almost sure it was Pennsylvania Station. I was chatting with some friends and suddenly, out of nowhere, there appeared before me none other than Freud himself, dressed as he was in some photograph in an issue of the Swiss *Du* dedicated to psychoanalysis. He did not join the conversation with my friends, which we interrupted, but he entered my own unac-knowledged thoughts and whispered in my ear in a manner that was friendly and somehow jocular: "What is it, Mr Lechoń wants to die?" And I replied: "And does immortality exist?" Freud became somewhat more serious and said very firmly: "Our will demands it." To which I said: "But the devil doesn't want it." Freud resumed his good-natured tone and asked me like a good doctor: "And does Mr Lechoń have anything to do with the devil?" I said: "Yes." And here's the unexpected but, in my opinion, logical conclusion of this dialogue. Freud says, as if making up a prescription: "Write one page every day." (p. 471)

In emigration, Bychowski continued his research from before the war. He published *Psychotherapy of Psychosis* (1952) and a number of minor studies. One of his interests in Poland used to be drug-induced psychoses, and now he turned to studying psychoses triggered by LSD.[41] He also continued to apply Freudian theory to literature and art, writing articles on figures such as Walt Whitman and the eighteenth-century German historian J. J. Winckelmann.[42] In 1965 he joined the editorial board of *American Imago*, which continued the tradition of the prewar *Imago* in Vienna, i.e. the application of psychoanalysis to the humanities. Mieczyslaw Wallis recalls Bychowski's lively interest in art and culture in *Ruch Filozoficzny*:

> Being a man of immeasurable vitality and energy, with a powerful élan vital, he also had an insatiable curiosity about the world. His intellectual thirst knew no bounds. He was interested in almost everything. He was a voracious reader of books, an avid museum-goer, a passionate traveller (he must have visited all the major countries of our globe). An extremely lively, dynamic, impulsive and expansive man, he easily connected with people of the most varied nationalities and backgrounds. In his flat, he had many valuable works of art – a Madonna and Child by the workshop of Filippo Lippi, acquired at a sale of part of the Metropolitan Museum's collection, works by Kandinsky and Chagall, paintings by Boznańska and Rembowski, miraculously saved from before the war, works of pre-Columbian and Polynesian sculpture. The shelves in this flat were heavy not only with books and magazines on psychiatry and psychoanalysis, neurology and psychology, ethnology and cultural history, but also with masterpieces of world literature and works by leading contemporary writers, as well as publications on art from all eras and continents. He also had a considerable record collection with the most outstanding world music performed by the best interpreters.[43]

Bychowski died unexpectedly, during a two-week trip to Morocco, on 3 April 1972, at the age of seventy-six.

41 Cf. J. Barchilon, "Gustav Bychowski (1895–1972)", *IJP* 1973, no. 54, p. 112.

42 G. Bychowski, "Walt Whitman: A Study in Sublimation", *PSS* 1951, no. 3, pp. 223–261; G. Bychowski, "Platonic Love and the Quest for Beauty: The Drama of J. J. Winckelmann", *AI* 1964, no. 21, pp. 80–94. For a full bibliography of Bychowski's work see P. Rubinton, "Bibliography of Gustav Bychowski (1895–1972)", *AI* 1972, no. 30, pp. 113–120.

43 M. Wallis, "Gustaw Bychowski, psychoanalityk i humanista (1895–1972)", p. 108.

One effect of the exodus of psychoanalysts that followed the public burning of Freud's works in 1933 – an effect that the Nazis neither foresaw nor desired – was that Freud's ideas were disseminated even more broadly throughout the world.[44] The price, however, was that psychoanalysis was purged of its most revolutionary aspects, reduced to a more or less effective therapeutic method and immersed in the American discourse of self-realisation and coping. The year 1933, when Hitler came to power and the IPA reacted by renouncing the political potential of psychoanalysis, followed by the departure of psychoanalysts from Germany, ends the era in which psychoanalysis was an emancipatory cultural project. The Nazis' entry into Vienna on 12 March 1938 and Freud's escape to London, where he died of assisted suicide in the face of terminal cancer, marks the end of this phase of disintegration. The key players' emigration to the United States completes the process in which Freudianism appears to have abandoned some of its most important features.

One crucial question that preoccupied the movement in the United States was lay psychoanalysis and the training of candidates without a medical degree. For Freud, medicine had been neither the sole nor the best path towards psychoanalysis. He often discouraged his followers from studying psychiatry, which is why the VPS represented a cross-section of the intelligentsia at large.[45] Hermann Nunberg recalls:

> It is striking that, at the beginning and even later on, more discussion was devoted to art, literature, mythology, religion and education than to problems of psychiatry [...]. The members of the group saw far more in psychoanalysis than a method of treating sick people. They found it necessary to concern themselves not only with the sick human being but also with literature, religion, philosophy, etc.[46]

In 1926, when the Viennese lay psychoanalyst Theodor Reik was sued for harmful treatment, Freud wrote *The Question of Lay Analysis* (*Die Frage der*

---

44 See e.g. *Freud in Exile: Psychoanalysis and its Vicissitudes*, ed. by E. Timms and N. Segal (New Heaven: Yale University Press, 1988), pp. 1–15.

45 "The group was heterogenous; it consisted of physicians, educators, writers, and others. In short, its members represented a cross-section of the intellectuals at the beginning of the century" (H. Nunberg, "Introduction", in *Minutes of the Vienna Psychoanalytic Society*, no. 1, p. xx).

46 H. Nunberg, *Memoirs*, p. 105.

Laienanalyse) in Reik's defence. This text, presented as a dialogue, argues that medical training is neither a necessary nor a suffi-cient prerequisite to practice psychoanalysis. The institutes that had emerged in the 1920s had developed their own training programmes, which were accessible to candidates from different professional back-grounds. At the Congress in Innsbruck in 1927, the American dele-gation proposed that only medical doctors ought to be admitted to practice psychoanalysis. Freud was vehemently opposed this idea, so the American Psychoanalytical Association (APA) split off from the IPA. This moment also marks the beginning of the gradual absorption of the IPA into APA. In early 1935, the APA still welcomed European analysts with open arms, but various restrictions were successively put into place. One condition for admission was that the European candidate had to be accepted by one of the local psychoanalytical societies that constituted the APA. European analysts suddenly found themselves in the position of petitioners. This signified the end of European hege-mony within the movement, even if in 1948 one in three APA mem-bers continued to be an émigré.

In accordance with the strict laws that the US legislature had passed on the practice of therapeutic work by people without a degree in medicine, the local associations refused to admit laypeople; at best, they were allowed as honorary members, without the right to treat clients. Of the VPS members, less than 64% were medical professionals – even before World War I. This is why many European analysts who arrived in the States were faced with difficulties. Some of them had never studied medicine (Siegfried Bernfeld, for instance, turned to theoretical work on Freud); others had difficulties with the accreditation of their degrees in America. What is more, there was no uniform regulation across the different states. One case in point is Hermann Nunberg, who moved from Philadelphia to New York in 1934 because in Pennsylvania he was required to pass examinations to get his European training re-cognised; there was no need for such a procedure in New York State.[47] Otto Fenichel, who settled in L.A. in 1938, decided to study for an American diploma so that he could support the concept of lay analysis as a medical professional, thus lending

47 Cf. H. Nunberg, *Memoirs*, p. 62.

credence to his argument. In 1946, six months into his mandatory hospital internship, he collapsed and died.[48] He was 48 years old.

Another circumstance that contributed to the distortion of Freud's original message was the fact that the English translation of his work gained so much traction. Bruno Bettelheim has argued that the Standard Edition edited by James Strachey introduces far-reaching changes; compared to the original, it makes Freud's writing appear more complex and dogmatic, and it gives the reader little reason to think that Freud was "a humanist in the best sense of the word".[49] The word *Seele* [soul], for instance, is rendered as "mind" or "intellect"; the adjective *seelisch* appears as "mental". Bettelheim goes so far as to suggest a telling difference between the German compound noun *Psychoanalyse*, which accentuates the first component, and its English equivalent, psychoanalysis, where the stress is on the second part; this shift in accents, he argues, explains why in the Anglo-American world Freudian therapy is often thought to hinge on analysing other people, whereas the primary endeavour according to Freud was to get to know oneself. The English translation sacrifices the rich semantic shades of the original because the translators often propose purely technical and unambivalent terms where Freud uses everyday words that suggest metaphorical layers. Finally, the dense allusions to the canon of European literature, easily legible to alumni of the classical *Gymnasium*, remain inaccessible to most American readers. Freud's English translators were motivated by the perceived need to anchor his theory in the field of medicine; they cloaked Freud's ideas in scientific terms, so that *Mutterleib* (here Bettelheim suggests "womb") was rendered as "uterus," *Zerlegung* ("taking apart" in Bettelheim) as anatomy, *Besetzung* ("occupation") as cathexis, while Freud's first-person comments were rendered in a dry, impersonal style that recalls a handbook. Most consequentially, the English translators' efforts to reintroduce psychoanalysis into the field of the exact sciences was that their versions of Freud's terms for the psychic apparatus became permanent fixtures of the English language. While

48 "The cause was attributed to a ruptured cerebral aneurysm. If the aneurysm was congenital, immediate circumstances may have been decisive in ending his life. He was working rotating night shifts as an intern. He complained frequently of fatigue; and he hoped to transfer to a hospital where night duty was not required" (R. Jacoby, *The Repression of Psychoanalysis*, p. 132).

49 Bruno Bettelheim, *Freud and Man's Soul* (London: Chatto & Windus, The Hogarth Press, 1983), p. xi.

Freud's original *Es*, *Ich* and *Über-Ich* are rooted in everyday language, the versions used in English, *id*, *ego* and *super-ego* draw on Latin terms connoting accuracy. For Bettelheim, this is the root of many misunderstandings, such as the tendency to critique psychoanalysis from a scientific perspective. Freud's failure to conform to scientific principles or methodologies, Bettelheim argues, is not a liability but an advantage: "If behaviouristic studies could prove Freud right, his would no longer be an introspective psychology that tries to elucidate the darkest recesses of the soul – the forces least accessible to our observation" (p. 108).

In postwar America, psychoanalysis was generally viewed with scepticism. Many leading intellectuals were suspicious about the influx of Central European migrants. Their vague concerns were echoed, decades later, in Allan Bloom's bestselling *The Closing of the American Mind.* The new arrivals, Bloom suggests, spread German philosophy on the other side of the Atlantic: "the *echt Deutsch* label has been replaced by a *Made in America* label; and the new American life-style has become a Disneyland version of the Weimar Republic for the whole family".[50] One writer who agreed with Bloom was Nabokov, who never missed an opportunity to deride "the Viennese delegation"; in the 1940s and 50s, he wrote, the psychoanalysts from Central Europe were spreading "Freudian voodoo" across American culture.[51]

Another factor that shaped the development of psychoanalysis in the United States – effectively leading to the abandonment of its social commitment – was the Second Red Scare (1947–1957). Even before the onset of McCarthyism, the former members of the Kinderseminar in Berlin were in a particularly difficult situation. As Jews and psychoanalysts they had been repressed by the Nazi authorities, but as Marxists they experienced harassment by the psychoanalytic establishment in postwar America. Until 1945, they continued their research at the intersection of psychoanalysis and politics in secret, using "Rundbriefe," a clandestine system of circulars devised before their emigration. The regular recipients included Berta Bornstein as well as Emanuel Windholz, the widower of her sister Stephanie. Having emigrated in 1937, he became a founding member and training analyst of the San Francisco Psychoanalytic Society; later he held a professorship in psychiatry at the University of California. The "Rundbriefe" worked as follows: Fenichel would send a letter to each of his colleagues; they were only allowed to reply

50 A. Bloom, *The Closing of the American Mind: How Higher Education Has Failed Democracy and Impoverished the Souls of Today's Students* (New York: Simon & Schuster, 1987), p. 147.

51 Cf. E. J. Rolnik, *Freud in Zion*, p. 100.

directly to him, and he would then quote or discuss their responses in the next letter. The documents were to be destroyed after reading, but some of the addressees failed to conform to this rule, allowing later editors of the correspondence to assemble a complete set.[52] Fenichel's secret group, a kind of underground psychoanalytic society, is reminiscent of Freud's secret committee, which operated among his closest collaborators in the 1920s: they also kept quiet about their very existence and communicated only through circulars.[53] The mission of Fenichel's group, active for twelve years, was to defend what they saw as the core of psychoanalysis and to prevent it from turning into something entirely different; as Fenichel put it, "the theme 'Freud vs. Freud' is the central theme of our critical work".[54] Unlike Wilhelm Reich, who was put on trial and imprisoned in the US, the members of the Kinderseminar never officially distanced themselves from the standards of the IPA and the APA but combined public compliance with private heresy. Nor did they acknowledge their Marxist past. Berta Bornstein, for example, added to her American visa application a letter from Lawrence S. Kubie, president of the New York Psychoanalytic Society, in which he vouches that "she has never taken an active part in or affiliated herself with any political activities".[55] In his last circular, dated 14 July 1945, shortly before his death, Fenichel voices his doubts about their raison d'être; the priority at present should not be social psychoanalysis, he suggests, but the defence of classical Freudianism against the American reformers of psychoanalysis.[56]

---

52 The editors Elke Mühlleitner and Johannes Reichmayr sourced individual letters from several library archives across the USA as well as from private document collections (e.g. Annie Reich's and Randi Markowitz's). In some cases, several copies of a letter survive, in other cases it is only one; sometimes the original was found (i.e. a typescript with Fenichel's handwritten corrections), sometimes it was a clean copy or photocopy of such a document.

53 Cf. P. Grosskurth, *The Secret Ring*.

54 O. Fenichel, *119 Rundbriefe*, vol. 1, p. 72.

55 Leo Baeck Institute, Joseph Bornstein Collection 1917–1952, catalogue number AR 4082/MF 650, < http://findingaids.cjh.org/?pID=121524 > [accessed on 22/08/2022].

56 The work of the Kinderseminar has certain parallels with that of the Frankfurt School, i.e. the Institute for Social Research founded at the University of Frankfurt in 1923. It was dissolved in 1933 and operated in New York from 1935 to 1949 before returning to Frankfurt. Unlike the psychoanalysts from Berlin, Adorno and his colleagues had official positions in the US, as well as financial resources and access to publication channels and a geographical centre. Fenichel's colleagues, meanwhile, were dispersed and not institutionalised, and the precarious status of immigrants forced them to focus on meeting their basic needs. Cf. R. Jacoby, *Otto Fenichel*, pp. 151-152.

Helene Deutsch, who survived all of Freud's early disciples, was able to observe the development of psychoanalysis in America until 1982, and she often spoke of her disappointment with the direction it had taken there. She was among those who spearheaded the institutionalisation of psychoanalysis, and for many of her colleagues she epitomised its official current. (For instance, Wilhelm Reich spoke of a campaign against him organised by "the most prominent members of the Vienna Society," specifically mentioning Deutsch and Nunberg.[57]) It was only in an interview shortly before her death that she admitted what had attracted her to psychoanalysis in the first place, namely its promise of social emancipation: "I always saw Freud as the greatest revolutionary."[58] Initially, she was thrilled by the freedom offered by America, but later she came to regret the commercialisation of psychoanalysis there. Her new colleagues' services tended to be tailored not to the clients' needs but to maximising their own profits, which explains the popularity of short-term analysis in the States. Students, too, were regrettably materialistic, allowing economic factors to guide their career choices, rather than pursuing their ideals or following a desire to change the world. Finally, therapy in the US was evidently aimed at restoring the patient to their social functions – a strikingly conservative approach when compared to the mission of European analysts before the war. Deutsch also points out that in the US, students of psychoanalysis were not selected on the basis of a suitable personality, as was the norm at the Vienna training institute in her time. (She mentions that among the candidates she had dissuaded from psychoanalysis was Esti Freud, the wife of Sigmund Freud's eldest son Martin. She eventually became an excellent speech therapist.) Deutsch's greatest regret, according to her 1973 autobiography, is that so few women opted for psychoanalytic training, although it was "par excellence a profession for women".[59] In fact, the processes discussed above pushed women out of the profession. Medicine was a highly masculinised field in the postwar United States; in the 1960s, only 7% of all doctors were female.[60] Although 30 % of émigré analysts were women, by 1958 women accounted for only 8 % of students in psychoanalysis.[61]

57 O. Fenichel, *119 Rundbriefe*, vol. 1, p. 71.

58 S. Gordon, "Helene Deutsch and the Legacy of Freud", *NYT* 30/07/1978, p. 23.

59 H. Deutsch, *Confrontations with Myself*, p. 209.

60 R. Jacoby, *Otto Fenichel*, p. 170.

61 L. Fermi, *Illustrious Immigrants*, p. 170.

Regarding the strict institutionalisation of psychoanalysis, Deutsch wrote: "More and more, I feel like someone who has been working in an artist's studio and suddenly finds himself in a factory" (p. 244). Siegfried Bernfeld expressed a similar disappointment in his last lecture in November 1952, a few months before his death.[62] Perhaps, he said, his argument would come as a shock, being uttered at a psychoanalytic society, but in his opinion, the way psychoanalysis was taught in the United States falsified what was most valuable about it.

According to Laura Fermi, "at the outbreak of World War II, European psychoanalysis found itself in the unenviable position of being the only discipline [...] that Hitler virtually exterminated in continental Europe".[63] When Jewish psychoanalysts started to flee Nazism in the 1930s, two-thirds of them ended up in the United States, shifting the epicentre of psychoanalysis from Central Europe to America. It is true that Anna Freud expressed her reservations about any American colleague becoming president of the IPA as late as February 1936; she insisted that under no circumstances should European psychoanalysis become just an outpost of the American movement.[64] Within a few decades, however, Central Europe lost its position as the homeland of psychoanalysis. In the statutes of the International Psychoanalytical Association, adopted in 1977 and still in force today, the realm of its activity was defined precisely as "America and the rest of the world". This document was highlighted by Jacques Derrida in one of his lesser-known texts. He calls for "a sort of mapreading approach to psychoanalysis" and suggests that geography could be an important tool for understanding its history and politics.[65]

My book follows Derrida's lead: I tracked the trajectories of some of the movement's early participants, who flocked from the Habsburg Empire's provinces to its Viennese heartland in the early twentieth century, only to find themselves in America in the aftermath of the Second World War; in terms of psychoanalysis, the United States were something of a Wild West, a lawless frontier region, when the Central European analysts arrived, but with their help it grew, within a few decades, into a new global hub, pushing the former centre to the margin. As a group, psychoanalysts may

62 S. Bernfeld, "On Psychoanalytic Training", *TPQ* 1962, no. 4, pp. 453–482.

63 L. Fermi, *Illustrious Immigrants*, p. 142.

64 Cited in R. Steiner, "'It is a New Kind of Diaspora...'", p. 58.

65 J. Derrida, "Geopsychoanalysis: '...And the Rest of the World'", trans. by D. Nicholson-Smith, *AI* 1991, no. 48, pp. 199–231.

have been the most successful Central European immigrants to the United States. But the fact that they assimilated remarkably quickly, that some of them enjoyed obvious professional success implementing psychoanalysis on the other side of the Atlantic – all this also obscures the end of psychoanalysis as a movement with cultural and socio-political potential.[66]

66 See R. Jacoby, *Otto Fenichel*, p. 14.

CODA

What have you against Doctor Krokowski?

Working on the project that culminated in this book, I kept returning to Thomas Mann's *Magic Mountain.* Although this novel, published in 1924, is not the only one to feature a psychoanalyst, it would be hard to find a character who has captured the collective imagination more powerfully than Dr Krokowski. While reconstructing the traces of the lives and work of Central Europe's Freudians, I kept asking myself why this paradigmatic psychoanalyst of the literary interwar period was cast as a Polish Jew. Dr Krokowski gave me no peace, so I decided to devote a separate part of my study to him. Taking the place of a conclusion, this section proposes to examine the meanings which the figure of the Polish psychoanalyst has acquired in Europe.

Hans Castorp, the protagonist of *The Magic Mountain*, arrives at the sanatorium in the Swiss Alps to visit his tubercular cousin, Joachim Ziemssen. As Joachim explains to Hans, the psychoanalyst Dr Krokowski is "the sanatorium's main attraction".[1]

> He was about thirty-five years old, broad-shouldered, stout, considerably shorter than the two men across from him, so that he had to tip his head back to look them in the eye, and extraordinarily pale – there was almost a translucence, even phosphorescence, to his pallor, and it was enhanced by dark, glowing eyes, black eyebrows, and a rather long beard that already showed a few gray strands and ended in two diverging points. He wore a black, rather worn, double-breasted business suit and black open-worked shoes, almost sandals really, over gray woollen socks. (p. 18)

As Yahya Elsaghe notes, Mann's portrayal of Krokowski parallels his representations of Jews in his early work. Described primarily as economic competitors and erotic rivals of German characters, they bear typical Jewish names and their appearance has much in common with racist

1 Thomas Mann, *The Magic Mountain*, trans. by John E. Woods (New York: Knopf, 2005), p. 778.

stereotypes; still, they are never explicitly referred to as Jews.[2] For Elsaghe, these characters demonstrate that before World War I, Mann was not immune to the influence of the anti-Semitic discourses that emerged in Germany during the last decade of the nineteenth century.

In *The Magic Mountain*, words like "Jew" or "Jewish" can be found only about a dozen times. Mostly they are used with reference to the Jesuit Naphta, whose Jewish origins Mann is keen to emphasise, as well as in a chapter on anti-Semitism. But the novel certainly presents more Jewish characters. As is the case with Krokowski, they are not directly identified as Jews; readers' speculations are, however, fuelled by a number of textual clues that engage stereotypes of Jewishness. The psychiatrist's Jewishness is suggested not only by his Semitic features and bizarre attire, but also by his profession (while Jews represented about 20% of German doctors at the time, in Mann's novels about every other doctor happens to be Jewish[3]) and his East European accent. As Sander L. Gilman has argued, what turn-of-the-century anti-Semites hated most was Jewish language – not just Yiddish (at least not primarily), but also the supposedly "Jewish" manner of speaking German, of thinking and formulating statements.[4] The doctor's "consciously affected, drawling accent had an exotic, palatised *r* – not a rolled *r*, but simply a single tap of the tongue just behind the upper front teeth" (p. 226). Whenever he said "regards," his greeting sounded "ghastly," like "d'gods" (p. 434). Krokowski speaks in Russian with a couple from Russia, and he takes to addressing Castorp in ways that suggest familiarity or identification ("comrade", p. 434).

Even as he portrayed the doctor as an unmistakable Eastern European Jew, Mann gave him a typically Polish – but not typically Jewish – surname with the suffix -ski.[5] Before Krokowski became a fully developed character in *The Magic Mountain*, his name had a first appearance in an outline for a novella titled "Ein Elender" [A Miserable Man]. Mann toyed with this project around 1910, envisioning it as a literary reckoning with a

2 Y. Elsaghe, "'Edhin Krokowski aus Linde bei Pinne, Provinz Posen': Judentum und Antisemitismus im *Zauberberg* und seiner Vorgeschichte", *MH* 2009, no. 1, pp. 56-59.

3 Y. Elsaghe, "Edhin Krokowski", p. 66.

4 See S. L. Gilman, *Jewish Self-Hatred, passim.*

5 Surprisingly, Polish critics seem to have overlooked Dr Krokowski's Polish-Jewish heritage. The character is not discussed in any of the prewar Polish reviews of *The Magic Mountain* reprinted in the collection *Thomas Mann w krytyce i literaturze polskiej: Antologia tekstów i dokumentów*, ed. by R. Dziergwa (Poznań: Wydawnictwo Poznańskie, 2003).

recently published pamphlet by Theodor Lessing.[6] In this pamphlet Lessing used his amateurish understanding of psychoanalysis to disparage Mann and his protector, the critic Samuel Lublinski.[7] Lessing portrays Mann as being torn between life and art – quite like the character Tonio Kröger from Mann's eponymous novella of 1903. Surviving documents suggest that Mann had also intended "Ein Elender" to settle the score with the influential writer and theatre critic Alfred Kerr, who had torn to pieces the premiere of Mann's drama *Fiorenza* and other of his publications, including *Buddenbrooks*. Elsewhere Mann pointed out that his enemies Lessing and Kerr, both of them Jews, shared a certain "self-loathing" (*Selbstverachtung*), as their writing was characterised by unbridled anti-Semitism.[8]

The protagonist of Mann's planned novella was to be Edhin Krokowski from Lipka near Pniewy ("Linde bei Pinne, Provinz Posen"). This place name alludes to a passage from Lessing's lampoon, where Samuel Lublinski is said to come from "Pinne in Posen" (Lublinski was actually born in East Prussia). Mann never realised his project, and no further information about it has been found in his notes. The title does appear, however, in *Death in Venice* (1912), with its author being protagonist Gustav von Aschenbach. This is how the narrator of *Death in Venice* describes von Aschenbach's "famous story *A Miserable Man*":

> [It was] an outburst of disgust with the indecent psychological leanings of the era as embodied in the figure of that week and foolish semi-scoundrel who fraudulently acquires a destiny by driving his wife into the arms of a beardless youth out of helplessness, out of depravity, out of an ethical caprice, and who believes that it is his profundity that permits him to commit despicable actions.[9]

---

6 Theodor Lessing, *Samuel zieht die Bilanz und Tomi melkt die Moralkuh oder Zweier Könige Sturz* (Hannover: Antirüpel, 1910).

7 Cf. J. Finck, *Thomas Mann et la psychanalyse* (Paris: Les Belles Lettres, 1982), pp. 50-52.

8 Thomas Mann, "Der Doktor Lessing", *Das Literarische Echo*, 1910, no. 13, pp. 977-980, reprinted in Thomas Mann, *Essays*, ed. by Heinrich Detering, Große kommentierte Frankfurter Ausgabe, vol. 14 (Frankfurt a.M.: Fischer, 2002), pp. 112-118. Many years later, Lessing would help establish the notion of the "self-hating Jew". See Theodor Lessing, *Der jüdische Selbsthaß* (Berlin: Jüdischer Verlag, 1930).

9 Thomas Mann, *Death in Venice*, trans. by Stanley Appelbaum (Mineola: Dover Publications, 1995).

It is impossible to tell whether the "miserable man" in the title referred to Krokowski or if Mann intended to cast Krokowski as the victim of another character, as suggested by the parallel between his surname and that of Lubinski, the butt of Lessing's jokes.

In *The Magic Mountain* Krokowski's name is another sign of his difference. His opponent, the Italian Lodovico Settembrini, an embodiment of Western culture and the ideals of the Enlightenment, "pretended the name was a tongue twister".[10] Krokowski's first name, Edhin – whose only mention appears towards the end of the book – is not listed in any German name dictionaries.[11] The fact that it sounds Scandinavian, thus "hyper-Germanic," suggests an effort to assimilate, as is the case with other Jewish characters in Mann's fiction (Hermann Hagenström in *Buddenbrooks*, Detlev Spinell in *Tristan*, Siegmund Aarenhold in *Wälsungenblut*).[12]

Krokowski's work as a psychoanalyst also associates him with the abject. Joachim tells his cousin: "'They make special note of his services in the brochure. He dissects the patients' psyches.' 'He what? Dissects their psyches? That's disgusting!' Hans Castorp cried".[13] In the original, this reference to psychoanalysis appears as *Seelenzergliederung* – a German translation of the term *Psychoanalyse*, borrowed from the Greek. At the time, this tendentious expression was commonly used by opponents of Freudianism.[14] While *Seele* is an accurate German equivalent of the Greek ψυχή (*psyche*), however, the connotations of the word *Zergliederung* are quite different from the Greek ἀνάλυσις (*analysis*). The use of the verb *zergliedern*, whose first meaning is "to dissect," is essentially restricted to inanimate objects; the particle *glied* (link, member, limb) implies fragmentation, and the prefix *-zer* denotes the process by which the object is destroyed. *Seelenzergliederung* suggests a soul being sliced or quartered – which is probably why the idea of such a practice strikes Castorp as "disgusting" (*widerlich*) and induces his nervous fit of laughter.

10 Thomas Mann, *The Magic Mountain*, p. 113.

11 See Eliza Pieciul, "Literarische Personennamen in deutsch polnischer Translation: Eine kontrastive Studie aufgrund der Prosawerke von Thomas Mann (*Buddenbrooks*, *Der Zauberberg*, *Doktor Faustus*)", unpublished doctoral thesis defended at the Adam Mickiewicz University in Poznań in 2000, pp. 224-228.

12 Y. Elsaghe, "Edhin Krokowski", pp. 66-67.

13 Thomas Mann, *The Magic Mountain*, p. 10.

14 Cf. J.-F. Laplénie, "Puissances voisines: Études pour une histoire structurelle de la réception de la psychanalyse dans les milieux littéraires germanophones (1900-1930)", unpublished doctoral thesis (Université de la Sorbonne Nouvelle – Paris III, 2004), pp. 203-205.

Mann's writings are peppered with references to psychoanalysis as "a Jewish science" – here both terms, "Jewish" and "science," are pejorative expressions – as a rationalist force in the service of destruction. In his article "Mein Verhältnis zur Psychoanalyse" [My Views on Psychoanalysis], written shortly after the publication of *The Magic Mountain*, he describes psychoanalysis as "a curious outgrowth [*merkwürdiges Gewächs*] of the scientific-civilisational spirit," expressing an obsession with discovery and liable to become a tool for "malicious enlightenment" in conflict with culture.[15] The realisations provided by Freudianism are essentially melancholic, especially when it comes to the psychology of the artist and the essence of art. Mann, like many writers of the time, mistrusted the psychoanalysts' ambitions to uncover the secret of creativity, worrying that a rational explanation of the mechanism would make further creative work impossible.[16] He rejects the scientistic objectivity claimed by psychoanalysts such as his fictional Dr Krokowski; science always struck him as the opposite of life. It is no coincidence that Krokowski's ideological opponent in *The Magic Mountain* is Peeperkorn, a representive of pantagruelic vitalism.

The sanatorium proudly advertises Dr Krokowski's services in its prospectus, apparently regarding psychoanalysis as a marker of modernity – on a par with radiological diagnostics, formaldehyde disinfection, electric razors, a gramophone, film screenings and a bobsleigh track.[17] At the same time, Freudian therapy is surrounded by an aura of darkness and mystery. The reader never crosses the threshold of the doctor's "analytical chamber" (p. 158) but is left with Joachim, who sees his cousin "vanish into the twilight of Dr Krokowski's analytical pit".[18] Behind its doors one might expect something like Faust's study or Dr Frankenstein's "workshop of filthy creation"[19] rather than an austere scientific laboratory.

When it comes to a representation of Mann's own views in *The Magic Mountain*, we may cite Settembrini, who dislikes Dr Krokowski. To Castorp's question, "What do you have against him,"[20] the Italian replies:

15 T. Mann, "Mein Verhältnis zur Psychoanalyse", *ADI*, 1926, p. 32.

16 J. Finck, *Thomas Mann et la psychanalyse*, p. 58.

17 Cf. M. Łukasiewicz, *Jak być artystą: Na przykładzie Tomasza Manna* (Warsaw: Towarzystwo "Więź", 2011), p. 82.

18 Thomas Mann, *The Magic Mountain*, p. 436.

19 Mary Wollstonecraft Shelley, *Frankenstein: Or, the Modern Prometheus* (London: Penguin Classics, 1985), p. 102.

20 Thomas Mann, *The Magic Mountain*, p. 264.

> Analysis is good as a tool of enlightenment and civilisation – to the extent that it shakes stupid preconceptions, quashes natural biases, and undermines authority. Good, in other words, to the extent that it liberates, refines, and humanises – it makes slaves ripe for freedom. It is bad, very bad, to the extent that it prevents action, damages life at its roots, and is incapable of shaping it. Analysis can be very unappetizing, as unappetizing as death, to which it may very well be linked – a relative of the grave and its foul anatomy. (*Ibid.*)

Settembrini sees a duality in psychoanalysis, which in his view resembles a cognitive tool but is also associated with night or death; he takes issue with the way it appears to vacillate between enlightenment and mysticism. This duality returns in Mann's later writings, although with a positive, rather than negative, connotation: in 1929 he describes it as a perfect synthesis of irrationalism and rationalism, "Romanticism turned natural science" [Naturwissenschaft gewordene Romantik].[21] In the late 1920s Mann came to feel rueful about his portrayal of psychoanalysis in *The Magic Mountain*. He had regrets especially about the glaring contrast between Krokowski's grotesque eccentricity and the great mind of Freud, with whom he had become personally acquainted.[22] Mann wrote about Freud several times, most importantly in 1929 and in 1936. The first occasion was his lecture titled "Die Stellung Freuds in der modernen Geistesgeschichte" [Freud's Position in Modern Intellectual History] given at the University of Munich; the second his laudation "Freud und die Zukunft" ["Freud and the Future"] celebrating Freud's eightieth birthday in 1936.[23] In both of

21 This translation is by T. Bhambry and L. Magnone. H. T. Lowe-Porter's translation of Mann's article ("natural science divested of mysticism and become romanticism," p. 196) is incorrect. See T. Mann, "Freud's Position in the History of Modern Thought", in *Past Masters and Other Papers*, trans. by H. T. Lowe-Porter (London: Martin Secker, 1933). Originally published as "Die Stellung Freuds in der modernen Geistesgeschichte", *Psychoanalytische Bewegung*, 1929, pp. 3-32.

22 As Jean Finck points out, Mann began to appreciate Freud when he discovered elements of psychoanalytic theory that were not linked to sexuality; *Totem and Taboo* would have a profound impact on Mann's novel *Joseph and His Brothers* (J. Finck, *Thomas Mann et la psychanalyse*, p. 79).

23 T. Mann, "Freud's Position in the History of Modern Thought", pp. 167-198; T. Mann, "Freud und die Zukunft", *I* 1936, no. 3, pp. 257-274, English version: "Freud and the Future", *TSR* 25/07/1936, pp. 3-4 and pp. 14-15.

these texts Mann compares Freudianism to Nietzscheanism and Schopenhauerism; the same triad appears on other occasions, such as in the essay "Schopenhauer" of 1938.[24]

Having read "Die Stellung Freuds in der modernen Geistesgeschichte," Freud remarked that when Mann was asked to write the lecture he must have pulled from his drawer a finished article on Romanticism and added a beginning and a conclusion on psychoanalysis.[25] The article's point of departure is Nietzsche's aphorism "The German Hostility to Enlightenment".[26] Mann argues that underneath its scientific form, psychoanalytic thought is deeply Romantic and that it is one of the theories which are hostile to the Enlightenment and yet turn out to be most conducive to it – if by "Enlightenment" we mean revolution, development and renewal of life. He goes on: "Its emphasis on the daemonic in nature, its passion for investigating the night side of the soul, makes it as anti-rationalistic as any product of the new spirit that lies locked in victorious struggle with the mechanistic and materialistic elements of the nineteenth century".[27] It is telling that Mann can pay full homage to Freud only at the cost of tying him to the tradition of German Romanticism, by treating psychoanalysis as a return "back into the night, the sacred primitive, the fore-known, the life-bearing; backward into the romantical, prehistorical mother-womb".[28]

In *The Magic Mountain*, Krokowski is not only inclined to vague mysticism, he also embodies the pansexualism stereotypically attributed to psychoanalysis. Here the accusation, so often levelled at Freud himself, is uttered by the Italian humanist, who says of the sanatorium doctor: "The man has but one thought in his head, and it is a filthy one."[29] Krokowski

24 Mann writes: "Schopenhauer, as psychologist of the will, is the father of all modern psychology. From him the line runs, by way of the psychological radicalism of Nietzsche, straight to Freud and the men who built up his psychology of the unconscious and applied it to the mental sciences" and "Schopenhauer's sinister domain of the will is entirely identical with what Freud calls the unconscious, the 'id' – as, on the other hand, Schopenhauer's intellect entirely corresponds to the Freudian ego, that part of the soul which is turned outwards to the world." Thomas Mann, "Schopenhauer", in *Essays of Three Decades*, trans. by H. T. Lowe-Porter (London: Secker & Warburg, 1947), p. 408.

25 Sigmund Freud and Lou Andreas-Salomé, *Letters*, ed. by Ernst Pfeiffer, trans. by William and Elaine Robson-Scott (London: The Hogarth Press, 1972), pp. 181-182.

26 See Friedrich Nietzsche, *The Dawn of Day*, trans. by J. M. Kennedy (London: Allen & Unwin, 1924), pp. 198-200.

27 T. Mann, "Freud's Position in the History of Modern Thought", p. 191.

28 T. Mann, "Freud's Position in the History of Modern Thought", p. 173.

29 Thomas Mann, *The Magic Mountain*, p. 73.

is also called a "shameless father confessor", in whose presence women blush because he knows all their secrets (p. 113). According to Director Behrens, the job of his deputy, Dr Krokowski, is to help patients keep their drives in check, although he is bound to fail:

> The damn libido [...]. Can I help it if phthisis is accompanied by increased concupiscence [...]? I didn't arrange things this way, but before you know what's happened you're running a cathouse [...]. We provide analysis, a chance to talk things out – and a hell of a lot of good it does. The more the rhonchial pack talks things out the more lecherous they become. (p. 493)

Every other Monday, Krokowski gives lectures before the Berghof residents, who assemble in the dining room to hear him read from his series "Love as a Force Conductive to Illness" (p. 137). Mann's descriptions focus on the female members of the audience, who listen with "eager eyes and downy red spots on both cheeks" (p. 147). Their faces have an expression of "ignorant ecstasy" (*ibid.*), while their chests are rising and falling. Hans is embarrassed: "How did one go about discussing such a delicate subject, something of such a private nature, here in broad daylight, before an audience of both ladies and gentlemen?" (p. 148). He barely takes notice of Krokowski's central thesis, that organic disease is a secondary symptom of the suppression of sexual desire, and can be cured by transforming the pathological changes back into conscious affects.

Mann pays particular attention to Krokowski's ability to manipulate his audience. He seems to suggest that Krokowski not only fails to cure his patients of their inhibitions, but actually promotes debauchery, stepping into the role of a "libertine messiah".[30] He is explicitly compared to Christ:

> Dr Krokowski concluded his lecture with a grand advertisement for psychic dissection – he spread his arms wide, and invited them to come unto him. Come unto me, he said, though not exactly in those words, all ye that labor and are heavy laden! And he left no doubt of his certainty that they all, without exception, labored and were heavy laden. He spoke of hidden suffering, of shame and affliction, of the redemptive effects of analysis; he praised the effects of light piercing the dark unconscious,

30 J. Finck, *Thomas Mann et la psychanalyse*, p. 83.

> explained that illness could be transformed again into conscious emotion, admonished them to trust, promised recovery.[31]

After the lecture, the patients followed Krokowski and gathered in concen-tric circles around him, so that "it was as if they were thronging after him – hesitant, without a will of their own, and yet in dazed unanimity, like a swarm of rats behind the Pied Piper" (*ibid.*); the doctor turns out to be a modern incarnation of Grimm's *Flutist of Hameln*, the prototype of the terrifying hypnotist. In this he resembles the hero of Mann's later novella, *Mario und der Zauberer* [*Mario and the Magician*]. Cipolla the magician, who uses "a riding-whip with a silver claw-handle"[32] to lull his victims to sleep, gives a performance that attacks the will-power, resulting in "the loss or compulsion of volition" (p. 201); he humiliates the audience by demanding total obedience. His manipulations are "horrible and incredible" (p. 202). A grotesque scene in which Cipolla convinces the young Mario that he, Cipolla, is Mario's beloved Silvestra and makes him kiss him ends with the boy killing the magician. The novella is set in Italy, in a holiday resort on the Tyrrhenian Sea. Even before the hypnotist arrives, the guests are confronted with the rise of nationalism, and the magician, who performs the fascist salute several times during his performance and forces others to do the same, brings to mind Mussolini himself. Mann compares the crowd devoted to its leader to a state of collective hypnosis – an argument that echoes Freud's *Group Psychology and the Analysis of the Ego* (1921).[33] Mann expanded on his argument in his essay "Bruder Hitler" ["That Man is My Brother"] of 1939:

> Lately, on the films, I saw a ritual dance of the Bali Islanders. It ended in the complete trance condition, with frightful twitchings of the bodies of the exhausted youths. Where is the difference between these practices and the procedure in the European mass meeting? There is none – or rather, there is one: the difference between the exotic and the repellent.[34]

Cipolla's sorcery in *Mario and the Sorcerer* is as perilous as that of Doctor Krokowski in *The Magic Mountain*. From the outset, the establishment's

---

31 Thomas Mann, *The Magic Mountain*, pp. 152-153.

32 Thomas Mann, "Mario and the Magician", in *Stories of a Lifetime*, trans. by Helen T. Lowe-Porter, vol. 2 (London: Mercury Books, 1916), p. 185.

33 S. Freud, *Group Psychology and the Analysis of the Ego*, SE XVIII, pp. 114-116.

34 Thomas Mann, "That Man is My Brother," *Esquire*, 01/03/1939, p. 133.

chief magician represents negative forces. The motif of darkness recurs in his portrayal: his eyes are said to have an "exotic" glow,[35] his eyebrows and beard are black, his clothes are black and his office is steeped in a "murky twilight, deep dusk" (p. 158). According to Settembrini, "his particular speciality is the night" (p. 73). When Krokowski visits Castorp in his room, he enters unnoticed, through the balcony door, "creating the impression that he had materialised out of thin air" (p. 226). He is stylised somewhat like the psychiatrists from the Expressionist horror films made shortly before the novel's publication, i.e. Robert Wiene's cunning Dr Caligari (1920) and Dr Mabuse from Fritz Lang's *Dr Mabuse the Gambler* (1922).[36] His yellow teeth and waxy pallor are frequently mentioned, bringing to mind Nosferatu, Friedrich Wilhelm Murnau's vampire (1920), though in a burlesque version.[37]

In Siegfried Kracauer's well-known interpretation, all these films, especially *The Cabinet of Dr Caligari*, reflect the collective unconsciousness during Weimar Germany and foreshadow Hitler's coming to power. An accomplished psychiatrist by day, Dr Caligari is a demonic hypnotist by night, carrying out murders through an unwitting medium. He "is a very specific premonition in the sense that he uses hypnotic power to force his will upon his tool – a technique foreshadowing, in content and purpose, that manipulation of the soul which Hitler was the first to practice on a gigantic scale".[38] The film's makers, Kracauer argues, "must have been driven by one of those dark impulses which, stemming from the slowly moving foundations of a people's life, sometimes engender true visions" (p. 73). In the original version of the screenplay, the film was intended as an indictment of the all-powerful state: Caligari, like the modern state, mercilessly violates all human laws and values to satisfy his lust for dominion, while the murderer, under hypnosis, is in fact an innocent victim, like an ordinary man who learns to kill under compulsory military service. In the final film version, the story ends by revealing that the entire plot was a mental

35 Thomas Mann, *The Magic Mountain*, p. 783.

36 As I wrote in the chapter on the avant-garde, it is no coincidence that films portraying demonic soul-doctors emerged with the popularisation of psychoanalysis.

37 Cf. J. Darmaun, *Thomas Mann, Deutschland und die Juden* (Tübingen: De Gruyter, 2003), p. 141.

38 Siegfried Kracauer, *From Caligari to Hitler: A Psychological History of the German Film* (Princeton: Princeton University Press, 2004), pp. 72-73.

patient's hallucination; he mistakes the establishment's director, a gentle and understanding man, for a demonic figure from his dreams.

> While the original story exposed the madness inherent in authority, Wiene's *Caligari* glorified authority and convicted its antagonist of madness. A revolutionary film was thus turned into a conformist one [...] to be in harmony with what the less educated felt and liked. (pp. 66-67)

At the same time, Kracauer argues, the film preserved and amplified the revolutionary original as a madman's fantasy. Caligari's failure became a psychological phenomenon:

> In this way Wiene's film does suggest that during their retreat into themselves the Germans were stirred to reconsider their traditional belief in authority. Down to the bulk of social democratic workers they refrained from revolutionary action; yet at the same time a psychological revolution seems to have prepared itself in the depths of the collective soul. The film reflects this double aspect of German life by coupling a reality in which Caligari's authority triumphs with a hallucination in which the same authority is overthrown. There could be no better configuration of symbols for that uprising against the authoritarian dispositions which apparently occurred under the cover of a behaviour rejecting uprising. (p. 67)

Is Krokowski, like Caligari, "a premonition of Hitler" (p. 72), or does he rather, like Dr Mabuse, represent a pre-Nazi tyrant who secretly exercises control over society, embodying opposing meanings such as relativism, Jewry, Bolshevism? According to one Polish film scholar, the fraudster Dr Mabuse is essentially a psychoanalyst, despite his many different incarnations. It is in this role that we see him every time before he puts on another guise, or when he gets rid of a particularly ostentatious costume; he is also listed as a psychoanalyst in the telephone directory.[39] Lang also engages the stereotype in as far as the financial crisis was thought to have been caused by the same people whom it eventually benefitted.[40] The *Ostjude*, the Jewish psychoanalyst, the speculator and money forger also

39 T. Kłys, *Dekada doktora Mabuse: Nieme filmy Fritza Langa* (Łódź: Wydawnictwo Uniwersytetu Łódzkiego, 2006), p. 167.

40 Some German psychoanalysts, paid in dollars by foreign patients, were among those who benefited from the financial crisis.

become allegories of inflation. Mabuse's lecture "Psychoanalysis as a Factor in Modern Therapy" is attended mostly by old scholars with caricatured Semitic features. Just like Mann's novel, therefore, Lang's film discredits psychoanalysis as a "Jewish science". In another scene, Lang presents the analyst as "a charismatic 'superman' who uses the dark, occult powers of hypnosis, telepathy and suggestion";[41] a charlatan who manipulates the crowd and seduces the masses.

In *The Magic Mountain,* too, the psychoanalyst's lectures take an unexpected turn. Although they "had always had a subterranean character, the whiff of the catacomb", they eventually turn "toward magical, arcane matters," exploring "the abstruse oddities of hypnotism and somnambulism, the phenomena of telepathy, prophetic dreams, and second sight" (pp. 778-779). At the end of the novel, Dr Krokowski replaces his readings with spiritualistic séances featuring Ellen Brand, a young Dane, in the role of the medium. Hans Castorp breaks with the analyst when the latter tries to summon Joachim's ghost. He interrupts the séance by turning on the lights:

> [He] walked over to Krokowski, who stood there protesting loudly, came up very close to him, tried to say something, but no words would come from his lips. With a brusque, demanding gesture he held out his hand. Taking the key, he nodded menacingly several times directly in the doctor's face, turned on his heels, and left the room. (p. 813)

Mann himself had taken part in a séance attempting to make contact with the dead. He described the experience in "Okkulte Erlebnisse"[Occult Experiences] in 1924.[42] The séance was organised by Albert von Schrenck-Notzing, an eccentric baron whose works include *Materialisations-Phänomene*, a study on mediumistic teleplasty published in 1914 [*Phenomena of Materialisation*, 1923]. In fact, Mann's portrayal of the host has much in common with Julian Ochorowicz, the Polish fringe psychologist discussed at length in the earlier parts of the present study:

> A medical practitioner by training, specialising in nervous diseases and sexual pathologies, he arrived at occult studies early, more than thirty years

41 T. Kłys, *Dekada doktora Mabuse*, p. 168.

42 Thomas Mann, "Okkulte Erlebnisse", *Gesammelte Werke in zwölf Bänden* (Frankfurt a. M.: Fischer, 1960), vol. X, pp. 135-171.

> ago, via hypnotism and somnambulism, and it seems that for a time he was inclined towards spiritualism, while today he rejects this theory; to account for all the inexplicable phenomena he evokes and observes he refers to still unknown but gradually understood natural forces. (p. 140)

Mann acknowledges his own "theoretical affinity" (p. 143) with the occult. He recounts that during a visit to the Baron he was able to observe mediums lifting objects by force of will, even when any possibility of deception had been ruled out. He describes these phenomena as "*Gaukelei*" (p. 166), a term that lacks an exact equivalent in English; possible translations range from "jugglery" or "street entertainment" to "magic" and "trickery" to "delusion" and "deception". Mann justifies his use of the term as follows: "*Gaukelei* is one of these words whose depth is obscured by murkiness. Concepts of reality and illusion are mingled in it, and perhaps this mixing and ambiguity have a real raison d'être, which are less alien to nature than to our conventional thinking" (pp. 166-167).

Several aspects of Mann's description of von Schrenck-Notzing's séance reappear in the chapter "Highly Questionable" in *The Magic Mountain*. Castorp's feelings as he makes his way to the meeting – a mixture of "nervousness, playfulness, curiosity, disgust, and awe"[43] – remind him of his mood when he approached a brothel for the first time in his life. The same comparison can be found in Mann's account of his own experience at the séance. His participation also has many parallels: like Mann, Castorp acts as a sort of assistant or controller at the event, and the séance leaves them with a similar distaste. Mann could have copied his words into the novel almost unchanged:

> No, I shall not go Schrenck-Notzing's anymore. It leads to nothing, at least nothing good. I love what I used to call the moral overworld, I love the human poem, the clear and intelligent idea. I despise cerebral contorsions and mental cesspools.[44]

At the same time, like Hans, the writer confesses that he would still like to relive that experience: "Just one more time I should like to see, my neck stretched, the nerves of my stomach quivering from the absurdity, the impossible as it happens, despite everything" (p. 171).

43 Thomas Mann, *The Magic Mountain*, p. 800.

44 Thomas Mann, "Okkulte Erlebnisse", p. 171.

These obvious analogies have inspired researchers to highlight similarities between Krokowski and Albert von Schrenck-Notzing.[45] Other inspirations have also been proposed, such as Schopenhauer's philosophy[46] or Freud's *Three Essays on the Theory of Sexuality*, published in 1905, i.e. two years before Castorp's arrival in Davos.[47]

A more interesting suggestion, however, was put forward by Wolfgang Martynkewicz, who has drawn attention to a number of parallels between Mann's fictional Krokowski and one of the most famous dissidents of the Freudian movement – Georg Groddeck.[48] No evidence has been found that Mann was personally acquainted with Groddeck. He might have heard of him from their shared publisher, Georg Hirzel, or, more likely, from Oscar A. H. Schmitz, one of Munich's bohemians. Mann met Schmitz several times, including at least once, on 5 March 1920, when Schmitz gave him a horoscope and then talked to him at length about philosophy, medicine, physiology and psychoanalysis.[49] Schmitz was one of Groddeck's patients. He describes the doctor as a prehistoric magician or sorcerer [*vorzeitlicher Zauberer*], and regards his psychoanalytic lectures as an introduction to the "secret doctrine" [*Geheimlehre*] of the demonic origins of life.[50]

Georg Groddeck completed his studies under Ernst Schweninger, Bismarck's personal physician, before he became owner and chief physician of the Marienhöhe sanatorium in Baden-Baden in 1900. The establishment has

45 M. Dierks, "Dr Krokowski und die Seinen: Psychoanalyse und Parapsychologie in Thomas Manns *Zauberberg*", in *Das "Zauberberg"Symposium 1994 in Davos*, ed. by T. Sprecher (Frankfurt am Main: Klostermann, 1995), pp. 173-195.

46 Cf. D. Pakalski, *Pytanie o ideę kultury w "Czarodziejskiej górze" Tomasza Manna* (Toruń: Wydawnictwo Tako, 2012), pp. 36-64 and pp. 120-123. Pakalski points out that Krokowski's lectures coincide with the 44th chapter of Schopenhauer's *The World as Will and Representation* ("Metaphysics of Sexual Love"), while his physical appearance is associated with a portrait of the philosopher by Ludwig S. Ruhl.

47 J. Finck, *Thomas Mann et la psychanalyse*, p. 62.

48 W. Martynkewicz, *Georg Groddeck: Eine Biographie* (Frankfurt am Main: Fischer, 1997), p. 155. See also T. Anz, W. Martynkewicz, "Thomas Manns Psychoanalytiker Dr Krokowski und Georg Groddeck: Dokumentation eines Mailwechsels und eine Einladung zur Spurensuche" literaturkritik.de, 2005, no. 8, <http://www.literaturkritik.de/public/rezension.php?rez_id=8416 > [accessed on 23/05/2013].

49 T. Mann, *Tagebücher 1918-1921* (Frankfurt am Main: Fischer, 1979), p. 392.

50 O. A. H. Schmitz, *Tagebücher*, ed. by W. Martynkewicz (Berlin: Aufbau, 2006-2008). Cf. also W. Martynkewicz, *Salon Deutschland: Geist und Macht, 1900-1945* (Berlin: Aufbau, 2009).

much in common with the one in Mann's *Magic Mountain.* As in many similar centres at the time, treatments were initially limited to therapeutic baths, restrictive diets and massages. Over time, Groddeck, unaware of Freud's work, made parallel discoveries about issues such as the importance of talking to patients about their repressed experiences, the crucial role of childhood sexuality as well as phenomena described by Freud in terms of resistance and transference. Unlike Freud, Groddeck came to these conclusions by studying not nervous but organic diseases.[51] He took a holistic approach, believing that one ought to treat not individual ailments but the person who is sick. Groddeck's most important discovery was that many patients were reluctant to be cured; what they were looking for was not an alleviation of their suffering but its confirmation and the doctor's empathy.

Groddeck was an exceptionally charismatic man, and he believed that the doctor's personality played a key role in the healing process.[52] From the outset, patients were impressed by his physiognomy. His powerful physique commanded respect, while his physical strength crushed all resistance. He was wont to apply muscular force in his massages, perching on top of his patients – the vast majority of whom were women – to knead their stomachs, at the same time demanding that they confess the true cause of their illness. He reportedly had large protruding ears, prominent lips and a hooked nose. His dark eyes and penetrating gaze added to the diabolic image (p. 9). His authoritative attitude was complemented by great kindness and a sincere desire to help. For many of the patients this special combination turned out to be addictive. The sisters Anna and Elie de Bruyn, for instance, sold off their property in the Netherlands to be near the doctor at all times (pp. 156-159). For them, Groddeck was not only a skilful masseur but a ruler of souls; they likened him to a devil and a god (p. 142).

Like Krokowski, Groddeck wanted to instruct his patients. Between 1916 and 1919 he gave one-hour lectures to his patients every Wednesday afternoon, understanding these sessions as an integral part of their therapy. Like Mann's protagonist, he saw illness as being rooted in repressed phantasms. One of the first sentences uttered by Krokowski in Mann's

51 Today Groddeck is considered a forerunner of psychosomatics. See G. Danzer, *Der wilde Analytiker: Georg Groddeck und die Entdeckung der Psychosomatik* (München: Kösel, 1992); H. Will, *Die Geburt der Psychosomatik: Georg Groddeck, der Mensch und Wissenschaftler* (München: Urban & Schwarzenberg, 1984).

52 W. Martynkewicz, *Georg Groddeck: Eine Biographie*, p. 141.

novel – "I've never met a perfectly healthy person before"[53] – could easily have been written by Groddeck. Illness is a substitute formation which allows for the realisation – although a crippled and imperfect one – of a shameful dream, most often an erotic one.[54] In Groddeck's view, the process of becoming aware of the hidden meaning of an illness leads to its cure. This is why he considered his lectures to be the most important remedy. It was with the same aim in mind that the sanatorium began to publish its own periodical, featuring mostly texts by Groddeck himself. Over time, the magazine's suggestive title, *Satanarium*, also came to stand for the establishment as such.[55]

Groddeck's lectures, like Krokowski's, were "a blend of poetical and academic styles".[56] Both usually spoke ad lib; their arguments were based on fleeting associations rather than any linear presentation of a system of thought. They used performance to inspire their audience, staging a self-analysis to encourage listeners to do the same.[57] Groddeck built the framework of his theory through these lectures. He was not yet familiar with Freud's ideas when he was basically trying to establish psychoanalysis, and when he finally did read Freud, he was unable to appreciate him. Hans Castorp's fear of *Seelenzergliederung* in the opening of *The Magic Mountain* echoes Groddeck's objections in *Nasamecu*, a book published in 1913, while Mann was beginning to gather material for the novel. Before he had actually become familiar with psychoanalysis, Groddeck had already attacked it as a *Seelenzergliederung* centred on sexuality.[58] Four

---

53 Thomas Mann, *The Magic Mountain*, p. 19.

54 G. Groddeck, *Conférences psychanalytiques à l'usage des malades prononcées au sanatorium de Baden-Baden*, trans. by R. Lewinter (Paris: Champ libre, 1981), vol. 3, p. 156.

55 C. M. Grossman, S. Grossman, *The Wild Analyst: The Life and Work of Georg Groddeck* (New York: Braziller, 1965), p. 90.

56 Thomas Mann, *The Magic Mountain*, p. 148.

57 Many years later, Jacques Lacan's listeners at his Parisian seminars would similarly find themselves in the position of the analysts rather than the analysands. On the parallels between Groddeck's lectures and Lacan's see e. g. J. Chemouni, *Georg Groddeck, psychanalyste de l'imaginaire* (Paris: Payot, 1984), p. 65. J.-B. Pontalis compares Groddeck and Lacan in *Perdre de vue* (Paris: Gallimard, 1988), esp. the chapter "Entre Groddeck et Freud", pp. 157-171, as well as M. Mannoni, *La théorie comme fiction: Freud, Groddeck, Winnicott, Lacan* (Paris: Seuil, 1979).

58 G. Groddeck, *Nasamecu: Der gesunde und kranke Mensch gemeinverständlich dargestellt* (Leipzig: S. Hirzel, 1913), p. 108. Cf. W. Martynkewicz, *Georg Groddeck: Eine Biographie*, p. 146.

years later he apologised to Freud, adding that he had now read *The Psychopathology of Everyday Life* and *The Interpretation of Dreams*; he was greatly impressed by these books, which had drawn his attention to the way his own clinical experiences overlapped with the form of therapy used by psychoanalysts.[59]

Even as he paid homage to the Viennese psychiatrist, Groddeck expressed his reservations about referring to his own practice in terms of psychoanalysis. His unease was fuelled by Freud's *On the History of the Psycho-Analytic Movement* (1914). Freud's account of the frequent schisms in the movement's early history carried the mark of his resentment against dissidents such as Adler and Jung. Groddeck wrote to Freud: "I do not want to call myself a follower of a movement when I have to run the risk of being rejected by the leader of that movement as an intruder who does not belong to it" (p. 48). He added that he was particularly troubled by the fact that his understanding of the unconscious was much broader than Freud's (at the time). For Groddeck, the unconscious was not merely a collection of elements repressed from consciousness. He defined it as *das Es* ("It"), of which both body and soul were emanations.[60] In his very first letter to Freud, written in May 1917, he asserts that it is through this governing force that "we are lived";[61] it determines the shape of our nose and hands, our thoughts and emotions. It can express itself through pneumonia or cancer just as well as through obsessive neurosis or hysteria. Each of these maladies "is also a symbol, a representation of something going on within, a drama staged by the It" (p. 117), which is why all of them should be treated in a similar way – although Groddeck was reluctant to use the term "treatment," convinced that no doctor can make a sick person well: only the patient's It has such power. The It is also, in Groddeck's view, what causes a person's health to fail gradually, so that "he alone will die who wishes to die, to whom life is intolerable".[62] Groddeck

59 *Briefwechsel Sigmund Freud–Georg Groddeck*, pp. 45-56.

60 In English translations of Freud, the term *Es*, which Freud had borrowed from Groddeck, was rendered as "id," while translations of Groddeck's writings render his *Es* as "it". This inconsistency obscures the terminological origin of Freud's concept.

61 A similar formulation can be found in *The Book of the It* [*Das Buch vom Es*]: "The affirmation 'I live' is only conditionally correct, it expresses only a small and superficial partly of the fundamental principle: "Man is lived by the It'." See Georg Groddeck, *The Book of the It: Psychoanalytic Letters to a Friend* (London: The C. W. Daniel Company, 1935), p. 16.

62 Georg Groddeck, *The Book of the It*, p. 116.

regarded every illness as a work of the "It" made with the help of the human body. In his lectures, for instance, he compared contracting pneumonia to writing an essay or painting a picture. Such a parallel is possible because an illness is above all a metaphor, a way of expressing matters that could not find any other outlet, or a means of fulfilling a particular desire. The doctor, therefore, is to be above all an interpreter of the expression of the "It".[63] For the members of the psychoanalytic movement, Groddeck's name itself became a sort of metaphor; in Freud's correspondence, the ironic expression "Totally Groddeck" ("Ganz Groddeck") – sums up the meaningful coincidences that seemingly prove his theory.[64]

Freud's reaction to Groddeck's first letter was enthusiastic. He responded that he sensed Groddeck's wish to be declared a heretic, but that he must disappoint him:

> I must lay claim to you, must insist that you are an analyst of the first order who has grasped the essence of the matter once for all. The man who has recognised that transference and resistance are the hubs of treatment belongs irrevocably to the "Wild Hunt." Whether he gives the "UCS" [unconsciousness] the name of "Id" as well makes no difference.[65]

In 1920 Freud invited Groddeck to the Sixth International Psychoanalytic Congress in The Hague, where the latter delivered an impromptu talk

---

63 Susan Sontag repeatedly refers to this part of Groddeck's argument in her essay *Illness as Metaphor* (New York: Farrar, Straus and Giroux, 1978), p. 19, p. 23, p. 44, p. 46, p. 48, p. 56. For Sontag, Groddeck is among the first theorists responsible for shifting the blame for illness onto the patient. What is more, Sontag cites several passages from Mann's *Magic Mountain* to demonstrate that tuberculosis is among the most metaphor-laden diseases ("For over a hundred years TB remained the preferred way of giving death a meaning", p. 16). She points out that tuberculosis was com-monly associated with excessive appetite and sexual excitability – a stigma that also informs Mann's novel.

64 In a letter to Ferenczi dated 06/11/1917 Freud writes:
"Yesterday I smoked away my last cigar, and since then I have been grumpy and tired, got heart palpitations and an increase in the painful swelling of my gums [...]. Then a patient brought me fifty cigars, I lit one, became cheerful, and the gum irritation rapidly abated! I wouldn't have believed it, if it weren't so striking. Totally Groddeck". (*The Correspondence of Sigmund Freud and Sándor Ferenczi*, vol. 2, p. 245.)

65 S. Freud, *Letters of Sigmund Freud 1873-1939*, ed. by Ernst L. Freud (London: The Hogarth Press, 1961), pp. 316-317.

entitled *Über die psychoanalytische Behandlung organischer Krankheiten* [On the Psychoanalytical Treatment of Organic Diseases]. He opens with an ironic remark: "I am a wild analyst."[66] This was a blatant challenge to the psychoanalytic establishment, as the Freudians had long been troubled by self-proclaimed (or "wild") psychoanalysis practised by individuals with no specialist training. As early as 1910 Freud had published the cautionary essay "Über 'wilde' Psychoanalyse" ["'Wild' Psycho-Analysis"], and in the following years he rushed to put down the principles of his original technique. The need for greater control and the establishment of rigid rules for professional training was the movement's most important task at the time and the main topic of the deliberations in The Hague.

Groddeck was also the author of the first psychoanalytic novel, or rather the first literary work promoting Freud's discoveries. *Der Seelensucher* [*The Seeker of Souls*] was published in 1921. Mann must have heard of it, for despite an enthusiastic review by one of the most important literary critics of the time, Alfred Polgar, in the *Berliner Tageblatt*,[67] Groddeck's novel caused a resounding scandal and was widely regarded as obscene. Groddeck's aim was to create a character who embodied the unconscious. The protagonist, Thomas Weltlein, follows all his impulses in words and actions, completely unhampered by social norms. For many years, no one dared to publish his book, and finally the Internationaler Psychoanalytischer Verlag took it on – not without resistance from Ernest Jones, Oscar Pfister and other members of the movement, who deemed it obscene.[68]

Apart from Freud, who compared Groddeck's novel to Cervantes' *Don Quixote* and its humour to that of François Rabelais, its supporters included Otto Rank, the head of the publishing house at the time (he also came up with the title), and Sándor Ferenczi. The Hungarian psychoanalyst reviewed the novel in *Imago*;[69] what is more, he went to Marienhöhe for treatment the same year and became close friends with the

66 C. M. Grossman, S. Grossman, *The Wild Analyst*, p. 97.

67 A. Polgar, "Der Seelensucher", *BT* 1921, no. 585, p. 2. The review was reprinted in *ADI*, the same yearbook in which Mann's "Mein Verhältnis zur Psychoanalyse" was published.

68 *Psychoanalysis and Faith: The Letters of Sigmund Freud and Oskar Pfister*, ed. by H. Meng, E. L. Freud, trans. by E. Mosbacher (New York: Basic Books, 1963), p. 81. On Pfister's initiative, the Swiss Society for Psychoanalysis issued an official protest against this publication. See W. Martynkewicz, *Georg Groddeck: Eine Biographie*, p. 273.

69 *I* 1921, no. 3, pp. 356-359.

author. From 1921 until his death in 1933, Ferenczi would spent every summer at Groddeck's sanatorium in Baden-Baden. The two men, who exchanged many letters between Ferenczi's visits, had much in common. First of all, they both saw themselves as marginal in relation to the psychoanalytical mainstream (Groddeck embraced his position as a "wild analyst" while Ferenczi was keen on recognition and kept emphasised his allegiance with classical Freudianism, even if his originality, in both theory and technique, branded him the movement's *enfant terrible*). Both men considered themselves physicians first and foremost, motivated by a desire to help others, and both believed it was necessary to constantly analyse themselves. Their family backgrounds differed considerably: Groddeck was born into a traditional Catholic family that experienced financial decline after the father's death, while Ferenczi came from the liberal Jewish bourgeoisie, his family having made a considerable fortune starting from nothing. Still, Groddeck and Ferenczi found many similarities on a personal level. As children they had both lacked love, which is why, in their own view, they looked to Freud for a maternal figure.[70] Thanks to Ferenczi, Hungarian writers also took an interest in Groddeck's ideas: in 1925 the owner of the "Satanarium" was interviewed by Dezső Kosztolányi for the magazine *Pesti Hírlap*, while Milán Füst, whom Groddeck had analysed in Baden-Baden in 1928, wrote a moving obituary after Groddeck's death in 1934.[71]

Although Groddeck had been a member of the Berlin Psychoanalytic Society for a number of years (he coincided with the Bornstein sisters, Otto Fenichel and Siegfried Bernfeld), he did not undergo analysis himself and was not officially recognised as a psychoanalyst. He would always oppose the idea that psychoanalysis should be restricted to nervous diseases, believing that all organic ailments were physiological expressions of unconscious emotional conflicts and should therefore be subjected to psychoanalytic therapy. (Groddeck went so far as to suggest to Freud that if he wanted to, he could rid himself of his cancer.[72]) He presented his

70 J. Dupont, "Introduction", in *The Sándor Ferenczi–Georg Groddeck Correspondence 1921-1933*, ed. by C. Fortune (London: Open Gate Press, 2002), pp. xxi-xxiii.

71 Cf. M. Babits, G. Csáth, M. Füst, F. Karinthy, D. Kosztolányi, G. Krúdy, *Cure d'ennui: Ecrivains hongrois autour de Sándor Ferenczi*, pp. 86-94 and pp. 197-200.

72 *Briefwechsel Sigmund Freud–Georg Groddeck*, p. 204. Cf. Georg Groddeck, "Von der psychischen Bedingtheit der Krebskrankheit," in *Psychoanalytische Schriften zur Psychosomatik*, ed. by Günter Clauser (Wiesbaden: Limes-Verlag, 1966), pp. 380-385.

ideas in *Die Arche,* a self-published biweekly magazine launched in the mid-1920s.[73] Shortly before Groddeck's death, the International Psychoanalytic Press published his last book, *Der Mensch als Symbol* [The Human as Symbol]. He explores humankind's tendency to create symbols as a primordial drive, presenting linguistic analyses, especially etymological ones, which indicate that every word is a metaphor. The "corpus of speech" (*Körper der Sprache*), Groddeck argues, can be compared to the human "corpus" or body – humans use their bodies in the same way as they use words.[74] Towards the end of his life, Groddeck developed delusions of grandeur and sent letters to Hitler, proposing to cure him of his death drive, evil tendencies and anti-Semitism; indeed, Groddeck saw himself as the only person who might save the world.

Groddeck's most important work is the epistolary novel *Das Buch vom Es* [*The Book of the It*], consisting of letters by Patrick Troll to a female friend. It was published in 1923, a year before *The Magic Mountain*. The fictional Patrick Troll not only expounds Groddeck's version of psychoanalytic theory, but also takes on the role of an analyst, interpreting his friend's words and behaviour, and performs a self-analysis of a similar kind to that which Freud undertook in his correspondence with Fliess – except that here the object of transfer is not the addressee of the letters, but the reader of the book.[75]

The idea for this novel emerged from Groddeck's correspondence with Freud, which can also be read as a kind of *Briefroman*. Freud read the manuscript, and his comments had a great influence on the final version. The author's alter ego ironically writes in his third letter: "But for my letters you shall have herewith the key; everything in them that sounds reasonable, or perhaps only a little strange, is derived from Professor Freud of Vienna and his colleagues; whatever is quite mad, I claim as my own spiritual property."[76]

---

73 G. Groddeck, *Die Arche: Vollständiger photomechanischer Nachdruck der Zeitschrift (1925-1927)*, ed. by O. Jägersberg (Frankfurt am Main: Stroemfeld, 2001). Groddeck's biographer sees this publication as having a therapeutic aim above all, since the author documents and analyses his own experiences, memories, dreams and symptoms. See W. Martynkewicz, *Georg Groddeck: Eine Biographie*, p. 316.

74 For a collection of Groddeck's writing on literature and culture see G. Groddeck, *Psychoanalytische Schriften zur Literatur und Kunst* (Frankfurt am Main: Fischer, 1978).

75 Cf. Peter L. Rudnytsky, *Reading Psychoanalysis*, pp. 164-165.

76 G. Groddeck, *The Book of the It*, p. 26.

By the time he began exchanging letters with Freud, Groddeck had already formulated his theory of the *Es* or It. The *Es* was the new term for the greatest riddle of the world – the creative principle. In his book *Hin zu Gottnatur* [Toward God Nature], published in 1909, he had still called it *Gott-Natur* or God-Nature, after the poem attributed to Goethe, which had made as strong an impression on Groddeck as it had on the young Freud.[77] But it is in *The Book of the It* that its essential points are set out most comprehensively.

A few weeks after Groddeck's novel, Freud's *The Ego and the Id* (*Das Ich und das Es*) appeared – a landmark text that introduced the so-called second topic, i.e. the division of the psyche into the "id", the "ego" and the "super-ego," replacing the previous three instances (consciousness, pre-consciousness and unconsciousness). This work is largely based on a long exchange of letters with Groddeck (Freud uses a drawing he had first sketched in one of his letters to his colleague, explaining his discovery that the repressed is also part of the ego, and therefore that the ego itself is to some extent unconscious). Freud notes that he owes the concept of the id to Groddeck, but he does so in a particular way:

> I think we shall gain a great deal by following the suggestion of a writer who, from personal motives, vainly asserts that he has nothing to do with the rigours of pure science. I am speaking of Georg Groddeck, who is never tired of insisting that what we call our ego behaves essentially passively in life, and that, as he expresses it, we are "lived" by unknown and uncontrollable forces.[78]

Freud annotates this passage with a bibliographical reference to Groddeck's novel, and later in the paragraph proposes to do him justice by calling "the other part of the mind, into which this entity [the ego] extends and which behaves as though it were Ucs., the 'id'" (p. 23). (In the original German, Freud's "id" – das *Es* – is identical with Groddeck's "it".)

While acknowledging the debt, Freud also minimised its significance, for he added that in choosing this term, "Groddeck himself no doubt followed the example of Nietzsche, who habitually used this grammatical term for whatever in our nature is impersonal and, so to speak, subject to

77 W. Martynkewicz, *Georg Groddeck: Eine Biographie*, p. 206. Cf. also J. Chemouni, *Georg Groddeck, psychanalyste de l'imaginaire*, pp. 160-169.

78 S. Freud, *The Ego and the Id*, SE XIX, p. 23.

natural law" (*ibid*).[79]

As most researchers now agree, Groddeck was inspired by Wilhelm Bölsche rather than by Nietzsche.[80] But Freud's remark is also striking because he rarely mentioned the philosopher and maintained that he had not read Nietzsche, presumably to avoid being accused of plagiarism of a theory that in many respects might have seemed precursory to his own.[81] To associate the notion of *Es* with Nietzsche's works would have required in-depth reading, as Nietzsche never presents it in any systematic way; there are only a few passages in which Nietzsche alludes to a concept that might foreshadow Freud's "id".[82] It seems that Freud either wanted to put the responsibility for borrowing from Nietzsche on Groddeck, or that he preferred to take an established philosopher as a precursor, rather than the infamous owner of the "Satanarium".

The entire correspondence between Freud and Groddeck is permeated by their shared anxiety of influence. In his first letter Groddeck confesses that his attack on Freud in 1913 was due to the fact that he wanted to be a creator, not an imitator; he also asserts that he was unable to read any of Freud's books to the end.[83] At the same time, he plays with possessive pronouns, writing, for example, about "my – or should I say your – views,"[84] to which Freud sternly replies that he is bothered by Groddeck's "banal ambition which hankers after originality

79 Freud also mentions Groddeck in the *New Introductory Lectures on Psycho-Analysis*, and again reduces him to a mere link between himself and Nietzsche: "Following a verbal usage of Nietzsche's and taking up a suggestion by Georg Groddeck, we will in future call it the 'id'. This impersonal pronoun seems particularly well suited for expressing the main characteristic of this province of the mind – the fact of its being alien to the ego." *New Introductory Lectures*, SE XII, p. 72.

80 Cf. e.g. W. Martynkewicz, *Georg Groddeck: Eine Biographie*, pp. 206-208.

81 On the relationship between Freud and Nietzsche see P.-L. Assoun, *Freud et Nietzsche* (Paris: PUF, 1982) and R. Gasser, *Nietzsche und Freud* (Berlin: De Gruyter, 1997). See also B. Nitzschke, "Zur Herkunft des 'Es': Freud, Groddeck, Nietzsche, Schopenhauer und E. von Hartmann", *Psyche* 1983, no. 37, pp. 769-804.

82 One of them is paragraph 17 in *Beyond Good and Evil: Prelude to a Philosophy of the Future*, trans. by Judith Norman (Cambridge: Cambridge University Press, 2001), pp. 53-54. The second is Zaratustra's speech "On the Despisers of the Body" in *Thus Spoke Zaratustra*, where "the self" (*das Selbst*) appears: *Thus Spoke Zarathustra: A Book for All and None*, trans. by Adrian del Caro (Cambridge: Cambridge University Press, 2006), pp. 68-69.

83 Cf. *An Autobiographical Study* (SE XX, pp. 59-60.)

84 *Briefwechsel Sigmund Freud–Georg Groddeck*, p. 48. In the case of correspondence that has not been included in *Letters of Sigmund Freud* I draw on the German edition, *Briefwechsel Sigmund Freud–Georg Groddeck* of 2008.

and priority".[85] He goes on to ask: "If you feel assured of the independence of your discoveries, why should you want to claim originality?" (*ibid.)*, then suggests that Groddeck, being many years his junior, may have "absorbed the leading ideas of psychoanalysis in a cryptomnemonic manner" (*ibid.)*, i.e. becoming acquainted with these ideas and then forgetting them, as happened in his own case with Nietzsche.

From the very beginning, Freud systematically accused Groddeck of mysticism. While accepting his texts for publication in psychoanalytic journals, he tried to persuade him to give up the more daring elements of his theory. He did this even as he conceded that at some point – namely where the personal self begins – everyone becomes mystical.[86] He was particularly opposed to Groddeck's "panpsychism" (*Panpsychismus*, p. 167) and his "mythology of the It" (*Es-Mythologie*, p. 233). He wrote: "in your It I naturally do not recognise my Id, which is civilised, bourgeois and deprived of all mysticism".[87]

Freud alludes to Groddeck, without mentioning him by name, in *Inhibitions, Symptoms and Anxiety* (1926), noting that his own notion of the ego's relative weakness as compared to the id and the super-ego, outlined in *The Ego and the Id* (1923), has found a strong response among his colleagues: "many writers have laid much stress on the weakness of the ego in relation to the id and of our rational elements in the face of daemonic forces within us; and they display a strong tendency to make what I have said into a corner-stone of a psycho-analytic *Weltanschauung*".[88] For Freud, such an interpretation expresses "an extreme and one-sided view"; he adds that he himself is not "partial to the fabrication of *Weltanschauungen*" (p. 96), as "such activities may be left to philosophers" (*ibid.*). Indeed, although Freud restricts the ego's autonomy, he nevertheless preserves it to the end, whereas for Groddeck the ego is entirely dependent on the *Es*. Groddeck often uses theatrical metaphors. The ego plays a role written by the *Es*, it is a marionette, a comedian, a mask of the *Es* that can be changed

85 S. Freud, *Letters of Sigmund Freud*, p. 317.

86 *Briefwechsel Sigmund Freud–Georg Groddeck*, p. 128. One compromise that Groddeck was willing to make can be found in the 30th letter of *The Book of the It*, in which the narrator modifies the concept of the It, indicating that it does not exist in the form previously presented. He admits that it was his own invention and takes back the notion of the It having no gender differentiation, introducing a separate It for men and women. (*The Book of the It*, pp. 255-264)

87 *Briefwechsel Sigmund Freud–Georg Groddeck*, p. 223.

88 S. Freud, *Inhibitions, Symptoms and Anxiety*, SE XX, p. 95.

at will. In one of his first letters to Freud he wonders why psychoanalysts insist on distinguishing between the conscious and the unconscious as separate instances or forces. In his opinion consciousness is merely one manifestation of the unconscious, an instrument that essentially serves communicative purposes. Groddeck even wonders whether consciousness, which gives us a feeling of omnipotence, might not be "a very funny but cruel game" on the part of the unconscious.[89]

The difference between Groddeck's *Es* and Freud's becomes clearer thanks to Agata Bielik-Robson's recent work on Freud and her notion of "Erros". "Erros" stands for the excessive, objectless libido in Freud's early works (above all *Three Essays on the Theory of Sexuality*), while the procreative and self-preserving "Eros" appears as a rival to the death drive (*Beyond the Pleasure Principle*). Revisiting Freud's early speculations (which he later renounced as if horrified by his own discovery), Bielik-Robson proposes a new interpretation of psychoanalysis in which sexuality is only one of many possible forms of the primordial, undifferentiated but exclusively human creative energy, a drive that strives for "augmented life".[90]

Groddeck, who sometimes used the terms *Es* and *Eros* interchangeably, and after reading *Beyond the Pleasure Principle* accused Freud of distancing himself from eroticism, was happy to compare himself to a form of libido working to satisfy the pleasure principle.[91] One could easily apply to Groddeck a description of Dr Krokowski in *The Magic Mountain*, namely that he "constantly used the word 'love' in a gently irresolute sense, so that one was never quite sure whether he meant its sanctified or more passionate and fleshy forms".[92] Groddeck's certainly endows his *Es* with a divine nature, presenting it as a sexually undifferentiated force that precedes humankind, creates humans, and then "lives" them, determining their fate.

Groddeck wrote a remarkable letter to Freud after reading *The Ego and the Id.* He compares himself to a plough that the farmer uses for his own purposes.[93] He develops this parable: while the farmer intends to sow and harvest, he, the plough, is only concerned with loosening the soil. It is

89 *Briefwechsel Sigmund Freud–Georg Groddeck*, p. 94.

90 A. Bielik-Robson, *Erros: Mesjański witalizm i filozofia*, pp. 277-278.

91 *Briefwechsel Sigmund Freud–Georg Groddeck*, p. 194.

92 Thomas Mann, *The Magic Mountain*, p. 148.

93 *Briefwechsel Sigmund Freud–Georg Groddeck*, p. 192.

incomprehensible to him why the farmer insists on ploughing the stony plot of the ego, which lies right next to the fertile fields of the *Es*. This parable is fairly easy to read. As Mircea Eliade has shown, the invention of the plough divides the history of primitive religions into two eras.[94] During the Neolithic Revolution – the transition from hunting and gathering to agriculture and settlement – the dominant belief was in chthonian maternity and self-fertilisation, and agriculture was a typically female occupation. It was only when the physiology of reproduction was discovered that working the land became a masculine domain. The plough took the place of the primitive spade and work on the land began to be compared to the act of fertilisation (p. 258). The association of agriculture and gender dynamics was first developed in the early twentieth century. One influential study in this domain was Albrecht Dieterich's *Mutter Erde: Ein Versuch über Volksreligion* [Mother Earth: An Essay on Folk Religion], first published in 1905, with a second edition in 1913. Dieterich presents a considerable number of images depicting the identity of plough and phallus on the one hand, and female genitalia and ploughed furrow or fertile land on the other. This book was known among Freud's early followers; Ludwig Jekels' 1914 study on Napoleon, for instance, contains a quotation from Dieterich.[95]

It seems that Groddeck, too, referred to this concept. Even while Freud's understanding of sexual difference evolved, he remained attached to the idea of primordial bisexuality and considered the child's relationship with the mother more important than the Oedipus complex. For Groddeck, every patient was a child in search of a mother, and the doctor should play her role. He also theorised men's jealousy of female reproductive capabilities, and suggested that the most important manifestation of sexuality was onanism – a self-reflexive, narcissistic, objectless eroticism; heterosexual intercourse, in comparison, is only an adaptation to socially useful forms. Incidentally, these themes in *The Book of the It* may have led Thomas Mann to Groddeck's other writings. Mann, too, believed that the opposition of the sexes was not a binding law and that the homosexual complex "can contain what is most sacred and culturally fertile".[96] In his essay *Über die Ehe,* written shortly after

94 M. Eliade, *Patterns in Comparative Religion*, trans. by Rosemary Sheed (London: Sheed and Ward, 1958). See especially the chapter "The Earth, Woman and Fertility", pp. 239-264.

95 L. Jekels, "Der Wendepunkt im Leben Napoleons I", p. 341.

96 Thomas Mann, "On the German Republic", trans. by Lawrence S. Rainey, *Modernism/Modernity*, vol. 14, no. 1, January 2007, p. 130.

the publication of *The Magic Mountain,* he presents Freud's discovery of humankind's primordial and natural bisexuality as the most important achievement of psychoanalysis.[97]

Mann often stressed that he became acquainted with psychoanalysis very late, namely only after the publication of Freud's *Collected Works* in the mid-1920s. It is difficult to take these assertions at face value. Mann's intellectual curiosity makes such a delay highly unlikely; he was a passionate reader of Schopenhauer and Nietzsche, an admirer of Dostoyevsky's psychological novels, he had an interest in medicine. What is more, his denial is highly inconsistent. As Jean Finck reminds us, Mann also admitted that *Death in Venice*, written between 1911 and 1912, was directly influenced by Freud.[98] The influence of Freud's interpretation of Jensen's *Gradiva* on the shape of Mann's novella has also been demonstrated; according to Manfred Dierks, Freud's text can be seen as a sort of narrative instruction manual for *Death in Venice.*[99]

Jensen's 1903 novella is the story of a young archaeologist's repressed childhood love, which returns in his fantasies under the influence of a bas-relief depicting a woman walking – he names her Gradiva. Following a dream about the eruption of Vesuvius and the destruction of Pompeii, the protagonist travels to the ruins of the ancient city. There he meets the girl he used to love. He addresses her in Latin, seeing in her a revived Gradiva. In Freud's interpretation of 1906, the novella proves that repressed unconscious content becomes active when one tries to escape from them. He also picks up on Jensen's metaphor of Pompeii to explain the mechanism of repression. Mann's *Death in Venice* was inspired by Jensen's work, while Freud's comments helped him structure his novella. Particularly important, of course, are the two narrative levels, one of which refers to an ancient myth. According to Dierks, Aschenbach's famous dream was also modelled on the dreams of Norbert Hanold of *Gradiva.*

Mann began writing *The Magic Mountain* soon after finishing *Death in Venice*. He outlined the novel's autobiographical origins in a lecture at

97 Cf. Thomas Mann, "Über die Ehe", *GW* vol. X, pp. 191-207.

98 Cf. J. Finck, *Thomas Mann et la psychanalyse,* pp. 37-49.

99 M. Dierks, "Der Wahn und die Träume in *Der Tod in Venedig*: Thomas Manns folgenreiche Freud-Lektüre im Jahr 1911", *PSY* 1990, no. 5, pp. 240-268; M. Dierks, "Traumzeit und Verdichtung: Der Einfluss der Psychoanalyse auf Thomas Manns Erzählweise", in *Thomas Mann und seine Quellen: Festschrift für Hans Wysling,* ed. by E. Heftrich, H. Koopmann (Frankfurt am Main: Klostermann, 1991), p. 132.

Princeton, explaining that his wife had spent six months at the sanatorium in Davos in 1912. He joined her for a three-week visit, but after ten days the doctor examined his lungs and suggested he, too, should stay for a six-month cure. "If I had followed his advice," Mann quips, "who knows, I might still be there!"[100] It was in Davos that he completed *Death in Venice* and began writing *The Magic Mountain*. He intended the latter to be another novella, "a humorous companion-piece to *Death in Venice*" and "a sort of satire on the tragedy just finished" (p. 722).

As in *Death in Venice*, the novel presents love as the actualisation of an old, repressed feeling. However, whereas in Jensen's work the culture of antiquity plays an important role, Mann consistently locates the objects of his protagonists' desire in the East (Tadzio, a young Pole, in *Death in Venice*; the Russian Clawdia Chauchat in *The Magic Mountain*). Mann's notion of the East essentially covers the eastern borders of the German Empire and Russia, and is always associated with the irrational, with violent passions, erotic secrets, as well as laziness and rejection of the bourgeois way of life.[101] In *The Magic Mountain*, the androgynous Frau Chauchat is the female embodiment of Castorp's boyhood crush, Pribislav Hippe, described as "the product of an ancient mixing of races, the blending of Germanic blood with Slavic-Wendish, or vice versa".[102] They both have wide-set, slightly slanted, grey-blue "Kyrgyz" eyes, high cheekbones, a husky voice; "the long-forgotten Pribislav had reappeared up here as Frau Chauchat" (p. 173). Driven by a kind of repetition compulsion, Castorp borrows a pencil from her – a gesture full of erotic connotations – just as he had done from his Eastern schoolmate.

Of the mechanisms of orientalisation described by Edward Said, one characteristic element is the interweaving of the East and the erotic. This suggests that what Castorp displaces are not only sexual desires, but also a longing to colonise. It is worth recalling that in *Civilisation and Its Discontents* Freud compares repression to colonial violence: "Civilisation behaves towards sexuality as a people or a stratum of its population does which has subjected another one to its exploitation".[103] Similarly, in Mann's "Freud and the Future" the relationship between the ego and the

100 Thomas Mann, "The Making of the Magic Mountain", in Thomas Mann, *The Magic Mountain*, trans. by H. T. Lowe-Porter (London: Minerva, 1996), p. 721.

101 D. Pakalski, *Pytanie o ideę kultury w "Czarodziejskiej górze"*, p. 96.

102 Thomas Mann, *The Magic Mountain*, p. 141.

103 S. Freud, *Civilisation and Its Discontents*, SE XXI, p. 104.

id in the second topic is compared to parts of the world: the ego is the "enlightened" part of the id, an island of reason and self-control within the unconscious, just as Europe is part of Asia, a small part of a vast continent, but one in which all culture and civilisation are concentrated. Beyond it lies the vast expanse of savagery and barbarism.[104]

This dimension of Mann's novel has been exploited by the Polish prose writer Paweł Huelle in *Castorp* (2004), his prequel to *The Magic Mountain*, which expands on a brief mention of Hans Castorp's having spent four semesters at the Danzig Polytechnic.[105] For Dariusz Skórczewski, the Polish novel is a postcolonial polemic with the portrayal of the province in a work rooted in the discourse of an imperial culture, similar to Jean Rhys's dialogue with Charlotte Brontë's *Jane Eyre* in *Wide Sargasso Sea*.[106] Huelle is writing back to Mann, but also to the entire discursive field in which *The Magic Mountain* is anchored. In this ideological and symbolic system, which informs much of turn-of-the-century German literature, an important role is played by "the East," understood as an imagined object of German imperial aspirations. Compensating for the relatively late acquisition of overseas colonies, Europe's eastern regions were at the same time a tangible goal for expansion, to be realised by political, military, economic and demographic means.[107] Huelle's protagonist Castorp arrives in Danzig imbued with the German colonisation project. Over the course of his stay, however, he comes to reject imperialism. In fact, his fascination with oriental otherness makes him succumb to what his uncle Tienappel had warned him about in the opening of the novel: he "goes native".

In *The Magic Mountain*, Dr Krokowski, the Polish-Jewish pansexual, represents an ironic counterpoint to Mann's orientalism. While coding the unconscious as oriental, Mann also portrays the newcomer from the East as the one who has understood the enigma of the unconscious. Kro-

---

104 "Freud and the Future", *TSR* 25/07/1936, p. 4.

105 Paweł Huelle, *Castorp*, trans. by Antonia Lloyd-Jones (London: Serpent's Tail, 2007). Incidentally, it is at the moment of Hans's first meeting with Krokowski that the city of Danzig – now Gdańsk – is first mentioned in the novel. "Hans Castorp had seen a soft, floppy collar like that only once before – sported by a photographer in Danzig" (p. 18).

106 Dariusz Skórczewski, *Polish Literature and National Identity: A Postcolonial Perspective*, trans. by Agnieszka Polakowska (Rochester: University of Rochester Press, 2020). See esp. the chapter "Identity as an Object of Inquiry (Paweł Huelle's *Castorp*)", pp. 136-159.

107 Cf. I. Surynt, *Postęp, kultura i kolonializm: Polska a niemiecki projekt europejskiego Wschodu w dyskursach publicznych XIX wieku* (Wrocław: Wrocławskie Wydawnictwo Oświatowe, 2006), p. 13.

kowski's central claim – "Any symptom of illness was a masked form of love in action, and illness was merely transformed love"[108] – is, however, not just a statement that could have been Groddeck's, it is also possibly the most succinct description of *The Magic Mountain*. After all, the novel's crux is the chapter "Analysis": Hans barely listens to Krokowski's lecture, as he is busy observing Clawdia, in whom he has just discovered Pribislav. Based on Mann's non-fictional work we might say that he shares Castorp's aversion to psychoanalysis and that, like his protagonist, he rejects doctors' attempts to rationalise mental mechanisms. Nonetheless, the entire plot of his novel seems to mirror Krokowski's lecture "Love as a Force Conductive to Illness" (p. 137). Illness in *The Magic Mountain* is indeed a form of erotic life, and Hans is ill with the return of repressed desire. In Krokowski's lecture, therefore, Mann caricatures the structural idea of his own work. In "Mein Verhältnis zur Psychoanalyse" he admitted that the bizarre figure of the psychoanalyst was a mere compensation for the far-reaching concessions he made to psychoanalysis in his novel.[109] Krokowski thus also stands in for the author who, almost in spite of himself, became naturalised to Freudianism.

Huelle's novel presents prototypes of two characters from *The Magic Mountain*. First, there is Wanda Pilecka, a Polish woman who represents an early incarnation of Hans Castorp's later love for Clawdia Chauchat (who, in Mann's version, reminds him of Pribislav Hippe). Huelle also imagines a prototype of Krokowski: tormented by his repressed desire for a Slavic woman, Castorp ends up on a psychoanalyst's couch. Just as in *The Magic Mountain*, he initially avows his aversion to analysis: "Are you suggesting I should bare my soul to you? Or undergo analysis, as you people call it? Please believe me, I count myself the type of person that feels a horror of such modern things."[110] Ultimately, however, he makes a complete confession.

The story of Castorp's analyst, invented by Huelle, is best illustrated by his name change. Born a Russian citizen, Piotr Ankiewicz was studying in Paris when "he got involved in one of those émigré political conspiracies that with their characteristic recklessness the Poles often used to form" (p. 131). Unable to return home under threat of being deported to Siberia, he completed his doctoral studies at an Austrian university; his thesis,

108 Thomas Mann, *The Magic Mountain*, p. 151.

109 T. Mann, "Mein Verhältnis zur Psychoanalyse", p. 33.

110 Paweł Huelle, *Castorp*, p. 137.

Treating hysteria according to the theories and practice of Professor Charcot (p. 132), drew on his experience in France. Having tried unsuccessfully to establish himself in Vienna, he finally became a German citizen, changing his name to Peter Ankewitz in the process. He settled in Gdansk and started treating patients with nervous disorders and insomnia. His office was in the immediate vicinity of Mrs Hildegard Wybe's boarding house, where Hans Castorp took up lodgings the same year. He had very few clients besides Castorp until he changed his name once again, this time to Dr Anke: "thanks to this undeniably sensible operation, he now had a consulting room in the city centre with a nurse and lot of patients" (p. 226). The portrayal of a Polish Freudian in Danzig in 1905 is clearly an anachronism, but Dr Anke's biography still shows remarkable parallels with the lives of Freud's Polish emissaries. Huelle's oriental Other embodies the suppression of Polishness by representatives of the first generation of Freudians.

Thus the Polishness of Dr Krokowski in *The Magic Mountain* is literally symptomatic: what has been displaced from Polish culture returns in an exaggerated form in the great European novel. To create a character recognisable as a "typical" psychoanalyst, Mann endowed him with a background that was characteristic of Freud's first followers, even if Dr Krokowski's actual prototype, Georg Groddeck, was not a Polish Jew but a Catholic from Saxony. But why did Krokowski have to be a Polish Jew and a fictional Georg Groddeck at the same time? In the light of my research there can be only one answer. In the early days, psychoanalysis had been a great emancipatory project and a vehicle of cultural rebellion, but by the mid-1920s, when Mann was writing his novel, it had already passed through a stage of professionalisation and institutionalisation, and it was poised to become a bureaucratised international movement. At the moment when "the dream became a system," to paraphrase Jerzy Szacki's definition of utopia,[111] Groddeck came to personify "wild" psychoanalysis, its untamed, dissident and marginal splinter group, which no longer had a place in the mainstream – even if the original core of Freudianism had been exactly there. By giving the character inspired by Groddeck the name of "Dr Krokowski," Mann unambiguously associated this subversive dimension of psychoanalysis with Polishness.

Indeed, the members of the Vienna Psychoanalytic Society depicted in this study were for the most part rebels who dramatically felt the need to

111 J. Szacki, *Spotkania z utopią* (Warsaw: Sic!, 2000), p. 27.

change the world, or at least its sexual and social codes. In their eyes, therapeutic practice did not exhaust the potential of psychoanalysis, which they saw not so much as a professional activity but as a cultural and political force. They believed in the emancipatory dimension of the Freudian project and were equally committed to radical socialism, Zionism, women's emancipation and non-authoritarian pedagogy. They never defied Freud's movement, which is why they were never banned in the manner of Wilhelm Reich and other open dissidents, but they were certainly the movement's ex-centrics. It was the new arrivals from the provinces – those who never obtained any prominent positions in the international structures of psychoanalysis and whose traces can now be found almost exclusively in the footnotes to the movement's history – who carried the subversive potential of Freudianism. This, however, was lost along the way of international expansion with its inherent compromises. Forced to give up their earlier ideals in emigration, they became, in spite of themselves perhaps, the architects of a fundamental shift within psychoanalysis. With their passive consent or active participation, the Central European cultural project was transformed into an American therapeutic technique.

Although the psychoanalytic establishment's victory over its dissidents can ultimately be seen as the demise of psychoanalysis itself, the story presented here is not one of defeat. After all, the efforts of Freud's emissaries were anything but fruitless, even if cultural history in Poland appears to do without them at first sight. Examining the transformations that shaped Polish culture in the first four decades of the twentieth century, we frequently come across evidence of their effectiveness. By 1939 the transfer of psychoanalysis to Polish culture was fully accomplished. My study not only recalls the names of those to whom we owe this fact, but it also lays the ground for future research on the reception of Freudianism in Polish literature and culture. The project I had initially envisaged should, in fact, begin exactly where this book ends.

Journals & periodicals

AAI	Anaïs: An International Journal
ADI	Almanach des Internationalen Psychoanalytischen Verlages (Almanac of the International Psychoanalytic Press)
ADP	Almanach der Psychoanalyse (Almanac of Psychoanalysis)
AE	Archiwum Emigracji: Studia – Szkice – Dokumenty (Emigration Archive: Studies – Notes – Documents)
AES	Annales: Économies, Sociétés, Civilisations (Annals: Economies, Societies, Civilisations)
AHR	American Historical Review
AI	American Imago
AJO	American Journal of Orthopsychiatry
AK	Ateneum Kapłańskie (The Priestly Athenaeum)
AN	Art News
AR	Arkusz (Broadsheet)
AS	Archeus: Studia z bioetyki i antropologii filozoficznej (Archeus: Studies in Bioethics and Philosophical Anthropology)
AT	Ateneum (The Athenaeum)
AZ	Allgemeine Zeitung (General Newspaper)
BAP	Bulletin of the American Psychoanalytic Association
BM	Bunt Młodych (Youth Revolt)
BPI	Bulletin of the Polish Institute of Arts and Sciences in America
BT	Berliner Tageblatt (Berlin Daily Paper)
BW	Biblioteka Warszawska (Warsaw Library)
CAG	Cahiers André Gide (André Gide Journal)

CDR	Cahiers de recherche de sciences des textes et documents (Scientific Journal of Studies of Texts and Documents)
CH	Chimera
CHO	Chowanna (*In Slavic mythology, a goddess of protection*)
CHW	Chwila (Moment)
CI	Critical Inquiry
CZ	Czas (Time)
D	Diacritics
DI	Dialog (Dialogue)
DL	Dziennik Ludowy (People's Daily)
DLE	Das literarische Echo (The Literary Echo)
DP	Dziennik Polski (Polish Daily)
DPB	Die Psychoanalytische Bewegung (The Psychoanalytical Movement)
DPL	Dzień Polski (Polish Day)
DR	Droga (The Way)
DRV	Deutsche Revue (German Review)
DS	Der Sturm (The Storm)
DW	Die Waage (The Balance)
DZ	Dzień (Day)
E	Ewa (Eve)
EIS	Ekran i Scena (Screen and Scene)
EP	Echo Przemyskie (Przemyśl Echo)
EPIŁ	Echa Płockie i Łomżyńskie (Płock and Łomża Echo)
ER	Europäische Revue (European Review)
ET	Echo Tatrzańskie (Tatra Echo)
EW	Echo Warszawskie (Warsaw Echo)

FP	Forum Psychologiczne (Psychological Forum)
FS	Feminist Studies
GE	Genèses (Origins)
GG	Głos Gminy Wilkowice (The Voice of the Municipality Wilkowice)
GH	Gazeta Handlowa (Trade Journal)
GL	Gazeta Lekarska (Medical Gazette)
GLP	Gazeta Polska (Polish Gazette)
GLW	Gazeta Lwowska (Lviv Gazette)
GŁN	Głos Narodu (The Nations' Voice)
GN	Gospodarka Narodowa (The National Economy)
GNA	Gazeta Narodowa (The National Gazette)
GP	Ginekologia Polska (Polish Gynaecology)
GR	Głos Robotnika (The Labour Voice)
GS	Głos Stolicy (Voice of the Capital)
GWP	Gazeta Warszawska Poranna (Warsaw Morning Gazette)
GZ	Głos Zakopiański (Voice of Zakopane)
GZF	Germanoslavica: Zeitschrift für germano-slawische Studien (Germanoslavica: Journal for Germanic and Slavic Studies)
HA	Haszomer: pismo młodzieży szomrowej (The Watchman: Journal of the Shomer Youth), a supplement to *Moriah* (MO)
HAR	Harcerstwo (Scouting)
HIA	History of Anthropology
HP	Higiena Psychiczna (Mental Hygiene)
I	Imago
IFP	International Forum of Psychoanalysis
IJOS	International Journal of Sex Economy and Orgone Research

IKF	Ilustrowany Kalendarz Filmowy (Illustrated Film Calendar)
IR	Ilustrowana Republika: Dodatek Literacko-Naukowy (Illustrated Republic: A Literary-Scientific Supplement)
IZAP	Internationale Zeitschrift für ärztliche Psychoanalyse (International Journal of Medical Psychoanalysis)
IZP	Internationale Zeitschrift für Psychoanalyse (International Journal of Psychoanalysis)
JAA	Journal of the American Academy of Psychoanalysis
JAM	Journal of American Medical Association
JAP	Journal of Abnormal Psychology
JDP	Jahrbuch der Psychoanalyse (Yearbook of Psychoanalysis)
JNM	Journal of Nervous & Mental Disease
JOC	Journal of Contemporary History
JOCP	Journal of Contemporary Psychoanalysis
JOO	Journal of the Otto Rank Association
JPP	Jahrbuch für Psychoanalytische und Psychopathologische Forschungen (Yearbook of Psychoanalytical and Psychopathological Research)
JS	Janetian Studies
K	Konteksty (Contexts)
KC	Kurier Codzienny (Daily Courier)
KF	Kwartalnik Filozoficzny (Philosophy Quarterly)
KIE	Kultura i Edukacja (Culture and Education)
KKS	Kwartalnik Kliniczny Szpitala Starozakonnych w Warszawie (Clinical Quarterly of the Jewish Hospital in Warsaw)
KL	Kurier Lwowski (Lviv Courier)
KLN	Kurier Literacko-Naukowy (Literary Studies Courier)
KMP	Książka: Miesięcznik poświęcony krytyce i bibliografii polskiej (The Book: Monthly of Polish Criticism and Bibliography)

KP	Kwartalnik Pedagogiczny (Pedagogy Quarterly)
KPIŚ	Kronika Polski i Świata (Chronicle of Poland and the World)
KPL	Kurier Polski (Polish Courier)
KPO	Kurier Poranny (Morning Courier)
KPOZ	Kurier Poznański (Poznań Courier)
KPS	Kwartalnik Psychologiczny (Psychology Quarterly)
KR	Kronos
KRR	Kronika Ruchu Rewolucyjnego w Polsce (Chronicle of the Revolutionary Movement in Poland)
KS	Księgarz (The Bookseller)
KW	Kurier Warszawski (Warsaw Courier)
L	Literatura (Literature)
LA	Luzifer-Amor (Lucifer-Amor)
LB	Leo Baeck Institute Year Book
LC	Literature Compass
LI	Linia (The Line)
LIE	Logos i Ethos (Logos and Ethos)
LIT	Littérature (Literature)
LNR	La Nouvelle Revue Française (The New French Review)
LNŚ	Literatura na Świecie (Literature in the World)
LPM	La Presse Médicale (The Medical Press)
LW	Lekarz Wojskowy (The Military Doctor)
M	Medycyna (Medicine)
MA	Maski (Masks)
MAR	Marchołt (Marcolf)
MDF	Mercure de France (Mercury of France)
MEJ	Múlt és Jövő (Past and Future)

MF	Médecine de France (Medicine in France)
MH	Monatshefte (Monthly Bulletin)
MIK	Medycyna i kronika lekarska: Czasopismo tygodniowe dla lekarzy praktyków (Medicine and Medical Chronicle: A weekly journal for practising physicians)
ML	Miesięcznik Literacki (Literary Monthly)
MN	Myśl Niepodległa (Independent Thought)
MNR	Myśl Narodowa (National Thought)
MO	Moriah
MU	Mucha (The Fly)
N	Nature
NC	Nowe Czasy (New Times)
ND	Nowy Dziennik (New Daily)
NF	Nowa Fantastyka (New Fantasy)
NFP	Neue Freie Presse (New Free Press)
NG	Nowa Gazeta (New Gazette)
NGP	Nowy Głos Przemyski (New Voice of Przemyśl)
NI	Niwa (The Field)
NIL	Nowości Ilustrowane (Illustrated News)
NK	Nowa Książka (The New Book)
NKP	Nowy Kurier Polski (New Polish Courier)
NKR	Nasz Kraj (Our Country)
NKU	Nowa Kultura (New Culture)
NL	Nowiny Lekarskie (Medical News)
NP	Nowiny Psychiatryczne (Psychiatry News)
NPD	Niepodległość (Independence)

NPK	Notatki Płockie: Kwartalnik Towarzystwa Naukowego Płockiego (Płock Notes: The Quarterly of the Science Society of Płock)
NPL	Neurologia Polska (Polish Neurology)
NPOL	Nauka Polska (Polish Science)
NPR	Nasz Przegląd (Our Review)
NR	Nowa Reforma (New Reform)
NS	Nowa Sztuka (New Art)
NU	Nurt (Current)
NW	Nasz Wyraz (Our Expression)
NYHT	New York Herald Tribune
NYT	New York Times Magazine
O	Ogniwo (The Link)
OO	Orędownik Ostrowski: Pismo na powiaty Ostrowski i Odolanowski oraz miast Ostrowca, Odolanowa, Sulmierzyc i Raszkowa (The Ostrów Advocate: Magazine for the districts of Ostrów and Odolanów and the towns of Ostrów, Odolanów, Sulmierzyce and Raszków)
OŚKA	Pismo Ośrodka Informacji Środowisk Kobiecych (Journal of the Information Centre of Women's Networks)
P	Prawda (Truth)
PA	Pro Arte
PAH	Psychoanalysis and History
PAP	Polskie Archiwum Psychologii (Polish Psychology Archive)
PAT	Pamiętnik Teatralny (Theatre Memoir)
PF	Przegląd Filozoficzny (Philosophy Review)
PFL	Przegląd Filozoficzno-Literacki (Philosophy and Literature Review)
PGL	Polska Gazeta Lekarska (Polish Physicians' Gazette)

PHO	Przegląd Historyczno-Oświatowy (History and Education Review)
PI	Pion (Perpendicular)
PK	Przegląd Katolicki (Catholic Review)
PKK	Psychoanalyse: Klinik und Kulturkritik (Psychoanalysis: Clinic and Cultural Criticism)
PL	Przegląd Lekarski (Physicians' Review)
PLA	Polonia (Polish Emigration)
PLI	Pamiętnik Literacki (Literary Memoir)
PLL	Pologne Littéraire (Literary Poland)
PM	Psychosomatic Medicine
PNL	Przegląd Naukowy i Literacki (Scientific and Literary Review)
PNW	Prace Naukowe Wyższej Szkoły Pedagogicznej w Częstochowie (Scientific Papers of the Higher School of Pedagogy in Częstochowa)
PO	Poezja (Poetry)
POD	Podtatrze (Low Tatras)
POL	Polonista (The Polonist)
POS	Papers of Surrealism
PP	Przegląd Psychologiczny (Psychological Review)
PPE	Przegląd Pedagogiczny (Pedagogical Review)
PPIN	Postępy Psychiatrii i Neurologii (Advances in Psychiatry and Neurology)
PPO	Przegląd Powszechny (General Review)
PR	Psychoanalytic Review
PRZ	Przegląd Społeczny (Social Review)
PS	Psychotechnika (Psychotechnology)
PSIA	Przegląd Sądowy i Administracyjny (Judicial and Administrative Review)

PSO	Psychoanalytic Study of the Child
PSP	Psychiatria Polska (Polish Psychiatry)
PSPL	Poznańskie Studia Polonistyczne: Seria Literacka (Poznań Polonist Studies: Literary Series)
PSS	Psychoanalytical Social Sciences
PSY	Psyche
PT	Przegląd Tygodniowy (Weekly Review)
PTD	Poetics Today
PTIM	Przegląd Teatralny i Muzyczny (Theatre and Music Review)
PW	Psychologia Wychowawcza (Educational Psychology)
PWS	Przegląd Współczesny (Contemporary Review)
PZ	Polska Zbrojna (Polish Armed Forces)
PZM	Prosto z Mostu (literally "straight off the bridge"; idiomatically "straight from the shoulder")
R	Robotnik (The Worker)
RDL	Revue des Littératures de l'Union Européenne (Journal of European Union Literature)
RE	Republika (Republic)
RF	Ruch Filozoficzny (Philosophical Movement)
RFP	Revue Française de Psychanalyse (French Review of Psychoanalysis)
RH	Rethinking History
RHL	Revue d'Histoire littéraire de la France (Review of French Literary History)
RIH	Revue Internationale d'Histoire de la Psychanalyse (International Review of the History of Psychoanalysis)
RKH	Rocznik Komisji Historycznoliterackiej PAN (Yearbook of the Literary-Historical Commission of the Polish Academy of Sciences)

RLIT	Rocznik Literacki (Yearbook of Literature)
RN	Revue Neurologique (Neurology Review)
RND	Rocznik Naukowo-Dydaktyczny WSP w Krakowie (Research and Teaching Yearbook of the Pedagogical University of Cracow)
RP	Ruch Pedagogiczny (Pedagogical Movement)
RPF	Revue philosophique de la France et de l'Etranger (Philosophical Review in France and Abroad)
RPS	Rocznik Psychiatryczny (Yearbook of Psychiatry)
RPZ	Rocznik Przemyski (Przemyśl Yearbook)
S	Skamander
SAN	Schweizer Archiv für Neurologie und Psychiatrie (Swiss Archive for Neurology and Psychiatry)
SCP	Scena Polska (The Polish Stage)
SDU	Schriftenreihe des Universitätsarchivs Universität Wien (University Archive of the University of Vienna, a series)
SEM	Semen: Revue de sémio-linguistique des textes et discours (Sement: Linguistic Review of Texts and Discourses)
SF	Sfinks (Sphinx)
SH	Studia Historyczne (Historical Studies)
SI	Silesia
SL	Svenska Laekartidn (Swedish Medicine)
SŁ	Słowo (The Word)
SP	Szkoła Powszechna (Public School)
SPL	Słowo Polskie (The Polish Word)
SPM	Słowo Pomorskie (The Word of Pomarania)
SPO	Społeczeństwo (Society)
SPR	Scandinavian Psychoanalytic Review
ST	Studio

SZS	Szkoła Specjalna (Special Education)
Ś	Świat (The World)
T	Teksty (Texts)
TA	Tygodnik Artystów (Artists' Weekly)
TCM	The Century Magazine
TD	Teksty Drugie (Second Texts)
TF	The Forum
TI	Tygodnik Ilustrowany (Illustrated Weekly)
TIR	The International Review of Psycho-Analysis
TLS	Times Literary Supplement
TPQ	The Psychoanalytic Quarterly
TRA	Tytuł roboczy: Archiwum (Working Title: The Archive)
TSR	The Saturday Review of Literature
TW	Twórczość (Creativity)
TZ	Tygodnik Zakopiański (Zakopane Weekly)
V	Verbum
W	Wiadomości (News)
WC	Wiadomości Codzienne (Daily News)
WCL	Warszawskie Czasopismo Lekarskie (Warsaw Journal of Physicians)
WIŻ	Wiedza i Życie (Knowledge and Life)
WL	Wiadomości Literackie (Literary News)
WMP	Wiener Medizinische Presse (Vienna Medical Press)
WN	Wiek Nowy (New Age)
WS	Women's Studies
WW	Wici Wielkopolskie (Threads from Greater Poland)
Z	Zdrój (Spa)

ZD	Zdrowie (Health)
ZFP	Zentralblatt für Psychoanalyse (Central Journal for Psychoanalysis)
ZFPP	Zeitschrift für psychoanalytische Pädagogik (Journal for Psychoanalytical Pedagogy)
ZFS	Zeitschrift für Sozialforschung (Journal for Social Research)
ZH	Zeszyty Historyczne (History Journal)
ZL	Ziemia Lubelska (The Lublin Region)
ZLI	Zeszyty Literackie (Literary Journal)
ZN	Zeszyty Naukowe Wyższej Szkoły Pedagogicznej w Opolu (Research Journal of the College of Pedagogy in Opole)
ZP	Zeszyty Prasoznawcze (Press Studies Journal)
ZS	Ziemia Sądecka (The Sącz Region)
ZŚ	Zaranie Śląskie (Silesian Dawn)
ZT	Zet (Zed)
ŻD	Życie Dziecka (The Child's Life)
ŻIZ	Życie i Zdrowie (Life and Health)
ŻL	Życie Literackie (Literary Life)
Виив	Вопросы изучения и воспитания личности (Questions Relating to the Study of Personality and Its Formation)
ЖНиП	Журнал невропатологии и психиатрии им. С.С.Корсакова (Journal of Neuropathology and Psychiatry [named after] S.S. Korsakov)
ПЗ	Психічне здоров'я (Mental Health)
Пс	Психотерапия (Psychotherapy)

CHRONOLOGY

	Biographical facts	Psychoanalytical movement events	Publications by Freud	Publications by other authors
1856	Sigmund Freud born in Freiberg (Příbor)			
1867	Ludwig Jekels born in Lviv			
1876	Eugenia Kutner (later Sokolnicka) born in Warsaw			
1880	Salomea Kempner born in Płock			
1881	Freud becomes a medical doctor in Vienna			
1884	Hermann Nunberg born in Będzin			
	Otto Rank (Rosenfeld) born in Vienna			
	Mira Gincburg born in Łódź			
	Helene Rosenbach (later Deutsch) born in Przemyśl			
1885	Freud begins his internship under Jean-Martin Charcot at the Salpêtrière Hospital in Paris			
	Józef Reinhold born in Stryj			

1888	Salomea Rettich (later Gutmann, then Isakower) born in Oświęcim			
1890	Berta Grünspan (later Betty Beile) born in Międzybrodzie			
1892	Siegfried Bernfeld born in Lemberg			
	Ludwig Jekels becomes a medical doctor in Vienna			
1895	Gustav Bychowski born in Warsaw		*Studien über Hysterie* (*Studies on Hysteria*), with Josef Breuer	
1896	Beata Münzer (later Rank) born in Nowy Sącz	First appearance of the word "psycho-analysis" in the article "L'Hérédité et l'étiologie des névroses" ("Heredity and the Etiology of Neuroses")		
	Berta Bornstein born in Cracow			
1897	Ludwig Jekels becomes director of a sanatorium in Bystra			
1899			*Die Traumdeutung* (*The Interpretation of Dreams*)	
1901			*Zur Psychopathologie des Alltagslebens* (*The Psychopathology of Everyday Life*)	
1902	Eugenia Kutner finishes her studies of natural sciences in Paris	Creation of the Psychological Wednesday Society (Psychologische Mittwoch-Gesellschaft)		

1903	Ludwig Jekels starts following Freud's lectures at the University of Vienna	First foreign translation of a work by Freud: *Über den Traum* appears in Russian		
	Eugenia Kutner marries Michał Sokolnicki			
1905			*Der Witz und seine Beziehung zum Unbewußten* (*The Joke and Its Relationship with the Unconscious*), *Drei Abhandlungen zur Sexualtheorie* (*Three Essays on the Theory of Sexuality*)	
1906	Ludwig Jekels starts participating in the meetings of the Psychological Wednesday Society			
1907	Helene Rosenbach starts her medical studies in Vienna	Freuds presents his lecture "Der Dichter und das Phantasieren" ("Creative Writers and Day-Dreaming") in Hugo Heller's art salon		*Der Künstler* (*The Artist*) by Otto Rank
1908	Salomea Kempner becomes a medical doctor in Zurich	Creation of the Vienna Psychoanalytic Society (Wiener Psychoanalytische Vereinigung)		
		1st international psychoanalytical congress in Salzburg		
1909	Ludwig Jekels presents psychoanalysis at the Congress of Polish Neurologists, Psychiatrists and Psychologists in Warsaw	Foundation of the *Jahrbuch für psychopathologische und psychoanalytische Forschungen*, editor-in-chief: Carl G. Jung		

		Freuds gives five lectures on psychoanalysis at Clark University		
		Psichoterapija founded in Russia		
		The first woman, Ludwika Karpińska, participates in a meeting of the VPS		
1910	Ludwig Jekels officially joins the VPS	The Berlin Psychoanalytic Society is founded	*Über "wilde" Psychoanalyse* (*"Wild" psychoanalysis*)	
	Freud's family spend their summer vacation in Bystra	The Zurich Psychoanalytic Society is founded	*Über psychoanalyse* (*Five Lectures on Psycho-Analysis*)	
	Hermann Nunberg becomes a medical doctor in Zurich	2nd International psychoanalytic congress in Nuremberg, creation of the International Psychoanalytical Association with Carl G. Jung as president		
	Helene Rosenbach completes a medical internship at Emil Kraepelin's clinic in Munich	*Zentralblatt für Psychoanalyse* is founded (editors: Alfred Adler and Wilhelm Stekel)		
	Józef Reinhold becomes a VPS member			
	Eugenia Kutner completes an internship with Carl G. Jung in Zurich			
1911	Mira Gincburg becomes the first woman to join the Berlin Psychoanalytic Society	The New York Psychoanalytic Society is founded		Ludwig Jekels publishes the first Polish translation of Freud (*Five Lectures on Psycho-Analysis*) in Lviv

		American Psychoanalytic Association is founded		
		Alfred Adler leaves the Vienna Psychoanaly-tical Society		
		3rd Congress of the International Psychoanalytical Association in Weimar		
1912	Ludwig Jekels sells the Bystra sanatorium and settles in Vienna	*Imago. Zeitschrift für die Anwendung der Psychoanalyse auf die Geiste-wissenschaften* is founded (editors: Otto Rank and Hanns Sachs)	*Totem und Tabu: Einige Überein-stimmungen im Seelenleben der Wilden und der Neurotiker* (*Totem and Taboo: Resem-blances Between the Psychic Lives of Savages and Neurotics*)	*Szkic psychoanalizy Freuda* (An Outline of Freud's Psychoanalysis) by Ludwig Jekels
	Ludwig Jekels and Hermann Nunberg attend the Second Congress of Polish Neurologists, Psychiatrists and Psychologists in Cracow	Founding of the Secret Committee (Sigmund Freud, Ernest Jones, Karl Abraham, Sándor Ferenczi, Otto Rank, Hanns Sachs)		*Teoria snu Freuda* (Freud's Theory of Dreams) by Franciszka Baumgarten
	Helene Rosen-bach marries Felix Deutsch and graduates from the medical departement in Vienna	Wilhelm Steckel resigns from the Vienna Psychoanalytical Society		
		Rupture between Freud and Jung		
1913	Mira Gincburg marries Emil Oberholzer	*Zentralblatt für Psychoanalyse* is replaced by *Inter-nationale Zeitschrift für ärztliche Psycho-analyse* (editors: Sándor Ferenczi and Otto Rank)		*Die Bedeutung der Psycho-analyse für die Geisteswissen-schaften* ("The Significance of Psychoanalysis for the Human Sciences") by Otto Rank and Hanns Sachs

	Salomea Rettich marries Felix Gutmann and becomes a medical doctor in Cracow	The Budapest Psychoanalytic Society is founded		Ludwig Jekels and Helene Ivánka publish the Polish translation of *The Psychopathology of Everyday Life*
		4th Congress of the International Psychoanalytical Association in Munich		*Psychologiczne podstawy freudyzmu* (The Psychological Foundations of Freudianism) by Ludwika Karpińska
		The London Psycho-Analytic Society is founded		*Freud i freudyści* (Freud and the Freudians) by Karol Irzykowski
				"Niespełnione życzenia według nauki Freuda" (Unfulfilled Desires According to Freud), the sole text in Polish by Hermann Nunberg, appears in *Neurologia Polska*
1914	Hermann Nunberg moves to Vienna and starts attending the meetings of the VPS	Carl G. Jung resigns from the International Psychoanalytical Association. Karl Abraham is elected as provisional president.	*Zur Geschichte der psychoanalytischen Bewegung* (*On the History of the Psychoanalytical Movement*)	"Jeden z problematów psychoanalizy Freuda" [One Problem in Freud's Psychoanalysis] by Leopold Wołowicz
	Eugenia Sokolnicka starts taking part in the VPS meetings	*Jahrbuch für psychopathologische und psychoanalytische Forschungen* is replaced by *Jahrbuch der Psychoanalyse* (editors: Karl Abraham and Edward Hitschmann). Only one issue of the new journal is published.		

	Helene Deutsch starts following Freud's lectures at the University of Vienna			
	Siegfried Bernfeld finishes his philosophical studies in Vienna			
1916	Eugenia Sokolnicka becomes a VPS member		*Vorlesungen zur Einführung in die Psychoanalyse* (*Introductory Lectures on Psychoanalysis*)	
1917	Eugenia Sokolnicka attempts to establish a Polish Psychoanalytic Society in Warsaw	The Netherlands Society for Psychoanalysis is founded		
1918	Beata Münzer marries Otto Rank	5th Congress of the International Psychoanalytical Association in Budapest. Sándor Ferenczi elected president of the IPA.		
	Helene Deustch becomes a VPS member			
1919	Gustav Bychowski becomes a medical doctor in Zurich	The publishing house Interna-tionaler Psycho-analytischer Verlag is founded, with Otto Rank at its head		
	Mira Gincburg and Salomea Kempner become founding members of the Swiss Society for Psychoanalysis	The British Psycho-Analytical Society is founded		*Tagebuch eines halbwüchsigen Mädchens* (*A Young Girl's Diary*) by Hermine von Hug-Hellmuth

		The Swiss Society for Psychoanalysis is founded		
		Kinderheim Baumgarten founded by Siegfried Bernfeld		
		Max Eitingon joins the Secret Committee		
1920	Eugenia Sokolnicka starts her analysis with Sándor Ferenczi in Budapest	The Polyclinic for Psychoanalytical Treatment of Mental Illness is founded in Berlin	*Jenseits des Lustprinzips* (*Beyond the Pleasure Principle*)	"Analyse einer infantilen Zwangsneurose" ("Analysis of an Obsessional Neurosis in a Child") by Eugenia Sokolnicka
		6th Congress of the International Psychoanalytical Association in The Hague, Ernest Jones becomes the acting president of the IPA		
		The title of the *Internationale Zeitschrift für Ärztliche Psycho-analyse* is shortened to *Internationale Zeitschrift für Psychoanalyse*		
		International Psycho-Analytical Press, the English branch of the Internationaler Psychoanalytischer Verlag, is founded, with Ernest Jones at its head		
		International Journal of Psycho-Analysis starts to appear (editor: Ernest Jones)		

1921	Eugenia Sokolnicka settles in Paris	The New Library of Psycho-Analysis founded by Ernest Jones	*Massenpsychologie und Ich-Analyse* (*Group Psychology and the Analysis of the Ego*)	
	Gustav Bychowski starts to take part in the VPS meetings			
	Salomea Rettich-Gutmann moves to Vienna			
1922		The Indian Psycho-Analytical Society is founded in Calcutta		"Über die pathologische Lüge" ("On The Pathological Lie") by Helene Deutsch
		The Russian Psychoanalytic Society is founded. A psychoanalytic institute and clinic open in Moscow		
		The Berlin Psychoanalytical Institute comprised of a polyclinic and a training institute founded		
		Wiener Psycho-analytisches Ambulatorium (Vienna psycho-analytical poly-clinic) opens under Eduard Hitschmann's direction		
		7th Congress of the International Psychoanalytical Association in Berlin		

1923	Freud is diagnosed with cancer		*Das Ich und das Es* (*The Ego and the Id*)	Beata Rank launches the series "Polska Biblioteka Psychoanalityczna" (The Polish Psychoanalytical Library) in Internationaler Psychoanalytischer Verlag with her translation of Freud's *On Dreams* (*O marzeniu sennem)*
	Beata Rank becomes a VPS member			
	Helene Deutsch starts her psychoanalysis with Karl Abraham in Berlin			
	Gustav Bychowski settles in Warsaw			
	Salomea Kempner moves to Berlin			
1924	Berta Grünspan finishes her medical studies in Vienna	Secret Committee dissolved		*Das Trauma der Geburt* (*The Trauma of Birth*) by Otto Rank
		8th Congress of the International Psychoanalytical Association in Salzburg, for the first time in the absence of Freud		*Das Buch vom Es* (*The Book of the It*) by Georg Groddeck
		Karl Abraham becomes president of the IPA		Polish translation of *Three Essays on the Theory of Sexuality* by Ludwig Jekels and Marian Albiński appears with Internationaler Psychoanalytischer Verlag

				"Zur Rolle der Frau in der Entwicklung der menschlichen Gesellschaft" (On the Role of Women in the Development of Human Society) by Beata Rank
				The Magic Mountain by Thomas Mann
1925	Siegfried Berlin leaves Vienna for Berlin	The Italian Psychoanalytical Society is founded	*Selbstdarstellung* (*An Autobiographical Study*)	*Zur Psychologie der Weiblichen Sexualfunktionen* by Helene Deutsch
		9th Congress of the International Psychoanalytical Association in Bad Homburg, foundation of the Training Committee (Internationale Unterrichtskommission) with Max Eitingon at its head		*Sisyphos, oder die Grenzen der Erziehung* (*Sisyphus or the Limitations of Education*) by Siegfried Bernfeld
		Max Eitingon succeeds Karl Abraham in the presidency of the IPA		*The Counterfeiters* by André Gide
		Lehrinstitut der Wiener Psychoanalytischen Vereinigung (Training Institute of the Vienna Psychoanalytical Society) is created by the Vienna Psychoanalytical Society under the direction of Helene Deutsch, Anna Freud and Siegfried Bernfeld		

		Adolf Josef Storfer succeeds Otto Rank as director of the Internationaler Psychoanalytischer Verlag		
		Max Eitingon, Sándor Rado, and Sándor Ferenczi replace Rank at the editorial desk of the *Internationale Zeitschrift für Psychoanalyse*		
1926	Otto and Beata Rank move to Paris	*Geheimnisse einer Seele* (Mysteries of a Soul), first film on psychoanalysis, directed by G. W. Pabst	*Die Frage der Laienanalyse* (*The Question of Lay Analysis*)	
		The Berliner Psychoanalytische Vereinigung becomes the Deutsche Psychoanalytische Gesellschaft (German Psychoanalytic Association)		
		Foundation of the Paris Psychoanalytic Society		
		Foundation of the *Zeitschrift für psychoanalytische Pädagogik* by Heinrich Meng and Ernst Schneider		
		Almanach der Psychoanalyse starts to appear		
		London Clinic of Psychoanalysis is founded		

1927		*Revue française de psychanalyse* (French Review of Psychoanalysis) founded	*Die Zukunft einer Illusion* (*The Future of an Illusion*)	
		10th Congress of the International Psychoanalytical Association in Innsbruck		
		American Psychoanalytic Association splits off from the IPA		
1928	Salomea Rettich-Gutmann starts attending the VPS meetings	Tokyo Psycho-analytic Institute is founded		*Psychoanaliza* by Gustav Bychowski
				"Ein Frauen-schicksal: George Sand" ("George Sand: A Woman's Destiny") by Helene Deutsch
1929	Berta Bornstein leaves Berlin for Vienna	11th Congress of the International Psychoanalytical Association in Oxford		
		Die Psychoanalytische Bewegung starts to appear		
1930	Berta and Stephanie Bornstein become members of the German Psychoanalytic Association	The Russian Psychoanalytic Society halts its activities	*Das Unbehagen in der Kultur* (*Civilisation and Its Discontents*)	*Psychoanalyse der Neurosen* (*Psychoanalysis of the Neuroses*) by Helene Deutsch
	Freud awarded the Goethe Prize	Psychoanalytical Institute founded in The Hague		*Słowacki i jego dusza* (Słowacki and His Soul) by Gustav Bychowski

		The Washington-Baltimore Psychoanalytic Society is founded		
1931	Gustav Bychowski becomes a member of the VPS	The New York Psychoanalytic Institute is founded		
	A commemorative plaque is placed on Freud's birthplace at Freiberg (Příbor)	opening of the Budapest Psychoanalytical Polyclinic directed by Sándor Ferenczi		
		Wilhelm Reich founds the German Association for a Sexual Proletarian Policy (Sex-Pol)		
1932	Siegfried Bernfeld leaves Berlin for Vienna	*The Psychoanalytic Quarterly* founded		*Allgemeine Neurosenlehre auf psychoanalytischer Grundlage* (*Principles of Psychoanalysis*) by Hermann Nunberg
	Hermann Nunberg leaves Vienna for Philadelphia	12th Congress of the International Psychoanalytical Association in Wiesbaden. Ernest Jones is elected president of the IPA.		
	Berta Grünspan becomes a VPS member	The Boston Psychoanalytic Society and Institute is founded		
		The Chicago Psychoanalytic Society and Institute is founded		

1933	Salomea Kempner becomes a VPS member	The Sendai Psychoanalytical Society is founded	*Neue Folge der Vorlesungen zur Einführung in die Psychoanalyse* (*New Introductory Lectures on Psycho-Analysis*)	*Die Massenspsychologie des Faschismus* (*The Mass Psychology of Fascism*) by Wilhelm Reich
	Stephanie Bornstein leaves Berlin for Prague	Felix Boehm and Carl Müller-Braunschweig take the presidency of the Berlin Psychoanalytical Society, Max Eitingon having been dismissed as a Jew		"Das Märchen vom Dornröschen in psychoanalytischer Darstellung" (The Fairytale of the Sleeping Beauty in Psychoanalytic Presentation) by Stephanie Bornstein
		Max Eitingon leaves Berlin for Jerusalem, where he founds the Palestine Psychoanalytical Society		
		Carl G. Jung becomes president of the Allgemeine Ärztliche Gesellschaft für Psychotherapie		
		The Prague Psychoanalytical Study Group founded and directed by Frances Deri		
		Die Psychoanalytische Bewegung folds		
1934	Eugenia Sokolnicka dies on 19 May in Paris	Institute of Psychoanalysis inaugurated in Paris. Director: Marie Bonaparte		"Über einen Typus der Pseudoaffektivität ('Als ob')" (On a pseudo-affectivity type ('As if')) by Helene Deutsch
	Ludwig Jekeks sent on a psychoanalytic mission to Stockholm	13th Congress of the International Psychoanalytical Association in Lucerne. Wilhelm Reich is expelled from the IPA		

	Siegfried Bernfeld emigrates to France	The Danish-Norwegian Psychoanalytical Society and The Finnish-Swedish Psychoanalytical Society are founded		
	Hermann Nunberg leaves Philadelphia for New York			
1935	Helene Deutsch leaves Vienna for Boston	Otto Fenichel succeeds Frances Deri as the leader of the Prague Psychoanalytical Study Group		Polish translation of *Introduction to Psychoanalysis* by Salomea Kempner (*Wstęp do psycho-analizy*) appears with Przeworski Publishers in Warsaw
		The Jewish members of the Berlin Psycho-analytic Society are forced to resign		
1936	Beata Rank leaves Paris for Boston	The Internationaler Psychoanalytischer Verlag repository in Leipzig is sequestered by the Nazis		Polish translation of *An Autobiographical Study* by Henryk Załszupin (*Wizerunek własny*)
		Deutsches Institut für Psychologische Forschung und Psychotherapie founded under the direction of M. H. Göring		
		14th Congress of the International Psychoanalytical Association in Marienbad, The American Psychoanalytical Association obtains exclusive power over its composition in North America		
		Celebrations of Freud's eightieth birthday		

1937	Ludwig Jekels returns to Vienna	*Imago* ceases to appear	*Die endliche und die unendliche Analyse* (*Analysis Terminable and Interminable*)	
	Siegfried Bernfeld leaves Europe and settles in San Francisco	The Philadelphia Psychoanalytic Society founded		
	Stephanie Bornstein marries Emanuel Windholz			
1938	Freud leaves Vienna for London	Vienna Psychoanalytic Society dissolved		
	Jekels leaves Vienna for New York	*Almanach der Psychoanalyse* ceases to appear		
	Berta Bornstein leaves Vienna for New York	Hanns Sachs founds *American Imago* in Boston, MA		
	Berta Grünspan emigrates to Palestine and changes her name to Betty Beile	15th Congress of the International Psychoanalytical Association in Paris		
	Salomea Rettich-Gutmann marries Otto Isakower, both leave Vienna for London	Deutsche Psychoanalytische Gesellschaft is dissolved		
1939	Freud dies on 23 September in London	Philadelphia Association for Psychoanalysis founded	*Der Mann Moses und die monotheistische Religion* (*Moses and Monotheism*)	*Ichpsychologie und Anpassungsproblem* (*Ego Psychology and the Problem of Adaptation*) by Heinz Hartmann
	Otto Rank dies on 31 October in New York	The Detroit Psychoanalytic Society founded		
	Stephanie Bornstein dies on 15 July in Prague			

	Salomea Kempner deported to Warsaw ghetto			
	Gustav Bychowski leaves Warsaw for Vilnius			
1940	Salomea and Otto Isakower emigrate to the US and establish themselves in New York			
	Gustav Bychowski leaves Europe and emigrates to the US via Sweden and Japan			
1941	Jekels becomes a honorary member of the New York Psychoanalytic Society	*Internationale Zeitschrift für Psychoanalyse* ceases to appear		
1942	Berta Bornstein becomes a honorary member of the New York Psychoanalytic Society	The San Francisco Psychoanalytic Society founded		
		The Topeka Institute for Psychoanalysis founded		
1943	Salomea Kempner dies on 29 January in Warsaw	Finno-Swedish Psychoanalytic Society dissolved	Publication of the first volume of the *Standard Edition of the Complete Psychological Works of Sigmund Freud*	
	Gustav Bychowski becomes a member od the New York Psychoanalytic Society			
1944				*The Psychology of Women* by Helene Deutsch

1946		The Los Angeles Institute for Psychoanalysis founded		
1947	Licensed to practice medicine in New York State, Jekels becomes a full member of the New York Psychoanalytic Society			
	Josef Reinhold dies on 3 November in Jeseník			
1948		The Palestine Psychoanalytic Society becomes the Israel Psychoanalytic Society		*Dictators and Disciples from Caesar to Stalin: A Psychoanalytic Interpretation of History* by Gustav Bychowski
1949	Mira Gincburg dies on 12 December in New York			
	Salomea Isa-kower, licensed to practice medicine in the State of New York, becomes a member of the New York Psychoanalytic Society			
1950	Hermann Nunberg becomes president of the New York Psychoanalytical Society			
1952				*Selected Papers* by Ludwig Jekels
1953	Siegfried Bernfeld dies on 2 April in San Francisco			Publication of the first volume of *Life and Work of Sigmund Freud* by Ernest Jones

1954	Ludwig Jekels dies on 13 April in New York			
1957	Wilhelm Reich dies on 3 November in the Lewisburg penitentiary, Connecticut			
1962				First volume of the *Minutes of the Vienna Psycho-analytic Society* edited by Herman Nunberg appears
1967	Beata Rank dies on 11 April in Cambridge, MA			
1970	Hermann Nunberg dies on 20 May in New York			
1971	Berta Bornstein dies on 5 September in Vinalhaven, Maine			
1972	Gustav Bychowski dies on 13 April in Fez, Morocco			
1973				*Confrontations with Myself* by Helene Deutsch
1975	Berta Grünspan dies on 27 July in kibbutz Yfat			
1982	Helene Deutsch dies on 29 March in Cambridge, MA			

References

This selective bibliography is limited to the most important secondary sources. It does not include unpublished archival material or printed primary sources such as psychoanalytic studies, books and articles from before 1939, diaries, memoirs, letters or literary works.

Abel, Elizabeth. 1989. *Virginia Woolf and the fictions of psychoanalysis* (Chicago: University of Chicago Press)

Alnæs, Randolf. 1980. 'The development of psychoanalysis in Norway: An historical overview', *Scandinavian Psychoanalytic Review*, 3: 55–101

Andersson, Ola. 1962. *Studies in the prehistory of psychoanalysis* (Stockholm: Svenska Bokförlaget)

Andres, Zbigniew (ed.). 1985. *Szkice o twórczości Emila Zegadłowicza* (Rzeszów: Towarzystwo Naukowe)

Anz, Thomas, and Oliver Pfohlmann (eds). 2006. *Psychoanalyse in der literarischen Moderne 1: Eine Dokumentation* (Marburg: LiteraturWissenschaft.de)

Anzieu, Didier. 1959. *L'auto-analyse de Freud* (Paris: Presses Universitaires de France)

Appignanesi, Lisa, and John Forrester. 1992. *Freud's women* (New York: Basic Books)

Arendt, Hannah. 1944. 'The Jew as pariah: A hidden tradition', *Jewish Social Studies*, 6/2: 99–122

Aschheim, Steven E. 1982. *Brothers and strangers: The East European Jew in German and German Jewish consciousness 1800-1923* (Madison: University of Wisconsin Press)

Avanza, Martina, and Gilles Laferté. 2005. 'Dépasser la "construction des identités"?: Identification, image sociale, appartenance', *Genèses*, 61/4: 134–152

Babik, Marek. 2010. *Polskie koncepcje wychowania seksualnego w latach 1900-1939* (Kraków: Ignatianum University Press)

Babits, Mihaly, Géza Csath, Gyula Krúdy, Frigyes Karinthy, Milan Füst, and Dezsö Kosztolányi. 1992. *Cure d'ennui: Écrivains hongrois autour de Sándor Ferenczi* (Paris: Gallimard)

Bair, Deirdre. 1995. *Anaïs Nin* (New York: Putnam)

Baranowska, Małgorzata. 1984. *Surrealna wyobraźnia i poezja* (Warszawa: Czytelnik)

Barth, Daniel. 2010. *Kinderheim Baumgarten: Siegfried Bernfelds "Versuch mit neuer Erziehung" aus psychoanalytischer und soziologischer Sicht* (Gießen: Psychosozial-Verlag)

Bartosik, Marta. 2000. *Bruno Schulz jako krytyk* (Kraków: Universitas)

Bator, Joanna. 2002. *Feminizm, postmodernizm, psychoanaliza: Filozoficzne dylematy feministek drugiej fali* (Gdańsk: Słowo/Obraz Terytoria)

Beller, Steven. 1989. *Vienna and the Jews, 1867-1938: A cultual history* (Cambridge: Cambridge University Press)

Berman, Marshall. 1982. *All that is solid melts into air: The experience of modernity* (New York: Simon & Schuster)

Bernheimer, Charles, and Claire Kahane (eds). 1985. *In Dora's case: Freud - hysteria - feminism* (New York: Columbia University Press)

Bertin, Célia. 2009. *La Femme à Vienne au temps de Freud* (Paris: Stock)

Bettelheim, Bruno. 1982. *Freud and man's soul* (New York: Knopf)

Bielik-Robson, Agata. 2012. *Erros: Mesjański witalizm i filozofia* (Kraków: Universitas)

Bilewicz, Aleksandra. 1997. *Prywatne średnie, ogólnokształcące szkolnictwo żeńskie w Galicji w latach 1867-1914* (Wrocław: Wydawnictwo Uniwersytetu Wrocławskiego)

Bittner, Günther, and Willy Rehm (eds). 1964. *Psychoanalyse und Erziehung: Ausgewählte Beiträge aus der "Zeitschrift für psychoanalytische Pädagogik"* (Bern: Huber)

Błonski, Jan. 2003. *Witkacy na zawsze* (Kraków: Wydawnictwo Literackie)

Bohachevsky-Chomiak, Martha. 1988. *Feminists despite themselves: Women in Ukrainian community life 1884-1939* (Edmonton: Canadian Institute of Ukrainian Studies, University of Alberta)

Böhme, Hartmut. 2014. *Fetishism and culture: A different theory of modernity* (Berlin: de Gruyter)

Bojarska, Anna. 1978. 'Andrée Lynne: (Proza Stanisławy Przybyszewskiej)', *Przegląd Humanistyczny*, 22/11: 103–120

Bolecki, Włodzimierz. 2012. *Modalnosci modernizmu: Studia, analizy, interpretacje* (Warszawa: Instytut Badań Literackich)

——— 1996. *Poetycki model prozy w dwudziestoleciu międzywojennym* (Wrocław: Ossolineum)

Bolecki, Włodzimierz, Jerzy Jarzębski, and Stanisław Rosiek (eds). 2003. *Słownik Schulzowski* (Gdańsk: Słowo/Obraz Terytoria)

Borchers, Hans. 1987. *Freud und die amerikanische Literatur (1920-1940)* (München: Fink)

Borkowska, Grażyna, and Magdalena Rudkowska (eds). 2004. *Kwestia żydowska w XIX wieku: Spory o tożsamość Polaków* (Warszawa: Cyklady)

Borzym, Stanisław. 1980. 'Abramowski, filozof epoki modernizmu', in Edward Abramowski, *Metafizyka doświadczalna i inne pisma* (Warszawa: Państwowe Wydawnictwo Naukowe)

Bourdieu, Pierre. 1996. *The rules of art: Genesis and structure of the literary field* (Cambridge: Polity Press)

Brabant, Eva. 1993. *Ferenczi et l'école hongroise de psychanalyse* (Paris: L'Harmattan)

Brandell, Gunnar. 1967. *Freud enfant de son siècle* (Paris: Lettres modernes)

Brooks, Peter. 1984. *Reading for the plot: Design and intention in narrative* (Cambridge, MA: Harvard University Press)

Brzozowski, Tadeusz. 1993. 'Gra w psychoanalizę, czyli (de)konstrukcja podmiotu w "filmowo-fotograficznym" modelu poezji "Almanachu Nowej Sztuki"', in *Z problemów podmiotowości w literaturze polskiej XX wieku*ed. by Mirosław Lalak (Szczecin: Wydawnictwo Uniwersytetu Szczecińskiego)

Bujnicki, Tadeusz, and Tadeusz Kłak (eds). 1979. *Katastrofizm i awangarda* (Katowice: Wydawnictwo Uniwersytetu Śląskiego)

Burkot, Stanisław. 1978. 'Od psychoanalizy klinicznej do literackiej', *Rocznik Naukowo-Dydaktyczny*, 68: 133–157

Burnham, John C. 1967. *Psychoanalysis and American medicine, 1894-1918: Medicine, science, and culture* (New York: International Universities Press)

Bžoch, Adam. 2013. *Psychoanalyse in der Slowakei: Eine Geschichte von Enthusiasmus und Widerstand* (Gießen: Psychosozial-Verlag)

Cabaj, Jarosław. 2007. *Walczyć nauką za sprawę Ojczyzny: Zjazdy ponadzaborowe polskich środowisk naukowych i zawodowych jako czynnik integracji narodowej (1869-1914)* (Siedlce: Wydawnictwo Akademii Podlaskiej)

Cała, Alina. 1989. *Asymilacja Żydów w Królestwie Polskim (1864-1897): Postawy, konflikty, stereotypy* (Warszawa: Państwowy Instytut Wydawniczy)

———2012. *Żyd - wróg odwieczny?: Antysemityzm w Polsce i jego źródła* (Warszawa: Wydawnictwo Nisza)

Castel, Pierre-Henri. 1998. *La Querelle de l'hystérie: La formation du discours psychopathologique en France (1881-1913)* (Paris: Presses Universitaires de France)

Charbonel, Frédéric. 2008. 'Au delà de Paris et Nancy, "L'école de Charles Richet" selon Pierre Janet: Son impact et ses réseaux, ses membres et son hétérodoxie de l'appel à un congrès international de psychologie (1881) à la fondation d'un Institut Psychique (1990)', *Janetian studies*, 5

Chemouni, Jacquy. 1984. *Georg Groddeck, psychanalyste de l'imaginaire* (Paris: Payot)

Chertok, Léon, and Raymond de Saussure. 1979. *The therapeutic revolution, from Mesmer to Freud* (New York: Brunner-Mazel)

Chmurski, Mateusz. 2013. 'Modernizm(y) Europy Środkowej: Rekonesans', *Przegląd Filozoficzno-Literacki*, 43/1-2: 395–421

Chwalba, Andrzej. 2014. *Samobójstwo Europy: Wielka Wojna 1914-1918* (Kraków: Wydawnictwo Literackie)

Cohn, Dorrit. 1999. *The distinction of fiction* (Baltimore: Johns Hopkins University Press)

——— 1984. *Transparent minds: Narrative modes for presenting consciousness in fiction* (Princeton: Princeton University Press)

Cywinska, Marta. 2007. *Manufaktura snów: Rozważania o polskiej poezji nadrealistycznej* (Warszawa: Państwowe Wydawnictwo Naukowe)

Czachowska, Jadwiga. 1966. *Gabriela Zapolska: Monografia bio-bibliograficzna* (Kraków: Wydawnictwo Literackie)

Czajecka, Bogusława. 1990. *"Z domu w szeroki świat": Droga kobiet do niezależności w zaborze austriackim w latach 1890-1914* (Kraków: Universitas)

Czaplowa, Kazimiera (ed.). 1976. *Studia o prozie Brunona Schulza* (Katowice: Wydawnictwo Uniwersytetu Śląskiego)

Czarnecki, Bartholomaus Gregor. 2006. *Ludwig Jekels (1867–1954) und die Anfänge der Psychoanalyse in Polen* (Tübingen: Eberhard-Karls-Universität)

Czermińska, Małgorzata. 1987. *Autobiografia i powieść, czyli pisarz i jego postacie* (Gdańsk: Wydawnictwo Morskie)

Czubała, Henryk, Krzysztof Kłosiński, and Krystyna Latawiec (eds). 2015. *Emil Zegadłowicz: Daleki i bliski* (Katowice: Wydawnictwo Uniwersytetu Śląskiego)

Danek, Danuta. 2002. 'Gustaw Bychowski: Zapoznana postać z dziejów kultury polskiej', in Gustaw Bychowski, *Słowacki i jego dusza: Studium psychoanalityczne* (Kraków: Universitas)

———1997. *Sztuka rozumienia: Literatura i psychoanaliza* (Warszawa: Oficyna Wydawnicza Szkoła Główna Handlowa)

Danek-Wojnowska, Bożena. 1976. *Stanisław Ignacy Witkiewicz a modernizm: Kształtowanie idei katastroficznych* (Wrocław: Ossolineum)

Danto, Elizabeth Ann. 2005. *Freud's free clinics: Psychoanalysis and social justics 1918-1938* (New York: Columbia University Press)

Danzer, Gerhard. 1992. *Der wilde Analytiker: Georg Groddeck und die Entdeckung der Psychosomatik* (München: Kösel)

Darmaun, Jacques. 2003. *Thomas Mann, Deutschland und die Juden* (Tübingen: Niemeyer)

Datner, Helena. 2007. *Ta i tamta strona: Żydowska inteligencja Warszawy drugiej połowy XIX wieku* (Warszawa: Żydowski Instytut Historyczny)

Dąbrowski, Mieczysław. 1995. *Polska awangarda prozatorska* (Warszawa: Semper)

de Certeau, Michel. 1987. *Histoire et psychanalyse: Entre science et fiction* (Paris: Gallimard)

De Man, Paul. 1979. 'Autobiography as de-facement', *Modern Language Notes*, 94/5: 919–930

de Mijolla, Alain (ed.). 2005. *International dictionary of psychoanalysis* (Detroit: Thomson Gale)

Debreuille, Jean-Yves. 1994. 'La psychanalyse en question dans "Les faux-monnayeurs"', *Semen*, 9

Decker, Hannah. 1977. *Freud in Germany: Revolution and reaction in science, 1893-1907* (New York: International Universities Press)

———1991. *Freud, Dora, and Vienna 1900* (New York: Free Press)

Degenne, Alain, and Michel Forsé. 1994. *Les réseaux sociaux: Une analyse structurale en sociologie* (Paris: Armand Colin)

Degler, Janusz. 1973. *Witkacy w teatrze międzywojennym* (Warszawa: Wydawnictwo Artystyczne i Filmowe)

Delaperrière, Marie. 2004. *Polskie awangardy a poezja europejska: Studium wyobraźni poetyckiej* (Katowice: Wydawnictwo Uniwersytetu Śląskiego)

Delay, Jean. 1956. *La jeunesse d'André Gide 1* (Paris: Gallimard)

Didi-Huberman, Georges. 1982. *Invention de l'hystérie: Charcot et l'iconographie photographique de la Salpêtrière* (Paris: Macula)

Dierks, Manfred. 1990. 'Der Wahn und die Träume in "Der Tod in Venedig"', *Psyche*, 5: 240–268

Dobroczyński, Bartłomiej. 2005. *Idea nieświadomości w polskiej myśli psychologicznej przed Freudem* (Kraków: Universitas)

Dobrzycka, Urszula. 1991. *Abramowski* (Warszawa: Wiedza Powszechna)

Domagalska, Małgorzata. 2004. *Antysemityzm dla inteligencji?: Kwestia żydowska w publicystyce Adolfa Nowaczyńskiego na łamach "Myśli Narodowej" (1921-1934) i "Prosto z mostu" (1935-1939)* (Warszawa: Żydowski Instytut Historyczny)

Domagalski, Jerzy. 1995. *Proust w literaturze polskiej do 1945 roku* (Warszawa: Instytut Badań Literackich)

Domański, Cezary. 2011. 'Polacy w Wiedeńskim Towarzystwie Psychoanalitycznym w latach 1902-1938', in *Psychologia europejska w okresie międzywojennym: Sylwetki, osiągnięcia, problemy*ed. by Włodzisław Zeidler, and Helmut E. Lück (Warszawa: Vizja Press), pp. 223–235

Dorosz, Beata. 2013. *Nowojorski pasjans. Polski Instytut Naukowy w Ameryce: Studia o wybranych zagadnieniach działalności 1939-1969* (Warszawa: Biblioteka)

Doyle, Laura, and Laura Winkiel (eds). 2005. *Geomodernisms: Race, modernism, modernity* (Bloomington: Indiana University Press)

Dudek, Peter. 2012. *"Er war halt genialer als die anderen": Biografische Annäherungen an Siegfried Bernfeld* (Gießen: Psychosozial-Verlag)

———2002. *Fetisch Jugend: Walter Benjamin und Siegfried Bernfeld - Jugendprotest am Vorabend des Ersten Weltkrieges* (Leipzig: Klinkhardt & Biermann)

Dutkowa, Renata. 1995. *Żeńskie gimnazja Krakowa w procesie emancypacji kobiet (1896-1918)* (Kraków: Instytut Historii Uniwersytetu Jagiellońskiego)

Dybel, Pawel. 1996. *Freuda sen o kulturze* (Warszawa: Instytut Kultury)

———2014. 'Literatura i prawda, czyli Bruno Schulz i psychoanaliza', in *Schulz: między mitem a filozofią*ed. by Joanna Michalik, and Przemysław Bursztyka (Gdańsk: Słowo/Obraz Terytoria)

———2000. *Urwane ścieżki: Przybyszewski - Freud - Lacan* (Kraków: Universitas)

———2006. *Zagadka "drugiej płci": Spory wokół różnicy seksualnej w psychoanalizie i w feminizmie* (Kraków: Universitas)

Dziedzic, Anna. 2010. *Antropologia filozoficzna Edwarda Abramowskiego* (Wrocław: Wydawnictwo Uniwersytetu Wrocławskiego)

Eaglestone, Robert. 1998. 'The "fine risk" of history: Post-structuralism, the past and the work of Emmanuel Levinas', *Rethinking History*, 2/3: 313–320

Eksteins, Modris. 2000. *Rites of spring: The Great War and the birth of the modern age* (Wilmington: Mariner Books)

Ellenberger, Henri. 1970. *The discovery of the unconscious* (New York: Basic Books)

Ellmann, Richard. 1982. *James Joyce* (Oxford: Oxford University Press)

Elsaghe, Yahya. 2009. 'Edhin Krokowski aus Linde bei Pinne, Provinz Posen: Judentum und Antisemitismus im "Zauberberg" und seiner Vorgeschichte', *Monatshefte*, 101/1: 56–72

Espagne, Michel, and Michael Werner. 1998. 'Deutsch-französischer Kulturtransfer als Forschungsgegenstand: Eine Problemskizze', in *Transferts: Les relations interculturelles dans l'espace franco-allemand (XVIIIe-XIXe siècles)*ed. by Michel Espagne, and Michael Werner (Paris: Recherches sur les civilisations), pp. 11–34

———1987. 'La construction d'une référence allemande en France 1750–1914: Genèse et histoire culturelle', *Annales. Économies, Sociétés, Civilisations*, 42/4: 969–992

Espagne, Michel. 1999. *Les transferts culturels franco-allemands* (Paris: Presses Universitaires de France)

———1994. 'Sur les limites du comparatisme en histoire culturelle', *Genèses*, 17: 112–121

Etkind, Alexander. 1997. *Eros of the impossible: The history of psychoanalysis in Russia* (Boulder, CO: Westview Press)

Eustachowicz, Lesław. 1970. 'Komedie Antoniego Cwojdzińskiego', *Dialog*, 12: 123–128

Falkowska, Maria. 1989. *Kalendarz życia, działalności i twórczości Janusza Korczaka* (Warszawa: Nasza Księgarnia)

Fallend, Karl, and Johannes Reichmayr (eds). 1992. *Siegfried Bernfeld oder Die Grenzen der Psychoanalyse: Materialien zu Leben und Werk* (Frankfurt am Main: Stroemfeld)

Fallend, Karl. 1995. *Sonderlinge, Träumer, Sensitive: Psychoanalyse auf dem Weg zur Institution und Profession* (Wien: Jugend & Volk)

Fermi, Laura. 1968. *Illustrious immigrants: The intellectual migration from Europe 1930-1941* (Chicago: University of Chicago Press)

Fiała, Edward. 2001. 'O początkach i perspektywach psychoanalitycznej interpretacji literatury: Gombrowicz w optyce Freuda i Fromma', *Pamiętnik literacki*, 92/4: 75–96

Finck, Jean. 1982. *Thomas Mann et la psychanalyse* (Paris: Belles Lettres)

Fischer, René. 1975. 'Zur Geschichte der psychoanalytischen Bewegung in der Tschechoslowakei', *Psyche*, 29: 1126–1131

Fiut, Aleksander. 1994. 'Pojedynek o doktorową z Wilczej', in *Czytanie Schulza: materały międzynarodowej sesji naukowej Bruno Schulz - w stulecie urodzin i w pięćdziesięciolecie śmierci*ed. by Jerzy Jarzębski (Kraków: TIC)

Frąckowiak-Wiegandtowa, Ewa. 1973. 'Psychologizm - przezwa czy nazwa?', *Teksty*, 4/10: 193–200

Franczak, Jerzy. 2007. *Poszukiwanie realności: Światopogląd polskiej prozy modernistycznej* (Kraków: Universitas)

Freidenreich, Harriet Pass. 2002. *Female, Jewish, and educated: The lives of Central European university women* (Bloomington: Indiana University Press)

Frosh, Stephen. 2005. *Hate and the "Jewish science": Anti-semitism, nazism and psychoanalysis* (Basingstoke: Palgrave Macmillan)

Gawin, Magdalena. 2005. *Rasa i nowoczesność: Historia polskiego ruchu eugenicznego (1880-1952)* (Warszawa: Instytut Historii Nauki PAN)

Gay, Peter. 1987. *A godless Jew: Freud, atheism, and the making of psychoanalysis* (New Haven: Yale University Press)

———1988. *Freud: A life for our time* (New York: Norton)

———1978. *Freud, Jews and other Germans: Masters and victims in modernist culture* (New York: Oxford University Press)

Genette, Gérard. 1990. 'Fictional narrative, factual narrative', *Poetics Today*, 12/4: 755–774

Gifford, Sanford. 2001. 'Authorship of an adolescent diary, 1900-04', *Journal of Clinical Psychoanalysis*, 2: 293–298

———2003. 'Émigré analysts in Boston, 1930–1940', *International Forum of Psychoanalysis*, 12: 164–172

Gilman, Sander L. 1993. *Freud, race and gender* (Princeton: Princeton University Press)

Gilman, Sander L. 1986. *Jewish self-hatred: Anti-semitism and the hidden language of the Jews* (Baltimore: Johns Hopkins University Press)

Gilmore, Leigh. 1994. *Autobiographics: A feminist theory of women's self-representation* (Ithaca: Cornell University Press)

Głowala, Wojciech. 1972. *Sentymentalizm i pedanteria: O systemie estetycznym Karola Irzykowskiego* (Wrocław: Ossolineum)

Głowiński, Michał. 1973. *Gry powieściowe: Szkice z teorii i historii form narracyjnych* (Warszawa: Państwowy Instytut Wydawniczy)

——1968. *Porządek, chaos, znaczenie: Szkice o powieści wspólczesnej* (Warszawa: Państwowy Instytut Wydawniczy)

——1997. *Powieść młodopolska: Studium z poetyki historycznej* (Kraków: Universitas)

Głowiński, Michał, and Janusz Sławiński (eds). 1972. *Studia o Stanisławie Ignacym Witkiewiczu* (Wrocław: Ossolineum)

Goggin, James E., and Eileen Brockman Goggin. 2001. *Death of a "Jewish science": Psychoanalysis in the Third Reich* (Bloomington: Indiana University Press)

Goulet, Alain. 1986. *Fiction et vie sociale dans l'œuvre d'André Gide* (Paris: Association des amis d'André Gide)

Goux, Jean-Joseph. 1984. *Les monnayeurs du langage* (Paris: Galilée)

Gołębiewska, Maria. 2006. *Irzykowski: rzeczywistość i przedstawienie: O tezach filozoficznych Karola Irzykowskiego* (Warszawa: Wydawnictwo Instytutu Filozofii i Socjologii PAN)

Graczyk, Ewa. 1994. *Ćma: O Stanisławie Przybyszewskiej* (Warszawa: OPEN)

——2004. *Przed wybuchem wstrząsnać: O twórczości Witolda Gombrowicza w okresie międzywojennym* (Gdańsk: Słowo/Obraz Terytoria)

Grosskurth, Phyllis. 1986. *Melanie Klein: Her world and her work* (New York: Knopf)

——1991. *The secret ring: Freud's inner circle and the politics of psychoanalysis* (London: Cape)

Grossman, Carl M., and Sylvia Grossman. 1965. *The wild analyst: The life and work of Georg Groddeck* (New York: Braziller)

Guderian-Czaplińska, Ewa. 1998. *Szara strefa awangardy* (Warszawa: Wiedza o Kulturze)

Guesnet, François. 1999. 'Litwacy i Ostjuden', in *Tematy żydowskie: historia, literatura, edukacja*ed. by Elżbieta Traba, and Robert Traba (Olsztyn: Wspólnota Kulturowa Borussia)

Gutowski, Wojciech. 2008. *Konstelacja Przybyszewskiego* (Toruń: Marszałek)

Hale, Nathan G. 1971. *Freud and the Americans (1876-1917): The beginnings of psychoanalysis in the United States* (New York: Oxford University Press)

Hamburger, Käte. 1973. *The logic of literature* (Bloomington: Indiana University Press)

Hemecker, Wilhelm. 1991. *Vor Freud: Philosophiegeschichtliche Voraussetzungen der Psychoanalyse* (München: Philosophia)

Herman, Eufemiusz. 1958. *Neurolodzy polscy* (Warszawa: Państwowy Zakład Wydawn. Lekarskich)

Hermanns, Ludger M. 2019. 'Unsere letzte psychoanalytische Mohikanerin in Berlin: Die Berliner Jahre (1923–1939) der polnischen Psychoanalytikerin Salomea Kempner (1880–1943) und ihr "Verschwinden" in Warschau', in *Im Schatten von Krieg und Holocaust: Psychoanalyse in Polen im polnisch-deutsch-jüdischen Kontext* (Gießen: Psychosozial-Verlag), pp. 90–91

Hoffman, Frederick J. 1957. *Freudianism and the literary mind* (Baton Rouge: Louisiana State University Press)

Hoops, Reinald. 1934. *Der Einfluss der Psychoanalyse auf die englische Literatur* (Heidelberg: Carl Winter)

Huber, Wolfgang. 1977. *Psychoanalyse in Österreich seit 1933* (Wien-Salzburg: Geyer)

Hulewicz, Jan. 1962. 'Materiały do studiów Polek w Paryżu i Genewie w latach dziewięćdziesiątych XIX wieku', *Przegląd Historyczno-Oświatowy*, 2: 307–316

Irzykowski, Karol. 2021. 'List do Zygmunta Freuda', *Teksty Drugie*, 31/4: 169–181

Ivanyk, Stepan. 2014. *Filozofowie ukraińscy w Szkole Lwowsko-Warszawskiej* (Warszawa: Semper)

———2012. 'Psychoanaliza w Szkole Lwowsko-Warszawskiej: Stepan Baley o motywie endymiońskim w twórczości literackiej Tarasa Szewczenki i Juliusza Słowackiego', *Logos i Ethos*, 32: 43–62

Iwanczewska, Łucja. 2007. *"Muszę się odrodzić": Inne spotkania z dramatami Stanisława Ignacego Witkiewicza* (Kraków: Księgarnia Akademicka)

Jaccard, Roland (ed.). 1982. *Histoire de la psychanalyse* (Paris: Hachette)

Jacoby, Russell. 1983. *The repression of psychoanalysis: Otto Fenichel and the political freudians* (New York: Basic Books)

Jakowska, Krystyna. 1983. *Powrót autora: Renesans narracji auktorialnej w polskiej powieści międzywojennej* (Wrocław: Ossolineum)

Janicka, Anna. 2013. *Sprawa Zapolskiej: Skandale i polemiki* (Białystok: Uniwersytet w Białymstoku)

Janik, Allan, and Hans Veigl. 1998. *Wittgenstein in Vienna: A biographical excursion through the city and its history* (Wien-New York: Springer)

Jaworski, Stanisław. 1976. *Między awangardą a nadrealizmem: Główne kierunki przemian poezji polskiej w latach trzydziestych na tle europejskim* (Kraków: Wydawnictwo Literackie)

Jedlicki, Jerzy (ed.). 2015. *A history of the Polish intelligentsia* (Bern: Peter Lang)

Jensen, Reimer, and Henning Paikin. 1980. 'On psychoanalysis in Denmark', *Scandinavian Psychoanalytic Review*, 3: 103–116

Jones, Ernest. 1953. *Sigmund Freud: Life and work* (London: The Hogarth Press)

Juszczak, Wiesław. 1981. *Zasłona w rajskie ptaki albo O granicach "okresu powieści"* (Warszawa: Państwowy Instytut Wydawniczy)

Kapuscińska, Krystyna. 1968. *Twórczość komediowa Bruno Winawera i Antoniego Cwojdzińskiego: Przypomnienie i próba oceny* (Łódź: Łódzkie Towarzystwo Naukowe)

King, Pearl H. M., and Riccardo Steiner. 1990. *The Freud-Klein controversies in the British psycho-analytical society, 1941-45* (London: Routledge)

Kirsner, Douglas. 2007. 'Saving psychoanalysts: Ernest Jones and the Isakowers', *Psychoanalysis and History*, 9: 83–91

Klatka, Urszula. 2012. *Wyobraźnia w czasie: O poezji Jana Brzękowskiego* (Kraków: Collegium Columbinum)

Kloocke, Ruth. 2002. *Mosche Wulff: Zur Geschichte der Psychoanalyse in Russland und Israel* (Tübingen: diskord)

Kłak, Tadeusz. 1979. *Czasopisma awangardy* (Wrocław: Ossolineum)

Kłosinska, Krystyna. 1999. *Ciało, pożądanie, ubranie: O wczesnych powieściach Gabrieli Zapolskiej* (Kraków: eFKa)

———2010. *Feministyczna krytyka literacka* (Katowice: Wydawnictwo Uniwersytetu Śląskiego)

———1988. *Powieści o wieku nerwowym* (Katowice: Wydawnictwo Uniwersytetu Śląskiego)

Kłys, Tomasz. 2006. *Dekada doktora Mabuse: Nieme filmy Fritza Langa* (Łódź: Wydawnictwo Uniwersytetu Łódzkiego)

Kofman, Sarah. 1983. *L'énigme de la femme: La femme dans les textes de Freud* (Paris: Galilée)

Korniejenko, Agnieszka. 1998. *Ukraiński modernizm: Próba periodyzacji procesu historycznoliterackiego* (Kraków: Universitas)

Kostkiewicz, Janina. 2013. *Kierunki i koncepcje pedagogiki katolickiej w Polsce 1918–1939* (Kraków: Impuls)

Kracauer, Siegfried. 1947. *From Caligari to Hitler: A psychological history of the German film* (Princeton: Princeton University Press)

Krajewska, Anna. 2004. *Komedia polska dwudziestolecia międzywojennego: Tradycjonaliści i nowatorzy* (Poznań: Wydawnictwo Uniwersytetu Adama Mickiewicza)

Krasuska, Karolina. 2011. *Płeć i naród: Trans/lokacje. Maria Komornicka/Piotr Odmieniec Włast, Else Lasker-Schüler, Mina Loy* (Warszawa: Instytut Badań Literackich)

Kulczykowski, Mariusz Jan. 1995. *Żydzi-studenci Uniwersytetu Jagiellońskiego w dobie autonomicznej Galicji (1867–1918)* (Kraków: Księgarnia Akademicka)

Kundera, Milan. 1984. 'The tragedy of Central Europe', *The New York Review of Books*, 31/7: 33–83

Kuśmierczyk, Seweryn. 1983. 'Opis początków psychoanalizy w powieści Prusa?: (Przyczynek do wiedzy o powstawaniu "Lalki")', *Przegląd Humanistyczny*, 27/9-10: 151–168

Kut'ko, Igor' Ivanovič, Lenina Ivanovna Bondarenko, and Petr Todorovič Petrjuk (eds). 1996. *Istorija psichoanaliza v Ukraine* (Kharkiv: Osnova)

Kutter, Peter (ed.). 1992. *Psychoanalysis international I: A guide to psychoanalysis throughout the world* (Stuttgart-Bad Cannstatt: frommann-holzboog)

Kwiecień, Roma. 1998. 'Bolesław Miciński i psychoanaliza', *Teksty Drugie*, 9/1-2: 85–108

Laplénie, Jean-François. 2004. *Puissances voisines: Études pour une histoire structurelle de la réception de la psychanalyse dans les milieux littéraires germanophones (1900–1930)* (Paris: Université Paris III)

Le Rider, Jacques. 1994a. *Le cas Otto Weininger: Racines de l'antiféminisme et de l'antisémitisme* (Paris: Presses Universitaires de France)

——— 1994b. *Modernité viennoise et crises de l'identité* (Paris: Presses Universitaires de France)

Ledger, Sally. 1997. *The new woman: Fiction and feminism at the fin de siècle* (Manchester: Manchester University Press)

Leinwand, Artur. 1983. *Poseł Herman Lieberman* (Kraków: Wydawnictwo Literackie)

Lejeune, Philippe. 1989. *On autobiography* (Minneapolis: University of Minnesota Press)

Lewandowski, Tomasz. 1982. *Dramat intelektu: Biografia literacka Stanisławy Przybyszewskiej* (Gdańsk: Wydawnictwo Morskie)

Lieberman, E. James. 1985. *Acts of will: The life and work of Otto Rank* (New York: Free Press)

Liebermann, Guido Ariel. 2012. *La psychanalyse en Palestine 1918–1948: Aux origines du mouvement analytique israélien* (Paris: Campagne première)

Lubański, Marek. 2008. *Krytyka literacka i psychoanaliza: O polskiej psychoanalitycznej krytyce literackiej w okresie dwudziestolecia międzywojennego* (Warszawa: Eneteia)

Ludwig-Körner, Christiane. 1999. *Wiederentdeckt – Psychoanalytikerinnen in Berlin* (Gießen: Psychosozial-Verlag)

Łebkowska, Anna. 1998. *Fikcja jako możliwość: Z przemian prozy XX wieku* (Kraków: Universitas)

———2001. *Między teoriami a fikcją literacką* (Kraków: Universitas)

Łubieniewska, Ewa. 2007. *Czysta forma i bebechy* (Kraków: Universitas)

Magnone, Lena. 2022. 'Emisariusze Freuda raz jeszcze', *Kwartalnik Historii Żydów*, 1: 45–80

Mahony, Patrick. 1984. *Cries of the Wolf Man* (New York: International Universities Press)

———1982. *Freud as a writer* (New York: International Universities Press)

Maigné, Carole (ed.). 2013. *Formalisme esthétique: Prague et Vienne au XIXe siècle* (Paris: Vrin)

Maigné, Carole, and Céline Trautmann-Waller (eds). 2009. *Formalismes esthétiques et héritage herbartien: Vienne, Prague, Moscou* (Hildesheim: Olms)

Maigné, Carole. 2007. *Johann Friedrich Herbart* (Paris: Belin)

Majerski, Paweł. 1999. 'Boczny tor awangardowego eksperymentu (O powieściach Jana Brzękowskiego)', *Ruch Literacki*, 40/6: 649–662

Major, René (ed.). 1981. *Géopsychanalyse: Les souterrains de l'institution. Rencontre franco-latino-américaine* (Paris: Confrontation)

Mannoni, Maud. 1979. *La théorie comme fiction: Freud, Groddeck, Winnicott, Lacan* (Paris: Seuil)

Manson, Irina. 1991. 'Comment dit-on "psychanalyse" en russe?', *Revue Internationale d'Histoire de la Psychanalyse*, 4: 407–423

Marcinowski, Filip. 2014. '"(...) by popchnąć naprzód świadomość ducha i leczyć jego zboczenia": Pierwszy zjazd neurologów, psychiatrów i psychologów polskich w Warszawie w 1909 roku', in *Na drogach i bezdrożach historii psychologii III*ed. by Teresa Rzepa, and Cezary Domański (Lublin: Wydawnictwo UMCS), pp. 211–221

Marcus, Steven. 1975. *Representations: Essays on literature and society* (New York: Columbia University Press)

Margalit, Elkana. 1969. 'Social and intellectual origins of the Hashomer Hatzair youth mouvement 1913–1920', *Journal of Contemporary History*, 2: 25–46

Mariot, Nicolas, and Claire Zalc. 2010. *Face à la persécution: 991 Juifs dans la guerre* (Paris: Odile Jacob)

Markiewicz, Henryk. 1998. *Polskie teorie powieści: Od początków do schyłku XX wieku* (Warszawa: Państwowe Wydawnictwo Naukowe)

Markowski, Michał Paweł. 2005. *Czarny nurt: Gombrowicz, świat, literatura* (Kraków: Wydawnictwo Literackie)

Martynkewicz, Wolfgang. 1997. *Georg Groddeck: Eine Biographie* (Frankfurt am Main: Fischer)

Matuszek, Gabriela. 1996. *Der geniale Pole?: Niemcy o Stanisławie Przybyszewskim (1892–1992)* (Kraków: Universitas)

———2008. *Stanisław Przybyszewski – pisarz nowoczesny: Eseje i proza – próba monografii* (Kraków: Universitas)

May, Ulrike. 2007. 'Freud's patient calendars: 17 analysts in analysis with Freud (1910-1920)', *Psychoanalysis and History*, 9: 153–200

McCagg, William O. 1992. *A history of Habsburg Jews, 1670-1918* (Bloomington, Ind.: Indiana University Press)

Menaker, Esther. 1982. *Otto Rank: A rediscovered legacy* (New York: Columbia University Press)

Michalewicz, Jerzy (ed.). 2015. *Corpus studiosorum Universitatis Iagellonicae in saeculis XVIII-XX Tomus III: 1850/1851-1917/1918* (Kraków: Archiwum Uniwersytetu Jagiellońskiego)

Micińska, Anna. 2003. *Istnienie poszczególne: Stanisław Ignacy Witkiewicz* (Wrocław: Wydawnictwo Dolnośląskie)

Mijolla-Mellor de, Sophie (ed.). 1999. *Les femmes dans l'histoire de la psychanalyse* (Bègles: L'Esprit du temps)

Mikhalevitch, Alexandre. 1991. 'L'âge d'argent de la psychanalyse russe: Les premières traductions des œuvres de Freud en Russie prérévolutionnaire (1904–1914)', *Revue Internationale d'Histoire de la Psychanalyse*, 4: 399–406

Miller, Martin A. 1998. *Freud and the Bolsheviks: Psychoanalysis in Imperial Russia and the Soviet Union* (New Haven: Yale University Press)

Mitchell, Juliet. 1986. *Psychoanalysis and feminism: A radical reassessment of Freudian psychoanalysis* (London: Penguin)

Moore, Nigel. 1978. 'Psychoanalysis in Scandinavia I: Sweden and Finland', *Scandinavian Psychoanalytic Review*, 1: 9–64

Mühlleitner, Elke. 1992. *Biographisches Lexikon der Psychoanalyse: Die Mitglieder der Psychologischen Mittwoch-Gesellschaft und der Wiener Psychoanalytischen Vereinigung 1902–1938* (Tübingen: diskord)

Mühlleitner, Elke, and Johannes Reichmayr. 1997. 'Following Freud in Vienna', *International Forum of Psychoanalysis*, 6: 73–102

Mühlleitner, Elke. 2000. 'Steff Bornstein, Otto Fenichel und die psychoanalytisch-pädagogische Ausbildung der Psychoanalytischen Arbeitsgemeinschaft v. Č.S.R. (1933–1939)', *Luzifer-Amor*, 26: 64–77

Munsch, Matthias. 2004. *Psychoanalyse in der englischen Moderne* (Marburg: LiteraturWissenschaft.de)

Neumann, Daniela. 1987. *Studentinnen aus dem Russischen Reich in der Schweiz 1867–1914* (Zürich: Rohr)

Nicolas, Serge. 2004. *L'hypnose. Charcot face à Bernheim: L'école de la Salpêtrière face à l'école de Nancy* (Paris: L'Harmattan)

Nycz, Ryszard. 2012. *Poetyka doświadczenia: Teoria – nowoczesność – literatura* (Warszawa: Instytut Badań Literackich)

——1984. *Sylwy współczesne: Problem konstrukcji tekstu* (Wrocław: Ossolineum)

——2017. *The language of Polish modernism* (Frankfurt am Main: Peter Lang)

Opalska, Magdalena. 1990. '"Wiadomości Literackie" – dyskusje nad kwestią żydowską (1924–1939)', *Przegląd Humanistyczny*, 34/10: 77–88

Otto, Wojciech. 2007. *Literatura i film w kulturze dwudziestolecia międzywojennego* (Poznań: Wydawnictwo Poznańskiego Towarzystwa Przyjaciół Nauk)

Ovčarenko, Viktor, and Valerij Lejbin. 1999. *Antologija rossijskogo psichoanaliza* (Moskva: Flinta)

Ovčarenko, Viktor. 2000. *Rossijskie psichoanalitiki* (Sankt Peterburg: Akademičeskij proekt)

Oxaal, Ivar, and Walter R. Weitzmann. 1985. 'The Jews of pre-1914 Vienna: An exploration of basic sociological dimensions', *The Leo Baeck Institute Yearbook*, 30: 395–432

Paczkowska-Łagowska, Elżbieta. 2010. 'Georg Brandes: "Nasz człowiek" w Europie', in *Europejczyk w podróży*ed. by Ewa Ihnatowicz, and Stefan Ciara (Warszawa: Neriton), pp. 305–326

Paczkowski, Andrzej. 1980. *Prasa polska w latach 1918–1939* (Warszawa: Państwowe Wydawnictwo Naukowe)

Pakalski, Dariusz. 2012. *Pytanie o ideę kultury w "Czarodziejskiej górze" Tomasza Manna* (Toruń: Tako)

Panek, Sylwia. 2006. *Krytyk w przestrzeniach literatury i filozofii: O młodopolskich wypowiedziach polemicznych Karola Irzykowskiego* (Poznań: Poznańskie Studia Polonistyczne)

Papierowski, Andrzej Jerzy, and Jerzy Stefański. 2002. *Płocczanie znani i nieznani: Słownik biograficzny* (Płock: Książnica Płocka)

Paszek, Jerzy (ed.). 1982. *Studia o Zegadłowiczu* (Katowice: Wydawnictwo Uniwersytetu Śląskiego)

Pawlukiewicz, Ryszard. 1987. 'Psychologiczne ujęcie problematyki badawczej w polskiej nauce o literaturze do roku 1939', in *Z dziejów polskiej nauki o literaturze I*ed. by Henryk Markiewicz, and Gabriela Matuszek (Kraków: Wydawnictwo Uniwersytetu Jagiellońskiego)

Perkowska, Urszula. 1994. *Studentki Uniwersytetu Jagiellońskiego w latach 1894-1939: W stulecie immatrykulacji pierwszych studentek* (Kraków: Secesja)

———1990. *Uniwersytet Jagielloński w latach I wojny światowej* (Kraków: Universitas)

Pieszczachowicz, Jan. 1970. '"Dziurek" na tle epoki', *Dialog*, 12: 113–122

Planta, Vera von. 2010. '"Analysiere nie wieder einen jungen Menschen wie mich…": Emil Oberholzer und Mira Oberholzer-Gincburg, ein russisch-schweizerisches Analytikerpaar in der ersten Hälfte des 20. Jahrhunderts', *Luzifer-Amor*, 45: 70–104

———2006. 'Mira Oberholzer-Gincburg (1884–1949): Eine Analytikerin der ersten Stunde in der Schweiz', *Luzifer-Amor*, 37: 142–149

Podnieks, Elizabeth. 2000. *Daily modernism: The literary diaries of Virginia Woolf, Antonia White, Elizabeth Smart, and Anaïs Nin* (Montreal-Kingston: McGill-Queen's University Press)

Poirier, Jacques. 1998. *Littérature et psychanalyse: Les écrivains français face au freudisme 1914–1944* (Dijon: Éditions universitaires de Dijon)

Pontalis, Jean-Bertrand. 1988. *Perdre de vue* (Paris: Gallimard)

Porge, Erik. 1994. *Vol d'idées?: Wilhelm Fliess, son plagiat et Freud, suivi de Pour ma propre cause de Wilhelm Fliess* (Paris: Denoël)

Prokop, Jan. 1972. 'Sprawa nadrealizmu', in Jan Prokop, *Lekcja rzeczy* (Kraków: Wydawnictwo Literackie)

Prokop-Janiec, Eugenia. 2013. *Pogranicze polsko-żydowskie: Topografie i teksty* (Kraków: Wydawnictwo Uniwersytetu Jagiellońskiego)

——2003. *Polish-Jewish literature in the interwar years* (Syracuse: Syracuse University Press)

Quen, Jacques M., and Eric T. Carlson (eds). 1978. *American psychoanalysis: Origins and development* (New York: Brunner-Mazel)

Roazen, Paul. 1970. *Brother animal: The story of Freud and Tausk* (London: Routledge)

——1975. *Freud and his followers* (New York: Knopf)

——1985. *Helene Deutsch: A psychoanalyst's life* (New York City: New American Library)

——2001. *The historiography of psychoanalysis* (New Brunswick: Transaction Publishers)

——1990. 'Tola Rank', *Journal of the American Academy of Psychoanalysis*, 18/2: 247–259

Robinson, Paul. 1969. *The Freudian left: Wilhem Reich, Géza Róheim, Herbert Marcuse* (New York: Harper & Row)

Rodak, Paweł. 2009. 'Prawda w dzienniku', *Teksty Drugie*, 20/4: 23–38

Rogozik, Joanna. 1997. '"Nasz Przegląd" (Między "hajntyzmem" a "mechesyzmem")', *Zeszyty Prasoznawcze*, 40/3-4: 127–128

Rolnik, Eran J. 1997. *Freud in Zion: Psychoanalysis and the making of modern Jewish identity* (London: Karnac Books)

Rosińska, Zofia, Joanna Michalik, and Przemysław Bursztyka (eds). 2008. *Freud i nowoczesność* (Kraków: Universitas)

Rosman, Moshe. 2007. *How Jewish is Jewish history?* (Portland: The Litman Library of Jewish Civilization)

Roudinesco, Elisabeth. 2000. *Dictionnaire de la psychanalyse* (Paris: Fayard)

——2003. *Histoire de la psychanalyse en France* (Paris: Des Femmes)

——2005. *Jacques Lacan: Jego życie i myśl* (Warszawa: Wydawnictwo KR)

Royer, Clara. 2011. *Le Royaume littéraire: Quêtes d'identité d'une génération d'écrivains juifs de l'entre-deux-guerres. Hongrie, Slovaquie, Transylvanie* (Paris: Champion)

Rozenblit, Marsha L. 1983. *The Jews of Vienna, 1867-1914: Assimilation and identity* (Albany: State University of New York Press)

Rudnytsky, Peter L. 2002. *Reading psychoanalysis: Freud, Rank, Ferenczi, Groddeck* (Ithaca: Cornell University Press)

——2011. *Rescuing psychoanalysis from Freud and other essays in re-vision* (London: Routledge)

Rybicka, Elżbieta. 2008. 'Od poetyki przestrzeni do polityki miejsca: Zwrot topograficzny w badaniach literackich', *Teksty Drugie*, 19/4: 21–38

Ryłko, Zdzisław. 1975. 'Polska recepcja nadrealizmu francuskiego w okresie międzywojennym', *Poezja*, 9: 15–30

Rzepa, Teresa. 2009. *Historia polskiej myśli psychologicznej* (Warszawa: Państwowe Wydawnictwo Naukowe)

Rzepa, Teresa (ed.). 1997. *Psychologia w szkole lwowsko-warszawskiej* (Warszawa: Państwowe Wydawnictwo Naukowe)

Rzepa, Teresa. 1998. *Życie psychiczne i drogi do niego (Psychologiczna Szkoła Lwowska)* (Szczecin: Wydawnictwo Uniwersytetu Szczecińskiego)

Sadkowska, Katarzyna. 2007. *Irzykowski i inni: Twórczość Fryderyka Hebbla w Polsce 1890–1939* (Kraków: Universitas)

Sadowski, Lesław. 1988. *Polska inteligencja prowincjonalna i jej ideowe dylematy na przełomie XIX i XX wieku* (Warszawa: Państwowe Wydawnictwo Naukowe)

Sajewska, Dorota. 2005. *Chore sztuki: Choroba/tożsamość/dramat* (Kraków: Księgarnia Akademicka)

Sandauer, Artur. 2005. *On the situation of the Polish writer of Jewish descent in the Twentieth Century: It is not I who should have written this study...* (Jerusalem: Magnes)

Saunders, Max. 2010. *Self impression: Life-writing, autobiografiction, and the forms of modern literature* (Oxford: Oxford University Press)

Sayers, Janet. 1991. *Mothers of psychoanalysis: Helene Deutsch, Karen Horney, Anna Freud, Melanie Klein* (New York: Norton)

Schor, Naomi. 1985a. *Breaking the chain: Women, theory and French realist fiction* (New York: Columbia University Press)

——1985b. 'Female fetishism: The case of George Sand', *Poetics Today*, 6/1-2: 301–310

———1986. 'Reading double: Sand's difference', in *Poetics of gender*ed. by Nancy K. Miller (New York: Columbia University Press), pp. 248–269

Schorske, Carl E. 1979. *Fin de siècle Vienna: Politics and culture* (London: Weidenfeld)

Sdvižkov, Denis. 2006. *Das Zeitalter der Intelligenz: Zur vergleichenden Geschichte der Gebildeten in Europa bis zum Ersten Weltkrieg* (Göttingen: Vandenhoeck & Ruprecht)

Sengoopta, Chandak. 2000. *Otto Weininger: Sex, science, and self in Imperial Vienna* (Chicago: University of Chicago Press)

Sharaf, Myron R. 1994. *Fury on Earth: A biography of Wilhelm Reich* (New York: Da Capo Press)

Shepherd, Naomi. 1993. *A price below rubies: Jewish women as rebels and radicals* (Cambridge, MA: Harvard University Press)

Sienkiewicz, Barbara. 1992. *Literackie "teorie widzenia" w prozie dwudziestolecia międzywojennego* (Poznań: Obserwator)

———1997. 'Poezja z "Freudowskiego pnia" – w orbicie sporu o polski surrealizm', in *Przez znaki – do człowieka*ed. by Barbara Sienkiewicz, and Anna Legeżyńska (Poznań: Wydawnictwo WiS), pp. 228–248

Skórczewski, Dariusz. 2002. '"Sprawa Irzykowskiego i Boya": Wokół głośnego epizodu międzywojennego sporu o krytykę', *Teksty Drugie*, 12/3: 223–231

———2020. *Polish literature and national identity: A postcolonial perspective* (Rochester: University of Rochester Press)

Skwara, Marta. 1999. *Szczecińskie Witkacjana* (Szczecin: Wydawnictwo Uniwersytetu Szczecińskiego)

Sokolowsky, Laura. 2013. *Freud et les Berlinois: Du congrès de Budapest à l'Institut de Berlin 1918–1933* (Rennes: Presses universitaires de Rennes)

Sosnowska, Danuta. 2008. *Inna Galicja* (Warszawa: Elipsa)

Speina, Jerzy. 1998. *Literatura w perspektywie psychologii: Studia i szkice o polskiej prozie narracyjnej Dwudziestolecia i jej recepcji krytycznoliterackiej* (Toruń: Wydawnictwo Uniwersytetu Mikołaja Kopernika)

———1965. *Powieści Stanisława Ignacego Witkiewicza: Geneza i struktura* (Toruń: Państwowe Wydawnictwo Naukowe)

——1975. 'Psychoanaliza w badaniach literackich w Polsce okresu międzywojennego', in *Z dziejów nauki polskiej: Księga pamiątkowa Towarzystwa Naukowego w Toruniu*ed. by Artur Hutnikiewicz, and Leszek Janiszewski (Warszawa: Państwowe Wydawnictwo Naukowe)

Spencer, Sharon. 1982. 'Delivering the woman artist from the silence of the womb: Otto Rank's influence on Anaïs Nin', *The Psychoanalytic Review*, 69: 111–129

Spiro, Melford E. 1982. *Oedipus in the Trobriands* (Chicago: University of Chicago Press)

Stachura-Lupa, Renata. 2009. 'Prus o działalności naukowej Juliana Ochorowicza', in *Bolesław Prus: pisarz nowoczesny*ed. by Jakub Malik (Lublin: Wydawnictwo KUL), pp. 211–220

Stala, Marian. 1994. *Pejzaż człowieka: Młodopolskie myśli i wyobrażenia o duszy, duchu i ciele* (Kraków: Baran i Suszczyński)

Stanford Friedman, Susan. 2007. 'Cultural parataxis and transnational landscapes of reading: Toward a locational modernist studies', in *Modernism*ed. by Astraður Eysteinsson, and Vivian Liska (Amsterdam: Benjamins), pp. 35–52

Steedman, Carolyn. 2001. 'Something she called a fever: Michelet, Derrida, and Dust', *The American Historical Review*, 106/4: 1159–1180

Steel, David. 1977. 'Gide et Freud', *Revue d'histoire littéraire de la France*, 77: 48–74

——1987. 'Jacques Rivière et la pensée psychanalytique', *Revue d'histoire littéraire de la France*, 87/5: 901–915

——1979. 'Les débuts de la psychanalyse dans les lettres françaises: 1914–1922', *Revue d'histoire littéraire de la France*, 79/1: 62–89

Steiner, Riccardo. 1989. '"It is a new kind of diaspora"', *International Review of Psycho-Analysis*, 16: 35–78

——2000. *"It's a new kind of diaspora": Explorations in the sociopolitical and cultural context of psychoanalysis* (London-New York: Routledge)

Stocking, G. W. 1986. 'Anthropology and the science of the irrational: Malinowski's encounter with Freudian psychoanalysis', *History of Anthropology*, 4: 449–491

Suchmiel, Jadwiga. 2008. *Polki w Uniwersytecie w Wiedniu ze stopniem doktora filozofii i medycyny, 1897-1939* (Częstochowa: Wydawnictwo Akademii im. Jana Długosza)

Sulloway, Frank J. 1992a. *Freud, Biologist of the mind: Beyond the psychoanalytic legend* (Cambridge, MA: Harvard University Press)

——1992b. 'Reassessing Freud's case histories: The social construction of psychoanalysis', in *Freud and the history of psychoanalysis*ed. by Toby Gelfand, and John Kerr (London: The Analytic Press), pp. 153–192

Szarejko, Piotr. 2001. *Słownik lekarzy polskich XIX wieku* (Warszawa: Semper)

Szarota, Piotr. 2013. *Wiedeń 1913* (Gdańsk: Słowo/Obraz Terytoria)

Szary-Matywiecka, Ewa. 1979. *Książka–powieść–autotematyzm (od "Pałuby" do "Jedynego wyjścia")* (Wrocław: Ossolineum)

Szałek, Piotr. 1999. *Lewica freudowska: Od psychoanalizy do irracjonalizmu* (Łódź: Wydawnictwo Uniwersytetu Łódzkiego)

Szpakowska, Małgorzata. 2012. *"Wiadomości Literackie" prawie dla wszystkich* (Warszawa: Wydawnictwo W.A.B.)

——1976. *Światopogląd Stanisława Ignacego Witkiewicza* (Wrocław: Ossolineum)

Szymaniak, Karolina. 2006. *Być agentem wiecznej idei: Przemiany poglądów estetycznych Debory Vogel* (Kraków: Universitas)

Szymanowski, Kornel. 1986. *Narcyz: Rzecz o Zegadłowiczu-powieściopisarzu* (Kraków: Wydawnictwo Literackie)

Szymańska, Beata. 1991. *Mistycy i pesymiści: Przeżycia i uczucia jako wartości w filozofii polskiego modernizmu* (Wrocław: Ossolineum)

——1979. *Poeta i nieznane: Poglądy filozoficzne Antoniego Langego* (Wrocław: Ossolineum)

Szymański, Wiesław Paweł. 1973. *Neosymbolizm: O awangardowej poezji polskiej w latach trzydziestych* (Kraków: Wydawnictwo Literackie)

——1971. *Świadomość estetyczna polskiej awangardy* (Kraków: Polska Akademia Nauk)

Taft, Julia Jessie. 1958. *Otto Rank: A biographical study based on notebooks, letters, collected writings, therapeutic achievements and personal associations* (New York: Julian Press)

Thompson, Nellie L. 1987. 'Early women psychoanalysts', *International Review of Psycho-Analysis*, 14: 391–407

Tichy, Marina, and Sylvia Zwettler-Otte. 1999. *Freud in der Presse: Rezeption Sigmund Freuds und der Psychoanalyse in Österreich 1895-1938* (Wien: Sonderzahl)

Timms, Edward, and Naomi Segal (eds). 1988. *Freud in exile: Psychoanalysis and its vicissitudes* (New Haven: Yale University Press)

Tomkowski, Jan. 2001. *Pokolenie Gombrowicza: Narodziny powieści XX wieku w Polsce* (Warszawa: Czytelnik)

Treichel, Irena. 1972. *Słownik pracowników książki polskiej* (Warszawa: Państwowe Wydawnictwo Naukowe)

Tych, Feliks. 1992. *Słownik Biograficzny Działaczy Polskiego Ruchu Robotniczego* (Warszawa: Książka i Wiedza)

Ulicka, Danuta. 2007. *Literaturoznawcze dyskursy możliwe: Studia z dziejów nowoczesnej teorii literatury w Europie Środkowo-Wschodniej* (Kraków: Universitas)

Urbanowski, Maciej. 2002. *Oczyszczenie: Szkice o literaturze polskiej XX wieku* (Kraków: Arcana)

Utley, Philip L. 1979. 'Siegfried Bernfeld's Jewish Order of Youth 1914–1922', *Leo Baeck Institute Year Book*, 4: 349–368

Walicki, Jacek. 2005. *Ruch syjonistyczny w Polsce w latach 1926–1930* (Łódź: Wydawnictwo Uniwersytetu Łódzkiego)

Waśkiewicz, Andrzej K. 1983. *W kręgu "Zwrotnicy": Studia i szkice z dziejów krakowskiej Awangardy* (Kraków: Wydawnictwo Literackie)

———2003. *W kręgu futuryzmu i awangardy* (Wrocław: Oświatowe)

Wasserstein, Bernard. 1979. *Britain and the Jews of Europe, 1939-1945* (Oxford: Clarendon Press)

Weitz, Erich. 2007. *Weimar Germany: Promise and tragedy* (Princeton: Princeton University)

Werner, Michael, and Bénédicte Zimmermann. 2004. *De la comparaison à l'histoire croisée* (Paris: Seuil)

Wieser, Annatina. 2001. *Zur frühen Psychoanalyse in Zürich 1900 – 1914* (Zürich: Universität Zürich)

Will, Herbert. 1984. *Die Geburt der Psychosomatik: Georg Groddeck, der Mensch und Wissenschaftler* (München: Urban & Schwarzenberg)

Winklowa, Barbara. 1994. *Karol Irzykowski: Życie i twórczość* (Kraków: Wydawnictwo Literackie)

Wójcikowa, Sylwia. 1979. 'Świat komedii naukowych B. Winawera i A. Cwojdzińskiego', *Przegląd Humanistyczny*, 23/2: 133–140

Wójtowicz, Aleksander. 2010. *Cogito i "sejsmograf podświadomości": Proza Pierwszej Awangardy* (Lublin: Wydawnictwo UMCS)

Wolff, Larry. 1995. *Child abuse in Freud's Vienna: Postcards from the end of the world* (New York: New York University Press)

———2010. *The idea of Galicia: History and fantasy in Habsburg political culture* (Stanford: Stanford University Press)

Wójcik, Mirosław. 2005. *Pan na Gorzeniu: Życie i twórczość Emila Zegadłowicza* (Kielce: Wydawnictwo Akademii Świętokrzyskiej)

Wróbel, Szymon. 1997. *Odkrycie nieświadomości: Czy destrukcja kartezjańskiego pojęcia podmiotu poznającego?* (Wrocław: Leopoldinum)

Wysińska, Elżbieta. 1964. 'Uczony, marzyciel i pechowiec', *Dialog*, 4: 129–134

Wysłouch, Severyna. 1975. 'Twórczość Choromańskiego wobec międzywojennego psychologizmu', *Pamiętnik literacki*, 66/1: 61–84

Young, Michael W. 2004. *Malinowski: Odyssey of an anthropologist, 1884-1920* (New Haven: Yale University Press)

Zieliński, Jan. 1983. *Pępek powieści: Z problemów powieści autobiograficznej przełomu XIX i XX wieku* (Wrocław: Ossolineum)

Zimand, Roman. 1990. *Diarysta Stefan Ż.* (Wrocław: Ossolineum)

Zych, Justyna Magdalena. 1990. *L'influence de la psychanalyse sur la critique littéraire en France (1914-1939)* (Warszawa: Wydawnictwo Uniwersytetu Warszawskiego)

———2011. 'Sześciokąt antyfreudowski, czyli o recepcji psychoanalizy w międzywojennej Francji', *Przegląd Humanistyczny*, 55/2: 39–48

Żarnowski, Janusz. 1965. *O inteligencji polskiej lat międzywojennych* (Warszawa: Wiedza Powszechna)

———1964. *Struktura społeczna inteligencji w Polsce w latach 1918–1939* (Warszawa: Państwowe Wydawnictwo Naukowe)

Żółkiewski, Stefan. 1995. *Społeczne konteksty kultury literackiej na ziemiach polskich (1890–1939)* (Warszawa: Instytut Badań Literackich)

TEORIA

20TH CENTURY POLISH THOUGHT

In spite of the recent boom of interest for the intellectual history of Central and Eastern Europe in the first half of the 20th century, knowledge of Polish achievements in the field of theoretical humanities remains shockingly selective and distorted. This holds true even in Poland, where scholars concentrate on the reception of often oversimplified, impoverished Franco-American derivatives of the tradition which Polish thinkers played a significant role in shaping. As such, a slew of fascinating ideas and concepts formulated in Poland or by Polish scholars still await their rediscovery, especially in light of recent findings about the transfer of ideas in Central and Eastern Europe. The series "Teoria" intends all at once to compensate for the lack of recognition of Polish theory, to offer a more exhaustive image of it and to allow a revision of the Polish legacy.

www.ingramcontent.com/pod-product-compliance
Lightning Source LLC
Chambersburg PA
CBHW051336230926
51848CB00006B/230
9782940738090